The Use of Force against Ukraine and International Law

Sergey Sayapin · Evhen Tsybulenko
Editors

The Use of Force against Ukraine and International Law

Jus Ad Bellum, Jus In Bello, Jus Post Bellum

Editors
Sergey Sayapin
School of Law
KIMEP University
Almaty, Kazakhstan

Evhen Tsybulenko
Tallinn University of Technology
Tallinn Law School
Tallinn, Estonia

ISBN 978-94-6265-221-7   ISBN 978-94-6265-222-4   (eBook)
https://doi.org/10.1007/978-94-6265-222-4

Library of Congress Control Number: 2018945449

Published by T.M.C. ASSER PRESS, The Hague, The Netherlands www.asserpress.nl
Produced and distributed for T.M.C. ASSER PRESS by Springer-Verlag Berlin Heidelberg

Printed on acid-free paper

This T.M.C. ASSER PRESS imprint is published by the registered company Springer-Verlag GmbH, DE part of Springer Nature
The registered company address is: Heidelberger Platz 3, 14197 Berlin, Germany

Foreword

The current conflict in Ukraine has had tremendous repercussions both on the individuals living in the affected territory and around the world. The 'Maidan' protests which began in November of 2013 as a response to the decision of Ukraine's pro-Russian former President Viktor Yanukovych not to sign an association agreement with the European Union set off a chain of events that not only toppled Yanukovych from power, but also provoked a furious Russian response that ultimately led to Crimea's annexation by the Russian Federation[1] and a war in Eastern Ukraine.

The twenty chapters of this book, *The Use of Force against Ukraine and International Law: Jus ad Bellum, Jus in Bello, Jus post Bellum*, represent an impressive attempt to address the legal and practical challenges posed by this difficult state of affairs. This book nuances the readers' understanding of the conflict, taking the perspective of those on the receiving end. Instead of involving authors only from Russia and Ukraine, a choice justified perhaps by the rawness and ongoing nature of the conflict, this book assembles a wide variety of scholars from around the world to address the complexities of Crimea's sudden incorporation into the Russian Federation and the conflict in Eastern Ukraine. It goes beyond *complaining* about the international illegality of the Russian Federation's activities to *explaining* how the Russian Federation has, for the most part, not dismissed international law as irrelevant, but has indeed endeavoured to explain it away or even redefine it. As one of the editor's notes, this represents a real challenge to both the content and the relevance of international law today.

Russia's annexation of Crimea resulted in dramatic legal changes for all of its formerly Ukrainian citizens: their currency, passports, rules regarding medical and social services, freedom of migration, freedoms of the press and the rights of assembly all were modified by a new legislative regime. President Vladimir Putin and Crimea's leadership signed agreements on 3 April 2014 making Crimea and the

---

[1] Office of the Prosecutor, Rep. on Preliminary Examinations 2017, 84–87 (4 December 2017) [hereinafter 2017 Preliminary Examinations Rep.].

city of Sevastopol part of the Russian Federation, and Russian legislation on the annexation of Crimea and Sevastopol became the vehicle for the extension of the entire corpus of Russian domestic law to the territory. Henceforth, all matters taking place in or in relation to the territory were subject to Russia's domestic jurisdiction and governed by Russian administrative bodies including its law enforcement authorities, judicial system and legislature. After annexing Crimea, Russian authorities expedited the issuance of Russian passports for the residents of the peninsula. As several authors noted, individuals who refused to take Russian nationality were allegedly subject to discrimination, while those who opposed the annexation, and certain minority groups, were subject to persecution. The International Criminal Court Prosecutor's Preliminary Examination 2017 Report contains allegations of disappearances, killings, ill-treatment, forced conscription, deprivation of fair trial rights, transfer of population from the Russian Federation into Crimea, seizure of property and alleged harassment of the Crimean Tatar population.[2] Although the absorption of Crimea by the Russian Federation was rapid and the numbers of specific violent crimes are not high, the overall impact of Crimea's integration into the Russian Federation has been enormous, causing financial and psychological harm in addition to the specific harms detailed above.

In Eastern Ukraine, the struggle between government and anti-government forces (allegedly supported by the Russian Federation) has already resulted in more than 10,000 deaths and 25,000 injuries, including thousands of civilians, and the alleged commission of war crimes including illegal detentions, torture and ill-treatment, sexual and gender-based violence, and disappearances.[3] This conflict continues today and threatens Ukraine as well as its neighbours.

Given the scope and magnitude of this ongoing conflict, the importance of this timely volume cannot be overstated. The first seven chapters discuss issues relating to the *jus ad bellum*, or the legality and characterisation of the conflict itself. The next, and longest section, Chaps. 8 through 15, discusses issues involving the *jus in bello*, although there is some overlap between Parts I and II and some chapters are concerned less with the *laws of war* than with the conduct of war itself, particularly in terms of the use of information warfare and cyber-operations by the Russian Federation and its surrogates. Finally, Chaps. 16 through 20 address issues involving the *jus post bellum,* largely in terms of the potential activity of the International Criminal Court (ICC).

Chapter 1, written by Miras Daulenov, sets the stage with a classic exposition of the law of the UN Charter on the use of force, as well as specific international agreements between the Russian Federation and Ukraine regarding the inviolability of the latter's borders, as well as the 1994 Budapest Memorandum on Security Assurances with Ukraine, Belarus, Kazakhstan and the Russian Federation, USA and the UK. Both he and Oleksandr Merezhko in Chap. 5 address the thorny question of the conflict's characterisation as international or non-international. Both

---

[2] *Id.* 96–103.
[3] *Id.* 104–110.

authors conclude in the light of the facts, treaties and customary law at play that both the conflict in Eastern Ukraine and the annexation of Crimea are international in nature. The International Criminal Court prosecutor has agreed with this assessment as to the situation involving Crimea,[4] but has thus far demurred regarding the conflict in Eastern Ukraine which it found to be as 'non-international' in nature, even as it 'continues to examine allegations that the Russian Federation has exercised overall control over armed groups in eastern Ukraine'.[5]

All the authors in this section conclude that Russia's annexation of Crimea was unlawful and that the presence of several thousand troops of the Russian armed forces in the east of Ukraine not only violates international law but represents a serious threat to peace and stability in Europe, and to the continued territorial integrity of Ukraine. They observe that the international community has, nearly unanimously, refused to recognise any new States emanating from Ukraine, noting that only a handful of States have 'joined' Russia in either backing the Crimean 'referendum' or actively opposing measures supporting Ukraine's territorial identity.[6] (Tymur Korotkyi and Nataliia Hendel offer a reprise of this argument in Chap. 7.)

Valentina Azarova picks up this theme in Chap. 3, arguing that 'a third state that recognised as lawful the illegal situation [...] would itself attract responsibility in international law'. Her chapter focuses not so much on the status of the conflict (as international or non-international), but on the effect of the conflict on the obligations of third-party States, concluding that because the 'annexing state is not permitted to extend international treaties to which it is a party, or benefits thereunder, to the annexed territory', as a consequence, 'third states must ensure that their dealings with an annexing state do not extend to the foreign territory it seeks to illegally annex'. She concludes that international law's 'foremost concern is to reverse the situation of suffering that results in the continuous production of violations [...] States and international organisations are charged with the heavy lifting necessary to achieve these ends by upholding these obligations in their transactions with the occupying state and its subordinate authorities. Third states have a public right and duty to seek an end to such situations of foreign territorial control through international cooperation under a standard of due diligence; the mere refusal to admit unlawful revisions to the status of the occupied territory is insufficient to put an end to an illegal territorial regime'.

---

[4] *Id.* 88.

[5] *Id.* 95.

[6] One hundred countries voted for UNGA Resolution 68/262, which reaffirmed the General Assembly's commitment to the territorial integrity of Ukraine within its international recognised borders. Eleven States voted against, fifty-eight abstained and twenty-four were absent. G.A. Res. 68/262, 80th Plenary Meeting, U.N. Doc. A/RES/68/262 (March 27, 2014). As one author has noted, States supporting Putin's position were either isolated regimes such as Cuba, North Korea, Syria, Sudan and Zimbabwe or 'post-Soviet autocracies'. Casey Michael, *Will Trump Recognize Russian Annexation of Crimea?*, THE DIPLOMAT, (January 9, 2017), https://thediplomat.com/2017/01/will-trump-recognize-russian-annexation-of-crimea/.

In *Conferral of Nationality of the Kin State—Mission Creep?*, Sabine Hassler and Noëlle Quénivet take up another aspect of Russia's intervention in Crimea arguing that the Russian Federation's policy of facilitating acquisition of Russian nationality combined with a nationalist discourse has allowed it to intervene in the internal affairs of neighbouring States by conferring nationality on individuals with a view to offering them diplomatic protection, then using force under the idea of protection of nationals abroad and, finally, annexing a part of the territory of another State. They suggest that contemporary international law 'has constrained Russia in its long-standing ability to influence neighbouring States and create a buffer zone around it so much that it has reverted to a pre-WWII policy of kin-State activism through the use of "nationality", potentially threatening the end of the post-WWII order in Europe, and in particular the Baltic states'.

This thoughtful chapter illuminates the wisdom, as seen in hindsight, of *Nottebohm's* distinction between nationality as defined under municipal law and the international validity of a State's assessment regarding whom it may extend diplomatic protection. As the authors' note, 'there seems little doubt that Russia uses nationality as a political, economic, and cultural tool of expansionism'. They suggest three phases to this strategy: *first*, 'conferral of nationality by way of passportisation to those identifying as Russian in Baltic states and Georgia'; *second* the use of force to protect these 'new' nationals abroad, in Georgia, for example; and *third* 'the use of force to acquire neighbouring territory on which Russians are living in order to recreate zones of influence'. This chapter suggests that the tendency of other States to use a 'self-defence' rubric to justify protection of their nationals abroad, such as the Israeli evocation of it in the *Entebbe* case and the US arguments in favour of the invasion of Grenada, should be treated with the utmost caution, as incidents justified, if at all, by extreme necessity, as opposed to an inherent rule of customary international law under Article 51 of the UN Charter.[7] William Burke-White makes a similar point in *Crimea and the International Legal Order*, arguing

> In claiming the legality of its actions, but twisting the law in subtle (and not so subtle) ways, Russia is taking a card straight from America's playbook. [...] In Crimea, Russia is, perhaps for the first time since the Soviet Union, asserting itself as a renewed hub for a particular interpretation of international law, one that challenges the balance at the heart of the post-Second World-War order and the ability of the US to lead that order.[8]

In *Legal Challenges in Hybrid Warfare Theory and Practice: Is There a Place for Legal Norms at All?*, Gergely Tóth argues that the Russian Federation is using 'hybrid' or 'asymmetric warfare' to achieve its ends in Ukraine, thereby blurring the

---

[7] In a similar vein, Bill Bowring suggests that the justification for annexation of a 'right to self-determination by the people of Crimea' is unpersuasive. In his view, the only 'people' potentially having such a right would be the Crimean Tatars, who would potentially have such a right as an indigenous Turkic people. Bill Bowring, Chap. 2 in this Volume.

[8] William W. Burke-White, *Crimea and the International Legal Order*, U. Pa L. Sch. 2 (Fac. Scholarship Paper 1360, 2014).

space between war and peace. Unlike the so-called US 'war on terror' in which a small but feisty adversary who does not respect the traditions of the *jus in bello* is thought to asymmetrically attack a large, otherwise compliant adversary, the use of the term 'hybrid' or 'asymmetric' warfare in this volume, as also suggested by Olga Butkevych (Chap. 9), centres upon the fact that

> Military aggression is just one element of the Russian hybrid warfare against Ukraine. Other elements encompass: (1) propaganda based on lies and falsifications; (2) trade and economic pressure; (3) energy blockade; (4) terror and intimidation of Ukrainian citizens; (5) cyber-attacks; (6) a strong denial of the very fact of war against Ukraine despite large scope of irrefutable evidence; (7) use of pro-Russian forces and satellite states in its own interests; (8) blaming the other side for its own crimes.[9]

According to Toth and Butkevych, hybrid conflicts involve multilayered efforts designed to destabilise a functioning State and polarise its society. Unlike conventional warfare, the 'centre of gravity' in hybrid warfare is a target population. The adversary tries to influence influential policy-makers and key decision-makers by combining kinetic operations with subversive efforts. They argue that aggressors will often resort to clandestine actions, to avoid attribution or retribution.

Jozef Valuch discusses the conflict in terms of cyber-operations. As he notes in Chap. 10, non-destructive cyber-operations, like the attacks on the confidence of the national government, do not involve the use of force, at least according to the *Tallinn Manual on the International Law Applicable to Cyber Warfare*, which suggests that cyber-operations involve the use of force only when their 'scale and effects are comparable to a non-cyber operation rising to the level of a use of force'.[10] This does not mean, however, that cyber-operations which do not include the use of force are consistent with international law. They may be prohibited by rules such as the principle of non-intervention, which forms part of the principle of the sovereign equality of States and is embodied in Article 2(1) of the UN Charter. The principle of non-intervention is also part of customary international law and according to the *Nicaragua* case 'forbids all states or groups of states to intervene directly or indirectly in the internal or external affairs of other states'.[11] He distinguishes the attacks in Ukraine as involving largely 'political and ideological effect', from those carried out presumably by the Russian Federation in Georgia, which were more closely allied, in his view, with military operations and therefore more clearly fell within the ambit of the laws of war.

In Chap. 11, *Foreign Fighters in the Framework of International Armed Conflict between Russia and Ukraine*, Anastasia Frolova considers whether international humanitarian lawfully addresses the complexities presented by the high level of foreign nationals' involvement in the ongoing conflict on Ukrainian territory. The

---

[9] Olga Butkevych, Chap. 9 in this Volume.

[10] TALLINN MANUAL ON THE INTERNATIONA LAW APPLICABLE TO CYBER WARFARE, Rule 11 (Michael N. Schmitt ed., 2013).

[11] Military and Paramilitary Activities in and Against Nicaragua (Nicar. v. U.S.), Judgment, 1986 I.C.J. Rep. 14, at 202-05. (June 27).

chapter notes certain ambiguities in outlining the parameters of the term, as well as difficulties with the application of international humanitarian law in cases of foreign fighters taken into either Ukrainian or Russian units. She points out, for example, that Belarus nationals—who formed part of the so-called Pahonia unit fighting on behalf of Ukraine—might not have protected status under the Third or Fourth Geneva Convention if captured by Russia if it can be argued that Russia usually exercises diplomatic protection over them. In such cases, she notes that international human rights law may provide a 'safety net'.

The plight of children afflicted by the conflict in Ukraine is taken in Chap. 12, *Children and the Armed Conflict in Eastern Ukraine*, penned by Natalia Krestovska. She notes the toll of the war on children, many of whom have been killed or wounded, and thousands more have been internally displaced. Children's living standards, educational attainment, health and security have been negatively affected by the conflict in violation of international humanitarian law and human rights law.

In Chap. 13, on the *International Legal Dimensions of the Russian Occupation of Crimea*, Evhen Tsybulenko and Bogdan Kelichavyi develop further the complications of Russia's occupation in terms of the legal regimes applicable to the annexed territory and the lives of the inhabitants there. As Butkevych's earlier chapter notes, the legal relationship between Russia and Ukraine and between individuals living in Crimea and both governments has been upended by the war. Butkevych observes that there were more than 350 treaties between Ukraine and the Russian Federation, the operation of which has largely been suspended or terminated, in many cases wrongfully, as a result of the armed conflict between them. Tsybulenko and Kelichavyi note that this has imposed real challenges to individuals currently living in Crimea as well as those displaced, who may have lost their passports, property rights, rights to social services and even political freedoms. Moreover, in response, Ukraine derogated from both the European Convention on Human Rights and the International Covenant on Civil and Political Rights, invoking special restrictions to the right to liberty and security, right to a fair trial, right to respect for private and family life, right to an effective remedy, freedom of movement in the territory of 'certain areas of the Donetsk and Luhansk *oblasts* of Ukraine'. Thus, the protection of human rights for all the individuals living in Ukraine (including Crimea) has been compromised. A particular worry evoked by this chapter, as well as Bowring's earlier essay on the fate of the Crimean Tatars (Chap. 2), is that the Russian invasion has put the Tatars of Crimea again 'on the brink of extinction', evoking the possibility that violation of the Genocide Convention may be in play. Ukraine, as they note, has turned to international legal institutions to make its case, submitting two declarations to the International Criminal Court relating to the conflict; applying to the European Court of Human

Rights for relief; initiating proceedings against Russia under the UN Convention on the Law of the Sea; and filing a claim against the Russian Federation with the International Court of Justice.[12]

In Chap. 14, Sergii Pakhomenko, Kateryna Tryma and J'moul A. Francis note the importance of 'historical memory' as a weapon of war, explaining that the Russian Federation has characterised its annexation of Crimea as restoring a 'historical right' and its aggression in the Donbas region of Ukraine as part of a struggle against fascism (evoking the Soviet Union's struggle against Nazism during WWII). While it may or may not be correct, as the authors' claim, that the 'possible destructive effects' of this historical revisionism are more harmful than those which took place in other twentieth-century European conflicts, it is likely that they helped to solidify the aggression that did take place much more quickly than in the past.

Picking up on this theme, Sergey Sayapin discusses a legal effort by the Russian Federation to influence and distort history by investigating an alleged 'genocide of Russian-speaking persons' in Eastern Ukraine allegedly masterminded and carried out by Ukrainian's 'supreme political and military leadership, Ukraine's Armed forces, and Ukraine's national guard [...]'. Sayapin discusses the Russian Investigative Committee's 'faulty interpretation of groups protected by the definition of the crime of genocide and Russia's abusive exercise of jurisdiction in the case at hand'. As he notes, the Genocide Convention protects 'national' and 'ethnic' groups, and although language can be an indicator of nationality or ethnicity, 'Russian language speakers' as such are not a group protected under the Convention. Russia's strategy is also problematic in terms of its potential impact in other CIS States, as under Russian law, virtually all nationals and permanent residents in each of the CIS fifteen States that formerly comprised the Soviet Union could be considered 'compatriots abroad'. This permits Russia to promote and even insist upon the use of the Russian language in countries, such as Kazakhstan, which are challenging it and, combined with the (allegedly) extraterritorial application of Russian criminal law to this alleged 'genocide' in Ukraine, permits Russia to engage in a form of legal warfare (dubbed 'hybrid law enforcement' by the author) that accompanies the acts of physical violence and territorial conquest discussed in other chapters.

In Chap. 16, Gerhard Kemp and Igor Lyubashenko address the conflict in the Donbas region of Ukraine in terms of *International, regional and comparative perspectives of the* jus post bellum *options*. Their project is to canvas the broad fields of 'post-conflict justice and transitional justice', in considering responses to the conflict. They suggest that criminal remedies should be 'exceptional' rather than

---

[12]Subsequent to the writing of this chapter, the Court found that Russia must refrain from imposing limitations on the ability of the Crimean Tatar community to conserve its representative institutions, including the Mejlis, and ensure the availability of education in the Ukrainian language. Application of the International Convention for the Suppression of the Financing of Terrorism and of the International Convention on the Elimination of All Forms of Racial Discrimination (Ukr. v. Russ.), Request for the Indication of Provisional Measures, 2017 I.C.J. No. 166, 106 (April 19).

a primary response to serious violations of human rights and that peace and the right to truth are overriding objectives. They conclude that peace and justice are not contradictory and conflicting forces, but promote and sustain each other, and that both 'should play some role, with sustainable peace as the baseline outcome'. They worry that the hybrid nature of the conflict may be 'a significant constraint on the goal of peace' because it 'effectively conceals the international dimension of the conflict' and poses an obstacle to truth. The focus on truth as one of the primary casualties of the conflict is reinforced by the final chapter of this volume, *Post-Conflict Reconstruction of Trust in the Media*, written by Katrin Merike Nyman-Metcalf, who notes that creating trust in media, in a time of 'post-truth' and 'fake news' is particularly challenging. She catalogues the struggles Ukraine is facing with propaganda, intimidation of journalists, lack of access to information and other difficulties but concludes that the best response is to vigorously protect freedom of information.

Three chapters focus on the possibility of an International Criminal Court intervention into the situation in Ukraine. Beatrice Onica Jarka takes up the ICC's preliminary examination of the situation, noting the two Article 12(3) declarations filed by Ukraine regarding alleged crimes committed in its territory (i) from 21 November 2013 to 22 February 2014 in the first instance and (ii) from 20 February 2014 onwards in the second instance. Her analysis covers the Preliminary Examination Reports from 2014, 2015 and 2016. While she is sympathetic to the ICC's possible intervention, she suggests that by filing Article 12(3) declarations rather than ratifying the Statute as a whole, Ukraine may have hurt its cause and may have provoked the Russian Federation into formally withdrawing its signature from the Rome Statute.[13]

Rustam Atadjanov's chapter, *War Crimes Committed during the Armed Conflict in Ukraine: What Should the ICC Focus On?*, adds to Jarka's chapter by examining the possible violations of the laws of war that may have been—and continue to be —committed—as a result of the conflict. Atadjanov notes the temptation to see the conflict as 'frozen', dooming the region itself (particularly in Donbas) to becoming a 'long-term frozen zone' in which 'living standards are inferior, virtually no government support for the population can be found and no normal societal development is possible'. In Chap. 19, Ioannis Tzivaras complements Atadjanov by focusing on the possible application of the Rome Statute to crimes involving sexual violence in Ukraine. His chapter discusses the possibility not only of war crimes charges but the possibility of crimes against humanity as well.

This book reveals a complex and sad struggle for control of Eastern Ukraine and Crimea, pitting Ukraine's government on the one hand and the Russian Federation and its allies and surrogates on the other. While the picture it paints is incomplete—

---

[13]Russia withdrew its signature from the ICC Statute just days after the prosecutor issued a report stating that the conflict in Ukraine amounted to an international armed conflict with Ukraine and the Russian Federation with respect to Crimea that represents an 'ongoing state of occupation'. Robbie Gramer, *Why Russia Just Withdrew from the ICC*, FOREIGN POL'Y (November 16, 2016), http://foreignpolicy.com/2016/11/16/why-russia-just-withdrew-from-icc-putin-treaty-ukraine-law/.

capturing the conflict at a particular point in time and leaving out some of the historical and geopolitical context—it is an extraordinarily useful collection of essays on how international law and international legal institutions interact with the use of force. In making its case for the annexation of Crimea and the conflict in Eastern Ukraine, the Russian Federation used international law, twisting it to its advantage and often bending the facts to fit the law. Ukraine has responded with force where it can, but more importantly has sought refuge in international law, mustering a host of international legal institutions and strategies to shore up its position against a much larger and militarily more powerful adversary: actions before the International Criminal Court, the International Court of Justice, the UN General Assembly, the UN Tribunal on the Law of the Sea and human rights bodies in Europe and in Geneva. The ability of international law, international legal institutions and effective diplomacy to resolve the crisis in Ukraine will be a test of its efficacy and resiliency. Both States have tried to use the media to sway public opinion to them; Russia may have prevailed inside the Russian Federation, but it is clear that Ukraine has the sympathies of most of the rest of the world, at least for the time being. The conflict is currently considered a stalemate, and although fighting continues, sanctions on Russia, such as its removal from the G8 in 2014, and a tentative rapprochement of Ukraine with NATO have helped strengthen Ukraine's position. The election of US President Donald Trump, with his pro-Putin leanings, gave rise to speculation that the USA might recognise the annexation of Crimea by Russia, but thus far that has not happened. This book thus appears at a critical time in which the legal consequences of Russian activities are under scrutiny by courts and international organisations around the world, and these activities combined with effective international diplomacy might help to thaw this otherwise 'frozen' conflict and redress some of its more pernicious effects. The authors, and the two co-editors, are to be commended for this important contribution.

St. Louis, USA   Leila N. Sadat
James Carr Professor of International
Criminal Law, Director, Whitney R. Harris
World Law Institute, Washington
University in St. Louis

Preface

The effects of Crimea's occupation and illegal annexation by the Russian Federation since early 2014, and of the ensuing Russian aggression in Eastern Ukraine, extend far beyond Ukraine's borders. In the Commonwealth of Independent States (CIS), this ongoing armed conflict is dividing entire peoples into 'pro-Russians' and 'pro-Ukrainians'. Individuals' daily lives are affected by broken friendships, and new friendships are made on the basis of respective affiliations. A rephrased version of a well-known Russian proverb[14] emerged and became quite popular over the past three years: 'Tell me whom Crimea belongs to, and I will tell you who you are'. On the international plane, most States and international organisations—*inter alia*, the UN, PACE, OSCE—aligned themselves with Ukraine, and sanctions against the Russian Federation were introduced, notably, by the USA, the European Union, Japan and some other States. In response, the Russian Federation introduced so-called countersanctions against States, which had introduced the 'original' sanctions against it,[15] empowered its Constitutional Court, in violation of the European Convention on Human Rights, to authorise (or decline authorising) the enforcement of the European Court of Human Rights' decisions on its territory,[16] and put in question the validity of international law as such, as a threat to its national sovereignty.[17] Some commentators went even further and asserted that, at this time, 'international law was absolutely not there [and] only the law of the strong [would] work',[18] whereas others, including a co-editor of the present volume, by contrast, regarded the armed conflict between Russia and Ukraine as a challenge to international law, which could make this law ever stronger.[19]

---

[14]The original proverb is as follows: 'Tell me who your friend is, and I will tell you who you are'.

[15]See Reuters (2017).

[16]See Roudik (2016).

[17]See BBC (2015).

[18]See Knyazev (2014).

[19]See *passim* Sayapin (2015).

This volume's co-editors were lucky to assemble a diverse team of authors from Europe, Asia, Africa and the Caribbean, who agreed to share their expert opinions on selected legal issues related to the ongoing armed conflict between Russia and Ukraine, with a common understanding that (1) the resulting volume would represent both internal and external perspectives—that is, the conflict would be reflected upon by authors from within and outside Ukraine, for the sake of scholarly objectivity; (2) the volume would cover the armed conflict in its three international legal dimensions—*jus ad bellum, jus in bello* and *jus post bellum*—with a view to identifying challenges that 'hybrid warfare' is posing in each of these dimensions; and (3) the opinions reflected in the respective chapters would be expressed for the purpose of this book project and should not be identified with anything said or written by the authors or co-editors elsewhere. It is also understood that all contributing authors were guided by academic freedom, and hence the co-editors do not necessarily share the views expressed in individual chapters.

Part I considers, from a variety of perspectives, the illegality of Russia's use of force against Ukraine in Crimea and Donbas. Miras Daulenov's inaugurating chapter recalls Russia's fundamental obligation under applicable international law not to have used force against Ukraine. Bill Bowring's and Valentina Azarova's chapters focus on aspects of Russia's use of force in Crimea. In the next chapter, Sabine Hassler and Noëlle Quénivet test the validity of Russia's claim to use force against Ukraine to protect 'nationals' abroad. Oleksandr Merezhko and Evhen Tsybulenko with J'moul A. Francis conclude Part I by analysing Russia's breach of the prohibition of the use of force in Eastern Ukraine.

Part II deals with selected issues of *jus in bello*, as applicable to the armed conflict between Russia and Ukraine. Gergely Tóth analyses the legal challenges posed by 'hybrid warfare'—an idea echoed, in their respective chapters, by Ondrej Hamulak and Jozef Valuch (in the chapter on cyber-attacks in the light of applicable international law) and by Sergii Pakhomenko and Kateryna Tryma (in the chapter on historical memory as an instrument of information warfare). The other chapters in Part II deal with the operation of treaties and international contracts in the context of Russia's aggression against Ukraine (by Olga Butkevych); with the participation of foreign fighters in the armed conflict between Russia and Ukraine (by Anastasia Frolova); with the plight of children in the armed conflict in Eastern Ukraine (by Nataliia Krestovska); with the international legal dimensions of Russia's occupation of Crimea (by Evhen Tsybulenko and Bogdan Kelichavyi); and with the 'hybrid' application of international criminal law against Ukrainian nationals accused of a 'genocide of the Russian-speaking persons' in Eastern Ukraine (by Sergey Sayapin).

Part III seeks to look beyond the end of the conflict in that it deals with issues of *jus post bellum*. Gerhard Kemp and Igor Lyubashenko consider possible models of post-conflict justice, which could be used in Ukraine. Beatrice Onica Jarka and Rustam Atadjanov study, in their respective chapters, the International Criminal Court's jurisdiction with respect to the core crimes under international law (with a focus on war crimes) committed during the armed conflict in Ukraine. Ioannis Tzivaras identified sexual violence in the conflict as a challenge to international criminal justice. Finally, Katrin Merike Nyman-Metcalf's chapter considers the post-conflict reconstruction of trust in the media.

The Appendix contains links to the most significant resolutions adopted by international organisations and institutions and dealing with various aspects of the armed conflict between Russia and Ukraine, as well as Sergey Sayapin's *amicus* memorandum in defence of Nadiya Savchenko.

The co-editors take this occasion to thank all contributors wholeheartedly for their excellent work. English language editors at Academic Proofreading Services Ltd. trading as www.englishproofread.com were very helpful in proofreading selected chapters. The Department of Law of the Tallinn University of Technology should be credited for taking over a part of proofreading costs. A very special word of thanks is due to Professor Leila Sadat, Special Adviser on Crimes against Humanity to the Prosecutor of the International Criminal Court and James Carr Professor of International Criminal Law at Washington University School of Law, for her supportive Foreword.

Last but not least, the co-editors sincerely thank Mr Frank Bakker, Ms Kiki van Gurp and Ms Antoinette Wessels at T.M.C. Asser Press for their excellent support throughout the publication process.

This volume is dedicated to the memory of Professor Oleksandr Zadorozhny, former President of the Ukrainian Association of International Law. Professor Zadorozhny taught and inspired many scholars and practitioners of international law in Ukraine and abroad, including both co-editors of this volume and several contributing authors. Professor Zadorozhny was invited, and agreed, to contribute a chapter to this book but passed away before this book was completed. He will remain in our memory as a patriot of sovereign Ukraine and a brilliant scholar and mentor.

Almaty, Kazakhstan   Sergey Sayapin
Tallinn, Estonia   Evhen Tsybulenko
July 2018

References

BBC (2015) "Bastrykin predlizhil ubrat mezhdunarodnoye pravo iz konstitutsii" [Bastrykin suggested to remove international law from the Constitution], http://www.bbc.com/russian/rolling_news/2015/07/150724_rn_bastrykin_law. Accessed 10 August 2017

Knyazev A (2014) "Vozmozhen li eksport 'tsvetnoy revolyutsii' v Uzbekistan?" [Is the export of a "colour revolution" to Uzbekistan possible?], https://zonakz.net/2014/11/27/vozmozhen-li-ehksport-cvetnojj-revoljucii-v-uzbekistan/. Accessed 10 August 2017

Reuters (2017) "Putin extends Russian counter sanctions until end of 2018", http://www.reuters.com/article/us-ukraine-crisis-russia-sanctions-idUSKBN19L1P2. Accessed 10 August 2017

Roudik P (2016) "Russian Federation: Constitutional Court Allows Country to Ignore ECHR Rulings", http://www.loc.gov/law/foreign-news/article/russian-federation-constitutional-court-allows-country-to-ignore-echr-rulings/. Accessed 10 August 2017

Sayapin S (2015) "Neizvestnoe izvestnoe mejdunarodnoe pravo" [The Unknown Known International Law], Ukrainian Journal of International Law, 1:34–40

Contents

Contributors

Rustam Atadjanov LLB, LLM, is a Graduate of the Karakalpak State University, Uzbekistan, and University of Connecticut School of Law, USA, with the main focus on International Human Rights Law. Formerly a Legal Adviser at the Regional Delegation of the International Committee of the Red Cross (ICRC) in Central Asia (2007–2014) dealing with international humanitarian law and public international law issues. He presently is a Dr. iur. Candidate in International Criminal Law (with a focus on crimes against humanity) at the University of Hamburg, Germany.

Valentina Azarova LLB (Honours), CDT, Ph.D., is a Postdoctoral Fellow at the Centre for Global Public Law, Koç University, and a Legal Adviser to the Global Legal Action Network (GLAN), a collective challenging transnational government and corporate activities that contribute to abuses. She formerly was Director of the Human Rights Programme and Lecturer at Al-Quds Bard College, Al-Quds University and Birzeit University, Palestine. She has worked with and advised civil society working on Palestine for close to a decade and published extensively on international law issues including occupation and third-state responsibility with a focus on the context.

Bill Bowring is Professor of Human Rights and International Law at Birkbeck, University of London. His first degree was in Philosophy, from the University of Kent. He has been at Birkbeck since 2006. He previously taught at University of East London, University of Essex and London Metropolitan University. As a practising barrister since 1974, he has represented applicants before the European Court of Human Rights in many cases since 1992, especially against Turkey and Russia. He has over 100 publications on topics of international law, human rights, minority rights, Russian law and philosophy. His latest book is *Law, Rights and Ideology in Russia: Landmarks in the Destiny of a Great Power* (Routledge 2013). He is President of the European Lawyers for Democracy and Human Rights (ELDH), with members in 18 European countries.

Olga Butkevych Dr. habil. is Professor of International Law at the International Law Department of the Institute of International Relations of Taras Shevchenko National University of Kyiv. In 1999, she earned an LLM degree (with honours) in international law from the same Institute. She co-authored ten collective monographs and authored four individual monographs and a manual on the history of international law, as well as over 100 publications on the history and theory of international law and human rights.

Miras Daulenov LLB, LLM, Ph.D., earned a Doctorate in Law from the University of Wroclaw, Poland. In 2009–2012, he worked at the University of Wroclaw's Department of International and European Law. In 2012–2015, he was Head of the Department of International Law at the Kazguu University, Astana, Kazakhstan, and is now Provost at the same University. He is a Member of the Advisory Council under the Economic Court of the Commonwealth of Independent States (CIS), of the Advisory Council under the Supreme Court of the Republic of Kazakhstan and of the Council of External Experts at the Department of Law, Economics and Administration of the University of Wroclaw. He is a critical reviewer of the *Wrocław Review of Law, Administration and Economics*, Poland, and of the *Law and State Journal*, Kazakhstan.

J'moul A. Francis is an Antiguan and Barbudan Law Graduate (*cum laude*) of the Tallinn University of Technology (TUT), specialising in European Union and International Law. His research interests include Public International Law, International Humanitarian Law, European Union Law, European Comparative Law, Constitutional Law, Contract Law, Legal Philosophy and Foreign Policy. He is the recipient of many awards to include receiving the Prime Minister's Scholarship Grant (Antigua and Barbuda) in 2014, being recognised as one of the four best freshmen students at Tallinn Law School (TLS) in 2015, and receiving the Performance-based Scholarship in 2015 and 2017. In the 2015–2016 academic year, he completed his Erasmus Year at Maastricht University, the Netherlands, where he mainly focused on European Union Law and European Comparative Law studies. Upon his return to TUT in 2016, he was one of three pleaders from the Tallinn Law School team that won the All-European International Humanitarian and Refugee Law Moot Court Competition 2016 in Ljubljana, Slovenia. He is also a law blogger and serves as an adjunct contributor to the 'Big Issues' programme on Observer Radio, Antigua, on European and International Affairs. In the 2017–2018, he will be pursuing postgraduate studies and research in his field of interests.

Anastasia Frolova is a Ph.D. student, University of Bern (Switzerland) and holds an LLM Degree from the Geneva Academy of International Humanitarian Law and Human Rights.

Ondrej Hamulak is a Senior Lecturer in EU Law at Faculty of Law, Palacký University Olomouc, Czech Republic, Visiting Professor at Tallinn Law School, TTU, Estonia, and Researcher at Faculty of Law, Comenius University in Bratislava, Slovakia. He earned the MA (2006), JUDr. (2010) and Ph.D. (2013) degrees from the Faculty of Law, Palacký University Olomouc. In recent

years, he underwent research visits and internships at Institute of Advanced Legal
Studies, London University (March 2014); Institute of European Law, Košice,
Slovakia (October and November 2014); and Institute of European and
Comparative Law, University of Oxford (February 2015). He has been teaching at
the Faculty of Law, Palacký University Olomouc, since 2006. Between 2013 and
2016, he served as vice-dean for public relations and development, Faculty of Law,
Palacký University Olomouc. Between 2010 and 2016, he held a position of
editor-in-chief of an academic journal *Acta Iuridica Olomucensia*. Nowadays, he is
responsible as an editor-in-charge for another academic journal, *International and
Comparative Law Review*. In his research, he focuses on the relations and interactions between EU law and national law, the theoretical impacts of the membership in the EU on the state sovereignty, the legitimacy and rule of law within the
EU, in particular system of protection of fundamental rights at supranational level.
He worked on several research and development projects.

Sabine Hassler (LLB (Hons) in European Comparative Law, LLM in International
Law, Ph.D.) is a Senior Lecturer in Law at the Department of Law, UWE Bristol.
She is the author of *Reforming the UN Security Council Membership: The illusion
of representativeness* (Routledge, 2012) and has contributed to the edition of the
Georgetown Journal of International Affairs celebrating the UN's anniversary:
'Accessing the world's most exclusive club—influencing decision-making on the
UN Security Council', 16(2) *Georgetown Journal of International Affairs*, 19–27.

Nataliia Hendel holds a Ph.D. in Law and is an Associate Professor of
International Law and International Relations at the National University 'Odessa
Law Academy' and is a Member of the Ministry of Justice's Interdepartmental
Commission for the Implementation of International Humanitarian Law in Ukraine.

Bogdan Kelichavyi earned an LLM degree from Tallinn University of
Technology.

Gerhard Kemp BA, LLB, LLM (Stellenbosch), ILSC (Antwerp), LLD
(Stellenbosch) is Professor of Law at Stellenbosch University, South Africa, and
Senior Research Fellow at Robert Bosch Stiftung, Berlin, Germany (2016/2017).
He is an Advocate of the High Court of South Africa and member of the board of
directors, Institute for Justice and Reconciliation, Cape Town.

Tymur Korotkyi holds a Ph.D. in Law and is an Associate Professor of
International Law and International Relations at the National University 'Odessa
Law Academy'. and is a Member of the Ministry of Justice of Ukraine's
Interdepartmental Commission for the Implementation of International
Humanitarian Law and Head of the Board of the Fundamental Research Support
Fund.

Natalia Krestovska Dr. habil. is Professor and Head of the Department of Theory
and History of Law at International Humanitarian University (Odessa, Ukraine).

Igor Lyubashenko is an Assistant Professor at the University of Social Sciences and Humanities (SWPS) in Warsaw. He holds a Ph.D. in Political Science from the Maria Curie-Sklodowska University in Lublin. His academic interests are various aspects of transition to democracy in post-communist states, in particular Poland and Ukraine. Previously, he worked as an analyst at the Polish Institute of International Affairs, focusing on politics and international relations in Eastern Europe.

Oleksandr Merezhko Dr. habil. is Professor of International Law at O. P. Jindal Global University, India.

Katrin Merike Nyman-Metcalf Ph.D. is a visiting Professor of Law and Technology at Tallinn University of Technology and Head of Research of the Estonian e-Governance Academy. She is active as an international consultant primarily in the area of information and communication technology law including freedom of expression, as well as e-governance. She obtained her Ph.D. (1999) in Public International Law (the law of outer space) and master's (1986) from the Uppsala University, Sweden. Her research interests include how law and technology meet with special emphasis on IT and communications.

Beatrice Onica Jarka is an Associate Professor of International Public and Humanitarian Law at University Nicolae Titulescu (Bucharest Romania), Attorney at Law and Coordinator of the Romania National/International Competition of International Humanitarian Law and Refugee Law, organized in cooperation with Romanian Red Cross Society, UNHCR – Romania, Romanian Army Centre for Humanitarian Law and National Commission of Humanitarian Law, www.concurstitulescu.ro.

Sergii Pakhomenko Ph.D. is an Associate Professor at the Department of International Relations and Foreign Policy, and the Department of Public Communications of the Mariupol State University. In 2005–2006, he was a Research Associate at the Institute of history of Ukraine, National Academy of sciences of Ukraine (Kiev).

Noëlle Quénivet (BA IEP Strasbourg (France), LLM Nottingham (UK), Ph.D. Essex (UK)) is an Associate Professor in International Law at the University of the West of England, UK. She has published several articles in international humanitarian law and international criminal law, authored *Sexual Offences in Armed Conflict in International Law* and co-edited two books, one on the relationship between international humanitarian law and human rights law and another on international law in armed conflict.

Sergey Sayapin LLB, LLM, Dr. iur. is an Assistant Professor in International and Criminal Law at KIMEP University's School of Law, Almaty, Kazakhstan, since 2014, and Director of the LLB in International Law Programme. In 2000–2014, he held a number of posts at the Regional Delegation of the International Committee of the Red Cross (ICRC) in Central Asia. His areas of expertise include international conflict and security law, international human rights and humanitarian law, and international criminal law. He authored *The Crime of Aggression in*

International Criminal Law: Historical Development, Comparative Analysis and Present State (T.M.C. Asser Press/Springer, 2014) and over 50 academic and publicist articles, chapters and essays. He is the Founding Editor-in-Chief of the *Central Asian Yearbook of International and Comparative Law.*

Gergely Tóth is a Doctor of Law, Eötvös Loránd University of Sciences, Budapest, and a Ph.D. candidate, National Public Service University, Budapest. He previously worked as a Legal Advisor at the Regional Delegation for Central Europe of the International Committee of the Red Cross (ICRC) and currently serves at Hungarian Ministry of Defence's Department for Coordination of Public Relations.

Kateryna Tryma holds a Ph.D. in Political Science and is a Senior Lecturer at Mariupol State University's Philosophy and Social Sciences Chair, Ukraine. She currently teaches the Theory of Politics (Political Science), Corporate Social Responsibility, Religious Factor in International Relations and Social Policy.

Evhen Tsybulenko is an Estonian Legal Scholar of Ukrainian descent. In 2000, he earned a Ph.D. in International Law from Kiev National University, Ukraine, and carried out postdoctoral research at the International Human Rights Law Institute of De Paul University, USA, in 2002. In Ukraine, he worked at the International Committee of the Red Cross (ICRC) and the Kyiv International University where he is a Professor since 2009. In Estonia, he was elected as a Professor of Law (2005) and appointed Chair of International and Comparative Law Department at the Tallinn University of Technology's Law School (2005–2010). He has been a researcher at the same School since 2010. He was a Founder and Director of the Tallinn Law School's Human Rights Centre (2007–2014). He is also an Adjunct (Visiting) Professor and Senior Visiting Mentor at the Joint Command and General Staff Course (JCGSC) at Baltic Defence College. He published over 40 books and academic articles and more than 200 general interest articles, comments and interviews in 15 countries, mainly in Russian or Ukrainian, but also in English and other languages. He cooperates, as an external expert, with the ICRC, Estonian Red Cross, Estonian Integration Commission, Directorate-General for Education and Culture of the European Commission, and the Organization for Security and Co-operation in Europe (OSCE).

Ioannis P. Tzivaras earned the LLM and Ph.D. degrees from the Faculty of Law at Democritus University of Thrace, Greece. He is a Tutor at the Open University of Cyprus' Department of Economics and Administration, and Deputy Director of Hellenic Institute for the United Nations.

Jozef Valuch Ph.D. is an Assistant Professor and Deputy Head of the Department of International Law and International Relations, Faculty of Law, Comenius University in Bratislava. He is the head of the group of authors of several textbooks in the field of public international law. He took part in several research stays abroad (Salzburg, Austria, 2011; Waseda, Japan, 2012; Tel Aviv, Israel 2014; Kaohsiung, Taiwan, 2016). He is a Member of the Slovak Society of International Law.

Part I
Jus ad Bellum

Chapter 1
The Legal Nature of States' Obligations Towards Ukraine in the Context of *Jus Contra Bellum*

Miras Daulenov

Contents

Abstract The development of the fundamental principles of international relations, which flow from the UN Charter, other treaties and international custom, has changed the understanding of the legal nature of states' international obligations. In this context, the 1994 Budapest Memorandum on Security Assurances is also a source of international obligations for the states involved. Given the importance of international community interests that are protected by *jus contra bellum*, the prohibition of the use of force can be regarded as a norm of *jus cogens*. The inherent right of states to self-defence is not covered by the scope of the prohibition of the use of force and cannot be understood as a derogation from the *jus cogens* norm. Finally, unilateral declarations of states may also have the effect of creating certain legal obligations in the context of *jus contra bellum*.

Keywords *jus contra bellum* · prohibition of the use of force · treaty · international custom · *jus cogens* · general principle · unilateral declaration · *erga omnes* · Ukraine

Miras Daulenov, University Lecturer, Director of the Academy of Legal and Economic Research, both at KAZGUU University, Astana, Kazakhstan, email: m_daulenov@kazguu.kz.

M. Daulenov (✉)
Academy of Legal and Economic Research, KAZGUU University, Astana, Kazakhstan
e-mail: m_daulenov@kazguu.kz

© T.M.C. ASSER PRESS and the authors 2018
S. Sayapin and E. Tsybulenko (eds.), *The Use of Force against Ukraine and International Law*, https://doi.org/10.1007/978-94-6265-222-4_1

1.1 The Meaning of *Jus Contra Bellum* in Current International Law

Since the earliest times, states have employed military force to pursue their political and economic objectives.[1] The use of armed force was one of the common measures taken by states in order to pressure less militarily and economically developed states, as well as non-state entities, such as self-governing cities and provinces. Frequently, wars and other armed conflicts involving several states at once were conducted over many years. Moreover, various sovereigns and men of state have launched wars based exclusively on personal reasons, rather than on account of their respective state's interests.

Since St. Thomas Aquinas explained the doctrine of a 'just war' in his *Summa Theologica*', the authority of a sovereign by whose command the war is conducted has become a matter of moral concern.[2] In his 1625 opus magnus *The Rights of War and Peace*, Grotius proposed that "the justifiable causes generally assigned for war are three, defence, indemnity, and punishment".[3]

Successively, however, the definitive establishment of a European balance of power system after the Peace of Westphalia and the corresponding emergence of legal positivism at a global level removed the doctrine of a 'just war' from international law as such.[4] This happened because of the strengthening and development of the principle of the sovereign equality of states. More precisely, the 'just war' doctrine's weak position was caused by a lack of any recognized international or even supranational authority, which was empowered to monitor and, in particular cases, decide upon whether or not the ethical 'standards' of a just war are met. States are equal in respect of their appurtenant sovereign rights, while there exists no lawful and recognized international authority that is competent to determine any legal consequences for a state in the case of an unjust war. Moreover, in the same way as Grotius' *jus ad bellum* doctrine (like other *jus ad bellum* doctrines) included first use of force as a natural element,[5] states have tried to justify their military actions by giving various doubtful reasons.

The 1919 Covenant of the League of Nations imposed on member states an obligation "not to resort to war".[6] Despite the fact that any war or threat of war was declared a matter of concern to the whole league,[7] the prohibition on the use of force was not provided by general international law or particular treaties at that time. A major step forward was taken by US Secretary of State Kellogg and French Foreign Minister Briand. The 1928 General Treaty for the Renunciation of War as an

---

[1] Higgins 2010, p. 238.

[2] Aquinas 1256, Q 40.

[3] Grotius 1625, Chapter I.

[4] Brownlie 1963, p. 14; Shaw 2014, p. 813.

[5] Bring 2000, p. 60.

[6] See 1919 Covenant of the League of Nations, Preamble, Articles 12 and 13.

[7] Ibid., Article 11.

Instrument of National Policy, also known as the Kellogg-Briand Pact, led to a significant transition from *jus ad bellum* to *jus contra bellum*.[8] Article I of the treaty provided that:

> The high contracting parties solemnly declare in the names of their respective peoples that they condemn recourse to war for the solution of international controversies and renounce it as an instrument of national policy in their relations with one another.[9]

This assertion was a starting point for the formation of the customary rule precluding the use of force except in self-defence as 'the inherent right' of states. After the cataclysmic events of the Second World War, it was thought necessary to further clarify, in the UN Charter, that force could only be used in self-defence, and not to pursue legal rights or genuinely held notions of justice.[10]

Article 2(4) of the UN Charter provides the following:

> All members shall refrain in their international relations from the threat or use of force against the territorial integrity or political independence of any state, or in any other manner inconsistent with the purposes of the UN.[11]

As was mentioned by the International Court of Justice (ICJ) in the *Nicaragua* case, the prohibition on the use of force in the UN Charter corresponds, in essential terms, to those found in customary international law.[12] In this case, the ICJ also confirmed that the 'natural' or 'inherent' right to self-defence provided by Article 51 of the Charter[13] reflects general international law,[14] and that "it is hard to see how this can be other than of a customary nature, even if its present content has been confirmed and influenced by the Charter".[15] The UN Charter, having itself recognized the existence of this right, does not, however, go onto directly regulate all aspects of its content.[16] Since the existence of the right to self-defence is established in customary international law, the ICJ has also noted that "whether the response to the attack is lawful depends on the observance of the criteria of the necessity and the proportionality of the measures taken in self-defence".[17]

---

[8] See also Dinstein 2017, p. 87–88.

[9] See 1928 General Treaty for Renunciation of War as an Instrument of National Policy, LNTS XCIV.

[10] Higgins 2010, p. 238.

[11] See 1945 Charter of the United Nations, 1 UNTS XVI.

[12] ICJ, *Case Concerning the Military and Paramilitary Activities in and against Nicaragua (Nicaragua v. United States), Judgment, 27 June 1986*, ICJ Reports 1986, p. 99.

[13] See UN Charter (fn. 11), Article 51. "Nothing in the present Charter shall impair the inherent right of individual or collective self-defence if an armed attack occurs against a Member of the United Nations, until the Security Council has taken measures necessary to maintain international peace and security. Measures taken by Members in the exercise of this right of self-defence shall be immediately reported to the Security Council and shall not in any way affect the authority and responsibility of the Security Council under the present Charter to take at any time such action as it deems necessary in order to maintain or restore international peace and security."

[14] See the discussion on 'general international law' by Tunkin 1993, pp. 534–47.

[15] ICJ, *Nicaragua* (fn. 12), p. 94.

[16] Idem.

[17] Ibid., p. 103.

The ruling of the ICJ in the *Nicaragua* case is indeed crucial. It has been confirmed that the prohibition on the use of force, as envisaged in the UN Charter and reflected in customary international law, does not cover situations in which states exercise their right to self-defence. An additional exception to the ambit of Article 2(4) of the UN Charter is authorization by the UN Security Council, which allows the use of force in response to threats to the peace, breach of the peace, or act of aggression. In such cases, states are authorized to take all necessary measures on behalf of the UN as an international organization.

Whilst the ICJ has refrained from recognizing the prohibition on the use of force as a whole, it is equally clear that aggression is prohibited under general international law.[18] Moreover, the UN General Assembly in 1974 held that "a war of aggression is a crime against international peace".[19] The further development of *jus ad bellum* as "the law governing the right to use of force"[20] or "the right of going to war"[21] by the prohibition of aggression as such, while the admission of self-defence under the conditions enshrined in the UN Charter, is considered as the result of an evolutionary process of crystallization of the concept of *jus contra bellum*. This concept, however, is somewhat distinct from pacifism as its proponents continue to operate within the parameters of just war thinking.[22] International humanitarian law (*jus in bello*) and 'the law after war' (*jus post bellum*) have also been further refined.

The law against war[23] was recognized as a source of rules common to the international community as a whole. The continuing development of *jus contra bellum* as limiting the scope of the use of force can be stripped down to three basic elements. First, aggression is prohibited as a crime against international peace and security. No consideration of whatever nature, whether political, economic, military or otherwise, may serve as a justification for aggression.[24] As a second element of this concept, self-defence will be considered to be lawful only if directed against aggression,[25] if proportionate and necessary in what it is seeking to achieve. Moreover, "states must take environmental considerations into account when assessing what is necessary and proportionate in the pursuit of legitimate military objectives".[26] Third, as reaction to threats to the peace, breaches of the peace, or acts of aggression, the UN Security Council is able to authorize one or more states to use force, but, once again, only to restore international peace and security.

---

[18] For a more extensive understanding of the crime of aggression, see Sayapin 2014.

[19] See UN General Assembly 1974, Resolution, Definition of Aggression, *UN Doc*. A/RES/3314.

[20] McCaffrey 2006, p. 236.

[21] Kant 1887, p. 53.

[22] Sharma 2009, p. 218.

[23] The term 'the law against war' is used, e.g., in Corten 2010.

[24] UN General Assembly Resolution (see fn. 18).

[25] Idem, Article 1. "Aggression is the use of armed force by a State against the sovereignty, territorial integrity or political independence of another State, or in any other manner inconsistent with the Charter of the United Nations, as set out in this Definition."

[26] ICJ, *Legality of the Threat or Use of Nuclear Weapons, Advisory Opinion, 8 July 1996*, ICJ Reports 1996, p. 242.

1.2 Treaties as a Source of *Inter Partes* Obligations

As Higgins indicated, international law is not just a set of particular rules. It is rather a normative order, that is to say, a system of normative conduct, which is regarded by each actor, and by the group as a whole, as being obligatory, and with violations carrying a price.[27] Treaties are still the main source of international obligations of states and other subjects of international law.[28] Citing Lord McNair, however, it would be a mistake to assume that every agreement between states, which adopts the form and language of a treaty, creates or is intended to create international legal obligations and is therefore strictly entitled to be classified as a treaty.[29] This possibility cannot be dismissed out of hand.

Article 38, para 1a, of the Statute of the ICJ frames the issue as follows:

The Court, whose function is to decide in accordance with international law such disputes as are submitted to it, shall apply international conventions, whether general or particular, establishing rules expressly recognized by the contesting states.[30]

The general sense of the given definition is to provide substance to the requirement that both universal law-making treaties establishing "general patterns of behaviour for the parties over a certain period of time in certain areas"[31] and bilateral agreements with a special subject matter have to be recognized as sources of international obligations. Nevertheless, unlike law-making treaties, it could be difficult to consider all bilateral agreements as sources of international law. In any case, in practice, the ICJ applies all relevant international agreements without pausing to examine the question about whether they fall within the technical concept of a 'convention'.[32] As long as 'contesting states' recognize such agreements as sources of their obligations towards each other, the court remains willing and available to resolve disputes between them by applying these agreements.

There is also a general understanding about the meaning of the term 'treaty', which involves the definition given by the 1969 Vienna Convention on the Law of Treaties (VCLT). According to Article 2, para 1a of the VCLT, 'treaty' means an international agreement concluded between states in written form and governed by international law, whether embodied in a single instrument or in two or more related instruments, irrespective of its particular designation.[33]

The VCLT uses 'treaty' as a generic term, and so includes treaties that may be described as universal or regional, intergovernmental, interministerial or administrative.[34] It also confirms that the number of legal instruments and the particular

---

[27] Higgins 2010, p. 1.

[28] Czapliński and Wyrozumska 2014, p. 56. See also Fitzmaurice and Quast 2007, p. 11.

[29] McNair 1961, p. 6.

[30] See the 1945 Statute of the ICJ, 33 UNTS 993.

[31] Fitzmaurice and Quast 2007, p. 12.

[32] Waldock 1962, p. 74.

[33] See 1969 Vienna Convention of the Law of Treaties, 1155 UNTS 331.

[34] Aust 2005, p. 52.

designation of an agreement are not decisive. For the purpose of establishing whether states have concluded a treaty imposing upon them international obligations, the substance of obligations is a more important criterion.

It is worth emphasizing that the VCLT restricts its definition of treaties to a specific context.[35] The VCLT is applicable to treaties concluded only 'between states' 'in written form' and 'governed by international law'. The first two elements of the definition have no influence on the legal force of agreements concluded between states and other subjects of international law, e.g., international organizations, or between such other subjects of international law, or to international agreements not in written form.[36] On the contrary, as the International Law Commission (ILC) stipulated in its commentary on the draft VCLT, the phrase 'governed by international law' serves to distinguish between international agreements regulated by public international law and those that, although concluded between states, are regulated by the national law of one of the parties (or by some other national law system chosen by the parties).[37]

The intention to create obligations under international law also differentiates treaties from agreements between states governed by domestic law.[38] As the ICJ established in the *Maritime Delimitation and Territorial Questions (Qatar v. Bahrain)* case, the intention of states to create treaty obligations governed by international law is a matter of objective determination. It means that even the position of a state's foreign ministry cannot alter the legal nature of a treaty imposing upon the contracting parties obligations regulated by international law.[39] In addition, the intention of states to create legal obligations under the provisions of a treaty depends on "the nature of the act or transaction" to which an agreement gives expression.[40]

The combined weight of the VCLT's approach and the ICJ's line of argumentation rests on a balance between material and procedural aspects as the constitutive elements of the definition of treaties in general international law. In this sense, a treaty refers to an international agreement concluded between international legal persons with the intention to create legal obligations governed by international law. This leaves the door open to recognition of some international agreements concluded between Ukraine and other subjects of international law as treaties.

Ukraine became a member of the UN in 1945. At the same time, Belarus, the Soviet Union and other founding states recognized the UN Charter as being not only a source of their international obligations, but also 'the constitutive treaty' of the international community.[41] The special character of the UN Charter flows from Article 103, which stipulates that, in the event of a conflict between the obligations

---

[35] Hollis 2012, p. 13.

[36] See VCLT (fn. 32), Article 3.

[37] International Law Commission 1966, p. 189.

[38] Aust 2013, p. 17.

[39] ICJ, *Maritime Delimitation and Territorial Questions (Qatar v. Bahrain), Judgment, 1 July 1994*, ICJ Reports 1994, pp. 121–2.

[40] ICJ, *Aegean Sea Continental Shelf Case (Greece v. Turkey), Judgment, 19 December 1978*, ICJ Reports 1978, p. 39.

[41] Kwiecień 2011, p. 169.

of UN members under the Charter and their obligations under any other international agreement, their obligations under the UN Charter shall prevail. On the one hand, this provision only covers *expressis verbis* treaty obligations of the UN members. On the other hand, it could expose the extent of the supremacy of the UN Charter *vis-à-vis* international agreements, which have been concluded between UN members and third countries that are not members of this organization, or agreements concluded between UN members and international organizations.

As already mentioned, the UN Charter, in Article 2(4), provides for the prohibition of the threat or use of force against the territorial integrity or political independence of any state, or in any other manner inconsistent with the purposes of the UN. The scope of application of the cited provision is broader than the prohibition of aggression. It covers not only the use of force, but also the threat of the use the force, which is outside the scope of the notion of aggression itself. On the other hand, the substance of the provision in question is limited by the intention to act against 'the territorial integrity' or 'political independence' of any state, or "in any other manner inconsistent with the purposes of the UN".

Given the particular reference to the purposes of the UN in Article 2(4) of its charter, it is worth taking into consideration the subsequent practice of the UN.[42] The 1970 Declaration on Principles of International Law defines the failure to refrain from the threat or use of force, as envisaged under Article 2(4) of the UN Charter, as a violation of international law and of the Charter itself. Moreover, it was noted that a war of aggression constitutes a crime against the peace, for which there is responsibility under international law.[43] The scope of application of Article 2(4) requires the prohibition of the use of force to be interpreted as also encompassing the duty not to violate existing international boundaries of states in order to resolve international disputes, including territorial disputes and problems concerning frontiers of states.

Commenting on Article 2(4) of the Charter, the UN General Assembly in its 1970 Declaration on Principles of International Law took the view that every state has the duty to refrain from organizing or encouraging the organization of irregular forces or armed bands, including mercenaries, for incursion into the territory of another state. Moreover, states are under the obligation to refrain from organizing, instigating, assisting or participating in acts of civil strife or terrorist acts in another state, or acquiescing in organized activities, within its territory, which are directed towards the commission of such acts, when the acts referred to in the present paragraph involve a threat or use of force. Perhaps the most important interpretation of Article 2(4) of the UN Charter, which might be applicable to the situation in Ukraine, is the recognition that the territory of a state shall not be the object of military occupation resulting from the use of force. For this reason, no territorial acquisition resulting

---

[42] See VCLT (fn. 32), Article 31, para 3b.

[43] See UN General Assembly 1970, Resolution, Declaration on Principles of International Law Concerning Friendly Relations and Co-operation among States in Accordance with the Charter of the United Nations, *UN Doc*. A/RES/25/2625.

from the threat or use of force shall be recognized as legal.[44] This reflects *ex injuria jus non oritur* as a general principle of international law.[45]

The importance of such subsequent practice in the application of the Charter by UN members represented at the UN General Assembly, as an element of its interpretation, is obvious. It constitutes objective evidence of the parties' understanding about the meaning of this 'constitutive treaty' of the international community.[46]

At the same time, Ukraine has concluded treaties with other states in the context of *jus contra bellum*. Such treaties shall be interpreted in good faith in accordance with the ordinary meaning to be given to the terms of the treaty in their context, and in light of its object and purpose.[47] As stated above, within this process of interpretation, account should be taken, together with the context of each treaty's provisions, of any subsequent practice in the application of that treaty.

Perhaps the most famous example of agreement concluded by Ukraine with other states in respect of *jus contra bellum* is the 1994 Budapest Memorandum on Security Assurances.[48] Identical agreements were also concluded with Belarus and Kazakhstan as guarantees in exchange for the elimination of all nuclear weapons from the territory of these states within a specified period of time.[49] Those memoranda were addressed to the UN Secretary-General.[50]

The 1994 Budapest Memorandum in para 2 states the following:

> The Russian Federation, the United Kingdom of Great Britain and Northern Ireland and the United States of America reaffirm their obligation to refrain from the threat or use of force against the territorial integrity or political independence of Ukraine, and that none of their weapons will ever be used against Ukraine except in self-defence or otherwise in accordance with the Charter of the United Nations.

Despite the opinion of some authors[51] about the non-binding character of the 1994 Budapest Memoranda, it may be regarded as a treaty, granting substantive

---

[44] Idem.

[45] Crawford, Pellet and Olleson 2010, p. 677: "The obligation of non-recognition of an unlawful situation is in large part based on the well-established general principle that legal rights cannot derive from an illegal act (*ex injuria jus non oritur*)." See also ICJ, *Legal Consequences for States of the Continued Presence of South Africa in Namibia (South West Africa) Notwithstanding Security Council Resolution 276 (1970), Advisory Opinion, 21 June 1971*, ICJ Reports 1971, p. 46.

[46] ILC 1966, Draft Articles on the Law of Treaties with Commentaries (fn. 36), p. 221.

[47] See VCLT (fn. 32), Article 31, para 1.

[48] See 1994 Memorandum on Security Assurances in Connection with Ukraine's Accession to the Treaty on the Non-Proliferation of Nuclear Weapons, *UN Doc.* A/49/765.

[49] See 1994 Memorandum on Security Assurances in Connection with the Republic of Kazakhstan's Accession to the Treaty on the Non-proliferation of Nuclear Weapons. http://www.exportlawblog. com/docs/security_assurances.pdf. Accessed 11 March 2017. See also 1994 Memorandum on Security Assurances in Connection with the Republic of Belarus' Accession to the Treaty on the Non-proliferation of Nuclear Weapons. http://www.exportlawblog.com/docs/security_assurances. pdf. Accessed 11 March 2017.

[50] See, e.g., Letter Dated 7 December 1994 from the Permanent Representatives of the Russian Federation, Ukraine, the United Kingdom of Great Britain and Northern Ireland and the United States of America to the United Nations Addressed to the Secretary-General, UN Doc. A/49/765.

[51] Aust 2013, p. 46.

rights and imposing legal obligations regulated by international law. As previously mentioned, the most important criterion for establishing the existence of a treaty in a given situation is the parties' intention to create obligations governed by international law. Such an intention is a matter of objective determination. Moreover, a particular designation of the treaty and the number of instruments constituting the treaty are not decisive.

The 1994 Budapest Memoranda on Security Assurances, as concluded with Ukraine, Belarus and Kazakhstan, represent the source of those states' commitment to eliminate all nuclear weapons from their territory. On the other hand, Russia, the UK and the US, as UN Security Council permanent members and nuclear weapon states, undertook the obligation to "refrain from the threat or use of force against the territorial integrity or political independence of Ukraine". It is hard to imagine that Ukraine, Belarus and Kazakhstan decided to eliminate a significant part of their military potential in exchange for a mere political pledge from Russia, the UK and the US. Indeed, whereas memoranda of understanding usually result in political commitments from the parties concerned, this does not preclude considering some memoranda as treaties in specific circumstances.

Moreover, the Treaty on Friendship, Cooperation and Partnership (TFCP), which was concluded between Russia and Ukraine in 1997,[52] provides the following in Article 3:

High contracting parties build the relations with each other on the basis of the principles of mutual respect, sovereign equality, territorial integrity, inviolability of borders, peaceful settlement of disputes, the non-use of force or threat of force, including economic and different ways of pressure, the right of the people to dispose freely of the destiny, non-interference to internal affairs, respect for human rights and fundamental freedoms, the cooperation between the states, fair accomplishment of the undertaken international obligations, and also other universally recognized norms of international law.

The analysis of the above-mentioned provisions in the Budapest Memorandum and the TFCP makes it clear that they are sources of international treaty obligations of states towards Ukraine. Therefore, states, including Russia, must respect the obligation not to use or threaten force, not only as a general commitment taken in the frameworks of the UN, but also as a treaty-based obligation towards Ukraine.

1.3 Customary Nature of States' Obligations

Article 38, para 1b, of the Statute of the ICJ refers to international custom as evidence of a general practice accepted as law.[53] Unlike with treaties, international custom is not created by what states put down in writing, but rather what they do in practice. A rule of customary international law develops when states behave in a particular

---

[52] See 1997 Treaty on Friendship, Cooperation and Partnership between the Russian Federation and Ukraine. http://cis-legislation.com/document.fwx?rgn=4181. Accessed 11 March 2017. See also Sorokowski 1996, pp. 319–29.

[53] See 1945 Statute of the ICJ (fn. 29).

manner and come to accept behaviour that is required by law.[54] It is a well-recognized premise that customary law comprises two elements, the 'objective' or 'material' element (state practice) and the 'subjective' element, often referred to as *opinio juris sive necessitatis* (or *opinio juris*).[55] A state is not, however, under an obligation to follow international custom, if it has expressed itself as a persistent objector at the time of the formation of such a customary rule.[56]

The material element of international custom requires establishing "constant and uniform usage practised by the states in question".[57] However, as it was stated by Judge Lachs in his dissenting opinion on the ICJ's judgement in the *North Sea Continental Shelf* cases,[58] "for it to become binding, a rule or principle of international law need not pass the test of universal acceptance".[59] In this sense, international custom can be created by the practice of "states whose interests are specially affected".[60]

In contrast to the material element, it is more difficult to prove that particular states have accepted their practice as law.[61] When it comes to the subjective element in customary law, the ICJ's contribution has been less helpful.[62] In truth, however, the ICJ's impact on the development of international custom remains essential. For instance, in the *North Sea Continental Shelf* cases, the ICJ ruled as follows:

> Not only must the acts concerned amount to a settled practice, but they must also be such, or be carried out in such a way, as to be evidence of a belief that this practice is rendered obligatory by the existence of a rule of law requiring it. The need for such a belief, i.e., the existence of a subjective element, is implicit in the very notion of the *opinio juris sive necessitatis*. The states concerned must therefore feel that they are conforming to what amounts to a legal obligation.[63]

In the context of *jus contra bellum*, the ICJ has recognized the customary nature of the obligation to refrain from the threat or use the force. In its judgement in the *Nicaragua* case, the ICJ found the existence of *opinio juris* (states' belief in the customary character of Article 2(4) of the UN Charter) in the attitude of states towards the 1970 Declaration on Principles of International Law which clarifies the scope and content of the prohibition on the threat or use of force. As the ICJ has postulated in the *Nicaragua* case, the effect of consenting to the text of the 1970 Declaration on Principles of International Law and certain UN General Assembly

---

[54] Arend 1999, pp. 47–8.

[55] *International Law Association,* Final Report of the Committee: *Formation of Customary (General) International Law (1984–2000).* http://www.ila-hq.org/en/committees/index.cfm/cid/30, p. 7.

[56] Czapliński and Wyrozumska 2014, p. 118.

[57] ICJ, *Asylum Case (Colombia v. Peru), Judgment, 20 November 1950,* ICJ Reports 1950, p. 276.

[58] ICJ, *North Sea Continental Shelf (Federal Republic of Germany v. Denmark; Federal Republic of Germany v. Netherlands), Judgment, 20 February 1969,* ICJ Reports 1969, p. 3.

[59] See *Dissenting Opinion of Judge Lachs to the ICJ's Judgment in North Sea Continental Shelf Cases,* ICJ Reports 1969, p. 229.

[60] ICJ, *North Sea Continental Shelf* (fn. 57), p. 42.

[61] Czapliński and Wyrozumska 2014, pp. 113–4.

[62] Lowe and Fitzmaurice 1996, p. 70.

[63] ICJ, *North Sea Continental Shelf* (fn. 57), p. 44.

resolutions cannot be understood as merely that of a 'reiteration or elucidation' of the treaty commitment undertaken in the UN Charter. On the contrary, in the ICJ's opinion, this may even be understood as an acceptance of the validity of the rule or set of rules declared by the resolutions themselves.[64]

Since the 1970 Declaration on Principles of International Law was adopted without a vote, the UN members represented at the UN General Assembly have agreed with its text. Moreover, the absence of a persistent objection clearly expressed by Ukraine, Russia, Belarus or any other UN member against the substance of this declaration weighs in favour of its customary nature.

1.4 *Jus Cogens* Norms and *Erga Omnes* Obligations

In contrast to international custom, peremptory norms of general international law (*jus cogens*) and *erga omnes* obligations are new phenomena in the international legal system.[65] In the *Barcelona Traction* case, the ICJ held that an essential distinction should be drawn between the obligations of a state towards the international community as a whole, and those arising *vis-à-vis* another state. By their very nature, the former are the concern of all states. The court added: "in view of the importance of the rights involved, all states can be held to have a legal interest in their protection; they are obligations *erga omnes*."[66]

The primary reason for the existence of such an international legal concept as 'the international community as a whole' is to render the principle of the rule of law as more effective. International obligations are taken by states, not only on the basis of particular treaties, but also because of general international law. Given the absence of an international dispute settlement mechanism with obligatory jurisdiction, states could face problems with the implementation[67] of the state's responsibility concerning an internationally wrongful act it has committed. In order to ensure that the most important obligations in international law are performed in good faith, all members of the international community are able to protect such common interests, and, where appropriate, bring a claim against the responsible state before an international judicial organ or an arbitration.

As the ICJ stated in the *Corfu Channel* case, "such obligations are based, not on the Hague Convention of 1907, No. VIII, which is applicable in time of war, but on certain general and well-recognized principles, namely: elementary considerations of humanity, even more exacting in peace than in war; the principle of the freedom of maritime communication; and every state's obligation not to allow knowingly

---

[64] ICJ, *Nicaragua* (fn. 12), pp. 99–100.

[65] Kwiecień 2011, p. 170.

[66] ICJ, *Barcelona Traction, Light and Power Company, Limited (Belgium v. Spain), 5 February 1970, Judgment*, ICJ Reports 1970, p. 32.

[67] The term 'implementation' in the context of the international responsibility of a state was introduced by the ICL in its Draft Articles on Responsibility of States for Internationally Wrongful Acts. See UN General Assembly 2001, Responsibility of States for Internationally Wrongful Acts, UN Doc. A/RES/56/83.

its territory to be used for acts contrary to the rights of other states."[68] Despite the affirmation of the concept of 'the international community as a whole' in the successive ICJ's jurisprudence,[69] the Court has been maintaining a prudent approach *vis-à-vis jus cogens* norms.

The VCLT in Article 53 provides as follows:

> A treaty is void if, at the time of its conclusion, it conflicts with a peremptory norm of general international law. For the purposes of the present Convention, a peremptory norm of general international law is a norm accepted and recognized by the international community of states as a whole as a norm from which no derogation is permitted and which can be modified only by a subsequent norm of general international law having the same character.[70]

Following the interpretation of Article 53 of the VCLT, it is worth mentioning that a norm or a principle of the international legal system can be qualified as a norm of *jus cogens*, if all criteria defined in Article 53 are met cumulatively.

In its commentary to the VCLT, the ILC pointed out that the UN Charter provision concerning the prohibition of the use of force itself constitutes a conspicuous example of a rule in international law, having the character of a peremptory norm (*jus cogens*).[71] The ILC's position was cited by the ICJ in the *Nicaragua* case. As the ICJ stated, the prohibition of the use of force expressed in Article 2(4) of the UN Charter is "a fundamental or cardinal principle".[72] The peremptory character of the prohibition of the use of force has also been supported by some authors.[73] Orakhelashvili goes as far as affirming that *jus ad bellum*, on the whole, is peremptory, arguing that it concerns the right of states to use force and defines the circumstances of such use. In this regard, the outer limits of the very prohibition of the use of force and any judgement about to whether the use of force is legal relate to whether that use of force is justified under Article 2(4) of the UN Charter and its customary counterpart. Therefore, as Orakhelashvili states, if the very prohibition of the use of force is peremptory, then every principle specifying the limits on the entitlement of states to use force is also peremptory.[74]

While the importance of the prohibition of the use of force in general international law is obvious, declaring the peremptory character of this norm requires detailed

---

[68] ICJ, *The Corfu Channel Case, Judgment, 9 April 1949*, ICJ Reports 1949, p. 22.

[69] See, e.g., ICJ, *Jurisdictional Immunities of the State (Germany v. Italy: Greece Intervening), Judgment, 3 February 2012*, ICJ Reports 2012, p. 141, where the Court stated: "to the extent that it is argued that no rule which is not of the status of *jus cogens* may be applied if to do so would hinder the enforcement of a *jus cogens* rule, even in the absence of a direct conflict, the Court sees no basis for such a proposition. A *jus cogens* rule is one from which no derogation is permitted but the rules which determine the scope and extent of jurisdiction and when that jurisdiction may be exercised do not derogate from those substantive rules which possess *jus cogens* status, nor is there anything inherent in the concept of *jus cogens* which would require their modification or would displace their application."

[70] See VCLT (fn. 32).

[71] ILC 1966, *Draft Articles on the Law of Treaties with Commentaries* (fn. 36), p. 247.

[72] ICJ, *Nicaragua* (fn. 12), p. 100.

[73] Orakhelashvili 2012, pp. 50–1; see also Linderfalk 2008, p. 859.

[74] Orakhelashvili 2012, p. 51.

examination. In order to qualify a norm of international law as peremptory, the VCLT requires evidence that: (1) this norm is recognized by the international community as a whole; (2) no derogation or exception is permitted; and (3) the respective norm can only be modified by a subsequent norm of *jus cogens*.

As discussed above, Article 2(4) of the UN Charter on the prohibition of the use of force has a customary nature in international law. Hence, it is clear that the prohibition of the use of force forms a constant and uniform general practice accepted by the international community of states as law. It would be also possible to assume that granting all states the opportunity to use force in an unlimited manner requires the adoption of a new peremptory norm by the international community. Otherwise, the international legal system would become a chaotic order without rules, whose function is not legal governance, but rather merely playing political games. Furthermore, "the inherent right of individual or collective self-defence" provided by Article 51 of the UN Charter could not be regarded as a derogation from the prohibition of the use of force. Indeed, when a state suffers from an armed attack, it is allowed to use its armed forces in order to restore international peace. Nevertheless, this inviolable right of states is limited by the UN Security Council's competence to maintain international peace and security. Moreover, the right to self-defence is an exception to the prohibition of the use of force, that is to say, is out of the scope of *jus cogens*.

Whilst the prohibition of the use the force is a norm of *jus cogens*, it is difficult to accept Orakhelashvili's opinion that every element (principle) of *jus ad bellum* (or *jus contra bellum*) is peremptory. As has become clear, every potential norm of *jus cogens* is required to pass the test specified in Article 53 of the VCLT. If limitations of the use of force are not accepted by the international community as a whole, and subsequent derogations are acceptable, any such potential norm could not be defined as peremptory.

1.5 General Principles of International Law

The prohibition of the use of force is more often defined as a general principle of international law. Article 38, para 1c, of the Statute of the ICJ allows for "general principles of law recognized by civilized nations" to be applied. The formulation appeared in the *compromis* of arbitral tribunals in the 19th century, and similar formulae appear in draft instruments concerned with the functioning of various arbitral tribunals.[75] This acknowledgement of general principles of law enables their use to fill gaps or address weaknesses that could otherwise be left to the operation of custom and treaty. Moreover, this approach provides a background of legal principles in light of which custom and treaties have to be applied, which in turn could modify their application. General principles of law, however, do not simply play a complementary role, but may give rise to rules of independent legal force.[76] Despite this, there is a

---

[75] Brownlie 1998, p. 15.

[76] Jennings and Watts 1992, p. 40.

great deal of debate among scholars about defining general principles of law[77] and general principles of international law.

Jus contra bellum comprises not only the prohibition of the use of force itself, but also other general principles of international law, which make it possible to enforce international obligations undertaken by states in good faith. Some of them are the foundations of the legal systems of various states. In simple terms, the concept of *jus contra bellum* is based on meta-norms of the international legal system, without which the international community would not be able to ensure the effectiveness of the prohibition of the use of force.

A major step in the development of the prohibition of the use of force as a general principle of international law, and not only as a principle of the UN, as defined in Article 2(4) of its Charter, was made by the ICJ in the *Nicaragua* case. The Court did not accept the position of the US in respect of the relation between the UN Charter and international custom, stating that:

> [So] far from having constituted a marked departure from a customary international law which still exists unmodified, the Charter gave expression in this field to principles already present in customary international law, and that law has in the subsequent four decades developed under the influence of the Charter, to such an extent that a number of rules contained in the Charter have acquired a status independent of it. The essential consideration is that both the Charter and the customary international law flow from a *common fundamental principle* outlawing the use of force in international relations.[78]

The 'credibility' of the reasoning of the ICJ presented in the *Nicaragua* case is linked to the understanding of the prohibition of the use of force as a fundamental principle of international relations and, of course, the international legal system. It was also essential to determine a close relationship between this principle and other sources of international law. The prohibition of the use of force established in customary international law and reflected in the UN Charter flows from a core element of *jus contra bellum*, but not the other way around.

The pervasive nature of the prohibition of the use of force as a common fundamental principle outlawing the use of force in international relations opens the door to the acceptance of certain principles of fundamental fairness as elements of *jus contra bellum*. A particular importance can be ascribed to *pacta sunt servanda*, the principle of good faith and estoppel. Whilst the rationale of *pacta sunt servanda* is to ensure compliance with international obligations set out in the UN Charter and other treaties, the principle of good faith and estoppel are not restricted to treaties but apply to all international obligations.[79] As stated by the ICJ in the *Nuclear Tests* cases, good faith is "one of the basic principles governing the creation and

---

[77] Arend 1999, p. 49. See also the 1950 Convention for the Protection of Human Rights and Fundamental Freedoms, ETS No. 005, Article 7(2): "This Article shall not prejudice the trial and punishment of any person for any act or omission which, at the time when it was committed, was criminal according to the general principles of law recognised by civilised nations."

[78] ICJ, *Nicaragua* (fn. 12), pp. 96–7.

[79] Aust 2005, p. 9.

performance of legal obligations, whatever their source."[80] In the same manner as the principle of good faith, estoppel was also defined as an instrument for ensuring the performance of international obligations irrespective of their nature. In this regard, estoppel holds that, when a party acts in a particular way and a second party relies on the act of the first party, the first party cannot subsequently behave in a manner contrary to its original act.[81] As the ICJ held in the *Frontier Dispute* case, some of the essential elements required by estoppel are: a statement or representation made by one party to another and reliance upon it by that other party to his detriment or to the advantage of the party making it.[82] This suggests that both the principle of good faith and estoppel are able to be applied not only in situations of violations of the UN Charter and other treaties, but also in violations of promises concerning unilateral declarations of states.

1.6 Unilateral Declarations of States

States may find themselves bound, on the international stage, by their unilateral behaviour.[83] As the ILC specified in its 2006 "Guiding Principles Applicable to Unilateral Declarations of States Capable of Creating Legal Obligations", declarations publicly made and manifesting the will to be bound may have the effect of creating legal obligations. The binding character of declarations that meet such conditions is based on good faith.[84] Consequently, the states concerned may take them into consideration and rely on them, such that such obligations are respected.[85] Therefore, unilateral acts of states can be regarded as a source of international obligations, rather than a source of international law. In this context, it is difficult to agree with Arend, who argues that unilateral acts create international law.[86] Undoubtedly, some principles of international law, such as *pacta sunt servanda*, good faith and estoppel, are applicable to situations related to unilateral acts.[87] However, they cannot alter their legal nature. International legal norms are only able to exist because of the will of at least two states. This is not relevant in the case of a unilateral act, as the latter can be established by the will of one state.

---

[80] ICJ, *Nuclear Tests Case (Australia v. France), Judgment, 20 December 1974*, ICJ Reports 1974, p. 268; ICJ, *Nuclear Tests case (New Zealand v. France), Judgment, 20 December 1974*, ICJ Reports 1974, p. 473.

[81] Arend 1999, p. 49.

[82] ICJ, *Case Concerning the Land, Island and Maritime Frontier Dispute (El Salvador v. Honduras), Judgment, 13 September 1990*, ICJ Reports 1990, p. 118.

[83] ILC 2006, Guiding Principles Applicable to Unilateral Declarations of States Capable of Creating Legal Obligations, With Commentaries Thereto, ILC Report, UN Doc. A/61/10.

[84] Idem.

[85] Idem.

[86] Arend 1999, p. 58.

[87] See Kozłowski 2009, pp. 64–74.

The above-mentioned position of the ILC is based on its jurisprudence. In the *Nuclear Tests* cases, the ICJ stated:

> It is well recognized that declarations made by way of unilateral acts, concerning legal or factual situations, may have the effect of creating legal obligations. Declarations of this kind may be, and often are, very specific. When it is the intention of the state making the declaration that it should become bound according to its terms, that intention confers on the declaration the character of a legal undertaking, the state being thenceforth legally required to follow a course of conduct consistent with the declaration.[88]

The importance of the intention behind a unilateral act was also confirmed by the ICJ in the *Frontier Dispute* case.[89] Unilateral declarations may be formulated in different ways. Official representatives of states, especially heads of states, heads of governments and ministers of foreign affairs, are able to undertake international obligations *vis-à-vis* other states, either orally or in writing.[90] Thus, contraventions of the unilateral declarations of states, in the form of organizing or encouraging the organization of irregular forces and armed bands, or the military occupation of Ukraine's territory, are to be regarded as violations of international obligations.

References

Aquinas St. T (1256) Summa Theologica of St. Thomas Aquinas. Part I QQ I.-XXVI. Second and revised edition. Vol. 1. http://oll.libertyfund.org/titles/1979. Accessed 18 March 2017

Arend A (1999) Legal Rules and International Society. Oxford University Press, Oxford

Aust A (2005) Handbook of International Law. Cambridge University Press, Cambridge

Aust A (2013) Modern Treaty Law and Practice. Cambridge University Press, Cambridge

Bring O (2000) The Westphalian Peace Tradition in International Law From *Jus* ad *Bellum* to *Jus contra Bellum*. International Law Studies 75: 57–80

Brownlie I (1963) International Law and the Use of Force by States. Oxford University Press, Oxford

Brownlie I (1998) Principles of Public International Law. Clarendon Press, Oxford

Corten O (2010) The Law Against War: The Prohibition on the Use of Force in Contemporary International Law. Hart Publishing, Oxford

Crawford J, Pellet A, Olleson S (2010) The Law of International Responsibility. Oxford University Press, Oxford

Czapliński W, Wyrozumska A (2014) Prawo międzynarodowe publiczne. 3. wydanie. Wydawnictwo C.H. Beck, Warszawa

Dinstein Y (2017) War, Aggression and Self-Defence, 6th edition. Cambridge University Press, Cambridge

Fitzmaurice M, Quast A (2007) Law of treaties Section A: Introduction to the law of treaties. University of London, London

---

[88] ICJ, *Nuclear Tests Case (Australia v. France)* (fn. 79), p. 267; ICJ, *Nuclear Tests Case (New Zealand v. France)* (fn. 79), p. 472.

[89] ICJ, *Frontier Dispute (Burkina Faso v. Republic of Mali), Judgment, 20 December 1986*, ICJ Reports 1986, p. 573.

[90] ICJ, *Armed Activities on the Territory of the Congo (New Application: 2002) (Democratic Republic of the Congo v. Rwanda) Jurisdiction of the Court and Admissibility of the Application, Judgment, 3 February 2006*, ICJ Reports 2006, p. 27.

Grotius H (1625) The Rights of War and Peace, including the Law of Nature and of Nations. http://oll.libertyfund.org/titles/553. Accessed 18 March 2017

Higgins R (2010) Problems and Process. International Law and How We Use It. Oxford University Press, Oxford

Hollis D (2012) The Oxford Guide to Treaties. Oxford University Press, Oxford

International Law Commission (1966) Draft Articles on the Law of Treaties with commentaries, Yearbook of the ICL, vol. II.

Jennings R, Watts A (1992) Oppenheim's International Law. Longman, London

Kant I (1887) The Philosophy of Law: An Exposition of the Fundamental Principles of Jurisprudence as the Science of Right. http://oll.libertyfund.org/titles/359. Accessed 18 March 2017

Kozłowski A (2009) Estoppel jako ogólna zasada prawa międzynarodowego. Wydawnictwo Uniwersytetu Wrocławskiego, Wrocław

Kwiecień R (2011) Teoria i filozofia prawa międzynarodowego: problemy wybrane. Difin SA, Warszawa

Linderfalk U (2008) The Effect of Jus Cogens Norms: Whoever Opened Pandora's Box, Did You Ever Think About the Consequences? EJIL 18: 853–871

Lowe V, Fitzmaurice M (1996) Fifty Years of the International Court of Justice. Essays in Honour of Sir Robert Jennings. Cambridge University Press, Cambridge

McCaffrey S (2006) Understanding international law. LexisNexis, Newark/San Francisco/ Charlottesville

McNair A (1961) The Law of Treaties. Clarendon Press, Oxford

Orakhelashvili A (2012) Peremptory Norms in International Law. Oxford University Press, Oxford

Sayapin S (2014) The Crime of Aggression in International Criminal Law: Historical Development, Comparative Analysis and Present State. T.M.C. Asser Press, The Hague

Shaw M (2014) International Law, 7th edn. Cambridge University Press, Cambridge

Sharma S (2009) The Legacy of Jus Contra Bellum: Echoes of Pacifism in Contemporary Just War Thought. Journal of Military Ethics 8:3: 217–230

Sorokowski A (1996) Treaty on Friendship, Cooperation, and Partnership between Ukraine and the Russian Federation. Harvard Ukraine Studies 20: 319–329

Tunkin G (1993) Is General International Law Customary Only? European Journal of International Law 4: 534–541

Waldock H (1962) Recueil Des Cours. Collected Courses. Tome 106 de la Collection. The Hague Academy of International Law, The Hague

Chapter 2
Who Are the "Crimea People" or "People of Crimea"? The Fate of the Crimean Tatars, Russia's Legal Justification for Annexation, and Pandora's Box

Bill Bowring

Contents

Abstract This chapter does not seek to add to the already voluminous literature on the legality of Russia's annexation of Crimea. I agree with the many international organisations and scholars of international law who have insisted that the annexation was illegal in international law. I focus on the "Legal arguments for Russia's position on Crimea and Ukraine" published by the Permanent Delegation of the Russian Federation to UNESCO on 7 November 2014. This official document asserted that there had been "…the implementation of the right to self-determination by the people of Crimea". It is my contention that there is only one people with a right to self-determination in Crimea, namely the Crimean Tatar People, who assert the right to recognition as the main indigenous people of Crimea. First, I briefly describe the events of 2014–15. Next I turn to the origins and history of the Crimean Tatars in Crimea, including their fate in the first Russian annexation of Crimea in 1783. Third, drawing on my own experience from the 1990s onwards, I explain the difficulties faced by the Crimean Tatars in Ukraine, from their return from exile in Central Asia in the late 1980s, and in independent Ukraine from 1991, until the second annexation

Bill Bowring, School of Law, Birkbeck College, University of London, Malet Street, London WC1E 7HX, b.bowring@bbk.ac.uk, +44 207 631 6022.

B. Bowring (✉)
School of Law, Birkbeck College, University of London, Malet Street, London WC1E 7HX, UK
e-mail: b.bowring@bbk.ac.uk

© T.M.C. ASSER PRESS and the authors 2018
S. Sayapin and E. Tsybulenko (eds.), *The Use of Force against Ukraine and International Law*, https://doi.org/10.1007/978-94-6265-222-4_2

by Russia in 2014. Fourth, I turn to the question of the proper status of the Crimean Tatars in international law. Fifth, I return to the official position of Russia, and sixth to the analyses, consistent with the official Russian justification, of three leading Russian scholars.

Keywords Russia · Ukraine · Crimea · Crimean Tatars · Self-Determination · Human Rights · International Law · Annexation · Indigenous

2.1 Introduction

On 18 March 2014 President Putin addressed State Duma deputies, Federation Council members, heads of Russian regions and civil society representatives in the Kremlin.[1] He started his speech with the following words:

> We have gathered here today in connection with an issue that is of vital, historic significance to all of us. A referendum was held in Crimea on March 16 in full compliance with democratic procedures and international norms.

Mr. Putin said that the total population of Crimea is 2.2 million people, of whom almost 1.5 million are Russians, 350,000 are Ukrainians who predominantly consider Russian their native language, and about 290,000–300,000 are Crimean Tatars. He asserted that

> Crimea is a unique blend of different peoples' cultures and traditions. This makes it similar to Russia as a whole, where not a single ethnic group has been lost over the centuries. Russians and Ukrainians, Crimean Tatars and people of other ethnic groups have lived side by side in Crimea, retaining their own identity, traditions, languages and faith.

The clear implication of this assertion, referred to by one of the Russian professors whose work I examine below, is that this has always been the case. The further implication was that the population of Crimea can properly be described as "the Crimean people", that is a "people" entitled to exercise the right to self-determination in international law. I have described this right as the "revolutionary kernel" of international law.[2] I have more recently analysed the *travaux préparatoires* for the incorporation of the right into binding treaty law in the human rights Covenants of 1966, with a critique of recent scholarship.[3]

Mr. Putin acknowledged that "… there was a time when Crimean Tatars were treated unfairly, just as a number of other peoples in the USSR. There is only one thing I can say here: millions of people of various ethnicities suffered during those repressions, and primarily Russians." This was an oblique reference to a uniquely horrifying event, the genocide of the Crimean Tatar people in 1944, at the hands

---

[1] http://en.kremlin.ru/events/president/news/20603. Accessed 21 August 2017.

[2] See Bowring 2008a, Chapter 1; Bowring 2008b, a chapter in Marks (2008); see also Cassese 1995; Fisch 2015; Teson 2016.

[3] Bowring forthcoming.

of Stalin, and their mass deportation from their homeland to Uzbekistan in Central Asia, from which they were only permitted to begin to return home in the late 1980s.

He asserted "great respect for people of all the ethnic groups living in Crimea. This is their common home, their motherland, and promised that Crimea would have three equal national languages: Russian, Ukrainian and Tatar." This was presented as a significant concession to the Crimean Tatars: their language enjoyed no such status when Crimea was part of Ukraine. Most important for this chapter, he referred to "the choice the Crimean people made", and to the "Crimean people".

In his Presidential Address to the Federal Assembly on 4 December 2014 Mr. Putin celebrated "the historical reunification of Crimea and Sevastopol with Russia".[4] He emphasised the "strategic importance for Russia as the spiritual source of the development of a multifaceted but solid Russian nation and a centralised Russian state. It was in Crimea, in the ancient city of Chersonesus[5] or Korsun, as ancient Russian chroniclers called it, that Grand Prince Vladimir[6] was baptised before bringing Christianity to Rus." In this speech Mr. Putin referred to "the people of Crimea and Sevastopol."[7]

The last two footnotes show that Mr. Putin's claim to a special relationship between Russia and Crimea extending back to the 10th century is controversial. Masha Lipman wrote as follows:[8]

> Putin's statement, one of many intended to prove the "Russianness" of Crimea, is controversial in several ways. The theory that Grand Prince Vladimir (whose death a thousand years ago was marked by the Kremlin this month) was baptized in Chersonesus is not the only version of this event. Another, equally well-known theory has it that Vladimir was baptized in Kiev, the birthplace of the history of Old Rus', but Kiev, for obvious reasons, has become a politically inconvenient place of origin for Russian Orthodox Christianity. Even if Vladimir had been baptized in Chersonesus, Crimea in the tenth century lay far beyond Rus', in the Byzantine Empire. Finally, in the many centuries since Vladimir's conversion, Chersonesus has never been a special place of worship for Orthodox Christians.

---

[4] http://en.kremlin.ru/events/president/news/47173. Accessed 21 August 2017.

[5] An ancient Greek colony, founded in the 6th century BC. In the late 2nd century BC Chersonesus became a dependency of the Bosporan Kingdom. It was subject to Rome from the middle of the 1st century BC until the 370s AD, when it was captured by the Huns. In the 980s Vladimir the Great of Rus' agreed to evacuate the fortress only if Basil II's sister Anna Porphyrogeneta would be given him in marriage. As a pre-condition for the marriage settlement, Vladimir was baptized here in 988, thus paving the way to the Baptism of Kievan Rus'. Thereafter Korsun' was evacuated by Rus'.

[6] Vladimir the Great, c.958-1015, was a prince of Novgorod, grand prince of Kiev, and ruler of Kievan Rus' from 980 to 1015. Here is an alternative account to that given in the previous footnote: in 988, having taken the town of Chersonesos in Crimea, Vladimir boldly negotiated for the hand of Byzantine emperor Basil II's sister, Anna. Never before had a Byzantine imperial princess married a barbarian, and to marry the 27-year-old princess to a pagan Slav seemed impossible. Vladimir was baptized at Chersonesos taking the Christian name of Basil out of compliment to his imperial brother-in-law; the sacrament was followed by his wedding to Anna.

[7] Rossi 2015 at pp. 146–147 on President Putin's multiple justifications; and Rossi 2016.

[8] Lipman 2015.

I have already indicated a number of rather oblique references to the Crimean Tatars, or more properly the Crimean Tatar people. This is an important distinction for the purpose of international law, and the right of *peoples* to self-determination.

This chapter does not seek to add to the already voluminous literature on the legality of Russia's annexation of Crimea. I agree with the many international organisations and scholars of international law who have insisted that the annexation was illegal in international law. The special issues of the *Heidelberg Journal of International Law* in 2015,[9] and of the *German Law Journal* published in 2016[10] contain splendid articles by a wide range of distinguished scholars, and may be down-loaded freely.

Instead, I focus on the "Legal arguments for Russia's position on Crimea and Ukraine" published by the Permanent Delegation of the Russian Federation to UNESCO on 7 November 2014.[11] This official document asserted that there had been "…the implementation of the right to self-determination by the people of Crimea". The referendum of 16 March, referred to below, was said to reflect "… the will of the people of Crimea." There followed extensive references to international law and practice concerning the right of peoples to self-determination, enshrined in United Nations treaties (the two International Covenants on Human Rights), the 1970

---

[9] Marxsen, Peters, Hartwig 2015. This Symposium contains Marxsen C: "Territorial Integrity in International Law –Its Concept and Implications for Crimea" 7–26; Bílková V: "The Use of Force by the Russian Federation in Crimea" 27–50; Oeter S: "The Kosovo Case – An Unfortunate Precedent" 51–74; Christakis T: "Self-Determination, Territorial Integrity and Fait Accompli in the Case of Crimea" 75–100; Kapustin A "Crimea's Self-Determination in the Light of Contemporary International Law" 101–118; Tolstykh V: "Three Ideas of Self-Determination in International Law and the Reunification of Crimea with Russia" 119–140; Salenko V: "Legal Aspects of the Dissolution of the Soviet Union in 1991 and Its Implications for the Reunification of Crimea with Russia in 2014" 141–166; Merezhko O: "Crimea's Annexation by Russia – Contradictions of the New Russian Doctrine of International Law" 167–194; Douhan A: "International Organizations and Settlement of the Conflict in Ukraine" 195–214; Milano E: "Russia's Veto in the Security Council: Whither the Duty to Abstain under Article 27(3) of the UN Charter?" 215–231. I discuss the Russian scholars' contributions below. Table of contents at http://www.zaoerv.de/75_2015/75_2015_1_a_1_2.pdf.

[10] "Special Issue on Crimea" vol. 16, no. 3 (2015) *German Law Journal* No. 3 (2015), http://www.germanlawjournal.com/volume-16-no-03. Accessed 21 August 2017. This contains: Oklopcic Z "Introduction: The Crisis in Ukraine Between the Law, Power, and Principle"; Vidmar J "The Annexation of Crimea and the Boundaries of the Will of the People"; Roth B "The Virtues of Bright Lines: Self-Determination, Secession, and External Intervention"; Fabry M "How to Uphold the Territorial Integrity of Ukraine"; Özsu M "Ukraine, International Law, and the Political Economy of Self-Determination"; Korhonen O "Deconstructing the Conflict in Ukraine: The Relevance of International Law to Hybrid States and Wars"; Mamlyuk B "The Ukraine Crisis, Cold War II, and International Law"; Tierney S "Sovereignty and Crimea: How Referendum Democracy Complicates Constituent Power in Multinational Societies"; Roznai Y & Suteu S "The Eternal Territory? The Crimean Crisis and Ukraine's Territorial Integrity as an Unamendable Constitutional Principle"; Catala A "Secession and Annexation: The Case of Crimea"; Banai A "Territorial Conflict and Territorial Rights: The Crimean Question Reconsidered"; Malcolm MacLaren "Trust the People"? Democratic Secessionism and Contemporary Practice"; Oklopcic Z "The Idea of Early-Conflict Constitution-Making: The Conflict in Ukraine Beyond Territorial Rights and Constitutional Paradoxes"; Arato A "International Role in State-Making in Ukraine: The Promise of a Two-Stage Constituent Process".

[11] http://russianunesco.ru/eng/article/1637. Accessed 21 August 2017.

Declaration on Principles of International Law concerning Friendly Relations and Cooperation among States in Accordance with the Charter of the United Nations, the case-law of the International Court of Justice, and other sources.[12]

The really controversial argument of the document was as follows:

> Concerning the situation around Crimea, it is a fact that Crimea's secession from Ukraine and its accession to Russia took place in extreme conditions of impossibility to implement the right to self-determination within the framework of Ukraine. These extreme conditions were exacerbated by the unlawful rise to power of those who do not represent the entire Ukrainian people. During its more than 20-year history as a part of Ukraine, the people of Crimea failed to realize their right to self-determination within the framework of this State.

It is my contention that there is only one people with a right to self-determination in Crimea, namely the Crimean Tatar people, who assert through their representative institutions, the Qurultay and Mejlis, the right to recognition as the main indigenous people of Crimea. According to the definition contained in Article 1 of the International Labour Organisation's 1989 *Convention concerning Indigenous and Tribal Peoples in Independent Countries*,[13] to which I return below, the Crimean Tatars are an indigenous people. I note that Ukraine only recognised the Crimean Tatars as an indigenous people in March 2014, after Russia's annexation.

First, I briefly describe the events of 2014–15. Next I turn to the origins and history of the Crimean Tatars in Crimea, including their fate in the first Russian annexation of Crimea in 1783. Third, drawing on my own experience from the 1990s onwards, I explain the difficulties faced by the Crimean Tatars in Ukraine, from their return from exile in Central Asia in the late 1980s, and in independent Ukraine from 1991, until the second annexation by Russia in 2014. Fourth, I turn to the question of the proper status of the Crimean Tatars in international law. Fifth, I return to the official position of Russia, and sixth to the analyses, consistent with the official Russian justification, of three leading Russian scholars in the special issue of the *Heidelberg Journal*.

2.2 The Events of February-March 2014

Here is a brief summary of events.

---

[12] *Legal Consequences for States of the Continued Presence of South Africa in Namibia (South West Africa), notwithstanding Security Council resolution 276 (1970)*, Advisory opinion, I.C.J. Reports 1971, pp. 31–32, paras 52–53; *East Timor (Portugal v Australia)*, Decision, ICJ Reports 1995, p. 102, para 29; *Legal Consequences of the Construction of a Wall in the Occupied Palestinian Territory*, Advisory opinion, ICJ Reports 2004 (I), pp. 171–172, para 88; *Accordance with International Law of the Unilateral Declaration of Independence in respect of Kosovo*, Advisory opinion, I.C.J. Reports 2010, p. 37, para 72.

[13] Adoption: Geneva, 76th ILC session (27 Jun 1989), into force 5 Sept 1991, at http://www.ilo.org/dyn/normlex/en/f?p=NORMLEXPUB:12100:0::NO::P12100_ILO_CODE:C169. Accessed 21 August 2017.

On 22 February 2014 President Yanukovych of Ukraine abandoned his post in the face of the Maidan protests, and fled from the capital, Kiev.[14] The following day, pro-Russian demonstrations were held in the capital of the Autonomous Republic of Crimea, Simferopol, and following clashes between rival demonstrations, on 27 February 2014 Russian special forces seized key government buildings in Simferopol. The existing government of Crimea was removed by force and replaced by a government headed by Sergey Aksyonov. Within days the whole of the Crimean peninsula had been secured by Russian troops, although it was not until 17 April 2014 that President Putin acknowledged that the Russian military had backed Crimean separatist militias, stating that Russia's intervention was necessary "to ensure proper conditions for the people of Crimea to be able to freely express their will."[15]

On 11 March 2014 the Supreme Council of Crimea and the City Council of Sevastopol declared their independence from Ukraine, citing the right of peoples to self-determination and the Advisory Opinion of the International Court of Justice concerning Kosovo. If the result of the referendum to be held on 16 March 2014 would be in favour of joining Russia, Crimea would be declared a sovereign and independent state.[16] Voters were given a choice between two questions in the referendum:[17]

1: Do you support the reunification of Crimea with Russia with all the rights of the federal subject of the Russian Federation?

2: Do you support the restoration of the Constitution of the Republic of Crimea in 1992 and the status of the Crimea as part of Ukraine?

Many commentators have noted that the voters were not given the choice of maintaining the status quo as it obtained prior to annexation by Russia, namely the Autonomous Republic of Crimea within the unitary Ukrainian state.[18]

On 17 March, following the official announcement of the referendum results, the Supreme Council of Crimea declared the formal independence of the Republic of Crimea, and on the same day President Putin signed an Executive Order recognising the Republic of Crimea 'as a sovereign and independent state'[19] and approved the

---

[14] See BBC: Ukraine Crisis Timeline, at http://www.bbc.com/news/world-middle-east-26248275. Accessed 21 August 2017.

[15] http://en.kremlin.ru/events/president/news/20796. Accessed 21 August 2017.

[16] https://web.archive.org/web/20140312060543/http://www.rada.crimea.ua/app/2988. Accessed 21 August 2017.

[17] http://www.kryminfo.net/pri-vossoedinenii-s-osiyey-krymchane-diskomforta-ne-pochustvuyut/. Accessed 21 August 2017. The original in Russian read:

1: Вы за воссоединение Крыма с Россией на правах субъекта Российской Федерации?

2: Вы за восстановление действия Конституции Республики Крым 1992 года и за статус Крыма как части Украины? Sayapin 2015 notes that "… an inquisitive researcher should see that its Ukrainian equivalent does fairly match the Russian original but the Crimean Tatar translation contains a fundamental semantic fault, which must be taken as a sufficient ground for recognising the outcome of the referendum as illegitimate".

[18] See for a thorough analysis of the anomalous formation of an autonomous republic within a unitary state, Bowring 2005.

[19] http://en.kremlin.ru/events/president/news/20596. Accessed 21 August 2017.

admission of Crimea and Sevastopol as federal subjects of Russia. The Treaty on Accession of the Republic of Crimea to Russia was signed between representatives of the Republic of Crimea (including Sevastopol, with which the rest of Crimea briefly unified) and the Russian Federation on 18 March 2014 to lay out terms for the immediate admission of the Republic of Crimea and Sevastopol as federal subjects of Russia and part of the Russian Federation.[20] Following a determination of the Constitutional Court of the Russian Federation on 19 March 2014,[21] it was ratified by the upper house of the Russian Parliament on 21 March and signed by President Putin on 21 March 2014.[22]

2.3   The Crimean Tatars

In 1995, when I began to work with the Crimean Tatars, David Marples and David Duke provided a concise history of the Crimean Tatars, and I paraphrase relevant parts of it in the next paragraphs.[23]

The Crimean Tatars are descended from Turkic members of the Golden Horde founded by Batu Khan in the early thirteenth century.[24] Following the conquest of Crimea by the Golden Horde in the mid-thirteenth century – Crime was until then inhabited by mixed population including Slavs, Greeks and other ethnicities now extinct - a Turkic population was encouraged to settle there. They displaced the Slavs and others living there, and exacted tribute from a number of Italian trading settlements located along the southern coast of the peninsula.[25] The region was ruled by a series of governors appointed by the Tatar khans based in the city of Saray on the lower Volga, from which they also extracted tribute from the Russians, the so-called and much mythologised "Tatar yoke". By the end of the fourteenth century, however, the Tatar governors of Crimea began to establish an entity which was independent of Saray.

An independent Crimean Tatar Khanate appeared under Khan Haci Giray in the 1440s, but was conquered by the Ottoman Turks in the 1470s and appears[26] to have been absorbed into the Ottoman Empire as a semi-autonomous province.

The Crimean Tatar Khanate prospered in the 300 years that followed, building an economy based on trade and in particular on the slave trade. The source of the slaves was the Slavic-populated land to the north of the Crimean peninsula.

---

[20] http://kremlin.ru/events/president/news/20605. Accessed 21 August 2017; BBC: Ukraine crisis: Putin signs Russia-Crimea treaty http://www.bbc.com/news/world-europe-26630062. Accessed 21 August 2017.

[21] http://doc.ksrf.ru/decision/KSRFDecision155662.pdf. Accessed 21 August 2017.

[22] https://www.rt.com/news/russia-parliament-crimea-ratification-293/. Accessed 21 August 2017.

[23] Marples and Duke 1995.

[24] Fisher 1978, p. 2.

[25] Marples and Duke 1995, p. 262.

[26] This is disputed: see Fisher 1978, pp. 8–16.

Alan Fisher writes:

> From 1468 … until the end of the seventeenth century, Tatar raiders made almost annual forays into Slavic agricultural communities in the north searching for captives to sell as slaves.[27]

In Fisher's account, which is not universally accepted, slavery provided the means by which the Tatars created a flourishing and elaborate culture centered in Crimea, represented by and reflected in significant architecture and literature.

In the Great Russo-Turkish War of 1768–1774 Russia began to displace the Ottoman Turks from the north coast of the Black Sea. In 1771 a Russian force invaded Crimea and forced the Ottoman governor to flee.[28] The Treaty of Karasu Bazaar, signed between Russia and the Tatars in November 1772, created an independent Crimean state under the supervision and protection of Russia. Russian "supervision and protection" meant in reality three more Russian invasions of Crimea in the next ten years. Without Ottoman support, Crimea suffered a complete annexation in 1783, its first annexation by Russia.[29]

Andrew Wilson described the history of the Crimean Tatars since the first annexation of Crimea by Catherine II in 1783 as follows:[30]

> In 1783, when the Russian Empire annexed the peninsula, the Crimean Tatars who had been the leading force in Crimea since the fourteenth century, were still the majority population, at just over 80%. Successive waves of out-migration reduced their number to 19% (218,000) on the eve of their mass Deportation by the NKVD in 1944. Almost half perished during the Deportation and in the difficult years in Central Asia that followed.

There was a brief period of revival of the fortunes of the Crimean Tatars. On October 18, 1921, Lenin personally decided on the creation of a Crimean Autonomous Soviet Socialist Republic (ASSR)[31] within the Russian Socialist Federation of Soviet Republics (RSFSR), and within this entity, especially in the 1920s, the Crimean Tatars enjoyed a significant degree of autonomy in cultural and linguistic affairs.[32]

2.4 The Crimean Tatars in Independent Ukraine

In 1991 the Qurultay (Assembly) of the Crimean Tatar people passed a 'Declaration of National Sovereignty of the Crimean Tatar People' in 1991, which claimed that

---

[27] Ibid., p. 27.

[28] Fisher 1970, pp. 82–84.

[29] Fisher 1978.

[30] Wilson 2013, p. 418.

[31] Декрет ВЦИК и СНК от 18.10.1921 «Об Автономной Крымской Советской Социалистической Республике»: Facsimile of the Decree, at https://pravo.ru/store/interdoc/doc/464/18.10_Crimea.pdf. Accessed 21 August 2017.

[32] Marples and Duke 1995, p. 265; and Kirimal 1952.

'Crimea is the national territory of the Crimean Tatar people, on which they alone have the right to self-determination'.[33] Wilson noted that the 1996 Ukrainian Constitution refers vaguely to the rights of 'rooted [indigenous] peoples', but does not say who they are (the rights of ethnic Ukrainians are separately defined).[34]

Nevertheless, as Alexander Osipov showed in detail in an ECMI Brief:[35]

> In the course of return to their homeland the Crimean Tatars encountered huge problems concerning housing, employment, property, schooling and social security.[36] No compensation or property restitution has been envisaged by Ukrainian law, and the housing programmes for the repatriates were insufficient.[37] This led to illegal seizure of land and squatting that in turn repeatedly provoked tensions and even violent clashes.

I first visited Crimea in 1995 and worked with the Crimean Tatars in connection with the vitally important issue of citizenship. I was recruited by the United Nations Development Programme (UNDP) to act as legal expert for the Crimea Integration and Development Programme (CIDP). CIDP was established at the invitation of the Ukraine government in order "to promote sustainable human development in a manner that contributes to the maintenance of peace and stability in the Crimean peninsula though initiatives aimed at preventing interethnic conflicts and enhancing integration among different ethnic groups."[38]

Lord Ponsonby, Rapporteur for the Council of Europe Committee on Migration, Refugees and Demography, reported in 2000[39] that

> 17. Upon gaining independence, Ukraine granted citizenship to all persons residing in Ukraine on 13 November 1991 who were not citizens of other states. Thousands of Crimean Tatars who arrived after that date were faced with the requirement to pass the Ukrainian language test, produce proof of lawful employment, proof of having relinquished any other citizenship and pass an AIDS test.

> 18. The demand of Crimean Tatar leaders that all returnees should be automatically granted Ukrainian citizenship remained unheeded by the authorities. ... As a result, until very recently, a sizeable proportion of the returnee population not only did not have Ukrainian citizenship, but was, de facto, stateless.

> 21. Statelessness has severe implications. Stateless persons cannot be employed in the civil service, higher education is more expensive with certain faculties closed to the stateless (e.g. law school), they cannot participate in the privatisation of household plots and enterprises, travel abroad (Russia included) is restricted to those with post-Soviet passports, and, finally, such persons cannot participate in national or regional elections.

---

[33] Wilson 2013, p. 424.

[34] Ibid., p. 428.

[35] Osipov 2014.

[36] Kotigorenko 2005.

[37] Shevel 2001.

[38] http://www.un.org.ua/en/information-centre/news/415-2006-10-12-15-57-02.   Accessed   21 August 2017.

[39] "Repatriation and integration of the Tatars of Crimea" 18 February 2000, Doc. 8655 http://www.assembly.coe.int/nw/xml/XRef/X2H-Xref-ViewHTML.asp?FileID=8863&lang=EN. Accessed 21 August 2017.

It should be noted that in the Summary to his report, Lord Ponsonby, who met a great many protagonists during his visit from 13–17 September 1999, refers to the Crimean Tatars as "a Turkic people", "the Crimean Tatar people", and "this long-suffering people", even if he said the following (para 4 of his report):

> They lay claim to the status of indigenous people. Although this Rapporteur could not get an answer as to what that status implies in legal terms he was led to believe that this is a euphemism for titular nation. As such, it could be viewed by Crimean Tatar extremists as a first step to national autonomy. Many Crimean Tatars, while making a decision to return to Crimea, were guided by unrealistic expectations fostered by some of their political leaders.

Lord Ponsonby did not mention that the Ukrainian legislation prohibited double citizenship, and that renunciation of the Uzbek citizenship with which many Crimean Tatars found themselves after the collapse of the USSR in 1991 often turned out to be an insurmountable obstacle.

As Osipov explained:[40]

> … Ukrainian legislation does not allow double citizenship, and while Uzbekistan regarded most of the repatriates as its nationals, denunciation of the Uzbek citizenship often turned out to be an insurmountable obstacle. Besides, residence registration is in fact a requirement for citizenship applications, and this also barred many people from naturalization in Ukraine. Fortunately, Uzbekistan and Ukraine managed to resolve the citizenship issue for Crimean Tatars in 1998–99[41] under the aegis of the OSCE High Commissioner on National Minorities and the UN High Commissioner for Refugees.[42]

Indeed, Osipov commented, correctly, that

> In fact, the Ukrainian government has striven to use the Crimean Tatar movement, but has done very little to convince the Crimean Tatars that strategically they had substantive reasons to be loyal to the Ukrainian state. …The Ukrainian Law on the rehabilitation of the repressed people has been adopted too late - on 17 April 2014 - while the 1991 national Law on individual victims of political repressions has offered only symbolic benefits and compensations.[43]

My own experience of intensive work with UNDP from 1995, and later with UNHCR and the HCNM was that the Ukrainian authorities were at the very least unenthusiastic about assisting the returning Crimean Tatars, on the question of citizenship or any of the other burning issues confronting them. I vividly recall one high level meeting with senior Ukrainian functionaries at which John Packer, at that time the Legal Advisor to the HCNM, reminded his Ukrainian counterparts, to their evident consternation, that Ukraine had ratified and was bound by the provisions of the UN Convention on the Rights of the Child.[44] In particular Article 7:

---

[40] Osipov 2014, p. 5.

[41] Seniushkina 2001; and Shevel 2001, note 16.

[42] Seniushkina 2001, pp. 375–377; and Shevel 2001, note 16; and Uehling 2004.

[43] Osipov 2014, p. 6.

[44] Adopted and opened for signature, ratification and accession by General Assembly resolution 44/25 of 20 November 1989, entry into force 2 September 1990, at http://www.ohchr.org/EN/ProfessionalInterest/Pages/CRC.aspx. Accessed 21 August 2017.

Article 7

1. The child shall be registered immediately after birth and shall have the right from birth to a name, the right to acquire a nationality and. as far as possible, the right to know and be cared for by his or her parents.

2. States Parties shall ensure the implementation of these rights in accordance with their national law and their obligations under the relevant international instruments in this field, in particular where the child would otherwise be stateless.

By deliberately allowing the continuation of a situation, which was within the power of Ukraine to remedy, in which many Crimean Tatar children were stateless, Ukraine was blatantly violating its binding treaty obligations. Recognition of this fact was a significant contribution to inducing Ukraine to make concessions itself and to prevail upon Uzbekistan to change its requirements. But I repeat that without the intervention of UNHCR, which interpreted its mandate creatively to assist the Crimean Tatars, and the High Commissioner on National Minorities, who was constantly reminded by the Crimean Tatars that they were not a minority, much less a national minority with a kin state, but an indigenous people, the problem of citizenship would not have been resolved.

In conclusion, Ukraine did little or nothing to recognise the plight of the Crimean Tatar people or to respond to their claims until after the second annexation by Russia in 2014 had taken place.[45]

In my opinion, the Crimean Tatars are indigenous people of Crimea, with the right to self-determination. In the next part of this article I explore various aspects of the status, not often recognised, of the Crimean Tatar people.

2.5   The Status of the Crimean Tatar People

From 1991 onwards the Mejlis of the Crimean Tatar People had campaigned for ratification by Ukraine of International Labour Organisation Convention No. 169 of 1989,[46] which came into force in 1991. In my view the second part of the definition section, Section 1, defining "indigenous peoples" fits exactly the Crimean Tatar people:

(b) Peoples in independent countries who are regarded as indigenous on account of their descent from the populations which inhabited the country, or a geographical region to which the country belongs, at the time of conquest or colonisation or the establishment of present State boundaries and who, irrespective of their legal status, retain some or all of their own social, economic, cultural and political institutions.

As does the next provision:

2. Self-identification as indigenous or tribal shall be regarded as a fundamental criterion for determining the groups to which the provisions of this Convention.

---

[45] See for a discussion of the position up to 2002 Bowring 2002.

[46] Convention concerning Indigenous and Tribal Peoples in Independent Countries 1989 (ILO No. 169), 72 ILO Official Bull. 59, entered into force 5 September 1991.

It should also be noted that under this definition the Russian population of Crimea cannot be considered an indigenous people: they carried out the conquest and colonisation, and were never subjected to it.[47]

Despite vigorous lobbying by the Mejlis, two of whom, Mustafa Dzhemiloglu and Refat Chubarov were members of Ukraine's Verkhovna Rada, and its supporters, Ukraine never came close to ratification. Nor did it endorse the United Nations Declaration on the Rights of Indigenous People[48] until May 2014.

Nevertheless, the status of the Crimean Tatars as an indigenous people, by far the most numerous in Crimea, is beyond doubt.

However, as Borys Babin and Anna Prikhodko of the Crimean Tatar Resource Centre[49] have shown in detail,[50] international organisations including the United Nations have been very reluctant even to use the correct name of the "Mejlis of the Crimean Tatar People", practically never refer to them as a people, instead using terms such as "Crimean Tatars and other minorities", the "Crimean Tatar community", "Crimean Tatar population", "indigenous inhabitants", and so on.

Even the UN's International Court of Justice Order for Provisional Measures of 19 April 2017,[51] adopted by 13 votes to 3, that Russia must "Refrain from maintaining or imposing limitations on the ability of the Crimean Tatar community to conserve its representative institutions, including the Mejlis", refers to the "Crimean Tatar community", and only to the "the Mejlis". This would appear to be a compromise formulation which has been robbed of legal meaning.

There have been some exceptions. On 4 February 2015 the European Parliament for the first time referred to the Crimean Tatars as "indigenous people".[52] On 4 August 2005 Mr. Julian Burger, Coordinator of the Indigenous and Minorities Unit at the Office of the UN High Commissioner for Human Rights, officially confirmed by his letter of that date that the Mejlis of the Crimean Tatar People had been accredited to take part in the activity of the Working Group on the UN Draft Declaration on the Rights of Indigenous Peoples, as the Representative Body of Indigenous People of Crimean Tatars.[53] The representatives of the Mejlis of the Crimean Tatar People,

---

[47] I follow Oliver Loode in taking the view that the Krymchaks and Karaites, even if indigenous to Crimea, cannot really be considered indigenous peoples with the right to self-determination since, unlike the Crimean Tatars, they have not developed representative institutions that would enable exercise of the right to SD. Communication to the author.

[48] Resolution adopted by the General Assembly [without reference to a Main Committee (A/61/L.67 and Add.1)] 61/295, 13 September 2007 at http://www.un.org/esa/socdev/unpfii/documents/DRIPS_en.pdf. Accessed 21 August 2017.

[49] http://ctrcenter.org/en/news. Accessed 21 August 2017.

[50] Crimean Tatar Resource Centre (2017), "UN Legal Standards' Application Towards the Indigenous Peoples of Crimea", on file with the author.

[51] http://www.icj-cij.org/files/case-related/166/19394.pdf. Accessed 21 August 2017.

[52] http://www.europarl.europa.eu/sides/getDoc.do?type=TA&reference=P8-TA-2016-0043 &language=EN&ring=P8-RC-2016-0173. Accessed 21 August 2017. And see the blog comment by Oliver Loode of Minority Rights Group International "A Window to Europe for Crimean Tatars" at http://minorityrights.org/2016/02/11/a-window-to-europe-for-crimean-tatars/. Accessed 21 August 2017.

[53] On file with the author.

notably Mr. Nadir Bekir, played an active role in the deliberations of the Working Group, but Mr. Burger's letter cannot be taken as an authoritative determination of status.

On 12 May 2016, the EU Parliament adopted a strongly worded resolution on the Crimean Tatars.[54] This stated that "...the Russian Federation has illegally annexed Crimea and Sevastopol and is therefore an occupying state which has violated international law."

The resolution characterised the Crimean Tatars in the following way: "the indigenous community of Crimean Tatars, a majority of whom oppose the Russian takeover of the peninsula and boycotted the so-called referendum on 16 March 2014";[55] and "the entire population of Crimean Tatars, an indigenous people of Crimea, was forcibly deported to other parts of the then USSR in 1944, with no right to return until 1989".[56] The resolution condemned the banning of the representative body of the Crimean Tatars, describing it as "... this democratically elected decision-making body representing the Crimean Tatar people...",[57] and the "Mejlis of the Crimean Tatar People, which is the legitimate and recognised representative body of the indigenous people of Crimea".[58]

There can therefore be no question but that the European Parliament recognises the Crimean Tatars as an indigenous people of Crimea, their "historic homeland", and puts beyond doubt their status as a "people" for the purposes of the right to self-determination.

The position of the Prosecutor of the International Criminal Court, Fatou Bensouda, on 14 November 2016, is unequivocal as to the status of Crimea:[59]

> The information available suggests that the situation within the territory of Crimea and Sevastopol amounts to an international armed conflict between Ukraine and the Russian Federation. This international armed conflict began at the latest on 26 February when the Russian Federation deployed members of its armed forces to gain control over parts of the Ukrainian territory without the consent of the Ukrainian Government. The law of international armed conflict would continue to apply after 18 March 2014 to the extent that the situation within the territory of Crimea and Sevastopol factually amounts to an on-going state of occupation. A determination of whether or not the initial intervention which led to the occupation is considered lawful or not is not required. For purposes of the Rome Statute an armed conflict may be international in nature if one or more States partially or totally occupies the territory of another State, whether or not the occupation meets with armed resistance.[60]

---

[54] http://humanrightshouse.org/Articles/21611.html. Accessed 21 August 2017.

[55] Ibid., at B.

[56] Ibid., at F.

[57] Ibid., at 1.

[58] Ibid., at 2.

[59] Report on Preliminary Examination Activities 2016, at https://www.icc-cpi.int/iccdocs/otp/161 114-otp-rep-PE_ENG.pdf. Accessed 21 August 2017.

[60] Ibid., para 170.

However, in her summary of alleged crimes committed in Crimea,[61] she refers only to the "Crimean Tatar population".

2.6 The Official (and an Unofficial) Russian Position

In addition to the "Legal Arguments" document referred to above, the official Russian position has been consistent. On 17 March 2014, commenting on the statements of the UN Assistant Secretary-General, Ivan Šimonović, during his visit to Ukraine, the Russian Ministry of Foreign Affairs (MID) stated: "The people of Crimea are the bearers of the sovereignty of Crimea and they expressed their will at the referendum of the 16 March."[62]

In his speech to the State Duma on 20 March 2014, Mr. Lavrov, the Russian Minister of Foreign Affairs said: "Against the backdrop of the events in Kiev and in Western regions of Ukraine, the attempts to do the same in South-East regions of Ukraine, the Crimeans took the decision that it was impossible for them to exercise their right to self-determination within the Ukrainian state."[63] Which necessarily implied that "the Crimeans" constituted a "people" for the purposes of international law.

On 20 May 2015 Mr. Lavrov repeated that "… the people of Crimea made their choice, which we supported, despite the fierce campaign to question the freedom of their choice."[64]

Most recently, in the Comment by Russian Foreign Ministry Spokesperson Maria Zakharova of 16 March 2017 "on the occasion of the three-year anniversary of Crimea's unification with Russia", she said the following, which I cite at some length:[65]

> The proclamation in March 2014 of the independence of the Republic of Crimea and its unification with the Russian Federation were a legitimate exercise of the right of the people of Crimea to self-determination following an armed coup in Ukraine and the mayhem wreaked by radical national forces that did not hesitate to use terror and intimidation on both political opponents and the population of entire regions of that country.
>
> In these circumstances, on March 17, 2014, the Supreme Council of the Republic of Crimea, based on the results of the general referendum in Crimea on March 16, decided to proclaim Crimea an independent sovereign state, the Republic of Crimea. On March 18, the Republic

---

[61] Ibid., paras 172–176, under the headings Harassment of Crimean Tatar population, Killing and abduction, Ill-treatment, Detention and fair trial, Compelled military service.

[62] http://www.mid.ru/en/web/guest/maps/ua/-/asset_publisher/ktn0ZLTvbbS3/content/id/70290. Accessed 21 August 2017.

[63] http://www.mid.ru/en/web/guest/foreign_policy/news/-/asset_publisher/cKNonkJE02Bw/content/id/69626. Accessed 21 August 2017.

[64] http://www.mid.ru/en/web/guest/kommentarii_predstavitelya/-/asset_publisher/MCZ7HQuMdqBY/content/id/2687592. Accessed 21 August 2017.

[65] http://www.mid.ru/en/web/guest/foreign_policy/news/-/asset_publisher/cKNonkJE02Bw/content/id/2687802. Accessed 21 August 2017.

of Crimea signed an international treaty to join the Russian Federation. As a result, the Russian Federation gained two new constituent entities, the Republic of Crimea and the federal city of Sevastopol.

The future has proved the legitimacy of the decision to reunite with Russia taken by Crimeans three years ago. The legality and validity of this exercise of the right to self-determination are on graphic display today, in light of the disgraceful bloody campaign waged by the Kiev regime against its own people.

The Russian official position is clear and consistent: the right to self-determination was exercised by "the people of Crimea", "the Crimeans". My contention is that Russia has quite simply got it wrong. The only "people" with a right to self-determination in Crimea is the Crimean Tatar people, an indigenous people of Crimea.

A flavour of the unofficial but highly influential Russian discourse concerning Ukraine and Crimea is given by an article, "The USA is hanging by a thread", which appeared on 3 February 2016 in the mass-circulation weekly *Argumenty i Fakty*.[66] The author was Leonid Reshetnikov, a retired Lieutenant General of the SVR, Russia's MI6, and Director of the research institute of the Russian Secret Services, RISI, Russian Institute for Strategic Research, appointed by President Putin in 2009.[67]

In part, his rather hysterical article read as follows:

We are living through the fruits of the bomb, of which V. Putin spoke, which Lenin placed under our State.[68]

The Soviet authorities created on sacred Russian territory a geopolitical monster, Ukraine. This took place through the special services of the Kaiser's Germany and the Bolsheviks.

They created Ukraine, and cut away from Russia the Russian city of Kharkov (founded by Alexei Mikhailovich), Donetsk (founded by Tsar Aleksander II), Nikolaev, Dnepropetrovsk and Odessa (all three founded by the Empress Catherine II). And Khrushchev also gave away Crimea.

What is Ukraine for? It was needed for one purpose – to become anti-Russian. And until our Little Russian brothers cease to be zombified monsters, their new owners the USA will be ready to fight to the last Ukrainian.

Indeed the idea that Ukraine is a fabricated state, created by those hostile to Russia, is widespread in the Russian media. If, on this argument, the purpose of Ukraine is indeed to attack Russia, then the predominantly ethnic Russian and Russian speaking population of Crimea had no choice but to secede.

---

[66] http://www.aif.ru/politics/world/leonid_reshetnikov_ssha_visyat_na_voloske (accessed on 14 July 2017.

[67] https://riss.ru/. Accessed 21 August 2017.

[68] This is a reference to Lenin's very clear theory and practice of the right of nations to self-determination.

2.7 Russian scholars on Crimea

Conveniently for my purposes, three leading Russian scholars contributed to the 2015 Heidelberg Journal special issue referred to above.

In his contribution,[69] Professor Anatoly Kapustin of the Peoples Friendship University in Moscow, correctly wrote as follows:

> ...the principle of self determination of peoples has developed into a generally accepted norm of international law, which has the character of a customary norm of international law.[70]

As to what constitutes a "people", Kapustin referred to a short passage from the work of James Summers:[71]

> At the same time, international legal scholarship recognizes that the right to self-determination is of a collective nature, so that "only groups that qualify as such, can access the right". However, in the broadest sense of the word peoples are considered as "large, anonymous human groups possessing certain national characteristics".[72]

Kapustin also drew from the doyen of Russian international legal scholarship, Stanislas Chernichenko,[73] for the following:

> Links to national traits bring the concept of the "people" close to the concept of the "nation", allowing some scholars to argue that a people, like the nation, is characterized by the following: accommodation in a common area, economic integrity of the population and related social integrity, the presence of certain elements of a common culture and an awareness of this fact. Additional factors that stimulate integrity may be racial or linguistic proximity, common religion, etc.[74]

After sketching the history of Crimea, somewhat tendentiously, Kapustin turned briefly to the heart of the matter: do the "people of Crimea" qualify as a "people" for the purpose of the exercise of the right to self-determination? His answer was:

> Moreover, there is no doubt that the people of Crimea may be considered a people by the standards of international law. They have developed a political-ethnic community, which is the bearer of the right to self determination. Earlier we referred to the wording that defines people as large, anonymous group of people who have certain national characteristics. This definition is quite applicable to the people of Crimea, which in its composition is poly-ethnic.[75]

And he cited in support the words of President Putin in his speech of 18 March 2017, already set out above: "Crimea is a unique blend of different peoples' cultures and traditions. This makes it similar to Russia as a whole, where not a single ethnic

---

[69] Kapustin 2015.

[70] Ibid., p. 104.

[71] Summers 2014.

[72] Ibid., pp. 7 et seq.

[73] Chernichenko 1999.

[74] Ibid., pp. 174, 177.

[75] Kapustin 2015, p. 115.

group has been lost over the centuries. Russians and Ukrainians, Crimean Tatars and people of other ethnic groups have lived side by side in Crimea, retaining their own identity, traditions, languages and faith".

It will be seen that Kapustin gratefully adopts Summers's words as to "anonymous group" but ignores the words which immediately follow: "certain national characteristics". He has failed to show that the "people of Crimea" have any such characteristics. As to the right to secession, he adds: "In the Crimean situation the physical existence of the people was at stake and therefore a secession from Ukraine was justified under the requirements of "remedial secession"."[76] Even if it is accepted that there is or was a "people of Crimea", Kapustin does not remotely show how their physical existence was at stake.

In his erudite contribution to the same issue of the Heidelberg Journal, Professor Vladislav Tolstykh of Novosibirsk State University settled on a novel interpretation of Rousseau's theory of the "general will".[77] When self-determination is considered in the light of the general will, Tolstykh argued, the "people" can be understood as a "political union". In which case "the right to self-determination, including in the form of secession, can be used by the groups excluded from political communication (excluded from the people) who, as a result, find themselves in a state of nature."[78] This line of reasoning lead to the following analysis: "... consideration of the Crimean situation in the context of the general will leads to... conclusions [differing from those of most scholars], according to which the winter coup in Kiev resulted in the breaking of the social contract and the exclusion of the Crimean population from political communication."[79] And a startling conclusion: "Being excluded from the political communication, the population of Crimea found itself in natural state, and formed its own general will, aiming at reunifying with Russia."[80] For Tolstykh it further followed that "... the behavior of the Western states in Ukraine in the winter 2013/2014 may be considered as interference in the formation of the general will and thus – as a violation of the principle of non-intervention."[81]

But this entire argument depends on an unusual and counter-intuitive understanding of which groups should qualify as "peoples". In this case, Tolstykh nominated "the population of Crimea".

Alexander Salenko of the Immanuel Kant Baltic Federal University in Kaliningrad was the author in the same issue of an even more unusual proposal.[82] He investigated the legitimacy of the dissolution of the Soviet Union, taking into consideration the results and legal effect of two referenda which took place in 1991: the Soviet Union Referendum on the preservation of the USSR on 17 March 1991 in which large majorities in 9 Union Republics – but not Ukraine - voted in favour of retaining

---

[76] Ibid., p. 117.

[77] Tolstykh 2015.

[78] Ibid., p. 124.

[79] Ibid., p. 135.

[80] Ibid., p. 136.

[81] Ibid., p. 136.

[82] Salenko 2015.

the USSR and the All-Ukrainian Independence Referendum on 1 December 1991. On this basis he proposed an analysis of the causes of the "Reunification of Crimea with Russia" on 21 March 2014.[83] He pointed out that in the opinion of Mikhail Gorbachev the "adventurist dissolving of the Soviet Union" was the prime cause.

Following a detailed although rather tendentious account of the relevant events, Salenko asserted that the liquidation of the Soviet Union was illegal and unconstitutional, and did not comply with the existing law. He concluded that "a "warped legal groundwork" was laid for the foundation of statehood of the new independent states (the former Soviet Union republics) because the elite of nine republics consciously violated the will of the people. And now we witness in Crimea and in the East of Ukraine that the "legal foundations have settled", and the walls of the "Ukrainian house" are beginning to crack."[84]

This is in effect an argument that Ukraine lacks legitimacy.

2.8 Conclusion

The purpose of this article, I repeat, has not been to rehearse or to repeat the many convincingly scholarly articles, and indeed the predominance of the views of the international community, that Crimea was illegally annexed by Russia in early 2014. Instead, I have focused on Russia's legal justification for its actions, and in particular its reliance on the alleged right of the "Crimean people" or "people of Crimea" to self-determination, and to "remedial secession". I hope to have shown in detail that there is one "people" which such a right in Crimea, namely the Crimean Tatar people, who are an indigenous people of Crimea.

My title contains the words "Pandora's Box". Russia's invocation of the right to self-determination of sits oddly with the denunciation, noted above, of Lenin's consistent call for the right of nations to self-determination. As early as 1991, the year of the collapse of the USSR, Mr. Putin denounced Lenin, and was filmed doing so. A YouTube clip contains a number of such statements by him over the years.[85] On 25 January 2016 President Putin accused Lenin of placing an 'atomic bomb'[86] under Russia. He was particularly critical of Lenin's concept of a federative state with its entities having the right to secede, saying it had heavily contributed to the 1991 breakup of the Soviet Union. He added that Lenin was wrong in his dispute with Stalin, who, in Mr. Putin's words, advocated a unitary state model. He also said that Lenin's government had whimsically drawn borders between parts of the USSR,

---

[83] Ibid., p. 141.

[84] Ibid., p. 162.

[85] https://www.youtube.com/watch?v=lIoEwESh320. Accessed on 21 August 2017.

[86] See also the transcript of a meeting of the President's Council on Science and Education, on 21 January 2016, at http://kremlin.ru/events/councils/by-council/6/51190. Accessed on 21 August 2017.

placing Donbass under the Ukrainian jurisdiction in order to increase the percentage of proletariat in a move Mr. Putin called "delirious".[87]

However, Russia's ethnic and linguistic diversity is impressive if not unique. Russia has stated that "The Russian Federation is one of the largest multinational states in the world, inhabited by more than 170 peoples, the total population being about 140 million." Russia also reported that "The education in Russia's schools is now available in 38 languages… As many as 75 national languages are a part (including languages of national minorities) of the secondary schools curricula." The Volga Tatars are the largest such minority, with 5½ million members, and there are large populations of Cherkassians, Buryats, Chechens, and many others. They are certainly peoples with a right to self-determination – and to remedial secession?

References

Bowring B (2002) Between a (Russian) rock and a (Crimean Tatar) hard place? Ethnic, linguistic and minority issues. In: Lewis A (ed) Ukraine and the EU: Neighbours, Friends, Partners? The Federal Trust, London, pp. 61–70

Bowring B (2005) The Crimean autonomy: innovation or anomaly? In: Weller M, Wolff S (eds) Autonomy, Self-governance and Conflict Resolution: Innovative approaches to institutional design in divided societies Routledge, Abingdon, pp. 75–97

Bowring B (2008a) The Degradation of the International Legal Order? The Rehabilitation of Law and the Possibility of Politics. Routledge, Abingdon

Bowring B (2008b) Positivism versus self-determination: the contradictions of Soviet international law. In: Marks S (ed) International Law on the Left: Re-examining Marxist Legacies. Cambridge University Press, Cambridge, pp. 133–168

Bowring B (forthcoming) The Contradictions of Soviet Diplomacy and Foreign Policy in the Era of Decolonization. In: Dann P, von Bernstorff J (eds) The Battle for International Law in the Decolonization Era. Oxford University Press, Oxford

Cassese A (1995) Self-Determination of Peoples. A Legal Reappraisal. Cambridge University Press, Cambridge

Chernichenko SV (1999) Teoriya mezhdunarodnovo prava. t.2 Starye i novye teoreticheskie problemy (Theory of International Law, Vol. II – Old and New Theoretical Problems), NIMP Publisher, Moscow

Fisch J (2015) The Right of Self-Determination of Peoples. The Domestication of an Illusion. Cambridge University Press, Cambridge 2015 (originally published as Das Selbstbestimmungsrecht der Völker (Verlag C. H. Beck oHG, München))

Fisher A (1970) The Russian Annexation of the Crimea, 1772–1783. Cambridge University Press, Cambridge

Fisher A (1978) The Crimean Tatars. Hoover Institution Press, Stanford

Kapustin A (2015) Crimea's Self-Determination in the Light of Contemporary International Law. Heidelberg Journal of International Law (Zeitschrift für ausländisches öffentliches Recht und Völkerrecht, ZaöRV) 75: 101–118 at http://www.zaoerv.de/75_2015/75_2015_1_a_101_118.pdf. Accessed 21 August 2017

Kirimal E (1952) Der nationale Kampf der Krimtürken [The National Struggle of the Crimean Turks]. Lechte, Emsdetten

---

[87] https://www.theguardian.com/world/2016/jan/25/vladmir-putin-accuses-lenin-of-placing-a-time-bomb-under-russia. Accessed on 21 August 2017.

Kotigorenko V (2005) Кримськотатарські репатріанти: проблема соціальної адаптації [The Crimean Tatar Repatriates: The Problems of Social Adaptation] Svitogliad, Kiev

Lipman M (2015) A Museum Survives in Crimea *The New Yorker* 3 August 2015, at http://www.newyorker.com/news/news-desk/a-museum-survives-in-crimea. Accessed 21 August 2017

Marks S (2008) (ed) International Law on the Left: Re-examining Marxist Legacies. Cambridge University Press, Cambridge

Marples D, Duke D (1995) Ukraine, Russia and the Question of Crimea. Nationalities Papers 23: 261–289

Marxsen C, Peters A, Hartwig M (eds) Symposium: The Incorporation of Crimea by the Russian Federation in the Light of International Law at http://www.zaoerv.de/75_2015/vol75.cfm and http://www.zaoerv.de/75_2015/75_2015_1_a_1_2.pdf. Accessed 21 August 2017

Osipov A (2014) What do the Crimean Tatars face in Crimea? European Centre for Minority Issues (ECMI) Brief #32, at http://www.infoecmi.eu/index.php/ecmi-issue-brief-crimean-tatars/. Accessed 21 August 2017

Rossi C (2015) Ex Injuria Jus Non Oritur, Ex Factis Jus Oritur, and the Elusive Search for Equilibrium After Ukraine. Tulane Journal of International and Comparative Law 24: 143–73,

Rossi C (2016) Impaled on Morton's Fork: Kosovo, Crimea and the *Sui Generis Circumstance*. Emory International Law Review 30: 353–390

Salenko A (2015) Legal Aspects of the Dissolution of the Soviet Union in 1991 and Its Implications for the Reunification of Crimea with Russia in 2014 Heidelberg Journal of International Law 75:1 141–166, at www.zaoerv.de/75_2015/75_2015_1_a_141_166.pdf. Accessed 8 July 2018

Sayapin S (2015) The United Nations General Assembly Resolution 68/262 in the context of general international law. European Political and Law Discourse 2: 19–30

Seniushkina T (undated) *Управление местными сообществами в Крыму* [Management of local communities in Crimea]. In: Tishkov V, Filippova E (eds) *Местное управление многоэтничными сообществами в странах СНГ* [Local Governance of Multi-ethnic Communities in the CIS Countries] Aviaizdat, Moscow, pp. 353–384

Shevel O (2001) Crimean Tatars and the Ukrainian state: the challenge of politics, the use of law, and the meaning of rhetoric. Krimski Studii, 1:109–129. At: http://www.iccrimea.org/scholarly/oshevel.html. Accessed 21 August 2017

Summers J (2014) Peoples and International Law, 2nd edn. Martinus Nijhoff

Teson F (2016) The Theory of Self-Determination. Cambridge University Press Cambridge

Tolstykh V (2015) Three Ideas of Self-Determination in International Law and the Reunification of Crimea with Russia Heidelberg Journal of International Law 75:1 119–139 at www.zaoerv.de/75_2015/75_2015_1_a_119_140.pdf. Accessed 8 July 2018

Uehling G (2004) Evaluation of UNHCR's programme to prevent and reduce statelessness in Crimea, Ukraine EPAU/2004/03, at http://www.unhcr.org/405ab4c74.pdf. Accessed 21 August 2017

Wilson A (2013) The Crimean Tatars: A Quarter of a Century after Their Return. Security and Human Rights 24: 418–431

Chapter 3
An Illegal Territorial Regime? On the Occupation and Annexation of Crimea as a Matter of International Law

Valentina Azarova

Contents

Abstract What happens to the international law of occupation when the de facto administrator not only subjectively rejects its applicability, but maintains the occupation with the intention to acquire or transform territory? What effects does it have on the de facto administrator's status? And what implications on the welfare of the civilian population? Is it appropriate for international law to regulate such situations as belligerent occupations? Russia's occupation of Crimea exemplifies the regulatory challenges created by contemporary situations of occupation qua annexation, which

Post-Doctoral Fellow, Center for Global Public Law, Koç University Law School, Istanbul. Koç University, Sariyer, Istanbul 34450, Turkey. She is also a strategic and legal advisor to the Global Legal Action Network (GLAN), a collective that works to challenge exploitative transnational dealings, and has over a decade of experience working with and advising international and local rights groups. The author owes thanks to Bill van Esveld, Szymon Zaręba and Antal Berkes for their insights and comments on earlier drafts. All errors remain the author's own. Email: vazarova@ku.edu.tr.

V. Azarova (✉)
Koç University Law School, Center for Global Public Law, 34450 Sariyer, Istanbul, Turkey
e-mail: vazarova@ku.edu.tr

V. Azarova
Koç University, 34450 Sariyer, Istanbul, Turkey

© T.M.C. ASSER PRESS and the authors 2018
S. Sayapin and E. Tsybulenko (eds.), *The Use of Force against Ukraine and International Law*, https://doi.org/10.1007/978-94-6265-222-4_3

this chapter argues are a form of illegal territorial regime. To address them, the chapter explores the place of occupation law and its mutually-reliant relationship between the international norms of conflict management (*jus in bello*), which includes occupation law, and those of conflict prevention and resolution (*jus ad bellum*). It argues that such illegal situations are incommensurable with the legal category of belligerent occupation in international law: they necessitate the diligent application of the *jus ad bellum* to appropriately regulate occupying states seeking territorial aggrandisement and foreign domination. The operation of the consequence of invalidity in such cases means that third party States and international organisations are made to undertake the enforcement and protection of the civilian population under the aegis of the foreign power.

Keywords Belligerent Occupation · Use of Force · Annexation · Foreign Territorial Control · Illegal Territorial Regime · Invalidity · De Facto Entities · Crimea

> Life goes on in the territory concerned for its inhabitants. That life must be made tolerable and be protected by the de facto authorities [...] the acts of these authorities related thereto cannot be simply ignored by third States or by international institutions.[1]
>
> European Court of Human Rights

> But fictions of law hold only in respect to the ends and purposes for which they were invented; when they are urged to an intent and purpose not within the reason and policy of the fiction, the other party may show the truth.[2]
>
> Lord L. J. Mansfield

3.1 Introduction

Russia's activities in Crimea raise urgent questions about the international law applicable to the facts of the case and, more broadly, about the appropriateness[3] of the use of the legal category of 'belligerent occupation' in contemporary situations of foreign control over territory. The international legal system has appeared unable to fully capture, much less accommodate, the consequences of Russia's conduct in Crimea, just as it has failed to bring an end to other situations of belligerent occupation that pursue the permanent displacement of the legitimate sovereign of the

---

[1] *Cyprus v. Turkey*, Application No. 25781/94, judgement of 10 May 2001, para 96.

[2] Lord L.J. Mansfield in Morris v Pugh (1761) 3 Burr. 1242, 1243; quoted by Lon L. Fuller, Legal Fictions (Stanford University Press 1967) at 51.

[3] Zhu Xi's ethical philosophy advocated "the need for people, as prospective moral agents, to notice the fine details, the distinguishing features of particular situations and to fashion on that basis the most discerning, appropriate response.", see Thompson 2015.

occupied territory, including through the territory's illegal annexation.[4] This work refers to such cases as having the effect of producing an illegal territorial regime.[5] In such situations, the international legal system is caught up in a dilemma: the classical operative premises of the international law of belligerent occupation (hereinafter occupation law) seem incommensurable[6] with the premises of other bodies of international law that apply to situations of annexation and permanent transformation of 'occupied territory'.[7] Occupation law seeks to fill a governance vacuum in territory from which the sovereign has been ousted, by imposing rights and obligations on the foreign power as occupying power. But these perquisites are at odds with the objective consequence of invalidity of the acts and effects of the authorities of an illegal territorial regime in cases where the invading state claims sovereign authority over the occupied territory.

Since the law of occupation (*jus in bello*) is a subset of the law of administration,[8] it and the law on the use of force (*jus ad bellum*) are in fact mutually dependent, and should be interpreted systemically.[9] Indeed, a common mistake is to apply occupation law, which has its place in the international law of conflict management, in isolation rather than in conjunction with the international law of conflict resolution and prevention (the *jus ad bellum*).[10] The misperception that these two bodies of law can operate at cross-purposes, in terms of the protection of the civilian population, is evidenced by the practice of international law in cases of occupation that pursue annexation. But the inter-reliance between these bodies of law can also generate productive synergies for the enforcement of international law, which have been overlooked.[11]

Crimea is an illegal territorial regime based on an objective illegality that results from violations of peremptory norms of international law (*jus cogens*) intended to change the international status of the territory, as well as its government system and demographic characteristics. In an occupation[12] maintained for the purpose of undertaking the annexation of the occupied territory, such violations of peremptory

---

[4] Other situations of unlawfully prolonged occupation referenced throughout the chapter include: Western Sahara, Palestine, Golan Heights, Abkhazia and South Ossetia, Transnistria, northern Cyprus, and Nagorno-Karabakh.

[5] The term was coined by Ronen 2011 based on criteria of legality for territorial regimes noted by Crawford 1979, which include principally the prohibition on the use of force to acquire territory including for the creation of a new state.

[6] Drawing on Thomas Kuhn's idea of incommensurability, see Bird 2011.

[7] Wrange 2015.

[8] See Wilde 2009.

[9] Vienna Convention on the Law of Treaties 1969 1155 U.N.T.S. 331, Article 31(3).

[10] Azarova 2018.

[11] Wright 1961.

[12] I use this term to refer to situations of occupation maintained through illegal force in pursuit of the territory's acquisition or secession. While occupation law applies equally to all situations of occupation, the pursuit of territorial acquisition renders the continued presence of the occupying state in the territory unlawful. See Azarova 2017a.

norms are systemic and structural such that the regime whose existence is premised on
the unlawful territorial situation,[13] is itself illegal. The chapter explores international
legal remedies for such illegal territorial regimes:[14] de facto authorities controlling
broadly defined territory, without either being a state or being formally recognised as
part of a state since their establishment is premised on violations of peremptory norms
of international law.[15] The constitutive features of an illegal territorial regime include
legislative and administrative acts that purport to revise the international legal status
of the territory, bestow political agency and sovereign title on a governing authority
other than the legitimate sovereign, change the territory's demographic composition,
and demote the status of its local population.[16] Taken as a whole, these factual features
have normative implications: they reveal the way the de facto administrator defines
its status in the territory and relates to its *de jure* obligations as an occupying power,
and to the rights of the ousted sovereign and its population.

The aim of this chapter is to interrogate the dissonance between the consequences
of an illegal territorial regime, particularly under the law on the use of force, and the
normative premises of the post-colonial law of belligerent occupation. Crimea, which
shares some characteristics with other ongoing situations of foreign occupation qua
annexation such as the West Bank, Golan Heights and Western Sahara,[17] marks a
departure from the traditional approach to the regulation of situations of belligerent
occupation. The purpose of insisting that the status of the territory is occupied as a
matter of international law is to nullify the claims being pursued through the use of
force by the annexing state. Here, the application of occupation law serves a normative
purpose. Understanding Russia's unlawfully-prolonged occupation of Crimea as an
illegal territorial regime – extra-legal to the law of occupation – helps expose the
limits of the remedial nature of occupation law and reveals the effects of the *ipso
jure* remedies assigned as part of the legal consequences of peremptory norms of
international law.[18] But, as we observe, it may also create protection gaps.[19]

In approaching this contemporary problematique of the relevance of occupation
law, the chapter observes the normative interplay between the law of belligerent
occupation[20] and other international law norms.[21] As a regime of *lex specialis* under
international humanitarian law (IHL), occupation law operates as mutually interac-

---

[13] See for the definition of an 'unlawful territorial situation' Milano 2006, at 5–10.

[14] Ronen 2011, at 1.

[15] Ibid., Milano 2006, at 5–10.

[16] On the processes of status demotion, Gross 2017, Chapter 5.

[17] Wrange 2015. It is not merely a situation governed by IHL, but also one that triggers the jus ad
bellum norms it violates.

[18] Costelloe 2017.

[19] See for a sequence of events concerning the annexation of Crimea Tancredi 2014. See for a
different perspective on the distortive effects of occupation law Sayed 2014.

[20] Contemporary occupation law is authoritatively conceived of as a legal framework drawn from
both IHL and IHRL; Arai-Takahashi 2009, Part II. Benvenisti 2013, at 102–105.

[21] See, on the international law of territoriality, Shaw 1982, at 61–91.

tive law:[22] while the correct interpretation and application of international human rights law (IHRL) provisions must be premised on the full implementation of IHL rules, the full implementation of IHL depends on the occupying state's respect of its obligations under the law on the use of force (the *jus ad bellum*). The chapter undertakes to address the as yet underdetermined practical and normative implications of this matrix of mutual interaction between IHRL, IHL and the *jus ad bellum* – with an emphasis on the consequence of invalidity triggered by the latter. It uses it as a point of departure for an analysis of the international law applicable to the illegal territorial regime maintained by Russia in Crimea. Complementing other accounts of the legal framework applicable to the situation in Crimea included in this volume, the chapter takes a consequentialist approach to the assessment of the international law response to situations like Crimea. It applies a heuristic to reconcile the seeming incommensurability and incoherence between the traditional approach to the regulation of occupation in international law, and the legal characteristics of an illegal territorial regime. In so doing, it signals a way forward in the regulation of the kind of predatory practices taking place in the context of Russia's occupation of Crimea.

The situation in Crimea emblematises the protection gaps and anomalies that result from the failure to systematise the application of the *jus ad bellum*.[23] The chapter begins with an appraisal of the appropriateness of the application of occupation law in situations like Crimea, in line with the widely-held view that the territory remains subject to regulation by the law of occupation despite its annexation.[24] Against this backdrop, we critically examine whether, and if so to what extent, contemporary international law is equipped to handle cases of illegal territorial regimes such as Crimea. Section 3.3 discusses the dilemmas of illegal *ipso jure*, by operation of the consequence of invalidity of certain internationally unlawful acts.[25] Section 3.4 analyses the institutions, acts, and effects of Russia's continued presence in Crimea. Section 3.5 discusses the consequences and costs of such remedies for the civilian population under an illegal territorial regime. The chapter's postscript reflects on the regulatory challenge presented by cases of foreign territorial control like Crimea as a function of long-standing questions of regime design in international law.

3.2 'Crimea': The End(s) of Occupation Law

The inappropriateness of the contemporary approach to the regulation of *sui generis* situations of belligerent occupation such as Crimea in international law results from the incommensurability of the phenomenon of colonial domination with the

---

[22] I owe this term, which denotes the mutual dependence and cross-fertilisation between the specialised law of occupation and other regimes of international law, to Basak Çali.

[23] Ohlin 2015.

[24] Tancredi 2014.

[25] Orakhelashvili 2003, at 19–56.

managerial law of occupation.[26] In post-colonial international law, the progressive abolition and exclusion of such practice has resulted in the dilution of the law prohibiting colonial domination, subjugation,[27] and exploitation which was replaced by the law of self-determination,[28] the law on the use of interstate force, the law on belligerent occupation under IHL and IHRL.[29]

3.2.1 Defying Ends

In the colonial era, occupation law was deemed inapplicable to 'colonial occupations', since a 'civilised' nation was allowed to claim sovereignty and acquire parts of the uncivilised world.[30] Today, international law has outlawed such colonial practices. The international law of conflict management, i.e. IHL and IHRL, was never intended to be able to disincentivise 'colonial occupants' from acting in contempt of the prohibition on colonial domination.[31] It relies on the prohibition to this effect in conflict prevention law (i.e. the UN Charter), which outlaws such acts and can be used to elicit responses to them in international circles. A recent example is found in the HRC's March 2017 resolution on Israeli settlements, affirming that settlements entail the "de facto annexation" of Palestinian territory and that it cannot be recognised as lawful by third parties, while calling on Israel "to accept the de jure applicability" of the 1949 Fourth Geneva Convention.[32] HRC and SC resolutions often stop short of assessing the international legal consequences that follow from the annexation; implying that the priority for regulating the situation that emerges from its continued presence in Palestinian territory is to entrust the regulation of its symptoms to occupation law. The result is that occupation law has been made into a trope at the whims of 'colonial occupiers'.

---

[26] Not all puzzles that could be tackled in the old paradigm will be solved by the new one—this is the phenomenon of "Kuhn loss".

[27] See for a similar case of dilution the abolition of slavery through international law, which formally marked the abolition of such a cardinal abuse, i.e. a breach of a peremptory norm of international law, yet also occurred in such a way that the safeguards and disincentives for its recurrence have subsequently weakened; McGeehan 2011, 436–460.

[28] Korman 1996.

[29] ICJ 2004, pp. 187–189, paras 127–131 and pp. 191–192, para 134. See also ECHR, Loizidou v. Turkey, Judgment, Application No. 15318/89, paras 54, 57; ECHR, Al-Skeini and others v. United Kingdom, Case No. 55721/07, Judgment, 7 July 2011, paras 138–142; ECHR Chiragov v. Armenia, Application No. 13216/05, judgement of 16 June 2015. See on human rights in prolonged occupation, Koutroulis 2012, 165–205. See, on the particularities of the interaction and the shortcomings of the application of IHRL in occupied territory, Gross 2015.

[30] Arai-Takahashi 2012, 51–80; Megret 2006.

[31] Carcano 2015.

[32] Human Rights Council, Israeli settlements in the Occupied Palestinian Territory, including East Jerusalem, and in the occupied Syrian Golan, UN Doc. A/HRC/34/L.41, adopted on 21 March 2017 (by 36 votes in favour, including the Netherlands, Germany, Switzerland and Belgium).

Foremost, this practice appears to set aside a basic point concerning the normative premises and predicates of occupation law noted above. Since a state's ability to respect occupation law depends on its compliance with *jus ad bellum* rules,[33] a state's compliance with occupation law is predicated on its intention to occupy (in the normative sense) foreign territory in accordance with international law.[34] When the actions of the occupying state have the effect of permanently excluding the ousted sovereign and permanently revising the *status quo ante bellum* in the occupied territory through annexation or other forms of regime change,[35] the changes it undertakes rupture the protective function and currency of occupation law.

Since Russia never intended to act in accordance with the law of occupation in Crimea, the trajectory of its invasion of Ukrainian territory manifests in its political will to permanently displace the Ukrainian sovereign and its authorities from the territory.[36] After its initial "indirect use of force" through assistance to local paramilitary groups,[37] in February 2014 Russian forces engaged in a direct armed intervention to bring the territory under Russia's effective control. The following month, its unilateral annexation of the territory followed a dubious referendum, conducted in the context of what members of the Security Council[38] and the European Union condemned as 'acts of aggression'.[39] The Russian government wrapped its *deliberate* acts of conquest in claims that it was protecting its nationals and their right to self-determination, which manifested in an act of remedial secession *a la* Kosovo.[40]

Given its evident intention to act in contempt of the restricted duty-bound mandate of an occupying power, the source and ends of Russia's governmental authority in Crimea is its territorial aggression. The long-standing distinction between the law on the conduct of hostilities (*jus in bello*) and the law on the resort to force (*jus ad bellum*) insists that the *applicability* of occupation law remain unaffected by the likelihood of compliance therewith in such situations, or its practical *relevance* thereto.[41] The fact that contemporary conquerors have enjoyed cover from the legal

---

[33] An occupying power that rejects the ousted sovereign's rights, necessarily also rejects the normative underpinnings of occupation law; Ben-Naftali et al. 2005, at 551–614.

[34] Ben-Naftali 2012, at 129–200.

[35] See, on support to secessionist movements in contravention of international law, Borgen 2007, at 477–534.

[36] As others in this volume discuss [??].

[37] Such conduct is proscribed by General Assembly Resolution 2625 (XXV) Declaration on Principles of International Law concerning Friendly Relations and Co-operation among States in accordance with the Charter of the United Nations, UN Doc. A/RES/25/2625, adopted 24 October 1970.

[38] See, for the interventions of the United States (5), and Australia (10), Security Council Verbatim Record, UN Doc S/PV.7124, 1 March 2014.

[39] The Council of the European Union, Foreign Affairs Council, Council Conclusions on Ukraine, 3 March 2014, www.consilium.europa.eu/uedocs/cms_data/docs/pressdata/EN/foraff/141291.pdf. Accessed 10 April 2017.

[40] While notably muddying its own arguments with irredentist historical claims to title over the territory. See, on the justifications put forward by the Russian government, Tancredi 2014, 10–13.

[41] See for a reproach of the viability of this distinction in situations of occupation, Giladi 2008, at 246–301.

consequences commensurate with the nature of their actions is a category error that has undermined the capacity of international law to protect vulnerable populations in such situations. Put to the test in Crimea, the law of occupation has proven to be incapable of regulating the source and severity of the wrongs such situations entail and their consequences for the international rule of law.[42]

3.2.2   Category Error

The proposition that contemporary situations of foreign territorial control are incommensurate with the kind of situations that were envisaged by occupation law suggests that the application of occupation law to illegal territorial regime is a category error. This mal-classification can be summarised as three uncertainties inherent to occupation law: (1) the uncertainty concerning the temporal scope and expiry-date of a lawful situation of occupation (uncertainty of duration); (2) the uncertainty concerning the scope of governing powers and authority and of the nature of the international 'mandate' granted implicitly to legitimate Occupying Powers under international law (uncertainty of governance powers); and (3) the uncertainty concerning the manner in which it executes this authority through the structures of the occupying power's administration of the occupied territory (uncertainty of administrative structures). The following considers each in turn, as a prelude to the discussion of the situation in Crimea.

First, while occupation law implies its own temporariness and exceptionality, and although occupation law's conflict-management task is at least in theory guided by – and intended to be interpreted in conjunction with[43] – the need to bring all occupations to an end at the earliest possible occasion, occupation law provides no normative instruction on the qualities of a situation of foreign territorial control. Duration alone is not a sufficient basis for adjudicating the lawfulness of the prolongation of an occupation, nor grounds for winding down the application of occupation law. Nonetheless, the length of time an Occupying Power can lawfully maintain effective control over an occupied territory hinges on the reasons for its sojourn in the territory.

The reasons for the prolongation of an occupation must meet an overall qualitative test of legality under the *jus in bello* principle of military necessity: the measures prolonging it are actually necessary to accomplish a legitimate military purpose.[44] Hence, the legitimacy of the justification for occupation, as a matter of military necessity, wears off over time, as the national security of the occupying state can be achieved by means other than foreign domination and the full displacement of another sovereign. An occupying state operating extra-legally of this theory of

---

[42] General Assembly Resolution 1514 (XV), Declaration on the Granting of Independence to Colonial Countries and Peoples, 14 December 1960.

[43] Vienna Convention on the Law of Treaties 1969, Article 31(1).

[44] Hampson F (2011) Military Necessity, Crimes of War. www.crimesofwar.org/a-z-guide/military-necessity/. Accessed 22 April 2017.

reality – one that alike Russia cannot claim to be acting in pursuit of any lawful military objective – comes *ipso jure* under an obligation to bring the occupation to an end. When occupation is prolonged beyond what is required by military necessity, the very maintenance of a situation of occupation inevitably entails violations of the international law protections for sovereigns rights, including the laws on the use of interstate force and on the self-determination of peoples.

Secondly, occupation law does not clearly delineate the material scope of the occupying power's governance powers: the matters and manner in which an Occupying Power – which enjoys international recognition of its belligerency in this capacity[45] – is authorized to interfere, albeit under a duty-bound mandate, in the domestic affairs of the occupied territory.[46] Since the occupying state is not accountable to the popular will of the local population, and does not formally wield authority on its behalf actions that it purportedly takes "for the benefit of the local population" should be reviewed under a subjective test based on the ends of occupation.[47] Absent political agency and accountability, an Occupying Power is duty-bound solely to "ensure and maintain" civil life and public order in line with the indigenous ecosystem of that territory, irrespective of the ends of its pursuits.[48] In Crimea, Russia undertook wholesale revisions as a consequence of establishing an administration subject to its domestic jurisdiction in the territory,[49] where it self-defines as a sovereign (and not a belligerent).[50]

In sum, occupation law creates a degree of uncertainty regarding the structure of the administering authority in occupied territory. The requirement in Article 42 of the 1907 Hague Regulations that the territory is "actually placed under the authority of the hostile army" is understood to be a factual criterion to be interpreted functionally[51] – intended to determine the applicability of occupation law, and not a normative test as to whether the occupier is entitled to continue to hold the foreign territory under its control. The "effective control" test implies a *direct* territorial element of control as a condition precedent for continuing the occupation, but does not explicitly prohibit

---

[45] Contemporary recognition of belligerency is different to its traditional use to denote the political status of the non-state actor; Azarova and Blum 2015.

[46] The occupying power's is based on the balancing between humanity and necessity in Laws and Customs of War on Land, 18 October 1907 (Hague Regulations 1907), Article 43.

[47] Israeli authorities have used this as a catch-all phrase to justify its stone quarrying in excess of what is otherwise permitted by occupation law, and to build roads for the benefit of both Israeli settlements and Palestinian villages. See HCJ 2164/09 Yesh Din v. The Commander of the IDF Forces in the West Bank, judgement of 26 December 2011; HCJ 281/11 Head of Beit Iksa Village Council v. Minister of Defense et al., Judgment, 6 September 2011, available in Hebrew. elyon1. court.gov.il/files/11/810/002/m12/11002810.m12.pdf. Accessed 13 May 2017. See also Kretzmer 2012, at 207–236.

[48] Occupation law assumes and mandates that the occupying state permits the operation of local authorities, courts and laws; e.g., Articles 56 and 64 of Geneva Convention IV. See Dinstein 2009, Chapter 5.

[49] Human Rights Watch (2015) Rights in Retreat: Abuses in Crimea.

[50] Ohlin 2015.

[51] Darcy and Reynolds 2010, at 211–243.

the establishment of 'puppet' governments acting as the occupying power's agent.[52] Such wholesale revisions to the political order would likely flout occupation law's rule on conservation;[53] rendering such re-structuring by the de facto authorities invalid as a matter of international law.[54] Occupation law places all subordinate authorities within the formal administrative domain – and as such the paramount responsibility – of the occupying state.[55] An occupying state that delegates control to a 'secessionist' local authority not only purports to revise these formal command structures, but also to do away with the normative predicates of occupation law that are intended to guarantee the continuity of the ousted sovereign's rights as a matter of international law. Occupation administrations acting as domestic authorities of the annexing state and 'puppet' regimes with the effect of transforming the territory's legal and political order and demographic characteristics, have the concomitant effect of politically subjugating the population in the territory. It follows that they also increase the likelihood, frequency and severity of violations of the 'fundamental guarantees of protected persons'[56] and are a systemic cause of widespread abuses of the human rights of the population of the ousted sovereign (often at the cost of protecting the rights of the annexing state's nationals).

All three reasons point to a mismatch – or incommensurability – between the legal category of belligerent occupation and unlawful situations that are maintained through illegal force (based on an unlawful *casus belli*); particularly given the objective legal character of the legal and administrative regime they underpin. Occupation law is not tasked with the regulation of the consequences of illegal territorial regimes[57] and situations[58] that do not align with its normative predicates. A vital predicate, to which we return below, is the full implementation of the *jus ad bellum* i.e. the UN Charter rules on the use of interstate force. Occupation law has little ability to prevent internationally-prohibited acts such as the annexation and transformation of the territory, when these become the underlying reasons for maintaining the occupation. Yet, in an apparently short-sighted international practice, the juridical move of insisting on the *de jure* applicability of occupation law has backgrounded the operation of other significant yet under-applied aspects of the responsibility and remedies prescribed in international law for illegal territorial regimes.[59]

While the precise nature of the effects of violations of the law on the use of force on the operability of occupation law remains unclear, it is evident that unlawfully

---

[52] Geneva Convention IV, Article 29.

[53] Geneva Convention IV, Articles 64 and 47. Sassòli 2005.

[54] Insofar as it is aimed at absolving the occupying power of its paramount responsibility; Dinstein 2009, para 134.

[55] See e.g., the practice of the ECtHR who considers the likes of the TRNC as 'subordinate authorities'; Loizidou v. Turkey (preliminary objections), 23 March 1995, para 62; Cyprus v. Turkey, Application No. 25781/94, paras 75–80; Ilaşcu and Others v. Moldova and Russia, Application No. 48787/99, paras 314–316.

[56] Article 27 GC IV.

[57] Ronen 2011.

[58] Milano 2006, chapter 2.

[59] Geiss 2015, at 425–449.

prolonged occupations are regulated in international law. The regulatory objective of the international legal system is to bring situations that denote a "par excellence challenge to the international legal and political order" to an end.[60] Significantly, neither the political status nor the legality of the Russian authorities' activities in the territory of Crimea, which has been formally annexed and integrated into Russia under Russian domestic law, can be adequately redressed by the "war crimes"-oriented conflict management framework of occupation law (which assumes impermanence and intention to bring the occupation to an end where none exists).[61] As the next section observes, the nature of the remedies provided in such situations by operation of objective international law can affect the remedial capacity of occupation law, and the practicality of placing the burden on the de facto administrator to comply with the law governing occupying powers. As a "par excellence challenge to the international legal and political order", such situations demand a more robust regulatory framework.[62]

3.3 Illegal Territorial Regimes: The Operation of the Consequence of Invalidity

The application of occupation law without accounting for the effects of violations of the *jus ad bellum* taking place in the context of situations of foreign territorial control is inappropriate and at cross-purposes with the systemic coherence of international law and its core values of conflict prevention and resolution. In a situation of occupation qua annexation, the operation of the international law doctrine on objective illegality is a function of the application of the *jus ad bellum* (i.e. the international law of conflict resolution and prevention). This section considers how the structural characteristics of the illegal territorial regime in Crimea can be understood in terms of their objective, or *ipso jure* illegality by operation of international law.[63] Further, the doctrine of objective illegality is the basis for the operation of the consequence of invalidity: it invalidates the rights, titles, and entitlements created by the illegal situation created by the continued reality of foreign territorial control, and obliges third parties to exclude the de facto authorities activities from their dealings with the occupying state so as to make sure that they do not give legal effect to the status of these authorities. This section synthesises the legal principles and doctrines that give rise to these consequences. The following section will then apply them to the situation in Crimea.

---

[60] Giladi 2008.

[61] The application of IHL in isolation from the *jus ad bellum* is often justified on the basis that doing so is necessary to maintain some authority even over outlawed belligerents in the context of a war of aggression; Bugnion 2003, at 4–16.

[62] Giladi rightly maintains that the legitimate objective that the occupying power may pursue in the occupied territory cannot "be justified (or justify vesting in the occupant legal powers) in normative terms if occupation endangers international peace and security." Giladi 2008.

[63] Orakhelashvili 2003, at 26–32.

3.3.1 Objective Illegality

Acts that violate *jus cogens* norms are objectively illegal. An important consequence of their status is that they do not need to be invoked by the wronged state. The case of an objective illegality is the exception to the usual determination of reparations and state responsibility in international law as a matter of *jus dispositivum* whereby the directly injured state must itself invoke the wrongdoing state's duty to make reparations.[64] Instead, since the operation of the non-derogable regime of *jus cogens* protects the common interests of all states, violations of *jus cogens* have *erga omnes* effect.[65] Their illegality exists independently of the harm done to, or claims made by, any given state because "the right injured is the public right of a member of the society to have the law maintained."[66] According to Rozakis, "objective illegality means the objective recognition of an illegality, as such, which can, therefore, be invoked with a view of its extinction by all members of the international community regardless of whether there is a particular damage sustained by the invoking state."[67] Since all states have a legal interest in their respect, states are not only expected to invoke the illegal status of acts and titles, but must expel them from international life.[68] That is, the burden of bringing an end to such wrongs is thereby placed on international law-observing states and international actors, through both unilateral measures of abstention and multilateral cooperation.

The duty to make reparation for a breach of *jus cogens*, according to Orakhelashvili, arises from "the objective circumstances underlying an actual situation of a given breach."[69] In the case of Russia's presence in Crimea, the underlying objective circumstance is its continued use of force to remain in the foreign territory.[70] Since Russia's use of force is directed at acquiring title to that territory[71] – its acts of force and their effects are considered to be objectively, *ipso jure* unlawful. In these circumstances, the regime of foreign occupation itself is an objective circumstance that maintains a breach of international law. The practice of this determination is however sparse and undocumented. This logic was upheld by the ECtHR's first and as yet only interstate award judgment in *Cyprus v Turkey*, which ordered Turkey to pay 90 million Euros to Cyprus for the serious human rights violations resulting from Turkey's use of force against Cyprus since 1974.[72] For Judge Pinto de Albuquerque, "[t]he message to member States of the Council of Europe is clear: those member States that wage war, invade or support foreign armed intervention in other member

---

[64] ILC Draft Articles on the Responsibility of States for Internationally Wrongful Acts 2001, Article 43.

[65] Orakhelashvili 2003.

[66] Chen 1951, at 424.

[67] Orakhelashvili 2003, 26; Rozakis 1976, at 24; Rozakis 1974, at 150–193.

[68] Orakhelashvili 2003, at 29.

[69] Ibid.

[70] Hague Regulations 1907, Article 42. See also the New commentary to Article 2 common to GCs.

[71] Crawford 2012a, b, at 595, at fn. 37; Costelloe 2017.

[72] Cyprus v. Turkey, Application No. 25781/94, Just Satisfaction Award, 20 May 2014, para 4.

States must pay for their unlawful actions and the consequences of their actions."[73] UNSC resolution 687 (1991) similarly ordered Iraq pay reparations for injury and harm caused by its illegal occupation of Kuwait.[74]

The capacity of certain international norms to invalidate actions that are for instance premised on the unlawful use of force is intended to perform a conflict-restraining function by bringing the law to bear on the resolution of disputes (in a pre-adjudicative manner).[75] In line with the principle of *ex iniuria ius non oritur*, unlawful acts and factual predicates arising from the illegal territorial regime cannot be a source of legal rights to the wrongdoer or to others.[76] In a similar vein, the ICJ upheld in its Namibia opinion that while the non-recognition of South Africa's administration of the territory should not have the effect of depriving the people of Namibia from any advantages derived from international cooperation, as a matter of exception under IHRL, official acts performed by the Government of South Africa after the termination of the mandate are illegal and invalid.[77] In the case of an illegal territorial regime, there are two types of international wrongs: those predicating the foreign occupation (*ex ante* or predicate wrongs), such as the pursuit of territorial aggrandizement, and those that emerge from the continuation and maintenance of this illegal territorial regime (*ex post* or perquisite wrongs), and entail abuses of the civil and political rights of the local population. Both types of acts are null and void, or legally invalid, and hence cannot be recognised as a lawful basis for the constitution of any further rights or entitlements and other perquisites or as a lawful predicate fact in national legal systems.[78] The effects of such wrongs can neither be subjectively justified, nor negotiated away.[79]

These two types of objective illegality (*ipso jure*) establish a threshold for assessing the legal character of the entities established under the auspices of an unlawfully prolonged situation of foreign territorial control, the status of their acts, and the legal implications of their purported effects. The consequences of legal invalidity extend to the constitutive elements of Russia's exercise of jurisdiction in the territory (invalidity of status), due to its unlawful effects on the ousted Ukrainian sovereign, and on Ukrainian nationals and entities. The consequence of invalidity also affects the rights, entitlements, and benefits of public and private entities contributing to or benefiting from the unlawful exercise of jurisdiction by the de facto authorities and the appropriation and allocation of property rights (through the invalidity of perquisites). Since the titles and rights accrued in the context of business activities – e.g. the production and sale of goods and services – under the jurisdiction of the

---

[73] Ibid., para 24.

[74] Security Council Resolution 687 (1991), UN Doc. S/Res/687, adopted 8 April 1991, para 16,

[75] Bothe 2015, para 4. See also Krieger 2016; Sztucki 1974, at 27.

[76] Crawford 2012a, b, at 594.

[77] Legal Consequences for States of the Continued Presence of South Africa in Namibia (South West Africa) notwithstanding Security Council Resolution 276, Advisory Opinion, ICJ Rep. 16, 1971, para 56.

[78] ILC Special Rapporteur, Gaetano Arangio-Ruiz cited in Talmon 2005.

[79] See on the challenges to the enforcement of compensation, Satkauskas 2003.

de facto authorities are arguably also invalid *ipso jure*, they are at risk of repudiation within third states' jurisdictions.[80]

De facto authorities possess authority to the extent that other states permit. A third state that recognised as lawful the illegal situation – the titles, rights, and entitlements purportedly created and consolidated through serious breaches of peremptory norms – that is the illegal territorial regime[81] would itself attract responsibility in international law.[82] States' obligations of abstention extend to their diplomatic relations as well as other forms of interstate cooperation and engagement with the wrongdoing state and its subordinate authorities, to ensure that illegality and illegitimacy prevail over effectiveness.[83] Its logic resonates that of the principle of territoriality, which is a source of stability in international affairs and interstate relations, whereby states are necessitated to ensure appropriate reliance on the practice of their partner countries in the definition of their domestic jurisdiction (as a form of extension of comity). In line with this principle, an annexing state is not permitted to extend international treaties to which it is a party, or benefits thereunder, to the annexed territory.[84] A treaty cannot affect the rights and responsibility of a third party sovereign without its consent.[85] Consistent with these rules, third states must ensure that their dealings with an annexing state do not extend to the foreign territory it seeks to illegally annex.

International law's foremost concern is to reverse the situation of suffering that results in the continuous production of violations. In cases of foreign territorial control, the need to redress human security considerations through the protection of past, present, and the future right of the sovereign, which are formally in a state of abeyance, but in practice under threat of erosion through effectiveness (*ex factis ius oritur*).[86] In the case of an illegal territorial regime, the continuation of foreign territorial control is the source of the violation of these rights and the cause of injury and harm to the civilian population. In the absence of an internationally recognised duty-bearer or addressee of obligations, the foremost task of international law is to eliminate the illegal territorial regime.

The consequence of invalidity is intended to contribute to these ends: it penalises the wrongdoer in hopes of deterring wrongful acts, and it provides a forward-looking basis for the reversal of the situation and restitution of rights to rightful titleholders, including individuals, entities, and sovereigns after the end of occupation. States and international organisations are charged with the heavy lifting necessary to achieve these ends by upholding these obligations in their transactions with the occupying

---

[80] Azarova 2017b.

[81] Crawford 2012a, b, at 591.

[82] ICJ Namibia, at 16.

[83] Crawford 2012a, b, at 598–9; Brownlie 1963, at 422; Orakhelashvili 2003, at 37.

[84] Chen 1951, at 431.

[85] Vienna Convention on the Law of Treaties 1969, Article 29. See also Costelloe 2016. See the case law of the European Court of Justice on the EU's agreements with Morocco: C-104/16 *Council v. Front Polisario*, Judgment, Grand Chamber, 21 December 2016; C-266/16 *Western Sahara Campaign UK v. Commissioners for Her Majesty's Revenue and Customs*, 27 February 2018.

[86] See on the threat of effectiveness, Milano 2006, Chapter 5.

state and its subordinate authorities. Third states have a public right and duty to seek an end to such situations of foreign territorial control through international cooperation; since the mere refusal to admit unlawful revisions to the status of the occupied territory is insufficient to put an end to an illegal territorial regime.[87]

3.3.2 Undercutting Occupation Law?

In a situation of foreign territorial control predicated on the pursuit of annexation, the administrative mandate that the law of occupation grants to the foreign power is incommensurable with the urgency to terminate the illegal territorial regime. It would seem inappropriate to grant the same predatory power that seeks the annexation of the territory a mandate to protect and act for the benefit of the vulnerable population there.[88] In international practice, such occupying states have in fact enjoyed cover under occupation law's 'mandate' to remain in the territory and wrongfully avail themselves of the rights of a legitimate occupying power. This approach has significant sociological, political, and normative implications.[89]

The very structures of administration in an occupation qua annexation are predicated on the illegal force and hence invalidated by operation of international law. But occupation law turns a blind eye precisely to the legality of the status of the authorities in the territory and the territorial regime their continued presence establishes and maintains. The vulnerable population as rights-holders become in effect unable to claim rights under occupation law. The exclusion and invalidation of wrongs under the doctrine of objective illegality may also have an effect on the validity of the very 'mandate' that a *de facto* administrator qua Occupying Power enjoys under occupation law – by invalidating ex post the acts it adopts in reliance on said mandate. South Africa's trusteeship mandate was repudiated as part of the determination by international bodies that the continued presence of South Africa in the territory maintained an "illegal situation".[90] Since the occupying state subjectively reject its status as occupying power, the predicate acts for its continued control over the occupied territory may objectively preclude it from being able to avail itself of an occupying power's authority. The question becomes, what protective framework would appropriately address the governance vacuum and deter the violations taking place under an illegal territorial regime.[91]

---

[87] A declarative role traditionally entrusted to international and regional institutions, which have in turn been increasingly deployed to serve political ends. Krieger 2016, at 21 et seq.

[88] Crawford 2012a, b, at 600.

[89] It bears recalling that IHL takes a conflict management approach to struggles against colonial domination. Protocol additional to the Geneva Conventions of 12 August 1949, and relating to the protection of victims of international armed conflicts (Protocol I), adopted 8 June 1977, Article 1(4).

[90] General Assembly, Question of Namibia, UN Doc. A/RES/S-14/1, 20 September 1986.

[91] Gross 2015.

The legal category of occupation in international law does productive ideological and bureaucratic work, organizing international responses in ways that structure social outcomes.[92] For occupation law to function in the international legal system, certain situations must *ipso jure* be excluded from its purview.[93] The abolition of colonial practice implies that "belligerent occupation" is distinct from "foreign domination" – and hence that occupation law is triggered not only by a factual test of effective control,[94] but also depends on qualitative criteria that factor in the motivations behind the maintenance of a situation of foreign territorial control. In line with the duty not to recognise changes made through illegal force as lawful, all third states must deny legal effect to the laws and administrative acts of illegal territorial regimes and to the claims that arise from the operation of the legal system in the occupied territory. We might say that the theory of reality that occupation law relies on for its proper function is empirically and conceptually at odds with both the structural and normative implications of the maintenance of an illegal territorial regime.

Contemporary international law contends with the suspension of sovereignty entailed by foreign territorial control, as a manifestation of armed conflict, and offers a formal mandate to this effect under occupation law,[95] which refocuses protection concerns on the individual.[96] Since the special-purpose law of occupation is not charged with the regulation or deterrence of colonial practices of foreign domination relies for this purpose on other international law.[97] Permitting aggressors that pursue annexation to act under an occupation law-based mandate makes the exception (of temporary foreign control justified by military necessity) swallow the rule (prohibiting aggression and territorial conquest). Maintaining the indeterminacies of occupation law, discussed above, without the diligent co-application of the *jus ad bellum* and its remedies of invalidity, the application of occupation law also permits wrongful measures to diminish rights protection that can only be justified on the basis of legitimate security objectives.[98] Such measures would themselves, however, likely be invalidated under the consequence of invalidity in international law.[99]

The need to assess the legality of the foreign territorial control arose during the occupation of Iraq,[100] notwithstanding the indeterminacies generated by subordinate

---

[92] See on the consequences of classification Bowker and Star 1999; Douglas and Hull 1992.

[93] Bowker and Star 1999, at 10–11.

[94] See for a discussion of the elements of the factual test in Article 42 of the Hague Regulations 1907, Dinstein 2009, chapter 2.I.

[95] Nicolosi 2011, at 165–187.

[96] Arai-Takahashi 2012.

[97] While occupation law is preoccupied with the need to manage and restrain violence, the law on the use of force is concerned with bringing the ongoing cause of the violence to an end. Arai-Takahashi 2012, at 51.

[98] Azarova 2018.

[99] Crawford 2012a, b, at 603.

[100] Thurer 2006, at 13–15.

administrations.[101] It also remains an issue of concern for the long-arm occupations of northern Cyprus (by Turkey-controlled TRNC authorities), Nagorno Karabakh (Armenia-controlled NKR authorities), South Ossetia, Abkhazia and Transnistria (Russia-controlled local governments).[102] The referenda in Transnistria (2006), Crimea (2014) and Nagorno Karabakh (2017), and other administrative and legislative measures adopted in these contexts, are null and void as a matter of international law,[103] and yet these determinations have had no demonstrable practical effect on the way that the international community addresses concerns for the protection of the civilian population subject to the control and authority of illegal territorial regime.

The ECtHR[104] and the UN[105] have grappled with the normative and operational difficulties and precariousness of rights protection in these contexts, but have not addressed the incoherence in the current legal practice surrounding such situations – especially given the deficiencies in the enforcement of the *jus ad bellum*. To fill these gaps, a differentiated approach to illegal territorial regimes is in demand. This does not require any reforms but rather a need to judiciously re-focus international law's regulatory objectives to make up for the effective mootness of occupation law. This would not mean either disabling or winding down the application of the *jus in bello*, and the protections it formally affords the local population, but rather entails taking on a long-view on the protection agenda for future and collective rights; an issue to which we return. Since it is beyond the scope of this chapter to venture such a framework, suffice it to note that the application of existing international law should be adjusted to account for the potential consequence of invalidity of the de facto authorities' actions, and for their status in international law.[106]

3.4 The Illegal Territorial Regime in Crimea

The invalidity of acts and facts in an illegal territorial regime implies that the attempt to manage such a situation under occupation law is counter-intuitive as it might inadvertently entrust the authorities of an illegal territorial regime with powers they do not possess.[107] But the law of occupation can also help inventory objectively unlawful changes introduced by the foreign de facto administrator, in order for the occupied state to be able to fulfil its duties to reverse such changes and restore

---

[101] See for an analysis of CPA status and responsibility in light of Iraq transfer of authority, Carcano 2015, at 147–158.

[102] See, e.g., Hammarberg 2013.

[103] ICJ on referendum for independence based on illegal force; Accordance with international law of the unilateral declaration of independence in respect of Kosovo, Advisory Opinion, ICJ Reports 2010, para 84.

[104] See review of relevant case law, Gross 2015.

[105] Hammarberg 2013.

[106] Afsah argues that occupation law is not the tool for introducing democratic changes in Iraq; Afsah 2006.

[107] Wilde 2008.

rights after the end of occupation.[108] Such an inventory can also be used by third parties to ensure they do not 'normalise' rights violations and permit perpetrators to benefit from their wrongdoing in contravention of the obligation of third states not to recognise as lawful serious breaches of peremptory norms of international law. Third parties should screen out and exclude illegal territorial regime authorities and the facts they produce from international transactions.[109] These acts and facts include: (1) the public institutions installed in the territory; (2) decisions of such bodies; and (3) the rights and entitlements granted to legal entities in or related to the territory. This section examines each of these categories in relation to Crimea.

First, the structures and basis of authority for the institutions in the territory. On 18 March 2014, Russian President Vladimir Putin signed a decree recognizing Crimea as an independent state.[110] Putin and Crimea's leadership then signed agreements on 3 April 2014 making Crimea and the city of Sevastopol part of the Russian Federation[111] through full integration into Russia's Southern Military District, which, with their addition, comprises 25 administrative regions. The Russian legislation on the annexation of Crimea and Sevastopol, adopted by the Duma Constitutional Law Committee, became the vehicle for the extension of the entire corpus of Russian domestic law to the territory. Henceforth, all matters taking place in or in relation to the territory became subject to Russia's domestic jurisdiction and governed by Russian administrative bodies including its law enforcement authorities, judicial system, and legislature.[112] These authorities cannot be recognized as having any status in the territory, given the consequences of their continued presence in the foreign territory as a matter of international law. Third parties have an implicit obligation to exclude unlawfully-established government authorities in Crimea from international and transnational dealings, so as not to give effect to the legal and political rights they unlawfully claim over Ukrainian territory.

The second category pertains to the acts adopted in the course of the administration of the territory by local authorities, whose formal source of authority under both domestic and international law is Russia's monopoly on the use of force in the territory. The Russian government proceeded to nationalise the ownership of strategic enterprises, and subject all enterprises to Russian domestic private laws. In July 2015, Russian President Medvedev declared that Crimea had been fully integrated into Russia – politically, economically and socially.[113] Notable examples include the

---

[108] Morgenstern 1951, at 291.

[109] See on exclusion as enforcement, Hathaway and Shapiro 2011.

[110] Office of the High Commissioner for Human Rights, Report on the Human Rights Situations in Ukraine 16 February to 15 May 2016, para 19.

[111] A de facto annexation signifies a state of complete dependence; Talmon 1999, at 534.

[112] Since local government authorities in Crimea were the subject of wholesale transformation before the formal annexation, the same 'secessionist' authorities became the local government of the territory following annexation.

[113] McHugh J (2015) Putin Eliminates Ministry of Crimea, Region Fully Integrated Into Russia, Russian Leaders Say. International Business Times, 15 July. Under Russian law, all decisions delivered by the Crimean branches of the judiciary of Ukraine up to its annexation remain valid. Including sentences (for "encroaching on Ukraine's territorial integrity and inviolability") for

law establishing 'special economic zones' in Crimea with benefits and incentives to encourage the operations of Russian and foreign businesses in the territory under Russian law; and Russian immigration and personal status laws that require all legal persons in the territory to hold Russian-issued identification documents, and which have negatively affected the continued stay of certain individuals and discriminated national minorities in the territory.[114] The object of such laws is to absorb and integrate the territory into Russia, as well as economically exploit its resources for the benefit of the Russian market; in contravention of the usufruct rule of occupation law, the law on self-determination of people, and the prohibition on the use of force against the territorial integrity of another state.

The operation of the consequence of invalidity entails that Russian laws and decisions adopted in or in relation to the territory or its population as though it were part of Russia,[115] must be deemed null and void both during and after occupation; third states and the returning sovereign may not enforce belligerent legislation and administrative acts.[116] In light of the proposed analysis in this chapter, whereby an aggressor's administrative mandate as occupying power is considered to be repudiated by operation of international law, all acts of pubic authority in Crimea by Russian executive, judicial, and legislative bodies would be deemed *ultra vires*. Acts of the occupying state that are rendered illegal by operation of international law, Morgenstern remarks, "are considered to have been executed by an incompetent organ and to lack legal force".[117] In belligerent occupation, the Occupying Powers authority hinges on its legitimate use of force. It would contradict this aim to permit the acts of the de facto authorities of an illegal territorial regime to have legal effect as any other sovereign authority within its exclusive jurisdictional domain,[118] and to expect that the population in occupied territory obeys them.[119]

The third category of acts affected by the regulation of illegal territorial regimes concerns the effects of acts under Russia's internationally unlawful legal and administrative regime on individuals and other legal persons such as transnational corporations. After annexing Crimea, Russian authorities expedited the issuance of Russian passports for the residents of Sevastopol.[120] People who refused to take

---

pre-2014 calls for an incorporation of Crimea into Russia; Pro-Russian Activist Falls On Hard Times In Annexed Crimea, Radio Free Europe, 16 January 2016.

[114] Human Rights Watch 2015. Shapovalova N (2016) The Situation of National Minorities in Crimea following its Annexation by Russia. European Parliament www.europarl.europa.eu/RegData/etudes/STUD/2016/578003/EXPO_STU(2016)578003_EN.pdf. Accessed 10 April 2017.

[115] See also Fraleigh 1949.

[116] Morgenstern 1951, at 317.

[117] Ibid., 306.

[118] Acts that the occupant is entitled to execute produce legal results; Morgenstern 1951, at 296 citing Foro Italiano, 1947, ii, at 133.

[119] That would mean placing the vulnerable population at the whims of the law of the occupant, since it is the occupant who is concerned with punishment for disobedience; Morgenstern 1951, at 296.

[120] By July 2015, 20,000 Crimeans had renounced their Ukrainian citizenship; de Waal 2015.

Russian nationality were subject to discrimination,[121] while those who opposed the annexation, including targeted minority groups, were subject to group persecution.[122] In addition to discriminatory practices, forcible transfer and deportation became widespread, as well as other measures threatening the personal integrity, health, and livelihood of Ukrainians in the territory.[123] While such policies and practices constitute human rights abuses and prima facie amount to violations of IHL's grave breaches regime, the hard and fast consequence of such acts is that they are invalid. They preclude third parties from recognising the rights of Russian residents unlawfully transferred into the territory of Crimea under Russian law, or of Ukrainian nationals as Russian nationals or domestic subjects of Russian law.[124] Unlike the indigenous Ukrainian population, the Russian population does not enjoy the right to habitual residence in the territory, and cannot therefore be treated in ways that would give effect to their habitual residence in that territory.

The ICJ's 'humanitarian exception' in its Namibia Opinion held that measures necessary to uphold basic rights should not be subject to the consequence of non-recognition, as a matter of exception under IHRL.[125] The exception extends solely to acts that "relat[e] to commercial obligations or matters of private law between individuals or matters of routine administration such as the registration of births, marriages or deaths."[126] Costelloe suggests that the humanitarian exceptions to non-recognition, set out in the ICJ's Namibia opinion, may permit certain treaty provisions to be extended to annexed territory.[127] While the returning sovereign is in theory obliged to annul the occupying authorities' acts, Ronen argues that in practice transitions from illegal regimes have accommodated and maintained a wider range

---

[121] See, e.g. they are barred from holding government and municipal jobs; Stewart P (2014) Ukraine human rights 'deteriorating rapidly'. Al Jazeera English, 3 December 2014 www.aljazeera.com/news/europe/2014/12/ukraine-human-rights-201412210270208204.html. Accessed 10 April 2017. Muravalev M (2014) Disappearing Crimea's anti-Russia activists, Al Jazeera English, 4 December 2014. www.aljazeera.com/indepth/features/2014/12/disappearing-crimea-anti-russia-activists-201412110405525656.html. Accessed 10 April 2017.

[122] See also in this volume, Bowring 2017, Chapter 2.

[123] See e.g., one of three complaints lodged before the ECtHR, Ukraine v. Russia I (no. 20958/14) in March 2014, alleged that the civilian population on the territory of Ukraine was at risk of measures by Russia that might threaten their life and health. Human Rights Watch 2014. Wrange 2015, at 24.

[124] The March 2014 law "On the Acceptance of the Republic of Crimea into the Russian Federation and the Creation of New Federal Subjects – the Republic of Crimea and the City of Federal Significance Sevastopol," required any permanent resident of Crimea who held Ukrainian citizenship to undergo a process of declaring intent to maintain Ukrainian citizenship, after which all Ukrainian passport holders who resided in Crimea were deemed Russian citizens. HRW Rights in Retreat (2014).

[125] See for the Namibia exception, ICJ Namibia 1971, para 122–124. ECHR Loizidou extended recognition transactions and acts such as the registration of various civic acts, e.g. marriages, births and deaths. An important limitation to the principle of nullity may also bear on its effects for instance on bona fide purchasers, in specific cases that should be examined by the returning sovereign; Morgenstern 1951, at 309.

[126] Caglar v. Billingham (Inspector of Taxes) [1996] STC (SDC) 150, para 121; cited in Crawford 2012a, b, para 113.

[127] Costelloe 2017, at 343–378.

of changes than required by law.[128] Nonetheless, as Crawford cautions, the principle of legality must be enforced in a way that both guarantees the protection of the population and ensures that "generally public act[s]" do not fall within the scope of the Namibia exception.[129] While occupation law assumes that a situation of foreign territorial control accords with the *jus ad bellum*, an illegal territorial regime is a form of foreign control of territory that is subject to an absolute prohibition. The regime in Crimea lacks a valid legal basis, and hence is the source of unlawful acts including systemic violations of collective and individual rights.

3.5 Consequences and Costs: The Challenge of Illegal Territorial Regimes

According to Milano, contemporary international law faces the dilemma of "matching a genuine effort to lead those territories to 'normalcy' with the diplomatic reluctance to enter 'into business' with [unrecognisable] authorities."[130] With its complex web of de facto institutions, whose acts have no recognisable effect. In operationalising the principle of *ex injuria jus non oritur*,[131] the consequence of invalidity offers situations like Crimea a rigid toolbox for disrupting and rendering unsustainable the foreign power's presence in the territory. States and international actors are required, as part of their obligations to participate in the observance of international law, to ensure that such facts do not enjoy legal effect. Such obligations of abstention from recognising such acts as lawful, and permitting wrongdoers to benefit from their wrongs, are based on "the community interest and reaction underlying the collective response to a violation of a fundamental norm of the international community."[132] A cohesive collective response to such cardinal international wrongs is assumed to be a default mode of participation in the observance of international law.[133]

The invalidity of the acts adopted by the de facto authorities of an illegal territorial regime is based on a different logic than the coercive sanctions adopted by the EU and the US, inter alia, in response to Russia's use of force against Ukraine's territorial integrity and political independence through the annexation of Crimea.[134] This chapter does not attempt to undertake a detailed assessment of the measures adopted against Russia. But it is intent to point out that sanctions are, unlike respect for the consequence of invalidity through non-recognition, neither mandated by inter-

---

[128] Ronen 2011.

[129] Crawford 2012a, b, paras 48 et seq.

[130] Milano 2007.

[131] See Lagerwall 2016.

[132] Milano 2007.

[133] Milano refers to the 'monist view' of the relationship between international and domestic legal systems, on which this assumption is based; Milano 2006, at 135. See also Nollkaemper 2010.

[134] European Commission, Commission Guidance note on the implementation of certain provisions of Regulation, Notice, (EU) No. 833/201425 September 2015.

national law nor are they a preferable mode of enforcement in many cases. Although the EU's measures bear the misleading label of a "non-recognition policy,"[135] they are in fact a set of sanctions par excellence, which are intended to exact a price and force Russia's hand into compliance. States are within their rights to adopt *lawful* coercive enforcement measures[136] – so long as these are neither disproportionate nor indiscriminate in effect.[137] However, measures of this nature are not always effective in the enforcement of international law[138] – as might be predicted given the volatility and shifting alliances characteristic of illegal situations. By contrast, measures of abstention denote a social process of (passive) enforcement that *all* international law-abiding states are expected to diligently apply.

The consequence of invalidity, which triggers third parties' obligations of non-abstention through non-recognition comes with a host of costs and complications. The principal function of this law of "minimum resistance"[139] is to lead such territories back to "normalcy" through normative rigidity.[140] The consequence of invalidity of the regime's legislative and administrative acts has the effect of suspending the subjects of this regime from the international juridical order.[141] Such an isolationist tactic however can be damaging from the perspective of the wellbeing of the indigenous local population at the whims of the annexing state.[142] The consequence of invalidity therefore has a major shortcoming: the effects of exclusion on the protection of rights can contribute to the emergence of an international governance gap.[143] Sanctions are not immune to a similar criticism: in Crimea, they are likely to impact the population under its control as well as Ukraine and its nationals, more than they do Russia, the principal perpetrator.

Since by its very nature an illegal territorial regime limits the possibilities for the enforcement of occupation law, arguably rendering it anomalous (even though the law of occupation remains de jure applicable to the territory subject to the illegal territorial regime),[144] a differentiated approach is necessary to fill the governance and protection

---

[135] See Information Note to EU business operating and/or investing in Crimea/Sevastopol., SWD (2014) 300 final/3, 10 June 2015.

[136] It remains unclear whether the concept of responsibility (in our case erga omnes) is a decisive driver behind such decisions, Nollkaemper 2017.

[137] For the law on countermeasures intended to bring the state into compliance with international law, ILC Draft Articles on the Responsibility of States for Internationally Wrongful Acts 2001, Articles 48–49. Basic Principles on the Use of Restrictive Measures (Sanctions), 10198/1/04 REV 1, PESC 450, 7 June 2004; Guidelines on the implementation and evaluation of restrictive measures (sanctions) in the framework of the EU Common Foreign and Security Policy, 15 June 2012, 11205/1. See also Wrange 2015, at 47–9; Public Defender of Georgia 2017.

[138] Thompson 2009, 307 et seq. See also Bradford, Ben-Shahar 2012, at 376 et seq.

[139] Lauterpacht 1948, at 431; Elsuwege 2009, para 20.

[140] Milano 2014.

[141] Agamben 2006, at 4.

[142] Human Rights Watch 2016.

[143] On the role of the UN in rights protection in situations of military occupation, Roberts 2005, at 458 et seq.

[144] McMahan 2011. See also Chehtman 2015, at 25 et seq.

gaps to which it gives rise.[145] IHRL no doubt forms the basis for a protection regime for individuals and groups subject to discrimination and persecution by an illegal territorial regime.[146] The question is, who is to be entrusted with this protection mandate? And whether and to what extent the annexing state is precluded from relying on its authority and availing itself of the rights of a legitimate Occupying Power, when its obligations to withdraw take precedence?

The IHRL framework for illegal territorial regime also places obligations on the occupied state. Both the Republic of Cyprus and the Georgian government monitor and protect the rights of nationals residing in occupied parts of their territories.[147] The ECtHR jurisprudence on occupied territories has pioneered, in a rather chequered fashion,[148] an understanding of the overlapping responsibilities of occupying states and occupied states.[149] It has upheld the occupied state's residual and primary obligations vis-à-vis the population subject to an illegal territorial regime, to actively attempt, where possible, to protect their nationals' rights, or to engage in diplomatic protest to contest violations by illegal de facto authorities and solicit international cooperation with respect to protection.[150] The Court has even allowed the occupying state to remedy a human rights concern in the territory through the de facto authority, whose remedies the Court proceeded to require the residents of the Turkish Republic of Northern Cyprus to exhaust.[151] De facto authorities have been "partially acknowledged" as incurring obligations under IHRL, based on their capacity for governance and control. But the exhaustion of local remedies under such regimes remains a matter of controversy for the ECtHR, who has been criticised for its jurisprudence due to its arguably overall negative effect on the protection of rights by setting aside the invalidity of the status and actions of the de facto authorities.[152]

In many cases, international bodies that have adjudicated the obligations of de authorities have considered them to be standalone duty-bearers; whereby their violations are not necessarily attributable to a controlling state.[153] This approach has been adopted in the documentation and reporting work of the UN, the Organisation for Security and Co-operation in Europe, and international groups like Human Rights Watch, whose researchers were told explicitly of the "new realities" being built in Abkhazia by its de facto President; part and parcel of which are the restrictions and

---

[145] See, on the grey areas in the interaction between occupation law and human rights law, Campanelli 2008, 653–668.

[146] Ratner 2005, at 709.

[147] See e.g. Ministry of Foreign Affairs of Georgia 2016.

[148] Gross 2015.

[149] It has however avoided discussing the status and obligations of de facto authorities. Ronen 2013, at 42.

[150] See, among recent cases on the obligations of occupied states: Sargsyan v. Azerbaijan Application No. 40167/06, judgement of 16 June 2015; Mozer v. The Republic of Moldova and Russia, Application No. 11138/10, judgement of 23 February 2016.

[151] According to Cullen and Wheatley this is in line with the subsidiary of the Convention; Cullen and Wheatley 2013, 711–2. See also Solomou 2010, at 633.

[152] Tomuschat et al. 2009. See also Lagerwall 2014.

[153] Ronen 2013, 43–4; Schoiswohl 2001, at 45 et seq.

limits on the rights of Georgian residents of the territory, as well as on their ability to remain in and return to it.[154] In the famous Carl Zeiss decision, Lord Wilberforce held that recognition can be given to such "actual facts or realities" in the territory if it accords with "the interests of justice and common sense", and only "where no consideration of public policy to the contrary has to prevail."[155] De facto authorities have effectively been treated as 'third parties' to the ECHR.[156]

Although the de facto authorities in illegal territorial regimes are in fact a proxy of the foreign (occupying) state, they do not enjoy the status of a state agent in international law. They are nevertheless bound by customary IHRL obligations as a non-state actor.[157] Its organs may enjoy functional recognition for the purpose of protecting the rights of the population under their control.[158] While this proposition may be controversial, it is not unprecedented. Irrespective of how broadly or narrowly the effects of non-recognition are construed,[159] the "ability and willingness to fulfil international obligations" may be a reasonable basis for offering even the de facto authorities of an illegal territorial regime functional recognition to undertake certain protection measures. The very fact that such authorities gain the ability to infringe upon rights justifies the need to scrutinise their exercise of authority.[160] The competing need to avert against the political recognition of the territorial situation maintained by force, and the effectiveness their actions may gain in the domestic and international domain,[161] however, means that such authorities' should also be subject to strict scrutiny actors that are innately hostile to the rights of others by UN bodies and states.[162] The imperative to do so arises from states individual and collective non-recognition responsibilities, as well as separately those of international organisations, to act diligently to provide legal and political clarity on the way that such situations could be brought to an end, and on how they should be treated in the interim.

To ensure that an illegal territorial regime in the occupied territory does not gain effectiveness, the addressees of IHRL obligations to the local population in such

---

[154] Human Rights Watch's Europe and Central Asia director called on Abkhazia to respect human rights: Williamson H (2011) Abkhazia must raise its game on human rights. The Guardian, 19 November. See also Hammarberg 2013. The European Committee for the Prevention of Torture and Inhuman and Degrading Treatment or Punishment (CPT) conducted visited and reported on detention conditions in Abkhazia and Transnistria: https://www.coe.int/en/web/cpt/georgia and https://www.coe.int/en/web/cpt/republic-of-moldova?desktop=true.

[155] Carl Zeiss Stiftung v. Rayner & Keeler Ltd (No. 2), House of Lords (England), Judgment of 18 May 1966,43 ILR 23, 66. Oguebie and Another v. Odunwoke and Others, Nigerian Supreme Court, Judgment of 19 April 1979, 70 ILR 17, at 20 et seq. These and others are cited and discussed in Schoiswohl 2001, at 73.

[156] This unsatisfactory approach is discussed by Cullen and Wheatley 2013, at 692.

[157] See Murray 2016.

[158] Chen 1951, at 429. See also on 'acquired rights', Berkes 2015; Frowein 2013.

[159] Milano 2007.

[160] Schoiswohl 2001, at 88–9.

[161] Brown 1950, 627 et seq. Cf. using a doctrine of implied mandate, Schoiswohl 2001, at 74.

[162] Peterson 1997, 68–71; van Essen 2012, 48; Buchanan 1999, at 46–47.

situations need to be carefully defined with the relevant caveats with regards to their informal status in international law.[163] At present, both a supervisory practice, and a coherent policy approach to such situations are in demand. A more granular understanding of the effects of such regimes on international law could significantly enhance third states' awareness of the effects of such regimes on domestic legal orders, and of their role as both enforcers and enablers of protection of the populations subject to such regimes. While a more granular appreciation of the tension between various actors in such territorial situations can appropriately attribute responsibility and authority to protect rights. Protection in such cases should be addressed through a more sophisticated approach.[164]

3.6 Postscript: Regime Design Matters

This paper's aim is to clarify the international law framework applicable to illegal territorial regimes, and to expose the potentially harmful consequences of the governance gap that emerges in illegal territorial regimes such as Crimea as a result of the operation of international law. Russia's absorption and integration of Crimea into its domestic jurisdiction marks a clear rupture from the category of belligerent occupation in international law. And, yet, occupation law, which is unable to regulate such situations, persist as if in a legal fiction.[165] In turn, the law on the interstate use of force (the *jus ad bellum*) which is a vital precursor to the full implementation of occupation law, has been relatively silent (and perhaps silenced). This problematique is akin to the question of 'regime design': the legal and political implications of choosing to pursue one regime framing over another. These legal challenges, and of course the real life situations they maintain also have the public duty to eliminate the kind of egregious violations such cases entail, including by ensuring that internationally wrongful acts do not percolate into their domestic laws.[166]

The case of Crimea is unique in that it has both effectuated a rupture in the status of the Occupying Power in the territory and its proxy de facto authorities that administer the illegal territorial regime, and triggered third party state responses that have the purpose of bringing about the *in casu* application of the *jus ad bellum* – which is too often neglected in other ongoing situations of occupation that pursue the transformation of the territory through annexation or secession; including the West Bank, northern Cyprus, Western Sahara, Nagorno-Karabakh, Transnistria and South Ossetia and Abkhazia. Yet even the response to Crimea indicates that international

---

[163] Draper 1983, at 264.

[164] The logic of treating non-state actors as duty-bearers irrespective of the legitimacy or legality of their political pursuits is not new: Sivakumaran 2009, at 489–513.

[165] Del Mar and Twining 2017, ix–xi. See also Gross 2017.

[166] See on the scope of non-recognition as an international duty; Talmon 2005. See also Crawford 2012a, b. See on obligations of abstention as community interests, Krieger 2016.

law in practice lacks a coherent policy and enforcement framework to which states can readily turn in addressing such situations. Such a framework would need to address both sources and content of the applicable obligations of different actors, and the overarching concern that legality can be trumped by effectiveness. As noted, the volatile character of illegal territorial regime means that certain forms of coercive intervention are likely to be counterproductive.

Key to addressing the multidimensional reality of an illegal territorial regime is a more diligent application of the primary rules of the law on the interstate use of force (including its prohibition on aggression), and a more rigorous commitment to the implementation of the consequences of the secondary rules on invalidity and abstention. To enable coordinated, non-coercive protection initiatives states must re-examine the scope of their duties of cooperation.[167] Such efforts must rest on an approach to rights protection that can, with the help of relevant inter- and non-governmental organisations (in cooperation with the authorities of the occupied state), fill the international governance gap that emerges from the invalidity of the acts of such types of regimes in international law.

It is evidently – and perhaps justifiably – beyond the capacity of international law to establish a normative framework for external regime change, whatever the harm that a given regime inflicts on the civilian population or the international legal order. International legal argument has notoriously been used to pursue political agendas: experts in the application of the law on international territorial administration have detected a trend of abusing international protection mandates, with insidious effects.[168] Lest we permit uncoordinated politicised responses to fill the governance vacuum and to provide for the local population's protection, a more dedicated and granular analysis of the dilemmas that arise from the conflicting objectives of different bodies of international law is necessary to reconcile the normative rigidities of isolation and invalidity prescribed by international law with concurrently applicable protection modalities that seek to redress the hardships faced by indigenous populations living under an illegal territorial regime.

Addressing such wrongful situations calls for the revision of some of the working assumptions for the application of certain norms of international law over others. A heuristic approach appears to be in demand to pre-empt the erosive effects that such realities can have on the relevance and effectiveness of international law. These crisis-focused conversations about Crimea also often come at the cost of issues of global justice (e.g. the role of non-state actors in rights protection), restricting the scope and nature of our enquiries and reductionist accounts of 'fundamental' questions that produce an "impoverished set of substantive principles".[169]

With a view to recasting both the nature and scope of the international law framework currently applicable to Crimea as a matter of international law – by acknowledging its human costs, in the short and long term, including beyond Crimea – we

---

[167] See for a critique of the thesis of cooperation, Hakimi 2017.

[168] See, e.g., on the danger of the return of the 'civilising mission' by other means, Wilde 2008. See also, on the use of human rights as pretext for transformative measures, Fox 2008.

[169] Charlesworth 2002.

cannot but revisit and perhaps also seek to re-awaken the proper normative force of the prohibition of colonial domination as a contemporary international value protected by international law. The fact that a notable number of ongoing situations of foreign territorial control maintain operative similarities with the illegal territorial regime in Crimea, signals the re-emergence of practices of (neo-)colonial domination,[170] and validates the capacity of post-colonial international law to address their effects. Illegal territorial regimes are a prototype of the category of situations that call for a rethinking of conventional approaches to the regulation of such situations through conflict management law (i.e. IHL and its rules on occupation). That being the case, international law would be itself at fault if we allow for a response to the Crimea 'crisis' that entrenches the "spatial and conceptual boundaries made real by international law" and remain indignant to its compromising effects on the local population of Crimea.[171]

References

Afsah E (2006) Limits and Limitations of Power. German Law Review
Agamben G (2006) State of Exception. University of Chicago Press, Chicago
Arai-Takahashi Y (2009) The Law of Occupation: Continuity and Change of International Humanitarian Law and Its Interaction with International Human Rights Law. Brill, The Hague
Arai-Takahashi Y (2012) Preoccupied with occupation: critical examinations of the historical development of the law of occupation. International Review of the Red Cross 94
Azarova V (2017a) Israel's Unlawfully Prolonged Occupation: Consequences Under an Integrated Legal Framework. European Council on Foreign Relations. www.ecfr.eu/page/-/ISRAELS_UNLAWFULLY_PROLONGED_OCCUPATION_ECFR216.pdf. Accessed 10 June 2017
Azarova V (2017b) The Bounds of (Il)legality: Home-State Regulation of Overseas Business and the Legal Risks of Transnational Corporate Wrongs. In: Yahyaoui E (ed) Taming Power in Times of Globalisation. Brill, The Hague
Azarova V (2018) Towards a Counter-Hegemonic Law of Occupation: On the Regulation of Predatory Interstate Acts in Contemporary International Law. Yearbook of International Humanitarian Law 20 (forthcoming)
Azarova V, Blum I (2015) Belligerency. In: Max Planck Encyclopaedia of Public International Law. Oxford University Press, Oxford
Ben-Naftali O (2012) PathoLAWgical Occupation: Normalizing the Exceptional Case of the Occupied Palestinian Territory (OPT) and Other Legal Pathologies, In: Ben-Naftali O (ed) International Humanitarian Law and International Human Rights Law. Cambridge University Press, Cambridge
Ben-Naftali O, Gross A, Michaeli K (2005) Illegal Occupation: Framing the Occupied Palestinian Territory. Berkeley Journal of International Law 23
Benvenisti E (2013) The International Law of Belligerent Occupation. Oxford University Press, Oxford
Berkes A (2015) "Grey Zones": The Protection of Human Rights in Areas Out of the Effective Control of the State. Unpublished thesis, Université Paris 1 Panthéon-Sorbonne
Bird A (2011) Thomas Kuhn. In: Zalta E (ed) The Stanford Encyclopedia of Philosophy. plato.stanford.edu/archives/fall2013/entries/thomas-kuhn/. Accessed 10 April 2017

---

[170] Gross reproaches occupation law for enabling such practices in modern time, Gross 2017, Chapter 1.

[171] See also the invasion of Kuwait after the UN resolution, Charlesworth 2002, at 389, 392.

Borgen CJ (2007) Imagining Sovereignty, Managing Secession: The Legal Geography of Eurasia's 'Frozen Conflicts'. Oregon Review of International Law 9

Bothe M (2015) Neutrality. In: Max Planck Encyclopedia of Public International Law. Oxford University Press, Oxford

Bowker G, Star S (1999) Sorting Things Out: Classification and Its Consequences. MIT Press, Cambridge MA

Brown P (1950) The Legal Effects of Recognition. American Journal of International Law 44

Brownlie I (1963) International Law and the Use of Force by States. Clarendon Press, Oxford

Buchanan A (1999) Recognitional Legitimacy and the State System. Philosophy and Public Affairs

Bugnion F (2003) Just War, Wars of Aggression and International Humanitarian Law. International Review of the Red Cross 18

Campanelli D (2008) The Law of Military Occupation Put to the Test of Human Rights Law. International Review of the Red Cross 90(871)

Carcano A (2015) The Transformation of Occupied Territory in International Law. Brill, The Hague

Charlesworth H (2002) International Law: A Discipline of Crisis. Modern Law Review 65(3):377–392

Chehtman A (2015) Occupation Courts, Jus Ad Bellum Considerations, and Non-States Actors: Revisiting the Ethics of Military Occupation. Legal Theory 21(1)

Chen T (1951) The International Law of Recognition. Praeger, New York, p. 424

Costelloe D (2017) Legal Consequences of Peremptory Norms of International Law. Cambridge University Press, Cambridge

Council of the European Union, Foreign Affairs Council, Council Conclusions on Ukraine, 3 March 2014, www.consilium.europa.eu/uedocs/cms_data/docs/pressdata/EN/foraff/141291.pdf. Accessed 10 April 2017

Crawford J (1979) The Creation of States in International Law. Oxford University Press, Oxford

Crawford J (2012) Third Party Obligations with respect to Israeli Settlements in the Occupied Palestinian Territories, Opinion. www.tuc.org.uk/sites/default/files/tucfiles/LegalOpinionIsraeliSettlements.pdf. Accessed 10 May 2017

Crawford J (2012) Brownlie's Principles of Public International Law. Cambridge University Press, Cambridge

Cullen A, Wheatley S (2013) The Human Rights of Individuals in De Facto Regimes under the European Convention on Human Rights. Human Rights Law Review 13(4)

Darcy S, Reynolds J (2010) An enduring occupation: The status of the Gaza Strip from the perspective of international humanitarian law. Journal of Conflict Security Law 15(2)

de Waal T (2015) The New Siege of Crimea. Carnegie Endowment for International Peace

Del Mar M, Twining W (2017) Legal Fictions in Theory and Practice. Springer Switzerland

Dinstein Y (2009) The International Law of Belligerent Occupation. Cambridge University Press, Cambridge

Douglas M, Hull D (1992) How Classification Works: Nelson Goodman Among the Social Sciences. Edinburgh University Press, Edinburgh

Draper G (1983) Humanitarian Law and Internal Armed Conflict. Georgia Journal of International and Comparative Law 13:253–277

Elsuwege P (2009) Baltic States. In: Max Planck Encyclopaedia of Public International Law. Oxford University Press, Oxford

European Commission (2014) Information Note to EU business operating and/or investing in Crimea/Sevastopol., SWD (2014) 300 final/3, 10 June 2015

European Commission (2015) Commission Guidance note on the implementation of certain provisions of Regulation, Notice, (EU) No 833/201425 September 2015

European Council (2012) Guidelines on the implementation and evaluation of restrictive measures (sanctions) in the framework of the EU Common Foreign and Security Policy, 15 June 2012, 11205/1

Fox G (2008) Humanitarian Occupation. Cambridge University Press, Cambridge

Fraleigh A (1949) The Validity of Acts of Enemy Occupation Authorities Affecting Property Rights. Cornell Law Quarterly 35

Frowein JA (2013) De Facto Regimes. In: Max Planck Encyclopedia of Public International Law. Oxford University Press, Oxford

Geiss R (2015) Russia's Annexation of Crimea: The Mills of International Law Grind Slowly but They Do Grind. International Legal Studies 91

Giladi R (2008) The Jus Ad Bellum/Jus in Bello Distinction and the Law of Occupation. Israel Law Review 41

Gross A (2015) Righting the Law of Occupation, In: Bhuta N (ed) The Frontiers of Human Rights. Oxford University Press, Oxford

Gross A (2017) The Writing on the Wall: Rethinking the International Law of Occupation. Cambridge University Press, Cambridge

Hakimi M (2017) The Work of International Law. Harvard Journal of International Law 58

Hammarberg   T   (2013)   Report   on   Human   Rights   in   the   Transnistrian Region of the Republic of Moldova. United Nations. md.one.un.org/content/dam/unct/moldova /docs/pub/Senior_Expert_Hammarberg_ReportTN_Human_Rights.pdf. Accessed 10 April 2017

Hathaway O, Shapiro S (2011) Outcasting: Enforcement in Domestic and International Law. Yale Law Journal

Human Rights Watch (2016) Ukraine: Fear, Repression in Crimea. New York

ICJ (2004) Legal Consequences of the Construction of a Wall in the Occupied Palestinian Territory

Tomuschat C (2009) International Jurists Opinion on Exhaustion of Local Remedies, 4 December www.law.gov.cy/Law/…nsf/0/…/Expert_Opinion_on_Local_Remedies_(3.12.09). doc. Accessed 10 April 2017

Korman S (1996) The Right of Conquest: The Acquisition of Territory by Force in International Law and Practice. Clarendon Press, Oxford

Koutroulis V (2012) The application of international humanitarian law and international human rights law in situation of prolonged occupation: Only a matter of time? International Review of the Red Cross 855

Kretzmer D (2012) The law of belligerent occupation in the Supreme Court of Israel. International Review of the Red Cross 94

Krieger H (2016) Rights and Obligations of Third Parties in Armed Conflicts. KFG Working Paper Series 5

Lagerwall A (2014) The duty not to recognise unlawful territorial situations and the European Court of Human Rights. In: Binder C, Lachmayer K (eds) The European Court of Human Rights and Public International Law – Fragmentation or Unity? Nomos, Vienna

Lagerwall A (2016) Le Principe Ex Injuria Jus Non Oritur en Droit Internationale. Bruylant, Brussels

Lauterpacht H (1948) Recognition in International Law. Cambridge University Press, Cambridge

McGeehan N (2011) Misunderstood and Neglected: The Marginalisation of Slavery in International Law. The International Journal of Human Rights 15

McMahan J (2011) Individual Responsibility and the Law of Jus ad Bellum. In: Benaji Y, Sussman N (eds) Reading Walzer. Routledge, London

Megret F (2006) From 'Savages' to 'Unlawful Combatants': A Postcolonial Look at International Humanitarian Law's 'Other'. In: Orford A (ed) International Law and Its 'Others'. Cambridge University Press, Cambridge, pp. 265–317

Milano E (2006) Unlawful Territorial Situations in International Law. Martinus Nijhoff, The Hague

Milano E (2007) The doctrine(s) of non-recognition: Theoretical underpinnings and policy implications in dealing with de facto regimes. Agora, European Society of International Law www. esil-sedi.eu/fichiers/en/Agora_Milano_060.pdf. Accessed 10 April 2017

Milano E (2014) The Non-recognition of Russia's Annexation of Crimea: Three Different Legal Approaches and One Unanswered Question. Questions of International Law. Editoriale Scientifica, Naples

Ministry of Foreign Affairs of Georgia (2016) First Quarterly Report (January - March 2016) of the Ministry of Foreign Affairs of Georgia on the Human Rights Situation in the Occupied Regions of Georgia

Morgenstern F (1951) Validity of the Acts of the Belligerent Occupant. British Yearbook of International Law 28

Murray D (2016) Human Rights Obligations of Non-State Armed Groups. Hart, Oxford

Nicolosi S (2011) The Law of Military Occupation and the Role of De Jure and De Facto Sovereignty. Polish Yearbook of International Law 31

Nollkaemper A (2010) The Power of Secondary Rules of International Law to Connect the International and National Legal Orders. In: Broude T, Shany Y (eds) Multi-Sourced Equivalent Norms. Hart, Oxford

Nollkaemper A (2017) Responsibility. In: D'Aspremont J, Singh S (eds) Fundamental Concepts for International Law: Constructing Intelligibility in International Legal Studies. Edward Elgar, Cheltenham

Ohlin J (2015) The Doctrine of Legitimate Defense. International Law Studies 91:119–154

Orakhelashvili A (2003) Peremptory Norms and Reparations for Internationally Wrongful Acts. Baltic Yearbook of International Law 3

Peterson M (1997) Recognition of Governments: Legal Doctrine and State Practice 1815–1995. Palgrave Macmillan, London

Public Defender of Georgia (2017) Analysis of the Law of Georgia "On Occupied Territories" and Recommendations. www.ombudsman.ge/uploads/other/4/4316.pdf. Accessed 10 May 2017

Ratner S (2005) Foreign Occupation and International Territorial Administration. European Journal of International Law 16(4)

Roberts A (2005) Transformative Military Occupation. In: Schmitt M, Pejic J (eds) International Law and Armed Conflict: Exploring the Faultlines. Brill, The Hague

Ronen Y (2011) Transition from Illegal Regimes in International Law. Cambridge University Press, Cambridge

Ronen Y (2013) Human Rights Obligations of Territorial Non-State Actors. Cornell International Law Journal 46

Rozakis C (1974) The Law on the Invalidity of Treaties. Archiv des Völkerrechts 16(2)

Rozakis C (1976) The Concept of Jus Cogens in the Law of Treaties. North Holland Publishers, Amsterdam

Sassòli M (2005) Legislation and Maintenance of Public Order and Civil Life by Occupying Powers, European Journal of International Law 16

Satkauskas R (2003) A Bill for the Occupants or an Issue to Negotiate? The Claims of Reparations for Soviet Occupation. Baltic Yearbook of International Law

Sayed H (2014) The Fictions of the 'Illegal' Occupation in the West Bank and Gaza. Oregon Review of International Law 16

Schoiswohl M (2001) De Facto Regimes and Human Rights Obligations. Austrian Review of International and European Law 6

Shapovalova N (2016) The Situation of National Minorities in Crimea following its Annexation by Russia. European Parliament www.europarl.europa.eu/RegData/etudes/STUD/2016/578003/EXPO_STU(2016)578003_EN.pdf. Accessed 10 April 2017

Shaw M (1982) Territory in International Law. In: Netherlands Yearbook of International Law 13

Sivakumaran S (2009) Courts of Armed Opposition Groups: Fair Trials or Summary Justice? Journal of International Criminal Justice 7

Solomou A (2010) Demopoulos and others v Turkey (Admissibility). American Journal of International Law

Sztucki J (1974) Jus Cogens and the Vienna Convention on the Law of Treaties: A Critical Appraisal. Springer-Verlag, Vienna/New York

Talmon S (1999) Who Is A Legitimate Government in Exile? In: Goodwin-Gill G, Talmon S (eds) The Reality of International Law. Oxford University Press, Oxford

Talmon S (2005) The Duty Not to 'Recognize as Lawful' a Situation Created by the Illegal Use of Force or Other Serious Breaches of a Jus Cogens Obligation: An Obligation without Real Substance? In: Tomuschat C, Thouvenin J (eds) The Fundamental Rules of the International Legal Order: Jus Cogens and Obligations Erga Omnes. Martinus Nijhoff, The Hague

Tancredi A (2014) The Russian Annexation of Crimea: Questions Relating to the Use of Force, Questions of International Law. Editoriale Scientifica, Naples

Thompson K (2015) Zhu Xi, In: Zalta E (ed) The Stanford Encyclopedia of Philosophy, Fall Edition, plato.stanford.edu/archives/fall2015/entries/zhu-xi/. Accessed 10 April 2017

Thurer D (2006) Current Challenges to the Law of Occupation. Collegium 34

van Essen J (2012) De Facto Regimes in International Law. Utrecht Journal of International and European Law.

Wilde R (2008) International Territorial Administration. Oxford University Press, Oxford

Wilde R (2009) From Trusteeship to Self-Determination and Back Again: The Role of the Hague Regulations in the Evolution of International Trusteeship, and the Framework of Rights and Duties of Occupying Powers. Loy. L.A. Int'l & Comp. L. Rev. 31

Wrange P (2015) Occupation/Annexation of a Territory: Respect for International Humanitarian Law and Human Rights and Consistent EU Policy, Directorate General for External Policies, www.europarl.europa.eu/RegData/etudes/STUD/2015/534995/EXPO_STU(2015)534995_EN.pdf. Accessed 10 April 2017

Wright Q (1961) The Role of International Law in the Elimination of War. Manchester University Press, Manchester

Chapter 4
Conferral of Nationality of the Kin State – Mission Creep?

Sabine Hassler and Noëlle Quénivet

Contents

Abstract Nationality is a surprisingly complex and emotive issue. At a time when global events appear increasingly threatening, the individual desire to align with a solid State is stronger than ever. While the acquisition of nationality is commonly not subject to much controversy, this chapter looks at Russia's escalating process of conferring nationality on individuals in States that used to form part of the Soviet Union. In order to be able to discuss whether such conferral of nationality is a permissible course of action to consequently justify the forcible protection of nationals abroad, this chapter discusses to what extent the conferral of nationality is an absolute exercise of State sovereignty and looks at the means and methods by which nationality may be acquired and/or conferred, both in general and in the Russian context. This

The author is a Senior Lecturer at the Bristol Law School of the University of the West of England, Bristol. sabine2.hassler@uwe.ac.uk.
The author is an Associate Professor in International Law at the Bristol Law School of the University of the West of England, Bristol. noelle.quenivet@uwe.ac.uk.

S. Hassler (✉) · N. Quénivet
Bristol Law School, University of the West of England, Bristol, UK
e-mail: sabine2.hassler@uwe.ac.uk

N. Quénivet
e-mail: noelle.quenivet@uwe.ac.uk

© T.M.C. ASSER PRESS and the authors 2018
S. Sayapin and E. Tsybulenko (eds.), *The Use of Force against Ukraine and International Law*, https://doi.org/10.1007/978-94-6265-222-4_4

allows the chapter to then explore the consequences of nationality and to what extent, if any, an individual or a group of individuals can expect protection from their 'home' State when abroad. It would appear that such State protection is entirely discretionary and subject to political and other considerations. What, then, is Russia's objective in declaring individuals in its near abroad as nationals? By exploring its activities, the chapter takes particular note of the experiences in the Baltics, Georgia, and Ukraine to conclude that Russia is in the process of attempting to rewrite the rules carefully crafted post-1945 to revive kin-State activism and so allowing for interference in neighbouring States to become an established international custom.

Keywords nationality · acquisition and/or conferral of nationality · passportisation · consequences of nationality · use of force · protection of nationals abroad · territorial integrity und non-intervention in internal affairs · privileged interest doctrine

4.1 Introduction

Most people take their nationality and citizenship rights for granted, not overly concerned with precise meanings and relying on official documentation that assure their status and rights. In everyday usage, thus, there is a tendency to use the terms interchangeably although how exactly these terms are interpreted can vary significantly.[1]

Nationality, by definition, refers to an individual's State of origin, commonly by birth, and thus imbues that individual with an innate connection with that State, regardless of his/her current residence, and implies that State's protection on grounds of his/her nationality.[2] In international law, specifically, the term 'nationality' is used to refer to the 'legal bond between an individual and a sovereign [S]tate'[3] which, in turn, not only implies a legal bond but also a political tie with the State as an entity, defined as a 'human group based on the need of civilised men for an organisation which will maintain and defend their civil rights and liberties'.[4]

An associated concept with nationality is citizenship; while often used synonymously, the latter is usually taken to specifically mean the legal status an individual enjoys as part of an entity's (such as a State's or the EU's) political framework. Thus,

---

[1] See Koessler 1947, p. 63. For an instructive overview of traditions, see European Union Democracy Observatory on Citizenship 2016a. Also European Convention on Nationality, opened for signature 6 November 1997, ETS No. 166 (entered into force 1 March 2000), (European Convention on Nationality), Article 2a.

[2] For a discourse on the meaning behind 'nationality', see Bisschop 1942, p. 151.

[3] European Union Democracy Observatory on Citizenship 2016a.

[4] Fawcett as cited by Bisschop 1942, p. 154. Of course, ethnically, a national of a State living within its territory may have different origins, be that because of cultural, religious and/or linguistic traditions but while 'nationality' is a legal concept, 'ethnicity' defines a group by way of certain characteristics which may confer specific rights under a State's internal or domestic laws, for example as part of anti-discrimination legislation.

broadly speaking, nationality is a 'status independent of residence' while citizenship is a 'as a bundle of rights granted only to nationals residing' within a State's territory.[5] Consequently, it is not advisable to use these terms interchangeably; they may be related but are nonetheless distinct from each other. For the purposes of this chapter, it is the concept of nationality and the protection it affords rather than citizenship rights that will be explored (though at times, as the sources cited do use the terms interchangeably, this chapter might do so too).

Nationality and respective modes of acquisition are rarely an issue as both the individual seeking nationality and the State conferring such nationality are 'in agreement'. However, when it comes to instances of a group of individuals who are nationals of State A but whose loyalty lies with another State (State B) and with that State reciprocating the desire to bring these individuals within its fold against State A's, and most likely the international community's, wishes, matters become complex, complicated and fraught. Claims that a whole class of individuals is in need of and must be afforded State B's protection against the 'oppressor' (home) State A have been advanced on the grounds of 'nationality', notably by Russia with regard to 'ethnic' Russians now living outside of the territory of the Russian Federation. This raises a number of important questions which, in turn, inform the structure of this chapter. First, what is nationality and how, if at all, is it possible to acquire, change or award nationality, on what grounds, and to what effect (both on part of the individuals seeking change and the States 'losing', 'gaining' that individual respectively)? Secondly, what are the legal consequences of granting nationality? And, finally, how far does a State's reach in protecting its nationals stretch?[6] Does it, indeed should it, go as far as allowing the State to use force?

The International Law Commission has clearly spelled out that while a State may invoke lawful and peaceful means to offer diplomatic protection to 'a natural [...] person that is a national' and who has suffered an 'injury caused by an internationally wrongful act' of another State, the use of force cannot be invoked to protect nationals abroad.[7] Yet, it appears that this is exactly the basis of Russia's actions in States such as Georgia and more recently Ukraine. Baltic States are in fact afraid that they might be the next targets of this policy.

We argue that Russia's policy of facilitating acquisition of Russian nationality combined with a nationalist discourse has allowed it to intervene in the internal affairs of its neighbouring States and that this has been carried out in three stages. It started with conferring nationality on individuals with a view to offering them diplomatic protection, then moved to using force under the idea of protection of nationals abroad, to finally annexing a part of the territory of another State. We contend that the contemporary international law framework has constrained Russia in its long-standing ability to influence neighbouring States and create a buffer zone

---

[5] European Union Democracy Observatory on Citizenship 2016a.

[6] As Koessler noted, the 'distinctions between personal and territorial sovereignty are flexible and not clearly delineated.' While the former is a matter of domestic law, the latter is one of international law. Koessler 1947, p. 70.

[7] ILC 2006a, Article 1. See also ILC 2006b, Article 1, para 8.

around it so much that it has reverted to a pre-WWII policy of kin-State activism through the use of 'nationality'.[8] If this were allowed to continue unrestrained, does that sound the end of the post-WWII order in Europe inasmuch as permitting such acts would set a dangerous precedent in international law?

4.2 Conferral of Nationality: An Absolute Exercise of State Sovereignty

As sovereign entities, States are free to 'determine under [their] own law who are its nationals'.[9] Generally, the rules on nationality are based on the following principles that (a) everyone has the right to a nationality or at the very least the right to acquire a nationality;[10] (b) statelessness shall be avoided;[11] (c) no one shall be arbitrarily deprived of his or her nationality;[12] and (d) neither marriage nor the dissolution of a marriage between a national of a State Party and an alien, nor the change of nationality by one of the spouses during marriage, shall automatically affect the nationality of the other spouse.[13] Thus, 'nationality is within the domestic jurisdiction of the State'[14] which implies that the State prescribes when, by whom, and how nationality may be acquired.

However, while it is the State which holds ultimate power to decide whether 'any individual shall be entitled to enjoy any, and what, rights',[15] it must be noted

---

[8] There is a clear delineation between internal struggles for independence and a State's perspective on conferring or extending 'nationality'. We are concerned with the latter and will not look at or explore self-determination.

[9] Note that the discussion of nationality has 'consequences on both the international and the municipal planes of law'. See e.g. Convention on Certain Questions Relating to the Conflict of Nationality Laws, opened for signature 13 April 1930, LNTS vol. 179 (entered into force 1 July 1937), Article 1; European Convention on Nationality, above n. 1, Chapter II, Article 3(1).

[10] E.g. Universal Declaration of Human Rights, 10 December 1948, 217A (III), Article 15; International Covenant on Civil and Political Rights, opened for signature 16 December 1966, UNTS vol. 999 (entered into force 23 March 1976), Article 24(3); United Nations Convention on the Rights of the Child, opened for signature 20 November 1989, UNTS vol. 1577 (entered into force 2 September 1990) (hereinafter UNCRC), Article 7; Helsinki Document 1992, 9–10 July 1992, VI: The Human Dimension (Helsinki Document 1992), paras 55–56; OSCE Istanbul Document 1999, Charter for European Security: III. Our Common Response (Istanbul Document 1999), para 19.

[11] See Convention on the Reduction of Statelessness, opened for signature 30 August 1961, UNTS vol. 989 (entered into force 13 December 1975), Preamble: 'considering it desirable to reduce statelessness by international agreement'.

[12] Helsinki Document 1992, above n. 10, paras 55–56; Istanbul Document 1999, above n. 10, para 19.

[13] All these principles are contained in European Convention on Nationality, above n. 1, Chapter II, Article 4.

[14] ICJ, *Nottebohm Case (Liechtenstein v. Guatemala)*, Second Phase, Judgment, 6 April 1955, ICJ Reports 1955 (*Nottebohm* 1955), p. 20.

[15] Bisschop 1942, p. 152.

that international law does place constraints on both the conferral and the removal of nationality though removal is more tightly regulated due to its impact on individuals.[16] Effectively conferral of nationality is dependent on the 'development of international relations'[17] as some States might or might not recognise the nationality of an individual and thus create customary rules which 'impose certain limits on the broad powers enjoyed by the States' to the extent that conferral of nationality 'cannot today be deemed within their sole jurisdiction'.[18] Indeed, as explained in Article 4 of the ILC Draft on Diplomatic Protection '[f]or the purposes of the diplomatic protection of a natural person, a State of nationality means a State whose nationality that person has acquired, in accordance with the law of that State, by birth, descent, naturalization, succession of States, or in any other manner, *not inconsistent with international law*.'[19] States are undoubtedly 'limited in their discretion to grant nationality by their obligations to guarantee equal protection before the law and to prevent, avoid and reduce statelessness'.[20]

4.2.1 Methods of Conferral of Nationality Under International Law

There are a multitude of modes of acquiring nationality as well as losing or renouncing it.[21] This chapter will concentrate on acquisition based on *jus soli* and *jus sanguinis* as foundational principles, and on modes of naturalisation in particular. While for the former two an individual's birth determines nationality, the latter allows for nationality to be acquired at any time after birth through 'attribution, declaration, option or application'.[22] *Jus soli*, or 'law of the soil', determines nationality by way of birth on the soil of a particular State. The right is conferred irrespective of the

---

[16] Pre-WWII the State exercised its absolute sovereignty with regard to the removal of nationality (as well as citizenship) such as the reprehensible and shameful Nürnberger Gesetze that stripped German Jews of their citizenship and relegated them to 'Staatsangehörige' without political rights in 1935. Die Nürnberger Gesetze 1935. Contemporary instances such as the Israeli government revoking Nahad Abu Kishaq's, a native-born Israeli of Arab descent, nationality in 2002 for his alleged involvement in suicide bombings are rare and controversial. See M. Mualem and J. Bana, 'Yishai revokes citizenship of Israeli Arab', *Ha'aretz*, 10 September 2002.

[17] PCIJ, *Nationality Decrees Issued in Tunis and Morocco*, Advisory Opinion, 7 February 1923, Ser. B. No. 4, p. 23.

[18] Inter-American Court of Human Rights, *Proposed Amendments to the Naturalization Provision of the Political Constitution of Costa Rica*, Advisory Opinion, 19 January 1984, OC-4/84, Series A No. 4.

[19] ILC 1976, p. 31 (emphasis added); and commentary on pp. 33–34.

[20] Butcher 2006, p. 10. Butcher refers to the case of the Inter-American Court of Human Rights, *Dilcia Yean and Violeta Bosico v. Dominican Republic*, Judgment, 8 September 2005, Series C No. 130.

[21] For a comprehensive overview see European Union Democracy Observatory on Citizenship, Comparative Typology of Modes of Acquisition and Loss of Citizenship.

[22] European Union Democracy Observatory on Citizenship 2016b.

parents' status or their birthplace. *Jus sanguinis*, or 'law of blood', on the other hand, determines nationality not by birthplace but rather by the individual's parents' nationality (either both, or exclusively the mother's or the father's nationality). This may either be automatically at the time of birth (*ex lege*) or, in some cases, after birth. This may occasionally raise a conflict when a child is born of parents with a different nationality (e.g. French) in a State that adopts the *jus soli* principle (e.g. the US) and may lead to that individual enjoying dual nationality (insofar as that is permissible).[23] In case conflicts arise, e.g. in case of military service, it is commonly resolved by considering the individual's habitual residence and 'close connection' with a particular country.[24]

Apart from 'birth rights', nationality may be acquired by naturalisation. In that case, an individual may take the decision to renounce his/her nationality in favour of another owing to 'stronger links acquired elsewhere, changes in family status, a move to another country, or requirements of another country in allowing access, for example, to the labour market'.[25] While an individual may opt for naturalisation based on an application to the relevant public authority of the adopted State, there are various mechanisms and modes by which a person may be naturalised; some are automatic, some are based on entitlements, and some are based on the discretion of the relevant State. First, ordinary naturalisation by way of application can be based on certain entitlement criteria such as continuous residency for a minimum period of time (usually not exceeding ten years of lawful residence),[26] evidence of secure dwelling and sufficient income, limitations where there have been criminal convictions, (elementary) knowledge of the language, evidencing knowledge of history and societal order of the adopted State, for the applicant to not pose any danger to security and defence, for the applicant to take an oath of allegiance or make a declaration of loyalty, and the provision of a good character reference to list but a few.[27] Second, naturalisation may be owing to cultural affinity – naturalisation under this heading is usually discretionary but can also be automatic. In Germany, for instance, naturalisation for reasons of cultural affinity may be automatic,[28] discretionary[29] or

---

[23] See Convention on the Reduction of Cases of Multiple Nationality and on Military Obligations in Cases of Multiple Nationality, opened for signature 6 May 1963, ETS 43 (entered into force 28 March 1968). There are instances of allowing naturalisation of individuals of a particular ethnic background without losing their original nationality, e.g. ethnic Turks in Germany. See Boll 2005, p. 37.

[24] Protocol Relating to Military Obligations in Certain Cases of Double Nationality, opened for signature 12 April 1935, LNTS vol. 178, no. 4117 (entered into force 25 May 1937), Article 1.

[25] Butcher 2006, p. 16.

[26] See European Convention on Nationality, above n. 1, Article 6(3).

[27] Note that this is a non-exhaustive list and varies from State to State.

[28] The person 'is an emigrant of German ethnic origin from Eastern Europe who has suffered from discrimination due to his or her descent, who has admission to Germany and has obtained a special certificate'. Based on StAG (Staatsangehörigkeitsgesetz) 1913, as amended 13 November 2014. See also European Union Democracy Observatory on Citizenship 2016b.

[29] Where the person 'is a citizen from another area in Europe (not Eastern Europe) where German is the official or colloquial language and has been resident in Germany for 4 years, or person is an emigrant of German ethnic origin and resident abroad'. Ibid.

it may be an entitlement.[30] Third, other reasons include the discretionary exercise of naturalisation owing to a person's special and unusual hardship (as in Canada),[31] because there is a genuine connection with the State (as in Germany) or the exercise of special grants such as the Israeli Aliyah, or the Law of Return,[32] which permits applications to settle in Israel based on being Jewish (i.e. the right to come to Israel as an Oleh) and fulfilling some additional conditions.[33]

All of the above, *jus sanguinis* and *jus solis* as well as modes of naturalisation, feed to some extent into and are supported by the ideas of 'identity',[34] 'loyalty' and 'allegiance'. 'Identity' and nationality are linked, although not mutually dependent, on a domestic legal plane through the use of identity cards which in particular evidence and record one's 'national identity' but also foster a 'feeling of belonging' both on registration of a child's birth and/or, later on, as an important instrument of both identity and evidence of nationality.[35] It should be noted, nonetheless, that there are individuals who, without apparent sense of allegiance or loyalty change their nationality status, as Boll notes, 'purely on the basis of subjective self-interest' such as sports people.[36]

As a matter of terminology, 'allegiance' as a factor is not free from controversy. In *Tadić* it was considered in the context of armed conflict and protected persons under Article 4 Geneva Convention IV, especially in the context of 'modern inter-ethnic armed conflicts as that in the former Yugoslavia'. Here, allegiance to a party to a conflict was emphasised as the crucial test rather than nationality; consequently, 'ethnicity rather than nationality may become the grounds for allegiance' in which case 'the requirement of nationality is even less adequate to define protected persons'.[37] Academic writers, however, are more careful and point to the feudal notions that, in the context of allegiance, connoted 'the duty owed by the individual to his lord or sovereign as the correlative of his claim of protection upon such superior.'[38] Hence, 'allegiance' in the sense of it having been a duty of obedience is to be differentiated from its modern interpretation, which includes an 'obligation of loyalty'

---

[30] Where the person 'is a citizen from another area in Europe (not Eastern Europe) where German is the official or colloquial language and has been resident in Germany for 4 years, or person is an emigrant of German ethnic origin and resident abroad'. Ibid.

[31] Canadian Citizenship Act 1985.

[32] Israel Ministry of Foreign Affairs, Law of Return 5710-1950 (as amended).

[33] Eligibility for Aliyah 2014.

[34] See Article 8 UNCRC, and a child's right to preserve its identity. The inclusion of this particular provision is due to Argentina's experience of 'disappeared children': Doek 2006, p. 29.

[35] The symbolic value of citizenship as a 'signal of common belonging on the part of both the holder and the granter of citizenship' has been acknowledged. See OSCE High Commissioner on National Minorities 2012, Principle 32.

[36] Boll 2005, p. 37.

[37] International Tribunal for the Prosecution of Persons Responsible for Serious Violations of International Humanitarian Law Committed in the Territory of the Former Yugoslavia since 1991, *Prosecutor v. Duso Tadic*, Judgment, 15 July 1999, IT-94-1-A, para 166.

[38] Parry et al. 1986, p. 16. Also, Koessler 1947, p. 68.

to the State.[39] 'Loyalty' and 'allegiance' as the emotional connections must not be underestimated, however.[40] Much like in human relationships where the emotional connection between a cohabiting couple conventionally is sought to be legally evidenced through a marriage certificate, the desire of an individual of State A to become a national of State B may eventually be confirmed and evidenced through naturalisation. Identity, loyalty, and allegiance are thus, arguably, strong factors in the nationality discourse and should not be ignored, especially in the context of this chapter. While there is an expectation that a national is loyal to his/her State in return for civil and political rights, even to the point of defending the State and its integrity against threats, both external and internal, to what extent a State owes a duty of loyalty, if any, to its nationals in return is a matter of debate.[41]

The above shows that it is not outside the realms of possibility to acquire, or indeed be granted, nationality for a variety of reasons, including for protective purposes. How far this may be extended in terms of actually conferring nationality and thus offering protection, and subject to which conditions and limitations, will need to be assessed in light of Russian practice.

4.2.2   Russian Practice Relating to Conferral of Nationality

While in international law 'nationality' is used to refer to the legal bond between an individual and a sovereign State, in Russian domestic law this definition is applied to the term 'citizenship'.[42] Thus, according to the Constitution of the Russian Federation, 'citizenship' (grazdanstvo - гражданство) under Article 6 is different from 'nationality' (national'nost' - национальность) under Article 26(1).[43] Accordingly, the former shall be acquired and terminated according to domestic law; it shall be one and equal, irrespective of the grounds of acquisition.[44] At the same time, the term 'nationality' appears to be wider, less easily defined and much more personal as Article 26 makes it clear that '[E]veryone shall have the right to determine and indicate his nationality. No one may be forced to determine and indicate his or her nationality.' Thus, the term nationality refers to individual membership in a nation (нация)

---

[39] For a more detailed discussion see Boll 2005, p. 37. In law, the duty of obedience is expressed in legislation that criminalises treason, see e.g. 18 U.S. Code § 2381. Disloyalty or treason are among potential reasons for the non-voluntary loss of citizenship. See 'New head of Ukraine's navy defects in Crimea', *BBC Europe*, 2 March 2014.

[40] While an individual's obligation of loyalty to the State is firmly anchored in domestic law it is accepted that it does have a role to play in international law. Boll 2005, p. 37.

[41] Koessler 1947, p. 68.

[42] See Federal Law on Russian Federation Citizenship (No. 62-FZ of 31 May 2002).

[43] The Constitution of the Russian Federation (adopted at national voting on 12 December 1993).

[44] Article 6(1); and a citizen of the Russian Federation may not be deprived of his or her citizenship or of the right to change it (Article 6(3)).

as determined by cultural, linguistic, and historic links.[45] By way of identifying the Russian diaspora as a 'nation', consequently, Russian nationality encompasses those who live within the territory of the Russian Federation, i.e. those with citizenship, and those who live outside the territory of the Russian Federation and who may be nationals of another State, e.g. Ukraine,[46] but are because of their links to Russia identified as compatriots.[47] The link between Russian citizens and Russian compatriots as Russian nationals, thus, appears to be not because of legal and/or political factors of identification but rather for other reasons. In fact, considerable efforts have gone into maintaining the 'Russian ethno-cultural space, and consolidating the Russian community' as such a 'consolidated Russian community abroad meets Russia's national interests'.[48] Incidentally, the definition of compatriot has undergone some changes.[49] While formerly a compatriot was a person who was any citizen of the former Soviet Union (SU), even if he or she, or their forebears, never lived in the Russian Federation,[50] more recently the definition appears to have changed so that it no longer automatically applies to all persons who in the past lived in the former SU.[51] Rather, it is now by the principle of self-identification by which a compatriot is to be recognised. In that regard, acquisition of citizenship for those who speak Russian and 'have documented proof that at least one of his or her direct ancestors was a permanent resident of the Soviet Union or the Tsarist Russian Empire who lived on the territory of the current Russian Federation' has become 'simpler and faster'.[52] Russian policy with regard to compatriots was designed around supporting them abroad and to 'facilitate their voluntary resettlement to the Russian Federation'.[53] Hence, the primary aim pointed to repatriation of those identified as compatriots with its immediate advantages of integration obvious: knowledge of the Russian language and culture, and their recognition of Russia as their homeland.[54] Moreover, as

---

[45] European Union Democracy Observatory on Citizenship 2016a. Also, Koessler noted that nationality 'has at least two accepted denotations: (1) the status of belonging to a state; (2) the quality of membership in an ethnological group.' Koessler 1947, p. 61.

[46] It is estimated that 'persons of Russian heritage constitute a substantial proportion of the population' in Ukraine: about 17.3 per cent. See 'Ukraine', CIA World Factbook 2017. Moreover, Russian's profound attachment to Ukraine is rooted in Russian civilisation having older roots in Ukraine than in Russia. House of Commons Library 2014, p. 31.

[47] While Vykhovanets and Zhuravsky assert that 'no ethnic considerations are or can be applicable here', Biersack and O'Lear refer to 'ethnicity' as an identification factor. Vykhovanets and Zhuravsky 2013. Biersack and O'Lear 2015, p. 250.

[48] Chepurin 2009, p. 68.

[49] For an analysis of the legal scope of 'compatriot' as part of crafting a Russian identity, see Kozin 2015, p. 286.

[50] Articles 1 and 3(3), About the state policy of the Russian Federation concerning compatriots abroad, Federal Law of the Russian Federation of 24 May 1999 (No. 99-F3) as amended on 24 July 2010. See Vykhovanets and Zhuravsky 2013.

[51] Amendment to the law on state policy towards compatriots living abroad (24 July 2010).

[52] Ibid. See President of Russia 2014 and V. Timkiv, 'New citizenship shortcut for Russian-speakers of Soviet', *RIA Novosti*, 21 April 2014.

[53] Vykhovanets and Zhuravsky 2013.

[54] Ibid.

Vykhovanets and Zhuravsky posit, the Russian State's socio-economic future was intended to benefit from 'improved age, sex and occupational population structure achieved at minimal expense'.[55] The policy and its implementation, however, never quite achieved its intended aims, not least owing to 'strategic disparities'.[56]

The above is clearly predicated on compatriots repatriating to Russia. In the context of this chapter, the question however is about the protection of so-called nationals abroad. This requires an understanding how nationality, or in the Russian understanding citizenship, is acquired and to what extent the Russian policy of extending citizenship is accompanied by legal validation rather than purely by way of what can be termed a symbolic declaration.

According to Russian Federal Law, citizenship 'means a stable legal relation of a person with the Russian Federation that manifests itself in an aggregate of their mutual rights and duties'.[57] As a corollary, a citizen who is staying outside the Russian Federation territory 'shall be granted the Russian Federation's defence and protection'.[58] Citizenship may be acquired, *inter alia*, as a result of being admitted for citizenship or on 'other grounds set out in the present Federal Law or an international treaty of the Russian Federation'.[59] Admission to citizenship may be on general terms[60] or in a simplified manner.[61] While in both instances individuals may ask for naturalisation, in the latter instance the residency aspect under the general terms heading need not be observed if certain conditions as listed are fulfilled. One of the conditions is that the individuals had USSR citizenship, and having resided and are residing in the States that have formed part of the USSR, have not become citizens of these States and as a result remain stateless persons.[62] In case of a change in State borders, an individual residing 'in the territory which switched its state shall have a right to choose citizenship (right of optation) in the manner and within the term established by a relevant international treaty of the Russian Federation'.[63] While normally the individual looking for citizenship has to make an application in person,[64] where an 'applicant cannot file the application in person due to circumstances of an exceptional nature as confirmed by documents, the application and the necessary documents may be forwarded for consideration through the services of another person

---

[55] Ibid.

[56] Ibid.

[57] Article 3, Federal Law on Russian Federation Citizenship (No. 62-FZ of 31 May 2002). While dual citizenship is possible, interestingly this is interpreted as the individual having 'allegiance' of a foreign State. Ibid.

[58] Ibid., Article 7(1).

[59] Ibid., Article 11.

[60] Ibid., Article 13.

[61] Ibid., Article 14.

[62] Ibid., Article 14(1)(b).

[63] Ibid., Article 17.

[64] Ibid., Article 32(1) and (2).

or sent by post.[65] Official certification of such citizenship is a passport.[66] Any issues relating to citizenship are within the powers of the President to resolve.[67]

This shows that, on the face of it, Russian citizenship is acquired in line with the modes outlined above. While officially there have been suggestions that acquisition of citizenship by naturalisation would be expedited by simplifying citizenship procedures,[68] there is evidence that Russia has employed so-called passportisation to create facts by converting existing documentation into Russian authorised documentation almost *carte blanche*.[69] While more easily accomplished in Abkhazia and South Ossetia owing to the majority of individuals there identifying as Russian, in Ukraine the situation is less clear as those identifying as Russian and desirous of citizenship are more dispersed.[70] Moreover, in Ukraine dual citizenship is likely to be banned outright.[71] Thus, anyone taking up the Russian offer could potentially be stripped of Ukrainian nationality which might well 'hand Russia an additional argument in the (largely false) narrative that Russians are being oppressed in Ukraine'.[72]

Understanding the leeway granted to States in conferring nationality allows us to accept that nationality is an important tool for States to shape their relationship with specific individuals as well as their relationship with other States. States will only grant nationality to individuals they consider their 'own'.

4.3 Nationality Under International Law: Recognition and Legal Consequences

Whilst granting nationality to individuals is no doubt a sovereign right of States, albeit to some extent constrained by international law, its concept as considered under international law and the political, economic and especially legal reach and consequences of the conferral of nationality must be fully understood. As outlined previously, an individual's nationality depends on the State granting and making available the trappings as well as the consequences of nationality by demanding evidence of the individual's entitlement by birth or, in case of naturalisation, by professions of allegiance and/or loyalty amongst other things; this, to some extent,

---

[65] Ibid., Article 32(3).

[66] Ibid., Article 10. See also Decree of the President of the Russian Federation No. 232 of March 13, 1997 on the Main Document Serving as the Personal Identity Document of a Citizen of the Russian Federation on the Territory of the Russian Federation.

[67] Articles 29 and 35(1), Federal Law on Russian Federation Citizenship (No. 62-FZ of 31 May 2002).

[68] 'Russia to make citizenship easier for native Russian speakers', *Reuters*, 7 March 2014. Also P. Kenyon, 'Russia may expedite passports for Ukraine's ethnic Russians', *NPR*, 6 May 2014.

[69] See A. Blomfield, 'Russia 'distributing passports in the Crimea', *The Telegraph*, 17 August 2008. Also V.M. Artman, 'Annexation by passport', *AlJazeera America*, 14 March 2014.

[70] V.M. Artman, 'Annexation by passport', *AlJazeera America*, 14 March 2014.

[71] 'Poroshenko proposes bill to ban dual citizenship in Ukraine', *RadioFreeEurope*, 14 March 2017.

[72] Spiro 2014.

raises a legitimate expectation on part of the individual that the State offers protection at home and potentially even abroad.[73] Once the link between a State and an individual is established and this link is recognised, the State *can* extend its protection to its nationals whether they are within or outside its territory.

4.3.1 Recognition of the Genuine Connection

Under international law, nationality is viewed as and only recognised as such if there is a 'genuine connection', i.e. a legal bond based on 'existence, interests and sentiments, together with the existence of reciprocal rights and duties'[74] between the individual and the State. This 'genuine connection' concept can be divided into two components: the legal element of the bond that involves reciprocal rights and duties and the 'social fact of attachment' and 'connection of existence, interests and sentiments'. Under international law, both components must be fulfilled. Although this seems to be relatively straightforward in its application, the reality is that it is not.

Whilst the legal component is simple to explain as it reflects a formal status provided by the law, the contours of the second component are difficult to discern. Indeed '[t]his legal relationship involves rights and corresponding duties upon both—on the part of the citizen no less than on the part of the State. If the citizen leaves the territory of this sovereign State and goes to live in another country, the duties and rights which his nationality involves do not cease to exist [...].'[75] To demonstrate this legal relationship, any documentation (e.g. a consular certificate, baptismal certificate) is permissible.[76] After all such documentation can be rebutted by another State by proving that the individual has lost his/her nationality by e.g. acquiring another one which does not allow dual nationality or by renouncing his/her nationality. Also, this legal relationship can be proven through the actual exercise of the rights and duties. The second component relates to the way the individual has incorporated him/herself into the State (the notion of 'social fact of attachment' is translated into 'family ties', 'participation in public life')[77] as well as to the degree the individual has integrated into the State's culture and values ('genuine connection of existence, interests and sentiments' is translated into 'closely connected with the population of the State').[78] The vagueness of these concepts and their subjective application have led scholars

---

[73] In this regard, it is important to keep the consequences of nationality in international law separate from those rights and duties derived from domestic law.

[74] *Nottebohm* 1955, above n. 14, p. 23.

[75] British-Mexican Claims Commission, *Lynch Claim (Great Britain v. Mexico)*, Decisions and Opinions, 8 November 1929, Vol. V RIAA 1929, p. 18.

[76] Ibid., p. 19.

[77] *Nottebohm* 1955, above n. 14, p. 22.

[78] Ibid., p. 23.

to criticise it.[79] As the *Nottebohm* jurisprudence is borne out of a dispute relating to a naturalisation procedure, it may be argued that the ICJ was looking to establish a threshold for 'actively' rather than 'passively' acquired nationality and thus raised the bar higher than it should be or maybe simply added a component that is not relevant in other circumstances.[80] In fact Article 4 of the Draft Articles on Diplomatic Protection does not make any reference to such a genuine link inasmuch as it only specifies that a legal bond should exist between the State and the individual.[81] Yet, in the very specific context of 'Russians' and 'Russian nationals' this component is of particular relevance.

Indeed, Russia identifies individuals as 'Russian' even if they only fulfil one of the components of nationality, and that is the one that is least supported in scholarly writings and in the jurisprudence. By extending rights to those identified as 'Russian', Russia acknowledges that there is a bond, a 'social fact of attachment', between these individuals and itself often recognized via knowledge of the Russian language and culture.[82] However, under international law these individuals do not qualify as Russians and thus cannot, as explained later in this chapter, benefit from the legal consequences derived from nationality. To what extent, if at all, is it utilitarian, even beneficial, for Russia to symbolically declare a group of individuals who are either dispersed (e.g. in Latvia or Estonia) or on an identified stretch of another State's territory (e.g. Georgia or Ukraine) as 'Russian nationals' and thus, without further conferral of nationality attributes, extend its reach for their protection? While a symbolic act does serve some purpose of fostering a sense of belonging and identity, the practical and legal act of converting such symbolic connection automatically raises such considerations as the issue of relevant identification documentation and the impact of such documentation on existing evidence of nationality.[83] If such declaration was meant to be, and to remain, purely of symbolic nature, any legal justification for diplomatic protection or 'protection of nationals abroad' arguably loses its foundation; if the declaration was meant to be followed up by the practical process of conferring nationality, and thus was meant to be of real legal, as opposed to purely symbolic, consequence, the next step is to understand the legal consequences of nationality and whether this has allowed Russia to use nationality as a leverage to meddle in the affairs of other States and eventually to annex a part of another State's territory.

---

[79] See e.g. Gulati 2014, p. 559; Van Panhuys 1968, p. 942.

[80] In *Mergé* the Italian-United States Conciliation Commission also dealt with a case of dual nationality and stressed the principle of 'effective nationality' and 'dominant nationality'. Italian-United States Conciliation Commission, *Mergé Case*, Decision, 10 June 1955, Vol. XIV RIAA 1955, pp. 241–242. It should be noted that in cases of dual nationalities tribunals are required to balance the strengths of competing nationalities (Report of the International Law Commission, 58th session (1 May–9 June and 3 July–11 August 2016), UN Doc A/31/10, page 46).

[81] ILC (1976), p. 31. See commentary on pp. 32–33.

[82] See discussion on Russians in South Ossetia, see in Natoli 2010, pp. 412–413.

[83] 'Poroshenko proposes bill to ban dual citizenship in Ukraine', *RadioFreeEurope*, 14 March 2017.

4.3.2 Legal Consequences of Nationality

From a legal point of view, the moment an individual becomes a national of a State it means that this individual has rights, entitlements, and privileges within and against the State but also obligations that do not apply to aliens.[84] After all, as Kesby puts it, nationality is the 'right to have rights'.[85]

An important benefit of nationality is the ability to enter, remain in, and exit the State of nationality[86] whereas non-nationals' movements can be restricted. Likewise, the State has a duty under customary law to readmit its nationals[87] which inevitably shows this physical belonging of the individual to the State. Also, a State can protect its nationals by refusing to comply with an extradition request on the basis that this individual is a national.[88]

Nationality also allows States to exercise sovereignty over individuals wherever they are in the world. Through the use of the nationality principle and the passive personality principle the State can stretch its reach beyond its territory, obliging individuals to comply with domestic law.[89] This application of national law abroad is uniquely accepted by foreign States.[90] That being said, a State does not incur responsibility for unlawful acts carried out by its nationals unless these acts can be imputed to the State.[91]

Further, it can offer its protection through the well-established concept of diplomatic protection which is a classic process of international law by which a State asserts that another State has treated the national of the former in violation of international law,[92] most commonly a human rights violation. There are in fact two sides in the application of this concept: the rights of the individual and the rights of the State. On the one hand, nationality is the gateway through which individuals 'can enjoy the

---

[84] See Boll 2005, p. 37.

[85] Kesby 2012, p. 142.

[86] See Higgins 1973, p. 341.

[87] See Perruchoud 2012, p. 147.

[88] See the German constitution that does not allow for the extradition of nationals: Grundgesetz, Article 16(2). The supremacy of this article was underlined by the German Constitutional Court (Bundesverfassungsgericht) in 2005: BVerfG, Urteil des Zweiten Senats vom 18. Juli 2005 - 2 BvR 2236/04 - Rn. (1-201). Also Article 4(5), Federal Law on Russian Federation Citizenship (No. 62-FZ of 31 May 2002).

[89] See ILC 1976, p. 522.

[90] For example, in the United Kingdom, War Crimes Act 1991, s 1, Sexual Offences Act 2003, s 72 and Cluster Munitions (Prohibitions) Act 2010, s 4(3) apply to British nationals abroad. See also Arnell 2012.

[91] In strict terms, States can only be held liable for acts of its agents and not of private persons or entities. Tomuschat argues that States cannot assume 'full accountability for the actions of their citizens who, in the exercise of their human rights, are not subject to governmental control.' Tomuschat 1999, p. 274.

[92] In exceptional circumstances, States may exercise diplomatic protection for non-nationals. See ILC 2001, Article 39, para 6; and PCIJ, *Panevezys-Saldutiskis Railway Case (Estonia v. Lithuania),* Judgment, 28 February 1939, PCIJ Rep Ser A/B No. 76, p. 16.

benefits from the existence of the Law of Nations'.[93] On the other hand, diplomatic protection is a right of the State, for a State can take action against another State on the basis that 'whoever ill-treats a citizen indirectly injures the State'.[94] Indeed, nationality is 'the justification in international law for the intervention of one government to protect persons and property in another country'.[95] Consequently and ultimately, the protection of nationals is an inter-State business that dates back to the time when nationals were considered as subjects of the State.[96] First, and provided that the local remedies have been exhausted,[97] the State makes diplomatic representations on behalf of a national vis-à-vis the foreign State that has violated international law and can be held responsible for this violation. The ICJ stated that 'within the limits prescribed by international law, a State may exercise diplomatic protection by whatever means [...] it thinks fit'.[98] The individual is not taking part in these discussions. In fact, the individual concerned cannot prevent his/her State of nationality from taking up his/her claim or from (dis)continuing the procedures.[99] Second, nationals do not have the right to request their State to protect them. Diplomatic protection is exercised at the discretion of the State and legal challenges to transform this into an obligation of the State have so far failed.[100] It would indeed impinge on the sovereign right of the State to decide upon how to conduct its international affairs and could potentially lead to a legal dispute with another State.[101]

A State can also go a step further than negotiations and bring a claim against a State that has injured one of its nationals before an international tribunal.[102] A number of applications to the ICJ show that this mechanism is still in use and offers a genuine possibility for States that have accepted the ICJ's jurisdiction to bring a legal claim to protect their nationals.[103] However, owing to the admissibility rules

---

[93] Oppenheim 1912, para 291.

[94] Peters 2016, p. 390.

[95] United States-Mexican Special Claims Commission, *Naomi Russell Case (United States v. Mexico)*, Decision, Vol. IV RIAA 1931, p. 811.

[96] Weis 1979, p. 4; Lie 2004, p. 131.

[97] See ICJ, *Diallo Case (Republic of Guinea v. Democratic Republic of the Congo)*, Preliminary Objections, Judgment, ICJ Rep 2007, para 44. As Künzli explains, '[a]fter exhaustion of local remedies [diplomatic protection] is no longer a dispute between an individual and a state but between two states. It is thus not an internal affair but an international dispute'. Künzli 2006, p. 333.

[98] ICJ, *Barcelona Traction, Light and Power Company, Limited*, Judgment, 5 February 1970, ICJ Reports 1970, para 78. On the different ways to make representations, see Künzli 2006, pp. 321–350.

[99] See Künzli 2006, p. 337.

[100] *Bertrand Russell Peace Foundation v. United Kingdom* (App 7597/76) (1978) 14 DR 117; *R (Abassi & Anor) v. Secretary of State for Foreign and Commonwealth Affairs and Secretary of State for the Home Department* [2002] EWCA Civ 1598; *Canada (Prime Minister) v. Khadr* [2010] 1 SCR 44; See discussion in Prochaska 2009.

[101] See discussion in Wellens 2014, pp. 19–151.

[102] In *Nottebohm,* the ICJ distinguished between 'diplomatic protection and protection by means of international judicial proceedings'. *Nottebohm* 1955, above n. 14, p. 24.

[103] ICJ, *Diallo Case (Republic of Guinea v. Democratic Republic of the Congo)*, Merits, Judgment, 30 November 2010, ICJ Reports 2010, p. 639; ICJ, *Avena and Other Mexican Nationals (Mexico v. United States of America)*, Judgment, 31 March 2004, ICJ Reports 2004 (*Avena* 2004), p. 12; and

relating to the nationality of claims, a State must demonstrate that there is a 'genuine connection of existence, interests and sentiments' between the individual and the State which 'assumes the defence of its citizens'.[104]

While diplomatic protection has traditionally been an exercise of State sovereignty, it has nonetheless at its heart the protection of individuals' rights,[105] which means that occasionally a State may act 'extraterritorially in order to assert its legal interest'.[106] It is generally assumed that the benefits of nationality, its pursuance as well as its acquisition, are primarily in the interests of individuals, not necessarily the State's.[107] In fact, it is an old fashioned way for States to protect the human rights of their nationals abroad. However, in a modern world of customary norms of and treaties on international (and regional) human rights law the concept of diplomatic protection might be viewed as redundant. This is compounded by the existence of a plethora of individual petition mechanisms on the international and regional level. So, why would the State wish to take on the case of an individual when such individual can in fact him/herself raise his/her claim before a petition mechanism, be that a committee in the case of e.g. the Human Rights Committee of the International Covenant on Civil and Political Rights, or a court in the case of e.g. the European Court of Human Rights of the European Convention on Human Rights?[108] Moreover, exercising diplomatic protection can be very costly towards a State's international relations, so exercising it for every injured party could prove disastrously damaging. For example, in the European context the *Ireland v. United Kingdom* case[109] contributed to further frictions between the two States. This explains why very few States have made the claims of their nationals their own.

So, what is the utility and what are the benefits for a State to increase the number of nationals they can protect through the means of diplomatic protection? There is an array of potential answers. First, it might be that the State does not trust the mechanisms in place to provide effective remedies to the individuals whose rights have been violated. In the case of human rights violations in Europe this justification does not hold much ground as the European Court of Human Rights offers a robust individual petition mechanism whose decisions are legally binding and enforced. Second, and relatedly, it might be a way for the State to pinpoint a sizeable number of nationals affected or a pattern of breaches of international law suffered by their nationals[110] and thus raise the issue as one that affects 'their nationals', i.e. a collectivity rather than

---

ICJ, *LaGrand case (Germany v. United States of America)*, Judgment, 27 June 2001, ICJ Reports 2001 (*LaGrand* 2001), p. 466.

[104] *Nottebohm* 1955, above n. 14, p. 23.

[105] It is acknowledged that individuals are increasingly able to assert their rights in person without having to rely on the State. Leys 2016, pp. 1–2.

[106] Leys 2016, p. 4.

[107] For a discussion on this assumption, see Boll 2005, p. 37.

[108] Convention for the Protection of Human Rights and Fundamental Freedoms, opened for signature 4 November 1950, ETS No. 005 (entered into force 3 September 1953).

[109] Ireland v. United Kingdom, Application No. 5310/70, 18 January 1978.

[110] See e.g. *Avena*, above n. 103, p. 12.

a collection of individuals. After all, as Künzli explains 'a claim brought on behalf of a state usually carries more weight than one brought on behalf of individuals' and therefore 'states should not feel restrained to exercise diplomatic protection if they have an interest in proving the human rights situation of their nationals abroad'.[111] Maybe the clue is that it is at the State's discretion to act and not because it must. Such applications are often only lodged when the State wishes to make a point.[112] In that case, the State decides when to intervene and so nationality becomes a tool at the hands of the State should it be needed.

This bond of nationality can go beyond its mere protective objective; it can become a political tool by influencing one's nationals in a State where they have the right to vote and thus the opportunity to shape the policies and laws of that foreign State.[113] Likewise, this bond can be used to repatriate these nationals when the socio-economic future of the State is bleak, the State thus relying on them to boost falling population numbers and skills gaps. Some scholars argue that '[o]nce the veil could be lifted, President Putin admitted the presence of Russian troops to make sure the Crimean people could hold a supposedly democratic referendum.'[114]

Overall, it could be argued that the diplomatic protection of nationals is as much about maintaining a political sphere of influence as it is about historical reasons and for the protection of securing the State's socio-economic future.[115]

4.4 Russia's Use of Nationality – Mission Creep

There seems little doubt that Russia uses nationality as a political, economic, and cultural tool of expansionism. Examining its behaviour over the past decades, it is possible to contend that there are three phases in this strategy (whether it was premeditated or is a piecemeal approach is unknown). The first one was the conferral of nationality by way of passportisation to those identifying as Russian in Baltic States and Georgia; the second was the use of force to protect nationals abroad, i.e. in Georgia; and the third was/is the use of force to acquire neighbouring territory on which Russians are living in order to recreate zones of influence.

---

[111] Künzli 2006, p. 350.

[112] See e.g. *LaGrand,* above n. 103, p. 466.

[113] See discussion in Bauböck 2007, pp. 2293–2447.

[114] Biersack and O'Lear 2015, p. 255.

[115] Vykhovanets and Zhuravsky 2013.

4.4.1 The Baltics and Georgia I: Conferral of Russian Nationality

To understand what motivates a State to confer nationality for reasons other than 'birth rights' two pertinent justifications, linked by history, might be adduced. The motivation might stem either from a historical sense of responsibility and obligation, or the creation of a State. The legacy of WWII led, in the former instance, to Germany adopting a policy of entitlement to apply for German nationality for those who despite their German descent were absorbed, for instance, by the Soviet Union (Russlanddeutsche) or Czechoslovakia (Sudetendeutsche).[116] In the latter instance, it led to the creation of Israel and its policy of Aliyah.[117] In the Russian context and its 'near abroad', a historic link based on a sense of responsibility could be, tentatively, advanced. Such a proposition would be based on the fact that Russians were during the existence of the Soviet Union encouraged to settle in non-Russian republics as part of the so-called Russification policy.[118] When the Soviet Union collapsed, they found themselves in 'alien' territory. Thus, a Russian sense of obligation and responsibility towards those it feels morally obligated to may be advanced. 'Russian-speaking minorities were seen as stranded and marginalised in the nationalizing states of the former Soviet multi-ethnic empire, while the policies of national governments started to prioritise native languages and citizens over minorities'.[119] Altruistically speaking, it may be argued that Russia is providing those without a 'home' with a sense of identity.

This rather legitimate justification might be used in the context of the Baltic States' (Latvia and Estonia, and to a lesser extent Lithuania) experience and their complex and complicated relationship with Russia.[120] While all three Baltic States have, since the breakup of the Soviet Union, become members of the EU and NATO,[121] they all have one inexorable link with what is now the Russian Federation: a number of ethnic Russians living within their borders owing to the Russification policy. As Patsiurko and Wallace explain, the 'Baltic states [...] were a particular flashpoint in these tendencies.'[122] The bone of contention concerns those who have for various reasons not been 'naturalised'[123] following the implementation of strict laws on

---

[116] See Article 116 Abs. 2, Grundgesetz and StAG (Staatsangehoerigkeitsgesetz) 1913, as amended 13 November 2014.

[117] Israel Ministry of Foreign Affairs, Law of Return 5710-1950 (as amended).

[118] See Krūma 2015, p. 1.

[119] Patsiuko and Wallace 2014, p. 187.

[120] See Krūma 2015.

[121] NATO has made it clear that the alliance is on alert to a possible Russian military operation. See Warsaw Summit Communiqué 2016, para 40. However, it should be noted that the RAND Corporation assessed NATO's chances of successfully defending the territories of its most exposed members as low to bad. See Shlapak and Johnson 2016.

[122] Patsiuko and Wallace 2014, p. 188.

[123] See Krūma 2015, p. 2.

nationality.[124] They are now classified as 'non-citizens' with limited rights to work or vote, receive a different type of passport, the so-called 'grey passport', because they do not speak the native language[125] and are, consequently, denied full citizenship.[126] In Latvia, the policy is based on the State continuity principle according to which 'only those who were Latvian citizens and their descendants could restore their citizenship *de facto*, leaving Soviet era immigrants in legal limbo'.[127] Similar, albeit different, legislation was adopted in Estonia resulting in many individuals becoming stateless.[128] While expulsion was and is not possible for political (and moral) reasons and owing to limitations in international human rights law, the steps taken to maintain the distinction and the 'labels' of citizen and non-citizen inevitably attracted Russia's attention. Indeed, Russia has expressed its concern over 'the unresolved problem of mass statelessness in the Baltic region',[129] an issue ascribed to 'lack of political will and discrimination' and, in part, due to the perceived reluctance on part of the EU to fully back the UN Human Rights Council's efforts on arbitrary deprivation of nationality.[130] Russia did not officially raise the issue with the Baltic States; after all, these individuals were not its nationals and it could thus not use the legal tool of diplomatic protection. Despite being the kin-State, Russia was unable to protect its people abroad. Indeed, while the symbolic declaration underlines the political expression of power,[131] procedurally there are real, practical limitations on a State declaring an identified group of individuals on another State's territory as its 'nationals'. They were in fact viewed as minorities in the classic sense of the term[132] which means that their existence and rights must be primarily protected by the State on whose territory they live. That being said, it is accepted that States

---

[124] See Lottmann 2008, pp. 503–521.

[125] R. Milne, 'Latvia's Russians express dissatisfaction', *The Financial Times*, 30 March 2014; Tsybulenko and Amorosa 2012, pp. 85–90.

[126] Roudik 2013.

[127] See Krūma 2015, p. 1.

[128] See discussion in Zinchenko 2014, pp. 19–20.

[129] 'Moscow concerned over statelessness in Baltics', *The Voice of Russia*, 6 October 2012.

[130] UN Human Rights Council 2013. See Kohn 2012.

[131] There is an implicit expectation that Russia exercises its superior power. Thus, '[T]his perception of a forceful Russia is particularly prevalent in the states of the former Soviet Union, wherein Russia is widely seen as a having a prerogative to intervene in and influence'. Biersack and O'Lear 2015, p. 251. See also Kozin who posits that forging the Russian national identity through 'the Law of Compatriot, demonstrated its allegiance to the paternalistic model of a strong state which considers compatriots as its juridical subjects'. Kozin 2015, p. 298.

[132] Whilst there is no internationally agreed definition as to the concept of minority, the United Nations Declaration on the Rights of Persons Belonging to National or Ethnic, Religious and Linguistic Minorities refers to their 'national or ethnic, cultural, religious and linguistic identity' in its Article 1. General Assembly 1992. A probably more elaborate definition is part imparted by Francesco Capotorti, the then Special Rapporteur of the United Nations Sub-Commission on Prevention of Discrimination and Protection of Minorities: 'A group numerically inferior to the rest of the population of a State, in a non-dominant position, whose members - being nationals of the State - possess ethnic, religious or linguistic characteristics differing from those of the rest of the population and show, if only implicitly, a sense of solidarity, directed towards preserving

cooperate in questions relating to persons belonging to minorities but this is, in modern international law, often limited to 'exchanging information and experiences, in order to promote mutual understanding and confidence'[133] unless there are special arrangements by way of treaties in place.

Unable to protect its non-nationals Russia decided to ease citizenship requirements in various laws passed between 1999 with the Law on Compatriots Living Abroad and 2002 with the Law on Russian Federation Citizenship. To some extent, it might be argued that Russia offered stateless individuals a way to acquire nationality. In 2002, the law was made less stringent and the procedure simplified to the effect that individuals had to submit an application to a Russian consulate in the State of their permanent residency to receive Russian travel passports as proof of their Russian citizenship.[134] In this case, one could even make a case that Russia was answering a genuine human rights demand based on Article 15 UDHR which specifies that '[e]veryone has the right to a nationality' which had been denied by the Baltic States' strict citizenship laws.

A similar pattern can be established with regard to Russian 'nationals' in Georgia though it must be underlined that the situation is different inasmuch as shortly before/after the breakup of the Soviet Union, Abkhazia and South Ossetia declared their independence and, although they were not recognised as States, managed to maintain factual autonomy from Georgia. Those inhabiting these areas technically held Georgian nationality but were unwilling, rather than unable as in the case of the Baltic States, to obtain Georgian documentation and the passports delivered by the local authorities were not internationally recognised. The 2002 change in Russia's citizenship laws allowed these individuals to obtain Russian nationality all the more as some support groups simply took their papers to a nearby Russian city for processing, thereby relieving them of the burden to travel to a nearby Russian consulate[135] located in Georgia. Reportedly, after the change in the law on citizenship, 90% of South Ossetians had acquired Russian nationality.[136] A similar flood of applications and naturalisation was observed in Abkhazia.[137] It is thus possible to contend that Russia offered these individuals a way to acquire an internationally recognised passport. However, in this specific situation it was not the bad faith of the territorial State that was the trigger for this en masse conferral of Russian nationality but the unwillingness of the population to acquire the documentation of nationality of the (under international law) territorial State. After all, in the specific context of State succession, individuals belonging to minority groups can, within the framework of

---

their culture, traditions, religion or language.' United Nations Sub-Commission on Prevention of Discrimination and Protection of Minorities 1979, para 568.

[133] General Assembly 1992, Article 6.

[134] Roudik 2008.

[135] Ibid.

[136] Ibid.

[137] A. Osipovich, 'Controversial passport policy led Russians into Georgia: Analysts' *Agence France Press*, 21 August 2008.

the right of self-determination, choose their nationality.[138] How this applies to newly independent States is however subject to debate.[139]

While it is possible to offer to and confer nationality on those desirous of such status, the unilateral conferral by a State of such status, even if welcomed by the relevant group of individuals, is questionable and the motivations behind such a step need to be explored and carefully considered. From a legal viewpoint, it is recognised that States may accord benefits to persons who belong to national minorities abroad with regard to nationality. Thus, the 2008 Bolzano Recommendations[140] acknowledge a State's discretion to 'take preferred linguistic competencies and cultural, historical or familial ties into account in their decision to grant citizenship to individuals abroad.'[141] This is, however, subject to the principles of friendly relations among nations[142] and 'should refrain from conferring citizenship en masse, even if dual citizenship is allowed by the State of residence.'[143] While a State may exercise its discretion in that regard, the protection of minorities' rights remains 'primarily the obligation of the State in which they reside'.[144] Hence, there are limits on a State's discretion in formulating policies with regard to access to citizenship.[145] The question is whether it is practically possible to demand from a State to stand back and witness individuals it considers for historical reasons its own being deprived of the basic right to have a nationality. In the specific context of Russia and Russian 'nationals', the Alma Ata Protocol to the Minsk Agreement adopted on 21 December 1991 specified that the States emerging from the Soviet Union would 'develop [...] relations on the basis of [...] the principle[s] of [...] non-intervention in internal affairs, of abstention [...] from economic or other means of applying pressure and of settling of controversial issues through agreement'.[146] The conferral of Russian nationality to large swathes of individuals in Georgia can be viewed as a violation of the principle of non-intervention in internal affairs. Unlike in the Baltics, where individuals are scattered, the Russian nationals in Abkhazia and South Ossetia are located within the confines of a specific, delimited territory whose governments have declared their independence from Georgia. Recognising, even if only in practical terms, the South Ossetian and Abkhazian authorities when dealing with individuals on their territory is without a doubt a breach of the principle of non-intervention. Further, aware of

---

[138] Pellet 1992, p. 184.

[139] See discussion in Natoli 2010, pp. 408–409.

[140] OSCE High Commissioner on National Minorities 2008.

[141] Ibid., para 9.

[142] General Assembly 1965; General Assembly 1970.

[143] OSCE High Commissioner on National Minorities 2008, para 9. This is reflected in Principle 36 in The Ljubljana Guidelines on Integration of Diverse Societies, OSCE High Commissioner on National Minorities 2012.

[144] OSCE High Commissioner on National Minorities 2012, Principle 36.

[145] Ibid., Principle 33.

[146] Protocol to the Agreement Establishing the Commonwealth of Independent States (1991) signed at Minsk on 8 December 1991, paras 3 and 4. It should be noted that Georgia did not ratify the Protocol.

the situation, Russia could have acted as an honest broker between Georgia and its 'reluctant nationals'.[147] Rather, it chose to solve the problem itself in a way that increased tensions with a neighbouring State and has thus breached the principle of friendly relations and good neighbourhood.

As a result, it does appear that in Realpolitik terms Russia is creating a new sphere of influence in its near abroad by whatever means necessary in areas that had become part of Soviet Russian understanding of (territorial) identity. As Brubaker already predicted in 1996 a 'shifting and ambiguous vocabulary of homeland' would enable Russia to advance jurisdictional claims in the near abroad by targeting a broader population than the nationals stricto sensu.[148]

4.4.2 Georgia II: Use of Force to Protect Nationals Abroad

Indeed, the next phase was that of Russia using its military, rather than political, power to protect those it identifies as its nationals. The 'protection of nationals' narrative at home led to an atmosphere that encouraged Russia to intervene militarily abroad, in breach of international law; that is, unless an expansive interpretation is espoused.

The 'protection of nationals abroad' argument can be interpreted as a type of passive 'aggression' designed to engineer escalation, for example through the use of media[149] to intensify debate on the position of minority ethnic Russians abroad, and to consequently extending Russian State sovereignty through those identified as ethnic Russian nationals, if not by law at least by symbolic extension of nationality, to the territory they live on. Kozyrev argued already in 1995 that 'in exceptional cases, to protect its citizens and interests abroad, [Russia] is prepared to use all the necessary means, including military force, in keeping with the UN Charter and international norms'.[150]

The 'protection of nationals' discourse is based on two related elements. First, as mentioned above, there is a constant rhetoric of Russian nationals viewed as a collectivity of individuals sharing the same language, culture and religion. The discourse is that of bonding. Second, in Russia the Russians abroad are portrayed as oppressed people whose rights are denied because they are Russians. The combination of these two elements led to a growing sentiment that Russians abroad must be, even forcefully, protected by Russia. Speaking about the military intervention in Georgia in 2008, President Medvedev explained: 'Russia will not allow anyone to compromise the lives and dignity of its citizens, Russia is a nation, which will

---

[147] It should be noted that in fact it was not until Georgia's more hostile attitude towards the South Ossetian authorities that the inhabitants of this territory decided to adopt Russian nationality. Natoli 2010, p. 409.

[148] Brubaker 1996, p. 145.

[149] The media, and access to media outlets, is used by all sides as part of an 'informational propaganda struggle'. See Biersack and O'Lear 2015, pp. 249 and 253.

[150] As cited in Royal Institute of International Affairs 2000, p. 95.

continue to be reckoned with', which leads him to state that 'we defended our legitimate interests, and these decisive steps were supported not only by Russian society, but also by the millions of people abroad who praised them as well' and eventually 'no country in the world would stand by as its citizens [...] were being killed. Russia was obliged to save lives, to uphold law and justice.'[151] Russia supported the South Ossetians, 'emphasi[zing] an obligation to protect the large number of Ossetians to whom it had given Russian passports'.[152] Also, in an interview with the BBC Lavrov recalled that Medvedev stressed that 'under the Constitution [the President] is obliged to protect the life and dignity of Russian citizens, especially when they find themselves in the armed conflict.'[153] Article 61(2) of the Russian Constitution proclaims that the 'Russian Federation shall guarantee its citizens defence and patronage beyond its boundaries'. This 'expansive politics of citizenship, finally, enables Russia to combine the traditional (and from the point of view of international law more legitimate) rhetoric of protecting citizens in other states with homeland nationalist claims to protect noncitizen co-nationals'.[154] It was this link of nationality that was used and exploited by Russia to intervene in Georgia.

It is Russia's duty to protect those it identifies as 'its nationals'. In the post-Soviet era, and with the collapse of the Soviet Union and its subsequent break-up, the drive to reunify Russians and protect them, especially if located in a breakaway entity, if necessary by a display of force, has been evidenced in the 2008 intervention in Georgia to protect 'Russians' in South Ossetia. Clearly, when the forcible protection of those identified as 'nationals' abroad is declared as a 'rescue mission'[155] established principles, their interpretation, and application in context as well as their subsequent impact as a potential precedent on international relations generally must be borne in mind. The legality of Russia's intervention in Georgia can be considered from a variety of perspectives such as the right of self-defence, intervention by invitation, protection of peacekeepers, responsibility to protect,[156] etc.[157] but this chapter focuses on one justification: the doctrine of protection of nationals abroad.

The doctrine of the protection of nationals abroad is highly controversial. Under the restrictionist theory, States are not allowed to use force for this purpose. Three core arguments are advanced to underpin this position. First, the primary aim of the United Nations is the maintenance of peace. Second, if force is used it must be authorised by the United Nations barring the exception of clear cases of self-defence under Article 51 of the UN Charter. Third, to tolerate the unilateral use of force by States would be tantamount to opening the door to interventionism on

---

[151] President of Russia 2008b. Elsewhere Medvedev further argued that Russia's actions were necessary to 'protect [...] the Russian citizens living in [South Ossetia]'. President of Russia 2008a.

[152] Human Rights Watch 2009, p. 20.

[153] As cited in Global Centre for the Responsibility to Protect 2008, p. 1.

[154] Brubaker 1996, p. 145.

[155] See Solomon and Salako 2016, p. 152.

[156] J. Rubin, 'Russia's poor excuse for invading Georgia', *The New Republic*, 8 November 2008.

[157] See for example Lott 2012, pp. 4–21.

the basis of (geo)political interests.[158] It is the combined interpretation of Articles 2(4) and 51 of the UN Charter that informs the restrictionist view. While Article 2(4) includes a broad prohibition of the use of force,[159] Article 51 only offers States a very narrow window of opportunity to claim for the right to self-defence. Consequently, restrictionist theorists argue that due to the infinite opportunities for abuse, the right to use force to protect nationals abroad cannot seriously be considered to have survived the UN Charter.[160] The main thrust of this theory is that the UN Charter has created an entire new system regulating the use of force and that '[t]he intention in 1945 was to formulate the prohibition to use force in as absolute terms as possible.'[161] More modern interpretations do not confer authority on individual States to take action for the protection of nationals abroad; rather, they stress the Member States' commitments to multilateralism.[162]

Whilst there might be some legal worth in considering the restrictionist theory, there is no doubt that powerful States, willing and able to protect their nationals abroad, have consistently acted in contravention of it. As a result, intervention for the protection of nationals abroad must fall within the purview of two lawful exceptions to the use of force in international law, the right of self-defence under Article 51 of the UN Charter and actions of the UN Security Council under Chapter VII.

First, these interventions are by nature unilateral and thus without UN Security Council backing and so unlawful according to this exception. Second, a classic approach towards Article 51 UN Charter is to argue that it can solely be invoked in cases of actual armed attack against the territory of the State.[163] Consequently, an attack against nationals on foreign soil does not constitute an armed attack within the meaning of Article 51, thereby not triggering the right to self-defence.[164] However, it may be argued that the 'defence of nationals, whether within or without the territorial jurisdiction of the state, is in effect the defence of the state itself.'[165] An additional contentious issue is the threshold of force that must be employed to characterise a certain act as an armed attack against nationals abroad. In other words, did the Georgian operation fall within the remit of the definition of an 'armed attack' that takes into account the gravity of the attack,[166] and notably the amount of human

---

[158] Brownlie 1973, p. 146.

[159] Schrijver refers to Article 2(4) as the 'mother of all use of force provisions in the Charter.' Schrijver 2005, p. 34.

[160] Brownlie 1963, p. 301. Yet, it must be recalled that the possibility of abuse is not unique to the right to protect nationals abroad but is endemic to any use of force.

[161] Bowett 1958, p. 87; Henkin 1979, p. 137.

[162] At the 2005 World Summit. See General Assembly 2005.

[163] Brownlie 1963, p. 278.

[164] Henkin 1979, p. 145.

[165] Bowett 1958, p. 92. The US has been a strong proponent of this position. Sofaer 1991, p. 286. For example, it was the violence committed upon American citizens in Panama that led to the American intervention in 1989. Franck 2002, p. 92.

[166] '[T]here may be occasions when the threat of danger is great enough, or wide enough in its application to a sizable community abroad, for it to be legitimately construed as an attack on the state itself.' Bowett 1958, p. 93. Elaraby also argues that '[t]hese actions can be justified only if one

casualties and/or the seriousness of the destruction of property?[167] The operations mounted by Georgia are likely to be seen as indeed having crossed that threshold, thereby raising a legitimate right of self-defence on Russia's side.

An alternative view on the right of self-defence is to adopt a customary, rather than treaty, law approach in which case the armed attack is not of a territorial nature. The State is still entitled to protect its nationals as a matter of self-defence because of the bond between a State and its citizens.[168] 'Political theories of the social contract gave rise to the view that protection, as the duty of the state, afforded the consideration of the *pactum subjectionis*, and that protection of the nationals of the state was, in effect, protection of the state itself. Within the definition of the state the requirement of a community is essential, and without nationals, without the community, the state ceases to exist.'[169] Hence, actual physical harm of nationals can be considered as analogous to an armed attack and thereby trigger the same response: the use of force in self-defence.[170] In this context, the premise is that an injury to nationals in a State that is either *unable* or *unwilling* to protect them is tantamount to an injury to the State itself.[171] The breach of the State in which nationals are being harmed entitles the aggrieved State to protective intervention[172] because of the failure or inability of the local sovereign to protect foreign citizens,[173] in accordance with international law. Indeed, as aforementioned, States are under a duty to protect foreign citizens and failure to do so entails State responsibility. Moreover, it can be argued that if

---

agrees that because population is an essential element of a state, a massive attack on one's nationals aboard is equal to an attack on one's territory.' Elaraby 2003, p. 50.

[167] Danish Institute for International Studies 2005, p. 57.

[168] See discussion in Wingfield 1999–2000, pp. 441–444.

[169] Bowett 1958, p. 91. See also 'Under our system of government, the citizen abroad is as much entitled to protection as the citizen at home. The great object and duty of government is the protection of the lives, liberty and property of the people composing it, whether abroad or at home; and any government failing in the accomplishment of the object, or the performance of the duty, is not worth preserving.' US Circuit Court of Appeals, *Durand* v. *Hollins*, 4 Blatch, p. 454.

[170] Danish Institute for International Studies 2005, p. 59. For example the ICJ referred to the taking of US embassy staff as hostages in Iran as an armed attack (ICJ, *United States Diplomatic and Consular Staff in Tehran*, Merits, 24 May 1980, ICJ Reports 1980, paras 57 and 91) and also qualified an attack on US merchant and warships as armed attack (ICJ, *Oil Platforms (Islamic Republic of Iran v. United States of America)*, Judgment, 6 November 2003, ICJ Reports 2003, paras 51–62). See contrary opinion by Gray 2004, pp. 118–119, thereby implicitly recognising that it may trigger the right of self-defence.

[171] 'A State has the right to use limited force to rescue its nationals where the territorial state is unable or unwilling to do so.' Wood 2005, p. 82. See also Bowett 1957, p. 117; Schrijver 2005, p. 38.

[172] Bowett 1957, p. 116.

[173] See Statement by Foreign Secretary Lloyd, Parliamentary Debates (Hanson), 5th series, vol. 199, House of Lords Official Report (31 October 1956); Statement of the US Ambassador to the United Nations in U.N. SCOR, 1196 mtg., para 14 (1965) as cited in Arend and Beck 1993, pp. 97–98; Statement by the US in the Security Council in UN SCOR, 1941 mtg, at 31 U.N. Doc. S/p.v. 1941 (1976); Department of State Bulletin, vol. 80, No. 2039 (1980). See also discussion in Henkin 1991, p. 297.

foreign nationals are being harmed, the State is in breach of human rights law.[174] The Georgian operation certainly breached the human rights of the Russian nationals in South Ossetia and thus, under this interpretation of international law, it would be possible to view the Russian intervention as one in self-defence. Whether the act in self-defence (the exercise of the right of self-defence) was lawful is however not the subject of this discussion, for it is irrelevant to understanding the link between a State and its nationals abroad.

Consequently, it is possible, through an expansive interpretation of the right of self-defence, to allow for interventions for the protection of nationals abroad. However, this interpretation is not widely accepted. On the contrary, the great majority of States[175] and jurists support the viewpoint that the UN Charter has abrogated the right of States to intervene[176] unilaterally on foreign soil for the purpose of rescuing or protecting their nationals[177] though some recognise that 'international practice is showing a tendency to resurrect the law in existence before the UN Charter came into force'.[178] If indeed there is no right of protection of nationals abroad then it could be argued that Russia has not acted in self-defence and has in fact carried out an armed attack that is prohibited under both the UN Charter and customary law.

Moreover, a couple of notes of caution must be rung. First, and as previously noted, to tolerate the unilateral use of force by States opens the door to interventionism.[179] The later annexation of Crimea on even more tenuous grounds in fact shows the slippery road on which this concept is built. Second, it is argued that the doctrine of the protection of nationals abroad is a 'subterfuge used by the strong to interfere in the domestic affairs of the weak.'[180] Georgia, a former Republic of Soviet Union, was viewed by Russia as belonging to its sphere of influence. Its 'rebellion' and independent stance were thus considered as insubordination. Third, as noted by the Tagliavini report, individuals who had received Russian nationality in South Ossetia (as well as in Abkhazia) could not be deemed Russian nationals in terms of international law, mainly because they had retained their Georgian nationality unless they had renounced or lost it in regular ways.[181] This undoubtedly leads to raising the issue as to how genuine the attempt at offering 'nationality' is/was so as to provide an anchor of identity for such individuals. The fact that Russia intervened militarily in South Ossetia tends to show that the issuance of passports had maybe more sinister objectives. Yet, as Natoli explains, 'there does not seem to be a *legal* basis under international law for saying it cannot'[182] confer nationality en masse. He however

---

[174] See discussion in Margo 1977, pp. 317–318.

[175] See d'Angelo 1981, p. 487.

[176] Brownlie 1963, p. 278.

[177] See discussion in Ruys 2008, pp. 235–236.

[178] Simma 2012, p. 133.

[179] Brownlie 1973, p. 146.

[180] See Franck 2002, pp. 76–77. See Elaraby 2003, p. 46.

[181] International Fact-Finding Mission on the Conflict in Georgia ('Tagliavini Report'), Council of the European Union, 2009, p. 18.

[182] Natoli 2010, p. 413.

convincingly demonstrates that this conferral might be an abuse of rights as Russia is using a gap of norms in international law, as the conferral of nationality is not regulated by international law and remains within the *domaine réservé* of the State, and that 'Russia's actions violated international law and therefore the international community should not recognise Russia's right to protect the citizens of South Ossetia on the basis of their being Russian citizens'.[183]

4.4.3   Ukraine: Protection of Ethnic Russians

Indeed, when looking at the Russian motivation for its actions in the Baltics, Georgia (South Ossetia and Abkhazia), and Ukraine (Crimea and, more recently, eastern Ukraine) another explanation for identifying a group of individuals as Russian nationals, and consequently its assertion of protecting those nationals abroad, has been advanced: that of (re-)acquisition of territory by means other than the classic (as now prohibited)[184] use of force, followed by occupation and annexation.[185] Effectively, this policy facilitates an indirect (re-)expansionist strategy of re-unifying the former Soviet Union territories under the guise of protecting nationals.[186]

The case of the annexation of Crimea by Russia goes a step beyond the confines of Russia's intervention in Georgia. For those who might consider the intervention in Georgia lawful on the basis of the right of self-defence, the intervention in Crimea and later in eastern Ukraine indisputably show that many of the legal justifications propounded on the Russian side are to be taken with a pinch of salt. Three elements distinguish the interventions in South Ossetia and Crimea: first, Russia maintained at the time that it did not deploy troops in Crimea prior to the referendum; second, the 'nationals' to be protected did not have a Russian passport; third, the territory is occupied/annexed by Russia.[187]

In contrast to South Ossetia, where the great majority of the population held Russian passports, the urge to obtain such documents was less prominent in Ukraine. Thus, the 'legal' nationality link claimed by Russia for its intervention in South Ossetia could not be exercised in the case of Crimea and eastern Ukraine. However, by identifying ethnic Russians with Ukrainian nationality as Russian nationals, their

---

[183] Ibid., p. 416.

[184] Article 2(4), UN Charter. See also General Assembly 1970.

[185] In the Crimean context, the strategy was described as 'political technology of non-occupation'. Alexei Yurchak 2014 as cited in Biersack and O'Lear 2015, p. 249.

[186] Looking at the wider strategy, Biersack and O'Lear posit that while there is undoubtedly a rationale for reunifying the Soviet Union, there is a 'concomitant shift to the "east"', which however is effected rather more silently and in an effort to foster energy politics. Biersack and O'Lear 2015, p. 247.

[187] It should also be added that Crimea has a unique history and relationship with Russia as it used to be part of the Russian Republic and was gifted in 1954 to Ukraine. See Churkin in UN General Assembly 2014, p. 3.

de facto national 'identity' determined by 'ethnicity' which includes language,[188] 'allegiance' and 'loyalty' rather than by their *de jure* nationality,[189] Russia was able to forge a justification for, threatened, forceful intervention in arguing that the 'home' State is failing in its duty to protect ethnic Russians (compatriots) from, amongst other things, human rights abuses. This situation is particularly relevant in the case of Crimea as the only Russian-majority province in Ukraine.[190] Putin made Russia's position unequivocally clear

> Millions of Russians and Russian-speaking people live in Ukraine and will continue to do so. Russia will always defend their interests using political, diplomatic and legal means. But it should be above all in Ukraine's own interest to ensure that these people's rights and interests are fully protected. This is the guarantee of Ukraine's state stability and territorial integrity.[191]

From this it is clear that Russia believes it may legally intervene on behalf of ethnic Russians in danger abroad. Yet, despite the lack of this nationality link, is it still possible for Russia to claim that the intervention was lawful under the expansive interpretation of the right of self-defence? 'The claim to use force in self-defence is also occasionally advanced by a government on behalf of persons who are not its citizens but on whose behalf an historic protective relationship is claimed to exist.'[192] The intervention of Turkey in Cyprus in 1964 was not condemned by the UN Security Council whose members seemed to prefer to find a peaceful solution to the dispute without apportioning blame.[193] To some extent the provocative attitude of the Cypriot government was taken into account and probably explained the reluctance of the members of the Security Council to criticize the use of force. In the instant case, it might be argued that Russia also reacted to the perceived 'provocative' attitude of the Ukrainian State. Crimea was given substantial autonomy within Ukraine[194] and a 1997 treaty between Russia and Ukraine confirmed the borders of Ukraine and thus the fact that Crimea was a territory of Ukraine.[195] The Maidan revolution in Ukraine was no doubt a catalyst for Russia's involvement[196] but it brewed for a long time as Russia disliked the fact that Ukraine was looking towards the West.[197] Russia claimed that ethnic Russians were in danger in Crimea, yet there was no tangible

---

[188] Indeed, language is a unifying factor. Kozin notes that '[I]n the Soviet Union, native languages of the republics other than the Russian SSR were neither promoted, nor excluded, which created a strong impression of diversity amidst cohesion, which in a great part, was based on the national language – Russian.' Kozin 2015, p. 290.

[189] As Biersack and O'Lear describe it: it is predicated on 'an essentialist belief in civilizational uniqueness and a penchant for reclaiming lost prestige'. Biersack and O'Lear 2015, p. 251.

[190] See discussion in Mastroianni 2016, p. 642 and Burke-White 2014, p. 6.

[191] President of Russia 2014.

[192] Franck 2002, p. 79.

[193] See discussion in Franck 2002, pp. 79–81.

[194] Menon and Rumer 2015, p. 4.

[195] Treaty on Friendship, Cooperation, and Partnership between Ukraine and Russia 31 May 1997.

[196] See Churkin in UN General Assembly 2014, pp. 3–4.

[197] General Assembly/Security Council 2014, pp. 7 and 9. See also Trenin 2009, p. 11.

evidence of this.[198] It was a draft law to revise the language policy in Ukraine that appeared to have been viewed by Russia as a violation of human rights.[199] In fact, the alleged violations of the rights of ethnic Russians seemed to be 'neither widespread nor systemic.'[200] In other words, even if there were allegations of violations, that threshold of harm was so low that it could certainly not trigger the right of self-defence as discussed earlier.

In 2014, in reaction to the ousting of the pro-Russian regime by protesters, pro-Russian demonstrations began in Crimea, setting the scene for Russia's involvement in the region. Despite Russia initially denying that it directly entered the territory of another State, President Putin eventually conceded that the 'little green men' present during the annexation of Crimea were Russian soldiers.[201] While ethnic Russians in Crimea had not suffered a military attack Russia no doubt helped create the physical[202] and mental[203] conditions for an independence referendum leading to the secession of Crimea from Ukraine. Russia, by stating that it was allowed to deploy troops in Ukraine, breached the principle of non-intervention notably because the 'prohibition of intervention also applies to premature forms of recognition of secessionist movements in terms of separate statehood'[204] as well as the principle of territorial sovereignty because of the presence of Russian armed forces on Ukrainian territory without the consent of the territorial State. Again, Russia used the ethnic bond to meddle in the affairs of another State.

If we accept, for argument's sake, that Crimea had seceded from Ukraine and, as such, it could 'freely consent' to a reunification with Russia,[205] in light of the foregoing it remains nothing short of an attempt at annexation.[206] Yet, the development of this complex 'legal' situation makes it difficult to declare the reunification as unlawful *prima facie* as an independent State is allowed to merge with another, though a shadow is cast over the lawfulness of the independence and the referendum.[207] As

---

[198] Walter 2014, p. 309; Grant 2015, pp. 73–75.

[199] General Assembly/Security Council 2014, p. 5; see Burke-White 2014, p. 7.

[200] OHCHR 2014, Report on the Human Rights Situation in Ukraine, para 73.

[201] Kondrashev 2015, and S. Walker, 'Putin admits Russian military presence in Ukraine for first time', *The Guardian*, 17 December 2015.

[202] In February-March 2014 unidentified uniformed troops appeared throughout Crimea. Whilst Russia denied any involvement prior to the referendum there are reports that Russian forces (additional to the ones already posted as part of the Black Sea Fleet Agreement between Ukraine and Russia) were in fact present on the territory. See discussion in Mastroianni 2016, p. 645; Walter 2014, p. 302.

[203] The Russian Duma authorised President Putin to deploy Russian troops. 'Russian parliament approves troop. deployment in Ukraine' *BBC News,* 1 March 2014. See also General Assembly/Security Council 2014, p. 5.

[204] Oeter 2014, p. 51.

[205] Mastroianni 2016, p. 647.

[206] General Assembly 2017. It is not the purpose of this chapter to offer a full examination of the legal situation in Crimea, rather it is only teasing out the elements relating to nationality and the protection of nationals abroad. To this effect, see Grant 2015, p. 68.

[207] See Grant 2015, p. 85.

stated in the 1970 Friendly Relations Declaration 'no territorial acquisition resulting from the threat or use of force shall be recognized as legal'.[208] This is where,
besides the fact that the referendum is in itself highly questionable from a legal point
of view[209] which this chapter cannot due to space constraints tackle, the concept
of legitimacy can be used to question the supposed legality of an act. The speed
with which all these events happened casts a major shadow over the legitimacy of
this involvement,[210] all the more as Russia amassed troops near the Ukrainian border quickly thereafter and it appeared that it was supplying pro-Russian Ukrainians
with weapons and various types of logistical support and later supporting the self-
proclaimed republics.[211]

Further, this rather 'sneaky' approach adopted by Russia in sending military elements whose presence on the ground can be denied appears to have been repeated in
eastern Ukraine, thereby again questioning the acts of Russia in Crimea whilst in fact
showing the emergence of a pattern of intrusion of Russia in various neighbouring
States on the grounds that its nationals in a broad sense of the term are in actual or
perceived danger. One may even question whether Russia's strategy has not entered
a fourth phase, that of covert (or maybe not so covert as Russian troops have been
sighted in eastern Ukraine)[212] operations, as it realised that it could plausibly deny
its early involvement in Crimea. Indeed, the 'effective control' test spelled out in the
Nicaragua Case[213] is too high a threshold of attribution for State responsibility to
link Russia to the activities of armed groups. Burke-White concedes that this 'relatively forgiving, and likely outdated, legal standard for […] attribution' has been
exploited by Russia.[214] Whether Russia is indeed using the loophole is unclear (time
will tell as with its previous policies and activities); however, it must be noted that
the ICJ was not convinced by the evidence adduced by Ukraine in its application
for provisional measures of Russia's involvement in terrorist activities in Ukraine[215]
which may indeed lend credence to Burke-White's argument. Overall, it appears that
from overt distribution of Russian passports and overt military operations Russia has
gone into more covert involvement as it realised that its legal justifications were less
and less holding ground in classic international law.

---

[208] General Assembly 1970.

[209] It is not the purpose of this chapter to elaborate on the lawfulness and legality of the referendum
and its consequences. In that regard, see General Assembly 2014 and McDougal 2015. On the link
between the right of self-determination and referenda, see Cavandoli 2016.

[210] Burke-White 2014, p. 8.

[211] Menon and Rumer 2015, pp. 85–86.

[212] See OSCE Parliamentary Resolution 2015.

[213] ICJ, *Military and Paramilitary Activities in and against Nicaragua (Nicaragua v. U.S.A.)*, Merits,
Judgment, 27 June 1986, ICJ Reports 1986, p. 14.

[214] Burke-White 2014, p. 4.

[215] ICJ, *Application of the International Convention for the Suppression of the Financing of Terrorism and of the International Convention on the Elimination of All Forms of Racial Discrimination
(Ukraine v. Russian Federation)*, Order, 19 April 2017, para 75.

4.5   Conclusion

The UN Charter was meant 'to save succeeding generations from the scourge of war […] [and] to ensure, by the acceptance of principles and the institution of methods, that armed force shall not be used, save in the common interests'.[216] It established a framework for States to settle their disputes peacefully and to only use force in the narrow exceptions of the right of self-defence and collective security as exercised by the UN Security Council. The principles of territorial integrity and non-intervention in internal affairs are viewed as cornerstones of this UN legal order; both of them appear to be under attack by Russia's policy to protect its nationals abroad.

That being said, in all its interventions, Russia sought to justify its actions by reference to this specific legal order. It cannot thus be classified as a rogue State as such. In fact, often, Russia exploits a situation. Undoubtedly, Russia wishes to be seen as an international actor that comports with the norms of international law.[217] It is its interpretation of the law that is questionable. However, 'in many ways, Putin has joined a tradition of great-power interaction with international law: reinterpreting and redefining legal rules to serve present interests'.[218] In particular, Burke-White has expressed concern that Russia's renewed sense of asserting political power could set dangerous precedents by destabilising the 'tenuous balance between the protection of individual rights and the preservation of states' territorial integrity that undergirds the post-Second World War order'.[219]

By setting out a different approach to international law and its fundamental principles Russia is in fact creating practice supported by *opinio juris* that could lead to the formation of a customary norm.[220] After all, as Goldsmith and Posner posit '[i]nternational law emerges from states' pursuit of self-interested policies on the international stage. International law is, in this sense, endogenous to state interests. It is not a check on state self-interest; it is a product of self-interest.'[221] In this regard the Russian 'privileged interests' doctrine needs to be examined more closely. This doctrine dates back to 1968 when Brezhnev stated that Russia would provide military support to 'fraternal countries' dealing with military strife. This doctrine was revived in 2008 by Lavrov explaining that it simply meant that Russia wanted to keep relationships with their old friends[222] and Medvedev announcing that Russia had regions of privileged interests that it would pay particular attention to.[223] The 'privileged interest' doctrine was one of the core five principles of Russia's foreign policy as laid down after the conflict in Georgia.[224] It was then obvious that for-

---

[216] UN Charter, Preamble.

[217] Mastroianni 2016, p. 656.

[218] Burke-White 2014, p. 8.

[219] Ibid., p. 1.

[220] Mastroianni 2016, pp. 601 and 629.

[221] Goldsmith and Posner 2005, p. 13.

[222] Minister of Foreign Affairs of the Russian Federation 2008.

[223] Quoted in Toomey 2009, p. 473.

[224] Russell 2012, p. 112.

mer Soviet Republics, now independent States, slowly became less keen on keeping this 'old friend' relationship and turned more and more towards the West.[225] Russia could not accept this. This relationship was of particular political (in terms of security of Russia), cultural (in terms of ethnic Russians) and to some extent economic importance.

Conferring nationality on ethnic Russians in these States as well as offering a wide understanding of the definition of the concept of nationals as co-citizens opened a door for Russia, that of being able to assert its power and in fact intervene, forcefully or not, in the internal and external affairs of its 'old friends'.[226] It also confirmed Russia's status as an international power to be reckoned with, for protection of nationals abroad is limited to a handful of States that have the military and financial capacity to launch such interventions. Indeed 'the right to intervene is a right in which only strong states may partake.'[227] Russia presents itself as a regional guarantor of security.[228] Yet, 'by marrying the state's sovereign right to confer citizenship with the state's sovereign right to protect its citizens, the former right can be effectively transformed into a tool of State aggression'.[229] It is clear that '[a]lthough identifying Russia's passport policy as unlawful and illegitimate may not prevent it from continuing to carry out such policy, the international community should not allow Russia to aggressively re-establish its sphere of influence under the pretense of legal legitimacy.'[230] The combination of the russification of and passportisation in Russia's neighbouring States endangers regional, if not international, peace and security all the more as Russia has now seemingly established this doctrine, at least for itself, as 'compliant' with international legal principles. In other words, it is highly likely that Russia will continue to use these and similar legal arguments to assert further rights and claims in neighbouring States.[231] Consequently, this interpretation of the law cannot and should not be viewed as in compliance with the legal order created by the United Nations in 1945.

The doctrine of 'privileged interests' is in fact reminiscent of kin-State activism that was prevalent between the two world wars but has seen a revival in the past few decades.[232] A kin-State is defined as 'a generic, political category which can be constructed both in strictly ethnic terms and loosely in terms of linguistic, cultural, and

---

[225] As Russia's Deputy Foreign Minister at the time explained 'Georgia's and Ukraine's membership in [NATO] is a huge strategic mistake which would have most serious consequences for pan-European security'. As cited in Mearsheimer 2014, p. 79; see also Mastroianni 2016, p. 655.

[226] Mastroianni 2016, p. 634.

[227] Fichtelberg 2008, p. 120.

[228] Borgen 2009, p. 19.

[229] Natoli 2010, p. 416.

[230] Ibid., p. 417.

[231] For example, the Baltic States' fears, especially in light of the 2008 intervention in Georgia and the annexation of Crimea, concern a potential Russian campaign against them based on claims that the ethnic Russian communities within their borders are suffering from human rights abuses such as linguistic discrimination. T. Barber, 'Baltic states fear Kremlin focus on ethnic Russians', *Financial Times*, 2 September 2014.

[232] Sabanadze 2006, p. 245.

historical affinities',[233] the latter being the definition most suited to Russia's interpretation of 'Russians'. Kin-States are essentially 'external national homelands'[234] which act as supervisors and monitors of the rights of their nationals. By muddling concepts such as 'compatriots', 'Russian citizens', 'ethnic Russians' etc., Russia has expanded the range of individuals it can declare eligible for Russia's support and protection in its neighbouring States.[235] The problem is in fact not so much the protection of nationals abroad or of minorities abroad but the fact that there is a concomitant revival of nationalism in Russia that stirs up further sentiments of belonging to another group and thus increases domestic demands for protection of those compatriots allegedly mistreated abroad. 'There can be no doubt the public admittance of Russia's role in Crimea was not to confirm the reasoning behind Western sanctions, but rather was for domestic Russian consumption to boost the government's image as decisive and asserting Russian power in gathering lands and peoples imagined to be Russian.'[236] As Putin himself acknowledged, '[t]he most recent public opinion surveys conducted here in Russia show that 95 percent of people think that Russia should protect the interests of Russians and members of other ethnic groups living in Crimea [...]. More than 83 percent think that Russia should do this even if it will complicate our relations with some other countries.'[237]

Such kin-State activism falls within the 'nationalist' type whereby internal political considerations are taken into account. In the case of Russia it is combined with the second type, 'geopolitical', kin-State activism inasmuch as Russia is using it to affirm its political standing and regional influence.[238] From a legal perspective, as the Venice Commission explained, kin-States can adopt unilateral measures to protect their kin-minorities, yet these measures must respect the following principles: '(a) the territorial sovereignty of States; (b) pacta sunt servanda; (c) friendly relations amongst States, and (d) the respect of human rights and fundamental freedoms, in particular the prohibition of discrimination.'[239] From the above, it is clear that Russia has failed to comply with the principle of territorial sovereignty of States and the principle of friendly relations. Returning to the old times of kin-State activism where States felt 'free' to trample on these key principles of what is now UN legal order should be prevented at all costs. If kin-State interference becomes an established international custom it means that the security of neighbouring States with large swathes of 'nationals' is at stake and this will no doubt destroy the carefully crafted post-1945 international legal order.

---

[233] Ibid., p. 244.

[234] Brubaker 1995, p. 110.

[235] Sabanadze 2006, p. 247.

[236] Biersack and O'Lear 2015, p. 255.

[237] Letter dated 19 March 2014 from the Permanent Representative of the Russian Federation to the United Nations Addressed to the Secretary-General, UN Doc A/68/803-S/2014/202, 20 March 2014, p. 10.

[238] For a discussion on the different types of kin-State activism, see Sabanadze 2006, pp. 248–250.

[239] Venice Commission 2001, p. 49.

References

Amendment to the law on state policy towards compatriots living abroad (2010) 24 July 2010. http://en.kremlin.ru/events/president/news/8429. Accessed 28 February 2017

Arend AC, Beck RJ (1993) International law and the use of force. Routledge, Oxon

Arnell P (2012) Law across borders: The extraterritorial application of United Kingdom law. Routledge, Oxon

Bauböck R (2007) Stakeholder citizenship and transnational political participation: A normative evaluation of external voting. Fordham Law Review 75: 2293–2447

Biersack J, O'Lear S (2015) The geopolitics of Russia's annexation of Crimea: Narratives, identity, silences, and energy. Eurasian geography and economics 55(3): 247–269

Bisschop WR (1942) Nationality in international law. Transactions Grotius Soc'y 28: 151–168

Boll AM (2005) Nationality and obligations of loyalty in international and municipal law. Australian Yearbook of International Law 24: 37–63

Borgen C (2009) The language of law and the practice of politics: Great powers and the rhetoric of self-determination in the cases of Kosovo and South Ossetia. Chicago Journal of International Law 10: 1–33

Bowett D (1957) The use of force in the protection of nationals. Transactions of the Grotius Society 43: 111–126

Bowett D (1958) Self-defence in international law. Praeger, New York

Brownlie I (1963) International law and the use of force by States. Oxford University Press, Oxford

Brownlie I (1973) Thoughts on kind-hearted gunmen. In: Lillich R (ed) Humanitarian intervention and the United Nations, University Press of Virginia, Charlottesville, pp 139–148.

Brubaker R (1995) National minorities, nationalizing states and external national homelands in the new Europe. Daedalus 124: 107–132

Brubaker R (1996) Nationalism reframed: Nationhood and the national question in the new Europe. Cambridge University Press, Cambridge

Burke-White WW (2014) Crimea and the international legal order. University of Pennsylvania, Penn Law: Faculty Scholarship, Paper 1360

Butcher CA (2006) Transforming international legal principles into national law: The right to a nationality and the avoidance of statelessness. Refugee Survey Quarterly 25(3): 8–25

Canadian Citizenship Act (1985). http://laws-lois.justice.gc.ca/eng/acts/C-29/index.html. Accessed 1 March 2018

Cavandoli S (2016) The unresolved dilemma of self-determination: Crimea, Donetsk and Luhansk. International Journal of Human Rights 20(7): 875–892

Chepurin A (2009) Approaching the far away: Russian policy toward Russian communities abroad. Russia in Global Affairs 7(3): 68–80

CIA World Factbook (2017) http://www.cia.gov/library/publications/the-world-factbook/geos/up.html. Accessed 17 March 2017

Constitution of the Russian Federation (adopted at national voting on 12 December 1993) (1993). http://www.constitution.ru/en/10003000-01.htm. Accessed 28 February 2017

D'Angelo J (1981) Resort of force by states to protect nationals: The U.S. rescue mission to Iran and its legality under international law. Virginia Journal of International Law 21: 485–519

Danish Institute for International Studies (2005) New threats and the use of force. http://pure.diis.dk/ws/files/27176/new_threats_whole_web.pdf. Accessed 7 May 2017

Die Nürnberger Gesetze (1935) Lebendiges museum online. http://www.dhm.de/lemo/kapitel/ns-regime/ausgrenzung-und-verfolgung/nuernberger-gesetze-1935.html. Accessed 14 February 2017

Doek JE (2006) The CRC and the right to acquire and to preserve a nationality. Refugee Survey Quarterly 25(3): 26–32

Elaraby N (2003) Some reflections on the role of the Security Council and the prohibition of the use of force in international relations: Article 2(4) revisited in light of recent developments. In: Frowein J et al (eds) Verhandeln für den Frieden: liber amicorum Tono Eitel, Springer, Berlin, pp 41–67

Eligibility for Aliyah, The Jewish Agency for Israel, January 2014. http://www.jewishagency.org/first-steps/program/2016. Accessed 6 May 2017

European Union Democracy Observatory on Citizenship (2014) Comparative typology of modes of acquisition and loss of citizenship, July 2014. http://eudo-citizenship.eu/images/docs/EUDO%20CITIZENSHIP%20Modes%20Typology.pdf. Accessed 22 December 2016

European Union Democracy Observatory on Citizenship (2016a) Citizenship or nationality? http://eudo-citizenship.eu/databases/citizenship-glossary/terminology. Accessed 22 December 2016

European Union Democracy Observatory on Citizenship (2016b) The EUDO glossary on citizenship and nationality. http://eudo-citizenship.eu/databases/citizenship-glossary/glossary#Acqity. Accessed 22 December 2016

Federal Law on Russian Federation Citizenship (No. 62-FZ of 31 May 2002) (2002). http://ww.legislationline.org/documents/action/popup/id/4189. Accessed 11 March 2017

Fichtelberg A (2008) Law at the vanishing point. A philosophical analysis of international law. Ashgate, Aldershot

Franck T (2002) Recourse to force: State action against threats and armed attacks. Cambridge University Press, Cambridge

General Assembly (1965) Declaration on the inadmissibility of intervention in the domestic affairs of states and the protection of their independence and sovereignty, UN Doc. A/RES/20/2131

General Assembly (1970) Declaration on principles of international law concerning friendly relations and co-operation among states in accordance with the Charter of the United Nations, UN Doc. A/RES/25/2625

General Assembly (1992) Declaration on the rights of persons belonging to national or ethnic, religious and linguistic minorities, UN Doc. A/RES/47/135

General Assembly (2005) World summit outcome, UN Doc. A/RES/60/1

General Assembly (2014) Territorial integrity of Ukraine, UN Doc. A/RES/68/262

General Assembly (2017) Situation of human rights in the Autonomous Republic of Crimea and the city of Sevastopol (Ukraine), UN Doc. A/RES/71/205

General Assembly/Security Council (2014) Letter dated 19 March 2014 from the permanent representative of the Russian Federation to the United Nations addressed to the Secretary-General, UN Doc. A/68/803-S/2014/202

Global Centre for the Responsibility to Protect (2008) The Georgia-Russia crisis and the responsibility to protect: Background note, New York, 19 August 2008. http://www.globalr2p.org/publications/132. Accessed 6 May 2017

Goldsmith JL, Posner E (2005) The limits of international law. Oxford University Press, Oxford

Grant TD (2015) Annexation of Crimea. American Journal of International Law 109: 68–95

Gray C (2004) International law and the use of force. Oxford University Press, Oxford

Gulati R (2014) The relevance of nationality in the age of Google, Skype and Facebook, In: Jenkins F, Nolan M, Rubenstein K (eds) Allegiance and identity in a globalised world. Cambridge University Press, Cambridge, pp 542–567

Henkin L (1979) How nations behave, 2nd edn. Columbia University Press, New York

Henkin L (1991) The invasion of Panama under international law: A gross violation. Columbia Journal of Transnational Law 29(2): 293–317

Higgins R (1973) The right in international law of an individual to enter, stay and leave a country. International Affairs 49: 341–357

House of Commons Library (2014) Ukraine, Crimea and Russia, Research Paper 14/16. http://researchbriefings.files.parliament.uk/documents/RP14-16/RP14-16.pdf. Accessed 7 May 2017

Human Rights Watch (2009) Up in flames: Humanitarian law violations and civilian victims in the conflict over South Ossetia. https://www.hrw.org/sites/default/files/reports/georgia0109web.pdf. Accessed 7 May 2017

ILC (1976) Report, UN Doc. A/31/10

ILC (2001) Draft articles on responsibility of states for internationally wrongful acts, UN Doc. A/56/10

ILC (2006a) Draft articles on diplomatic protection, UN Doc. A/CN.4/L.684

ILC (2006b) Draft articles on diplomatic protection with commentaries. http://legal.un.org/ilc/texts/instruments/english/commentaries/9_8_2006.pdf. Accessed 11 March 2017

Israel Ministry of Foreign Affairs, Law of return 5710-1950 (as amended). http://www.mfa.gov.il/mfa/mfa-archive/1950-1959/pages/law%20of%20return%205710-1950.aspx. Accessed 31 January 2017

Kesby A (2012) The right to have rights: Citizenship, humanity and international law. Oxford University Press, Oxford

Koessler M (1947) 'Subject,' 'citizen,' 'national,' and 'permanent allegiance'. Yale Law Journal 56: 58–76

Kohn S (2012) Russia and the Baltics: The great statelessness game. European Network on Statelessness, 25 October 2012. http://www.statelessness.eu/blog/russia-and-baltics-great-statelessness-game. Accessed 9 February 2017

Kondrashev A (2015) Crimea. The way home (Documentary) Россия 24, 15 March 2015. https://www.youtube.com/watch?v=t42-71RpRgI. Accessed 28 May 2017

Kozin A (2015) The law of 'compatriot': Toward a new Russian national identity. Russian Journal of Communication 7(3): 286–299

Krūma K (2015) Country report on citizenship law: Latvia, EUDO Citizenship Observatory, January 2015. http://cadmus.eui.eu/bitstream/handle/1814/34481/EUDO_CIT_2015_06-Latvia.pdf?sequence=1. Accessed 9 February 2017

Künzli A (2006) Exercising diplomatic protection. The fine line between litigation, demarches and consular assistance. Zeitschrift für ausländisches und öffentliches Völkerrecht 66: 321–350

Leys D (2016) Diplomatic protection and individual rights: A complementary approach. Harvard International Law Journal Online 57: 1–14. http://www.harvardilj.org/wp-content/uploads/January-2016_Vol-57_Leys1.pdf. Accessed 2 March 2018

Lie J (2004) Modern peoplehood. Harvard University Press, Cambridge MA

Lott A (2012) The Tagliavini report revisited: Jus ad bellum and the legality of the Russian intervention in Georgia. Merkourios 28: 4–21

Lottmann A (2008) No direction home: Nationalism and statelessness in the Baltics. Texas International Law Journal 43: 503–521

Margo RD (1977) The legality of the Entebbe raid in international law. South African Law Journal 94(3): 306–326

Mastroianni M (2016) Russia running rogue? How the legal justifications for Russian intervention in Georgia and Ukraine relate to the U.N. legal order. Seton Hall Law Review 46(2): 599–659

McDougal T (2015) A new imperialism? Evaluating Russia's acquisition of Crimea in the context of national and international law. Brigham Young University Law Review 6:1847–1887

Mearsheimer J (2014) Why the Ukraine crisis is the West's fault. Foreign Affairs 93: 77–90

Menon R, Rumer E (2015) Conflict in Ukraine: The unwinding of the post-cold war order. Massachusetts Institute of Technology Press, Cambridge MA

Minister of Foreign Affairs of the Russian Federation (2008) Transcript of speech of Sergey Lavrov on 24 September 2008, Council on Foreign Relations. http://www.cfr.org/world/sergey-lavrov/p34440. Accessed 17 March 2017

Natoli K (2010) Weaponizing nationality: An analysis of Russia's passport policy in Georgia. Boston University International Law Journal 28(2): 389–417

Oeter S (2014) The role of recognition and non-recognition with regard to secession. In: Walter C, von Ungern-Sternberg A, Abushov K (eds) Self-determination and secession in international law. Oxford University Press, Oxford, pp 45–67

OHCHR (2014) Report on the human rights situation in Ukraine, 15 April 2014. http://www.ohchr.org/Documents/Countries/UA/Ukraine_Report_15April2014.doc. Accessed 7 May 2017

Oppenheim L (1912) International law, a treatise, Vol. 1, 2nd edn. Longmans, Green and Co, London

OSCE High Commissioner on National Minorities (2008) The Bolzano/Bozen recommendations on national minorities in inter-state relations and explanatory note, June 2008. http://www.osce.org/hcnm/33633. Accessed 11 March 2017

OSCE High Commissioner on National Minorities (2012) The Ljubljana guidelines on integration of diverse societies. http://www.osce.org/hcnm/integration-guidelines?download=true. Accessed 7 May 2017

OSCE Parliamentary Assembly (2015) Resolution on the continuation of clear, gross and uncorrected violations of OSCE commitments and international norms by the Russian Federation. Helsinki, 8 July 2015. https://www.oscepa.org/meetings/annual-sessions/2015-annual-session-helsinki/2015-helsinki-final-declaration/2282-07. Accessed 29 May 2017

Parry C, Grant JP, Parry A, Watts AD (eds) (1986) Encyclopaedic dictionary of international law. Oceana Publications, New York

Patsiuko N, Wallace C (2014) Citizenship, Europe and ethnic boundary making among Russian minorities in Latvia and Lithuania. Migration Letters 11: 187–205

Pellet A (1992) Opinions of the Badinter arbitration committee: A second breath for the self-determination of peoples. European Journal of International Law 3: 178–185

Perruchoud R (2012) State sovereignty and freedom of movement. In: Opeskin B, Perruchoud R, Redpath-Cross J (eds) Foundations of international migration law. Cambridge University Press, Cambridge, pp 123–151

Peters A (2016) Beyond human rights: The legal status of the individual in international law. Cambridge University Press, Cambridge

President of Russia (2008a), Joint press conference with Federal Chancellor Angela Merkel, 15 August 2008. http://en.kremlin.ru/events/president/transcripts/1102. Accessed 17 March 2017

President of Russia (2008b) Opening address at the meeting of the State Council on the situation around South Ossetia and Abkhazia, 6 September 2008. http://en.kremlin.ru/events/president/transcripts/statements/1314/print. Accessed 2 March 2018

President of Russia (2014), Address, 18 March 2014. http://en.special.kremlin.ru/events/president/news/20603. Accessed 24 February 2017

Prochaska E (2009) Testing the limits of diplomatic protection: Khadr v the Prime Minister of Canada. EJIL Talk!. https://www.ejiltalk.org/testing-the-limits-of-diplomatic-protection-khadr-v-the-prime-minister-of-canada/. Accessed 7 May 2017

Roudik P (2008) Russian Federation: Legal aspects of war in Georgia, Library of Congress, August 2008. https://www.loc.gov/law/help/russian-georgia-war.php. Accessed 17 March 2017

Roudik P (2013) Latvia: Extension of citizenship to emigrants, Global Legal Monitor, 25 October 2013. http://www.loc.gov/law/foreign-news/article/latvia-extension-of-citizenship-to-emigrants/. Accessed 9 February 2017

Royal Institute of International Affairs (2000) Russian peacekeeping strategies in the CIS: The cases of Moldova, Georgia and Tajikistan. Palgrave Publishers, New York

Russell J (2012) Whose 'near abroad'? Dilemmas in Russia's declared sphere of privileged interests. In: Freire MR, Kanet RE (eds) Russia and its Near Neighbours. Palgrave, Basingstoke, pp 109–128

Ruys T (2008) The 'protection of nationals' abroad doctrine revisited. Journal of Conflict and Security Law 13: 233–271

Sabanadze N (2006) Minorities and kin-states. Helsinki Monitor 17: 244–256

Schrijver NJ (2005) Challenges to the prohibition to use force: Does the straitjacket of Article 2(4) UN Charter begin to gall too much? In: Blokker NM, Schrijver NJ (eds) The Security Council and the use of force. Brill, Leiden, pp 31–45

Shlapak DA, Johnson MW (2016) Reinforcing deterrence on NATO's Eastern flank: Wargaming the defense of the Baltics. RAND Corporation. https://www.rand.org/content/dam/rand/pubs/research_reports/RR1200/RR1253/RAND_RR1253.pdf. Accessed 9 February 2017

Simma B (ed) (2012) The Charter of the United Nations: A commentary. Oxford University Press, Oxford

Sofaer A (1991) The legality of the United States action in Panama. Columbia Journal of Transnational Law 29(2): 281–292

Solomon E, Salako SE (2016) Forcible protection of nationals abroad and humanitarian intervention: Might or right? International Law Research 5(1): 152–167

Spiro P (2014) Russia's citizenship power-play in Ukraine is pretty weak. Opinio Juris, 7 March 2014. http://opiniojuris.org/2014/03/07/russias-citizenship-power-play-ukraine-pretty-weak/. Accessed 17 March 2017

Tomuschat C (1999) International law: Ensuring the survival of mankind on the eve of a new century. Recueil des Cours 281, Brill, Leiden

Toomey M (2009) The August 2008 battle of South Ossetia: Does Russia have a legal argument for intervention? Temple International and Comparative Law Journal 23: 443–477

Trenin D (2009) Russia's spheres of interest, not influence. Washington Quarterly 32: 3–22

Tsybulenko E, Amorosa P (2012) National minorities in Estonia: 20 Years of citizenship policies. L'Europe unie/United Europe, Revue d'études européennes 6: 85–90

UN Human Rights Council (2013) Human rights and arbitrary deprivation of nationality: Report of the Secretary-General, UN Doc. A/HRC/25/28

United Nations Sub-Commission on Prevention of Discrimination and Protection of Minorities (1979) Study on the rights of persons belonging to ethnic, religious and linguistic minorities, UN Doc. E/CN.4/Sub.2/384/Rev.1

Van Panhuys HP (1968) The 'genuine link doctrine' and flags of convenience. American Journal of International Law 62: 942–943

Venice Commission (2001) Report on the preferential treatment of national minorities by their kin-state, Venice, 19–20 October 2001, CDL-INF(2001)019-e. http://www.venice.coe.int/webforms/documents/?pdf=CDL-INF(2001)019-e. Accessed 7 May 2017

Vykhovanets O, Zhuravsky A (2013) Compatriots: Back to the homeland, Russian International Affairs Council, 31 May 2013. http://russiancouncil.ru/en/inner/?id_4=1908#top-content. Accessed 28 February 2017

Walter C (2014) Postscript: Self-determination, secession and the Crimean crisis 2014. In: Walter C, von Ungern-Sternberg A, Abushov K (eds) Self-determination and secession in international law. Oxford University Press, Oxford, pp 293–312

Warsaw Summit Communiqué (2016), issued by the Heads of State and Government participating in the meeting of the North Atlantic Council in Warsaw 8–9 July 2016. http://www.nato.int/cps/en/natohq/official_texts_133169.htm. Accessed 9 February 2017

Weis P (1979) Nationality and statelessness in international law, 2nd edn. Sijthoff and Noordhoff International Publishers B.V., Alphen aan den Rijn

Wellens K (2014) Negotiations in the case law of the International Court of Justice: A functional analysis. Ashgate Publishing Limited, Farnham

Wingfield TC (1999–2000) Forcible protection of nationals abroad. Dickinson Law Review 104: 439–469

Wood MC (2005) Towards new circumstances in which the use of force may be authorized? The cases of humanitarian intervention, counter-terrorism, and weapons of mass destruction. In: Blokker NM, Schrijver NJ (eds) The Security Council and the use of force. Brill, Leiden, pp 75–90

Zinchenko E (2014) Passportisation policy of Russia and new old concerns of the Baltics. Cultural Relations Quarterly Review 16. http://culturalrelations.org/Review/CRQR_01_03/CRQR_01_03_Ekaterina-Zinchenko_Passportisation-policy-of-Russia-and-new-old-concerns-of-the-Baltics.pdf. Accessed 2 March 2018

Chapter 5
International Legal Aspects of Russia's War Against Ukraine in Eastern Ukraine

Oleksandr Merezhko

Contents

Abstract The war in Eastern Ukraine, from the perspective of international law, should be qualified as Russian aggression and Russia's war against Ukraine. This qualification is corroborated by a number of international documents. Russia's aggression against Ukraine should also be legally qualified as both direct and indirect aggression because the former not only mobilized and sent its mercenaries into the territory of Ukraine, but also directly invaded Ukrainian territory using its regular armed forces. Not only should Russia's leaders be accused of committing war crimes and crimes against the peace in Ukraine, but the Russian State and its people should also bear international legal and moral responsibility for this war against Ukraine.

Keywords war · aggression · international legal responsibility · aggression against Ukraine

Oleksandr Merezhko, Dr. Hab., Professor, O.P. Jindal Global University.

O. Merezhko (✉)
O.P. Jindal Global University, Sonipat, India
e-mail: amerezhko@yahoo.com

© T.M.C. ASSER PRESS and the authors 2018
S. Sayapin and E. Tsybulenko (eds.), *The Use of Force against Ukraine and International Law*, https://doi.org/10.1007/978-94-6265-222-4_5

5.1 War in Ukraine: Internal or International Armed Conflict?

In his speech on the occasion of the annexation of Crimea, Russian President Vladimir Putin described Russia as "one of the biggest, if not the biggest, divided nation in the world".[1] In the same speech, Putin also referred to the right to self-determination as justification for Russia's aggression against Ukraine and Crimea's annexation.[2]

Professors of international law Evhen Tsybulenko and Sergey Pakhomenko wrote that "Russian aggression in Ukraine directly threatens European security as it violates the existing principles of international law, destabilizes the system of international relations, sets a precedent for the use of force in the realization of geopolitical interests, opens the possibility of not complying with 'the rules of the game' for individual subjects of international relations. Thus, the possible destructive effects of the Ukrainian crisis are clearly superior to the past conflicts in Europe of the second half of the twentieth century, including the conflicts in the former Yugoslavia".[3]

But how does Russia view what is euphemistically called 'a conflict in Eastern Ukraine?'. According to Russia, it is not an international but an internal conflict within Ukraine: a civil war between the government in Kiev, on the one hand, and local 'rebels' on the other. Russia also categorically denies the presence of its military servicemen in Donbas, despite abundant proof to the contrary.

Let us consider the Russian position on the war in Eastern Ukraine from an international legal perspective. From this angle, Crimea's annexation by Russia and the ongoing war in Eastern Ukraine should be treated not as two separate events, but as one aggressive war waged by Russia against Ukraine. This war has been carefully preplanned by Russia, perhaps since the Orange Revolution in 2004; and, even though it is sometimes referred to as a "hybrid war," in reality, and from the standpoint of international law, it is still an aggressive war in violation of international law.

In this context, the concept of "hybrid war," a war of the 21st century, was clearly articulated in an article by Russian Chief of General Staff Valery Gerasimov, which was published in *Voenno-promyshlennyi kur'er* (*Military-Industrial Courier*).[4] According to General Gerasimov, "in the 21st century [sic], we have seen a tendency toward blurring the lines between the states of war and peace. Wars are no longer declared and, having begun, proceed according to an unfamiliar template. The experience of military conflicts – including those connected with the so-called coloured revolutions in North Africa and the Middle East – confirm that a perfectly thriving state can, in a matter of months and even days, be transformed into an arena of fierce armed conflict, become a victim of foreign intervention, and sink into a web of chaos, humanitarian catastrophe and civil war".[5] In this article, Gerasimov

---

[1] Address by the President of the Russian Federation 2014.

[2] Ibid.

[3] Tsybulenko and Pakhomenko 2016, pp. 167–80.

[4] See Gerasimov 2013; Galeotti 2013.

[5] Ibid.

also refers to the hybrid war by stating that "the focus of applied methods of conflict has altered in the direction of the broad use of political, economic, informational, humanitarian and other non-military measures – applied in coordination with the protest potential of the population. All this is supplemented by military means of a concealed character, including carrying out actions of informational conflict and the actions of special operations forces. The open use of force – often under the guise of peacekeeping and crisis regulation – is resorted to only at a certain stage, primarily for the achievement of final success in the conflict".[6] As a matter of practice, these hybrid wars were used by Russia in Georgia and Ukraine.

In terms of international law, the actions by Russia against Ukraine, starting with the military occupation of Crimea, its subsequent and ongoing annexation can be qualified as (1) an act of aggression (in accordance with the Definition of Aggression of 1974), (2) war (in both a technical and a material sense), (3) an armed attack (in the sense of Article 51 of the UN Charter) and (4) the illegal use of force in international relations (in the sense of Article 2(4) of the UN Charter, Declaration on Principles of International Law of 1970 and the Helsinki Final Act of 1975).

Under the Definition of Aggression adopted by the UN General Assembly (Article 3(g)) Russia's actions in Crimea and in the east of Ukraine can be qualified as "indirect aggression", which presupposes the "sending by or on behalf of a State of armed bands, groups, irregulars or mercenaries, which carry out acts of armed force against another State".[7] The International Court of Justice in *Nicaragua v. United States*, "sees no reason to deny that, in customary law, the prohibition of armed attacks may apply to the sending by the State of armed bands to the territory of another State, if such an operation, because of its scale and effects, would have been classified as an armed attack rather than as a mere frontier incident had it been carried out by regular armed forces".[8] Krzysztof Skubiszewski, a Polish international lawyer, states that "it appears to be beyond doubt that an armed attack has occurred when armed forces of one state, regular, irregular, or armed bands composed of private individuals controlled by, and in fact remaining under the orders of, the state using violence in or against … another state."[9]

Besides, under The Hague Convention (IV), respecting the laws and customs of war, of 18 October 1907, the laws, rights, and duties of war apply to armies, militia and volunteer corps fulfilling, *inter alia*, such conditions as having a fixed distinctive emblem recognizable at a distance and conducting their operations in accordance with the laws and customs of war. From this perspective, Russian troops during Crimea's invasion and invasion into Eastern Ukraine also committed a violation of international humanitarian law.

At the same time, Russia's actions in Crimea and Eastern Ukraine constitute not only "indirect", but also direct aggression and a fully fledged war because Russia's armed forces directly invaded and occupied Crimea, directly invaded the territory of

---

[6] Ibid.

[7] UN General Assembly, Definition of Aggression 1974.

[8] ICJ Reports 1986, p. 103, para 195.

[9] Skubiszewski 1968, p. 777.

Ukraine in the east of the country in summer 2014, and directly subjected Ukrainian territory to shelling from Russian territory. Interestingly enough, in the 2016 Report of the International Criminal Court (ICC) Prosecutor, Crimea's annexation was qualified as an international armed conflict between Ukraine and Russia. According to this report: "the information available suggests that the situation within the territory of Crimea and Sevastopol amounts to an international armed conflict between Ukraine and the Russian Federation. This international armed conflict began at the latest on 26 February when the Russian Federation deployed members of its armed forces to gain control over parts of the Ukrainian territory without the consent of the Ukrainian Government."[10]

The ICC Prosecutor's report also recognized Russia's war against Ukraine, noting that "additional information, such as reported shelling by both States of military positions of the other, and the detention of Russian military personnel by Ukraine, and vice-versa, points to direct military engagement between Russian armed forces and Ukrainian government forces that would suggest the existence of an international armed conflict in the context of armed hostilities in eastern Ukraine from 14 July 2014 at the latest, in parallel to the non-international armed conflict".[11] In Resolution 2067 (2015), the Parliamentary Assembly of the Council of Europe recognized Russian aggression in Ukraine and urged Russia to "release all prisoners illegally captured in Ukrainian territory".[12] It also recognized the presence of Russian troops on Ukrainian soil and called on "the Russian Federation to withdraw its troops from the territory of Ukraine and stop military supplies to the separatists" in Resolution 2132 (2016).[13]

Of particular importance is the report of the Parliamentary Assembly of the Council of Europe, entitled *Legal Remedies to Human Rights Violations on the Ukrainian Territories Outside the Control of the Ukrainian Authorities*, which states that "the annexation of Crimea by the Russian Federation and the military intervention by Russian forces in eastern Ukraine violate international law and the principles upheld by the Council of Europe",[14] thereby not only explicitly recognizing the fact of Russia's military invasion of Ukraine, but also, in effect, acknowledging that its annexation of Crimea and its war in Donbas constitute one war, and one international armed conflict. Furthermore, according to the report, Russia's effective control over the so-called "Donetsk People's Republic" (DPR) and the "Luhansk People's Republic" (LPR), which Russia created to camouflage its military presence in Ukraine, is "based on the well documented crucial role of Russian military personnel in taking over and maintaining control of these regions, against the determined resistance of the legitimate Ukrainian authorities and on the complete dependence of the 'DPR' and 'LPR' on Russia in logistical, financial and administrative terms".[15]

---

[10] International Criminal Court, Office of the Prosecutor 2016.

[11] Ibid.

[12] See Parliamentary Assembly 2015.

[13] See Parliamentary Assembly 2016

[14] See Committee on Legal Affairs and Human Rights 2016.

[15] Ibid.

The UN Human Rights Committee, in its Concluding Observations on the Seventh Periodic Report of the Russian Federation, recognized that Russia exercises effective control over part of Donbas and thus occupies part of Ukrainian territory when it stated that: "the Committee is concerned about reports alleging serious violations of the Covenant in the Donbas region of Ukraine by forces over which the State party appears to have considerable influence, which may amount to effective control. It is also concerned about reports that allegations of serious violations of the Covenant committed during the armed conflict in the South Ossetia region of Georgia in 2008 were not fully investigated (art. 2)... The Committee, in line with the interpretation of Article 2(1) of the Covenant in its general comment No. 31 (2004) on the nature of the general legal obligation imposed on States parties to the Covenant, calls on the State party to ensure the application of the Covenant in respect of acts perpetrated by armed groups and proclaimed authorities of the self-proclaimed 'Donetsk people's republic,' 'Luhansk people's republic,' and 'South Ossetia,' to the extent that it already exercises influence over these groups and authorities which amounts to effective control over their activities."[16]

In the Organization for Security and Cooperation in Europe (OSCE) Parliamentary Assembly's Resolution on the Continuation of Clear, Gross and Uncorrected Violations of OSCE Commitments and International Norms by the Russian Federation, the Assembly unequivocally condemned Russia's aggression against Ukraine, not only in Crimea, but also in Donbas, by stating that it considered that "the actions by the Russian Federation in the Autonomous Republic of Crimea and the city of Sevastopol, as well as in certain areas of the Donetsk and Luhansk regions of Ukraine, constitute acts of military aggression against Ukraine".[17] In the same resolution, the OSCE Parliamentary Assembly recognized the presence of Russian regular armed forces in the territory of Ukraine, calling upon "the Russian Federation to stop the supply and flow of heavy weaponry, ammunition, units of the Russian Armed Forces and mercenaries across the Russian border into eastern Ukraine".[18] Some international non-governmental organizations have also recognized Russia's war against Ukraine as an international armed conflict. For example, Amnesty International considers the war to be "an international armed conflict" and presented independent satellite photo analyses to confirm the involvement of the regular Russian Army in the conflict.[19]

Strangely enough, despite these international documents and obvious facts confirming Russia's aggression against Ukraine in Donbas, some Western institutions have promoted Russia's propaganda lies by referring to "the conflict in Ukraine" as an internal, not an international, armed conflict. A case in point is the Heidelberg Institute for International Conflict Research, which, in its *Conflict Report* (2016), falsely claims that, "[as] in the previous year, the only highly violent conflict in Europe took place in Ukraine, where the war in the Donbas region between the

---

[16] See Human Rights Committee 2015.
[17] See OSCE Parliamentary Assembly 2017.
[18] Ibid.
[19] See Amnesty International 2014.

Donetsk People's Republic and the Luhansk People's Republic, on the one hand, and the Ukrainian government as well as Ukrainian nationalist volunteer battalions, on the other, continued in its third consecutive year".[20] This statement stands in stark contrast to the documents issued by international organizations, which recognize the presence of Russian troops on Ukrainian territory and direct Russian aggression in Donbas. The Heidelberg Institute has released further misinformation about "Ukrainian nationalist volunteer battalions", because the volunteer battalions were integrated into the forces of the Ukrainian Ministry of Internal Affairs and there are no volunteer battalions in the zone of "the antiterrorist operation".[21] With regard to Russia's war against Ukraine in Donbas, Lithuanian Minister for Foreign Affairs *Linas Linkevičius* correctly states that: "This is not a conflict in Ukraine (sometimes we hear such a term). But I always try to correct [this conclusion]: this is an external aggression; this is not an internal conflict, not a civil war."[22]

5.2 The Issue of Russia's International Legal Responsibility for War Crimes Committed in Eastern Ukraine

What is the purpose of Russia's war against Ukraine?

The answer to this question can be found in an interview with Russian citizen Aleksandr Borodai, self-proclaimed prime minister of the DPR. In this interview with the Russian newspaper *Zavtra* (*Tomorrow*), Borodai openly acknowledged that Russia's goal in its war against Ukraine was to re-establish the Russian Empire.[23] In his view, Ukraine does not deserve to be an independent state for it is only a part of the authoritarian Russian Empire.[24] Putin himself considers Ukraine to belong to Russia and has talked about "Novorossiya", which, in his view, includes southern regions of Ukraine.[25]

In this author's opinion, the Russian state, by waging an aggressive war against Ukraine, committed acts falling within the scope of the "state terrorism" definition contained in the Geneva Declaration on State Terrorism of 1987.[26] According to this declaration, state terrorism, in particular, manifests itself in: military exercise manoeuvres or war games conducted by one state in the vicinity of another state for the purpose of threatening the political independence or territorial integrity of that other state; the armed attack by the military forces of a state on targets that put at risk the civilian population residing in another state; the creation and support of armed mercenary forces by a state for the purpose of subverting the sovereignty of

---

[20] See Conflict Barometer 2016.

[21] See Ukrinform 2015.

[22] See Linkiavichus 2017.

[23] See Fefelov 2014.

[24] Ibid.

[25] See Palmer 2009.

[26] UN General Assembly 1987.

another state; covert operations by "intelligence" or other forces of a state, which are intended to destabilize or subvert another state, national liberation movements, or the international peace movement; and disinformation campaigns by a state, whether intended to destabilize another state or to build up public support for economic, political or military force or intimidation directed against another state. All these manifestations of state terrorism are present in the case of Russia's war against Ukraine.

The issue could arise concerning Russia's international legal responsibility for the mass killings of Ukrainians in the East of Ukraine. Russia's occupying forces in Eastern Ukraine consist of the following elements: (1) Russian regular military forces heavily armed by Russia (despite not always wearing military insignia, so as to obscure the fact they belong to the Russian Army); (2) bands of terrorists controlled, financed, trained and equipped by Russia (Russian citizens, including leaders of the self-proclaimed DPR and LPR); and (3) mercenaries and collaborators from among the local population.[27]

There are numerous factual and legal pieces of evidence corroborating the Russian Army's presence in Eastern Ukraine. Among this evidence is a confession by Aleksandr Zakharchenko, one of the terrorist leaders, according to whom 3,000 Russian military servicemen fought in Donbas, a resolution of the Council of Europe calling upon Russia to withdraw its troops from Ukraine, and numerous testimonies of Western journalists. These armed forces are controlled and equipped by Russia. For this reason, they should be treated as *de facto* organs of Russia, and it is the Russian state that bears international legal responsibility for their actions and crimes. As Israeli author Yoram Dinstein put it, "When terrorists are sponsored by Arcadia against Utopia, they may be deemed 'de facto organs' of Arcadia".[28]

It is noteworthy that the Western mass media is sometimes misled by Russian propaganda in this respect, especially when it uses terms such as "pro-Russian separatists" or "rebels" in Eastern Ukraine, instead of using legally correct designations such as "Russian troops" or "Russian military servicemen". Additionally, crimes committed by the DPR and LPR terrorist organizations should be attributed to Russia because, under Article 8 of the Articles on the Responsibility of States for Internationally Wrongful Acts, drafted by the International Law Commission, "The conduct of a person or group of persons shall be considered an act of a State under international law if the person or group of persons is in fact acting on the instructions of, or under the direction or control of, that State in carrying out the conduct".

These international crimes committed by Russia lead to the issue of how, and in what form, Russia and its leaders should bear responsibility for their crimes. Russian leaders, beginning with current Russian President Vladimir Putin, should be brought to criminal justice, either before the ICC or before a specially created international *ad hoc* tribunal. Russia itself, as a state, should also be brought to international

---

[27] Historically and legally, the presence of collaborators among the local population has never turned the external invasion or aggression into an internal conflict. It has always been common practice for foreign invaders to use certain representatives of the local population in their aggression.

[28] Dinstein 2003, p. 182.

justice. Even though the concept of the criminal responsibility of states for serious international crimes is still a controversial issue in international legal doctrine,[29] the case of Russia's heinous crimes clearly indicates that, without this form of legal responsibility, it is impossible to prevent Russia from committing such crimes again.

5.3 Subjects of International Legal Responsibility for Crimes Committed by Russia Against Ukraine

One of the key legal questions that must be answered, in order to restore peace and international legal order in Europe, concerns the subjects of international legal responsibility for international crimes committed by Russia against Ukraine.

The following subjects of legal responsibility are:

(1) Individuals responsible for crimes against the peace (i.e., for planning, starting and waging war against Ukraine), crimes against humanity (the terrorist act against Malaysia Airlines flight MH17, which was shot down by Russian troops), and war crimes (numerous crimes committed against civilians in Ukraine by the Russian Army). These individuals are well known, starting with Putin (the Russian Army's Commander-in-chief), the Minister of Defence etc, and should be subject to legal responsibility. Additionally, Russia's propagandists actively involved in a campaign of hatred and lies against the Ukrainian people on Russian TV (including the infamous Russia Today channel) and other Russian mass media should be brought to international justice.

(2) Russia's organizations and state structures responsible for war crimes and atrocities committed against Ukraine and its people should be held accountable, including, but not limited to: the Russian political police (the FSB), which tortured Ukrainian political prisoners; the General Staff and High Command of the Russian Army, which planned and conducted an aggressive war against Ukraine; Russia's Ministry of Foreign Affairs, which provided propagandistic support for war against Ukraine; and Russia's Foreign Intelligence Service (the SVR) and Military Intelligence Service (the GRU), which conducted subversive operations against Ukraine.

(3) Russia, as a state, should be answerable. In the doctrine of international law, there is the concept of criminal responsibility of a state for aggression and other international crimes. In the Western doctrine of international law, the proponents of this concept have been authors such as Pelta, Donnedieu and de Vabres.[30] In Polish doctrine, there has been the book *Criminal Nation* by Emil Stanislaw Rappaport (*Naród-zbrodniarz, Łódź,* 1945). In other words, Russia as a state should bear full international criminal responsibility for its heinous crimes against Ukraine. The future international tribunal on Russia's crimes

---

[29] See Rappaport 1946.
[30] Bierzanek 1982, p. 110.

should not only be a criminal tribunal prosecuting Putin and his regime, but also a tribunal prosecuting Russia as a criminal state.

(4) The Russian people should also be held liable for the crimes of Putin's regime, because 86% of Russian population support Putin and more than 90% support Crimea's annexation, i.e., support Putin regime's crimes against Ukraine. Interestingly enough, some Russian international lawyers have been in favour of the concept of the people's international legal responsibility. For example, Fiodor Kozhevnikov stated in his textbook, *International Law* (1982), that, "Any people bears responsibility for the actions of its government in international relations".[31] Nikolai Ushakov, a member of the UN International Law Commission from the Soviet era, considered peoples along with states to be subjects of international law.[32]

Russian scholars Givi V. Sharmazanashvili and Anatoliy K. Tsikunov, in their book *The Right of the Peoples and Nations to Freedom and Independence*, wrote that: "Dictatorial, fascist, aggressive-imperialistic regimes constitute by themselves a potential threat to the whole of mankind. It is especially dangerous, when such regimes possess contemporary kinds of weapons of mass destruction. For this reason, in the contemporary world, the people of each state are obliged not to put their will against the will of other people; their political status should not be based upon militarism. The duty of each people is to strictly secure that its government strictly acts in the spirit of the fundamental principles of the UN Charter and the Helsinki Final Act in its international relations, and would not put into jeopardy peace and security of the other peoples."[33]

From the perspective of Russia's constitutional law, the Russian people are "the bearer of sovereignty and the only source of power in the Russian Federation" (Article 3(1) of the Constitution of the Russian Federation); hence, Russian people are also responsible for all the international crimes committed by the Russian state. The results of Russia's crimes (its state and its people) against Ukraine (its state and its people) are well documented: thousands of Ukrainian citizens (many of them civilians, including women and children) have been brutally killed by the Russian occupying army in Donbas, while around two million Ukrainian citizens have been forced by Russia's war against Ukraine to leave their homes and became displaced persons. Furthermore, many factories in the east of Ukraine have been deliberately destroyed or stolen by Russia, and Russian occupation authorities have unleashed a campaign of terror and repression against Crimean Tatars and Ukrainians in occupied Crimea. Economic losses suffered by Ukraine as a result of Russia's war are estimated to be in the dozens of billions of US dollars.

In his book, *National Responsibility and Global Justice*, David Miller writes that: "My argument [is] that national identity entails national responsibility. By virtue of identifying with compatriots, sharing their values, and receiving the benefits that national communities provide, we are also involved in collective responsibility for

---

[31] See Sharmazanashvili and Tsikunov 1987, p. 45.

[32] Ushakov 1983, pp. 7–8.

[33] Sharmazanashvili and Tsikunov 1987, p. 45.

the things that nations do. This extends to include things that our ancestors have done – national responsibility includes responsibility for the national past."[34] In other words, not only Russia's leaders, who are accused of committing war crimes and crimes against the peace in Ukraine, but also the Russian state and its people should bear international legal and moral responsibility for their country's war against Ukraine.

Russia's ambassador to the UN, Leonid Skotnikov, once said, "I'd like to stress that international law is more than simply a tool; it is part of very powerful process that has real ramifications. We might not pay for today's violations of international law, but our children will".[35] Of course, future generations of Russians will have to pay, in full, for the current crimes now being committed by Russia against Ukraine, but the international community should do everything in its power to stop Russia's aggressive war against Ukraine and bring all those war criminals to full justice, starting with Russia's President, Vladimir Putin, and its government, who continue to commit heinous crimes against the Ukrainian people with impunity.

References

Address by President of Russian Federation (2014) http://en.kremlin.ru/events/president/news/20603. Accessed 7 March 2017

Amnesty International (2014). Ukraine: Mounting evidence of war crimes and Russian involvement. https://www.amnesty.org/en/latest/news/2014/09/ukraine-mounting-evidence-war-crimes-and-russian-involvement/. Accessed 7 March 2017

Bierzanek R (1982) Wojna a prawo miedzynarodowe. Wydawnictwo Ministerstwa Obrony Narodowej, Warsaw

Committee on Legal Affairs and Human Rights (2016) Legal remedies to human rights violations on the Ukrainian territories outside the control of the Ukrainian authorities. http://website-pace.net/documents/19838/2192213/20160906-RemediesViolationsUkraine-EN.pdf/3e52694a-26f8-4f7e-8eb6-cfa220ea32f6. Accessed 7 March 2017

Conflict Barometer (2016) https://www.hiik.de/en/konfliktbarometer/pdf/ConflictBarometer_2016.pdf. Accessed 7 March 2017

Dinstein Y (2003) War, Aggression and Self-Defence, 3rd edn. Cambridge University Press, Cambridge

Fefelov A (2014) Kazhdyj neset svoi krest http://zavtra.ru/content/view/kazhdyij-nesyot-svoj-krest/. Accessed 7 March 2017

Galeotti M (2013) The 'Gerasimov Doctrine' and Russian Non-Linear War http://inmoscowsshadows.wordpress.com/2014/07/06/the-gerasimov-doctrine-and-russian-non-linear-war/. Accessed 7 March 2017

Gerasimov V (2013) Tsennot' nauki v predvidenii. http://vpk-news.ru/sites/default/files/pdf/VPK_08_476.pdf. Accessed 7 March 2017

Human Rights Committee. Concluding observations on the seventh periodic report of the Russian Federation (2015) http://docstore.ohchr.org/SelfServices/FilesHandler.ashx?enc=6QkG1d%2FPPRiCAqhKb7yhstWB5OJfDOQhMEkiX20XNhIfwS44vVjDCG9yOfCaGgJ%2B4aMVruPFpyUaMYJvfEOEBQCPHWJdUArBGlBJo5DzI4ZqOZa12FMGUZJqFSjwcIYP. Accessed 7 March 2017

---

[34] Miller 2007, p. 265.

[35] See Scharf and Williams 2010, p. 179.

ICJ Reports (1986) http://www.icj-cij.org/docket/files/70/6503.pdf. p. 103, para. 195. Accessed 7 March 2017
International Criminal Court. The Office of the Prosecutor (2016). Report on Preliminary Examination Activities 2016. https://www.icc-cpi.int/iccdocs/otp/161114-otp-rep-PE_ENG.pdf. Accessed 7 March 2017
Linkiavichus L (2017) «Na shodi Ukrainy ja stav svidkom porushen' Mins'kuh ugod» [In the east of Ukraine, I became a witness to violations of the Minsk arrangements] http://ukrainian.voanews.com/a/linas-ukraine/3743775.html. Accessed 7 March 2017
Miller D (2007) National Responsibility and Global Justice. Oxford University Press, Oxford
OSCE Parliamentary Assembly (2017). Resolution on the Continuation of Clear, Gross and Uncorrected Violations of OSCE Commitments and International Norms by the Russian Federation. https://www.oscepa.org/meetings/annual-sessions/2015-annual-session-helsinki/2015-helsinki-final-declaration/2282-07. Accessed 7 March 2017
Palmer R (2009) Putin Confirms: Ukraine is Russia's https://www.thetrumpet.com/article/6218.2.0.0/europe/eastern-europe/putin-confirms-ukraine-is-russias. Accessed 7 March 2017
Parliamentary Assembly (2015) Resolution 2067. Missing Persons during the Conflict in Ukraine http://assembly.coe.int/nw/xml/XRef/Xref-XML2HTML-en.asp?fileid=21970&lang=en. Accessed 7 March 2017
Parliamentary Assembly (2016) Resolution 2132. Political Consequences of the Russian Aggression in Ukraine. http://assembly.coe.int/nw/xml/XRef/Xref-XML2HTML-en.asp?fileid=23166&lang=en. Accessed 7 March 2017
Rappaport E (1946) Naród-Zbrodniarz : przestępstwa hitleryzmu a naród niemiecki : szkic analityczny przestępczości i odpowiedzialności osobowo-zespołowej. Spółdzielnia Dziennikarska "Prasa, Lodz
Scharf M, Williams P (2010) Shaping Foreign Policy in Times of Crisis. The Role of International Law and the State Department Legal Adviser. Cambridge University Press, Cambridge
Sharmazanashvili Givi V, Tsikunov Anatolij K (1987) Pravo narodov i natsiy na svobodu i nezavisimost'. Kritika burzhuaznykh kontseptsiy. Izdatel'stvo Universiteta Druzhby Narodov, Moscow
Skubiszewski K (1968) Use of Force by States. Collective Security. Laws of War and Neutrality. In: Sorensen M (ed) Manual of Public International Law. Macmillan, London
Tsybulenko E, Pakhomenko S (2016) The Ukrainian Crisis as a Challenge for the Eastern Partnership. In: Tanel Kerikmäe T, Chochia A (eds) Political and Legal Perspectives of the EU Eastern Partnership Policy. Springer, Berlin
United Nations General Assembly. Definition of Aggression (1974), A/RES/29/3314 http://www.un-documents.net/a29r3314.htm. Accessed 7 March 2017
Ukrinform (2015). U zoni ATO nemaje dobrovol'chykh batalioniv – Natsgvardija. http://tyzhden.ua/News/134072. Accessed 7 March 2017
UN General Assembly (1987). The Geneva Declaration on Terrorism (http://i-p-o.org/GDT.HTM). Accessed 7 March 2017
Ushakov N (1983) Osnovanija mezhdunarodnoj otvetstvennosti gosudarstv. Mezhdunarodnye otnoshenija. Moscow

Chapter 6
Separatists or Russian Troops and Local Collaborators? Russian Aggression in Ukraine: The Problem of Definitions

Evhen Tsybulenko and J'moul A. Francis

Contents

Abstract This chapter analyses how incorrect definitions accredited to individuals behind the Russian aggression in Ukraine can lead to falsifications at the international level. Such incorrect definitions include the mistaken classification of the conflict as a non-international armed conflict and the inaccurate characterizations of individuals fighting in Donbas as 'rebels' and 'separatists'. As a result, this definitional problem has led to a distorted view of the conflict in Donbas. Hence, this chapter firstly argues that the conflict is an international armed conflict under international law and that the notion of the existence of both international and non-international armed conflicts ought to be debunked. Secondly, this chapter examines the nature and role of individuals fighting in Donbas, evidencing their manner of participation and true characterization. Attention is also given to the relationship between Russian troops and local collaborators whose cohesive effort sustains Russian aggression in Donbas. Thirdly, this chapter assesses the root of the definitional problem stemming from the incorrectly ascribed classifications being disseminated throughout the world, which

Evhen Tsybulenko, Department of Law, School of Business and Governance, Tallinn University of Technology, Tallinn, Estonia, email: evhen.tsybulenko@ttu.ee.
J'moul A. Francis, Department of Law, School of Business and Governance, Tallinn University of Technology, Tallinn, Estonia, email: jmoulfrancis@icloud.com.

E. Tsybulenko (✉) · J. A. Francis
Department of Law, School of Business and Governance,
Tallinn University of Technology, Tallinn, Estonia
e-mail: evhen.tsybulenko@ttu.ee

J. A. Francis
e-mail: jmoulfrancis@icloud.com

© T.M.C. ASSER PRESS and the authors 2018   123
S. Sayapin and E. Tsybulenko (eds.), *The Use of Force against Ukraine and International Law*, https://doi.org/10.1007/978-94-6265-222-4_6

form part of the distorted language around the conflict. Furthermore, consideration is given to the issues regarding how distortions are 'creeping' into reports and other publications, which form part of the pool of information used at public, legal, and diplomatic levels. Fourthly, this chapter analyses the consequential issues concerning the normative backlash, the attribution of responsibility, and the manner of response to the conflict from the international community. The analysis then focuses on the argument that the use of distorted information could be used to influence future decisions, inevitably resulting in futile solutions. Finally, this chapter concludes by discussing the propagation of incorrect definitions, which has an undermining effect on the principles and doctrines of international law. Moreover, emphasis is given to the importance of the responsibility of definitional accuracy during times of perilous conflict.

Keywords Ukraine · Donbas · Russian aggression · international armed conflict · definitions · accuracy · public international law · international humanitarian law · reporting

6.1   Background

The conflict in Ukraine presents a unique challenge, in that there is a general lack of understanding about the players on the ground and the conflict itself. The situation entails Russian aggression in two zones: Crimea and the Donetsky Bassein (Donbas), located in Eastern Ukraine. A corollary of the aggression is the occupation and unlawful annexation of Crimea[1] and the unlawful occupation,[2,3] or at least effective control, of Donbas.[4] Much is known, to a degree, about the unlawful annexation of Crimea that took place on 20 March 2014; however, little is known about the continuous unlawful activities taking place in Donbas. Despite the fact that varying specific international resolutions and statements defined constitutive elements of the conflict within their right contexts, such as naming the situation as Russian aggression[5] and identifying the presence of Russian regular troops,[6] there are varying alternative and misleading terms utilized to tell the story of the conflict. On the one hand, some label

---

[1] UN General Assembly 2016. See also, *inter plurima alia*, UN General Assembly 2014; Parliamentary Assembly of the Council of Europe 2016a, b; OSCE Permanent Council of the European Union 2016.

[2] Permanent Mission of Ukraine to the UN 2017.

[3] Parliamentary Assembly of the Council of Europe 2018.

[4] Parliamentary Assembly of the Council of Europe 2016b.

[5] OSCE Permanent Council of the European Union 2016.

[6] Parliamentary Assembly of the Council of Europe 2016b; see also OSCE Parliamentary Assembly 2015.

the collaborators and even Russian troops as "rebels"[7] and "separatists";[8] hence why some view the situation in Donbas as a "civil war",[9] "separatist action"[10] or a "hybrid war".[11] Conversely, others label the collaborators as "Russian-backed forces"[12] or "Kremlin-backed militants",[13] among other similar terms; hence, why others view the situation as much more than an internal conflict. In other words, in the case of the former characterizations, the conflict would be viewed as a non-international armed conflict (NIAC). In the case of the latter, however, the conflict would be viewed as an international armed conflict (IAC). With the intermingling of Russian regular forces and local fighters, the lines between the conflicting labels are blurred and may create a degree of definitional doubt. As such, this clash of labels could affect how international law is accurately viewed and applied. This diametrical tension of definitions is reflected in a 2016 preliminary examination report published by the International Criminal Court (ICC).[14] If the tensions are not resolved, there could be undesirable results in relation to attribution, liability and responsibility under international law. Hence, it is important for the parties to the conflict to be properly defined in the eyes of the public and the international community. Moreover, there is a duty not to introduce and incorporate alternative definitions of critical terms into the language around any international conflict. The primary objective of this duty is to combat and repel the spread of distorted information, unfounded claims, baseless evidence and mistaken policy positions, which could arise during times of conflict. Therefore, the problem of definitions around the conflict in Donbas ought to be resolved before it is too late to correct the distorted information.

6.2 Defining the Separatists, Russian Troops and Local Collaborators

The collaborators rose to power through the seizure of Ukrainian government buildings in Donbas.[15] In fact, Russian special troops captured some buildings, which

---

[7] Voice of America 2017, 'Russia to supply power to rebel-held parts of Eastern Ukraine'. https://www.voanews.com/a/russia-to-supply-electricity-to-rebel-held-areas-in-eastern-ukraine/3824981.html. Accessed 2 April 2017. See also, *inter plurima alia*, Corder 2017; BBC News 2016, 'Ukraine crisis: new ceasefire "holding with eastern rebels"'. http://www.bbc.com/news/world-europe-37243434. Accessed 2 April 2017.

[8] Goodenough 2017. See also, *inter plurima alia*, Reuters 2017; Channel News Asia 2017; Jurist 2017.

[9] Howard 2014. See also, *inter plurima alia*, Damien 2016.

[10] Chifu and Tutuianu 2016, p. 28.

[11] Toler and Haring 2017.

[12] Grytesenko 2017. See also Chicago Tribune 2017.

[13] Coyness 2017.

[14] ICC-OTP 2016.

[15] Balaban et al. 2017, p. 33.

enabled them to gain 'effective control' over the local government administration.[16] These buildings are located in the major cities in Donbas including, most importantly, Donetsk and Luhansk oblasts.[17] Due to their *de facto* control in those oblasts, the collaborators decided to declare those areas independent from the rest of Ukraine via the infamous 'referendum' process.[18] As a result, the Donetsk and Luhansk oblasts were self-declared as the "Donetsk People's Republic" ("DPR") and the "Luhansk People's Republic" ("LPR"), respectively.[19] The first prime minister of the "DPR" was Alexander Borodai, a Russian citizen with close connections to the Russian intelligence services.[20] However, the Ukrainian Alexander Zakharchenko is currently leading the "DPR",[21] while the "LPR" is currently led by another Ukrainian, Igor Plotnitsky.[22] Furthermore, these 'leaders' and their associates have admitted that thousands of Russian citizens and soldiers are supporting the fulfilment of their agenda.[23]

The vehicles, machinery and weaponry utilized by Russian troops and collaborators in the "DPR" and "LPR" include infantry mobility vehicles, BTR and BMP armoured personnel carriers, battle tanks, self-propelled and towed howitzers and guns, armoured trucks, multiple launch rocket systems, battlefield surveillance radars, surface-to-air missile systems, and air reconnaissance drones.[24] Moreover, some of the weapons employed were produced in the Russian Federation after the collapse of the Soviet Union, which were never supplied to Ukraine. Furthermore, the weapons could not be seized from the Ukrainian forces, as the local collaborators claim, because those weapons were never part and parcel of the Ukrainian Army. Specifically, such weapons, *inter alia*, include: T-72BA, T-72B3 and T-90A main battle tanks; a BTR-82A armoured personnel carrier; GAZ-233014 Tigr, GAZ-39371 Vodnik and KAMAZ-43269 Vystrel infantry mobility vehicles; a Mustang KamAZ-5350 armoured truck; a 2B26 Grad-K multiple launch rocket system; 1RL232-2M Leopard battlefield surveillance radar; 9K332 Tor M-2 tactical surface-to-air missile systems; a 96K6 Pantsir-S1 surface-to-air missile and gun system; RB-341V Leer-3 and Rtut-BM electronic warfare (EW) systems; and Granat-1, Granat-2, Forpost, Orlan-10, Eleron-3SV and Zastava unmanned aerial vehicles (UAVs).[25] As such, the specified weaponry used in Donbas confirm the support given by the Russian

---

[16] Bukkvoll 2016, p. 18. See also Asymmetric Warfare Group 2016.

[17] Ibid.

[18] BBC News 2014, 'Ukraine rebels hold referendums in Donetsk and Luhansk'. http://www.bbc.com/news/world-europe-27360146. Accessed 22 April 2017.

[19] Ibid.

[20] Miller 2014.

[21] Ibid.

[22] BBC News 2016, 'Ukraine crisis: blast injures Luhansk rebel leader Plotnitsky. http://www.bbc.com/news/world-europe-37000601. Accessed 7 June 2017.

[23] BBC News 2014, 'Ukraine crisis: key players in eastern unrest. http://www.bbc.com/news/world-latin-america-27211501. Accessed 23 April 2017.

[24] Balaban et al. 2017, *supra* fn. 16, pp. 73–81.

[25] Ibid., See also the Office of the United Nations High Commissioner for Human Rights (OHCHR) 2016.

Federation to the militant agenda of those leading the charge in the "DPR" and "LPR".

Behind the Russian-made and -supplied military equipment is an organized military command, which supports Russian military personnel in waging war against the Ukrainian military. Such was the case when the Russian 58th Army Command posted military personnel from Russia's 136th Motorized Rifle Brigade to fight against the Ukrainian Army in Donbas.[26] One such fight against this army took place in 2014, during the Battle of Ilovaisk, in an attempt to gain control of the city of Ilovaisk and divide the "rebels" in Donbas.[27] This battle saw a number of Ukrainian military personnel killed as a result of Russian military personnel opening fire on a previously agreed "live corridor" for treating Ukrainian soldiers.[28] Another battle near Debaltseve in 2015 saw not only the loss of life of a number of Ukrainian troops, but also the flagrant breach of the Minsk II Agreement.[29] As with the Battle of Ilovaisk, it was also reported that regular Russian troops were actively engaged in the Battle of Debaltseve, fighting alongside local collaborators. Furthermore, according to the commander of a separatist "special forces" detachment, "Russian tanks and soldiers have been "decisive" in winning key battles against government troops in eastern Ukraine".[30] These are two from among a plethora of examples, which give credence to the fact that Ukraine is facing an enemy with highly trained personnel and vast military resources. Hence, it would be a mistake to merely limit Russian aggression in Donbas to participation through the supply of weaponry and agents, i.e., a proxy war. Furthermore, regular paratroopers from Russia were captured and later exchanged, with Russia claiming that the paratroopers entered Ukraine by "accident".[31] However, this claim of crossing the border by "accident" contradicts reports of the mobilization of 1,200 military personnel and 150 pieces of military equipment from Russia. "On March 2, 2015, U.S. Army Europe Commander Ben Hodges estimated that 12,000 Russian soldiers, including 'military advisers, weapons operators and combat troops,' are active in eastern Ukraine."[32] What is also apparent in the wider context is that the actions of the Russian military are not only concentrated in Donbas, but also on the Russian side of the Ukrainian border near Donbas. This

---

[26] Inform Napalm 2017. 'Signal troops of Russian Army's 136th Brigade in Donbas: lists, documents, orders (photos). https://informnapalm.org/en/signal-troops-russian-army-s-136th-brigade-donbas-lists-documents-orders-photos/. Accessed 23 April 2017.

[27] Kim 2014. See also, *inter plurima alia*, BBC News 2014, 'Ukraine conflict: fierce battle for town of Ilovaisk. http://www.bbc.com/news/world-europe-28866283. Accessed 23 April 2017. See also UNAIN Information Agency 2016, 'Kyiv honoring soldiers killed in 2014 Ilovaisk battle. https://www.unian.info/kiev/1490359-kyiv-honoring-soldiers-killed-in-2014-ilovaisk-battle.html. Accessed 23 April 2017.

[28] Ibid.

[29] BBC News 2015, 'Ukraine crisis: fierce fighting after Minsk. http://www.bbc.com/news/world-europe-31449981. Accessed 23 April 2017.

[30] Parfitt 2015. See also Harress 2015.

[31] BBC News 2014, 'Ukraine and Russia exchange captured troops'. http://www.bbc.com/news/world-europe-29002147. Accessed 7 June 2017.

[32] Luhn 2015a, b. See also, Czuperski et al. 2015a, b.

is evident through the movement of Russian military personnel and weaponry into Donbas to fight against Ukrainian resistance. The placement of Russian military personnel in this manner also highlights a military agenda, which seeks the sustainability of hostilities. As such, the identification of Russian military apparatus and personnel further proves that labelling the participants of the conflict as "rebels" and "separatists" is irreconcilable with the reality of the conflict. It is to be noted at this point that the full list of regular Russian troops taking part in active hostilities in Donbas can be retrieved from the Inform Napalm database.[33]

The sustainability objective is not only limited to the supply of personnel and equipment; it also includes the use of local personnel who are used for strategic military advantages in order to harness their local knowledge. Thus, this cooperation presents another dimension of the Russian aggression whereby Russian troops, with the assistance of local collaborators, wage war against the Ukrainian state on Ukrainian soil. The collaboration between local Russian sympathizers and Russian troopers could be viewed as a 'proxy war'; however, both state actors – the Russian and Ukrainian military – are directly fighting each other. Thus, the conflict cannot be labelled, classified or defined as a 'proxy war'. However, there are non-state actors playing a significant secondary role in the conflict. As mentioned, alongside the military personnel are Russian voluntary fighters. Indeed, it is reported that over 10,000 individuals were enlisted to fight in Donbas through the "Union of Donbas Volunteers" organization.[34] Thus, the policy employed by the Russian Federation is one that also guarantees the destabilization of Donbas through the supply of sustained levels of personnel through collaborating recruitment agencies. A further policy implication is the expansion of the Russian military to reinforce its direct resistance against the Ukrainian Army on Ukrainian territory. This is made possible through the idea of a "Greater Russia" which appeals to many young local Russian nationalists,[35] who also form part of the military command. As such, this results in the further expansion of Russian military personnel, whilst establishing relations with Russian sympathizers, in order to utilize their local knowledge to assist in the execution of military objectives. Hence, local fighters are said to be paid to fight as mercenaries, working alongside imported fighters in the same vein.[36]

It is important to note that local fighters form part of a very small minority in a region where the appetite for separation or reconnection with Russia is very low.[37] Thus, it is of no surprise that the extent of local collaborators' participation is miniscule in the larger scheme and hierarchy of Russia's operations in Donbas. Therefore, military personnel and local collaborators are part and parcel of what is effectively the Russian agenda of open aggression in Donbas. Based on the evidence concerning the *de facto* power of the Russian military in Donbas, it is clear that local collaborators are subordinate to the command of the Russian military and its agenda. However, there

---

[33] Inform Napalm 2017.

[34] OSCE, Permanent Mission of Ukraine to the International Organizations in Vienna 2016.

[35] Yekelchyk 2015, p. 7.

[36] Ibid.

[37] Ibid.

is a mistaken view that active collaborators, whether local or Russian, are deemed to be "rebels" and "separatists". Therefore, it is necessary to examine how such terms ought to be construed in a conflict.

As terms or labels, "rebels" and "separatists" infer the presence of an agenda of independence, theoretically free of the military support and apparatus of another state. As such, it is important to engage with the definitions of "rebels" and "separatists" in order to determine whether local collaborators are acting in their own right. Rebels are defined as militant organizations fighting against a central government employing confrontational and violent methods.[38] Moreover, rebels can be classified as "armed opposition groups", "guerrillas", "freedom fighters", "non-state armed groups" or even "parties to an international armed conflict".[39] Rebels primarily fight for political causes, independence and the rights of minorities in society.[40] Separatists are similar to rebels, but they fight for a cause in connection with a specific territory, the value of land and the security of an area of economic interest.[41] Therefore, the use of "rebels" and "separatists" interchangeably translates into local collaborators being viewed as fighting for a political cause, rights and independence, premised upon the significance of the land in Donbas. This notion falsely implies that the situation in Donbas is an internal conflict over political and civil rights, which also gives the impression that the conflict existed in a subtle form before the Euromaidan Revolution. Therefore, it is important to determine whether the conflict was triggered by the existing sociopolitical intricacies of Donbas.

The fact is that the situation in Donbas before Euromaidan was one of peace and normalcy, rather than years of suppressed political tensions over independence. As such, the inaccurate labels would lead one to conclude that the fight for independence, and other political and social rights, would entail pre-existing issues of territoriality, language and economics. However, those three issues cannot be regarded as contributing factors of the conflict. There have also been no issues in relation to territorial demarcation because the delineation of the border occurred without conflict when the USSR collapsed.[42] In fact, the border was established according to the old border of the Ukrainian Soviet Socialist Republic (UkrSSR).[43] Additionally, Ukrainians represent the ethnic majority in Donbas; however, Russian is the predominant native language.[44] Despite this fact, the majority of individuals residing in Donbas are fluent in both Ukrainian and Russian.[45] In relation to economic issues, even though Donbas was at an economic disadvantage compared to the rest of Ukraine, it had a viable economy due to its output of steel and agricultural products.[46] It is important to note

---

[38] Jo 2015, pp. 36–7.

[39] Ibid., p. 37.

[40] Ibid.

[41] Walter 2009, pp. 4–7.

[42] Balaban et al. 2017, *supra* fn. 16, p. 19.

[43] Ibid., p. 18.

[44] Ibid., pp. 22–3.

[45] Ibid., p. 23.

[46] Ibid., p. 22.

that the conflict only came into being after Euromaidan, i.e., national protests against Russian influence over the then government and its intervention in Ukraine's future economic realignment with the EU. The pre-existing Russian influence is evident from the pressure placed on the then pro-Russian President Viktor Yanukovych, who succumbed to pressure and made the decision not to sever ties with Russia in favour of the EU.[47] Due to the political force of Euromaidan, President Yanukovych fled the state, which effectively ended any Russian influence over subsequent Ukrainian administrations. Therefore, the causes that are purported to inspire "separatism" or "independence" in Donbas are not compatible with factual history and current statistics. As such, one may reflect on the reasons why the terms "rebels" and separatists" were incorporated into the language around the conflict in Donbas.

The uniqueness about the actions of Russian collaborators at this juncture is that they tend to resurrect themselves in former Soviet states during times of diminishing Russian influence. As such, these Russian collaborators take on the persona of "rebels and "separatists" as a cover for a geopolitical and military strategy. This strategy fits in with the "Grachev Doctrine", which holds that Russia must maintain a degree of political and economic influence over its 'close neighbourhood'.[48] Similar tactics were used in Georgia in 2008 when Russia was losing its grip on its sphere of influence in the Caucuses. Furthermore, it has been said that Russia's actions were also triggered by the thought of NATO being on its doorstep.[49] In such cases, the doctrine demands that Russia must act to protect its 'legitimate interests', which is then used as justification for aggression.[50] This was the same excuse used to justify the invasion of Georgia, which, like Ukraine, sought to shift its attention towards the West. As in Georgia and Crimea, Russia tends to justify its occupation on the grounds of 'protecting' its citizens.[51] From another perspective, involving another Russian border region, the Baltic States (Estonia, Latvia and Lithuania) are starting to see subtle movements by Russia similar to those used in Georgia and Ukraine.[52] As a result, the Baltic States are extremely fearful that Russia may eventually pursue a similar agenda against them.[53] Thus, one can see an emerging pattern, whereby the events in Donbas do not relate in any way to mere internal strife. What is playing out in Donbas is part of a large-scale plan and a policy of maintaining the "Grachev Doctrine" in an effort to remain as a regional superpower. The collaborators on the ground are the ones giving effective assistance to the doctrine, and not pursuing a cause for liberalization, independent of both Ukraine and Russia. Therefore, consideration must now turn to whether the collaborators acted under directions from or control of the Russian state.

---

[47] Ibid., p. 26. See also the interview with a former US Ambassador to Ukraine on PBS News in 2013.

[48] Ágh 1998, p. 31.

[49] Rodrigues and Dubovyk 2010, p. 64.

[50] Saakashvili 2014.

[51] Ibid., See also Lally and Englund 2004.

[52] Larrabee et al. 2017, pp. 7–11.

[53] Ibid., p. 7.

Regarding the Russia's over agenda, the default rule for state involvement is enshrined in Article 2(4) of the UN Charter. According to this provision:

> All Members shall refrain in their international relations from the threat or use of force against the territorial integrity or political independence of any state, or in any other manner inconsistent with the Purposes of the United Nations.[54]

Article 2(4) ought to be interpreted as being applicable not only to direct actions, but also indirect actions through private actors. If no such actions can be attributed to a state, one can conclude that the collaborators acted independently. Article 2 of General Assembly Resolution 56/83[55] emphasizes this view by confirming that a state is liable for an internationally wrongful act when there is an act or omission, attributable to the state under international law, which constitutes a breach of an international obligation. Furthermore, in Article 8 of the same resolution, attribution to a state will be found if the conduct in question was "directed or controlled" by the state through a person or group of persons.[56] With regard to a breach of international obligations, a violation of Article 2(4) of the UN Charter (*jus cogens*) will suffice when considered with Article 12 of General Assembly Resolution 56/83. Therefore, the link between Russia's large-scale plan and policy and its collaborators must be established to dispel the notion of the collaborators being "rebels" and "separatists" under international law. Such was the contention in the International Court of Justice (ICJ) *Nicaragua v. United States* case,[57] which established the "effective control" test to determine the degree of control over collaborators violating Article 2(4) of the UN Charter. Moreover, Article 3(g) of General Assembly Resolution 3314 (XXIX) on the Definition of Aggression defines aggression as sending armed bands, groups, irregulars or mercenaries to conduct acts of armed forced against another State, even to a substantial degree of involvement.[58] Thus, the aforementioned ICJ case held that the threshold of state responsibility for groups acting upon the territory of another must go beyond encouraging, supporting, supplying, training and assistance.[59]

Going beyond that threshold is linked with the hurdle in Article 8 of General Assembly Resolution 56/83, which requires the conduct by persons or a group of persons to be "directed or controlled" by the state. The ICJ *Nicaragua* case and its "effective control" test requires that the collaborators "participated in the planning, direction, support, and execution" of unlawful actions.[60] In this case, however, the US was not held liable because its military personnel did not take part in the "execution" of unlawful actions. To apply this concept to the Russian collaborators, it can be

---

[54] Charter of the United Nations – opened for signature on 26 June 1945 (Trb. 1979 Nr. 37); entry into force on 24 October 1945.

[55] UN General Assembly 2001.

[56] Ibid.

[57] ICJ, *Case Concerning Military and Paramilitary Activities in and Against Nicaragua (Nicaragua v. United States of America), Judgment on Merits, 1986*, ICJ Reports 14, 27 June 1986, paras 105–115 (*Nicaragua* 1986).

[58] UN General Assembly 1974.

[59] Dixon 2014, p. 262.

[60] *Nicaragua* 1986, *supra* fn. 53, para 86.

argued that Russia cannot be held liable for the collaborators' actions because its military personnel did not participate 'directly' in the execution of acts in Donbas, i.e., took command of the actions. As such, credence would be given to the terms "rebels" and "separatists". However, as discussed above, there is evidence of regular Russian military personnel actively engaged on the ground in Donbas taking command of many military operations.[61] Thus, the "effective control" of Donbas by the military actions of the Russian Federation can be established upon the basis of the *Nicaragua* case. It must be noted that the "effective control" test presents a hurdle requiring command, rather than a direct mandate.

If command cannot be established, the International Criminal Tribunal for the Former Yugoslavia (ICTY) established the much preferred and more realistic "overall control" test in the *Tadić* case.[62] This test requires not only equipping, financing, training and support, but also "coordinating or helping" in the general execution of the act.[63] Based on the evidence, Russia is not only equipping, financing, training and supporting the collaborators, but it also organizing and assisting in the execution of unlawful actions in Donbas. This is evident through the continuous supply of weapons, machinery, vehicles and so-called 'humanitarian assistance' in the occupied region.[64] Moreover, Russia is paying the salaries and pensions of individuals, including its collaborators, living on what is lawfully Ukrainian territory.[65] Therefore, it is suggested that the collaborators are not fighting for the separation of a race, creed, or religious minority for the purpose of succession to independence. The collaborators are in fact fighting for Russia and the maintenance of its sphere of influence. What is striking is the fact that Russia's overall control of Donbas is maintained through collaborators who are acting as the enforcement personnel of the "Grachev Doctrine".

6.3 Defining the Conflict

To all intents and purposes, the situation in Donbas is an armed conflict according to customary international humanitarian law. This is premised on the fact that, according to the definition of an armed conflict given in the *Tadić* case,[66] collaborators on the ground resorted to armed force in the pursuit of their objectives. Additionally, Common Article 2 of the Geneva Conventions holds that, where a territory is occupied,

---

[61] See also Luhn 2015a, b.

[62] ICTY, *Prosecutor v. Dukso Tadić, Judgement of the Appeals Chamber, 15 July 1999, Case No. IT-94-1-A. (Tadić* 1999).

[63] Ibid., paras 131–137.

[64] Fox News 2016, 'In Ukraine, feeling grows that the east is lost to Russia'. http://www.foxnews.com/world/2017/05/05/in-ukraine-feeling-grows-that-east-is-lost-to-russia.html. Accessed 25 April 2017.

[65] Ibid.

[66] *Tadić* 1999, *supra* fn. 58, para 10.

an armed conflict is deemed to exist. However, the issue that arises from the previous section is whether the situation in Donbas is a NIAC or an IAC. One may conclude, based on the analysis in the previous section, that the situation is indeed an IAC; however, it would not be so simple to establish such a fact. In order to determine whether the conflict in Donbas is one between Russia and Ukraine, or between Ukraine and Russian collaborators, Article 2(4) of the UN Charter (the prohibition on the use of force) is once again the default starting point. Further, another sacred default rule that can be extrapolated from that provision is the "principle of non-intervention". This principle derives from every state's right to political independence, sovereignty and territorial integrity.[67] Moreover, this principle is restated in Article 2(7) of the UN Charter prohibiting nations from intervening in the domestic jurisdiction of any other state. Therefore, the implication of these principles is that, where there is a conflict between two states, the aggressor state has very little grounds to justify its actions.

NIACs entail situations where belligerent forces are a product of a purely domestic crisis. Thus, such conflicts will be within the remit of the jurisdiction of the state and should be free from external intervention. However, some authors argue that the only exception to this rule is that any intervention must be pursued with the aim of upholding imperative treaty obligations and to protect the nationals of the intervening state.[68] It must be noted that this exception is disputed by jurists,[69] which results in doctrinal and interpretative uncertainty about it. The latter justification (protecting nationals) is the one in which Russia sought to legitimize their military actions in Georgia, Crimea and Donbas. However, in the Donbas region, Russian citizens are not in the majority.[70] Furthermore, Russian citizens were not under any form of threat from the anti-Russian protests due to the fact of their peaceful coexistence during the protests and prior to the conflict.[71] Moreover, there was no appetite in the region for separatism, reunification with Russia or independence, because Donbas was fully represented in the Ukrainian Parliament.[72] Russia submitted to the contrary view that 'radical extremists' linked to Euromaidan threatened its citizen; however, these 'extremists' were protesters who enjoyed national and international support.[73] Again, this is the same line that Russia used in South Ossetia and Crimea, i.e., under the guise of protecting Russia's interests.[74]

It seems that the collaborators are using NIAC tactics as a cover for a greater IAC agenda. It must be noted that the situation in Donbas was first triggered by the actions of the Russian Federal Security Service (FSB) through an FSB colonel,

---

[67] Jennings and Watts 2008, p. 428.

[68] Crawford and Pert 2008, p. 58.

[69] Ibid.

[70] Balaban et al. 2017, *supra* fn. 16, p. 22.

[71] Ibid., p. 32.

[72] Ibid., pp. 25–30.

[73] BBC News 2014, 'Ukraine crisis: does Russia have a case? http://www.bbc.com/news/world-europe-26415508. Accessed 26 April 2017.

[74] Killingsworth et al. 2015, p. 101.

Igor Strelkov, also known as 'Igor Girkin', who confessed to being the own who "fired the trigger for the war".[75] His rationale for being instrumental in starting the conflict in Donbas was to take control of populated areas and stop the "rebellion" from expanding.[76] As such, this can be read as a covert IAC intended to stop Ukraine from rebelling against the "Grachev Doctrine". Over time, the situation was joined by a host of collaborators engaging in disturbances before an armed conflict came into being. Subsequently, the collaborators took on the persona of belligerents with an agenda. In turn, they have sought to be recognized as belligerents, a status that enjoys legal benefits and consequences ranging from the conferral of rights to the ascription of neutrality.[77] This endeavour has been embodied in the creation of the "DPR" and "LPR" "independent states".

As such, both "states" seek to solidify their possession of parts of legitimate Ukrainian territory, establish a form of 'government' and conduct their objectives against a legitimate government.[78] This approach is gravely mistaken because of the overwhelming evidence that the declared 'separatism' is not of the kind faced by Israel (with Palestine), the UK (with Scotland), China (with Tibet), Spain (with Catalonia) etc. With Russian political "tourists" and regular military personnel propping up the "DPR" and "LPR" to the total exclusion of the Ukrainian Government, the conflict, *ipso facto*, became international *ab initio*. Therefore, against this backdrop, the situation is Donbas ought to be classified as an IAC.

Under international law, an IAC exists when states resort to armed force against each other.[79] This definition, when read alongside Common Article 2 of the Geneva Conventions, expresses that an IAC will come into being when a state, *inter alia*, occupies the territory of another state through armed force. Hence, that is why there is an IAC between Ukraine and Russia, which started at the time of the occupation of Crimea. From another prospective, prior to Euromaidan, Donbas was not subjected to Ukrainian colonial domination, racism, nor alien domination; nor was it pursuing independence. Some would argue that the movement behind the 'restoration of Novorossiya' was the basis for the start of the conflict in Donbas.[80] However, based on the discussion above, it is evident that the 'restoration of Novorossiya' was simply a Kremlin propaganda exercise. Later, with the shooting-down of Malaysia Airlines flight MH17 (a Boeing 777 jet) and other grisly criminal activities, it became clear that the conflict in question was not one of self-determination.[81] In relation to MH17, the Dutch-led Joint Investigation Team, in their report, stated that there is "irrefutable evidence" that the Malaysian jet was shot down by a Russian-made BUK missile from the 9M38 series.[82] Furthermore, it was the 69th Separate Logistics Brigade

---

[75] Chekalkin 2017. See also Dolgov 2014.

[76] Ibid.

[77] Crawford and Pert 2008, p. 59.

[78] Jennings and Watts 2008, p. 101, *supra* fn. 63.

[79] *Tadić* 1999, para 10.

[80] Loiko 2016.

[81] See also ibid.

[82] Openbaar Ministerie 2016.

from Unit 11385 from the Russian military that transported the BUK unit vehicles around the time when the Boeing 777 was shot down.[83] After the missile was fired, the vehicles were then transported back to Russia over the border.[84] In addition to shooting down flight MH17, there is damning evidence that Russia used its territory to fire its military artillery into Ukraine.[85] According to US intelligence, weapons were supplied not only to target Ukrainian military positions, but also to boost the resources of "pro-Russian rebels".[86] These abhorrent acts both highlight the brutishness of the so-called "rebels", and prove Russian responsibility in connection with an objective that is most unrelated to self-determination. Therefore, as a result of an absurd agenda, one can understand why the region has, in part, turned into a cesspit of criminality and corruption.[87]

The notion of a "civil war" or "separatist conflict" in Donbas has an unfounded premise in international law. Furthermore, with the absence of an agenda linked to liberalization and independence, there can be no parallel conflict. Thus, it is submitted that Russia has created a situation in which to destabilize Ukraine for its own 'advantage' and as a warning to other border states, should they attempt to look to the West. Thus, the conflict in Donbas has nothing to do with the people in that region; the conflict is about penalizing Ukraine, as was the case in Georgia, for ditching its pro-Russian government. Moreover, the military intervention has been to maintain a degree of control in Ukraine. As such, based on ICTY jurisprudence in the *Blaskic*, *Kordic* and *Rajic* cases, the situation in Donbas is an IAC on the basis of Russia's military intervention under the overall control of armed collaborators.[88]

6.4 Broadcasting Alternative Facts: The Effect of the Distortion

The distortions surrounding the definitions of the collaborators and the conflict have resulted in the distortion of the real conflict. The media portrayal of the collaborators as "rebels" and "separatists" gives the impression that the collaborators are seeking to be liberated, when, in fact, there is a greater agenda at hand. As such, the collaborators may take advantage of the distortion of definitions to solidify their 'justified' position in the eyes of the public. The Russian Government may even go further to create

---

[83] Daniel 2017.

[84] Openbaar Ministerie 2016, *supra* fn. 81.

[85] Elftheriou-Smith 2014.

[86] Ibid., See also Sky News 2014, 'US: Russian military 'firing into Ukraine'. http://news.sky.com/story/us-russian-military-firing-into-ukraine-10395472. Accessed 8 June 2017. See also Case 2014.

[87] Ibid.

[88] ICTY, *Prosecutor v. Tihomir Blaškić, Trial Judgement, 3 March 2000, IT-95-14-T*, paras 76, 83–94. See also: ICTY, *Prosecutor v. Dario Kordić and Mario Čerkez, Trial Judgement, 26 February 2001, IT-95-14/2-T*, paras 66–7, 79, 108–9; ICTY, *Prosecutor v. Ivica Rajić, Review of Indictment, 13 September 1996, IT-95-12-R61*, paras 10–21; and Crawford and Pert 2008, p. 86.

"alternative facts" about the reality of the conflict. One major source of alternative facts is the Kremlin's media machine, which is keen to portray its actions in Ukraine as being in conformity with international law. Broadcasters will then republish and even incorporate certain terms, such as "rebels", "separatists", "civil war" and "internal affair", into their mediated language. As a result, these terms feed into the everyday discourse about the conflict because the majority of individuals do not understand how such labels ought to be ascribed. This distortion of definitions has also infected the diplomatic realm, such that even Ukraine's UN Ambassador, Yuriy Sergeyev, saw the need to correct the distortions around the conflict.[89] Despite this correction, the distortions are continually republished in academic literature and the reports of certain international organizations.[90] This could only be a consequence of 'reporting language', which has a legitimizing effect on the terminologies around the conflict. In the spheres of international law, however, such distortions are now absent from the language used by international courts. For example, the ICC, in its preliminary report, refrained from ascribing such labels to the Russian collaborators in Ukraine.[91] This apparent policy is in fact due to the evidence of a larger Russian agenda, which goes beyond mere internal conflict between "separatists", "rebels" and the Ukrainian Government.

Another problem lies with how distorted broadcasts are translated and interpreted through their dissemination on social media. The manner in which armed conflicts are broadcast to the public has changed significantly over the years due to the rise in social media,[92] which gives everyone, regardless of their intention, the tools needed to address the public and mass media. Journalists who are active on social media will absorb the means by which conflicts are interpreted, which will then influence the composition of their reports. Such influence could stem from how terms are applied and used *en masse* during times of conflict. This form of newsgathering and interaction is evident with the increasing prominence of the social media editor in the field of journalism.[93] However, despite the evolution of this new form of journalism, many hold that the traditional principles of journalism ought to remain steadfast to ensure that accuracy continues to be the primary goal of reporting.[94] Even with the traditional model of journalism, conflicts, such as those in Rwanda and Yugoslavia, have been subjected to terminological inaccuracies and sensationalist reporting.[95] Thus, traditional problems coupled with new challenges posed by social

---

[89] UN Security Council 2014, Security Council Briefed on Fast-breaking Developments in Ukraine, as Political Official Warns Failure to Secure Russian-Ukrainian Border Obstructing Peace, UN Doc. SC/11645. https://www.un.org/press/en/2014/sc11645.doc.htm. Accessed 27 April 2017.

[90] For example, European Parliament 2016; see also Amnesty International 2016.

[91] International Criminal Court, Office of the Prosecutor (ICC-OTP) 2016.

[92] Dredge 2014.

[93] Bunz 2009.

[94] Dredge 2014, *supra* fn. 81.

[95] Sarkin and Fowler 2010, pp. 61, 84, 86.

media can even contribute to greater levels of violence in conflicts.[96] Therefore, the interaction between traditional and social media journalism can have a direct and indirect influence on the conflict and its participants.

Alternative facts are borne out of the tensions between authority and authenticity during times of international conflict. Since social media, in particular, provides a voice for everyone, individuals, including those in and around conflict zones, will publish information as they see fit. As such, some information may be deemed 'credible' in the eyes of the wider public because of the 'professional' manner in which it is published. Hence, the collaborators and the Kremlin will utilize social media in such a manner as to spread their propaganda, which in turn will be picked up by global broadcasters. When broadcasters republish inaccurate information and terminology (as they do with their definitions of the collaborators and the conflict), individuals and even experts will form their opinions based on the presumption of authority being equated to accuracy in the world of news. However, issues of credibility will arise when distorted definitions are challenged by more prudent experts, thus creating an environment of intellectual misunderstanding. Alternatively, a negative by-product of social media is that many individuals feel that they are an authority on issues because they absorb a plethora of publications available on social media. Some are even emboldened to challenge and discredit experts, who are qualified and spend most of their time in researching the area in question. This problem is made even worse because social media provides a platform, not only to share 'opinions' but to spread 'opinions' at frightening speed.[97] In turn, the collaborators and the Kremlin utilize social media to distribute their propaganda, which will consequently reach a vast audience who will think that the 'information' is credible. The 'information' will also incorporate twisted terms in an effort to divide public opinion and lessen the opposition against the situation in Donbas.[98] As it stands, the public and even diplomatic circles are divided over the conflict in Donbas because the Russian agenda has been effective to a degree. This is why the EU, in particular, is seeking to aggressively confront the problem of alternative facts.[99]

Therefore, it is the duty of the media to ensure that accuracy is given primacy over authority.[100] This disrupts the mission behind the distorted definitions, which seeks to galvanize a certain narrative about the conflict by the parties involved.[101] As demonstrated in Sects. 6.2 and 6.3, alternative definitions can alter the characterization of the participants in a conflict and the nature of the conflict. Moreover, persons who are not entrenched in research around the conflict could be intellectually led astray because they have no other sources of information. Therefore, it is incumbent upon the media to ensure that, during times of conflict, the views of prudent experts

---

[96] See BBC News 2015, 'Is Palestinian-Israeli violence being driven by social media?'. http://www.bbc.com/news/world-middle-east-34513693. Accessed 3 May 2017.

[97] Grey 2017.

[98] European Parliament 2015a; see also European Parliament 2015b.

[99] Ibid.

[100] Dredge 2014, *supra* fn. 81.

[101] Dougherty 2014. See also Czuperski et al. 2015a, b.

are given priority in broadcasting in order to combat the tide of alternative facts. Furthermore, journalists must not be too eager to compile reports based on material published on social media. As such, there should be a process of cross-checking and prudent expert-checking to ensure that everyone outside of a conflict is not led towards intellectual peril.

6.5   The Importance of Definitional Accuracy During International Conflicts

During times of international conflicts, especially regarding the conflict in Donbas, definitional accuracy is important for several reasons. Firstly, labelling collaborators as "rebels" and "separatists" has led to the notion that there is a "civil war" being waged in Ukraine. This is what the narrative of Russia's propaganda machinery wants to achieve; and, to a degree, it has been successful. The aim is to portray Russia as the great protector of its citizens and the high paragon of international virtue. As such, opinions are formed in line with that narrative, which in turn creates a degree of sympathy for the "Grachev Doctrine". Secondly, incorrect definitions that feed into the language surrounding the conflict legitimizes the role and actions of the collaborators. This builds upon the previous point, whereby flagrant violators of international law must be called out for all that they erroneously embody. By ascribing alternative definitions to them and their actions, their public image is softened and not regarded as a serious problem in international law. The use of such a Kremlin propaganda model equates to calling the Waffen-SS "rebels" and "separatists". History shows that such actions had dire consequences for the future of Europe and the rest of the world. From another angle, applying mistaken labels can also be likened to also referring to the Russian troops who fought for Germany during the Second World War against the Soviet Union as separatists and rebels. The point is that the presence of Russian military in Donbas cannot be classed as a situation involving "rebels" and separatists" in straightforward internal conflict. The conflict is one in which one country seeks to maintain a degree of control through unlawful methods over another, and should be framed as such. Therefore, the aim of definitional accuracy is to create a specific mindset, which ensures that the collaborators know that their time is short and that there will be consequences for their actions. Moreover, the information war waged by Russia and its enablers will fail if individuals become acquainted with the correct terminology and can ascribe them accordingly.

Building upon the third point, incorrect definitions have ultimately undermined the normative and moral treatment of the reality in Donbas. As it stands, even though Russian leaders are seen as corrupt and war-like, the response to their unlawful actions has been less than adequate.[102] This creates a dampening effect on the minds of not only onlookers, but also those living in Ukraine, and Donbas in particular. Due to the stand-off approach adopted by the international community, Ukraine has effectively

---

[102] Balaban et al. 2017, *supra* fn. 15, p. 58.

been weakened, while Russia has faced no consequences from its occupation of Donbas. Hence, some commentators are of the view that the Ukrainian Government 'gave up' on Crimea because it saw no incentive to do otherwise.[103] Moreover, coupled with Russia's focus elsewhere, the situation in Donbas is not seen as serious as the conflict in Syria.[104] As such, failing to attribute the correct terminology at the start of the conflict resulted in a temporary *de facto* win in terms of the Russian occupation in Donbas. This is based on the fact that the conflict was not viewed as it should have been because of the promulgation of alternative definitions creating alternative facts. As a result, divisions were created at all levels, where different standards and expectations clashed, causing the conflict to worsen. Therefore, the normative and moral treatment of the situation in Donbas must be recalibrated in order to prevent such future actions in other border states.

Finally, incorrect definitions ascribed to the conflict in Donbas will negatively affect the way in which the international community responds to similar conflicts in the future. This was the case with the woeful response to the Russian occupation of Georgia, which led to the conflict in Ukraine.[105] With reports from international broadcasters and organizations employing distorted definitions, the conflict was inaccurately framed, while policy responses were misguided. Hence, the general misunderstanding surrounding the conflict in Donbas contributed to a lacklustre response from certain national governments around the world.[106] Thus, with differing views based on differing definitions, it is inevitable that a lack of a common, accurate understanding will even impede diplomatic efforts to find a solution. Another explanation could be that any response would have led to direct conflict with Russia, for which there was no appetite.[107] Whatever the reason, the central point is that an improper attribution cannot invoke an appropriate response to a violation of international law. This is evidenced by the fact that the Office of the Prosecutor at the ICC is contemplating classifying the conflict as both an NIAC and an IAC. If accurate definitions had been ascribed *ab initio*, the ICC may not have had to conduct an additional attribution process. Russian foreign policy has been able to violate international law with impunity because the seeds of doubt had been planted. Embedded within the alternative facts concerning Donbas, are the seeds of definitional accuracies, which are wreaking havoc on a united and coherent solution to the conflict's end.

6.6   Conclusion

The labels "rebels", "separatists", "Russian-backed separatists" "civil war", "internal conflict" etc. are incompatible with the reality of the conflict in Donbas. Moreover, incompatible labels create problems when applying international law, where attri-

---

[103] Bershidsky 2016.
[104] Walker 2015.
[105] Sharkov 2016.
[106] Parliament of the United Kingdom 2015.
[107] Smith 2010.

bution and consequences hinge on accurate characterizations. Therefore, the reality is that the situation must be deemed to be an IAC, with the involvement of Russian regular and irregular troops aided by local collaborators. The collaborators' characterization of fighting for their own cause is a fallacy; what is true is that they are fighting to support Russian aggression on the sovereign territory of another state. Moreover, the collaborators are emissaries of the Russian Federation, who are fighting to preserve a zone of pro-Russian influence through the use of force. As such, the conflict cannot be classified as an NIAC for the simple fact that Russia exercises effective or even overall control over its collaborators. In fact, the collaborators are embedded with Russian military personnel, jointly and collectively, engaging in the active destabilization of Ukraine. To create a positive narrative, inaccurate labels have been ascribed to create an 'idealistic' picture of the conflict and its participants.

The sources of these inaccurate characterizations are those who flagrantly violate international law and norms. These labels are then incorporated into the broadcasts, reports and findings of international media and other organizations, which are then absorbed by the public and diplomats. Furthermore, the openness of social media further deepens the problem in which authority no longer means accuracy in the world of information. As a result, divisive opinions are formed over the conflict, which in turn produce a distorted and counterproductive view of the real conflict. Thus, the role of the media is, now more than ever, paramount in combatting alternative facts buoyed by alternative definitions. This is because incorrect labels undermine the realities of the conflict, contribute to the legitimization of aggressors' actions, erode moral and normative treatments of the conflict, and impede efforts to find an effective solution to the conflict. Moreover, established incorrect definitions will negatively affect the manner of response to similar conflicts in the future. International law is based on well-defined principles and norms that maintain the rule of law. If these principles and standards are distorted, the rule of law will be further weakened and give way to the further international violation conducted with impunity. This has been evident from Russia's actions around its borders for decades and decades. Therefore, definitional accuracies will ensure that conflicts are precisely described, such that violators of international law are duly held responsible in the courts of law and public opinion.

References

Ágh A (1998) The Politics of Central Europe. SAGE Publications Ltd, USA

Amnesty International (2016) Ukraine: "You Don't Exist": Arbitrary Detentions, Enforced Disappearances, And Torture In Eastern Ukraine https://www.amnesty.org/download/Documents/EUR5044552016ENGLISH.PDF. Accessed 27 April 2017

Asymmetric Warfare Group (2016) Russian New Generation Warfare Handbook. https://info.publicintelligence.net/AWG-RussianNewWarfareHandbook.pdf. Accessed 24 September 2017

Balaban M et al (2017) Donbas in Flames: Guide to the Conflict Zone. https://prometheus.ngo/wp-content/uploads/2017/04/Donbas_v_Ogni_ENG_web_1-4.pdf. Accessed 1 April 2017

Bershidsky L (2016) Why Russia Stopped at Crimea? https://www.bloomberg.com/view/articles/2016-02-22/why-russia-stopped-at-crimea. Accessed 7 May 2017

Bukkvoll T (2016) Russian Military Power: Russian Special Operations Forces in Crimea and Donbas. Accessed 22 April 2017, p 18. http://ssi.armywarcollege.edu/pubs/parameters/issues/Summer_2016/5_Bukkvoll.pdf

Bunz M (2009) What will the BBC's new social media editor do? https://www.theguardian.com/media/pda/2009/nov/19/bbc-social-media-editor-alex-gubbay. Accessed 3 May 2017

Case S (2014) Putin's Undeclared War: Summer 2014-Russian Artillery Strikes against Ukraine. https://www.bellingcat.com/news/uk-and-europe/2016/12/21/russian-artillery-strikes-against-ukraine/. Accessed 15 June 2017

Channel News Asia (2017) Ukraine readies project to jam separatists broadcasting. http://www.channelnewsasia.com/news/world/ukraine-readies-project-to-jamseparatist-broadcasting-8802958. Accessed 2 April 2017

Charter of the United Nations (1945) [opened for signature 26 June 1945]. Trb. 1979 Nr. 37 (entry into force 24 October 1945)

Chekalkin D (2017) How Russia invaded Ukraine as told by FSB colonel Girkin. http://euromaidanpress.com/2014/12/07/fsb-colonel-girkin-tells-details-of-how-russia-invaded-ukraine-in-twice-censored-interview/#arvlbdata. Accessed 8 June 2017

Chicago Tribune (2017) An on-the-ground look at the deadly surge of violence in Eastern Ukraine. http://www.chicagotribune.com/news/nationworld/ct-eastern-ukraine-violence-20170203-story.html. Accessed 2 April 2017

Chifu I, Tutuianu S (2016) Torn between East and West: Europe's Border States. Routledge, Abingdon

Corder M (2017) UN court rejects Ukraine request to block rebel funding. http://abcnews.go.com/amp/International/wireStory/court-rule-ukraines-case-russia-46881332. Accessed 2 April 2017

Coyness H (2017) Putin must go, Donbas must be freed for normalized relations with Russia. http://www.ukrweekly.com/uwwp/putin-must-go-donbas-must-be-freed-for-normalized-relations-with-russia. Accessed 2 April 2017

Crawford E, Pert A (2008) International Humanitarian Law, Cambridge University Press, Cambridge

Czuperski M et al (2015) Hiding in Plain Sight: Putin's War in Ukraine. http://www.atlanticcouncil.org/images/publications/Hiding_in_Plain_Sight/HPS_English.pdf. Accessed 5 May 2017

Czuperski M et al (2015) Putin's secret warriors: Russian soldiers sent to fight in Ukraine. http://www.newsweek.com/putins-secret-warriors-tales-three-russian-soldiers-sent-fight-ukraine-339665. Accessed 8 June 2017

Damien S (2016) 'NATO Dismisses Russian Claims of Civil War in Ukraine. http://www.newsweek.com/nato-dismisses-russian-claims-civil-war-ukraine 450617. Accessed 2 April 2015

Daniel R (2017) MH17-Drivers of the Russian June and July 2014 Buk Convoy Trucks. https://www.bellingcat.com/news/uk-and-europe/2017/06/05/mh17-drivers-russian-june-july-2014-buk-convoy-trucks/. Accessed 7 June 2017

Dixon M (2014) Textbook on International Law, 7th edn. Oxford University Press, Oxford

Dougherty J (2014) Everyone Lies: The Ukraine Conflict and Russia's Media Transformation. Shorenstein Center on Media, Politics and Public Policy Discussion Paper Series (July 2014). https://shorensteincenter.org/wp-content/uploads/2014/07/d88-dougherty.pdf Accessed 6 May 2017

Dredge S (2014) Social media, journalism and wars: 'Authenticity has replaced authority. https://www.theguardian.com/technology/2014/nov/05/social-media   journalism-wars-authenticity. Accessed 1 May 2017

Dolgov A (2014) Russia's Igor Strelkov: I Am Responsible for War in Eastern Ukraine. https://themoscowtimes.com/articles/russias-igor-strelkov-i-am-responsible-for-war-in-eastern-ukraine-41598. Accessed 8 June 2017

Elftheriou-Smith L (2014) US says new evidence shows Russia 'firing artillery into Ukraine'. http://www.independent.co.uk/news/world/americas/us-says-new-evidence-shows-russia-firing-artillery-into-ukraine-9628034.html. Accessed 8 June 2017

European Parliament (2015a) Russia's disinformation on Ukraine and the EU's response. http://www.europarl.europa.eu/RegData/etudes/BRIE/2015/571339/EPRS_BRI(2015)571339_EN.pdf. Accessed 7 April 2017

European Parliament (2015b) Russia's manipulation of information on Ukraine and the EU's response. http://www.europarl.europa.eu/RegData/etudes/BRIE/2015/559471/EPRS_BRI(2015)559471_EN.pdf. Accessed 7 April 2017

European Parliament (2016) Ukraine and the Minsk II agreement. On a frozen path to peace? http://www.europarl.europa.eu/RegData/etudes/BRIE/2016/573951/EPRS_BRI(2016)573951_EN.pdf Accessed 27 April 2017

Goodenough P (2017) Russian-Backed Separatists Blame Kiev For Death of US Observer in Rebel-Held Eastern Ukraine. http://www.cnsnews.com/news/article/patrick-goodenough/russian-backed-separatists-blame-kiev-death-us-observer-rebel-held. Accessed 2 April 2017

Grey R (2017) Lies, Propaganda, and Fake News: A Challenge for Our Age. http://www.bbc.com/future/story/20170301-lies-propaganda-and-fake-news-a-grand-challenge-of-our-age. Accessed 5 May 2017

Grytesenko O (2017) Russian-controlled Donbas splits further from Ukraine. https://www.kyivpost.com/ukraine-politics/russian-controlled-donbas-splits-ukraine.html. Accessed 2 April 2017

Harress C (2015) Russian Soldiers Were in Debaltseve Fighting Against Ukrainian Military, Claims Russian Newspaper. http://www.ibtimes.com/russian-soldiers-were-debaltseve-fighting-against-ukrainian-military-claims-russian-1822868. Accessed 23 April 2017

Howard A (2014) Ukraine Crisis: It's war, civil war. https://www.theguardian.com/world/2014/may/03/ukraine-crisis-war-odessa-fire. Accessed 2 April 2017

International Criminal Court-Office of the Prosecutor (ICC-OTP) (2016) Report on Preliminary Examination Activities (14 November 2016) https://www.icc-cpi.int/iccdocs/otp/161114-otp-rep-pe_eng.pdf. Accessed 1 April 2017

Inform Napalm (2017) Signal Troops of Russian Army's 136th Brigade in Donbas: lists, documents, orders (photos). https://informnapalm.org/en/signal-troops-russian-army-s-136th-brigade-donbas-lists-documents-orders-photos. Accessed 23 April 2017

Jennings R, Watts A (2008) Oppenheim's International Law, 3rd edn. Oxford University Press, Oxford

Jo H (2015) Rebel Groups and international Law in World Politics. Cambridge University Press, Cambridge

Jurist (2017) Ukraine asks ICJ to bar Russia from aiding Ukraine separatists. http://www.jurist.org/paperchase/2017/03/ukraine-asks-icj-to-bar-russia-from-aiding-ukraine-separatists.php. Accessed 2 April 2017

Killingsworth M, Sussex M, Pakulski J (2015) Violence and the State. Manchester University Press, Manchester

Kim L (2014) The Battle of Ilovaisk: Details of a Massacre Inside Rebel-Held Eastern Ukraine. http://www.newsweek.com/2014/11/14/battle-ilovaisk-details-massacre-inside-rebel-held-eastern-ukraine-282003.html. Accessed 8 June 2017

Lally K, Englund W (2004) Putin says he reserves right to protect Russians in Ukraine. https://www.washingtonpost.com/world/putin-reserves-the-right-to-use-force-in-ukraine/2014/03/04/92d4ca70-a389-11e3-a5fa-55f0c77bf39c_story.html?utm_term=.b339f16460da. Accessed 25 April 2017

Larrabee F et al (2017) Russia and the West After the Ukrainian Crisis (ed) European Vulnerabilities to Russian Pressures. RAND Corporation, pp 7–11

Loiko S (2016) The unravelling of Moscow's dream of "Novorossiya". http://www.ukrweekly.com/uwwp/the-unraveling-of-moscows-dream-of-novorossiya/. Accessed 26 April 2017

Luhn A (2015) 'Russian soldiers' captured in Ukraine to face trial on terrorism charges. https://www.theguardian.com/world/2015/may/18/russian-soldiers-ukraine-trial-terrorism-charges. Accessed 7 June 2017

Luhn A (2015) Russian Soldiers Have Given Up Pretending They Are Not Fighting In Ukraine. https://news.vice.com/article/russian-soldiers-have-given-up-pretending-they-are-not-fighting-in-ukraine. Accessed 25 April 2017

Miller C (2014) Russian resigns to make way for Ukrainian as new head of 'Donetsk People's Republic'. https://www.theguardian.com/world/2014/aug/08/russian-resigns-ukrainian-head-donetsk-peoples-republic. Accessed 7 June 2017

Office of the United Nations High Commissioner for Human Rights (OHCHR) (2016) Report on the human rights situation in Ukraine 16 February to 15 May 2016. http://www.ohchr.org/Documents/Countries/UA/Ukraine_14th_HRMMU_Report.pdf. Accessed 23 April 2017

Openbaar Ministerie (2016) JIT: Flight MH17 was shot down by a BUK missile from a farmland near Pervomaiskyi. https://www.om.nl/onderwerpen/mh17-crash/@96068/jit-flight-mh17-shot/. Accessed 7 June 2017

OSCE Permanent Council of the European Union (2016) Statement on "Russia's Ongoing Aggression against Ukraine and the Illegal Occupation of Crimea", PC.DEL/1558/16. http://www.osce.org/pc/299901?download=true. Accessed 1 April 2017

OSCE Permanent Mission of Ukraine to the International Organisation in Vienna (2016) Statement by the Delegation of Ukraine at the 832nd FSC Plenary Meetings, 13 October 2016, FSC. DEL/202/16. http://www.osce.org/fsc/276271?download=true. Accessed 25 May 2017

OSCE Parliamentary Assembly (2015) Resolution on the Continuation of Clear, Gross and Uncorrected Violations of OSCE Commitments and International Norms by the Russian Federation Helsinki, 5-9 July 2015 https://www.oscepa.org/meetings/annual-sessions/2015-annual-session-helsinki/2015-helsinki-final-declaration/2282-07. Accessed 2 April 2017

Parfitt T (2015) Separatist fighter admits Russian tanks, troops 'decisive in eastern Ukraine battles'. http://www.telegraph.co.uk/news/worldnews/europe/russia/11506774/Separatist-fighter-admits-Russian-tanks-troops-decisive-in-eastern-Ukraine-battles.html. Accessed 8 June 2015

Parliament of the United Kingdom (2015) The EU and Russia: Before and beyond the crisis in Ukraine. https://www.publications.parliament.uk/pa/ld201415/ldselect/ldeucom/115/115.pdf. Accessed 8 May 2017

Parliamentary Assembly of the Council of Europe (2018) Resolution 2198 (2018), Council of Europe Doc. 14463

Parliamentary Assembly of the Council of Europe (2016a) Resolution 2132 (2016), Council of Europe Doc. 14130 (PACE 2016, *Resolution 2132*)

Parliamentary Assembly of the Council of Europe (2016b) Resolution 2133 (2016), Council of Europe Doc. 14139

PBS Interview with a former U.S. Ambassador to Ukraine in PBS News (2013) Why did Ukraine's Yanukovych give in to Russian pressure on EU deal? http://www.pbs.org/newshour/bb/world-july-dec13-ukraine2_12-02/. Accessed 24 April 2017

Permanent Mission of Ukraine to the UN (2017) Statement by the delegation of Ukraine at the UN Security Council Briefing by the Chairperson-in-Office of the OSCE. http://ukraineun.org/en/press-center/171-statement-by-the-delegation-of-ukraine-at-the-un-security-council-briefing-by-the-chairperson-in-office-of-the-osce/. Accessed 1 April 2017

Reuters (2017) Austrian suspected of war crimes in Ukraine detained in Poland. https://www.reuters.com/article/us-austria-crime-ukraine-idUSKBN17W0NM. Accessed 2 April 2017

Rodrigues L, Dubovyk V (2010) Perceptions of NATO and the New Strategic Concept. IOS Press, Amsterdam

Saakashvili M (2014) Let Georgia be a lesson for what will happen to Ukraine. https://www.theguardian.com/commentisfree/2014/mar/14/georgia-lesson-for-ukraine-crimea-referendum-trick. Accessed 24 April 2017

Sarkin J, Fowler C (2010) The Responsibility to Protect and the Duty to Prevent Genocide: Lessons to Be Learned from the Role of the International Community and the Media during the Rwandan Genocide and the Conflict in Former Yugoslavia. Suffolk Transnational Law Review 33(1): 35–86

Sharkov D (2016) Ukraine Blames International Response to Georgia Crisis for Russian Intervention. http://www.newsweek.com/ukraine-blames-un-international-response-georgia-crisis-russian-intervention-488734. Accessed 8 May 2017

Smith B (2010) U.S. Pondered military use in Georgia. http://www.politico.com/story/2010/02/us-pondered-military-use-in-georgia-032487. Accessed 8 May 2017

Toler A, Haring M (2017) How Putin Funds and Commands the War in Ukraine. http://www.newsweek.com/how-putin-funds-and-commands-war-ukraine-589733. Accessed 2 April 2017

UN General Assembly (1974) Resolution 3314 (1974), UN Doc. A/RES/29/3314

UN General Assembly (2001) Resolution 83 (2001), UN Doc. A/RES/56/83.

UN General Assembly (2014) Resolution 262 (2014), UN Doc. A/RES/68/262

UN General Assembly (2016) Resolution 205 (2016), UN Doc. A/RES/71/205.

UN Security Council (2014) Security Council Briefed on Fast-Breaking Developments in Ukraine, as Political Official Warns Failure to Secure Russian-Ukrainian Border Obstructing Peace, UN Doc. SC/11645. https://www.un.org/press/en/2014/sc11645.doc.htm. Accessed 27 April 2017

UNAIN Information Agency (2016) Kyiv honoring soldiers killed in 2014 Ilovaisk battle. https://www.unian.info/kiev/1490359-kyiv-honoring-soldiers-killed-in-2014-ilovaisk-battle.html. Accessed 23 April 2017

Walker S (2015) As Russia enters war in Syria, conflict in Ukraine begins to wind down. https://www.theguardian.com/world/2015/oct/01/as-russia-enters-war-in-syria-conflict-in-ukraine-begins-to-wind-down. Accessed 8 May 2017

Walter B (2009) Reputation and Civil War: Why Separatists Conflicts Are So Violent, 1st edn. Cambridge University Press, Cambridge

Yekelchyk S (2015) The Conflict in Ukraine: What Everyone Needs to Know, 1st edn. Oxford University Press, Oxford

Chapter 7
The Legal Status of the Donetsk and Luhansk "Peoples' Republics"

Tymur Korotkyi and Nataliia Hendel

Contents

Abstract In this chapter, issues of legitimacy surrounding the creation/proclamation of the "Donetsk People's Republic" (DPR) and the "Luhansk People's Republic" (LPR) are considered. The international legal aspects of the recognition of the DPR and the LPR are also analysed. In addition, the position adopted by the Russian Federation and the international community towards these so-called people's republics is revealed.

Keywords legitimacy of the creation/proclamation · unrecognized state · separatist formation · recognition · territorial integrity of Ukraine · the "Donetsk People's Republic" · the "Luhansk People's Republic"

Tymur Korotkyi, Professor, Department of International Law and International Relations, National University "Odesa Law Academy", Ukraine, email: tymur_korotkyi@ukr.net.
Nataliia Hendel, Associate Professor, Department of International Law and International Relations, National University "Odesa Law Academy", Ukraine, email: n.v.hendel@gmail.com.

T. Korotkyi (✉) · N. Hendel
Department of International Law and International Relations,
National University "Odesa Law Academy", Odessa, Ukraine
e-mail: tymur_korotkyi@ukr.net

N. Hendel
e-mail: n.v.hendel@gmail.com

© T.M.C. ASSER PRESS and the authors 2018
S. Sayapin and E. Tsybulenko (eds.), *The Use of Force against Ukraine and International Law*, https://doi.org/10.1007/978-94-6265-222-4_7

7.1   Introduction

A state acquires full status in international relations and international law at the moment of its recognition. This concept of international law is not an example of active and progressive development and codification, but important to the existence of international relations. Its political and legal nature does not raise doubts. While not seeking to thoroughly analyse this concept, we note its main idea: the status of a state is inextricably connected with the presence of signs of a sovereign state and its recognition. The international legal recognition of a state relates to the above-mentioned features and lawfulness of its creation. Thus, lawfulness is an important criterion, without which any entity, despite possessing separate signs of a state, could not be considered a state, neither in a legal nor in a political sense. Such entities in terms of international relations are often called "unrecognized states".

When it comes to "unrecognized" or "puppet" states, we acknowledge that, although "unrecognized" states are not regulated by international law, there is still a certain status given to them, mainly *de facto* existence. Undoubtedly, it is more of a political than a legal characteristic. At the same time, we are aware that not all of them are "unrecognized states"; but, in many cases, in the absence of basic signs of statehood,[1] we should consider them as separatist formations.[2]

On the other hand, any "unrecognized" state (such as a separatist formation) iden-tifies itself as a state, as well as seeks the recognition as and status of a full member of the international community. These questions are, to some extent, connected with each other, since it is possible to speak not only about the recognition of an "un-recognized state", but also about the non-recognition of an "unrecognized state". The actual denial of a state's status as an "unrecognized", and thus the very fact of the formation of such a semblance of a state and the recognition of the territorial integrity of a "maternal" state, on whose territory this formation takes place, rather than claiming the status of a state, is why the status of an "unrecognized state" is given.

The "unrecognized" status generates a significant number of challenges concern-ing national and international security, the instability of international relations, and massive violations of human rights. In the modern world, there have been dozens of armed conflicts based on the "struggle for self-determination". They are charac-terized by varying degrees of activity – from non-permanent terrorist acts to regular armed actions under the leadership of separatist movements, which exercise par-tial or total control over a state's territory, up to the displacement of the central government.[3] As N. A. Tsyvadze observed, in relation to the existing differences between scientists and politicians in assessing the lawfulness of decisions made, the

---

[1] The presence of orderly management structures; attributes of statehood: constitution, parliament, lawfully elected heads of state and government; domestic legal, monetary and financial systems; adequate social security of the population.

[2] Daliavska 2016, pp. 32, 37.

[3] Hewitt et al. 2008, p. 33.

problem with unrecognized states is a challenge for nations and for the entire world community. [4]

Even though, in the modern world, there has been a significant number of unrecognized states, the question concerning their legitimization and universal delegitimization remains open. However, such legitimization is possible only within the framework of the existing international legal order; but most unrecognized states have emerged in violation of the fundamental principles of international law, which makes it impossible to recognize them.[5]

Do unrecognized states seek legitimization or transformation into an actual state? The answer is not as straightforward as it seems at first glance, because the uncertainty of unrecognized states can benefit many actors, especially those states that condone separatism and are interested in creating instability zones, escalating conflict, politically and economically degrading a "maternal" state, and achieving instability in a region or globally. These geopolitical interests are usually hidden behind a "mask" of the right to self-determination, human rights, and protecting national minorities and compatriots.

Nevertheless, the unrecognized state or the separatist formation seeks international recognition. According to G. G. Shynkaretska, "for so-called unrecognized states, it is highly desirable to obtain recognition from other states, thereby enabling them to become members of the UN. After becoming a member of the UN, a state loses its unrecognized status, even if it fails to establish official relations with all members of the international community.[6] This point of view is supported by James Crawford, who refers to the UN's prerogative in recognizing a new state through "The General Assembly, whether as the successor of the League of Nations with respect to the mandate system or by the virtue of the authority to recognize the new state".[7] It should be noted that the recognition of the Donetsk and Luhansk "People's Republics" in any form by the UN and other international organizations is lacking.

> Never consider yourself not to be what others do not consider you, and then others will not think you are not what you would like to seem to them.

> Lewis Carroll, *Alice's Adventures in Wonderland*

---

[4] Tsyvadze 2010, p. 175.

[5] In of Northern Cyprus" was invalid, called upon all states "not to recognize any Cypriot State other than the Republic of Cyprus". In Resolution No. Resolution No. 541 (1983) of 18 November 1983, the UN Security Council, noting that the attempt to establish a "Turkish Republic 550 (1984) of 11 May 1984, the UN Security Council condemned and declared illegal all acts of separatism, including the so-called "ambassadorial exchange" between Turkey and the Turkish Cypriot leadership, "and once again called upon all states" not to recognize the so-called "Turkish Republic of Northern Cyprus", created as a result of separatist actions.

[6] Shinkaretskaia 2010, p. 172.

[7] Crawford 2011, p. 308.

7.2 Legitimacy of the Creation/Proclamation of the Donetsk and Luhansk People's Republics

Undoubtedly, the lawfulness of the creation/proclamation (or simply its semblance) is an important component in the emergence of an "unrecognized state", as this is the first test of the ability to be recognized by other states. This lawfulness must comply with international law, especially its principles: the principle of territorial integrity, the principle of the inviolability of borders, the principle of non-interference, the legitimate use of the principle of peoples' right to self-determination. Violation of these principles presumes the legal insignificance of entities claiming the status of an "unrecognized state". International lawfulness is closely connected with the assessment of the creation of the "unrecognized state" according to the legislation of a "maternal" state, which tests the respect for the sovereignty of the maternal country.

This test – the test for lawfulness – has not been passed in respect of the "Donetsk People's Republic" (DPR) and the "Luhansk People's Republic" (LPR), created within the Donetsk and Luhansk oblasts of Ukraine (oblast are the administrative divisions of Ukraine). The proclamation of the DPR and LPR was accompanied by numerous violations of the above-mentioned principles of international law, as well as the national legislation of Ukraine, as evidenced in numerous publications,[8] including some sections of this edition. Of course, it is not worth talking about the emergence of unrecognized states on Ukrainian territory. Thus, on the basis of this criterion, these entities should be regarded as illegal from the point of view of international law, and as such remain under the jurisdiction of Ukraine and subject to internal qualifications. To the extent, their general description, according to Ukrainian legislation, as unlawful, separatist and terrorist entities is perfectly justified.[9] Such

---

[8] Zadorozhnii 2015c, pp. 3–19; Zadorozhnii 2014b, pp. 42–69; Zadorozhnii 2014a, pp. 172–6; Zadorozhnii 2014c, pp. 129–34; Zadorozhnii 2015b, p. 712; Zadorozhnii 2015f, pp. 231–46; Zadorozhnii 2015d, pp. 119–43; Zadorozhnii 2015a, pp. 17–32; Zadorozhnii 2015e, pp. 19–30; Zadorozhnii 2016b, pp. 605–15.

[9] See, e.g., (1) Resolutions of the Verkhovna Rada of Ukraine on the Statement on the Tragic Death of People as a Result of a Terrorist Act Over the Territory of Ukraine (22 July 2014). http://zakon3. rada.gov.ua/laws/show/1596-18. Accessed 31 July 2017. (2) On the Counteraction to the Spread of the International Terrorism Supported by the Russian Federation (22 July 2014). http://zakon2.rada.gov. ua/laws/show/1597-18. Accessed 31 July 2017. (3) On the Appeal of the Verkhovna Rada of Ukraine to the United Nations, the European Parliament, the Parliamentary Assembly of the Council of Europe, the NATO Parliamentary Assembly, the OSCE Parliamentary Assembly, the GUAM Parliamentary Assembly, the National Parliaments of the World for the Recognition of the Russian Federation as an Aggressor State (27 January 2015). http://zakon2.rada.gov.ua/laws/show/129-19. Accessed 31 July 2017. (4) Resolution on the Statement of the Verkhovna Rada of Ukraine on the Recognition by Ukraine of the Jurisdiction of the International Criminal Court Regarding the Commission of Crimes Against Humanity and War Crimes by Senior Officials of the Russian Federation and the Leaders of the Terrorist Organizations "DPR" and "LPR", Which Led to Particularly Grave Consequences and the Massacre of Ukrainian Citizens (4 February 2015). http://zakon3.rada.gov.ua/laws/show/145-19. Accessed 31 July 2017. (5) Draft Law on the Recognition of Self-proclaimed Organizations "Donetsk People's Republic" and "Luhansk People's Republic" as Terrorist Organizations (10 December 2014). http://w1.c1.rada. gov.ua/pls/zweb2/webproc4_1?pf3511=52808. Accessed 31 July 2017. (6) Resolution on the Appeal

qualifications are also given to these entities by foreign countries, such as the Minister of Foreign Affairs for the Visegrad Group and the UK Foreign Secretary.[10]

The second criterion is the compliance with at least the basic attributes of a sovereign state: not only their fictitious consolidation in virtual legal acts, but their actual implementation. This statement is confirmed by Matthew Craven, who points out that "international law does possess certain criteria that condition the 'existence' of the state".[11] These criteria are contained, for example, in Article 1 of the Inter-American Convention on the Rights and Duties of States of 1933, and include: (1) a permanent population; (2) a defined territory; (3) a government; and (4) a capacity to enter relations with other states. Regarding the DPR and LPR, they do not meet the criteria of statehood.[12] Firstly, the people and the citizenship of these "people's republics" are fictions, since the population of the Donetsk and Luhansk regions are citizens of Ukraine. The international community and nearly all states recognize the territorial integrity of Ukraine and the inviolability of its borders.[13] The only legitimate government on the territory of Ukraine, including the Donetsk and Luhansk oblasts, is the Ukrainian Government. The DPR and LPR are neither recognized by other states nor international organizations.

The third criterion concerns the reaction of the international community to the emergence of an entity that self-identifies itself as a state, its recognition or non-recognition by the international community, or the denial of its very existence and the reflection of another status of this entity, such as a terrorist organization. Recognition at an international level of the territorial supremacy of the "maternal" state, its right to prevent the separatist aspirations of any group on its territory and its qualification under national law allows us to speak about the reluctance and inadmissibility concerning identifying this group as even an unrecognized state. The DPR and LPR should be considered in this regard. The PACE Resolution of 12 October 2017 states that the DPR and LPR, created with the support and under the control of the Russian Federation, have no legitimacy in accordance with Ukrainian or international law.[14] This formula, in one form or another, is reproduced in the numerous statements of foreign states and international organizations.

---

of the Verkhovna Rada of Ukraine to Parliaments of Foreign States and International Organizations on Condemning the Escalation of Armed Aggression of the Russian Federation Against Ukraine (7 February 2017). http://zakon3.rada.gov.ua/laws/show/1837-viii. Accessed 31 July 2017. (7) Draft Law on Amendments to Certain Legislative Acts of Ukraine on the Improvement of the Mechanisms for Combating Terrorism (13 February 2015). http://w1.c1.rada.gov.ua/pls/zweb2/webproc4_1?pf3511=54044. Accessed 31 July 2017. (8) 'The General Prosecutor's Office of Ukraine recognized the self-proclaimed Donetsk People's Republic (DPR) and Luhansk People's Republic (LPR) terrorist organizations'; see LIGABusinessInform 2014.

[10] Interfax-Ukraine 2014.

[11] Craven 1998, p. 159.

[12] Zadorozhnii 2016c, pp. 7–14.

[13] See, e.g., General Assembly of the United Nations 2014; General Assembly of the United Nations 2017; Security Council of the United Nations 2015; European Parliament 2015; OSCE Parliamentary Assembly 2017; U.S. Department of State 2017.

[14] TSN.UA 2016.

The plan, to be sure, was excellent: simple and clear, it couldn't be better. It had only one drawback: it was completely unknown how to implement it.

Lewis Carroll, *Alice's Adventures in Wonderland*

7.3   Recognition of the Donetsk and Luhansk People's Republics

Regarding the process of recognizing new entities, of importance is the legal reaction of existing subjects of international law on the international legal status of such entities and, as a result, their international legal recognition.[15] Therefore, we will consider the general issues concerning the recognition of unrecognized states and the reaction of the international community to the proclamation of the DPR and LPR.

It should be noted that there have been certain dynamic attempts to endow the DPR and LPR with elements of subjects of international law, which are related to the geopolitical interests of the Russian Federation. Therefore, actions aimed at acquiring the status of subjects of international law relate to the external influence and the use of these entities as pawns on a geopolitical chessboard. The period 2014–2015 saw an attempt to create Novorossiya; in 2015–2016, there was an attempt to integrate the DPR and LPR as "Trojan horses" into the political and legal space of Ukraine; and 2017 saw an attempt by the Russian Federation to increase the legal capacity of the occupied territories by recognizing "passports" and other DPR and LPR documents.[16]

Extrapolating the general provisions concerning a desire of some entities to claim the status of a state, in the situation concerning the DPR and LPR, we should note that these entities have declared themselves as independent states, along with asserting a desire to establish relations with other states[17] and international organizations. In 2014, the LPR turned to 11 states (Armenia, Belarus, Venezuela, Kazakhstan, China, Cuba, Moldova, Nicaragua, the Russian Federation, Serbia and Syria), two unrecognized states (Abkhazia and South Ossetia) and even to subjects of the Russian Federation (the Republic of Ingushetia, the Chechen Republic),[18] inviting them to

---

[15] Mytsyk 2002, pp. 344–5.

[16] Oreshkin 2017; Voice of America 2017.

[17] Abkhazia, South Ossetia, the Nagorno-Karabakh Republic and Transnistria have recognized the independence of and closely cooperated with each other for a long time; see PanARMENIAN.Net 2010. The Donetsk People's Republic has recognized the independence of Abkhazia and South Ossetia; see RUSSIAN NEWSPAPER 2015.

[18] The document was addressed to: the head of the Government of Ingushetia, Abubakar Malsagov; the Chairman of the National Assembly of the Republic of Ingushetia, Magomed Tatriyev; the head of Chechnya, Ramzan Kadyrov; and the Speaker of the Parliament of the Chechen Republic, Dukuvas Abdurakhmanov. The appeal, in particular, stated the following: "The Supreme Council of the Luhansk People's Republic highly appreciates the activities of the Republic of Ingushetia [in another letter, the Chechen Republic]. Since the establishment of the LPR, our citizens were firm in their intention to build an independent state and consistent in their desire to share the fate of the Republic of Ingushetia [the Chechen Republic]." See News of Ingushetia Bakdar 2014.

recognize its independence. The text of the appeal was published on 11 June 2014 by the press service of the LPR.[19] On 22 May 2014, the so-called Supreme Council of the DPR also decided to appeal to the Russian Federation to recognize its independence.[20] However, despite these attempts, the DPR and LPR have still not been recognized by any state. The recognition of their independence by South Ossetia[21] is rather difficult to consider, given the lack of recognition of the latter. South Ossetia opened its diplomatic mission on the territory of the DPR and LPR.[22] On 11 May 2017, the DPR and South Ossetia signed a protocol on the establishment of diplomatic relations[23] and a treaty on friendship, cooperation and mutual assistance.[24] These diplomatic relations between South Ossetia and the so-called "people's republics" represent the only form of recognition for these entities at an international law. All these examples are absurd from a logic perspective, as all actors involved are unrecognized states and have no features of subjects of international law. This situation is perfectly captured in this quote from Lewis Carroll: "No matter how she tried, she could not find there a shadow of meaning, although all the words were completely understandable to her."

A number of states made statements of protest regarding the opening of pseudo-diplomatic missions by the DPR and LPR on their territories, such as the Czech

---

[19] The appeals on behalf of the Supreme Council (Parliament) of the LPR asked addressees "to decide on the recognition of the LPR as a sovereign independent state". Appeals were addressed to countries such as Russia, Abkhazia, Belarus, South Ossetia, Ingushetia, Chechnya, Kazakhstan, the Transnistrian Moldavian Republic, Armenia, Syria, Serbia, Venezuela, China, Cuba and Nicaragua; see RIA News 2014. In the case of Russia, the wording read: "The Supreme Council of the LPR, city councils, regional councils of people's deputies, public associations are appealing to the Russian Federation to decide on the recognition of the LPR as a sovereign independent state." Similar statements were sent to Armenia, Belarus, Kazakhstan, China, Serbia, Venezuela, Cuba and Nicaragua. The text of the appeals was published on 11 June by the press service of the LPR; see TASS News Agency 2014. For the full text, see Luhansk Online 2014.

[20] On 12 May, the self-proclaimed DPR addressed the Russian Federation with a request to include it in its composition: "We, the people of the Donetsk People's Republic, according to the results of the referendum held on May 11, 2014, and based on the Declaration of Independence of the DPR, announce that, from now on, the Donetsk People's Republic is a sovereign state. Based on the will of the people of the DPR and for the restoration of historical justice, we ask the Russian Federation to consider the entry of the DPR into the Russian Federation." The authorship of this statement was credited to the Chairman of the Presidium of the DPR's Supreme Council, Denis Pushylin. See TASS News Agency 2014.

[21] On 25 June 2014, the President of the South Ossetia, Leonid Tibilov, signed a decree on the recognition of the sovereignty and independence of the LPR, supported by the Parliament of the Republic, which stated: "Taking into account the will of the people and the appeal of the Supreme Council of the Donetsk People's Republic to the President of the South Ossetia to recognize the sovereignty of the Donetsk People's Republic, supported by the Parliament of the Republic of South Ossetia, I resolve: (1) To recognize the Donetsk People's Republic as a sovereign independent state." See Russian Legal Portal 2014; Russia Today 2014.

[22] Lenta.ru 2015.

[23] RBC.ru 2017.

[24] RIA News 2017.

Republic,[25] Greece,[26] Italy[27] and France.[28] The Ostrava Regional Court of the Czech Republic decided to initiate a procedure for the elimination of the "Representative Centre of the DPR" in the Czech Republic, while, on 28 June 2017, it decided to close down the self-proclaimed Honorary Consulate of the Donetsk People's Republic, recognizing its activity as illegal.[29] The head of the Foreign Ministry, Lubomír Zaorálek, said that the creation of this association contravened the norms of international law, as mentioned in the Constitution of the Czech Republic, namely, the obligation to respect the territorial integrity of other states.[30] These attempts to set up pseudo-diplomatic and pseudo-consular institutions of the DPR and LPR, contrary to the rules of the law of external relations and internal law, are null and void in terms of both international and domestic law, since they have no legal grounds or consequences.

Moreover, there is a reverse situation: many states claim the territorial integrity of Ukraine,[31] thus excluding even the occurrence of unrecognized states on Ukrainian territory. This fact should be interpreted in favour of the qualification of the so-called DPR and LPR as separatist entities.

> If you kept the small rules, you could break the big ones.

> George Orwell, *Nineteen Eighty-four*

7.4 The Russian Federation's Position on Recognizing the Donetsk and Luhansk People's Republics

The Russian Federation holds a separate position, as far as it can be recognized as a party to the conflict, as well as the state whose actions are considered to be armed aggression against Ukraine, alongside controlling anti-government armed groups and leaders of the DPR and LPR.[32] In the sense of defining the status of the so-called "people's republics", the Russian Federation, as already been indicated, is adopting a stance related to its own geopolitical interests and desires, which substantially violate the basic principles and norms of international law.

At the beginning of Russian aggression against Ukraine in 2014, statements and acts of Russian state authorities concerning the events in Ukraine were mostly

---

[25] 112 Ukraine 2017; Radio Liberty 2017a.

[26] Ukrainian Pravda 2017; Greek Reporter 2017.

[27] EuroPravda 2016.

[28] EuroPravda 2017a; Stopfake.org 2017.

[29] EuroPravda 2017c; The Prague Daily Monitor 2017; Radio Liberty 2017a.

[30] EuroPravda 2017d; The Prague Daily Monitor 2017.

[31] General Assembly of the United Nations 2014.

[32] Zadorozhnii 2015c, pp. 3–19; Zadorozhnii 2015b, p. 712; Zadorozhnii 2016a, p. 455; Korynevych 2015, p. 78; Reeves and Wallace 2015, pp. 361–401; Parliamentary Assembly of the Council of Europe 2016b; Parliamentary Assembly of the Council of Europe 2016a.

contradictory and inconsistent. Now and then, there were widely circulated publications[33] on the Internet that the Russian Federation *de facto*[34] recognized the DPR and LPR, because it used terms "DPR" and "LPR" in the resolutions on a criminal case initiated by the Main Investigation Department of the Investigative Committee of the Russian Federation.[35] It should be noted that, in accordance with international practice and Russian legislation, the Investigative Committee[36] (as well as any similar body in another state) has no authority to carry out external relations and does not bear responsibility (positive) for the implementation of the foreign policy of a state.[37] Moreover, further reports from the Main Investigation Department of the Investigative Committee referred to mentioned events in "South-eastern Ukraine", which contradict the previous statement.[38] These circumstances, however, do not exclude the responsibility of the Russian Federation for actions undertaken by its public authority. Thus, the Russian Federation, as represented by the Investigative Committee, is violating the principles of territorial integrity, non-interference in internal affairs, international obligations to combat terrorism, as well as the provisions of Articles 1–3 of the Treaty on Friendship, Cooperation and Partnership between Ukraine and the Russian Federation of 31 May 1997. Using the names of terrorist organizations as unrecognized territories in the official document issued by the Investigative Committee could also be interpreted as a violation of international law on the part of the Russian Federation according to Article 4 of the Articles on the Responsibility of States for Internationally Wrongful Acts.

Furthermore, the rhetoric of the Ministry of Foreign Affairs of the Russian Federation is far from consistent as well. According to the Department of Information and Press in the Russian Federation's Ministry of Foreign Affairs, regarding the

---

[33] "02/06/2014 On the official site of the Investigative Committee of Russia there was a message, which allows us to conclude that Russia has actually recognized the DPR and the LPR. Republics in the message were named, not areas, but the republics. Moreover, Ukraine, the DPR and the LPR were listed through commas as independent entities of international law"; see, Zamlelova 2014. "The Investigative Committee of Russia *de jure* recognized the Donetsk and Luhansk People's Republics as states"; see Pandora's Box 2014. "In fact, today, Russia *de facto* recognized the Luhansk and the Donetsk republics, and its own jurisdiction over the situation"; see SUMMER56 2014.

[34] "The *de facto* recognition of a new government is being formed in certain statements of competent government bodies, in the signing of agreements of a limited or temporary nature, and in maintaining relations with the new government in current trade, financial and other matters"; see Mytsyk 2002, p. 360.

[35] "Regarding still unidentified servicemen of the Armed Forces of Ukraine, as well as persons from the 'National Guard of Ukraine' and the 'Right Sector', involved in shelling the cities of Slavyansk, Kramatorsk, Donetsk, Mariupol and other settlements proclaimed by the Donetsk and Luhansk People's Republics, a crime is envisaged as per Part 1 of Article 356 of the Criminal Code (the use of prohibited means and methods of warfare)"; see Investigative Committee of the Russian Federation 2014b. "During this operation, during the shelling of the cities of Slavyansk, Kramatorsk, Donetsk, Mariupol and other settlements proclaimed by the Donetsk and Luhansk people's republics..."; see Investigative Committee of the Russian Federation 2014c.

[36] The State Duma 2010.

[37] "Recognition is carried out by a body competent, in accordance with the constitutional right of this state, to represent it in external relations"; see Mytsyk 2002, p. 346.

[38] Investigative Committee of the Russian Federation 2014a.

dismissal of Organization for Security and Cooperation in Europe (OSCE) observers in the east of Ukraine, "the direct appeal of the OSCE mission to representatives of the Donetsk and Luhansk People's Republics had a significant role, as they held direct negotiations with individuals detaining the OSCE observers".[39] However, in July 2014, in the content of the Daily Information Bulletin of the Ministry of Foreign Affairs of the Russian Federation, neither the DPR nor the LPR were mentioned in any form. At the briefing, Russian Foreign Minister Sergey Lavrov said that, "without a genuine desire to consider and reflect on the agreements in the interests of all citizens of Ukraine and all its regions, including the Donetsk and Luhansk regions and the south-east as a whole, relying on a political settlement, which would be stable, is impossible".[40] In other words, the territorial integrity of Ukraine is recognized. The names of the so-called DPR and LPR in these statements, as well as other names of separatist formations, were not used. Regarding illegal armed formations, the term "insurgents" was used.[41]

The official position of the Russian Federation, as of 2014, was expressed in statements of its Ministry of Foreign Affairs and speeches of its Foreign Minister,[42,43] in which where actions in south-eastern Ukraine were mentioned, but not in the so-called DPR and LPR. In public speeches and meetings with European diplomats, Russian diplomats used the expression "internal Ukrainian crisis", thus rejecting the presence of independent actors in the form of the DPR and LPR: "Today it is necessary to concentrate on the unconditional and immediate termination to the bloodshed and the use of force, and start a dialogue involving all regions of Ukraine to agree on the future of this state."[44,45]

Thus, in the reply of the Russian Federation Minister of Foreign Affairs to the question about Russian mass media reporting on the "Ukrainian crisis", Lavrov talked about the events in the Donetsk and Luhansk regions and the situation in the south-east of Ukraine. The DPR and LPR were not mentioned at all, while separatists were referred to as "insurgents" and "rebels"; negotiations "between the Ukrainian parties", however, were mentioned.[46] According to the aforementioned Department of Information and Press, at the start of OSCE observers' work at the "Donetsk" and "Hukovo" checkpoints on the Russia-Ukraine border: "On 29 July, the first

---

[39] Daily newsletter of the Ministry of Foreign Affairs of the Russian Federation 2014a.

[40] Daily newsletter of the Ministry of Foreign Affairs of the Russian Federation 2014b.

[41] Ibid.

[42] Ministry of Foreign Affairs of the Russian Federation 2014.

[43] Daily newsletter of the Ministry of Foreign Affairs of the Russian Federation 2014c.

[44] Daily newsletter of the Ministry of Foreign Affairs of the Russian Federation 2014d.

[45] "The main attention will be paid to the resolution of the acute domestic political crisis in Ukraine, the task of stopping bloodshed and realizing the mechanisms of an inclusive political dialogue in this country", commentary in the Daily newsletter of the Ministry of Foreign Affairs of the Russian Federation 2014e.

[46] Daily newsletter of the Ministry of Foreign Affairs of the Russian Federation 2014f.

OSCE observers arrived in the Rostov region and began to work at the 'Donetsk' and 'Hukovo checkpoints on the border with Ukraine."[47]

In the period 2015–2017, the rhetoric from the Russian public authorities and the statements of officials about the DPR and LPR fluctuated along with the "party line". That is, the position of the Russian Federation was centred on purely tactical issues, and on exploiting the recognition/non-recognition of the so-called "people's republic" for influence over Ukraine and blackmailing the international community. Particularly indicative was the official reaction of the Russian Federation to the statement of Alexander Zakharchenko, the leader of the DPR, regarding the creation of Malorossiya.[48] These actions by the Kremlin's puppet may be characterized as excessive, resulting in a negative reaction, as well as uncoordinated and inconsistent with the current interests of the Russian Federation.

In general, these statements and acts demonstrate how the DPR and LPR are only used as pawns and sacrificed without hesitation in the messy geopolitical game of the Russian Federation, whose aim is to trample over the existing international order; a game, in which separatist formations act as hooks, holding sovereign states in the orbit of the Russian Federation. In this game, the "status" of quasi-state structures provides an attempt to abuse the rules of recognition, rules that are used only in the international legal system as a whole, along with other principles and norms of international law.

An important example of such abuses of international law is the "Presidential Decree on the Recognition by the Russian Federation of Documents and Registration Numbers of Vehicles Issued to Citizens of Ukraine and Stateless Persons Permanently Residing in the Territories of Certain Districts of the Donetsk and Luhansk Regions of Ukraine". This decree represented an acknowledgement by the Russian Federation of "valid identity documents, documents on education and (or) qualifications, birth certificates, certificate of conclusion (termination) of marriage, change of name, death, vehicle registration certificates, registration plates of transport assets issued by the relevant bodies (organizations), operating in the mentioned areas, to citizens of Ukraine and stateless persons permanently residing in these territories" (Para 1a of the decree).

This decree includes a clear violation of the general principles of international law and Ukrainian legislation. Nothing in international humanitarian law, the reference to which is contained in the preamble to the decree, allows for accepting anything that is illegal from the point of view of international law. Furthermore, international humanitarian law does not recognize documents of separatist entities, which in the decree are referred to as "issued by the relevant authorities (organizations) actually operating in the territories of the mentioned areas". The decree itself stresses the absence of any subjectivity concerning the DPR and LPR, insofar as they were hardly mentioned in it. As we can see from its text, the decree mentions "separate districts of the Donetsk and Luhansk regions of Ukraine"; this once again confirms that this document violates the principle of non-interference in the internal

---

[47] Daily newsletter of the Ministry of Foreign Affairs of the Russian Federation 2014g.

[48] Apostrof 2017.

affairs of Ukraine.[49] The decree reaffirms the deliberate inconsistency of the Russian Federation's position on the status of the DPR and LPR, and its attempt to justify internationally wrongful acts by referring to abstract rules of international law. That is, the Russian Federation seeks the legitimacy of unlawful actions in international law, whose principles these actions have grossly violated.

This is why the adoption of this decree, an internal action on the part of the Russian Federation, has received a negative response from the international community, further indicating its international unlawfulness. The issue concerning violations of international law due to Russia's recognition of documents issued by the DPR and LPR was considered on 21 February 2017 at the 7,886th meeting of the UN Security Council. The position taken by the US was thus: "The recent recognition by Russia of so-called passports and other illegal documents distributed in the Donetsk and Luhansk regions of Ukraine by the separatists supported by Russia is another direct challenge to the efforts to establish peace in the east of Ukraine."[50] Meanwhile, the representative from France stated: "We also regret the decision of the Russian authorities to recognize the official documents adopted by authorities of *de facto* districts of Donetsk and Luhansk regions, which is contrary to the spirit of the Minsk Agreements."[51] However, the Russian Federation argued that "there is nothing wrong with the recognition of documents issued by the authorities in the Donetsk and Luhansk regions, which are not controlled by Ukrainian government".[52]

Lamberto Zannier, Secretary General of the OSCE, condemned Russia's recognition of DPR and LPR "documents".[53] In the resolution, Restoration of Ukraine's Sovereignty and Integrity, adopted on 9 July2017, the Parliamentary Assembly of the OSCE called on the Russian Federation "to revoke its decisions on the recognition of so-called 'documents' (passports, driving licences, birth certificates etc.) issued by illegal entities in certain areas of the Donetsk and Luhansk regions of Ukraine and on the full circulation of Russian currency in the temporarily occupied areas of Donbas region of Ukraine, and to return seized Ukrainian local, state, and private economic entities into Ukraine's jurisdiction".[54] In an interview with Radio "Svoboda", Zannier said that "Russia's decision to recognize certain 'documents' issued by separatist institutions in the occupied part of the Donbas would undermine the ability to strengthen the armistice". The OSCE Secretary General also emphasized that the decision to recognize such 'documents' "of course, actually means… recognition of those, who issue these 'documents'".[55]

The Secretary General of the North Atlantic Alliance, Jens Stoltenberg, also expressed concern regarding violations of the ceasefire in the south-east of Ukraine and criticized the Russian Federation's decision to recognize passports issued by

---

[49] The President of the Russian Federation 2017.

[50] Security Council of the United Nations 2017.

[51] Ibid.

[52] Ibid.

[53] Radio Liberty 2017b.

[54] OSCE Parliamentary Assembly 2017.

[55] ZIK.UA 2017.

the self-proclaimed DPR and LPR.[56] In turn, the Speaker of the European External Action Service of the EU, Maja Kocijančič, said that the decree on Russia's recognition of documents issued in the "republics" does not correspond with the spirit of the Minsk Agreements[57].

Ukraine's authorities also reacted to these events. Ukrainian President Petro Poroshenko responded as follows: "For me, this is further proof of the Russian occupation and Russian violation of international law."[58] According to Oleksandr Turchynov, Secretary of the National Security and Defence Council of Ukraine, by signing the decree, Putin had legally recognized quasi-state terrorist groups and left "the Minsk process". [59]

Foreign states also reacted to the Russian President's decree. The Polish Ministry of Foreign Affairs stated that the Russian Federation's decision to recognize documents issued by so-called separatists in parts of the Donetsk and Lugansk regions, not controlled by the Ukrainian Government, was another step that undermined the sovereignty and territorial integrity of Ukraine. "Despite numerous declarations of readiness for a constructive resolution of the conflict, Russia has repeatedly demonstrated that its goal is to destabilize Ukraine, but not the fulfilment of commitments envisaged by the Minsk Agreements," stressed the Polish Foreign Ministry.[60] The French Ministry of Foreign Affairs noted that "France has considered the decree of the President of the Russian Federation on the recognition of official documents issued by the actual authorities of some districts of Donetsk and Luhansk regions and regrets this decision, which is not in line with the spirit of the Minsk agreement".[61] A similar position was adopted by the US,[62] Australia,[63] Germany,[64] Belarus[65] and other states. The *Chargé d'Affaires* of Ukraine to the Republic of Macedonia, Rostislav Palagusynets, pointed out that Putin's issuance of the decree on recognition of pseudo-documents issued by fake quasi-state entities, namely, the DPR and LPR, was nothing more than another violation of the state sovereignty and territorial integrity of Ukraine and a demonstration of Moscow's intention to continue escalation of the armed conflict that began in Eastern Ukraine.[66] Thus, a legal action on the part of the President of the Russian Federation became an act that substantially violated the basic principles of international law, for which the Russian Federation would be held responsible in accordance with the general rules of such law.

---

[56] NEWSru 2017.

[57] Korrespondent.net 2017.

[58] UNIAN news agency 2017; ZIK.UA 2017.

[59] ZIK.UA 2017.

[60] Online Express 2017.

[61] KP.UA 2017b.

[62] Radio Liberty 2017c.

[63] Ukrinform 2017.

[64] EuroPravda 2017b; Deutsche Welle 2017.

[65] KP.UA 2017a.

[66] Embassy of Ukraine in the Republic of Macedonia 2017.

7.5 The International Community's Position on the Donetsk and Luhansk People's Republics

The attempt at recognition within the framework of the UN and other international organizations of the so-called DPR and LPR is also doomed to fail. This is evidenced by the words of the former UN Secretary-General U Thant: "The UN position is unambiguous. As an international organization, the United Nations had never recognized, does not recognize, and, I believe, will never recognize the lawful separation of part of the territory of its member under the pretext of self-determination."[67] However, the LPR made such an attempt by addressing UN Secretary-General Ban Ki-moon with a "request to consider recognition of its statehood – its natural right".[68]

The situation is exactly the opposite: the UN and other international organizations[69] consistently recognize the territorial integrity and sovereignty of Ukraine. In this regard, we should note that the following, for example, refer to the Donetsk and Luhansk regions of Ukraine:[70] Resolution of the Security Council 2202 (2015) on Complex of Measures to Implement the Minsk Agreements (12 February 2015);[71] Report of the UN Office of the High Commissioner for Human Rights (OHCHR) on the Human Rights Situation in Ukraine (16 November 2016 and 15 February 2017);[72] Report of the UN OHCHR on the Human Rights Situation in Ukraine (16 February-15 May 2017);[73] Report of the UN Office for the Coordination of Humanitarian Issues on the Situation in the Donetsk and Luhansk Regions of Ukraine (17 and 25 July 2014); Report of the UN OHCHR on the Status of Human Rights in Ukraine (6 May-15 August 2016);[74] Humanitarian Bulletin of the UN Office for the Coordination of Humanitarian Questions in Ukraine (1–30 June 2016,[75] 1–31 August 2016,[76] 1–30 September 2016,[77] 1 October–31 December 2016).[78] Furthermore, OSCE resolutions and documents refer to the Donetsk and Luhansk regions of Ukraine, for example, in the Resolution on the Restoration of Ukraine's Sovereignty and Territorial Integrity (5–9 July 2017).[79] Meanwhile, the Conclusions of the EU Council

---

[67] 'Speech on the attempts to divide Biafrey from Nigeria': see Emerson 1971, p. 460.

[68] UNIAN News Agency 2014.

[69] Office of the United Nations High Commissioner for Human Rights 2014a; Office of the United Nations High Commissioner for Human Rights 2014b; Council of Europe Parliamentary Assembly 2014.

[70] United Nations Office for the Coordination of Humanitarian Affairs 2014a; United Nations Office for the Coordination of Humanitarian Affairs 2014b.

[71] Security Council of the United Nations 2015.

[72] Office of the United Nations High Commissioner for Human Rights 2017a.

[73] Office of the United Nations High Commissioner for Human Rights 2017b.

[74] Office of the United Nations High Commissioner for Human Rights 2016.

[75] United Nations Office for the Coordination of Humanitarian Affairs 2016a.

[76] United Nations Office for the Coordination of Humanitarian Affairs 2016b.

[77] United Nations Office for the Coordination of Humanitarian Affairs 2016c.

[78] United Nations Office for the Coordination of Humanitarian Affairs 2016d.

[79] OSCE Parliamentary Assembly 2017.

on Foreign Affairs on Ukraine refer to the de-escalation of the conflict in the east of Ukraine,[80] EU statements confirm support for the territorial integrity, sovereignty and unity of Ukraine,[81] and resolutions of the European Parliament indicate a military situation in the districts of Luhansk and Donetsk regions.[82]

Moreover, in most cases, the DPR and LPR are identified not as unrecognized states (the DPR and the LPR, the representatives of the DPR and LPR, the governments of the DPR and LPR, i.e., not as an entity, even an illegal one, with a certain level of institutionalization), but as an "armed opposition groups",[83] "armed groups",[84] "rebels",[85] "separatist rebels",[86] "pro-Russian separatists",[87] "armed separatists"[88] and "insurgent fighters".[89] Thus, the international community, in the form of statements made by international organizations, does not even recognize the status of unrecognized states with regard to the DPR and LPR, primarily because of the international wrongfulness of their creation.

Since the beginning of the conflict, other states, both jointly and separately, have expressed support for the sovereignty and territorial integrity of Ukraine. In a Joint Declaration by Ministers of Foreign Affairs of Germany, the Russian Federation, Ukraine and France of 2 July 2014 "reaffirm[ed] their commitment to establishing lasting peace and stability in Ukraine. In this context, they emphasize the need for rapid agreement and compliance by all parties involved with a permanent ceasefire to put an end to violence in **Ukraine** [authors' own emphasis]."[90]

Australia claimed that its position regarding the sovereignty and territorial integrity of Ukraine is immutable.[91] The Czech Republic has declared its full respect for the territorial integrity and sovereignty of Ukraine, while considering the Russian annexation of Crimea and the presence of several thousand troops from the Russian armed forces in the east of Ukraine as flagrant violations of international law and serious threats to peace and stability in Europe.[92] The official representative of the Greek Foreign Ministry, Strátos Efthymíou, stated that "any actions that undermine the territorial integrity of Ukraine are in sharp contrast to the established position of the

---

[80] Ministry of Foreign Affairs of Ukraine 2014e.

[81] Korrespondent.net 2017.

[82] European Parliament 2015.

[83] UN News Centre 2014a.

[84] Security Council of the United Nations 2014; UN News Centre 2014b.

[85] Ministry of Foreign Affairs of Ukraine 2014d.

[86] Ibid.

[87] Mirror of the Week, Ukraine 2014c; Raidió Teilifís Éireann 2014; Mirror of the Week, Ukraine 2014a; The Telegraph 2016; Mirror of the Week, Ukraine 2014b.

[88] Ministry of Foreign Affairs of Ukraine 2014e.

[89] Ministry of Foreign Affairs of Ukraine 2014d.

[90] Embassy of the Russian Federation in the United Kingdom of Great Britain and Northern Ireland 2014.

[91] Ukrinform 2017; Embassy of Ukraine in Australia 2017; Ukraine News (UAZMI) 2017.

[92] 112 Ukraine 2017; The Prague Daily Monitor 2017; Radio Liberty 2017a.

Greek government".[93] The position of France remains loyal to Ukraine's sovereignty within its recognized borders.[94]

In some cases, supporters of the DPR and LPR have attempted to open "diplomatic institutions" on their behalf in several states. An analysis of the bizarre nature of these attempts, from the point of view of international law, has been presented above, but the attitude of foreign countries to these attempts to promote the DPR and LPR by opening fake "diplomatic institutions" deserves attention.

7.6   Conclusion

The concept of recognition as a legal requirement in international law is a rather conservative and politicized phenomenon. However, its functioning and implementation largely depend on external factors, including the level of development and the basic principles of international law in general, as well as the trends and challenges of international relations. Therefore, the political and legal nature of this concept has not only an internal nature (sources, the procedure of decision-making for recognition), but also an external nature, which is determined by the level of development of international law and international relations. Examples of the first group of factors of such influence are the emergence of basic principles of international law, the implementation of provisions of the UN Charter as criteria for recognition, and the use of international organizations as a platform for discussing specific cases of recognition. The second group includes processes of decolonization in the second half of the 20th century, the emergence of international terrorism and its institutionalization, and the application of hybrid methods as the dominant means of influence in international relations.

Changes in modern international law, along with the consolidation of imperative basic principles, have led to the possibility of abusing these principles for unlawful purposes, as well as creating and utilizing quasi-state entities to destabilize sovereign states and influence their domestic and foreign policies. These processes have intensified in the post-Soviet space to become a "hallmark" of the Russian Federation to keep sovereign states that found independence after the USSR's collapse within Russia's political orbit.

To ensure the external legalization of these actions to the maximum possible extent, particular norms and concepts of international law are used (the concept of recognition, the principle of self-determination of nations), but they are used beyond their connection with other principles and norms of international law, contrary to their essence, the principle of the rule of law, and international legality. These actions violate the modern international order and may be qualified as an abusive form of international law with illegal intent.

---

[93] Ukrainian Pravda 2017; Greek Reporter 2017.

[94] EuroPravda 2017a; Stopfake.org 2017.

This phenomenon is not unique to state practice of the 20th century; but, due to the democratization of international relations, the growing influence of society on foreign policy decision-making albeit with an insignificant degree of international legal awareness, and changes in the possibilities of informational influence on the public, international law is applied in a distorted form as a kind of informational weapon, which is used at different levels, namely, national, bilateral and multilateral, within the framework of international organizations in order to substantiate and justify actions that contradict international law.[95] This is one of the manifestations of the phenomenon, which, in modern discourse, is called a "hybrid war".

The attempt to recognize the so-called DPR and LPR illustrates precisely these examples. Their creation, contrary to international law and in violation of its fundamental principles, makes the attempts to legalize these internationally unlawful entities in the international arena untenable. For the same reason, the DPR and LPR cannot claim the status of unrecognized states: they have neither legal nor factual grounds to be named as such. These conclusions are the result of both international legal analysis and a generalization of the position adopted by the international community. Therefore, Ukraine's official position regarding the DPR and LPR, based on the qualification of these entities as terrorist organizations,[96] corresponds to the internationally recognized position regarding the territorial integrity and sovereignty of Ukraine over the whole of its territory within internationally recognized borders, including the territory of the Donetsk and Luhansk regions.

References

112 Ukraine (2017) Chehija zajavila o nelegitimnosti ljubyh predlozhenij ot "DNR" i "LNR" [The Czech Republic declared the illegitimacy of any proposals from the "DPR" and "LPR"]. https://112.ua/politika/chehiya-zayavila-o-nelegitimnosti-lyubyh-predlozheniy-ot-dnr-i-lnr-401855.html. Accessed 31 July 2017

Apostrof (2017) Glavar' DNR sdelal neozhidannoe zajavlenie o sozdanii "Malorossii" [The leader of DPR made an unexpected statement about the creation of "Malorossia"]. https://apostrophe.ua/news/politics/regional-policy/2017-07-18/glavari-dnr-i-lnr-sdelali-neozhidannoe-zayavlenie-o-sozdanii-malorossii/101806. Accessed 31 July 2017

Council of Europe Parliamentary Assembly (2014) The Humanitarian situation in Ukraine, Doc. 13550. http://assembly.coe.int/nw/xml/XRef/Xref-XML2HTML-en.asp?fileid=21044&lang=en. Accessed 31 July 2017

Craven MCR (1998) The Problem of State Succession and the Identity of States under International Law. European Journal of International Law 9(1):142–162

---

[95] Koval and Korotkyi 2014, pp. 875–83.

[96] Ministry of Foreign Affairs of Ukraine 2014b; Ministry of Foreign Affairs of Ukraine 2014c; Ministry of Foreign Affairs of Ukraine 2014a; "The General Prosecutor's Office of Ukraine, for their participation in the activities of terrorist organizations of the so-called 'Donetsk People's Republic' and 'Luhansk People's Republic, has declared the aforementioned persons as suspected of committing a criminal offense under Part 1 of Article 258-3 of the Criminal Code of Ukraine (Creation of a Terrorist Organization)"; see General Prosecutor's Office of Ukraine 2014.

Crawford J (2011) The Creation of States in International Law, 2nd edn. Oxford University Press, Oxford

Daily newsletter of the Ministry of Foreign Affairs of the Russian Federation (2014) Kommentarij Departamenta informacii i pechati MID Rossii v svjazi s osvobozhdeniem na Vostoke Ukrainy nabljudatelej OBSE 28 ijunja [Commentary of the MFA Information and Press Department regarding the release of OSCE observers in the East of Ukraine on June 28]. http://www.mid.ru/bl.nsf/. Accessed 31 July 2017

Daily newsletter of the Ministry of Foreign Affairs of the Russian Federation (2014) Brifing ministra inostrannyh del Rossii S. V. Lavrova dlja predstavitelej inostrannyh i rossijskih SMI [Briefing of Russian Foreign Minister Sergey V. Lavrov for representatives of foreign and Russian mass media]. http://www.mid.ru/bl.nsf/. Accessed 31 July 2017

Daily newsletter of the Ministry of Foreign Affairs of the Russian Federation (2014) Zajavlenie MID Rossii v svjazi s prodolzhajushhimisja karatel'nymi operacijami kievskih vlastej na Jugo-Vostoke Ukrainy [Statement by the Russian Foreign Ministry in connection with the ongoing punitive operations of the Kyiv authorities in the South-East of Ukraine]. http://www.mid.ru/bl.nsf/. Accessed 31 July 2017

Daily newsletter of the Ministry of Foreign Affairs of the Russian Federation (2014) Vystuplenie i otvety na voprosy SMI ministra inostrannyh del Rossii S. V. Lavrova v hode sovmestnoj press-konferencii po itogam peregovorov s ministrom inostrannyh del Pol'shi R. Sikorskim i ministrom inostrannyh del FRG F.-V. Shtajnmajerom [Speech and answers to questions by Russian Foreign Minister Sergey V. Lavrov at a joint press conference following negotiations with Polish Foreign Minister R. Sikorski and Foreign Minister of Germany F.-V. Steinmeier]. http://www.mid.ru/bl.nsf/. Accessed 31 July 2017

Daily newsletter of the Ministry of Foreign Affairs of the Russian Federation (2014) Kommentarij Departamenta informacii i pechati MID Rossii v svjazi so vstrechej ministrov inostrannyh del Rossii, Germanii i Pol'shi [Commentary of the MFA Information and Press Department regarding the meeting of the Ministers for Foreign Affairs of Russia, Germany and Poland]. http://www.mid.ru/bl.nsf/. Accessed 31 July 2017

Daily newsletter of the Ministry of Foreign Affairs of the Russian Federation (2014) Otvet ministra inostrannyh del Rossii S. V. Lavrova na vopros rossijskih SMI po tematike ukrainskogo krizisa [Russian Foreign Minister Sergey Lavrov's response to a question from Russian media on the subject of the Ukrainian crisis]. http://www.mid.ru/bl.nsf/. Accessed 31 July 2017

Daily newsletter of the Ministry of Foreign Affairs of the Russian Federation (2014) Kommentarij Departamenta informacii i pechati MID Rossii o nachale raboty nabljudatelej OBSE na punktah propuska «Doneck» i «Gukovo» na rossijsko-ukrainskoj granice [Commentary of the MFA Information and Press Department regarding beginning of work of OSCE observers at the checkpoints "Donetsk" and "Gukovo" on the Russian-Ukrainian border]. http://www.mid.ru/bl.nsf/. Accessed 31 July 2017

Daliavska T (2016) Fenomen nevyznanykh derzhav: politolohichnyi analiz [The phenomenon of unrecognized states: political analysis]. National Academy of Sciences of Ukraine, Koretsky Institute of State and Law, Kiev

Deutsche Welle (2017) Germany: 'Unacceptable' that Russia accepts separatist Ukraine passports. http://www.dw.com/en/germany-unacceptable-that-russia-accepts-separatist-ukraine-passports/a-37638344. Accessed 31 July 2017

Embassy of the Russian Federation in the United Kingdom of Great Britain and Northern Ireland (2014) Sovmestnaja deklaracija ministrov inostrannyh del Germanii, Rossii, Ukrainy i Francii, Berlin, 2 ijulja 2014 g [Joint Declaration of the Ministers for Foreign Affairs of Germany, Russia, Ukraine and France, Berlin, July 2, 2014]. http://rus.rusemb.org.uk/foreignpolicy/2298. Accessed 31 July

Embassy of Ukraine in Australia (2017) Russia's recognition of the documents of separate regions of Donetsk and Luhansk regions (ORDLO) is not the basis for their recognition by Australia. http://australia.mfa.gov.ua/en/press-center/publications/5362-viznannya-rf-dokumentiv-ordlo-ne-je-pidstavoju-dlya-jih-viznannya-z-boku-avstraliji. Accessed 31 July 2017

Embassy of Ukraine in the Republic of Macedonia (2017) Rosii brakuie shche vyznaty vevchanski pasporty [What if Russia recognizes the Vevčani passports]. http://macedonia.mfa.gov.ua/ua/embassy/ambassador/interview/5348-rosiji-brakuje-shhe-viznati-vevchansyki-pasporti. Accessed 31 July 2017

Emerson R (1971) Self-Determination. American Journal of International Law 65:459–475

European Parliament (2015) Resolution on the situation in Ukraine, 2014/2965(RSP). http://www.europarl.europa.eu/sides/getDoc.do?type=TA&language=EN&reference=P8-TA-2015-0011. Accessed 31 July 2017

EuroPravda (2016) Zhodnoho "predstavnytstva DNR" v Italii nemaie – posol [There is no "DPR" mission in Italy - the ambassador]. http://www.eurointegration.com.ua/news/2016/12/15/7058938/. Accessed 31 July 2017

EuroPravda (2017) Posolstvo Frantsii prokomentuvalo stvorennia "predstavnytstva "DNR" v Marseli [The French embassy commented on the creation of a "DPR" mission in Marseilles]. http://www.eurointegration.com.ua/news/2017/06/27/7067730/. Accessed 31 July 2017

EuroPravda (2017) Rishennia RF vyznaty pasporty ORDLO porushuie Minski uhody – uriad Nimechchyny [The decision of the Russian Federation to recognize the passports of the ORDLO violates the Minsk agreements - the government of Germany]. http://www.eurointegration.com.ua/news/2017/02/20/7061929/. Accessed 31 July 2017

EuroPravda (2017) Sud v Chekhii ostatochno likviduvav "predstavnytstvo DNR" yak nezakonne [The Czech court finally eliminated the "representation of the DPR" as illegal]. http://www.eurointegration.com.ua/news/2017/06/28/7067788/. Accessed 31 July 2017

EuroPravda (2017) Sud zakryv feikove "posolstvo DNR" u Chekhii za pozovom MZS [The court closed the fake "embassy of the DPR" in the Czech Republic on the lawsuit of the Ministry of Foreign Affairs]. http://www.eurointegration.com.ua/news/2017/04/7/7064200/. Accessed 31 July 2017

General Assembly of the United Nations (2014) Territorial Integrity of Ukraine: resolution, A/RES/68/262. http://www.refworld.org/docid/534502a14.html. Accessed 31 July 2017

General Assembly of the United Nations (2017) Situation of human rights in the Autonomous Republic of Crimea and the city of Sevastopol (Ukraine): resolution, A/RES/71/205. http://www.refworld.org/docid/589b4db11e.html. Accessed 31 July 2017

General Prosecutor's Office of Ukraine (2014) Sud nadav dozvil na zatrymannia samo-proholoshenykh kerivnykiv "DNR" ta "LNR" [The court granted permission to detain self-proclaimed leaders of the "DPR" and "LPR"]. http://www.gp.gov.ua/ua/news.html?_m=publications&_t=rec&id=140393&fp=50. Accessed 31 July 2017

Greek Reporter (2017) Greece Has Never Recognized the Self-Proclaimed Donetsk People's Republic - FM Spox Says. http://greece.greekreporter.com/2017/03/22/greece-has-never-recognized-the-self-proclaimed-donetsk-peoples-republic-fm-spox-says/. Accessed 31 July 2017

Hewitt JJ, Wilkenfeld J, Gurr TR (2008) Peace and Conflict 2008. Paradigm Publishers, London

Interfax-Ukraine (2014) "Vybory" "DNR" i "LNR" nezakonny – zajavlenie glav MID Vyshegradskoj chetverki ["Elections" in "DPR" and "LPR" are illegal - statement of the Foreign Ministers of the Visegrad Four]. http://interfax.com.ua/news/political/232014.html. Accessed 31 July 2017

Investigative Committee of the Russian Federation (2014) Sledstviem ustanovleny lica, prichastnye k voennym prestuplenijam na territorii jugo-vostoka Ukrainy [The investigation established the persons involved in war crimes in the territory of the southeast of Ukraine]. http://www.sledcom.ru/actual/407377/. Accessed 31 July 2017

Investigative Committee of the Russian Federation (2014) Vozbuzhdeno ugolovnoe delo po faktu primenenija zapreshhennyh sredstv i metodov vedenija vojny na territorii Doneckoj i Luganskoj Narodnyh Respublik [A criminal case was instituted on the use of prohibited means and methods of war on the territory of the Donetsk and Luhansk People's Republics]. http://www.sledcom.ru/actual/403388/. Accessed 31 July 2017

Investigative Committee of the Russian Federation (2014) Vozbuzhdeno ugolovnoe delo v otnoshenii Igorja Kolomojskogo i Arsena Avakova [A criminal case has been opened against

Igor Kolomoisky and Arsen Avakov]. http://www.sledcom.ru/actual/405159. Accessed 31 July 2017

Korrespondent.net (2017) Evropa otkazalas' priznavat' pasporta DNR i LNR [Europe refused to recognize passports of the DPR and LPR]. http://korrespondent.net/world/3828252-evropa-otkazalas-pryznavat-pasporta-dnr-y-lnr. Accessed 31 July 2017

Korynevych A (2015) Zastosuvannia mizhnarodnoho humanitarnoho prava do zbroinoho konfliktu na terytorii Ukrainy [Application of international humanitarian law to armed conflict in the territory of Ukraine]. Feniks, Odessa

Koval D, Korotkyi T (2014) Informatsiina viina Rosiiskoi Federatsii proty Ukrainy: otsinka mizhnarodnoho spivtovarystva [Information War of the Russian Federation against Ukraine: an assessment of the international community]. In: Antonovych M, Babin B, Baimuratov M (eds) Ukrainska Revoliutsiia hidnosti, ahresiia RF i mizhnarodne pravo [Ukrainian Revolution of Dignity, Russian aggression and international law]. K.I.S, Kiev, pp 847–885

KP.UA (2017) Belarus' ne budet priznavat' pasporta "DNR" i "LNR" [Belarus will not recognize the passports of "DPR" and "LPR"]. http://kp.ua/politics/567585-belarus-ne-budet-pryznavat-pasporta-dnr-y-lnr. Accessed 31 July 2017

KP.UA (2017) MID Francii: priznanie pasportov "DNR" ne sootvetstvuet duhu Minskih soglashenij [French Ministry of Foreign Affairs: recognition of "DPR" passports does not correspond to the spirit of Minsk agreements]. http://kp.ua/politics/567620-myd-frantsyy-pryznanye-pasportov-dnr-ne-sootvetstvuet-dukhu-mynskykh-sohlashenyi. Accessed 31 July 2017

Lenta.ru (2015) V Luganske otkrylos' dippredstavitel'stvo Juzhnoj Osetii [The diplomatic mission of South Ossetia was opened in Luhansk]. https://lenta.ru/news/2015/04/16/lugansk/. Accessed 31 July 2017

LIGABusinessInform (2014) Genprokuratura objavila DNR i LNR terroristicheskimi organizacijami [The General Prosecutor's Office declared DPR and LPR terrorist organizations]. http://news.liga.net/news/incident/1760339-genprokuratura_obyavila_dnr_i_lnr_terroristicheskimi_organizatsiyami.htm. Accessed 31 July 2017

Luhansk online (2014) Respublikanskoe sobranie Luganskoj Narodnoj Respubliki obratilos' v OON [The Republican Assembly of the Luhansk People's Republic appealed to the UN]. http://lugansk-online.info/news/respublikanskoe-sobranie-luganskoi-narodnoi-respubliki-obratilos-v-oon. Accessed 31 July 2017

Ministry of Foreign Affairs of the Russian Federation (2014) Zajavlenie MID Rossii otnositel'no silovoj operacii na Jugo-Vostoke Ukrainy [Statement by the Russian Foreign Ministry regarding the force operation in the Southeast of Ukraine]. http://www.mid.ru/brp_4.nsf/0/3E75E3F7753EE78A44257CCC003985B3. Accessed 31 July 2017

Ministry of Foreign Affairs of Ukraine (2014) Komentar Departamentu informatsiinoi polityky shchodo pidtrymky Rosiieiu terorystychnoi diialnosti v Donetskii ta Luhanskii oblastiakh [Commentary by the Department of Information Policy on Russia's support for terrorist activities in the Donetsk and Luhansk oblasts]. http://mfa.gov.ua/ua/press-center/comments/1512-komentar-departamentu-informacijnoji-politiki-mzs-ukrajini-shhodo-pidtrimki-rosijeju-teroristichnoji-dijalynostiv-donecykij-ta-lugansykij-oblastyah. Accessed 31 July 2017

Ministry of Foreign Affairs of Ukraine (2014) Komentar shchodo cherhovykh provokatsii z boku Rosii na ukrainsko-rosiiskomu derzhavnomu kordoni [Comment on another Russian provocation on the Ukrainian-Russian state border]. http://mfa.gov.ua/ua/press-center/comments/1990-komentar-mzs-ukrajini-shodo-chergovih-provokacij-z-boku-rosiji-na-ukrajinsyko-rosijsykomu-derzhavnomu-kordoni. Accessed 31 July 2017

Ministry of Foreign Affairs of Ukraine (2014) Komentar shchodo nelehalnoi peredachi Rosiiskoiu Federatsiieiu ozbroien terorystychnym uhrupovanniam, shcho diiut u Donetskii i Luhanskii oblastiakh [Commentary on the illegal transfer of arms by the Russian Federation to terrorist groups operating in the Donetsk and Luhansk oblasts]. http://mfa.gov.ua/ua/press-center/comments/1665-komentar-mzs-ukrajini-shhodo-nelegalynoji-peredachi-rosijskoju-federacijeju-ozbrojeny-teroristichnim-ugrupovannyam-shho-dijuty-u-donecykij-i-lugansykij-oblastyah. Accessed 31 July 2017

Ministry of Foreign Affairs of Ukraine (2014) Rezoliutsiia Yevropeiskoho Parlamentu shchodo sytuatsii v Ukraini vid 17 lypnia 2014 r [Resolution of the European Parliament on the situation in Ukraine of July 17, 2014]. http://mfa.gov.ua/ua/news-feeds/foreign-offices-news/25779-rezolyucija-jevropejsykogo-parlamentu-shhodo-situaciji-v-ukrajini-vid-17-lipnya-2014-roku. Accessed 31 July 2017

Ministry of Foreign Affairs of Ukraine (2014) Vysnovky Rady YeS u zakordonnykh spravakh shchodo Ukrainy, ukhvaleni za pidsumkamy zasidannia 23 chervnia 2014 r v Liuksemburzi [Conclusions of the EU Council on Foreign Affairs on Ukraine, adopted following the meeting of 23 June 2014 in Luxembourg]. http://mfa.gov.ua/ua/press-center/comments/1714-zajava-mzs-ukrajini-shhodo-visnovkiv-radi-jes-stosovno-ukrajini-vid-23-chervnya-2014-roku. Accessed 31 July 2017

Mirror of the week, Ukraine (2014a) Brytanske MZS zvynuvatylo RF u brekhni pro prychyny avarii "Boinha" [The British Foreign Ministry accused Russia of lying about the causes of the Boeing accident]. http://dt.ua/WORLD/britanskiy-mzs-zvinuvativ-rf-u-brehni-pro-prichini-avariyi-boyinga-147613_.html. Accessed 31 July 2017

Mirror of the week, Ukraine (2014b) Merkel ne bachyt alternatyvy dialohu z Putinym dlia myru v Ukraini [Merkel does not see an alternative to dialogue with Putin for peace in Ukraine]. http://dt.ua/WORLD/merkel-ne-bachit-alternativi-dialogu-z-putinim-dlya-miru-v-ukrayini-147093_.html. Accessed 31 July 2017

Mirror of the week, Ukraine (2014c) Obama: Malaiziiskyi litak zbytyi raketoiu, vypushchenoiu z kontrolovanoi terytorii boiovykamy [Obama: Malaysian plane was shot down by missile, released from the territory controlled by militants]. http://dt.ua/UKRAINE/obama-malayziyskiy-litak-zbitiy-raketoyu-vipuschenoyu-z-kontrolovanoyi-teritoriyi-boyovikami-147163_.html. Accessed 31 July 2017

Mytsyk V (2002) Vyznannia v mizhnarodnomu pravi [Recognition in international law]. In: Butkevych V (ed) Mizhnarodne pravo. Osnovy teorii [International law. Fundamentals of the theory]. Lybid, Kyiv, pp 344–365

News of Ingushetia Bakdar (2014) Luganskaja narodnaja respublika poprosila Ingushetiju priznat' ee nezavisimost' [The Luhansk People's Republic asked Ingushetia to recognize its independence]. http://bakdar.org/view_index.php?id=3597. Accessed 31 July 2017

NEWSru (2017) NATO raskritikovalo Rossiju za priznanie pasportov DNR i LNR [NATO criticized Russia for recognizing passports of DPR and LPR]. http://www.newsru.com/world/30mar2017/stoltenberg.html. Accessed 31 July 2017

Office of the United Nations High Commissioner for Human Rights (2014) Report on the human rights situation in Ukraine 15 May 2014. http://www.ohchr.org/Documents/Countries/UA/HRMMUReport15May2014.pdf. Accessed 31 July 2017

Office of the United Nations High Commissioner for Human Rights (2014) Report on the human rights situation in Ukraine 15 June 2014. http://www.ohchr.org/Documents/Countries/UA/HRMMUReport15June2014.pdf. Accessed 31 July 2017

Office of the United Nations High Commissioner for Human Rights (2017) Dopovid shchodo sytuatsii z pravamy liudyny v Ukraini 16 lystopada 2016 roku – 15 liutoho 2017 roku [Report on the human rights situation in Ukraine during November 16, 2016 - February 15, 2017]. http://www.ohchr.org/Documents/Countries/UA/UAReport17th_UKR.pdf. Accessed 31 July 2017

Office of the United Nations High Commissioner for Human Rights (2017) Dopovid shchodo sytuatsii z pravamy liudyny v Ukraini 16 liutoho–15 travnia 2017 roku [Report on the human rights situation in Ukraine during February 16-May 15, 2017]. http://www.ohchr.org/Documents/Countries/UA/UAReport18th_UKR.pdf. Accessed 31 July 2017

Office of the United Nations High Commissioner for Human Rights (2016) Report on the human rights situation in Ukraine 16 May to 15 August 2016. http://reliefweb.int/sites/reliefweb.int/files/resources/Ukraine15thReport.pdf. Accessed 31 July 2017

Online Express (2017) U MZS Polshchi vidreahuvaly na rishennia RF pro vyznannia "pasportiv L/DNR" [The Ministry of Foreign Affairs of Poland responded to the decision of the Russian

Federation to recognize "passports of L/DPR"]. http://expres.ua/news/2017/02/22/229325-mzs-polshchi-vidreaguvaly-rishennya-rf-vyznannya-pasportiv-ldnr. Accessed 31 July 2017
Oreshkin D (2017) Rashodimsja po domam: SShA poslali Rossii chetkij signal po Donbassu [Lets go home: the United States sent Russia a clear message regarding Donbass]. https://apostrophe.ua/article/politics/2017-05-07/rashodimsya-po-domam-ssha-poslali-rossii-chetkiy-signal-po-donbassu/12130. Accessed 31 July 2017
OSCE Parliamentary Assembly (2017) Rezoljucija "Vosstanovlenie suvereniteta i territorial'noj celostnosti Ukrainy" [Resolution "Restoration of the sovereignty and territorial integrity of Ukraine"]. https://www.oscepa.org/documents/all-documents/annual-sessions/2017-minsk/declaration-25/3557-declaration-rus/file. Accessed 31 July 2017
PanARMENIAN Network (2010) Vice-spiker parlamenta Abhazii: Vybory v NKR sootvetstvujut vsem mezhdunarodnym standartam [Vice Speaker of Abkhazian Parliament: Elections in NKR correspond to all international standards]. http://www.panarmenian.net/rus/world/news/49007/. Accessed 31 July 2017
Pandora's Box (2014) Juridicheskoe priznanie Rossiej Doneckoj i Luganskoj Narodnyh Respublik [The legal recognition of Donetsk and Luhansk People's Republics by Russia]. http://pandoraopen.ru/2014-06-01/yuridicheskoe-priznanie-rossiej-doneckoj-i-luganskoj-narodnyx-respublik/. Accessed 31 July 2017
Parliamentary Assembly of the Council of Europe (2016) Report of the Committee on Legal Affairs and Human Rights "Legal remedies for human rights violations on the Ukrainian territories outside the control of the Ukrainian authorities". http://assembly.coe.int/nw/xml/XRef/Xref-DocDetails-en.asp?FileID=23007&lang=en. Accessed 31 July 2017
Parliamentary Assembly of the Council of Europe (2016) Resolution 2133 "Legal remedies for human rights violations on the Ukrainian territories outside the control of the Ukrainian authorities". http://assembly.coe.int/nw/xml/XRef/Xref-XML2HTML-en.asp?fileid=23167&lang=en. Accessed 31 July 2017
Radio Liberty (2017) Court in Czech Republic closes Ukrainian separatist mission in Ostrava. https://www.rferl.org/a/court-czech-republic-closes-ukrainian-separatist-mission-donetsk-peoples-republic-ostava-/28585123.html. Accessed 31 July 2017
Radio Liberty (2017) OBSIe: vyznannia Rosiieiu "dokumentiv" ORDLO pidryvaie myrni zusyllia v Ukraini [OSCE: Russia's recognition of ORDLO "documents" undermines peaceful efforts in Ukraine]. https://www.radiosvoboda.org/a/news/28318870.html. Accessed 31 July 2017
Radio Liberty (2017) SShA: vyznannia Rosiieiu «dokumentiv» okupovanoho Donbasu superechyt Minskym uhodam [USA: Russia's recognition of "documents" of the occupied Donbass contradicts the Minsk treaties]. https://www.radiosvoboda.org/a/news/28318243.html. Accessed 31 July 2017
Raidió Teilifís Éireann (2014) Obama says pro-Russian separatists shot down MH17 https://www.rte.ie/news/2014/0718/631526-malaysia-airlines-ukraine/. Accessed 31 July 2017
RBC.ru (2017) DNR i Juzhnaja Osetija podpisali protokol ob ustanovlenii dipotnoshenij [DPR and South Ossetia signed a protocol on the establishment of diplomatic relations]. http://www.rbc.ru/rbcfreenews/59149e9a9a79473d099547c5. Accessed 31 July 2017
Reeves SR, Wallace D (2015) The Combatant Status of the "Little Green Men" and Other Participants in the Ukraine Conflict. International Law Studies 91:361–401
RIA News (2014) LNR obratilas' k 15 stranam i subektam RF o priznanii nezavisimosti [LPR has addressed to 15 countries and subjects of the Russian Federation about recognition of its independence]. http://ria.ru/world/20140611/1011694535.html#ixzz39d5rBIQ8. Accessed 31 July 2017
RIA News (2017) Juzhnaja Osetija i DNR podpisali dogovor o druzhbe i vzaimnoj pomoshhi [South Ossetia and DPR signed a treaty on friendship and mutual assistance]. https://ria.ru/world/2017 0511/1494077743.html Accessed 31 July 2017
Russian legal portal (2014) O priznanii Doneckoj Narodnoj Respubliki: Ukaz prezidenta Juzhnoj Osetii [On the recognition of the Donetsk People's Republic: Decree of the President of South Ossetia]. http://constitutions.ru/?p=10048. Accessed 31 July 2017

RUSSIAN NEWSPAPER (2015) DNR priznala nezavisimost' Abhazii i Juzhnoj Osetii [DPR acknowledged the independence of Abkhazia and South Ossetia]. https://rg.ru/2015/05/12/dnr-site-anons.html. Accessed 31 July 2017

Security Council of the United Nations (2014) Resolution on the downing of Malaysia Airlines flight MH17 on 17 July in Donetsk Oblast, Ukraine, S/RES/2166. http://www.refworld.org/docid/53 d63dd74.html. Accessed 31 July 2017

Security Council of the United Nations (2015) On the Package of Measures for the Implementation of the Minsk Agreements, S/RES/2202. http://www.refworld.org/docid/54eefb4155.html. Accessed 31 July 2017

Security Council of the United Nations (2017) The Report of the 7886th meeting, S/PV.7886. https://documents-dds-ny.un.org/doc/UNDOC/PRO/N17/045/61/PDF/N170456 1.pdf?OpenElement. Accessed 31 July 2017

Shinkaretskaia G (2010) Polozhenie fakticheski sushchestvuiushchikh rezhimov (nepriznannye gosudarstva) [The situation of the actual regimes (unrecognized states)]. RAS Institute of State and Law, Moscow

Stopfake.org (2017) Fake: Donetsk People's Republic Opens Offices in France. http://www. stopfake.org/en/fake-donetsk-people-s-republic-opens-offices-in-france/. Accessed 31 July 2017

SUMMER56 (2014) Sledstvennyj Komitet RF vozbudil delo po faktu metodov vedenija vojny na territorii DNR i LNR [The Investigative Committee of the Russian Federation initiated a case on the methods of warfare in the territory of DPR and LPR]. http://summer56.livejournal.com/13 0010.html. Accessed 31 July 2017

TASS news agency (2014) Provozglashennaja Luganskaja narodnaja respublika (LNR) obratilas' k Rossijskoj Federacii i eshhe 14 gosudarstvam s pros'boj priznat' ee nezavisimost' [The proclaimed Lugansk People's Republic (LPR) appealed to the Russian Federation and 14 other states with a request to recognize its independence]. http://itar-tass.com/mezhdunarodnaya-panorama/ 1253083. Accessed 31 July 2017

The Prague Daily Monitor (2017) Court dissolves group of alleged Donetsk honorary consul. http://praguemonitor.com/2017/06/29/court-dissolves-group-alleged-donetsk-honorary-consul. Accessed 31 July 2017

The President of the Russian Federation (2017) Ukaz o priznanii dokumentov, vydannyh grazhdanam Ukrainy i licam bez grazhdanstva, prozhivajushhim na territorijah otdel'nyh rajonov Doneckoj i Luganskoj oblastej Ukrainy ot 18 fevralja 2017 goda [Decree on recognition of documents issued to citizens of Ukraine and stateless persons residing in the territories of certain regions of Donetsk and Luhansk regions of Ukraine of February 18, 2017]. http://kremlin.ru/ events/president/news/53895. Accessed 31 July 2017

The State Duma (2010) O Sledstvennom komitete Rossijskoj Federacii: Federal'nyj zakon RF [On the Investigative Committee of the Russian Federation: Federal Law of the Russian Federation]. http://fzrf.su/zakon/o-sledstvennom-komitete-403-fz/. Accessed 31 July 2017

The Telegraph (2016) MH17 Investigation: Moscow denounces 'biased' investigation as prosecutors say missile came from Russia. http://www.telegraph.co.uk/news/2016/09/28/mh17-investigation-prosecutors-to-reveal-where-missile-that-down/. Accessed 31 July 2017

TSN.UA (2016) Vyznannia vtorhnennia RF na Donbas ta vykonannia minskykh uhod [Recognition of Russia's invasion in the Donbas and the fulfillment of the Minsk Treaty]. https://tsn.ua/politika/ viznannya-vtorgnennya-rf-na-donbas-ta-vikonannya-minskih-ugod-povniy-tekst-rezolyuciyi-parye-785901.html. Accessed 31 July 2017

Tsyvadze N (2010) O razvitii principa samoopredelenija v mezhdunarodnom prave [On the development of the principle of self-determination in international law]. RAS Institute of state and law, Moscow

Ukraine News (UAZMI) (2017) Australia does not recognize ORDLO "documents". http://uazmi. com/news/post/cIE8hwtXtnudCMo2e3CZhW. Accessed 31 July 2017

Ukrainian Pravda (2017) Vlasti Grecii postavili na mesto "predstavitel'stvo DNR" [The Greek authorities restrained a "representation of DPR"]. http://www.pravda.com.ua/rus/news/2017/03/ 22/7138882/. Accessed 31 July 2017

Ukrinform (2017) Avstralija ne priznaet dokumenty ORDLO [Australia does not recognize ORDLO "documents"]. https://www.ukrinform.ru/rubric-polytics/2181945-avstralia-ne-priznaet-dokumenty-ordlo.html. Accessed 31 July 2017

UN News Centre (2014) Navi Pilljej prizvala vooruzhennye gruppy v Ukraine slozhit' oruzhie [Navi Pillay called on armed groups in Ukraine to lay down their arms]. http://www.un.org/russian/news/story.asp?NewsID=21606. Accessed 31 July 2017

UN News Centre (2014) Vooruzhennye gruppy na vostoke Ukrainy pytajutsja navjazat' mestnomu naseleniju vlast' straha i terrora, govoritsja v doklade OON [Armed groups in the East of Ukraine are trying to impose on the local population the power of fear and terror, the UN report says]. http://www.un.org/russian/news/story.asp?newsID=22066. Accessed 31 July 2017

UNIAN news agency (2014) Luganskaja Narodnaja Respublika prosit OON priznat' ee nezavisimost' [The Luhansk People's Republic asks the United Nations to recognize its independence]. http://www.unian.net/politics/919654-luganskaya-narodnaya-respublika-prosit-oon-priznat-ee-nezavisimost.html. Accessed 31 July 2017

UNIAN news agency (2017) Poroshenko: Priznanie Rossiej "pasportov" "DNR" i "LNR" javljaetsja ocherednym dokazatel'stvom narushenija mezhdunarodnogo prava [Poroshenko: Russia's recognition of the "passports" of the "DPR" and "LPR" is yet another proof of a violation of international law]. https://www.unian.net/politics/1784492-poroshenko-priznanie-rossiey-pasportov-dnr-i-lnr-yavlyaetsya-ocherednyim-dokazatelstvom-narusheniya-mejdunarodnogo-prava.html. Accessed 31 July 2017

United Nations Office for the Coordination of Humanitarian Affairs (OCHA) (2016) Humanitarian Bulletin Ukraine. Issue 11, 1–30 June 2016. http://reliefweb.int/sites/reliefweb.int/files/resources/ukraine_-_issue_11_eng.pdf. Accessed 31 July 2017

United Nations Office for the Coordination of Humanitarian Affairs (OCHA) (2016) Humanitarian Bulletin Ukraine. Issue 13, 1–31 August 2016. http://reliefweb.int/sites/reliefweb.int/files/resources/humanitarian_bulletin_20160908_en.pdf. Accessed 31 July 2017

United Nations Office for the Coordination of Humanitarian Affairs (OCHA) (2016) Humanitarian Bulletin: Ukraine. Issue 14, 1–30 September 2016. http://reliefweb.int/report/ukraine/humanitarian-bulletin-ukraine-issue-14-1-30-september-2016-enru. Accessed 31 July 2017

United Nations Office for the Coordination of Humanitarian Affairs (OCHA) (2016) Humanitarian Bulletin: Ukraine. Issue 15, 1 October-31 December 2016. http://reliefweb.int/report/ukraine/humanitarian-bulletin-ukraine-issue-15-1-october-31-december-2016. Accessed 31 July 2017

United Nations Office for the Coordination of Humanitarian Affairs (OCHA) (2014a) Ukraine Situation report No.3, July 17 2014. http://reliefweb.int/sites/reliefweb.int/files/resources/SitRep-Ukraine_20140717_final.pdf. Accessed 31 July 2017

United Nations Office for the Coordination of Humanitarian Affairs (OCHA) (2014b) Ukraine Situation report No.4, July 25 2014. http://reliefweb.int/sites/reliefweb.int/files/resources/SitRep-Ukraine_20140725_final.pdf. Accessed 31 July 2017

U.S. Department of State (2017) Country Reports on Human Rights Practices for 2016. Ukraine. https://www.state.gov/j/drl/rls/hrrpt/humanrightsreport/#wrapper. Accessed 31 July 2017

Verkhovna Rada of Ukraine (2014) Postanova Pro Zaiavu Verkhovnoi Rady Ukrainy "Pro trahichnu zahybel liudei vnaslidok terorystychnoho aktu nad terytoriieiu Ukrainy" [Resolution on the Statement of the Verkhovna Rada of Ukraine "On the tragic death of people as a result of a terrorist act over the territory of Ukraine"]. http://zakon3.rada.gov.ua/laws/show/1596-18. Accessed 31 July 2017

Verkhovna Rada of Ukraine (2014) Postanova Pro Zaiavu Verkhovnoi Rady Ukrainy "Shchodo protydii poshyrenniu pidtrymuvanoho Rosiiskoiu Federatsiieiu mizhnarodnoho teroryzmu" [Resolution on the Statement of the Verkhovna Rada of Ukraine "On the counteraction to the spread of the international terrorism supported by the Russian Federation"]. http://zakon2.rada.gov.ua/laws/show/1597-18. Accessed 31 July 2017

Verkhovna Rada of Ukraine (2014) Proekt Zakonu pro vyznannia samoproholoshenykh orhanizatsii "Donetska narodna respublika" ta "Luhanska narodna respublika" terorystychnymy orhanizatsiiamy [Draft Law on the recognition of self-proclaimed organizations "Donetsk People's Republic" and "Luhansk People's Republic" as terrorist organizations]. http://w1.c1.rada.gov.ua/pls/zweb2/webproc4_1?pf3511=52808. Accessed 31 July 2017

Verkhovna Rada of Ukraine (2015) Postanova Pro Zaiavu Verkhovnoi Rady Ukrainy "Pro vyznannia Ukrainoiu yurysdyktsii Mizhnarodnoho kryminalnoho sudu shchodo skoiennia zlochyniv proty liudianosti ta voiennykh zlochyniv vyshchymy posadovymy osobamy Rosiiskoi Federatsii ta kerivnykamy terorystychnykh orhanizatsii "DNR" ta "LNR", yaki pryzvely do osoblyvo tiazhkykh naslidkiv ta masovoho vbyvstva ukrainskykh hromadian" [Resolution on the Statement of the Verkhovna Rada of Ukraine "On the recognition by Ukraine of the jurisdiction of the International Criminal Court regarding the commission of crimes against humanity and war crimes by senior officials of the Russian Federation and the leaders of the terrorist organizations "DPR" and "LPR", which led to particularly grave consequences and the massacre of Ukrainian citizens"]. http://zakon3.rada.gov.ua/laws/show/145-19. Accessed 31 July 2017

Verkhovna Rada of Ukraine (2015) Postanova Pro Zvernennia Verkhovnoi Rady Ukrainy do Orhanizatsii Obiednanykh Natsii, Yevropeiskoho Parlamentu, Parlamentskoi Asamblei Rady Yevropy, Parlamentskoi Asamblei NATO, Parlamentskoi Asamblei OBSIe, Parlamentskoi Asamblei HUAM, natsionalnykh parlamentiv derzhav svitu pro vyznannia Rosiiskoi Federatsii derzhavoiu-ahresorom [Resolution on the Appeal of the Verkhovna Rada of Ukraine to the United Nations, the European Parliament, the Parliamentary Assembly of the Council of Europe, the NATO Parliamentary Assembly, the OSCE Parliamentary Assembly, the GUAM Parliamentary Assembly, the national parliaments of the world for the recognition of the Russian Federation as an aggressor state]. http://zakon2.rada.gov.ua/laws/show/129-19. Accessed 31 July 2017

Verkhovna Rada of Ukraine (2015) Proekt Zakonu pro vnesennia zmin do deiakykh zakonodavchykh aktiv Ukrainy shchodo udoskonalennia mekhanizmiv borotby z teroryzmom [Draft Law on amendments to certain legislative acts of Ukraine on the improvement of the mechanisms for combating terrorism]. http://w1.c1.rada.gov.ua/pls/zweb2/webproc4_1?pf3511=54044. Accessed 31 July 2017

Verkhovna Rada of Ukraine (2017) Postanova Pro Zvernennia Verkhovnoi Rady Ukrainy do parlamentiv inozemnykh derzhav ta mizhnarodnykh orhanizatsii shchodo zasudzhennia eskalatsii zbroinoi ahresii Rosiiskoi Federatsii proty Ukrainy [Resolution on the Appeal of the Verkhovna Rada of Ukraine to parliaments of foreign states and international organizations on condemning the escalation of armed aggression of the Russian Federation against Ukraine]. http://zakon3.rada.gov.ua/laws/show/1837-viii. Accessed 31 July 2017

Voice of America (2017) US Lawmakers Include Several Measures Targeting Russia in Spending Bill. https://www.voanews.com/a/us-spending-bill-government-running-senate-trump/3840388.html. Accessed 31 July 2017

Zadorozhnii O (2014) Ahresiia Rosiiskoi Federatsii proty Ukrainy i mizhnarodno-pravovyi pryntsyp neporushnosti kordoniv [The aggression of the Russian Federation against Ukraine and the international legal principle of the inviolability of borders]. Naukovyi visnyk Mizhnarodnoho humanitarnoho universytetu. Seriia: Yurysprudentsiia [Scientific Herald of the International Humanitarian University: Jurisprudence] 12(2):172–176

Zadorozhnii O (2014) Mizhnarodno-pravovyi pryntsyp neporushnosti kordoniv u Yevropi ta ahresiia Rosiiskoi Federatsii proty Ukrainy [The international legal principle of the inviolability of borders in Europe and the aggression of the Russian Federation against Ukraine]. Naukovi pratsi NU "OUA" [Scientific works of the National University "Odesa Law Academy"] 14:42–69

Zadorozhnii O (2014) Mizhnarodno-pravovyi pryntsyp nezastosuvannia syly abo pohrozy syloiu v konteksti dii Rosiiskoi Federatsii proty Ukrainy [The international legal principle of non-use of force or threat of force in the context of the Russian Federation's action against Ukraine] Pravova derzhava [Legal state] 18:129–134

Zadorozhnii O (2015) Porushennia ahresiieiu RF proty Ukrainy mizhnarodno-pravovoho pryntsypu dobrosovisnoho vykonannia mizhnarodnykh zoboviazan [Violation of the international legal principle of the honest fulfillment of international obligations by Russian Federation's aggression against Ukraine]. Ukrainskyi chasopys mizhnarodnoho prava [Ukrainian Journal of International Law] 1:17–32

Zadorozhnii O (2015) Porushennia ahresyvnoiu viinoiu Rosiiskoi Federatsii proty Ukrainy osnovnykh pryntsypiv mizhnarodnoho prava [Violation of the fundamental principles of international law by the aggressive war of the Russian Federation against Ukraine]. Ukrainian association of international law, Taras Shevchenko National University of Kyiv, Kyiv

Zadorozhnii O (2015) Porushennia pryntsypu suverennoi rivnosti derzhav v ahresyvnii viini Rosii proty Ukrainy [Violation of the principle of sovereign equality of states in the aggressive war of Russia against Ukraine]. Almanakh mizhnarodnoho prava [Almanac of International Law] 7:3–19

Zadorozhnii O (2015) Porushennia Rosiiskoiu Federatsiieiu u 2014–2015 rokakh pryntsypu nevtruchannia u vnutrishni spravy derzhav stosovno Ukrainy [Violation of the principle of noninterference in the internal affairs of states by the Russian Federation in 2014–2015 in relation to Ukraine]. Naukovi pratsi NU "OUA" [Scientific works of the National University "Odesa Law Academy"] 15:119–143

Zadorozhnii O (2015) Pravova otsinka zastosuvannia RF syly proty Ukrainy v konteksti mizhnarodno-pravovoho pryntsypu nezastosuvannia syly [Legal assessment of the use of force by the RF against Ukraine in the context of international legal principle of non-use of force]. Ukrainskyi chasopys mizhnarodnoho prava [Ukrainian Journal of International Law] 2:19–30

Zadorozhnii O (2015) Stanovlennia i normatyvnyi zmist pryntsypu terytorialnoi tsilisnosti derzhav yak osnovnoho pryntsypu mizhnarodnoho prava [Formation and normative content of the principle of territorial integrity of states as the main principle of international law]. Universytetski naukovi zapysky [University scientific notes] 1:231–246

Zadorozhnii O (2016) Opravdat liuboi tcenoi. Agressivnaia voina Rossiiskoi Federatcii protiv Ukrainy i transformatciia rossiiskogo videniia mezhdunarodnogo prava [Justify at any cost. The aggressive war of the Russian Federation against Ukraine and the transformation of the Russian vision of international law]. Ukrainian association of international law, Taras Shevchenko National University of Kyiv, Kyiv

Zadorozhnii O (2016) Porushennia pryntsypu povahy osnovnykh prav i svobod liudyny ahresiieiu RF na Skhodi Ukrainy [Violation of the principle of respect for fundamental rights and freedoms by aggression of the Russian Federation in the East of Ukraine]. In: Zadorozhnii O, Poiedynok O (ed) Liber Amicorum do 60-richchia prof. V.V. Mytsyka [Liber Amicorum for the 60th anniversary of prof. V. Mytsyk]. Feniks, Kyiv, Odesa, pp 605–615

Zadorozhnii O (2016) Revisiting the "International Legal Personality" of DPR/LPR. European Political and Law Discourse 3(4):7–14

Zamlelova S (2014) Priznanie respublik [Recognition of republics]. http://www.zamlelova.ru/novosti/all/article_306/. Accessed 31 July 2017

ZIK.UA (2017) Hensek OBSIe zasudyv vyznannia Rosiieiu «dokumentiv» ORDLO [The OSCE General Secretary condemned Russia's recognition of the ORDLO "documents"]. http://zik.ua/news/2017/02/20/gensek_obsye_zasudyv_vyznannya_rosiieyu_dokumentiv_ordlo_0_1046599. Accessed 31 July 2017

Part II
Jus in Bello

Chapter 8
Legal Challenges in Hybrid Warfare Theory and Practice: Is There a Place for Legal Norms at All?

Gergely Tóth

Contents

Abstract The chapter introduces the theory and practical consequences of asymmetric and hybrid warfare, as observed in the crisis in Ukraine. It summarizes the legal problems arising from such methods of conducting an armed conflict and asks the question about whether this new type of warfare is compatible with the existing legal system concerning armed conflict, especially regarding the distinction between times of peace and times of conflict, as well as the distinction between combatants/military objectives and protected persons/installations. The conclusion is that if, as predicted by many, hybrid warfare becomes the 'new normal', then the current legal regime will have to change to remain meaningful.

Keywords asymmetric warfare · hybrid warfare · Russia · Ukraine · distinction

Gergely Tóth, Doctor of Law, Eötvös Loránd University of Sciences, Budapest; Ph.D. candidate, National Public Service University, Budapest. Previously a Legal Adviser with the Regional Delegation for Central Europe at the International Committee of the Red Cross. Currently based at the Hungarian Ministry of Defence, Department for Coordination of Public Relations, email: tothgergely@hm.gov.hu.

G. Tóth (✉)
Eötvös Loránd University of Sciences, Budapest, Hungary
e-mail: tothgergely@hm.gov.hu

© T.M.C. ASSER PRESS and the authors 2018
S. Sayapin and E. Tsybulenko (eds.), *The Use of Force against Ukraine and International Law*, https://doi.org/10.1007/978-94-6265-222-4_8

8.1 Introduction

Many chapters in this book deal with the numerous violations of the norms of international law, regulating not only *jus ad bellum* and *jus in bello*, but also international human rights, international criminal law provisions and other legal regimes regulating the relationship of states to each other. One is prompted to ask as to whether the source of this apparent "lawlessness" surrounding the conflict in Ukraine is a feature of the belligerent parties involved, or whether it is feature of the type (not in a legal, but rather in a military sense) of armed conflict that is taking place. While we can probably state that the persons taking part in hostilities are neither better nor worse than people we may find in any armed conflict, I believe the paradigm of conflict in which the Russian Federation made its first large-scale appearance, namely, hybrid (or, as it is sometimes called, asymmetric) conflict, is inherently less respectful towards existing international legal norms; and, because of this, it foreshadows a grim future of the law on armed conflict in such situations.

In the following, I will try to lay down some theoretical foundations for hybrid warfare, including, wherever possible, recent examples from the conflict in Ukraine in order to demonstrate its fundamental incompatibility with the law of war as it exists today.

We must understand the fact that the means of conflict has fundamentally changed. Von Clausewitz's paraphrased statement that war is a chameleon, which will change its aspects at each occurrence, is more relevant today than it has been ever before. New approaches, in this regard, include China's "unrestricted warfare" concept or Russia's novel approach to conflict, both of which have put the world on a "total war" footing, where everything is acceptable and nothing is off limits. As part of the changing characteristics, there is no longer any distinction between what is or what is not a battlefield. Physical spaces, including the ground, the sea, the air and outer space, are all potential battlefields, but social spaces, such as politics, economics, culture, cyberspace and the psyche, can also become territories for engagement.[1]

However, before conducting a deeper analysis of the current concept of hybrid warfare, we must ask the question, does *nomen est men* apply in this case? Will the name of this new method of warfare lead to its downfall? Does it really involve the combination of multiple new methods and their flexible use, or is it simply the employment of diplomatic, national security, military, economic, cyber, information technology and psychological methods in a new way? Is it really possible that a state may recklessly use all of the tools that are available to it? Can we really define hybrid warfare as a flexible type of warfare where the transition between regular and irregular warfare may happen at practically any time? If we examine the Russian military, diplomatic and media operations during the Crimean and Eastern Ukraine crisis, our answer must be a firm "yes".

---

[1] Tsybulenko and Pakhomenko 2016.

8.2 Hybrid Warfare

To understand the theoretical foundations of hybrid/asymmetric warfare, a few important works from military science must be mentioned because they can be understood as laying a partial foundation for the concept.

Emily Goldman suggests that nations have two fundamental choices when designing their defence frameworks. One choice is matching their adversaries, which is essentially what occurred during the Cold War between the US and the Soviet Union. The second option is to invest in offsetting capabilities, as the French did towards the end of the 19th century by using mines, cruisers and swarming torpedo boats, rather than try and match England's powerful battleships.[2] Along these lines, nations have two fundamental choices when designing their future defence framework: either matching it with those of possible future adversaries or offsetting capabilities. These arguments, taken together, provide nations with a robust starting point for justifying the need to abandon their conventional strategy and match their opponents' approaches.

If we approach the problem from a historic angle, we will find that Carl von Clausewitz[3] already recognized the importance of terrain when he argued that ground that is difficult to traverse or an area that is split up into smaller sections by roads, vegetation or other features makes it possible for irregular fighters on the weaker side to hide from regular forces on the stronger side, which is important when someone wages a "people's war" or employs modern guerrilla warfare. The importance of rugged terrain is mentioned in the works of Lawrence of Arabia[4] and also in the works on partisan warfare by Josip Broz Tito.[5] The theory of urban warfare has been refined by the publication of the *Minimanual of the Urban Guerrilla* in 1969 by the Brazilian Carlos Marighella,[6] who proved that, because the most important government functions are carried out in cities, an antagonist may in effect paralyze the whole state by attacking government buildings, police stations etc.[7]

The more recent literature on hybrid/asymmetric warfare is so robust that a comprehensive review would take a length of an entire book, so let us only look at a number of definitions. The term *asymmetry* first appeared in the United States Joint Doctrine in 1995. The concept was initially used in a very simplistic and limited sense. "The doctrine defined asymmetric engagements as those between dissimilar forces, specifically air versus land, air versus sea, and so forth."[8] Following the realization and the materialization of "asymmetric" conflicts in Iraq and Afghanistan, the United States Department of Defense (DoD) finally defined asymmetric warfare as "attempts to circumvent or undermine an opponent's strengths while exploiting his

---

[2] Goldman 2006.

[3] Von Clausewitz 1832.

[4] Lawrence 1922.

[5] Tito 1966.

[6] Marighella 2011.

[7] Rácz 2015.

[8] Metz and Johnson 2001.

weaknesses using methods that differ significantly from the opponent's usual mode of operation."[9] In addition to the DoD's definition, the Central Intelligence Agency (CIA), which has been heavily involved in recent conflicts, also defined the problem as "the use of innovative strategies, tactics, and technologies by a 'weaker' state or sub-state adversary that are intended to avoid the strengths and exploit the potential vulnerabilities of larger and technologically superior opponents. This includes: (1) The selective use of weapons or military resources by a state or sub-state group to counter, deter, or possibly defeat a numerically or technologically superior force. (2) The use of diplomatic and other non-military resources or tactics by a state or sub-state group to discourage or constrain military operations by a superior force."[10]

Most recently, the RAND Corporation added its own definition of asymmetric warfare to the literature in terms of "conflicts between nations or groups that have disparate military capabilities and strategies."[11]

As far as we know, the term *hybrid warfare* was coined by William Nemeth in his thesis, *Future War and Chechnya: A Case for Hybrid Warfare*, way back in 2002. The author wrote about a hybrid society, in which modern and ancient characteristics merged, that fights in a hybrid way, using a combination of contemporary and older methods. His primary example were the Chechens, who fought fiercely against Russian armed forces in 1994–95 and 1999–2000.

The concept of hybrid warfare – sometimes used interchangeably with asymmetric warfare, sometimes marking a subcategory within it – entered NATO's lexicon in the last couple of years. Increasingly, NATO officials are using the term. NATO Secretary General, Jens Stoltenberg, said that "hybrid warfare combines different types of threats, including conventional, subversion or cyber"[12] and that the organization has to adapt to the task at hand. Heidi Reisinger and Alexandr Golts, in a NATO research paper, describe Russian hybrid warfare methods as a "mix of military and non-military, conventional and irregular components that can include… cyber and information operations. None is new; it is the combination of different actions that achieves a surprise effect and creates ambiguity."[13] Today, the term *hybrid warfare* is mostly used in connection with the aforementioned Russian activities, while asymmetric warfare, in more general terms, is used to refer to many other actors (most notably, the so-called Islamic State).

Russian hybrid warfare is really nothing new in the sense that it is a revival and a modernization of the Cold War era's Soviet Active Measures – intelligence and paramilitary operations that were considered as part of a major weapons system for conducting covert warfare. Active Measures were utilized to influence and

---

[9] Wurzel et al. 1998.

[10] Central Intelligence Agency, Statement of Work for Asymmetric Warfare Threats to US Interests: Expert Panel Support (Washington, DC: CIA, May 1998), 2. https://www.hsdl.org/?view&did=439201. Accessed 14 October 2016.

[11] http://www.rand.org/topics/asymmetric-warfare.html. Accessed 15 November 2016.

[12] Garamone 2015, 'NATO focuses on combating hybrid warfare'. https://www.defense.gov/News/Article/Article/604638, Accessed 20 January 2017.

[13] Reisinger and Golts 2014.

manipulate events and behaviour in foreign societies through influencing the policies of other governments, undermining or building up leaders and groups in these states, and undermining opponents through support for opposition political and armed groups.[14]

The tools in the Active Measures toolbox included: forging documents to discredit opponents; employing agents of influence (foreign journalists, labour leaders, government officials, academics), whom "Lenin called 'useful idiots'… who would believe Soviet myths and repeat them endlessly to promote"[15] political goals; the creation of front groups to influence political developments; information operations (psychological warfare); support for opposition political movements in foreign countries; and support for insurgent and terrorist groups.

This concept was revived and polished during the reorganization and strengthening of Russia's security apparatus in the 2010s, with the Chief of the Russian General Staff, General Valery Gerasimov, describing this new approach as "blurring the lines between states of war and states of peace. Wars are no longer declared, and having begun, proceed according to an unfamiliar template… the very rules of war have changed significantly. The use of non-military methods to achieve political and strategic objectives has in some cases proved far more effective than the use of military force."[16] Its first public appearance took place during the 2008 Five-day War in Georgia.

The most important goal of the new Russian approach to war is not the destruction of the enemy, but its manipulation or internal subversion. Therefore, in addition to kinetic operations, Gerasimov recommends the use of cultural and communication (INFOOPs, PSYOPs) tools, while preferring the use of special forces instead of the deployment of conventional forces. War is not limited to the front lines; instead, the whole territory of the enemy can be targeted during the conflict when the use of military force is coordinated with political, diplomatic, economic, informational, technological and environmental operations.

According to András Rácz, who thoroughly analysed Russia's Crimean operations, a hybrid conflict can be divided into preparation, attack and stabilization phases.[17] The following table describes the actions, objectives and primary tools for each phase (Table 8.1).

8.3 Legal Implications

As was obvious reading through the above, there are fundamental problems with hybrid warfare from a legal point of view, since it denies most of the fundamental distinctions on which the law of armed conflicts is built.

---

[14] Schulz and Godson 1984.

[15] Friedman 2016.

[16] Berzenis 2014.

[17] Rácz 2015.

Table 8.1 Phases, content, aims and tools of a hybrid war (*Source* Rácz 2015)

Phases, content, aims and tools of a hybrid war

Phase	Actions	Objective	Tools
Preparation	**Strategic preparation**: • Loyal NGOs and media organizations • Finding vulnerable points • Building up diplomatic and media positions	• Preparing for the creation and/or expansion of a conflict by diplomatic methods • Intelligence organizations find the vulnerable points of the enemy	Diplomacy Intelligence
	Political preparation: • Increasing the level of unrest towards the central authority of the country • Corrupting or 'turning' professionals, leaders of the public administration, members of the military or police • Building contacts with criminal networks	Creating conditions within the hostile country, which may weaken the country's political (strategic) leadership	Political Diplomatic Intelligence
	Operational preparation: • Extensive political pressure on the country to be attacked • Mobilization of bureaucrats, police and military leaders, local criminals • Contacting local oligarchs	Increasing economic and political pressure on the target country	Diplomatic Intelligence Economic
Assault	**Launching the crisis**: • Widespread anti-government demonstrations • Special forces infiltrate their designated targets • Provocations and acts of sabotage • The media causes confusion	Entering an area and seizing it by attacking the hostile government and by using our own special forces	Diplomatic Intelligence Military Media INFOOPS PSYOPS
	Forcing out the central power: • Capturing administrative buildings and points of strategic importance • Media activities • Creating an information-communication superiority • Paralysing local armed forces	• Forcing the forces of the hostile government out of their own country • Influencing the international community	Diplomatic Intelligence Military Media INFOOPS PSYOPS

(continued)

Table 8.1 (continued)

Phases, content, aims and tools of a hybrid war

Phase	Actions	Objective	Tools
	Setting up an alternative centre of political power: • Proclaiming a new political centre • Setting up new political bodies • Media campaigns • Blocking military counterattacks	• Strengthening the *status quo* • Influencing the international community	Diplomatic Intelligence Military Media INFOOPS PSYOPS
Strategic exploitation of success	**Political stabilization of the success**: • Organizing a bogus referendum • Media campaign	• Creating the legal justification for the captured territories • Influencing the international community	Diplomatic Intelligence Military Media INFOOPS PSYOPS
	Taking an area from the hostile country: • The attacking country annexes the areas that it has occupied • Invading an area on the pretext of either peacekeeping activities or crisis management	• Military occupation of the selected areas • Setting up a military administration • Keeping the captured territory	Political Diplomatic Intelligence Military Media INFOOPS PSYOPS
	Limiting the political and strategic flexibility of the attacked country: • The loss of economic, infrastructural, and demographic resources causes serious economic difficulties and long-lasting internal imbalance • The loss of territorial integrity means that the attacked country cannot join any political or military organization, where it is a requirement for membership	Preventing the enemy country from joining international political or military organizations	Political Diplomatic Intelligence Media INFOOPS PSYOPS

First of all, there is no longer any real distinction between war and peace – in practice, this means continuous war, encompassing all aspects of civil life. Thus, *jus* and *bellum* distinctions become largely meaningless.

The struggle encompasses all aspects of life blurring the lines of conflict. It is worth comparing the above with the foreword in *Unrestricted Warfare*, an important Chinese work on future conflicts, which quotes one of its authors, Senior Colonel Qiao: "The first rule of unrestricted warfare is that there are no rules, with nothing forbidden."

The problem with this approach is that, similar to their current adversaries, nations that have been "playing by the rules" will have to consider the introduction of an "unrestricted" or "total" war-like national defence strategy and accept that there is no longer any dividing line between peace and war. If there has ever been a time in history when military strategist Frank Hoffman's statement, that "the incentives for states to exploit non-traditional modes of war are on the rise",[18] was true, then now is that time. Nations are forced to listen to Marshall McLuhan's words: "do no try to do today's job with yesterday's tools and yesterday's concepts."[19] Unfortunately, for many, concepts will not only include military, but also legal concepts. This new approach will probably provide an answer to Samuel P. Huntington's famous question about how to modernize a defensive system without Westernizing it.[20] However, we may need to ask the following question as well: does Westernization also mean accepting legal norms pertaining to the waging and conduct of hostilities, based on the Western, i.e., Clausewitzian, understanding of warfare?

Kenneth Waltz argues that, in the current competitive international environment, states "socialize" towards similar strategies. For Waltz: "The fate of each state depends on its responses to what her competitors do. The possibility that conflict will be conducted by force leads to competition in the arts and the instruments of force. Competition produces a tendency toward the sameness of the competitors."[21] This means that there are calls on Western military forces to follow the Russian example and transform themselves in the same way. That said, adopting these methods would require adopting the tendency to no longer adhere to legal regulations.

General Rupert Smith reminded NATO that it needs "a paradigm shift that necessitates both new assumptions and the reconstruction of prior assumptions."[22] To effectively counter the Russian approach, nations may have to start harvesting from the edges of strategic thinking, instead of trying to blindly follow the conventionally rooted ideas of the "mainstream".

This means that countries may have to break down decades-old – in some cases, centuries-old – military culture and traditions. Just as the phalanx, the heavy cavalry or the hussars, and the doctrines and weapon systems associated with these formations vanished hundreds of years ago, currently existing services, branches, formations, training structures and military rank systems may disappear in most nations as well. As Martin van Creveld suggested, "regular armed forces themselves change forms, shrink in size and wither away... regular forces degenerate into police-like forces or, in case the struggle lasts for very long, mere armed gangs. Over time uniforms will probably be replaced by mere insignia in the shape of sashes, armbands and

---

[18] Hoffmann 2009, p. 38.

[19] This is a common paraphrase of McLuhan's original sentence, which reads: "Our 'Age of Anxiety' is, in part, the result of trying to do today's job with tools – with yesterday's concepts." McLuhan and Fiore 1967.

[20] Huntington 1957.

[21] Waltz 1979, p. 127.

[22] Smith 2005, p. 4.

the like."[23] Furthermore, the new defence establishments "will not amount to armies as we understand the term today."[24] Formations can be based on military, police, secret or intelligence services, while organizational character should also incorporate the useful elements of terrorist groups and partisan and insurgent organizations. These future defensive formations may contain specialist members with engineering, medical, cyber, communication and media capabilities, among other. These new elements can also employ completely unexpected techniques, tactics and procedures, such as swarming,[25] in order to be effective against both a conventional and an unconventional adversary.

The obvious problem with the above is that it can hardly accommodate today's legal regime; for example, if rank systems (and maybe also the distinction between combatants and civilians) were to disappear, many provisions of the Third and Fourth Geneva Conventions would become meaningless, thus creating confusion.

There is also the problem of integrating non-violent means into the overall strategy of an operation. Russia itself has used civilian-based non-violent actions in Ukraine and made them an integral part of its military doctrine. To achieve this goal, Russia uses a wide array of political, diplomatic, secret service, economic and information tools, which are coordinated in almost real time. The greatest novelty of hybrid warfare is that it can achieve direct results, such as the annexation of territories, despite its use of asymmetric methods of warfare. As a countermeasure, NATO and its member states have also started to give serious consideration to the idea of employing these strategies, because they offer serious advantages over traditional military strategies by exploiting the political vulnerabilities of the enemy.

This results in the extreme fluidity of a hybrid war: it is extremely difficult to prove the involvement of the aggressor, while regular military units are only used during the latest phases of the conflict. This fact also calls into question the applicability of conventional defence guarantees. Regular armed forces do openly not attack the enemy, as proposed by Mao's "two arms theory".[26] Their role is to threaten the country with an attack, adding an extra element of political pressure and preventing the concentration of the defender's forces.

8.4 Conclusion

While books have been written about the theory of asymmetric and hybrid warfare, in most cases, they only analyse new developments from a military standpoint, as this phenomenon first has to be understood on factual and theoretical levels.

However, once we understand what is happening in the field, it is impossible not to talk about the legal implications, which are very serious, and probably the

---

[23] Van Creveld 1991, p. 207.

[24] Ibid., p. 209.

[25] Arquilla and Ronfeldt 2000.

[26] Tse-Tung 2007, p. 132.

most serious since the Second World War. Today, not only do fringe elements (rebel movements, separatists etc.) in the international community question the way that war is waged (in both *jus ad bellum* and *jus in bello* senses), but so do some of the strongest and most influential players, most notably the Russian Federation (and, to a lesser extent, China). Russia has already demonstrated in Georgia and Ukraine what this new type of war will look like, and we can already identify the legal challenges (and, in some cases, the failure to comply with legal regulations) that we will face.

The "mother of all problems" is the blurring of lines between war (armed conflict) and peace, as well as between combatants and civilians. The very idea of asymmetric/hybrid warfare demands the dismantling of the 'wall' between these situations and statuses; and. while it offers many new avenues for the parties to explore regarding their possible actions, it effectively annuls most of the protections afforded by international law to vulnerable persons and civilian objects.

Although it is hard to predict whether this new form of warfare will become the norm, it is possible that other nations will be hard-pressed by events to copy it, which may result in the necessity to review the current legal framework regulating armed conflicts. As it now seems, such a revision would probably result in less, not more, protection for all involved in such conflicts.

References

Arquilla J, Ronfeldt D (2000) Swarming and the Future of Conflict. RAND Corporation, Santa Monica

Berzenis J (2014) Russia's New Generation Warfare in Ukraine: Implications for Latvian Defense Policy. Policy Paper No 02. National Defence Academy of Latvian Center for Security and Strategic Research, Riga

Central Intelligence Agency (1998) Statement of Work for Asymmetric Warfare Threats to US Interests. Expert Panel Support, Washington DC

Friedman G (2016) The Soviet Union and Russia: Tragedy and Farce. Geopolitical Futures 29 December 2016

Garamone J (2015) NATO Focuses on Combating Hybrid Warfare." DoD News, https://www.defense.gov/News/Article/Article/604638. Accessed 17 February 2017

Goldman EO (2006 Cultural Foundations of Military Diffusion. Review of International Studies, Vol. 32, No. 1 (Jan. 2006), pp. 69–91

Hoffmann FG (2009) "Hybrid Warfare and Challenges". Small Wars Journal, 52, 1st Quarter 2009

Huntington SP (1957) The Soldier and the State: The Theory and Politics of Civil-military Relations. Harvard University Press

Lawrence TE ["Lawrence of Arabia"] (1922) Seven Pillars of Wisdom. Oxford

Marighella C (2011) Minimanual of the Urban Guerrilla. Create Space Independent Publishing Platform

McLuhan M, Fiore Q (1967) The Medium is the Message: An Inventory of Effects New York. Bantam Books

Metz S, Johnson DV II (2001) Asymmetry and U.S. Military Strategy: Definition, Background and Strategic Concepts (January 2001), 2. http://strategicstudiesinstitute.army.mil/pdffiles/PUB223.pdf. Accessed 16 February 2017

Rácz A (2015) Russia's Hybrid War in Ukraine: Breaking the Enemy's Ability to Resist. The Finnish Institute of International Affairs 2015. http://www.fiia.fi/en/publication/514/russia_s_hybrid_war_in_ukraine/. Accessed 15 February 2017

Reisinger H, Golts A (2014) "Russia's Hybrid Warfare Waging War below the Radar of Traditional Collective Defence". Research Paper, NATO Defense College, Rome. http://ftalphaville.ft.com/files/2014/11/rp_105.pdf. Accessed 18 February 2017

Smith R (2005) The Utility of Force: The Art of War in the Modern World, London, Allen Lane

Schulz R, Godson R (1984) Dezinformatsia: Active Measures in Soviet Strategy. Pergamon-Brassey's, Washington

Tito JB (1966) Selected military works. Vojnoizdavacki zavod

Tse-Tung M (2007) On Guerrilla Warfare. BN Publishing

Tsybulenko E, Pakhomenko S (2016) The Ukrainian Crisis as a Challenge for the Eastern Partnership. In: Kerimae T, Chochia A (eds) Political and Legal Perspectives of the EU Eastern Partnership Policy. Springer International Publishing, Switzerland

van Creveld M (1991) Transformation of War. The Free Press, New York

von Clausewitz C (1832) On War. (introduction Natusch Maude F, translator Graham JJ) http://oll.libertyfund.org/titles/clausewitz-on-war. Accessed 16 February 2016

Waltz KN (1979) Theory of International Politics. McGraw-Hill, New York

Wurzel DJ, McGruther KR, Murray WR (1998) A Survey of Unclassified Literature on the Subject of Asymmetric Warfare. Arete Associates, Sherman Oaks CA

Chapter 9
The Operation of International Treaties and Contracts in the Event of Armed Conflict: Problems Reopened by Russian Aggression Against Ukraine

Olga Butkevych

Contents

Olga Butkevych, Doctor of International Law and Professor of the Chair of International Law, Institute of International Relations, Taras Shevchenko National University of Kyiv, Olga Butkevych, Ukraine, Kyiv, Melnykova str. 36/1, email: olga_butkevych@ukr.net, tel.: +380674010156. In the present work, the terms *war* and *armed conflict* are used in accordance with their meaning in the appropriate historical period. Considering classical international law, we use *war* and *armed conflict* as interchangeable notions. With the formation of modern humanitarian law, we predominantly use the term *armed conflict* in the sense of the 1949 Geneva Conventions and other instruments pertaining to current international law and jurisprudence.

O. Butkevych (✉)
Institute of International Relations, Taras Shevchenko National University of Kyiv,
Melnykova str. 36/1, Kyiv, Ukraine
e-mail: olga_butkevych@ukr.net

© T.M.C. ASSER PRESS and the authors 2018   185
S. Sayapin and E. Tsybulenko (eds.), *The Use of Force against Ukraine and International Law*, https://doi.org/10.1007/978-94-6265-222-4_9

Abstract War has traditionally been regarded as an event that terminates the operation of treaties. After the prohibition of war by the UN Charter and under the influence of the process of globalization, an armed conflict is regarded as an event that does not *ipso facto* terminate or suspend the operation of treaties, either between states parties to the conflict or a state party to the conflict and a third state. Nowadays, the problem concerning the effect of war on the operation of international agreements, which was not solved by the 1969 Vienna Convention on the Law of Treaties, rather belongs to the domain of international customary law. The adoption of the Draft Articles on the Effects of Armed Conflicts on Treaties by the UN International Law Commission in 2011 (as well as a number of earlier, more or less doctrinal, documents such as the 1985 Resolution of the Institute of International Law on the Effects of Armed Conflicts on Treaties) has not solved this problem either, because the character of this document is one of "soft law". For a long time, states avoided solving this problem for political reasons. Settlement of the legal problem was inevitability revived after the start of the Russian aggression against Ukraine in 2014, which affected the operation of (a) bilateral treaties, (b) bilateral contracts and (c) multilateral treaties. A number of bilateral treaties of the parties has been terminated or suspended. Russian aggression has also revealed general trends in current international law, which seek to minimize the impact of war on the continuity of treaties and contracts.

Keywords international treaty · international contract · law of the treaties · Vienna Convention on the Law of Treaties · international customary law · armed conflict · aggression · *jus cogens* · *rebus sic stantibus*

9.1 Traditional Concept of the Effect of Armed Conflicts on International Agreements

9.1.1 Concept of the Effects of War Upon Treaties

The classical concept of the effects of war upon treaties has passed through three subsequent stages in its development. At first, war was regarded in international law as an event that ought to terminate the operation of treaties. This approach was influenced by the natural law doctrine, which established a clear division of the state of international relations into peace and war, whereby the latter excluded the mere possibility of any legal contacts that were characteristic of peacetime (economic, commercial, diplomatic, political and treaty relations): "the fact of the occurrence of war excludes the continuing operation of law."[1] According to the naturalist approach to international law, the commencement of hostilities between peoples puts to an end

---

[1] Delbrück 2000, p. 1368.

all kinds of peaceful interrelations. This idea was already known in ancient natural legal theory. Thus, according to Livy, "Laws passed in time of peace, war frequently annuls, and peace those passed in times of war" (speech by Licius Valerius, reported by Livy).[2]

Although natural law was based on the principle of *pacta sunt servanda* and good faith in international law, there was probably only one legal basis on which to withdraw from that commitment, namely, the commencement of hostilities. Of course, such a possibility was only attributed to a *bona fide* actor – a victim of war or aggression, and not to the aggressor as such.

However, classical theorists of international law (Suarez, Grotius, de Vattel et al.) have already deviated from such an approach and expressed new ideas about the possibility of complying with proper treaty commitments, which are minimally affected by war. This was done for the sake of the basic international legal principle of *pacta sunt servanda*. In this context, Grotius stated that, "least of all should that be admitted which some people imagine, that in war all laws are in abeyance. On the contrary, war ought not to be undertaken except for the enforcement of rights; when once undertaken, it should be carried on only within the bounds of law and good faith… between enemies. Written laws, that is, laws of particular states, are not in force, but that unwritten laws are in force, that is, those which nature prescribes, or the agreement of nations has established", i.e., the law of nations.[3]

Besides, Grotius emphasized the basic principle of good faith between enemies.[4] Moreover, according to Grotius, any war that terminates all other kinds of interstate conduct should activate treaty relations.[5]

In the 18th century, when a gradual transition to the authority of positivism began, ideas about the desirability of treaties' continuity between belligerents was expressed. In this respect Emer de Vattel argued that: "It would be an error equally abhorrent and disastrous to imagine that all duties cease and all ties of humanity are broken when two Nations go to war… all those duties, the exercise of which is not necessarily suspended by this conflict, continue in full force and are binding upon us both with respect to the enemy and to all other men. Now, the obligation of keeping faith, far from ceasing in time of war because of the precedence to be given to duties towards oneself, becomes more necessary than ever."[6]

The termination of treaties as a result of war should be regarded as an exception: "Conventions and treaties are broken or annulled when war breaks out between the contracting parties, either because such agreements imply a state of peace, or because each party, having the right to deprive the enemy of his property, may take from him such rights as have been given him by treaties. However, an exception is to be made of those treaties which contain provisions that are to take effect in

---

[2] Cited from: Scott 2002, p. 285.

[3] Grotius 1925, pp. 18–9.

[4] Ibid., 1925, pp. 800–1.

[5] Ibid., 1925, p. 631; see also: ibid., Book III, Chapter XXI ('On good faith during war'), pp. 832–44.

[6] de Vattel 1916, p. 296.

the event of war."[7] De Vattel considered that war generates special treaties reducing hostilities and improving the state of combatants and civilians, which should be faithfully observed by the belligerents.[8]

Indeed, war does not stop international relations. Sometimes, it even activates them, becoming a mighty catalyst for the arrival of a new era in international law (as was the case with the Peace of Westphalia, which terminated the Thirty Years' War and introduced a new historical period for this law, or the rapid development of international law after the Second World War). In this regard, we may agree with the statement that "state practice suggests that war does not mean the total disruption of all legal bonds between States and that the belligerents must observe basic rules of humanity towards each other and must also entertain some legal relations with each other as, for instance, in the case of armistice agreements, agreements on the exchange of the sick and the wounded, etc."[9] But this is only true for new treaties concluded as a result of war, but not already existing agreements signed before the outbreak of conflict.

Nevertheless, in the 17th and 18th centuries, the attitude to war as a terminating factor for international treaties was still influential. That period witnessed the struggle between emerging positivism and natural law, according to which "one feature of a state of war was held to be the automatic and total abrogation of all peaceful relations between the warring states. More specifically, it meant the automatic abrogation of all pre-war treaties."[10] In general, the first stage in the formation of this concept was marked by the predominance of natural law. Thus, we may conclude that, at that time, terminating most of the previous treaties led to invigorating treaty-making activity connected with waging hostilities.

The second stage in the development of the concept of the effect of war on treaties started at the end of the 19th and the beginning of the 20th centuries. This stage turned out to be more practically oriented and pragmatic under the influence of positivism, which dominated international legal theory of that time. War began to be treated as an inappropriate feature of international relations, whose impact on them should be reduced. Both legal (universalization of international law and order, appearance of first international organizations, interdependence of international relations and policy) and economic (the need to develop interstate trade) factors contributed to a shift in interpreting the influence of war to treaties. On the one hand, there was established "a belief that war is – or at least should be – a contest between the professional armed forces of the two societies, with minimal disruption of civilian life"; on the other hand, "in the materialistic nineteenth century, it was increasingly held that the world was – or at least was becoming – a single economic community, and that intermittent wars were merely, so to speak, temporary disturbances on the surface which should not affect that underlying unity".[11]

---

[7] de Vattel 1916, p. 296.

[8] See de Vattel 1916, pp. 269–301, 322–30 etc.

[9] Delbrück 2000, p. 1368.

[10] Neff 2004, p. 368.

[11] Ibid., 2004, pp. 370–1. See also Lesaffer 2012, pp. 71–94; O'Connell 2012, p. 272–93.

The general view was that international treaties should continue to operate, except in cases of essential influence of hostilities on their implementation or when they should be suspended during wartime (Cardozo, Westlake, Oppenheim). In this context, many scholars of that time were influenced by earlier thinkers, in particular, by Emer de Vattel's views.[12] According to Oppenheim, "the doctrine was formerly held, and a few writers maintain it even now, that the outbreak of war *ipso facto* cancels all treaties previously concluded between the belligerents, such treaties only excepted as have been concluded specially for the case of war. The vast majority of modern writers on international law have abandoned this standpoint, and the opinion is pretty general that war by no means annuls every treaty. But unanimity in regard to such treaties as are and such as are not cancelled by war does not exist."[13] At that time, an assumption prevailed that all political treaties, and even treaties on diplomatic relations, would terminate in the event of war, whereas treaties that were especially concluded in the case of war would continue to operate.

Both state interests and international relations had a rather serious impact on such an approach: "[Few] states deliberately place themselves in a belligerent attitude between whom treaty obligations of considerable importance are not in existence at the date of the rupture of friendly relations. These undertakings create mutual rights and obligations and some of them are of such serious importance that their unexpected abrogation would constitute a serious blow to their prosperity and to the health of the body politic."[14]

The same pragmatic approach was confirmed by the resolution of the Institute of International Law known as *Règlement concernant les effets de la guerre sur les traits* (*Institut de Droit International. Session de Christiana* – 1912),[15] which was probably the first, albeit somewhat doctrinal, document dedicated to the topic. This document not only summarized existing practices and approaches to the effect of war on treaties, but also had a powerful influence on further international lawmaking. According to this document, the commencement and waging of war do not influence concluded treaties and agreements except in the case of: (a) large-scale political treaties, treaties on alliances, protectorates, establishment of political control or economic regime, etc., and (b) any treaty whose application or interpretation has been the direct cause of the war or the treaties that were exclusively designed for times of peace (Article 2). All treaties that remain in force should be respected and observed by belligerent parties as strictly as possible (Article 4). Treaties with third parties should remain unaffected by the war; there is also a presumption of the continuity of multilateral treaties, when one or several parties to them are belligerents (Articles 8–11). Actually, here, the termination of treaties as a result of war is regarded more as an exception than a rule. Thus, the resolution demonstrated a shift in the attitude to war as a

---

[12] See Chetail and Haggenmacher 2011.

[13] Oppenheim 1935, p. 107–8.

[14] Davis 1912, pp. 124–5.

[15] See the text of the resolution in French here: http://www.idi-iil.org/app/uploads/2017/06/1912_christ_02_fr.pdf. Accessed 19 August 2017.

catastrophic disaster for international legal order, to its interpretation as an event that should ordinarily not affect international commitments of the belligerents.

During the interwar period, this problem received little scholarly attention. Only a few researchers dealt with it. A comprehensive analysis of international legal doctrine and practice concerning the effect of war on international treaties in the period before the Second World War was conducted by Arnold D. McNair, while some aspects of the problem were touched upon in the works of Wehberg, Descamps, Taube and Whitton.[16] Due to all the above factors, we arrive in our own age with a lack of theoretical reasoning on the operation of international treaties during armed conflict.[17]

The third stage in the development of this concept began with the prohibition of war by the UN Charter in the middle of the 20th century. Afterwards, it was also influenced by the process of globalization at the beginning of the 21st century. The shift in the understanding of war as a legal means of restoring justice, in relation to an illegal action or even a crime, defined the attitude to the effects of war on treaties and contracts.

A more detailed analysis of present-day attitudes to war and its effect on treaties is provided below.

Generally, in the course of history, two approaches interacted and finally defined the stages of the development of the doctrine, which is considered here. The first is the principle of strict compliance with international commitments. The second is the interpretation of war as an extraordinary phenomenon, which destroys the world order. In order to harmonize these approaches, a concept of fundamental change in circumstances (*rebus sic stantibus*) was developed, as well as the concept of the continuity of international treaties. Treaties have also been classified into those that are terminated due to war, those that suspend their operation, with their renewal after the end of hostilities, and those that continue to be applied and should be performed by the parties in good faith. In general, historically speaking, the concept of the effect of war on international treaties has developed from the notion of the termination of all international agreements to the modern view that treaties should continue to operate.

9.1.2   Concept of the Effect of Armed Conflicts on International Contracts

The concept of the effect of armed conflicts on international contracts has, to some extent, developed separately from the above theories. Taking into account the private character of such agreements and the minimal impact of the state on them, they

---

[16] McNair 1937, pp. 523–85. See also Wehberg 1928, pp. 147–306; Descamps 1930, pp. 393–559; Taube 1930, pp. 291–389; Whitton 1934, pp. 147–276.

[17] See De La Pradelle 1948; Rank 1953. The analysis of the problem of the effect of war on treaties is quite incomplete within or missing from rather thorough studies on international treaty law: Aust 2013; Villiger 2009; Dörr and Schmalenbach 2012.

were treated as being more independent from interstate interactions, including war relations. It is mainly at the discretion of the parties to determine to what extent war affects contracts. Traditionally, the negative impact of war on such agreements was treated from the point of view of the impossibility and economic impracticability of their performance. However, state control and the regulation of such transactions also remain somewhat significant (legislative prohibitions of some transactions with the enemy, state interference in cases of economic warfare, the legal status of enemy property etc.).[18]

The problem of the operation of international contracts during wartime was the subject of examination only at the end of the 19th and the beginning of the 20th centuries. The study of this problem intensified with the outbreak of the First World War. Oppenheim offered the following characteristics of the doctrine in question: "Following Bynkershoek all British and American writers and cases, and also some French and German writers assert the existence of a rule of International Law that all relations, and especially, trading, is *ipso facto* by the outbreak of war prohibited between the subjects of the belligerents, unless it is permitted under the customs of war, as, for instance, ransom bills, or is allowed under special licenses, and that all contracts concluded between the subjects of the belligerents before the outbreak of war become extinct or suspended. On the other hand, most German, French, and Italian writers deny the existence of such a rule, but assert the existence of another, according to which belligerents are empowered to prohibit by special orders all trade between their own and enemy subjects."[19]

This was a time when the nations of the world adhered to the three main approaches to the influence of interstate armed conflict on international private contracts. According to the first, the commencement of war terminates all contracts with the enemy (including those in which third parties take part); such termination is legalized by the relevant governmental decree. The second approach presumes that private agreements continue to operate unless specific contracts are forbidden by a special (individual) governmental act. The third group includes countries that strictly prohibit contractual relationships with the enemy, except in cases of special governmental permission.

International legal doctrine and legislative practice of states during that period already distinguished peculiarities in the application of contracts that were concluded before conflict and those that were concluded in wartime. This may be explained by the influence of judicial practice and an increasing number of complaints about the violation of pre-war contracts.

With the development of international private contacts in the late 20th century and the extended influence of transnational corporations on the world economy, the issue of international private agreements has gradually disappeared from the international public domain and the influence of the state. Today, one may notice a rather independent functioning of the system of international private contracts, and therefore a minimal impact of interstate armed conflicts on it. The commencement

---

[18] Davis 1912, pp. 129–32; Steimel 2000, pp. 1360–7.

[19] Oppenheim 1935, p. 152.

of an armed conflict may be regarded by parties as ordinary *force majeure*, more or less.

In general, an effect of armed conflicts on contracts today is mostly noticeable during so-called "economic warfare". Economic sanctions against a violator of international law, which have developed within modern international law, directly affect the performance of international contracts. The phenomenon of "humanitarian financial intervention" is thus formed. It is revealed in asset freezes and other financial penalties imposed on the violator.[20] Nowadays, each state establishes its own legislation that provides for the freedom to operate or limits the operation of private international contracts in wartime due to national interests and safety and economic requirements.

9.2 Transformation of the International Legal Concept of the Effect of War on the Operation of International Treaties and Contracts in the Late 20th Century and the Age of Globalization

9.2.1 Legal Problems with the Effect of Armed Conflict on the Operation of International Treaties and Contracts Revealed by the Russian Aggression Against Ukraine

Russian aggression against Ukraine, which openly began in February 2014, reopened a huge range of international legal problems, including the effect of armed conflict on the operation of international treaties and contracts.

Hereinafter, the notions of "Russian aggression against Ukraine" and "Russian occupation of Ukrainian territory" are grounded, *inter alia*, on the definition of aggression given in the UN General Assembly Resolution 3314 (XXIX) adopted on 14 December 1974 and the following documents: General Assembly Resolution of 19 December 2016 (No. 71/205) on the Situation of Human Rights in the Autonomous Republic of Crimea and the City of Sevastopol (Ukraine), in which the Russian Federation is recognized as an occupying power (particularly in Crimea); Resolutions of the Parliamentary Assembly of the Council of Europe (PACE) No. 2132 (2016) on the Political Consequences of the Russian Aggression in Ukraine, and No. 2133 (2016) on the Legal Remedies for Human Rights Violations on the Ukrainian Territories Outside the Control of the Ukrainian Authorities, adopted on 12 October 2016; PACE Resolution 1990 on the Reconsideration on Substantive Grounds of the Previously Ratified Credentials of the Russian Delegation, adopted 10 April 2014, which recognizes the "military occupation of the Ukrainian territory";

---

[20] Criddle 2013, pp. 583–615.

PACE Resolution No. 2145 (2017) on the Functioning of Democratic Institutions in Ukraine, which emphasizes "Russian aggression in eastern Ukraine and the illegal annexation of Crimea"; OSCE Parliamentary Assembly Resolution on the Continuation of Clear, Gross and Uncorrected Violations of OSCE Commitments and International Norms by the Russian Federation, adopted in Helsinki on 8 July 2015, which states that "the actions by the Russian Federation in the Autonomous Republic of Crimea and the city of Sevastopol, as well as in certain areas of the Donetsk and Luhansk regions of Ukraine, constitute acts of military aggression against Ukraine"; the International Criminal Court's (ICC's) Annual Report on Preliminary Examination Activities, issued on 14 November 2016 by the ICC Prosecutor, Fatou Bensouda, in which the situation in Ukraine (especially the annexation of Crimea) is recognized as "an international armed conflict between Ukraine and the Russian Federation", which began at the latest on 26 February 2014.

First and foremost, current international law considers aggression as one of the gravest crimes and does not recognize war as a means of dispute settlement and restoring rights. Such a shift in the legal treatment of armed conflicts has led to respective changes in attitude towards their effects on different domains of life, including treaty relations. Such logic suggests that peaceful relations should be maintained at most. At the same time, issues of national security and other national interests may keep the government from continuing its treaty relations with the enemy party. As a consequence, the problem concerning the effect of armed conflict on the operation of international treaties has become somewhat topical in current international law.

A wide range of problems results from the fact that, for the first time in recent history, a permanent member of the UN Security Council has committed direct aggression against another state, thereby completely blocking the peacekeeping activity of this body. The occurrence of such an offence turned out to be unexpected by the international community, which was unable to develop an appropriate legal attitude towards it.[21]

---

[21] International lawyers at the turn of the millennium were almost unanimously optimistic about ending the "Cold War", unblocking the UN Security Council and its effectiveness in the future. Such optimism *inter alia* led to the unreadiness of international law to react to the aforementioned challenges. See, for instance, Grewe: "The world changed completely between 1989 and 1991. The Soviet Union, one of the two superpowers, dissolved, leaving a collection of mostly medium-sized and minor independent States in Eastern Europe and Central Asia. The most important of these states were the Russian Federation and Ukraine. The Cold War faded away, and the United Nations Security Council was no longer paralyzed by the veto-power of its antagonistic permanent members" (Grewe 2000, p. 701); Johnston: "The end of the Cold War in 1989 restored hope that major problems in international relations could be dealt with effectively through the peaceful processes of international law and diplomacy… [The] Russian government could no longer afford its superpower status and the cost of daily confrontation with the United States. The game of veto-politics in the Security Council had lost most of its appeal" (Johnston 2008, p. 89); Frowein: "With the fall of Berlin wall in 1989 and the disappearance of the east-west conflict which had lasted for almost 50 years the United Nations system, as designed in 1945, could be, for the first time, tested as to its possibilities. While binding decisions by the Security Council under Chapter VII of the UN Charter were practically excluded during the east-west conflict they have become a normal occurrence since 1990" (Frowein 2000, pp. 1038–9).

Firstly, the huge complex of commitments has been violated by the aforementioned aggression in the context of Russia's obligations under the UN Charter, the Budapest Memorandum on Security Assurances in Connection with Ukraine's Accession to the Treaty on the Non-proliferation of Nuclear Weapons (1994) etc. Besides, there also occurs a problem with the fulfilment of regional – foremost in the framework of the Commonwealth of Independent States (CIS) – and bilateral treaties, especially in the domain of political, military and legal cooperation.

Secondly, the Russian-Ukrainian conflict is characterized as a "hybrid" war, which appears to be a recent phenomenon. Such a phenomenon relates to many fields of international and municipal life, covering different domains of human (not only state) activity, inevitably touching on treaty and private contractual relations. This includes the interconnection between public treaty and international commercial (private) relations during a hybrid war, which leads to a question as to the continuity of treaty commitments in wartime. The hybrid character of a conflict, which may only cover part of a country or its definite region, entails the problem of the territorial scope of a treaty.

Thirdly, the ban on the use of force and the prohibition of war in international law have resulted in a transition in the attitude towards the effect of armed conflicts on treaties and contracts. That shift manifested itself in the contents of the UN Draft Articles on the Effects of Armed Conflicts on Treaties (2011), which state that "the existence of an armed conflict does not *ipso facto* terminate or suspend the operation of treaties" (Article 3).

9.2.2 Changes in the Concept of War in International Law (Prohibition of Aggressive War and Transition from the Concept of "War" to the Concept of "Armed Conflict")

The transformation of the international legal conception of war manifests itself in the prohibition of aggressive war and the transition from the idea of a "just war" to the concept of "armed conflict". This may even be observed in the terminology: nowadays, most international legal instruments use the term *armed conflict*, rather than *war*. Another visible trend in international law is the increased influence of the law of international society (international civil society as a determining factor for international lawmaking). The idea of the continuity of international treaties and contracts in the event of a conflict continues to attract supporters, although it is quite important to define all possible exclusions from such a continuity.

As Cançado Trindade observes: "In the last decades, one has witnessed a true conversion of the traditional and surpassed *jus ad bellum* into the *jus contra bellum* of our days; this is one of the most significant transformations of the contemporary international legal order";[22] however, this seems too optimistic. Meanwhile, the international community did not get rid of hostilities and wars in the traditional meaning. After the atrocities of the Second World War, it only changed its attitude towards the same phenomenon, as well as its influence on international treaty law: "What the world really witnessed after 1945 was less the abolition of war than its reconceptualization. The pieces of the puzzle, so to speak, remained in existence: but they were assembled into somewhat different patterns of picture. [After] 1945 came a return to the enlightened idea of war in the service of peace and justice, coupled with the laying down of appropriate penalties for the resort to armed force for egoistical ends."[23] New branches of international law were created and replaced former laws concerning war (international humanitarian law, international security law, international criminal law etc.).

The ban on force also spreads to the financing or any other support of illegal armed groups abroad, which was confirmed by the ICJ in the *Nicaragua* case.[24] The latter position is extremely important in spite of the phenomenon of "hybrid war".

Due to these changes, armed conflict can no longer be regarded as a basis for non-compliance with one's obligations, nor as a legal continuation of peaceful relations. For the purpose of the effect on treaties and contracts, an armed conflict may be characterized as per the Draft Articles on the Effects of Armed Conflicts on Treaties:[25] "a situation in which there is resort to armed force between States or protracted resort to armed force between governmental authorities and organized armed groups" (Article 2). This reflects a rather general approach to the notion.[26] According to the commentary on this document, "it was desirable to include situations involving a state of armed conflict in the absence of armed actions between the parties. Thus, the definition includes the occupation of territory which meets no armed resistance." That is important to the legal interpretation of the Ukrainian situation. There was no direct military resistance in the course of the occupation of Crimea in 2014; meanwhile, it is recognized as an armed conflict. Thus, the ICC's Annual Report on Preliminary Examination Activities, issued on 14 November 2016, stated that "the information available suggests that the situation within the territory of Crimea and Sevastopol amounts to an international armed conflict between Ukraine and the Russian Federation. This international armed conflict began at the latest on 26 February when the Russian Federation deployed members of its armed forces to gain control over parts of the Ukrainian territory without the consent of the Ukrainian Government."

---

[22] Cançado Trindade 2011, pp. 106–7.

[23] Neff 2005, pp. 315–395.

[24] Ibid., pp. 317-8.

[25] http://legal.un.org/ilc/texts/instruments/english/commentaries/1_10_2011.pdf.   Accessed   19 August 2017.

[26] See Dudley 2016, p. 20.

9.2.3 Appearance of the Phenomenon of "Hybrid War" and Its Influence on the Operation of International Treaties and Contracts

In current international law and international relations, a new phenomenon of *hybrid war* has become more widespread. The formation of a "hybrid" type of conflict comes from the prohibition of the use of force and may be regarded as a kind of workaround. Since *hybrid war* is not of a purely military character, it is difficult to make a difference between military, political, economic and informational aspects of the conflict. The hybrid character of a conflict also complicates the settlement of treaty issues, since each sphere has its specific influence on the respective treaty and contractual relations in the domains of security, policy, human rights, the environment, finance and the economy, information, legal cooperation etc.

In the aforementioned Russian-Ukrainian conflict, the character of a "hybrid war" (interstate conflict where military, terrorist, economic, informational, political and diplomatic means are involved; armed conflict covering only a part of a state's territory, whereas most parts of the state and its economy remain "detached" by the war) has changed the factors of its effect on the operation of treaties and contracts. The issue of "economic aggression" is actualized; more attention should be paid to the question concerning the conclusion of a treaty "under the threat or use of economic force" and the validity of such treaty (this issue has been discussed at the UN Conference on the Law of Treaties, although it was not included in Article 52 of the Vienna Convention). Thus, the refusal to sign the Association Agreement with the EU in 2013, which sparked the Euromaidan Revolution in Ukraine, was made *inter alia* under economic pressure from the Russian Federation, and thus may be regarded as economic coercion. At the end of July 2013, Russia introduced a blockade of Ukrainian exports and the sale of Ukrainian products, which led to significant losses in the Ukrainian economy.[27]

The essence of the Russian-Ukrainian conflict as a "hybrid" war is implicit in the position adopted by the Ministry of Foreign Affairs of Ukraine: "Military aggression is just one element of the Russian hybrid warfare against Ukraine. Other elements encompass: (1) propaganda based on lies and falsifications; (2) trade and economic pressure; (3) energy blockade; (4) terror and intimidation of Ukrainian citizens; (5) cyber attacks; (6) a strong denial of the very fact of war against Ukraine despite large scope of irrefutable evidence; (7) use of pro-Russian forces and satellite states in its own interests; (8) blaming the other side for its own crimes."[28] Foreign scholars have also come to the same conclusions about this conflict: "As the conflict in Ukraine illustrates, hybrid conflicts involve multilayered efforts designed to destabilise a functioning state and polarize its society. Unlike conventional warfare, the 'centre of gravity' in hybrid warfare is a target population. The adversary tries to influence

---

[27] http://zik.ua/news/2015/12/03/tombinskyy_sanktsii_rosii_proty_650677; http://www.ji-magazine. lviv.ua/2015/Aslund_Vijna_Rosii_proty_ekonomiky_Ukrainy.htm. Both accessed 19 August 2017.

[28] Ministry of Foreign Affairs of Ukraine 2015, '10 facts you should know about Russian military aggression against Ukraine. http://mfa.gov.ua/en/page/open/id/5026. Accessed 19 August 2017.

influential policy-makers and key decision makers by combining kinetic operations with subversive efforts. The aggressor often resorts to clandestine actions, to avoid attribution or retribution."[29]

According to researchers, "contrary to the traditional view of war breaking out at a certain point in time, a conflict may *de facto* exist long before the international legal definition of armed conflict is satisfied".[30]

All this has a direct impact on the formation of a doctrine according to which an armed conflict does not *ipso facto* terminate a wide range of international treaties. Given the intensity and territorial proliferation of an armed conflict, which is crucial in its impact on treaties and contracts, hybrid war complicates this problem. Nowadays, a conflict may cover only part of a territory, which raises the question of the territorial scope of a treaty. Conversely, hostilities may have no or a minimal impact on the national economic system, thus provisions of economic treaties or private contracts etc. may not be suspended or terminated. It is important to consider the nature, territorial extent and intensity of a conflict and its effect on the international obligations of the aggressor party.

As the Russian-Ukrainian conflict contains all the main features of "hybrid war", it has minimal influence on the treaties, with many of them continuing to operate. It covers part of a territory and, according to official statements, its impact on the state economy has been minimized.

9.2.4 Change in the International Legal Approach to the Effect of Armed Conflict on International Treaties and Contracts

The Vienna Convention on the Law of Treaties has not solved the problem concerning an effect of armed conflicts on treaty obligations. The reason *inter alia* concerns the selection of rapporteurs: all four special rapporteurs, James Brierly, Hersch Lauterpacht, Gerald Fitzmaurice and Humphrey Waldock, were representatives of the British doctrine of international law, which does not combine issues of war and peaceful treaty obligations. It should be also mentioned that, in general, the Vienna Convention was influenced by the British approach in many aspects. Therefore, this problem has to be solved by international practice itself. However, treaty practice is of little help, given that states very rarely envisage cases of armed conflict between themselves in their treaties, as well as the possibility of their legal termination.

In the past, it was easier to solve the problem of the influence of war on the operation of international treaties, since there existed a distinct legal fact – a declaration of war (this was one of the main postulates of the "just war" concept). Today,

---

[29] 'Deterring hybrid warfare: a chance for NATO and the EU to work together? NATO review'. http://www.nato.int/docu/review/2014/Also-in-2014/Deterring-hybrid-warfare/EN/index.htm. Accessed 19 August 2017.

[30] Pronto 2013, p. 232.

most armed conflicts start without a declaration of war (because of the prohibition of war by international law, among other factors). That is why it is more difficult to determine a status for international treaties between conflicting parties.

In 1985, an attempt was made to codify this issue in the Institute of International Law's Resolution on the Effects of Armed Conflicts on Treaties.[31] Although this document is doctrinal in nature, it reflects current approaches to this problem. Returning to this problem after 75 years (its first resolution on the same issue was adopted in 1912) and two world wars, the institute referred to the lack of clarity about the effects of war on treaties. Thus, it was envisaged that "the outbreak of an armed conflict does not *ipso facto* terminate or suspend the operation of treaties in force between the parties to the armed conflict" between belligerents and parties to the conflict and any third parties and multilateral treaties (Articles 2, 5). The outbreak of hostilities should not affect treaties establishing international organizations (Article 6). However, a state that is a victim of aggression has the right to self-defence and "is entitled to suspend in whole or in part the operation of a treaty incompatible with the exercise of that right" (Article 7).

The above resolution had an influence on the work of the UN International Law Commission concerning the Draft Articles on the Effects of Armed Conflicts on Treaties, which were finalized in 2011. The latter documents repeat all the main approaches to the issue, although they are more solid and diverse.[32] Among the main ideas in them is the provision about the continuity of treaty obligations. As stated in the commentary to the draft articles, this provision was made for the sake of international legal stability and the *pacta sunt servanda* rule.[33] The same idea is reflected in the legal doctrine as well.[34]

Modern international law determines different regimes for international treaties in the event of armed conflict: some of them are terminated; others are partially suspended for the duration of the conflict (only those rules and articles for which peaceful relations were essential are suspended); treaties of the third group are entirely suspended with an opportunity to be reinstated after the end of the conflict; treaties of the fourth group continue to fully operate etc. It should also be borne in mind that the legal fact of the beginning of an armed conflict entails entry into the operation of international treaties concluded for the period of war (such as the 1949 Geneva Conventions on the protection of war victims and their Additional Protocols of 1977 and 2005, other agreements on international humanitarian law, armed conflict law, the international protection of human rights etc.). The general prohibition of aggression in international law leads to the formation of the principle, according to which the party to a treaty, which is an aggressor, should bear responsibility for the termination or suspension of a treaty as a result of an armed conflict, as well as for the

---

[31] The text is available in French here: http://www.idi-iil.org/app/uploads/2017/06/1985_hel_03_fr.pdf. Accessed 19 August 2017.

[32] See, for instance, Dudley 2016.

[33] See http://legal.un.org/ilc/texts/instruments/english/commentaries/1_10_2011.pdf. Accessed 19 August 2017.

[34] See Pronto 2013, p. 230.

consequences of such a termination or suspension. This includes responsibility for the violation of the principle of *pacta sunt servanda*, the breach of obligations before another contracting party, damages caused by such a termination or suspension, and the loss of profits caused by the non-application of a treaty. The presumption that follows from this principle suggests that the victimized party in the aggression should have the right to initiate a renewal of the agreement (as well as its termination or suspension). Additionally, another presumption follows from the above principle – that there is a common right of all member states of the international community (above all, third parties to the treaty, which are non-belligerents) to suspend any treaty with the aggressor state.

The issue of the effect of an armed conflict on international treaties, as well as the problem of aggressor states had already been discussed at the Vienna Conference on the Law of Treaties. However, it was decided to formulate a provision on the suspension of treaties in a rather general form, rather than include a norm about the effects of an armed conflict in the text of the document (Article 73). The problem of the influence of hostilities on international treaties was considered to be high risk and politically charged. While there was a proposition to involve the UN Security Council in resolving problems connected with the effects of armed conflicts on international agreements (Japan), there were also propositions to remove any mention of the notion of "aggression" from the convention, due to its legal uncertainty and the absence of a proper definition.

In order to understand the impact of an armed conflict on the enforcement of international treaties, it is important to determine the nature of such a conflict: whether it is an act of aggression or any other kind of military conflict. Although the Vienna Convention did not definitively settle the problem of the aggressor state, a rule was introduced, which provided for an aggressor state to be held responsible for the violation of a treaty (Article 75). Considering the lack of regulation, this problem has been settled in the domain of international customary law and by *opinio juris*, including doctrine. Any international agreements with an aggressor state may be terminated or suspended, except those that were concluded on humanitarian issues (treaties in the field of international humanitarian law and the protection of human rights). The international treaty-making capacity of an aggressor state may be limited as a sanction during an armed conflict or after its completion.

Altogether, the problem concerning the threat or use of force, leading to the invalidity of a treaty, failed to find general support at the Vienna Conference on the Law of Treaties. Many countries preferred to abstain from addressing such a sensitive question in the convention, since it could have affected the stability of international treaties and international law on the whole (Switzerland). Similarly, the issue of "economic coercion" in order to conclude a treaty was not included in the text of Article 52 (as proposed by Afghanistan) under the influence of developed countries. Therefore, coercion is here regarded only in terms of the threat or the use of military or political force. Economic pressure as a means of imposing a treaty was only condemned in the additional Declaration on the Prohibition of Military, Political or Economic Coercion in the Conclusion of Treaties, which was adopted as part of the Final Act of the Vienna Conference on the Law of Treaties.

Another specific problem is the issue of peace treaties (i.e., treaties with defeated parties), since they may be regarded as those concluded under coercion within the meaning of Article 52 of the Vienna Convention. However, the provisions of this article as grounds for the invalidity of a treaty are very rarely referred to in international legal practice. Instead, Article 52 should be interpreted in a broad sense – not as a mechanism for the protection of an injured party exclusively, but as a means of maintaining the normal international legal order. A post-conflict peace treaty with the aggressor, along with the relevant sanctions or provisions on retortions or reparations, should be recognized as valid. This is also confirmed by Article 48 of the UN Articles on the Responsibility of States for Internationally Wrongful Acts (2001), according to which each state may require the responsibility of the aggressor state, since aggression is a violation of the *erga omnes* rule and "the obligation breached is owed to the international community as a whole".

It is also important to clarify the intention of the contracting parties at the moment of the conclusion of the treaty (through means of interpretation). The situation is clearer when states parties to a treaty include provisions on the effects of armed conflict in its text.

On the whole, in current international law, the following consequences of armed conflict for the operation of international treaties between contracting parties may be identified. Some treaties are completely terminated (mainly agreements in the fields of security, military cooperation, political treaties on friendship and cooperation). Aggression is regarded as a violation of treaty commitments and the *jus cogens* rule by one of the contracting parties (i.e., the aggressor state). Therefore, the aggressor may not refer to the armed conflict as grounds for the termination of a treaty under Article 52 of the Vienna Convention. International treaties on the protection of human rights – as well as treaties in the field of environmental protection, which represent a new trend in international law and enshrined in the draft articles – cannot be terminated on the ground of armed conflict. Armed conflict does not affect treaty-founding documents of international organizations, as well as treaties on the status of borders. Hostilities may initiate the conclusion of special international agreements (armistice, ceasefire, exchange of prisoners of war, evacuation of civilians, diversion of military equipment, etc.). As a general rule, treaties of the belligerents with third parties continue to be in force.

Such opportunities and challenges as globalization, deepening economic interdependence of states, terrorism, environmental problems and disasters, and epidemics lead to the desirability of the maximum continuity of international treaties and contracts in the event of armed conflict. Thus, at the beginning of the 21st century, it became clear that "the basic idea underlining the present-day approach to the problem of the effects of war on treaties is to minimize the disruptive effects of war in the sphere of treaty law without overlooking the fact that in some areas of political and social relations between States, the continuing effectiveness of treaties is incompatible with a state of war".[35]

---

[35] Delbrück 2000, p. 1369.

9.3 Practical Effect of the Russian Aggression Against Ukraine on the Operation of International Treaties and Contracts

At the beginning of 2017, the legal framework for Ukrainian-Russian relations amounted to over 350 treaties. In general, Russian aggression against Ukraine, which manifested itself in the annexation of Crimea and the military intervention in the Donbas region in 2014, is an example of the violation of the basic principle of current international law: the observance of treaties in good faith, that is, the *pacta sunt servanda* principle, which is essential for the operation of (a) bilateral treaties, (b) bilateral contracts and (c) multilateral treaties.

9.3.1 Operation of Bilateral Treaties

According to current international practice, the outbreak of armed conflict suspends most bilateral treaties on economic and political issues and, less often, treaties regulating diplomatic relations.[36]

The situation is especially problematic when (a) the treaty itself contains no provision on its termination and (b) the parties, while concluding it, expressed no intention to admit the possibility of denunciation in accordance with Article 56 of the 1969 Vienna Convention on the Law of Treaties. That is true for the majority of bilateral treaties between Ukraine and the Russian Federation.

Nowadays, a number of bilateral treaties of the parties is being terminated or suspended. At the same time, most of them remain in force. Therefore, reasonable and baseless invocations of armed conflict as grounds for the termination of a treaty should be differentiated. In the case of treaties in the field of military cooperation or security issues, the impossibility of their performance is obvious. For instance, on 21 May 2015, Ukraine denounced the 1997 interstate Agreement on Cooperation in the Field of Military Intelligence.

Copious intergovernmental treaties, which were terminated by Ukraine or the Russian Federation during 2014–2016 period, can be divided into three main groups. The first group includes treaties dealing with security and military cooperation and exchanges of information in these fields (e.g., the 1993 Agreement Between the Government of Ukraine and the Government of the Russian Federation on Military-technical Cooperation was terminated by the Ukrainian Government on 20 May 2015; the 1995 Agreement on Military Cooperation was denounced by Ukraine on 21 May 2015; the 2000 Agreement Between the Government of Ukraine and the Government of the Russian Federation on Mutual Protection of Secret Information was also denounced by Ukraine on 21 May 2015; the 1993 Agreement Between the Government of Ukraine and the Government of the Russian Federation on Productive

---

[36] See Pronto 2013, pp. 227–8.

and Scientific-technical Cooperation Between Enterprises of the Defence Industry was terminated by the Ukrainian Government on 26 August 2015).

The second group includes treaties in the field of transport cooperation and migration: for example, on 4 March 2015, the Government of Ukraine introduced temporary restrictive measures on the realization of the 2011 Agreement Between the Cabinet of Ministers of Ukraine and the Government of the Russian Federation on the Procedure for Crossing the Ukrainian-Russian Border by Residents of the Border Regions of Ukraine and the Russian Federation; certain provisions of the Agreement Between the Government of Ukraine and the Government of the Russian Federation on Visa-free Travel for Citizens of Ukraine and the Russian Federation were suspended by Ukraine on 30 January 2015 in order to prevent Russian citizens from entering, exiting, transiting, staying and travelling in the territory of Ukraine on the basis of their internal passport; the 2013 Agreement on Joint Actions on the Organization of the Construction of a Transport Crossing Through the Kerch Strait was terminated by Ukraine on 1 October 2014.

The third group of treaties includes trade agreements, most of which were terminated by the Russian Federation in 2014 (e.g., the 1995 Agreement Between the Government of Ukraine and the Government of the Russian Federation on the Implementation of the Free Trade Regime; the 1993 Agreement Between the Government of Ukraine and the Government of the Russian Federation on Free Trade and Protocols to This Agreement).

Numerous interdepartmental agreements were terminated or suspended by the parties, including: the agreements on cooperation in different domains between the Security Service of Ukraine and the Ministry of Security of the Russian Federation and other Russian security and intelligence bodies; the agreements between the ministries of defence and transport of both parties; the agreements between the border services of Ukraine and the Russian Federation. Except for security and military cooperation, which normally terminates after the outbreak of conflict between parties, some ordinary "peaceful" agreements were also terminated. Thus, on 30 March 2016, the Cabinet of Ministers of Ukraine terminated the Agreement on Cooperation in the Field of Physical Culture and Sports between the Ministry of Youth and Sports of Ukraine and the Ministry of Sports of the Russian Federation. This is evidence of the overall influence of the armed conflict, even if a hybrid one, on a wide range of interstate relations

Very often, researchers and practitioners give rather ephemeral reasons for non-compliance with treaty commitments. Thus, for a long time, the concept of a fundamental change in circumstances as grounds for the termination or suspension of a treaty has been treated ambiguously.[37] Political and legal arguments have frequently been misrepresented. The unilateral termination of the Agreements Related to the Presence of the Russian Black Sea Fleet on the Territory of Ukraine by the Russian

---

[37] On this subject, see Haraszti 1975, pp. 1–94.

State Duma on 31 March 2014 was prompted by an ideological, rather than a legal, interpretation of the *rebus sic stantibus* clause.[38]

This decision was preceded by a statement made by the Russian Prime Minister, Dmitry Medvedev, on 4 April 2014, about the necessity to denounce the above-mentioned agreements, in which he said that, "taking into account the changed circumstances and the fact that now Crimea is a part of the territory of the Russian federation there are no grounds for continuation of this treaty. There is an international-legal principle according to which a treaty is in force until the circumstances that generated it exist."[39]

While presenting the draft Federal Law on the Termination of the Agreements Governing the Presence of the Russian Federation Black Sea Fleet on the Territory of Ukraine, the Deputy Minister of Foreign Affairs of the Russian Federation, Grigory Karasin, stated that the reason for terminating the agreements was the following: "From now, the territory of the Republic of Crimea and the federal city of Sebastopol is an integral part of the Russian Federation, over which, in accordance with article 4 of the Constitution, the sovereignty of the Russian Federation spreads. Therefore, today there are no grounds for the continuation of the legal relations on the location of the facilities and the personnel of the Black Sea Fleet of the Russian Federation in Ukraine, including the obligations of the Russian party to provide payment or any other compensation or reimbursement." It is obvious that this argumentation refers to the illegal act of the annexation of Crimea.

The actual reason for denouncing the agreements was the Federal Law on the Annexation of Crimea and the Federal City of Sebastopol by the Russian Federation, which was adopted by the State Duma on 20 March 2014. The reasons invoked for

---

[38] It should be noted that the Russian legal doctrine follows its Soviet predecessor on many issues concerning international treaty law, including the problem of the *rebus sic stantibus* clause. In the first decades after the creation of the Soviet Union, its lawyers insisted on this clause as grounds for the unilateral termination of a treaty, especially if such a change was the result of a social revolution. This was quite natural for the doctrine of the state, which came into being as a result of the Russian Revolution of 1917. It was a principal difference between early Soviet doctrine and Western science of that time. In the post-war period, Soviet lawyers were more careful in their recognition of a fundamental change in circumstances as grounds for a treaty termination. For them, the main reasons were the following: changes in political regimes, social revolutions etc. However, starting from the mid-1960s and into the 1970s, the Soviet doctrine changed its attitude towards *rebus sic stantibus* and began to treat it as an exception, including in terms of decolonization, the principle of the self-determination of nations and social revolutions. Soviet scholars of that time sharply criticized their Western counterparts for any wider interpretation of this clause. One of the founders of the post-war Soviet international legal school, Professor Grigory Tunkin (member of the UN International Law Commission) repeatedly argued that Article 62 of the Vienna Convention on the Law of Treaties prohibits the violation of international commitments on the grounds of *rebus sic stantibus* (Document A/CN.4/SR.697. Summary Record of 697 Meeting. Topic: Law of Treaties. Extract from the *Yearbook of the International Law Commission: 1963, Vol. 1*, pp. 157–8). Starting from the 1990s, the Russian doctrine of international law considered the clause as an exception and interpreted it in restrictive fashion. Practically, it rejected (or remained quite sceptical about) social revolutions being fundamental changes in circumstances. In general, Russian scholars maintained this position until the outbreak of the open conflict with Ukraine at the beginning of 2014.

http://state.kremlin.ru/security_council/20623. Accessed 19 August 2017.

[39] Ibid.

the adoption of this law included the illegal referendum in Crimea on 16 March 2014, the Declaration of Independence of Crimea and the City of Sebastopol and the Treaty on Accession of the Republic of Crimea to Russia.

> Thus, the reference to a fundamental change in circumstances, as the basis for the revision of international legal obligations before the aggression against Ukraine, is becoming increasingly popular in Russia. Another example of the misinterpretation of the fundamental change in circumstances is the 1997 Treaty on Friendship, Cooperation and Partnership between Ukraine and the Russian Federation. Russian scholars state that Ukraine cannot refer to this treaty, as it requires joint consultations to be held, whereas "there has been no request made asking Russia to hold any consultations. This affirmation is obvious because there is no legal entity in existence to do so... There is no legal entity to talk with."[40]

Here, the "lack of powers" of the official representatives of Ukraine and the validity of their applications are based on the thesis of the *coup d'état* and the illegal change of power. On the same grounds, Russian scholars and officials have justified the refusal of the Russian Federation to participate in previous consultations with Ukraine about the guarantor states of its territorial integrity.[41] Despite the fact that the 1997 agreement itself provides a mechanism of consultation for the settlement of any controversial issues (Articles 4, 5, 7, 37), it does not contain any indication of a change in the political situation in one of the states as a reason for its termination. The positive obligation of the parties towards the treaty under Article 7 is the following: "In the event of a situation which, in the opinion of one of the High Contracting Parties, poses a threat to peace, breaks the peace or affects the interests of its national security, sovereignty and territorial integrity, it may appeal to the other High Contracting Party to hold appropriate consultations promptly."

Russia's refusal to hold such consultations on the basis of a change of government in Ukraine, which it did not recognize, is a direct violation of the rules of the agreement and a denial of the principle of a fundamental change in circumstances as set out in Article 62 of the Vienna Convention. In fact, the change of government in Ukraine at the end of February 2014 has been interpreted as grounds for the violation by other parties of their obligations under agreements with Ukraine, despite the fact that this government was officially recognized by most states of the world and all main international organizations (such as the UN, the EU and all its members, NATO, Council of Europe) between March and May 2014.

At the same time, the Russian Association of International Law holds the same position.[42] In this context, two international instruments, which were violated by the

---

[40] Mezyaev 2014.

[41] Ibid.

[42] http://www.ilarb.ru/html/news/2014/5062014.pdf. Accessed 19 August 2017.

Russian Federation (after its annexation of Crimea and military occupation of the eastern regions of Ukraine), should be mentioned. The first is a universal document – the 1970 UN Declaration on Principles of International Law Concerning Friendly Relations and Co-operation Among States, which confirms that "Every State has the duty to refrain from the threat or use of force to violate the existing international boundaries of another State or as a means of solving international disputes, including territorial disputes and problems concerning frontiers of States… Every State [also] has the duty to refrain from organizing or encouraging the organization of irregular forces or armed bands including mercenaries, for incursion into the territory of another State." The other is the 1997 bilateral Treaty on Friendship, Cooperation and Partnership between Ukraine and the Russian Federation, which envisages that "Each High Contracting Party shall refrain from participating or maintaining any action against the other High Contracting Party" (Article 6).

The reference to the *rebus sic stantibus* clause concerning cases of Russia's denunciation of treaties with Ukraine is unlawful. Here, it is necessary to clarify the position of some Ukrainian specialists, who emphasize that: (a) the Agreement between Ukraine and the Russian Federation Related to the Presence of the Russian Black Sea Fleet on the Territory of Ukraine of 21 April 2010 does not contain any provisions for its denunciation, and therefore cannot be denounced unilaterally; (b) by the time of its conclusion, the parties had not expressed their intention regarding the so-called "denunciation provision" in accordance with Article 56 of the Convention on the Law of Treaties; (c) in the case of denouncing this agreement, the Russian Federation violated a number of procedural rules stipulated by Article 65 of the Vienna Convention (in particular, with respect to the prior notification of the other party of the intention to denounce the agreement, conducting appropriate joint consultations, negotiations etc.).[43] However, the invalidity of denunciation does not exclusively stem from procedural breaches. In this case, the invalidity of legal argumentation about a fundamental change in circumstances extends from the fact that the change referred to by the Russian Federation was the result of the violation of its obligations under bilateral agreements with Ukraine and the imperative norm of general international law (annexation of Crimea). Thus, it cannot be regarded as the *rebus sic stantibus* clause under Article 62 of the Vienna Convention.

9.3.2 Operation of Bilateral Contracts

The operation of international contracts in the event of armed conflict is treated rather liberally by Ukrainian laws. There is a general principle of the continued operation of these agreements under such circumstances. However, the execution of contracts with a hostile party in the field of exchanges of information or technologies, national security or state property is more problematic.

---

[43] http://gazeta.zn.ua/energy_market/rebus-medvedeva-k-voprosu-o-vzaimosvyazi-mezhdu-krymskim-krizisom-i-gazovym-cenoobrazovaniem-.html. Accessed 19 August 2017.

In accordance with the Agreement Between the Cabinet of Ministers of Ukraine and the Government of the Russian Federation on the Encouragement and Mutual Protection of Investments (1998), which remains in force until now, the State Bank of Ukraine (*Oschadbank*) claimed for compensation of losses caused by the annexation of Crimea. The same claims were filed by more than 20 private companies in Ukraine.[44] Under this agreement, an "investment" covers a wide range of goods and profits ("all kinds of property and intellectual values, which are put in by the investor of one Contracting Party on the territory of the other Contracting Party ... (a) movable and immovable property and any other rights of property therein; (b) monetary funds as well as securities, liabilities, deposits and other forms of participation; (c) rights to objects of intellectual property, including authors' copyrights and related rights, trade marks, the rights to inventions, industrial samples, models and technological processes and know-how; (d) rights to perform commercial activity, including rights to prospecting, development and exploitation of natural resources" – Article (1). After the annexation of Crimea and the illegal expropriation of Ukrainian goods therein by the Russian Federation, the provisions of the agreement on the resolution of disputes (Articles 9–10) should be based on a process of dispute settlement. They include the resolution of disputes by a competent court or an arbitration court of the contracting party, the Arbitration Institute of the Chamber of Commerce in Stockholm, an *ad hoc* arbitration tribunal, in conformity with the Arbitration Regulations of the UNCITRAL or a specialized arbitration tribunal (Articles 9–10).

The Russian Federation rejected all the claims, considering them to be "politically motivated". Alongside this, "it was for the first time in international practice that an issue of operation of the treaty on mutual protection of investments is considered as to the territory under occupation".[45] The problem becomes more complicated as the agreement deals with investments that are displaced on foreign territory. At the same time, according to international law, the Crimean Peninsula is regarded as a territory of Ukraine, although occupied, but Ukrainian goods have been confiscated by the Russian Federation within it ("The investments of investors of either Contracting Party, made on the territory of the other Contracting Party, shall not be subject to expropriation, nationalization or other measures, equated by its consequences to expropriation" – Article (5). A number of similar contractual commitments is currently being considered by different international judicial bodies.

On the whole, the impact of the Russian-Ukrainian armed conflict on private bilateral contracts is threefold. Firstly, many of them remain in force (mostly those connected with purely "peaceful" and issues, and thus not affected by the conflict). Secondly, there are many contracts related to military, transborder or security (quasi-state, private) cooperation: these have been terminated or suspended as a rule. Thirdly, contractual obligations, which were directly affected by the conflict (e.g., expropriation of property belonging to a Ukrainian company in the territory of Crimea as a result of annexation), are subject to consideration by the competent international commercial and judicial bodies.

---

[44] Zadorozhnii 2016, pp. 310–5.

[45] Ibid., p. 312.

9.3.3 Operation of Multilateral Treaties

With regard to multilateral treaties affected by the conflict, particularly noteworthy are at least the following three examples:

(a) *CIS Free trade Agreement and its unilateral suspension by Russia in relation to Ukraine*

The Russian Federation used to be Ukraine's largest trade partner. However economic pressure has become a major component of the Russian hybrid war against Ukraine. Thus, on 1 January 2016, Russia unilaterally suspended the application of the CIS Free Trade Agreement with regard to Ukraine. In turn, the Government of Ukraine introduced import duties on goods originating from Russia up to and including 31 December 2016.

The legal basis for a free trade area between Ukraine and Russia is the multilateral Free Trade Agreement, signed on 18 October 2011 between Ukraine and Russia, as well as Azerbaijan, Belarus, Armenia, Kazakhstan, Kyrgyzstan, Moldova, Tajikistan, Turkmenistan and Uzbekistan. This treaty was ratified by Ukraine on 30 July 2012 and came into force in the country on 20 September of the same year.

As a general rule, if consent to the obligation of a treaty is provided in the form of a law, its implementation should be stopped by law. However, para 4 of Article 37 of the Russian Law on International Treaties of the Russian Federation does not contain relevant norms. The Russian Federation, by its own decision, has violated both international and domestic laws; nor does it provide explanations for the suspension of the treaty, while the relevant regulatory acts do not contain grounds for its approval.

Although "economic aggression" is not a prevailing concept in international law, it is often a component of armed intervention. Moreover, its elements violate the rules of bilateral and multilateral international treaties and the basic principles of international law (e.g., the principle of cooperation). That is why international legal responsibility must be a consequence of unlawful pressure in the economic sphere.

(b) *Memorandum on Security Assurances in Connection with Ukraine's Accession to the Treaty on the Non-proliferation of Nuclear Weapons (Budapest Memorandum) 1994 (especially in terms of its effect on Ukraine and Russia, as well as adherence to it by third parties)*

At a press conference held on 4 March 2014, Vladimir Putin, as President of the Russian Federation, stated that Russia no longer regarded the Budapest Memorandum as obligatory. Putin's rationale was as follows: in the opinion of the Russian Federation, "an armed seizure of power took place [in Ukraine from late February to early March 2014]… contrary to the Constitution" and an "anti-constitutional *coup d'état* occurred", characterized in Ukraine as a revolution. Furthermore, "if it were a revolution… a new state would appear on this territory; as was the case with the collapse of the Russian Empire after the revolution of 1917 when a new state came into existence. And with this state and in respect of this state, we have not signed any obligatory documents."[46] That is a refrain of an early Soviet (Bolshevik) version of the doctrine of revolution as a fundamental change in circumstances in international law. Of course, political statements, even those made by heads of states, cannot be regarded as legal acts. However, further actions on the part of the Russian Federation (annexation of Crimea, military aggression against Ukraine in the Donbas Region, overall support for separatist and terrorist entities in the east of Ukraine) are evidence of its violation of basic provisions in the Budapest Memorandum: "The United States of America, the Russian Federation, and the United Kingdom of Great Britain and Northern Ireland, reaffirm their commitment to Ukraine, in accordance with the principles of the CSCE [Conference on Security and Co-operation in Europe] Final Act, to respect the Independence and Sovereignty and the existing borders of Ukraine... reaffirm their obligation to refrain from the threat or use of force against the territorial integrity or political independence of Ukraine, and that none of their weapons will ever be used against Ukraine except in self-defense or otherwise in accordance with the Charter of the United Nations" (paras 1–2).

The Ministry of Foreign Affairs of the Russian Federation, in response to accusations of violating the Budapest Memorandum, made on 1 April 2014, stated that "the common element of the Budapest Memorandum and the concept of 'the negative guaranties' in its classical interpretation is only an obligation not to use or to threat to use the nuclear weapon against non-nuclear weapon states. Such an obligation was not violated against Ukraine in any form." However, the statement is a clear distortion of the content of the memorandum, since the document does not limit these actions to the threat or use of nuclear weapons alone. The memorandum "was a unique international instrument in the sphere of nuclear disarmament. It enshrined legal obligations by nuclear powers (the USA, the United Kingdom, Russia, and China) with regard to Ukraine's national security; territorial integrity and inviolability of borders in accordance with the generally recognized principles of international law. Any economic pressure against Ukraine was also prohibited."[47]

Moreover, while agreeing to these commitments, the parties should refer to the CSCE Final Act, which reaffirms the general principles of international law related to nuclear or non-nuclear status of a state or other issues concerning the use or threat of use of nuclear weapons: "As far as the legally binding force of the Budapest Memorandum is concerned, it is a treaty because it meets all the criteria of a treaty as envisaged in the Vienna Convention on the Law of Treaties (1969)... By its actions in 2013-2015, Russia violated almost all of its obligations under the Budapest Memorandum, except for the obligation to seek immediate actions by the UN SC."[48]

On the same basis, the *rebus sic stantibus* clause cannot be asserted by the Russian Federation in order to explain its failure to comply with its obligations under other treaties (e.g., the 1997 Treaty on Friendship, Cooperation and Partnership Between Ukraine and the Russian Federation). Firstly, because the functioning of Ukrainian governments, which concluded these treaties, was not an essential condition for their

---

[46] http://kremlin.ru/news/20366. Accessed 19 August 2017.

[47] Zadorozhnii 2016, p. 90.

[48] Ibid.

conclusion (that is why the change of government, which took place in Ukraine in 2014 and which is referred to by Russia, is an issue of internal jurisdiction). Secondly, a fundamental change in circumstances is not grounds for the violation by a party of the imperative rule of international law (territorial integrity and inviolability of the borders, non-intervention into internal affairs). According to scholars, "a study of the Budapest Memorandum of 1994 proves the fallacy of its Russian interpretation shared by both Russia as a state and Russian academia, which regard it as a political-document of declaratory nature without any binding commitments. It is viewed as a document which only confirms the provisions of the Helsinki Final Act, prohibiting the use of nuclear weapons against Ukraine and the use of force in general but only in the meaning of direct hostilities and containing merely collective obligations of the assuring states... The Budapest Memorandum is a key treaty for the whole process of nuclear disarmament."[49]

(c) *European Convention on Human Rights (ECHR) (obligations derived from the effective control over occupied territories, interstate cases in the European Court of Human Rights etc.)*

On 21 May 2015, the Verkhovna Rada (Parliament) of Ukraine approved Resolution No. 462-VIII, by which it adopted the Declaration on the Derogation from Certain Obligations Under the International Covenant on Civil and Political Rights [ICCPR] and the Convention for the Protection of Human Rights and Fundamental Freedoms. This declaration stipulates that, "Due to the annexation and temporary occupation by the Russian Federation of the integral part of Ukraine – the Autonomous Republic of Crimea and the city of Sevastopol – as a result of armed aggression against Ukraine, the Russian Federation is fully responsible for the respect for human rights and implementation of the relevant treaties in the annexed and temporarily occupied territory of Ukraine... In order to ensure the vital interests of the society and the State in response to the armed aggression of the Russian Federation, the Verkhovna Rada of Ukraine, the Cabinet of Ministers of Ukraine and other authorities have to adopt legal acts, which constitute the derogation from certain obligations of Ukraine under the International Covenant on Civil and Political Rights and the Convention for the Protection of Human Rights and Fundamental Freedoms."[50] Therefore, Ukraine exercised the right of derogation from its obligations established in Article 2, para 3, and Articles 9, 12, 14 and 17 of the ICCPR, Articles 5, 6, 8 and 13 of the Convention for the Protection of Human Rights and Fundamental Freedoms (in the ECHR), in certain areas of the Donetsk and Luhansk Oblasts of Ukraine.

Both international treaties envisage derogation from some of their provisions in cases of war or other public emergencies threatening the life of the nation, the existence of which is officially proclaimed. The declaration is made under Article 15 of the ECHR and Article 4 of the ICCPR, and indicates that, in a state of public

---

[49] Ibid., p. 92.

[50] The text is available at: https://wcd.coe.int/com.instranet.InstraServlet?command=com. instranet.CmdBlobGet&InstranetImage=2833408&SecMode=1&DocId=2278178&Usage=2. Accessed 19 August 2017.

emergency, special restrictions can be imposed on the following rights, which are guaranteed by both international instruments: the right to liberty and security, the right to a fair trial, the right to the respect for a private and family life, the right to an effective remedy, and freedom of movement.

As to the territorial scope of derogation, it extends to "certain areas of the Donetsk and Luhansk *Oblasts* of Ukraine, which is determined by the Anti-Terrorist Centre of the Security Service of Ukraine in connection with the anti-terrorist operation, for the period until the complete cessation of the Russian Federation armed aggression, the restoration of constitutional order and orderliness in the occupied territory of Ukraine and until further notification to the Secretary-General of the United Nations and the Secretary General of the Council of Europe of the resumption of the application in full of the International Covenant on Civil and Political Rights and the Convention for the Protection of Human Rights and Fundamental Freedoms". Both depositaries of the above-mentioned documents are regularly informed about any changes to the territorial scope of derogation (i.e., exclusion or inclusion criteria for any new areas where the given rights are derogated in the face of armed conflict, expansion and the possibility to maintain control over respective territories).

Furthermore, the Secretary General of the Council of Europe and the Secretary-General of the UN had been notified by the Government of Ukraine of its decision to have recourse to Article 15 of the ECHR and Article 4 of the ICCPR, respectively.

According to Ukrainian analysts: "[We] are talking about an even greater level of responsibility that rests with our state... After all, by declaring the derogation, Ukraine gave the right to the Council of Europe (the controlling body concerning compliance with the Convention for the Protection of Human Rights and Fundamental Freedoms) and the United Nations (the controlling body concerning compliance with the International Covenant on Civil and Political Rights) to monitor the implementation of their restrictions. In addition, a state that derogates from individual obligations has an additional obligation to provide information regarding the fulfilment of its international obligations relating to the protection of human rights, in particular, in situations of emergency."[51]

Human rights activists consider the statement of the Verkhovna Rada of Ukraine as an "absolutely logical step", since it was issued due to the lack of physical access to the territory occupied by the Russian Federation. Furthermore, Ukraine cannot guarantee or protect human rights in the respective territories.[52] This case is an example of how an armed conflict affects unilateral obligations of the state under international treaties.

---

[51] For an analysis of this document, see: National Expert Institute (2016) Analytical reference on Derogation http://nei.com.ua/%D0%95%D0%9A%D0%A1%D0%9F%D0%95%D0%A0%D0% A2%D0%9D%D0%90-%D0%94%D0%A3%D0%9C%D0%9A%D0%90/. Accessed 19 August 2017.

[52] Coynash 2015. http://khpg.org/en/index.php?id=1432504574. Accessed 19 August 2017.

9.4   Conclusion

The annexation of Crimea and the armed conflict in the east of Ukraine expose general trends in international law as to the effect of an armed conflict on the operation of international treaties and contracts. The latter shows the formation of mechanisms aimed at minimizing the impact of conflict on the continuity of treaties and contracts. This reflects the lawlessness of war in a modern international legal context, as well as the increased role of the global community, which is interested in the evolutionary development of international law. One may observe the loss of the former decisive role of the state in international law, including treaty and contractual (private) relations.

The issue concerning agreements that should be terminated or suspended in response to armed conflict (agreements on military, criminal, civil cooperation, cooperation in the fields of security, exchange of information and technologies, etc.) requires dedicated research.

Nowadays, the situation is growing complex because many states have concluded a number of treaties with conflicting commitments, as well as many agreements, which provide no rules about their operation in the case of armed conflict. That is a systemic problem within national legislation and the practice of international treaties.

The entire legal framework of Ukrainian-Russian relations should be revised as a result of the Russian aggression against Ukraine. Many bilateral treaties are either affected by the conflict or not applicable. Ukraine should appeal to international judicial bodies and demand that the Russian Federation accepts responsibility for the violation of its treaties and contracts, as well as appropriate reparations.

References

Aslund A (2015) The Russian war against the economy of Ukraine [in Ukrainian: Аслунд А. Війна Росії проти економіки України]. http://www.jimagazine.lviv.ua/2015/Aslund_Vijna_Rosii_proty_ekonomiky_Ukrainy.htm. Accessed 19 August 2017

Aust A (2013) Modern Treaty Law and Practice, 3rd edn. Cambridge University Press, Cambridge

Cançado Trindade AA (2011) International Law for Humankind: Towards a new Jus Gentium. Martinus Nijhoff Publishers, Leiden/Boston

Chetail V, Haggenmacher P (eds) (2011) Vattel's International Law from a XXIst Century Perspective [Le Droit International de Vattel vu du XXIe Siècle] Brill/Martinus Nijhoff Publishers

Coynash H (2015) Ukraine's laws for military zone criticized. Information website of the Kharkiv Human Rights Protection Group, 28 May 2015. http://khpg.org/en/index.php?id=1432504574. Accessed 19 August 2017

Criddle EJ (2013) Humanitarian Financial Intervention. EJIL, Vol. 24, № 2: 583–615

Davis GB (1912) The Effects of War Upon International Conventions and Private Contracts. Proceedings of the American Society of International Law and Its Annual Meeting (1907–1917). Vol. 6: 124–132

De La Pradelle A (1948) The effect of war on private law treaties. International Law Quarterly, Vol. 2, No. 4: 555–576

de Vattel E (1916) The Law of Nations or The Principles of Natural Law Applied to the Conduct and to the Affairs of Nations and of Sovereigns In: Scott JB (ed) The Classics of International Law, Vol. three (translation of the 1758 edn.). Carnegie Institute of Washington, Washington

Delbrück J (2000) War, effect on treaties. In: Bernhardt R (ed) Encyclopedia of Public International Law, Vol. IV. North-Holland/Elsevier, Amsterdam

Descamps EEF (1930) Le droit international nouveau. L'influence de la condemnation de la guerre sur l'évolution juridique international. Recueil des Cours de l'Académie de Droit International, tome 31 de la collection, pp. 393–559

Dörr O, Schmalenbach K (eds) (2012) Vienna Convention on the Law of Treaties. A Commentary. Springer

Dudley L (2016) Until We Achieve Universal Peace: Implications of the International Law Commission's Draft Articles on the "Effect of Armed Conflict on Treaties". American University National Security Law Brief, Vol. 6, No. 1: 13–36

Frowein Jochen Abr. United Nations (2000). In: Bernhardt R (ed) Encyclopedia of Public International Law, Vol. IV. North-Holland/Elsevier, Amsterdam

Grewe WG (2000) The Epochs of International Law (translated and revised by Byers M). Walter de Gruyter, Berlin/New York

Grotius H (1925) De Jure Belli ac Pacis. Libri Tres (translation). In: Scott JB (ed) The Classics of International Law, Vol. two. At the Clarendon Press/Humphrey Milford, Oxford/London

Haraszti G (1975) Treaties and the Fundamental Change of Circumstances. Recueil des Cours de l'Académie de Droit International, tome 146 de la collection, 1975 / III : 1–94

International Law Commission (2011) Draft articles on the effects of armed conflicts on treaties, with commentaries. http://legal.un.org/ilc/texts/instruments/english/commentaries/1_10_2011. pdf. Accessed 19 August 2017

Johnston DM (2008) The Historical Foundations of World Order. The Tower and the Arena. Martinus Nijhoff Publishers, Leiden/Boston

Lesaffer R (2012) Peace Treaties and the Formation of International Law. In: Fassbender B, Peters A (eds) The Oxford Handbook of the History of International Law. Oxford University Press, Oxford pp. 71–94

McNair AD (1937) Les effets de la guerre sur les traits. Recueil des Cours de l'Académie de Droit International, tome 59 de la collection, 1937 / I : 523–585

Mezyaev A (2014) Is the New Ukrainian Government Legal? http://dissidentvoice.org/2014/03/is-the-new-ukrainian-government-legal/. Accessed 19 August 2017

National Expert Institute (2016) Analytical reference on Derogation [in Ukrainian: Аналітична довідка про дерогацію]. http://nei.com.ua/%D0%95%D0%9A%D0%A1%D0%9F%D0%9 5%D0%A0%D0%A2%D0%9D%D0%90-%D0%94%D0%A3%D0%9C%D0%9A%D0%90/. Accessed 19 August 2017

NATO (2014) Deterring hybrid warfare: A chance for NATO and the EU to work together? NATO review. http://www.nato.int/docu/review/2014/Also-in-2014/Deterring-hybrid-warfare/ EN/index.htm. Accessed 19 August 2017

Neff S (2004) Peace and prosperity: commercial aspects of peacemaking. In: Lesaffer R (ed) Peace Treaties and International Law in European History: From the Late Middle Ages to World War One. Cambridge University Press, Cambridge

Neff S (2005) War and the Law of Nations. A General History. Cambridge University Press, Cambridge

O'Connell ME (2012) Peace and War. In: Fassbender B, Peters A (eds) The Oxford Handbook of the History of International Law. Oxford University Press, Oxford, pp. 272–293

Oppenheim L (1935) International Law. Vol. II: Disputes, War, and Neutrality, 5th edn. Longmans/Green & Co., London

Pronto A (2013) The Effect of War on Law – What Happens to Their Treaties When States Go to War? Cambridge Journal of International and Comparative Law (2) 2: 227–241

Rank R (1953) Modern War and the Validity of Treaties. Cornell Law Review. Vol. 38, Issue 3: 511–540

Scott JB (2002) Law, the State and International Community, Vol. two. The Lawbook Exchange Ltd., Union, New Jersey

Steimel Ch (2000) War, Effect on Contracts. In: Bernhardt R (ed) Encyclopedia of Public International Law, Volume IV. North-Holland/Elsevier, Amsterdam, pp. 1360–1367

Taube M (1930) L'inviolabilité des traits. Recueil des Cours de l'Académie de Droit International, tome 32 de la collection, 1930 / II : 291–389

Villiger E (2009) Commentary on the 1969 Vienna Convention on the Law of Treaties. Brill

Wehberg H (1928) Le problème de la mise de la guerre hors la loi. Recueil des Cours de l'Académie de Droit International, tome 24 de la collection, 1928 / IV : 147–306

Whitton JB (1934) La règle "pacta sunt servanda". Recueil des Cours de l'Académie de Droit International, tome 49 de la collection, 1934 / III : 147–276

Zadorozhnii O (2016) International Law in relations between Ukraine and the Russian Federation. K.I.S., Kiev [In Ukrainian: Задорожній О.В. Міжнародне право у відносинах України та Російської Федерації. Київ: К.І.С.]

Chapter 10
Cyber Operations During the Conflict in Ukraine and the Role of International Law

Jozef Valuch and Ondrej Hamulak

Contents

Abstract The phenomenon of cyberspace and its definition and normative regulation represent a big challenge for contemporary international law. The cybersphere forms a fifth domain of activities where interactions between state and non-state actors could happen. Indeed, it has started to play an important role in conflicts and hostilities. Especially in these situations, international society does not have a unified view on the question as to how to deal with activities in cyberspace. Nevertheless, the fact is that cyber incidents are increasingly used to engage, harm or weaken enemies/counterparts. We can also see the different forms of abuse pursued in cyberspace during the conflict in Ukraine. This conflict is a productive example of the complexity of the legal approach and the (lack of) capability in relation to

Jozef Valuch, Assistant Professor, Faculty of Law, Comenius University in Bratislava, Slovakia, email: jozef.valuch@flaw.uniba.sk.
Ondrej Hamulak, Senior Lecturer, Member of Jean Monnet Chair, Faculty of Law, Palacký University Olomouc, Czech Republic and Visiting Professor in the Implementation of EU Law, School of Business and Governance, TTU Tallinn, Estonia, email: ondrej.hamulak@upol.cz.

J. Valuch (✉)
Faculty of Law, Comenius University in Bratislava, Bratislava, Slovakia
e-mail: jozef.valuch@flaw.uniba.sk

O. Hamulak
Faculty of Law, Palacký University Olomouc, Olomouc, Czech Republic
e-mail: ondrej.hamulak@upol.cz

O. Hamulak
EU Law, School of Business and Governance, TTU Tallinn, Tallinn, Estonia

© T.M.C. ASSER PRESS and the authors 2018   215
S. Sayapin and E. Tsybulenko (eds.), *The Use of Force against Ukraine and International Law*, https://doi.org/10.1007/978-94-6265-222-4_10

the legal understanding of cyber operations and attacks. The goal of this chapter is to highlight this complexity and determine the status of cyber incidents realized in Ukraine from the perspective of international law. Having considered the distinction between cyber attacks and cyber operations, our assumptions in the realms of conflict in Ukraine tend towards the latter notion.

Keywords Ukraine · conflict · cyberspace · cyber operations · cyber attacks · international law

10.1 Introduction

It is possible to observe the conflict in Ukraine from multiple angles. One may focus on the Euromaidan protests in Kiev, the occupation of the Crimean Peninsula by the Russian Federation, the hybrid war and the deployment of Russian troops in Ukraine's Donbas area,[1] the EU sanctions against Russia etc. through the prism of international politics, international relations, security and global studies, and of course international law. In addition, observations and opinions on the conflict in Ukraine vary among scholars, state leaders and representatives of international organizations. When we opt for the optic of contemporary international law, we learn that the evaluation and analysis of this complex conflict is considered to be highly complicated and controversial.[2]

In this chapter, we focus on a very narrow and particular question concerning the multifaceted topic of war in Ukraine. Hereafter, we devote particular attention to the use of cyberspace during the conflict from the perspective of international law.

Cyberspace is now at the centre of international law concerns. It is the focus of research being undertaken by a multitude of academic institutions, and international forums and other organizations. As an example, the Berkman Klein Center for Internet & Society at Harvard University carries out major research in this field and runs a cyber law clinic, which delivers high-level legal services to government entities, nonprofit organizations and individuals. Other examples of research centres focusing on cyber law and security are the Cybersecurity Law Institute at Georgetown University, the Center for Internet and Society at Stanford Law School and the NATO Cooperative Cyber Defence Centre of Excellence (CCDCOE) in Tallinn.[3] The study of this topic also forms an important part of research activities conducted by the UN Institute for Disarmament Research (UNIDIR). In addition, particular states are paying attention to cyberspace topics, especially focusing on the preservation of their own national security. In 2009, France established the National Agency of IT Security[4] and the UK created the Cyber Security Operations Centre as part of Government

---

[1] Tsybulenko and Pakhomenko 2016, p. 168.

[2] Bílková 2014, p. 1.

[3] Mrázek 2014, p. 538.

[4] French name: *Agence Nationale de la Sécurité des Systèmes d'Information* (ANSI).

Communications Headquarters. In 2010, the USA established the US Cyber Command (USCYBERCOM) as part of the US Department of Defense. In Germany, the Centre of Cyber Protection (*Cyber-Abwehrzentrum*) provides services in this field. In Russia, cybersecurity matters fall under the competence of the Ministry of Defence and the Federal Security Service (the FSB). In Ukraine the Ministry of Internal Affairs and the Security Service of Ukraine deal with cybersecurity problems, while, in 2007, the country's Computer Emergency Response Team was created.[5] In 2016, the establishment of the National Coordination Centre for Cyber Security as a working body of the National Security and Defence Council was announced. The aim of the centre will be the coordination of activities among the agencies involved in the national security and defence of Ukraine. It will also be responsible for searching and investigating potential and real threats to cybersecurity, studying international experience in cybersecurity etc.[6]

The topic covered by this chapter (and research devoted to it) involves special terminology, which needs to be presented at the very beginning of our paper. The use of incorrect terms or misunderstandings could lead to false conclusions. Not all operations and activities in cyberspace should be understood as cyber attacks. It is obvious that not all actors get legal protection in the same manner, that not all conflicts in the international field could be defined as war conflicts etc. The proper understanding of terminology and the differentiation of particular situations are prerequisites for the complex coverage of the topic. Therefore, we start this chapter with the outline of the main terms, phrases and definitions.

10.2 The Notion of Cyberspace

The crucial term for the purpose of our work is the notion of "cyberspace". As Tsagourias pointed out: "For international lawyers, their conception of cyberspace is influenced by their understanding of how spaces are represented in international law."[7] The concept of cyberspace was not originally a legal one. It appeared for the very first time in science fiction literature. This special term was invented by W. F. Gibson in his short story, "Burning Chrome", from 1982 and later used in his novel *Neuromancer*, from 1984.[8] The popularity of using this term quickly grew in parallel to the increasing speed and usage of the virtual space around the world. Cyberspace created a special communication network with a distinct status, which was non-dependent on any concrete state, legal system or jurisdiction. In the present world, cyberspace negates the classical understanding of public space. According to Karl Jaspers, the public voice and public influence are connected with the visibility

---

[5] Pakharenko 2015, p. 60.
[6] UNIAN Information Agency 2015.
[7] Tsagourias 2015, p. 15.
[8] Knorr 2005, p. 14.

of actors.[9] Cyberspace contravenes this approach. The Internet (the net of "interconnected networks") opens the space for electronic communication, where anyone can be heard without being seen. This is the basic feature of real "cyberspace".[10]

Other authors define cyberspace as a global, interconnected network of information technology and communication structures, including the Internet, telecommunication networks, computer networks and information included within these systems.[11] There are also some official or semi-official definitions of this notion. For example, in the US, the National Military Strategy for Cyberspace Operations in 2006 defined cyberspace as "a domain characterized by the use of electronics and the electromagnetic spectrum to store, modify, and exchange data via networked systems and associated physical infrastructures".[12]

Some armed forces understand cyberspace as a fifth domain (next to land, water, air and space) where it is possible to perform military operations and wage war. These views formed the basis of the definition of cyberspace, provided by the US Secretary of Defense, as a global domain within the information environment consisting of the interdependent network of information technology infrastructures and resident data, including the Internet, telecommunications networks, computer systems, and embedded processors and controllers.[13] It is clear that cyberspace, as a fifth domain, is distinct from the other four. It represents human creation and is administrated by human activity.[14] It has a global character; it erases the borders between the states and works independently of any political system. There is a wide range of actors performing their activities within this domain, both private (individuals, groups, associations) and the public (states and international organizations).[15] The above-mentioned autonomy of cyberspace leads to problems with its management and security threats. Absolute security in this domain is almost impossible or unimaginable. In comparison to the other four domains, cyberspace is also special due to its factual non-governability. Even with huge resources and capacities, no power would be able to seize or control a domain with so many actors, simple access and anonymity. Cyberspace is flexible and variable, simple and accessible to the masses. Nevertheless, all its advantages give rise to wide range of malicious intents and opportunities. Cyberspace is a new universe for information criminality and cyberthreats of a different degree of gravity (hacking, cyber espionage, distributed denial of service – or DDoS – attacks, propaganda and the dissemination of wrong or dangerous information, Internet fraud, misuse or abuse of personal data etc.). Current threats are coming from a wide range of entities including hackers, hacktivists (ideologically motivated hackers), states, criminal or terrorist groups with varied technical resources and backgrounds. The common feature of all cyber attacks is

---

[9] In *Stanford Encyclopedia of Philosophy* 2014; Thornhill 2002.

[10] Gábriš 2014, pp. 14–5.

[11] Melzer 2011, p. 4.

[12] United States Department of Defense 2006, p. 11.

[13] Roscini 2014, p. 9.

[14] Roscini 2014, p. 9. See also UNIDIR 2011.

[15] Melková and Sokol 2015, pp. 55–6.

the complicated process of identifying their real source.[16] With relevant skills and with the appropriate technology (which is now fairly accessible without requiring a major investment), it is possible to cause serious threats and immense damage, even to the states that have modern and significant conventional forces. The character and 'opportunities' of cyberspace blur the distinction between traditional threat actors and hackers, terrorists, organized criminal networks, industrial spies and foreign intelligence services,[17] which in turn complicates the identification of the attacker.[18]

The complexity of cyberspace itself gives rise to different views on the content of this domain. The common feature of particular definitions of cyberspace is the multilayered approach to its content. According to certain views, cyberspace comprises three layers: physical (composed of hardware, satellites, cables and other technical equipment), syntactic (software, applications and operating systems) and semantic (which includes concrete information, human activities, considerations and judgements).[19] Another perspective refers to a three-layered structure, but involves (in a more technical sense) a hardware layer, software layer and data layer. In all cases, all three layers (separately or as a whole) could be the target of cyber attacks.[20]

10.3 Cyberspace and International Law

The international law approach towards cyberspace must reflect the specific nature of this legal system. International law should be defined as "the standard of conduct, at a given time for states and other entities subject thereto".[21] It is mostly based on the coordination principle (contrary to the subordination principle, which is widely used in national law). States as traditional actors cooperate here on the principle of equality. They are the addressees of the legal norms (possessing rights and duties), but act together as the major rule-makers.[22] International law is therefore the result of compromises made by states. The normative content and quality of international law depends on the level of compromise that was necessary during the negotiation processes.[23] It is therefore logical that the approach taken in international law towards cyberspace and its regulation must be the result of compromise. We can see the consequences of these specifics in the context of the definitions of crucial terms such as cyber operations and cyber attacks.

Not all cyber operations should be considered as cyber attacks. The definitions of cyber attacks involve a narrower approach. According to the so-called *Tallinn*

---

[16] Melková and Sokol 2015, p. 57. See also Kramer et al. 2009, p. 664.

[17] Australian Cyber Security Strategy 2009.

[18] Roscini 2014, pp. 1–2. See also Australian Cyber Security Strategy 2009, p. 3.

[19] Sheldon 2016, pp. 182–3. See also Mrázek 2014, p. 541.

[20] Tobanksy 2011, pp. 75, 77–78. See also Tsagourias 2015, p. 15.

[21] Grant and Barker 2009, p. 300.

[22] Vršanský et al. 2012, p. 51.

[23] Ibid., p. 52.

Manual,[24] "A cyber attack is a cyber operation, whether offensive or defensive, that is reasonably expected to cause injury or death to persons or damage or destruction to objects". This classification has significant importance especially in connection with the restrictive notion of "attack" in the law of armed conflicts. The general restriction, whereby civilians and objects of a civilian nature shall not be subject to attacks, is also valid in the domain of cyberspace.[25] On the other hand, the *Tallinn Manual* accepts that a cyber attack can involve those who are not civilians, specifically members of armed forces, members of organized armed groups, civilians taking a direct part in the hostilities, and – in an international armed conflict – *levée en masse* conscripts.[26] In defining the notion of "attack", the *Tallinn Manual* refers to the First Additional Protocol to the Geneva Conventions, which defines *attack* in Article 49, para 1, as an "act or acts of violence against the adversary, whether in offence or defence". The violence here is determined by the results of the act. The use of violence against a target distinguishes attacks from other military operations.[27] Therefore, non-violent operations, such as psychological cyber operations or cyber espionage, are not qualified as cyber attacks.[28] In connection with this, we must deal with the question about whether cyber operations should be determined as a use of force in the meaning of international law. The prohibition of threat or use of force is part of the cogent norms of international law. According to the UN Charter, this prohibition relates to "attacks" on territorial integrity or political independence of any state, but also to any other conduct inconsistent with the purposes of the UN.[29] In this respect, according to the *Tallinn Manual*, "a cyber operation constitutes a use of force when its scale and effects are comparable to a non-cyber operation rising to the level of a use of force".[30] In an attempt to determine when cyber operations should be understood as a use of force in the meaning of Article 2(4) of the UN Charter, we ought to recall the *Nicaragua* case.[31] The use of the International Court of Justice (ICJ) findings for the purpose of cyberspace leads us to the conclusion that key factors are the effects and extent of the cyber operations. In this meaning, non-destructive cyber operations, such as attacks on the confidence of a national

---

[24] *Tallinn Manual on the International Law Applicable to Cyber Warfare Prepared by the International Group of Experts at the Invitation of the NATO Cooperative Cyber Defence Centre of Excellence* (hereinafter called the *Tallinn Manual*), Rule 30.

[25] *Tallinn Manual*, Rule 32: "The civilian population as such, as well as individual civilians, shall not be the object of cyber attack"; Rule 37: "Civilian objects shall not be made the object of cyber attacks. computers, computer networks and cyber infrastructure may be made the object of attack if they are military objectives".

[26] *Tallinn Manual*, Rule 34.

[27] Bruner 2015, p. 161.

[28] *Tallinn Manual*, Rule 30(2).

[29] UN Charter Article 2(4): "All members shall refrain in their international relations from the threat or use of force against the territorial integrity or political independence of any state, or in any other manner inconsistent with the purposes of the United Nations."

[30] *Tallinn Manual*, Rule 11.

[31] ICJ 1984, *Military and Paramilitary Activities in and Against Nicaragua (Nicaragua v. United States)*, ICJ Reports, 39.

government, could not be determined as attacks involving the use of force.[32] On the other hand, this does not mean that cyber operations, which do not include the use of force, are in harmony with international law. They could be covered by other international legal rules, e.g., the prohibition of intervention, which forms part of the principle of the sovereign equality of states (Article 2(1) of the UN Charter). The prohibition of intervention is also part of customary international law[33] while, according to the ICJ, the non-intervention principle "forbids all states or groups of states to intervene directly or indirectly in the internal or external affairs of other states".[34]

International law deals with activities in cyberspace mostly in connection to so-called "cyberwarfare" and therefore from the perspective of *jus ad bellum* and *jus in bello*. One of the most visible challenges to international law is the determination of the rules of cyber conflict. At present, there is no common accord between state representatives on the determination of this problem. For example, during negotiations of the Governmental Group of Experts in 2015, focusing on the possibility of the application of international legal rules on cyber conflicts,[35] this topic prompted the most questions and gave rise to the most complex discussions. There is a significant discord between the group of nations led by Russia and China, on the one hand, and members of NATO on the other. The crux of the disagreement lies in the possibility of using UN Charter rules (especially Article 2(4): "refrain from use of force"; and Article 51: "right to self-defence") in cyber conflicts.

One of the most crucial questions in connection with cyber conflicts concerns the dilemma of using or overcoming classical norms (included in the UN Charter and international treaties) on war conflicts, as well as the need to introduce new rules that are particularly applicable to this new and specific type of conflict. According to some authors, there is an option to extend the special UN Charter rules to explicitly determined cyber actions.[36] One of the most influential opinions promoting this view is connected with the work of Professor Harold H. Koh, who claims that that cyberspace is not a neutral sphere without legal regulation, where anyone can conduct hostile acts without any consequences. Contrary to that, he presents the view that traditional rules and principles of international law are valid and applicable, even within this domain.[37]

The relation between cyberattacks and rules on *jus ad bellum* and *jus in bello* was significantly covered by the work of the International Group of Experts at the invitation of the NATO CCDCOE, which prepared the above-mentioned *Tallinn Manual* in 2012. This manual, in its two sections, covers questions of cybersecurity (and *jus ad bellum*), as well as questions of armed conflicts (and *jus in bello*).[38]

---

[32] Šmigová 2013, p. 1226.

[33] *Nicaragua v. United States*, p. 202.

[34] *Tallinn Manual*, Rule 10 (6–7). See also *Nicaragua v. United States*, p. 205.

[35] GGE 2015.

[36] Lewis 2015, pp. 42–43.

[37] Koh 2012.

[38] Gábriš 2014, p. 174.

Although this document is the non-binding outcome of research by the expert group, it is inspiring and has significantly impacted developments in the field of cyber law.

Currently, there is a wide acceptance of the applicability of international law rules to activities within cyberspace. This confirmed by academia and international organizations. For example, NATO clearly recognizes the impact of general international law and international humanitarian law in the cybersphere.[39] Cybersecurity and potential threats in the field of information and communication technologies (ICT) also form a stabile part of the UN agenda. Since 1998, annual reports are presented by the Secretary-General to the General Assembly on ICT questions and international security. Additionally, four Groups of Governmental Experts (GGEs) (2004, 2009, 2011 and 2014; composed of representatives from 15–20 countries, including the US, Russia and China) were created to deal with questions of cyber-security, threats in cyberspace and developments in this field. All of these expert groups confirmed the necessity of applying international legal rules and especially the UN Charter to promote peace and stability and support open, safe, accessible and peaceful spaces for ICT. A significant contribution to addressing these questions was made by the fourth GGE. In its report from June 2015, it presented a set of norms, rules and principles applicable to the activities of states in cyberspace. This set of norms covered a wide range of questions about how international law should deal with ICT problems. The UN Office for Disarmament Affairs (UNODA) summary of this report sets out the key principles presented by the GGE:

- *"In their use of ICT, States must observe, among other principles of international law, State sovereignty, the settlement of disputes by peaceful means, and non-intervention in the internal affairs of other States.*
- *"Existing obligations under international law are applicable to the State use of ICT and States must comply with their obligations to respect and protect human rights and fundamental freedoms.*
- *"States must not use proxies to commit internationally wrongful acts using ICT and should seek to ensure that their territory is not used by non-State actors to commit such acts.*
- *"The UN should play a leading role in promoting dialogue on the security of ICT in their use by States, and in developing common understandings on the application of international law and norms, rules and principles for responsible State behaviour."*[40]

The identification of the main principles and the attempt to present some general rules are very important, but still insufficient, due to the lack of any binding force. There is a crucial open question about the applicability of these rules in practice.

---

[39] "Our policy also recognises that international law, including international humanitarian law and the un charter, applies in cyberspace." wales summit declaration (issued by the heads of state and government participating in the meeting of the North Atlantic Council in Wales)", 5 September 2014, para 72.

[40] UNODA 2015.

Another problem arises in connection with the promoted applicability of general international law norms to the particular features of cyberspace.[41]

It is clear that, in the absence of specific rules, we must look for solutions in general international law. However, the biggest problems here lie in the (non-)transferability of classical notions to cyberspace specifics. For example, the concepts of jurisdiction or the notion of state accountability for certain types of conduct is so general that their applicability *vis-á-vis* indeterminate cyberspace features is misconceived and almost impossible. Furthermore, the applicability of the concept of due diligence, as approved by the ICJ in the *Corfu Channel Case*,[42] may raise some doubts. Once we accept a broad understanding of the notion of state territory, including the infrastructure for ICT built into it, we can use the due diligence principle, even in connection with cyberspace.[43] On the other hand, we must always take the special character of cybersphere, which uses global networks and poses particular difficulty in searching for the source of concrete operations and attacks, into account. Another problem in connection with cyberspace is the non-existence of stable international executive structures, which could deal with its specifics. If we connect the above-mentioned inconsistencies with the principle of the autonomy and freedom of choice for all states (in situations where there is no international rule prescribing or prohibiting certain types of conduct), we must also deal with the risk of fragmentation and the incapacity of the international community to govern cyberspace effectively. For all these reasons, cyberspace represents one of the most visible challenges to contemporary international law.[44]

10.4 Cyber Operations and the Conflict in Ukraine

10.4.1 The Threat of Cyberspace Abuse: Examples

The conflict in Ukraine is far from being the first example of cyberspace abuse involving harmful operations. The fears and doubts about the misuse and exploitation of this virtual sphere have been present since the very early times of the Internet. Attacks and examples of malpractice have appeared in numerous forms, targeting webpages of governments, defence and security administrations, banks and financial institutions, media organizations etc. Furthermore, the scale of these threats is persistently growing. [45]

Before moving onto an analysis of cyber operations during the conflict in Ukraine, we will deal with the most visible and well-known examples of the misuse of

---

[41] Stinissen 2015, p. 124.

[42] *Corfu Channel Case (UK v. Albania)*, ICJ Reports, 1949. See also Buchta and Sýkorová 2016, pp. 13–4.

[43] Zimmermann 2014.

[44] Ibid.

[45] O'Connell et al. 2012.

cyberspace, which offer us a real insight into the gravity and (negative) potential of abuses in the cybersphere.

In the first example, we refer to a 2007 case from Estonia. In April of that year, Estonia faced serious DDoS attacks for almost three weeks. The attacks paralysed the webpages of important public authorities as well as some private service providers. The incentive for these attacks was the decision by the Estonian authorities to move the Soviet Army monument from Tallinn city centre to the military cemetery. This decision led to resistance and some unrest from members of the Russian minority in Estonia, who recognized the monument as a tribute to the victims of the Second World War. On the other hand, the majority Estonian community connected the monument with Soviet times and the occupation of their country. DDoS attacks was made on Internet sites of government agencies and later on those of newspapers, TV stations, banks etc. Webpages carrying Russian propaganda replaced many of the attacked sites, with false apology statements substituting some of them. However, most of the attacks were aimed at simply shutting down the existing sites. These attacks gave rise to serious protests and the spokesperson of the Estonian Defence Ministry even compared them to the '9/11' attacks on New York and Washington. According to the Estonian authorities, most of the attacks came from sources in Russia, although many of them stemmed from thousands of private personal computers (PCs) from around the world. There were several Russian websites publishing instructions on how to perform the DDoS attacks in practice. Some other attacks were made from computers infected by special PC viruses, which automatically involved the infected workstations in the attack structures without the awareness of their owners.[46] According to some sources, when the attacks occurred, they included more than one million computers based in more than 100 countries. Despite the mass character and impact of the attacks, only minor economic and ICT disturbances occurred, which did not cause any serious material damage, injury or loss of life.[47] Although Estonia is a member of NATO, there were no official countermeasures taken by this organization as a response to the attacks that Estonia suffered. Nevertheless, NATO established an Internet defence facility in Estonia known as the CCDCOE.[48]

Another example of relevant cyber operations occurred in summer 2008, both before and during the armed conflict between Georgia and the Russian Federation. The assaults targeted official sites of the Georgian Government and caused them to go offline or slow down the distribution of Internet services. Immediately before and after the interference of Russian troops in the territory of the Georgian province of South Ossetia, some of the Georgian Government's official website were brought down and their content replaced by anti-Georgian propaganda.[49] Some DDoS attacks also paralysed Georgia's ability to disseminate information, with the country accusing the Russian Federation of being responsible for these hostile operations. The Russian Federation denied this allegation and claimed that certain private parties,

---

[46] The Economist 2007.

[47] Roscini 2014, pp. 4–5.

[48] O'Connell et al. 2012.

[49] See Kerikmäe et al. 2014.

who had acted independently and without any connection to the Russian administration, were responsible. These cyber operations were also addressed in the Report
of the Independent Fact-finding Mission on the Conflict in Georgia from 2009.[50]
While this report failed to reach any concrete conclusions about accountability or
attribution, it nevertheless stated that, "if these attacks were directed by a government
or governments, it is likely that this form of warfare was used for the first time in an
inter-state armed conflict".[51] Some sources claim that four out of the five repositories
used for the operations and cyber blockade of official Georgian sites were located
on Russian territory (the fifth was based in Turkey), while all of them were under
the control of the criminal syndicate, the Russian Business Network.[52] The Georgian
experience is a clear example of the misuse of cyberspace during interstate conflicts,
offering powerful evidence of the growing importance of cyber operations, which
can achieve the same results as classical warfare methods.

In addition, Iran has had to counter a number of cyber incidents in the last few
years. Many of them were closely connected to Iran's nuclear programme. One
of the most well-known attacks used the so-called Stuxnet worm, one of the most
sophisticated and intelligent computer viruses, which inflected nuclear facilities. It
appeared in the second half of 2010. It is a hidden virus, which mostly inflects industrial software (especially with Siemens capabilities) and can spread very quickly
to attack the most important system capacities, e.g., control and monitoring processes or structures securing the communication between the system devices and
applications. Several proven Stuxnet attacks caused severe damage to the Iranian
nuclear programme.[53] This worm attack represents another example of the major
opportunities for malpractice offered by the open cybersphere. Although the damages were not officially quantified, we can see that cyberattacks using malware, such
as Stuxnet, are capable of producing real material harm and endangering human
lives.[54] Some opinions suggest that Stuxnet is the first example of a global cyber-
weapon with great geopolitical potential.[55] According to most of the allegations, the
US with the support of Israel are behind the creation and spread of Stuxnet. These
contestations assume that Stuxnet has to involve governmental support. "Private"
hackers do not have the sufficient technical and economic resources to develop such
a sophisticated cyberthreat.[56] However, there is no clear evidence to confirm these
accusations. Against this backdrop is the fact that the Stuxnet virus also attacked
other countries, such as India, Indonesia and Russia. Some sources state that more
than 40% of all infected computers came from outside Iran.

---

[50] Report of the Independent International Fact-finding Mission on the Conflict in Georgia 2009.

[51] Roscini 2014, pp. 7–8. See also Report of the Independent International Fact-finding Mission on
the Conflict in Georgia 2009, pp. 217–9.

[52] See Melková and Sokol 2015, p. 59. See also Smith 2014.

[53] Macková 2013.

[54] NATO Review 2011.

[55] Macková 2013.

[56] O'Connell et al. 2012.

Finally, we have been able to find another example of a cyber operation with a clear military aim/target, which involved an attack by Israel on the Syrian air defence system. During the so-called Operation Orchard, Israel conducted an airstrike on Syrian nuclear devices with the support of a cyber operation. This cyberattack allegedly led to the disruption of the Syrian air defence, which allowed the unimpeded flight of Israeli bombers over a considerable part of Syrian territory.[57] Israeli software had allegedly penetrated computer networks in Syria and copied recorded radar values, which were later displayed during the attack. Therefore, despite the fact that Israeli aircraft crossed the border and approached their target, Syrian monitors were showing data from the time when the sky was empty. There is also some speculation that Israel used Suter technology, which overwhelms radars with false targets and makes it impossible to identify the real fighters.[58]

10.4.2 Cyberspace and the Conflict in Ukraine

The conflict in Ukraine evolved through several phases, where more or less relevant events occurred: (1) at the end of 2013 and the beginning of 2014 – Ukrainian President Yanukovych's refusal to sign the association agreement between Ukraine and the EU, as a crucial part of the EU Eastern Partnership Policy,[59] which led to a mass wave of anti-government protests in Kiev; March 2014 – the declaration of independence of the Republic of Crimea and the occupation of Crimea by the Russian Federation; April/May 2014 – escalation of armed conflict in eastern parts of Ukraine; perpetual sanctions against Russia, peace and ceasefire negotiations and the continuation of attacks in 2016[60] and 2017. From the very beginning of the conflict, all the protests, riots, armed actions and other kinetic acts were accompanied by cyber operations of a different nature and relevance. The threats that these cyber incidents brought were all the more serious because Ukraine is among the most vulnerable countries in terms of cybersecurity. According to the Global Cybersecurity Index & Cyberwellness Profiles for April 2015, which reflect countries' readiness in connection to cyberspace and ICT risks, Ukraine was in 17th position; however, because one position could be held by several states, there were in fact 65 countries ahead of Ukraine.

The cyber incidents that occurred during the conflict in Ukraine are wide-ranging and include DDoS and website defacements, while cyber espionage tools have been discovered in Ukraine and NATO countries. Meanwhile, new and more menacing forms of malware have appeared, including Turla/Uroburos/Snake, RedOctober and MiniDuke. There have also been: cyberattacks against opposition servers,

---

[57] Lewis 2015, p. 46.

[58] Bruner 2015, p. 167.

[59] See Kerikmäe and Chochia 2016; Siskova et al. 2014.

[60] On the question of the use of force in international law, see Faix 2013, p. 115; on relations between Russia and Ukraine, see Vršanský 2014, pp. 106–37.

smartphones, websites and Internet accounts; continuous leaks of stolen sensitive information;[61] attacks targeting the mobile devices of Ukrainian members of parliament; and cyberattacks against the Ukrainian Central Election Commission in May 2014 (to undermine the credibility of the elections and present false election results). Furthermore, Eastern Ukraine has been isolated from the rest of the country by Internet censorship and regular forensic checks on citizens' computers and mobile devices etc.[62]

There is an important question about how to deal with these cyber activities, which are clearly connected to the ongoing conflict, and whether it is possible to include these cyber operations under the umbrella of international law on armed conflicts. The answer to this question depends on the gravity of their consequences. In the case where a cyber operation gives rise to injuries, deaths, damage or destruction, the law on armed conflicts should apply. This may occur, for example, when one country starts cyber operations against another country with the aim of destroying the latter's critical infrastructure, such as civil aviation control systems or national grids, which would lead to the malfunctioning of aircraft and in turn injuries, damage and deaths. When we take into consideration the consequences, there is no space for a distinction between conventional weapons and cyber operations.[63] It is clear from the above-mentioned *Tallinn Manual* that "cyber operations executed in the context of an armed conflict are subject to the law of armed conflict".[64] From this perspective, e.g., cyber operations, which were targeted at Estonia in 2007, were not subject to the law of armed conflicts, because the situation itself (and its consequences) did not reach the level of an armed conflict. On the other hand, in the Georgian situation from 2008, the law on armed conflicts covered cyber operations in this case, because they were carried out in order to support the conflict itself.[65]

The question now concerns how these conclusions affect the evaluation of the situation in Ukraine. Here, it is important to mention that all members of the expert group that worked on the *Tallinn Manual* unanimously agreed with the necessity to recognize the existence of a nexus between cyber activities and armed conflict. On the other hand, they failed to agree on the level and nature of this prescribed nexus. According to one group of experts, the law on armed conflicts is applicable to all cyber operations carried out by one side of the armed conflict against the enemy. According to another group, only operations undertaken in furtherance of the hostilities, that is, in order to contribute to the original aggressor's military effort, could be included under the regulation of armed conflicts.[66] These activities are connected to other military (hostile) operations against the enemy, while, at the same time, constituting acts of hostility by themselves.[67] Here, we are facing one of the stumbling blocks

---

[61] Geers 2015, p. 11.

[62] Ibid.

[63] O'Connell et al. 2012, p. 10.

[64] *Tallinn Manual*, Rule 20.

[65] *Tallinn Manual*, Rule 20(3).

[66] *Tallinn Manual*, Rule 20(5).

[67] Bruner 2015, p. 160.

within the evaluation of the nature of cyber incidents realized in Ukraine. The nexus between these incidents and the conflict itself could be considered as disputable and give rise to openly expressed doubts.

Another important circumstance of relevance is the question of accountability. In connection with cyber incidents, this notion is one of the most challenging. Cyberspace is open, flexible, full of actors, simple to enter and leave, and anonymous. The determination of responsible actors in the case of cyber operations is therefore very complicated. It raises many intertwined questions:

- Who performed the cyber operation and on what basis?
- If it is a non-state actor, is there any support or management by the state?
- If so, what is the level of state involvement or support?[68]

Moreover, we must always take the risk posed by the false use or misuse of devices, sources and connections of innocent owners by cyberattackers into account.

The conflict in Ukraine is described as a hybrid warfare situation. It is a mixture of non-conventional tactics and strategies, secret operations, cyber activities, the operation of irregular forces and political manipulations. One of the goals of all these mixed strategies is the attempt to avoid military reprisals. The activities are performed so as to avoid encroaching on the boundaries of the definition of the use of force. Here, static actions have the same importance as classical kinetic attacks. Conventional warfare is only one part of the broad set of actions[69] performed not only by states but also by non-state actors. Cyber operations are capable of producing comparable effects to kinetic weapons and their advantage is also their informational potential. These operations are able to manipulate public opinion and decision-making. They are mostly aimed at producing political and psychological effects, manipulating data and influencing knowledge and opinions, rather than causing physical damage and injuries. In addition, they offer benefits to one side of the conflict in the form of uncertainty and doubts on the part of the enemy. [70]

According to some authors, "cyber activities conducted as part of a wider conflict are governed by that conflict's legal framework".[71] Therefore, it is important to determine the nature of the conflict itself. The conflict in Ukraine is mixed and evolving, with different types of situations and views concerning their determination:

- The original riots in Kiev's Independence Square could be determined as demonstrations and violent clashes between protesters and police, rather than a military (armed) conflict. This first phase belonged to Ukrainian internal affairs, although it gave rise to events that developed into the armed conflict. Therefore, we cannot define this phase as an (international) armed conflict, and it is hard to include any cyber operations that occurred during this time within the legal framework of the law on armed conflicts.

---

[68] O'Connell et al. 2012, p. 11.

[69] Lewis 2015, p. 40.

[70] Ibid.

[71] Stinissen 2015, p. 124.

- The secession of Crimea from Ukraine and its connection to the Russian Federation do not find any support in current international law.[72] Thus, the Crimea situation can be determined as an occupation. The law on armed conflicts applies to a situation of total and also partial occupation, even if this occupation did not lead to armed resistance on the occupied territory.[73] Occupation is a hostile substitution of territorial power and authority, which exactly corresponds to the situation in Crimea, where Russia exercises territorial control without the consent of the Ukrainian Government.[74] The cyber operations related to this situation could be determined as military operations under the regime of the law on armed conflicts in its above-mentioned broad understanding.
- The situation in Eastern Ukraine was determined by an International Committee of the Red Cross in 2014 as a non-international armed conflict,[75] which is defined as an "armed conflict not of an international character occurring in the territory of one of the High Contracting Parties".[76] In addition, some academics support this approach. For example, Professor Robert Heinsch analysed the conflict in Ukraine from different perspectives (as an international armed conflict, a non-international armed conflict and an 'internationalized' armed conflict) and came to the conclusion that at least some acts belonging to the second category occurred within the conflict.[77]
- There are also numerous international resolutions that clearly define Russian actions in Eastern Ukraine as military aggression. For example, the OSCE Parliamentary Assembly Resolution of 8 July 2015, stated that "actions by the Russian Federation in the Autonomous Republic of Crimea and the city of Sevastopol, as well as in certain areas of the Donetsk and Luhansk regions of Ukraine, constitute acts of military aggression against Ukraine".[78]
- Further developments in understanding and defining this conflict occurred in 2016, when the Office of the Prosecutor of the ICC stated the following: "[The] information available suggests that the situation within the territory of the Crimea and Sevastopol amounts to an international armed conflict between Ukraine and the Russian Federation. This international armed conflict began at the latest on 26 February when the Russian Federation deployed members of its armed forces to gain control over parts of the Ukrainian territory without the consent of the Ukrainian Government. The law of international armed conflict would continue to apply after 18 March 2014 to the extent that the situation within the territory of Crimea and Sevastopol factually amounts to an on-going state of occupation. A determination of whether or not the initial intervention, which led to the

---

[72] Bílková 2014, p. 12.

[73] Geneva Conventions 1949, Common Article 2.

[74] Stinissen 2015, p. 128.

[75] International Committee of the Red Cross (ICRC) 2014.

[76] Geneva Conventions, Common Article 3.

[77] Heinsch 2015.

[78] OSCE Parliamentary Assembly Resolution 2015. See also the Parliamentary Assembly of the Council of Europe Resolution 2132 (2016) or Resolution 2133 (2016).

occupation, is considered lawful or not is not required. For purposes of the Rome Statute an armed conflict may be international in nature if one or more States partially or totally occupies the territory of another State, whether or not the occupation meets with armed resistance."[79] Notwithstanding the fact that Russia in not a party to the Rome Statute (and, most likely in reaction to the statement of the Office of Prosecutor, it withdrew from the process of accession to the ICC at the end of 2016), this opinion changes the view of the conflict in Eastern Ukraine, which is now defined as an international armed conflict and therefore could also cover cyberattacks and related operations.

We must point out that Russia firmly denies any responsibility or participation in the conducted or ongoing cyber operations. It is a fact that most of the agents of cyber operations in Crimea were non-state actors, e.g., the pro-Russian hackers group known as CyberBerkut. To further evaluate the cyber operations conducted in connection with the conflict in Ukraine, it is crucial to determine the status of these agents. If these agents were an integrated part of Russian military forces, we could easily determine them as the combatants. We could also determine them as combatants if they acted as a part of an armed group belonging to one of the parties of armed conflict and if they: (a) acted under the command of a person responsible for his subordinates; (b) wore a fixed distinctive sign recognizable at a distance; (c) carried arms openly; and (d) conducted their operations in accordance with the laws and customs of war. These are the key criteria by which to distinguish combatants and civilians. It is more than clear that any non-state hacker group, which is actively influencing the conflict in Ukraine, would not fulfil those criteria. They represent a virtual group, organized in cybersphere and only communicating via the Internet. They do not carry weapons, while acting anonymously, such that no distinctive sign can be observed. Therefore, we must determine them as civilians, but ones who (as direct participants in the activities of fighting parties) have lost the protection offered to civilians under the law on armed conflicts. In this situation, they may also be the target of any countermeasures by the opposing fighting party.[80]

Another important issue in attempts to determine cyber operations in light of international law is the notion of damage and injuries. Until now, we have not acknowledged any grave destructive consequences of cyber operations during the conflict in Ukraine. Several DDoS attacks occurred during fighting in Eastern Ukraine, while some operations led to a change in the content of official webpages and certain attacks affected the reliability and operability of communication channels. Some Internet sites of the Ukrainian government and Ukrainian embassies abroad were affected by spy software in order to gain access to secret information. Even though these operations complicated the operability of the state administration and endangered state security to a certain extent, most authors point out that they had no direct connection to the ongoing military conflict and, in the main, did not lead to any destructive consequences. Therefore, they refuse to accept the applicability of

---

[79] ICC 2016, pp. 35–6.
[80] Stinissen 2015, p. 132.

international law on armed conflicts, and in turn international humanitarian law, in these instances.[81]

Even though it is hard to classify the cyber operations in Ukraine in relation to the law on armed conflicts or humanitarian law, when we look at them from the wider perspective of international law, we may find some room for manoeuvre. One option would be to consider them as acts against rules on the protection of diplomatic information and communication. According to Rule 84 of the *Tallinn Manual*, diplomatic archives and communications are protected against cyberattacks in all cases. This rule has its basis in the Vienna Convention on Diplomatic Relations (1961) and the ICJ judgement in the *Tehran* case,[82] which refers to diplomatic relations as a "self-contained regime". We may find another example of the breach of international legal rules, e.g., the principle of non-interference in domestic affairs, during the Ukrainian conflict, especially in connection with the disruption of elections, albeit on the condition that these disruptions were operated or supported by a foreign state power. [83]

Until the present day, most cyber operations in Ukraine have been conducted in order to obtain strategic information and as the part of the "information war" between the two sides of the conflict. There have been no destructive consequences in connection with key infrastructure and no elimination of warfare equipment. Therefore, we may conclude that the operations instigated were neither forbidden by, nor in breach of international rules on armed conflicts. Of course, it would be a completely different situation if the cyber operations had been involved or interconnected with the kinetic war operations.[84]

When we try to compare the cyber operations carried out in connection with the conflict in Ukraine and those carried out in Estonia and Georgia, we must underline the different nature of all three situations. In Estonia, the cyber incidents were interconnected with civil unrest, and their aim was psychological and strategic in nature. They produced an atmosphere of uncertainty and were part of a power game or power expression, without any consequential military acts. In Georgia, the cyber operations were clearly linked to the ongoing armed conflict and, notwithstanding the uncertainty about the imputability of these incidents in relation to Russia, potentially represented the first time that this form of warfare was deployed in an interstate armed conflict.[85] The cyber operations in Ukraine, on the other hand, have mostly had a political and ideological effect. Their impact on the development and outcomes of the conflict itself has not been as significant, especially when we compare them to the impact and consequences of establishing support and military backup for pro-Russian separatist groups in Ukrainian territories, along with the outnumbered

---

[81] Bruner 2015, p. 169–70.

[82] *United States Diplomatic and Consular Staff in Tehran Case (US v. Iran)*, ICJ. Reports, 1980, paras 61–2, 77, 86. See also Buergenthal and Maier 1985, p. 210; Valuch 2013, p. 78.

[83] Stinissen 2015, p. 133.

[84] Stinissen 2015, p. 134.

[85] Roscini 2014, pp. 7–8. See also Report of the Independent International Fact-finding Mission on the Conflict in Georgia 2009, pp. 217–9.

Russian-speaking minority.[86] Of course, cyber operations could be also used for military purposes, but this is not the situation in Ukraine. To speak about the strategic or military impact of the cyber operations, some concrete requirements must be met: they must have a destructive impact, and be integrated into existing military structures, doctrine, planning and operations. An example of these types of military cyber operation can be seen in the attack by Israel on the Syrian air defence system, as mentioned above.

It is more than clear that Russia had an opportunity to penetrate Ukrainian ICT networks, thus presenting them with an important advantage in connection to tactics and planning kinetic operations. On the other hand, it is obvious, that this advantage was not exploited to its full potential. According to some commentators, Russia used this opportunity to test the possibilities and potential of cyber operations in gaining political benefits.[87] Therefore, negative damaging consequences were minimized.

10.5   Conclusion

Cyber space, often called the fifth domain for the performance of military operations, represents a major challenge for contemporary international law theory and practice, as we can see in the Ukrainian example. The application of international law to activities in this domain is widely accepted, but still unclear, due to a lack of specific international legal rules that are applicable to cyber warfare and cyber operations. In this regard, only general international legal rules are applicable, but they are very general and, as they were negotiated and adopted in the pre-cyber era, often non-applicable to cybersphere specifics.

Cyber operations are very broad, flexible and variable in nature. They can take different forms and intensities, and involve a variety of players, implementers, addressees etc. To determine whether cyber incidents are in fact cyberattacks that form part of warfare, they must either be comparable to the use of force with a destructive impact or form part of ongoing military operations. Without these attributes, they may simply be determined as other cyber operations, which are not forbidden by *jus in bellum*. The line between these two categories of incidents is often very thin and unclear. There are also significant discrepancies between representatives of doctrine.[88] Some authors claim that cyber operations that do not lead to any destructive consequences are more unacceptable than forbidden, which leads onto the creation of so-called customs about the permissibility of cyber operations.[89] Still, it is clear that, even in cases were cyber activities cannot be classified as military or warfare operations or attacks, they do not fall outside the interests and regulation of international law. Cyber operations could have different impacts and different consequences.

---

[86] Lewis 2015, p. 45.

[87] Lewis 2015, p. 47.

[88] Bruner 2015, p. 162.

[89] Brown and Poellet 2014. See also Bruner 2015, p. 166.

They could also be determined as breaches in the prohibition of intervention, diplomatic rules etc. In both cases – cyber warfare and cyber incidents that could not be determined as uses of force – there is still a major challenge for international law, specifically in relation to attribution and responsibility. Due to the fact that cyber space is an open domain, where many anonymous actors can enter with ease, these two questions very much remain open.

We have seen several cyber operations during the conflict in Ukraine, which provide useful examples of the complexity and difficulty of their determination. We are facing the heterogeneity of actors and different gravities of cyber incidents. Therefore, problems in identifying the responsible entity, as well as with the classification of operations under international law rules, are presented here. The conflict in Ukraine is classified as a hybrid warfare situation, mixing non-conventional tactics and strategies, secret operations, the operation of regular and irregular forces, and political manipulations. Cyber incidents are inevitably part of this hybrid situation. However, their classification is very complicated: they are more a part of an information war than a component of military actions, because they have not resulted in any destructive consequences and were not connected to any particular military operations. Therefore, they cannot be determined as cyberattacks in the sense of the *Tallinn Manual*.

References

Australian Cyber Security Strategy (2009). https://www.ag.gov.au/RightsAndProtections/CyberSecurity/Documents/AG%20Cyber%20Security%20Strategy%20-%20for%20website.pdf. Accessed 20 February 2017

Bílková V (2014) Mezinárodněprávní aspekty vývoje na Krymu [International law aspects of the developments in Crimea]. CSIL Working Papers 1:1–12

Brown G, Poellet K (2014) The customary law of cyberspace. Strategic Studies Quarterly 6:126–145

Bruner T (2015) K podmínkám a způsobu aplikace mezinárodního humanitárního práva na kybernetické operace [Conditions and ways of application of international humanitarian law in connection to cyber operations.] In: Bílková V (ed) Mezinárodní humanitární právo: vznik, vývoj a nové výzvy [International humanitarian law - the basis, developments and challenges]. Univerzita Karlova v Praze, Prague, pp. 159–171

Buchta T, Sýkorová M (2016) Najdôležitejšie rozsudky v medzinárodnom práve verejnom [The most important cases in international public law]. C. H. Beck, Bratislava

Buergenthal T, Maier HG (1985) Public International Law. West Publishing, St. Paul

Center for Strategic And International Studies, Cybersecurity And Cyberwarfare (2011) Preliminary Assessment Of National Doctrine And Organization (Unidir, 2011). http://www.unidir.org/Files/Publications/Pdfs/Cybersecurity-And-Cyberwarfare-Preliminary-Assessment-Of-National-Doctrine-And-Organization-380.Pdf. Accessed 12 January 2017

DoD - US Department of Defense (2006) National Military Strategy for Cyberspace Operations

Faix M (2013) Law of Armed Conflict and Use of Force. Part One. Securing International Pace and Security: International Law on the Use of Force. Univerzita Palackého, Olomouc

Gábriš T (2014) Cyber Law. Univerzita Komenského v Bratislave, Bratislava

Geers K (ed) (2015) Cyber War in Perspective: Russian Aggression against Ukraine. NATO CCD COE Publications, Tallinn

Grant JP, Barker JC (2009) Parry & Grant Encyclopaedic Dictionary of International Law, 3rd edn. Oxford University Press, Oxford

Group of Governmental Experts (2015) Report On Developments In The Field Of Information And Telecommunications In The Context Of International Security. http://www.un.org/Ga/Search/View_Doc.Asp?Symbol=A/70/174. Accessed 25 November 2016

Heinsch R (2015) Conflict Classification in Ukraine: The Return of The "Proxy War"? International Law Studies. 91:323–360

ICC (2016) Report on Preliminary Examination Activities 2016. https://www.icc-cpi.int/iccdocs/otp/161114-otp-rep-PE_ENG.pdf. Accessed 10 December 2016

ICRC (2014) Ukraine: ICRC calls on all sides to respect international humanitarian law. https://www.icrc.org/eng/resources/documents/news-release/2014/07-23-ukraine-kiev-call-respect-ihl-repatriate-bodies-malaysian-airlines.htm. Accessed 15 March 2017

Independent international fact-finding mission on the conflict in Georgia report (2009). http://www.mpil.de/files/pdf4/iiffmcg_volume_ii1.pdf. Accessed 14 December 2016

Kerikmäe T, Chochia A (eds) (2016) Political and Legal Perspectives of the EU Eastern Partnership Policy. Springer International Publishing, Cham

Kerikmäe T, Nyman-Metcalf K, Gabelaia D, Chochia A (2014) Cooperation of Post Soviets with the Aim of not being "Post" and "Soviets". In: Šišková N (ed) From Eastern Partnership to the Association. The Legal and Political Analysis (144–159). Cambridge Scholars Publishing, Newcastle upon Tyne

Knorr A (2005) The Stability of Cyberspace. http://xirdalium.net/wp-content/uploads/KNORR_2006_The_stability_of_cyberspace.pdf. Accessed 30 November 2016

Koh HH (2012) International Law in Cyberspace. Harvard International Law Journal Online 54:1–12

Kramer DF, Starr HS, Wentz L, Kuehl D (2009) Cyberpower and National Security. Potomac Books, Dulles VA

Lewis JA (2015) Compelling Opponents to Our Will: The Role of Cyber Warfare in Ukraine. In: Geers K (ed) Cyber War in Perspective: Russian Aggression against Ukraine. NATO CCD COE Publications, Tallinn, pp. 39–47

Macková V (2013) Cyber War of the States: Stuxnet and Flame Virus Opens New Era of War. CENAA Policy Papers 2:1–10

Melková M, Sokol T (2015) Kybernetický priestor ako nová dimenzia národnej bezpečnosti (Cyberspace as the new dimension of national security). Bezpečnostné fórum 2015. Belianum, Banská Bystrica, pp. 54–64

Melzer N (2011) Cyber Warfare and International Law. http://unidir.org/files/publications/pdfs/cyberwarfare-and-international-law-382.pdf. Accessed 16 February 2017

Mrázek J (2014) Mezinárodní právo v kybernetickém prostoru (International law in the cyberspace). Právník 153:537–561

NATO Cooperative Cyber Defence Centre of Excellence (2013) History. https://ccdcoe.org/history.html. Accessed 14 December 2016

NATO Cooperative Cyber Defence Centre of Excellence (2013) Tallinn Manual. https://ccdcoe.org/research.html. Accessed 5 January 2017

NATO Review (2011) Nové hrozby - kybernetické dimenzie. http://www.nato.int/docu/review/2011/11-september/cyber-Threads/SK/index.htm. Accessed 9 March 2017

O'Connell M E, Arimatsu L, Wilmshurst E (2012) Cyber Security and International Law. https://www.chathamhouse.org/sites/files/chathamhouse/public/Research/International%20Law/290512summary.pdf. Accessed 2 February 2017

OSCE (2015) OSCE Parliamentary Assembly Resolution 'The Continuation of Clear, Gross and Uncorrected Violations of OSCE Commitments and International Norms by the Russian Federation' (Helsinki, 08.07.2015). https://www.oscepa.org/meetings/annual-sessions/2015-annual-session-helsinki/2015-helsinki-final-declaration/2282-07. Accessed 26 May 2017

Pakharenko G (2015) Cyber operations at Maidan: a first-hand account. In: Geers K (ed) Cyber War in Perspective: Russian Aggression against Ukraine. NATO CCD COE Publications, Tallinn, pp. 59–66

Roscini M (2014) Cyber Operations and the Use of Force in International Law. Oxford University Press, Oxford

Sheldon JB (2016) Cyberwarfare. Encyclopaedia Britannica. https://www.britannica.com/topic/cyberwar. Accessed 27 January 2017

Šišková N (2014) From Eastern Partnership to the Association: A Legal and Political Analysis. Cambridge Scholars Publishing, Newcastle

Šmigová K (2013) Kybernetické útoky a medzinárodné právo [Cyber attacks and international law]. Bratislavské právnické fórum 2013. Univerzita Komenského v Bratislave, Bratislava, pp. 1224–1230

Smith JD (2014) Russian Cyber Strategy and the War Against Georgia. http://www.atlanticcouncil.org/blogs/natosource/russian-cyber-policy-and-the-war-against-georgia. Accessed 24 February 2017

Stanford Encyclopedia of Philosophy (2014) Entry: Karl Jaspers. https://Plato.Stanford.Edu/Entries/Jaspers/. Accessed 11 January 2017

Stinissen J (2015) A Legal Framework for Cyber Operations in Ukraine. In: Geers K (ed) Cyber War in Perspective: Russian Aggression against Ukraine. NATO CCD COE Publications, Tallinn, pp. 123–134

The Economist (2007) A Cyber-riot. http://www.economist.com/node/9163598. Accessed 10 December 2016

Thornhill Ch (2002) Karl Jaspers: Politics and Metaphysics. Routledge, London

Tobanksy L (2011) Basic concepts in cyber warfare. Military and Strategic Affairs 3:75–92

Tsagourias N (2015) Research Handbook on International Law and Cyberspace. Edward Elgar, London

Tsybulenko E, Pakhomenko S (2016) The Ukrainian Crisis as a Challenge for the Eastern Partnership. In: Kerikmäe T, Chochia A (eds) Political and Legal Perspectives of the EU Eastern Partnership Policy. Springer, Switzerland

Unian Information Agency (2015) Ukraine creates National Center for Cyber Security. http://www.unian.info/society/1369157-ukraine-creates-national-center-for-cyber-security.html. Accessed 3 December 2016

UNODA - United Nations Office for Disarmament Affairs (2015) Developments in the field of information and telecommunications in the context of international security. https://www.un.org/disarmament/topics/informationsecurity/. Accessed 23 February 2017

Valuch J (2013) Diplomatické výsady a imunity: sloboda jednotlivca alebo prerogatíva štátu? [Diplomatic privileges and immunities: individual freedom or state competences?]. Univerzita Komenského v Bratislave, Bratislava

Vršanský p. (2014) Analýza právnej úpravy použitia sily v medzinárodnom práve v kontexte vývoja vzťahov medzi Ruskom a Ukrajinou [Analysis of Regulation of Use of Force in International Law in the Context of Evolution of Relations between Russia and Ukraine]. Acta Facultatis Iuridicae Universitatis Comenianae. 33:106–137

Vršanský P, Valuch J et al. (2012) Medzinárodné právo verejné - Všeobecná časť [Public international law - general part]. Eurokódex, Bratislava

Zimmermann A (2014) International Law and 'Cyber Space'. ESIL Reflections 3:1–6

Chapter 11
Foreign Fighters in the Framework of International Armed Conflict Between Russia and Ukraine

Anastasia Frolova

Contents

Abstract The situation in which foreign nationals take part in armed conflicts in favour of one side or another is not new. The recent increase in the number of foreign nationals travelling abroad to take part in armed conflicts, such as in the Middle East, has attracted the attention of scholars as to the reasons for this phenomenon. More and more publications are dealing with issues related to the status of foreign fighters, as well as rights and obligations of different states towards them. However, neither a universal definition of the term *foreign fighter* has been proposed, nor does

Anastasia Frolova is a Ph.D. student, University of Bern (Switzerland) and holds an LLM Degree from the Geneva Academy of International Humanitarian Law and Human Rights. Contact details: Anastasia Frolova, University of Bern, Hochschulstrasse 6, 3012 Bern, Switzerland, email: anastasia.frolova@students.unibe.ch.
The author would like to thank Col. (ret.) Peter Hostettler for his valuable comments on the earlier drafts of this chapter, although any errors are my own.

A. Frolova (✉)
University of Bern, Hochschulstrasse 6, 3012 Bern, Switzerland
e-mail: anastasia.frolova@students.unibe.ch

a comprehensive analysis exist of the status of foreign fighters in the situation of an armed conflict. At the same time, reality continues to provide new challenges for international lawyers. The ongoing armed conflict on Ukrainian territory is characterized by a very high level of foreign nationals' involvement (on all sides), as well as other specific features that were not too common in previous conflicts. In the present chapter, we will try to answer the question about whether existing international humanitarian law is prepared for such challenges, and whether the introduction of a "foreign fighter" category makes sense in this context.

Keywords foreign fighters · Ukraine · Russia · armed conflict · international humanitarian law · nationality

11.1 Introduction

The situation in which foreign nationals take part in armed conflicts in favour of one side or the other is not new. History provides examples of the hiring of foreign troops,[1] the enlisting of foreign soldiers by armed forces[2] and many other similar precedents. In particular, foreign nationals were actively engaged in the revolutionary movements of the 18th century, including the French and American Revolutions.[3] There have been individuals who have literally made it their profession to fight in different armed conflicts around the globe for material reward or other incentives.

Lately, due to the increasing numbers of individuals travelling abroad to take part in an armed conflict, a new term has been coined to identify them: so-called "foreign fighters". This phenomenon started to attract closer attention from researchers, including international law specialists, especially in connection with the emergence of the so-called Islamic State (mostly known as ISIS) on battlefields[4] in the Middle East. Some key features have been noted that distinguish the new generation of "foreign fighters" from mercenaries, employees of private military and security companies, and other foreign actors. For example, it has been established that the primary motive for most people who joined ISIS was no longer the expectation of material reward, but ideological, religious and other reasons.

However, neither a universal definition of the term *foreign fighter* has been proposed, nor does a comprehensive analysis of the status of foreign fighters exist in the context of armed conflict. At the same time, reality continues to provide new challenges for international lawyers. Armed conflict on Ukrainian territory is characterized by a very high level of foreign nationals' involvement (on all sides), as

---

[1] Ditcham 1978, p. 2.

[2] Flores 2016, p. 37.

[3] Ibid., pp. 29–30.

[4] On ISIS, in general, see Warrick 2015.

well as other specific features that were not too common in previous conflicts.[5] In the present chapter, we will try to answer the question as to whether existing international humanitarian law (hereafter "IHL") is prepared for such challenges, and whether the introduction of a "foreign fighter" category makes sense in this context.

In the first part of the article, we briefly describe the contextual framework of the Ukrainian conflict and its specific features, and provide an overview of the applicable international law. In the second part, we analyse the existing definitions of the term *foreign fighter* and the possibility of its application within the framework of the mixed armed conflict taking place in Ukraine. It will be argued that existing definitions have not led to the creation of any new category of persons under international humanitarian law, nor are they constructed in such a manner whereby they could repeat the sad fate of the definition for *mercenary*, which has already become an example of how legal definitions should not be constructed. In the third part, we provide a more practical insight and try to apply the existing definitions of *foreign fighter* to actual events and situations in the armed conflict in Ukraine. Finally, in the fourth part, we discuss, whether foreign fighters enjoy (or deserve) any special status under IHL, international criminal law and international human rights law (hereafter "IHRL").

Some caveats need to be made. First, as reflected in its title, the present chapter is limited to the issues in the context of an international armed conflict (hereafter "IAC") between Russia and Ukraine. Thus, the legal relations deriving from the non-international armed conflict (hereafter "NIAC") between Ukraine and non-state armed groups (which definitely represent a very exciting research topic) will be put aside. Secondly, the main research subject of this chapter is *jus in bello*, thus the issues of *jus ad bellum*, state responsibility and states' obligations related to foreign fighters will not be touched upon. We mainly focus on IHL analysis and limit ourselves to some brief but necessary remarks on international and national criminal law, human rights law, and other applicable norms.

11.2   Situation in Ukraine: Legal Qualification

While no one seems to dispute the existence of armed violence and clashes taking place on Ukrainian territory, the legal qualification of the situation in Ukraine since 2014 still invites controversy. Once the situation reaches the threshold of an armed conflict (whether an IAC or an NIAC), IHL starts to apply. The criteria defining the threshold for IHL application are objective and do not depend on statements issued by the parties to the conflict, who may call it a "war" or an "anti-terroristic operation" or deny any involvement whatsoever.[6] Therefore, to avoid terminological ambiguities,

---

[5] For example, the deployment of individual members or units belonging to the state armed forces while taking measures to conceal their identity. See, e.g., ICC 2016, para 155.

[6] See Geneva Convention (III) Relative to the Treatment of Prisoners of War, 12 August 1949, 75 UNTS 135 ("GC III"), Articles 2, 3; Protocol Additional (I) to the Geneva Conventions of 12

we will further refer to the events in Ukraine as happening in the course of an IAC or NIAC, respectively.

Given that the legal norms applicable during an IAC and an NIAC are still significantly different, the first step in the analysis of any conflict concerns its legal qualification. Due to space constraints, we will not be able to examine this issue in detail;[7] therefore, in line with the preliminary findings of the International Criminal Court (hereinafter "ICC"),[8] we assume that there is an IAC between Russia and Ukraine and a parallel NIAC between Ukraine and a number of non-state armed groups, including the self-proclaimed Donetsk and Luhansk People's Republics.

An IAC has, most likely, existed since February 2014, when the actions of Russian military forces on the territory of Crimea, prior to the phony "referendum on secession" from Ukraine later in the same month,[9] almost certainly constituted an act of occupation.[10] Alternatively, it may be argued that, since mid-2014, members of the Russian armed forces (sometimes in the uniforms without insignia) have been seen fighting alongside rebels, while Russian weapons and military convoys have crossed the border to reinforce pro-Russian forces. This conclusion is supported by a number of international bodies, as well as reliable fact-finding reports.[11] Finally, in December 2015, Russian President Vladimir Putin admitted that Russian military intelligence officers were operating on the territory of Ukraine.[12] Given that the threshold for applying IHL to an IAC is relatively low, both sets of facts, if true, trigger its application.

As for the NIAC, which followed a deep political crisis in Ukraine,[13] between non-state armed groups (including the self-proclaimed Luhansk and Donetsk People's Republics and Ukraine), the thresholds of (1) the organization of non-state armed groups and (2) the intensity of armed clashes, established by IHL on NIACs[14] were presumably also fulfilled by April-May 2014.[15]

August 1949, and Relating to the Protection of Victims of International Armed Conflicts, 8 June 1977, 1125 UNTS 3 ("AP I"), Article 1(4).

[7] In general, see Grzebyk 2015, pp. 35–56.

[8] ICC 2016, para 169.

[9] Working Group on Mercenaries 2016, para 9.

[10] Despite the fact that particular Russian armed forces were legally present in Crimea, their actions aimed at taking over strategic infrastructure on the peninsula were contrary to existing agreements, and therefore can be considered as occupation. See, e.g., Agreement Between the Russian Federation and Ukraine on the Status and Conditions of the Black Sea Fleet's Presence on the Territory of Ukraine, 14 May 2010; Russian Bulletin of International Treaties October 2010 No. 10, pp. 74–5, Articles 6, 8 (no longer in force). See also Parliamentary Assembly of the Council of Europe 2016, para 4.

[11] See, e.g., UN General Assembly 2014; Parliamentary Assembly of the Council of Europe 2016, paras 2, 4; Working Group on Mercenaries 2016, para 10; Walker, Grytsenko and Ragozin 2014; OSCE 2014.

[12] Walker 2015.

[13] On economic issues related to the crisis, see Tsybulenko and Pakhomenko 2016, p. 173.

[14] In general, see ICRC 2008.

[15] Working Group on Mercenaries 2016, para 10.

Both Russia and Ukraine are state parties to the four Geneva Conventions and the two Additional Protocols thereto,[16] as well as to different human rights treaties. In addition, all the parties to the conflict are bound by customary international law (including customary IHL and customary IHRL).

11.3 Existing Definitions of the Term *Foreign Fighter*

There is no internationally accepted legal definition of whom can be considered a "foreign fighter". The Geneva Academy of International Humanitarian Law and Human Rights in *Academy Briefing No. 7* provides the following definition:

> A foreign fighter is an individual who leaves his or her country of origin or habitual residence to join a non-state armed group in an armed conflict abroad and who is primarily motivated by ideology, religion and/or kinship (hereinafter the "Geneva Definition").[17]

The UN Human Rights Council Working Group on the use of mercenaries as a means of violating human rights and impeding the exercise of the right of peoples to self-determination (hereinafter "Working Group on Mercenaries"), whose mandate also includes issues connected with foreign fighters, has more or less adopted a similar working definition:

> [The] term foreign fighter is generally understood to refer to individuals who leave their country of origin or habitual residence and become involved in violence as part of an insurgency or non-state armed group in an armed conflict (hereinafter "WG Definition").[18]

As it can be seen, the WG Definition is different in some important aspects: (1) it requires the foreign fighter to actually "become involved in violence", while (2) omitting the motivational criteria altogether. To inform the reader as to how complicated this issue is, we should also refer to the definition of *foreign terrorist fighters*, as adopted by the UN Security Council in Resolution 2178 (2014):

> [Individuals] who travel to a State other than their States of residence for the purpose of the perpetration, planning or preparation of, or participation in, terrorist acts, including in connection with armed conflict (hereinafter "SC Definition").[19]

While these definitions can broadly seem to objectively describe some aspects of the existing phenomena, their practical application can lead to a number of problems.

Firstly, the requirement of actual participation in hostilities provided for in the WG Definition could be too difficult to establish and prove, and its application may lead to unfair results. From the wording of the WG Definition, it follows that a person becomes a "foreign fighter" only after he commits his first act of violence. However,

---

[16] The list of the states parties is available from the ICRC website: https://ihl-databases.icrc.org/ihl. Accessed 28 February 2017.

[17] Kraechenmann 2014, p. 6.

[18] Working Group on Mercenaries 2016, para 19.

[19] UN Security Council Resolution 2178 2014, para 5.

it is very difficult (if not impossible) in some cases to actually prove whether a particular person participated in acts of violence.

Secondly, the Geneva Definition and the WG Definition seem to be unreasonably limited to NIAC situations. It is noteworthy, however, that all researchers (including the authors of the aforementioned definitions restricting the participation of foreign fighters to NIAC situations) agree that foreign fighters sometimes also participate in IACs,[20] thus the above limitation appears to be unfounded in our view.

Thirdly, the motivational criteria used in the Geneva Definition also prompts questions. The limitation to three possible motives (ideology, religion and/or kinship) by which to define the foreign fighter seems to us to be counterproductive. Besides somewhat practical difficulties that anyone could face when passing judgement on such a subjective and controversial category as "motive", this limitation appears to far from supported by the research. For example, a report prepared by the Institute for Strategic Dialogue includes the following reasons behind motivating individuals to become foreign fighters:

> [Boredom], intergenerational tensions, the search for greater meaning in life, perceived adventure, attempts to impress the local community or the opposite sex, a desire for increased credibility, to… gain peer acceptance, revenge, to redress local and regional grievances, family members encouraging each other or misguided conflict experience expectations.[21]

This report evidences that the motives of foreign fighters are not limited to ideology, religion and/or kinship. In addition, the Geneva Definition, if adopted, would exclude foreign fighters who are motivated by other reasons, such as pressure and/or support from their own government, non-monetary rewards (e.g., medals, promises of promotion), and wish to attain a particular status. In addition, the link to a motive in a legal definition may render the definition meaningless in practice, because it is unlikely that someone would openly admit to having motivation, which would ultimately make him subject to less privileged treatment (for example if a captured combatant admits that he is a mercenary).[22]

Finally, the criterion of "habitual residence" also seems to be too vague, as it is likely to override the criterion of "nationality", which retains importance under IHL with regard to civilians.[23] In addition, this criterion was developed in the literature dealing with the conflict in the Middle East. Under the Geneva Definition, a Syrian national who has lived in Switzerland, Germany or France for his whole life, and then decides to return to his country of origin to fight in an armed conflict, would be seen as a foreign fighter,[24] which is at least questionable as he still holds a passport of that state. In addition, the conflict in Ukraine can present a more challenging task, especially in terms of foreign fighters from neighbouring countries (Russia, Belarus and others).

---

[20] Kraechenmann 2014, p. 17.

[21] Briggs and Silverman 2014, p. 13.

[22] On the problems related to the status of "mercenary" under IHL, see ICRC 1987, paras 1794-1801

[23] See, e.g., Geneva Convention Relative to the Protection of Civilian Persons in Time of War, Geneva, 12 August 1949, 75 UNTS 287 ("GC IV"), Article 4 (A).

[24] For a discussion of this issue, see Kraehenmann 2016 pp. 235–6.

1. It is not clear what authors precisely regard as "habitual residence". If one can rely on an analogy, in international refugee law, the term *habitual residence* is most commonly interpreted as requiring a certain period of stay, but no *animus manendi* (intent to stay permanently).[25] This criterion, when applied to neighbouring countries that share much in common, can be rather tricky, and in some cases can lead to unfair results. The nature of pre-existing and current links between, for example, Ukraine and Russia (they formerly constituted one state, share a common history, language and traditions to a significant extent, have relatively well-established economic ties) is very complicated. Keeping this in mind, can a Ukrainian national, residing in Russia for working purposes only, having left his family in Ukraine, who then returns to Ukraine to take part in the armed conflict on the Ukrainian side, be considered a "foreign fighter"? Or a person with Belarus citizenship, who, due to business reasons, lives for half of the year in Russia and in Ukraine for the other half? It seems that, in these cases, as well as when applied to dual citizens, the criterion of "habitual residence" is not fair enough and does not provide a trustworthy criterion to establish the foreign fighter status.[26]

2. In addition, the introduction of a "habitual residency" criterion in the context of IHL can be problematic. IHL does not establish such a reason for distinguishing "permanent", "habitual" or any other type of "residence". Only "nationality" and "allegiance" can play a role in a number of situations.[27] The introduction of a liberal understanding of the term *habitual residence* in international refugee law was definitely aimed at widening the scope of protection, which is fully in line with the aims of this branch of law. However, introducing such a criterion within a definition applicable to the framework of IHL seems to lead to alternative results. Conversely, let us imagine that the definition of a foreign fighter includes the residency criterion. Then, two interpretations of the existing IHL rules are possible:

(1) Under a very progressive (and unlikely) interpretation, the criterion of "nationality" in IHL is interpreted to include "residency" (thus, logically, residency, if

---

[25] Robinson 1953, p. 90.

[26] These problems are recognized by the Working Group on Mercenaries. See Working Group on Mercenaries 2015, para 62.

[27] See, e.g., GC IV (fn. 23), Articles 68, 98, 105, 107, 135. One could argue that, while GC IV refers not only to "nationality", but also to "allegiance" criteria, the ICTY allowed a wider understanding of the "nationality" criteria, including the notions of "allegiance" and "effective protection", while discouraging reliance on "formal bonds and purely legal relations" (see ICTY, *The Prosecutor v. Dusko Tadić, Appeals Chamber Judgment, IT-94-1-A, 15 July 1999 (Tadić case)*, para 166; ICTY, *The Prosecutor v. Zejnil Delalić et al. Čelebići Camp, Appeals Chamber Judgment, IT-96-21-A*, 20 February 2001, para 73). However, there is a number of counterarguments to relying on this interpretation. Firstly, there is scarce evidence that this concept was applied in any context other than an ethnic or religious conflict, which does not seem to be the case in Ukraine. Secondly, *allegiance* is a vague term that is extremely difficult to establish. The absence of uniformity in interpretation and subjectivity can lead to abuse and hamper guarantees of protection. This position was implicitly confirmed by the ICRC, which noted the absence of any other criteria to determine the status of foreign fighters under IHL, other than nationality. See ICRC 2015, p. 19.

different from nationality, would have priority). In this case, civilians who are nationals of the party to the conflict, but residents of other states and thus enjoy the status of "protected persons" under Article 4(A) of GC IV on the basis of nationality in case they find themselves in the hands of the other party to the conflict, will now lose the protected persons status due to the residency criterion (if their state of residency has normal diplomatic representation in the state party to the conflict). The position of states on whether to provide diplomatic assistance to people who are their residents, but not their citizens is, to say the least, not uniform.[28] Furthermore, one cannot exclude the fact that the guarantees of protection for these people will be undermined.

(2) If the residency criterion is not taken into account by IHL (in accordance with the widely accepted position),[29] then it becomes obsolete, and the status of "foreign fighter" becomes nothing more than another name to the people on the ground (there are no rights or duties associated with it). Therefore, if the inclusion of the residency criterion means much in international refugee law, we argue that it is not the case for the definition of *foreign fighters* in the context of IHL.

Therefore, if we were to argue in favour of defining *foreign fighters* as a separate category of persons, we would suggest the following definition: **a foreign fighter is an individual who leaves his country of origin (nationality) to join a party to an armed conflict abroad**. The question remains, however, as to whether these individuals would really enjoy any specific status under the applicable international law, whereby such a categorization would be justified. We aim to provide an answer in the following sections.

11.4   Who Could Be a Foreign Fighter in Ukraine?

11.4.1   Basis for Analysis

As the notions listed above could appear to be rather theoretical, we believe it would be useful to give the reader more practical insights. Thus, who can be considered as a "foreign fighter" in the armed conflict in Ukraine? Newspapers and other media are constantly reporting about foreign fighters or even "mercenaries" fighting either for Ukraine[30] or for the Russian Federation,[31] as well as the rebels in Eastern Ukraine;[32] however, not all these reports are legally correct. In the framework of the armed

---

[28] For example, Switzerland does not provide diplomatic assistance to non-citizens, including those that have a temporary or permanent residence permit. Information provided by telephone by Swiss Federal Department of Foreign Affairs, 10 April 2016.

[29] ICRC 2015, p. 19.

[30] Soldier of Fortune Magazine 2016.

[31] Quinn 2016

[32] Centre for Research on Globalization 2016.

conflict in Ukraine (which, as we assumed, is an IAC with a parallel NIAC), both bodies of law are applicable.[33] The law on IACs distinguishes between "combatants" who have the right to participate directly in hostilities[34] and, in case of capture, enjoy prisoner of war (POW) status, and non-combatants (including medical and religious personnel of armed forces and civilians), who can be criminally prosecuted for directly participating in hostilities and do not enjoy POW status upon capture.[35] In contrast, the law on NIACs does not provide for the combatant (and, therefore, POW) status *stricto sensu*, as the difference in participants' status relates more to protection from attack (for civilians not taking direct part in hostilities), or the absence thereof (in the case of members of the armed units of the non-state party to the NIAC having continuous combat functions or civilians taking direct part in hostilities),[36] than to their treatment upon capture.

We argue that the general algorithms with which to determine the status of the person in question should include two steps: (1) determination of the applicable legal framework (IAC or NIAC); (2) determination of the status of the person with regard to the established framework. Below, we analyse the status of those who could be recognized as either Russian foreign fighters or third-state foreign fighters. Given that Ukraine is a party to both an IAC and an NIAC, Ukrainian nationals cannot be foreign fighters in the present conflict; thus, they will not be considered.

11.4.2 Russian Foreign Fighters

As described above, Russia's involvement in the Ukrainian conflict is twofold: (1) as a party to an IAC with Ukraine, and (2) as a supporter of separatist forces in the NIAC (arguably not reaching the degree of control necessary to turn the conflict into an IAC).[37] Given the definition of the term *foreign fighter*, no Russian national can be a "foreign fighter" within the framework of the IAC (as in this case, they represent nationals of the party to the conflict). However, this does not exclude the possibility of a Russian citizen acting without any reference to the Russian authorities and taking part in an NIAC on the side of the rebels. In this context, he could be considered a foreign fighter. Therefore, drawing the right distinction between the two frameworks

---

[33] ICJ, *Military and Paramilitary Activities In and Against Nicaragua (Nicaragua v. United States)*, *Judgment (Merits), 27 June 1986* (*Nicaragua* case), para 219.

[34] The "right" to participate directly in hostilities or combatant "immunity" means that combatants are immune from criminal prosecution for merely participating in hostilities, unless they committed a violation of IHL.

[35] Nishat 2015, p. 1079.

[36] Melzer 2009, Part 1, paras II–VII, X.

[37] In general, see Grzebyk 2015, pp. 35–56. The threshold of control is also relevant for the applicability of human rights norms. See, e.g., ICJ, *Legal Consequences of the Construction of a Wall in the Occupied Palestinian Territory, Advisory Opinion of 9 July 2004* (*The Wall* case), para 109. The jurisdiction of the ECHR is not yet settled; see, e.g., ECHR (2016).

(IAC and NIAC) becomes of critical importance. While the main distinction lies in the "nexus" of the party to the conflict, one can use *inter alia* the following criteria:[38]

1. *Membership of the Russian armed forces or other governmental bodies/continuous combat function in a non-state armed group.* Being a member of the armed forces or other governmental bodies (such as the Federal Security Service, or "FSB") of the Russian Federation leads to a strong presumption, under international law, that the actions of such a person shall be attributed to the state[39] (and thus fall under the IAC framework). The conditions that a person has to satisfy to be considered a member of the Russian armed forces are established by Russian law.[40] However, do Russia's actions, aimed at concealing their identity (taking off insignia, depriving soldiers of relevant documents, painting over signs of respective tactical units, and other similar measures),[41] result in turning these members of the armed forces into "foreign fighters" as per the framework of an NIAC? We would argue in the negative. Neither Russian law nor IHL makes the status of a person as an armed forces member (and, therefore, a POW) dependent on the existence of particular insignia or confirming documents. It is true that, under IHL, combatants (members of armed forces) are obliged to distinguish themselves from the civilian population,[42] but not to identify themselves as belonging to a particular nation. Therefore, the absence of insignia or documents, while definitely making the recognition and attribution of actions more difficult, does not influence the legal qualification of the status of the person – they continue to be combatants[43] and are entitled to POW status, if captured. The same conclusion shall be made for the members of Russian armed forces who are "on vacation" – their status as members of the armed

---

[38] The list of criteria given below should not be interpreted as closed. Given the complexity of the situation in Ukraine, the weight of each criterion should be assessed on a case-by-case basis.

[39] See, e.g., UNGA 2001, Articles 4–5.

[40] See, e.g., Federal Law of 27 May 1998 No. 76-FZ on the Status of the Members of Armed Forces, Article 2. Accessed 28 February 2017.

[41] Bellingcat 2016.

[42] AP I (see fn. 6), Articles 43–4.

[43] Ibid.; GC III, above n.6, Article 4.

forces is not suspended for the vacation period.[44] On the other hand, the incorporation or integration (official or *de facto*) of a Russian national into the units of a non-state armed group could signal the existence of a nexus between that individual and the non-state armed group, and, therefore, the applicability of the NIAC framework. Thus, for example, intelligence officers, whose participation in the Ukrainian conflict was recognized by Russian President Vladimir Putin,[45] as well as Russian military personnel allegedly operating Buk missiles during the incident with flight MH17,[46] will most likely fall under the IAC framework, while Igor Strelkov-Girkin, who (possibly while remaining an officer of the Main Intelligence Directorate of the General Staff of the Armed Forces, or "GRU")[47] held the position of the Minister of Defence in the self-proclaimed Donetsk People's Republic[48] and commander of its army should most likely be qualified as a foreign fighter in the NIAC framework.

2. *Control over the person/unit or subsequent approval of his/its actions.* Despite the fact that the threshold level of such control is somewhat disputed[49] and, according to some sources, different for private individuals and military units,[50] one should establish the strength of the nexus of the person in question with the parties to the conflict. The following criteria can be considered: the chain of command to which the person is subordinated, the source of military and financial support (e.g., whether Russia is paying the person a salary/compensation for the period when he is fighting in the conflict in Ukraine, providing him with weapons and other logistic services), the source and nature of instructions given to the person before sending him to the territory of the conflict (if any), the use of pressure to make sure he departs, etc. Thus, a person acting under official or de facto orders (or under other types of pressure, such as the threat of being fired), who

---

[44] Ibid., Federal Law of 27 May 1998 No. 76-FZ on the Status of the Members of Armed Forces, Articles 2(2), 2(8), 11(5).
Accessed 28 February 2017. Decree of the Plenum of the Supreme Court of the Russian Federation (2014), para 3. http://www.consultant.ru/cons/cgi/online.cgi?req=doc&base=LAW&n=200355&dst=0&profile=0&mb=LAW&div=LAW&BASENODE=69774703-4081201017&SORTTYPE=0&rnd=244973.169453460&ts=20790148832505220217&REFTYPE=CDLT_CHILDLESS_CONTENTS_ITEM_MAIN_BACKREFS&REFBASE=LAW&REFSEGM=-1&REFDOC=203456&REFDST=100459&REFPAGE=0&dirRefFld=65534%2C18%2C203456#0. Accessed 28 February 2017. Under the aforementioned provisions, citizens (foreign citizens) acquire the status of being members of the armed forces at the moment of starting military service (acquiring the rank of a private or entering into a military service contract or being accepted into a military educational institution), and lose this status after the end of the military service (official exclusion from the list of the members of the unit). Being granted a holiday (whether paid or unpaid) is not listed as grounds for losing the aforementioned status.

[45] Walker 2015.

[46] Dearden 2016; see also Openbaar Ministerie (The Netherlands Public Prosecution Service) 2016.

[47] European Council 2014.

[48] Mir24.tv 2014.

[49] UNGA 2001, Article 8; *Nicaragua* case (see fn. 27), paras 105-15; *Tadić* case (see fn. 27), para 405.

[50] *Tadić* case (see fn. 27), para 133.

continues to receive a salary related to his service in Russia, will most likely fall under the framework of the IAC (thus will not be qualified as a foreign fighter), while a private individual, unconnected to the Russian authorities in any way, who goes to Ukraine to fight on the side of the rebels or on the side of the Ukrainian Government, for example, for ideological reasons, becomes integrated in the local chain of command and subordinated thereunder will, most likely, be considered a "foreign fighter", engaged in the NIAC.

While not providing a universal solution, the criteria listed above could, in our view, help to bring some clarity to the complicated patchwork of various Russian actors in the Ukrainian conflict.

11.4.3 Nationals of Third States

The fact that foreign nationals have taken part in an armed conflict on Ukrainian territory, at least on the side of the Ukrainian Government, has been confirmed by reliable sources.[51] There is less verifiable data about the foreign nationals fighting in the IAC context for the Russian Government; however, such a possibility cannot be excluded. There are also plenty of websites, including blogs, social network profiles and video interviews of foreign fighters in the Ukrainian conflict.[52] Both Russia[53] and Ukraine[54] have allowed foreign nationals to serve in their respective armies. Aside from foreign nationals serving in the regular Ukrainian armed forces *per se*, the Working Group on Mercenaries reported on the existence of other units, subordinated to the Ukrainian Government and consisting of or including foreign nationals, such as "volunteer battalions", "territorial defence battalions", the "National Guard" and other similar armed units.[55]

As follows from the definition, all nationals of third states are foreign fighters in the framework of either the IAC or the NIAC. Thus, all foreign nationals fighting on the Russian side are automatically foreign fighters in the IAC. However, due to the mixed nature of the conflict, the determination of the framework applicable

---

[51] See, e.g., Working Group on Mercenaries 2016, para 7.

[52] See, e.g., the Belsat TV interview with Ben Fisher. https://www.youtube.com/watch?v=hI4 p0uyn19o. Accessed 28 February 2018. Intended to describe the Austrian foreign fighter's life in Ukraine, this TV programme on a Belarus channel started with the claim: "we know that there are dozens of Belarus volunteers fighting for Ukrainian integrity". Nezhivoi K (YouTube user), interview with Serbian nationals calling themselves Bata, Radomir and Djako. https://www.youtube.com/watch?v=hbn0jYRA3dE. Accessed 28 February 2017.

[53] Regulation on the Procedure of Military Service 1999, No. 1237, paras 1–3. http://base.garant.ru/180912/#block_1000. Accessed 28 February 2017.

[54] Decree (2016) No. 248/2016 on the Regulation on the Procedure of Military Service in the Ukrainian Armed Forces by Foreign Nationals and Stateless Persons.
http://www.president.gov.ua/news/prezident-pidpisav-ukaz-yakim-nadayetsya-mozhlivist-inozemcy-37343. Accessed 28 February 2017.

[55] Working Group on the use of mercenaries… (2016), para 24.

to the foreign nationals fighting on the Ukrainian side is trickier. Under a strict interpretation of IHL norms, once the foreign fighters fighting for the Ukrainian Government face individuals fighting for Russia in the framework of the IAC, IAC law applies. On the contrary, armed clashes between foreign fighters from the Ukrainian side and the rebels are regulated by NIAC law. This distinction may seem rather artificial; however, it is important to stress that, due to the development of IHL, the rules regulating the conduct of hostilities in IACs and NIACs were more or less harmonized, in particular, with the help of customary international law. This means that the fighters on the ground will not have to confront complicated legal issues about defining the law, which are applicable to every particular situation. As will be elaborated in the next section, it is mostly after an individual is captured that this distinction becomes important.

11.5 The Status of Foreign Fighters in an IAC Between Russia and Ukraine

In the previous section we showed that, if applied, the category of "foreign fighter", within the framework of the IAC, would encompass a significant number of individuals with different links to the states parties to the conflict, who are differently organized and have different statuses under the national laws of the relevant states. Now, we turn to the last part of our analysis, that is, whether it makes sense to identify a separate category of foreign fighters in the context of an IAC.

11.6 Status of Foreign Fighters Under International Humanitarian Law

As noted above, IHL with regard to IACs is based on the principle of distinction between certain categories of persons: members of armed forces (combatants and non-combatants) (4.1.1) and civilians (4.1.2). Combatants are protected against legal action as long as they do not commit acts contrary to IHL; however, they may be attacked by the opposing armed forces. Non-combatant members of armed forces may only use the amount of force necessary for their self-defence or defence of their patients against armed violence. They may not be attacked and may not resist their capture by armed forces of the enemy. Civilians are protected against attack as long as they do not take a direct (or active) part in hostilities. Otherwise, they may be attacked and, after capture by the enemy, prosecuted under the national law of the captor for mere acts of violence, as well as for eventual violations of IHL. Below, the different categories involved will be examined in more detail.

11.6.1 Combatants

The conditions for determining combatant/POW status are listed in Article 4 of GC III and Articles 43 and 44 of AP I. In particular, Article 43 of AP I states that the "armed forces of the Party to a conflict consist of all organized armed forces, groups and units which are under a command responsible to that Party for the conduct of its subordinates... Such armed forces shall be subject to an internal disciplinary system which, inter alia, shall enforce compliance with the rules of international law applicable in armed conflicts."

Article 44 provides for some specifications on the duty to ensure the distinction from civilians; notably, in order to enjoy POW status, a combatant must distinguish himself from the civilian population while "engaged in an attack or in a military operation preparatory to an attack", and, when this is impossible, at least openly carry arms in the situations listed above.[56] As previously stated, the status of a combatant does not depend on whether he identifies himself as belonging to a particular state, nor on the presence of documents confirming membership of the armed forces.

GC III does not provide for any distinction based on the nationality of the person in question, nor for establishing the combatant/POW status or for the following treatment of a POW (e.g., internment).[57] Thus, foreign fighters – members of Russian or Ukrainian armed forces, as well as members of (para)military organizations on the both sides (volunteer battalions, territorial defence battalions and the National Guard, which are under the command of the Ukrainian Government, on the Ukrainian side,[58] as well as members of the so-called "Kadyrov Army" (if not Russian nationals), on the Russian side) will be qualified as combatants under the same conditions as nationals of the relevant states serving in aforementioned units. The only consequence for the foreign fighter – a national of a neutral state – will be the loss of his neutral status "if he commits acts in favor of a belligerent, particularly if he voluntarily enlists in the ranks of the armed force of one of the parties. In such a case, the neutral shall not be more severely treated by the belligerent as against whom he has abandoned his neutrality than a national of the other belligerent State could be for the same act."[59] This provision leads effectively to the same result. Therefore, unless a foreign fighter satisfies the definition of a mercenary (Article 47 AP I), he must be treated in the same way as other POWs, without any distinction based on nationality.[60] This in turn brings us to the conclusion that the absence or existence of "foreign fighters" does not in any way change the scope of protection provided to combatants.

---

[56] AP I (see fn. 6), Article 44.

[57] In support of this position, see ICRC 2015, p. 19.

[58] On the status of the aforementioned units, see Butusov 2014.

[59] Convention (V) Respecting the Rights and Duties of Neutral Powers and Persons in Case of War on Land. The Hague, 18 October 1907, 36 Stat. 2310, Article 17. Russia has been a party to the aforementioned convention since 1909, while Ukraine only ratified it on 29 May 2015.

[60] Subject to the presumption of combatant status, stated in AP I (see fn. 6), Article 45(1).

11.6.2   Civilians

As discussed above, foreign fighters who do not satisfy the conditions listed in Article 4 of GC III and Articles 43–44 of AP I, are civilians. Under IHL, civilians enjoy immunity from attack unless and for such time until they participate directly in hostilities.[61] While participation in hostilities does not deprive such foreign fighters of their civilian status nor protection under GC IV, if applicable, they may, however (and, almost no doubt, will), be criminally prosecuted for crimes associated with participation in hostilities under the national law of the relevant state (for example, murder, illegally carrying arms). A productive example of a quasi-military organization, allegedly not satisfying the criteria of Article 4 of GC III and Article 43 of AP I, is the so-called "Ukrainian Volunteer Corps", formed under the auspices of "The Right Sector" political movement. According to media reports, at least some members of the Ukrainian Volunteer Corps, which is (or, at least until recently, was) not subordinated to the Ukrainian government, are foreign nationals.[62] Therefore, members of this unit should be considered as civilians under the IAC framework. Same qualification is allegedly relevant to the "Pahonia" volunteer unit, consisting of Belarusian nationals,[63] and the so-called "Georgian National Legion", before its integration into the Ukrainian armed forces.[64]

In contrast to combatants/POWs, the status of civilians in the IAC and the degree of their protection under IHL also depend on their nationality, one of the distinguishing criteria of a foreign fighter.

GC IV, which regulates the protection of civilians in times of armed conflict, provides for different degrees of protection to (1) "protected persons", satisfying the definition of Article 4 of GC IV and (2) all "populations" of the countries in conflict in general, without any regard to the existence or absence of a "protected person" status.[65] For the purposes of the present article, we abstain from any detailed analysis of the regime of an occupied territory (e.g., Crimea), as there is no substantial evidence of armed clashes involving foreign fighters in this context.[66]

11.6.3   Foreign Fighters: Protected Persons

Under Article 4 of GC IV, a protected civilian is an individual who:

---

[61] On the notion of direct participation in hostilities, see Melzer 2009.

[62] For example, the commanders of the corps have refused to comply with the ceasefire agreement reached with the Ukrainian Government. 112.ua (Ukrainian news portal) 2015.

[63] Guz 2014.

[64] Censor.Net (Ukrainian news portal) 2016.

[65] In particular, see GC IV (see fn. 23), Articles 13–26.

[66] Ibid., Articles 27–34, 47–78.

(1) finds himself in the hands of the party to the conflict or occupying power of which
he is not a national, provided that nationals of neutral states who find themselves
in the territory of a belligerent state shall not be regarded as protected persons,
while the state of which they are nationals has normal diplomatic representation
in the state in whose hands they are;

(2) is not a protected person under GCs I–III.

Protected civilians enjoy a significantly higher level of protection under GC IV,
including the right to apply to and be visited by representatives of humanitarian
organizations, such as the International Committee of the Red Cross (ICRC) (Article
30 of GC IV), the right to leave the territory after serving a sentence, if they are found
guilty of crimes or offences (Article 37 of GC IV), and the prohibition to transfer
them to states that are not parties to GC IV (excluding cases of repatriation, subject,
however, to the principle of non-refoulement).[67]

The first condition relating to nationality (i.e., not being a national of a party to the
conflict) is, by definition, satisfied in relation to foreign fighters. However, if a foreign
fighter possesses the nationality of a neutral state, he loses the status of a "protected
person" if the country of his nationality has normal diplomatic representation in the
relevant state party to the conflict. Unfortunately, there is no definition of "normal
diplomatic representation", in IHL or in other branches of international law, including
the Vienna Convention on Diplomatic Relations.[68] Jean Pictet, in his commentary to
GC IV, proposes that "normal diplomatic representation" can be established when:
"representations made by the diplomatic representative will be followed by results
and that satisfactory replies will be given to him. It would also seem essential for the
representatives in question to have sufficient liberty of action and liberty of movement
to be able to visit their fellow-countrymen and come to their help when circumstances
so require."[69]

Another term that needs clarification is the "neutrality" of the state of nationality
of the foreign fighter. "Neutral" states under Article 4 of GC IV presumably include
the states claiming permanent neutral status (for example, Switzerland), as well as
all other states not taking part in the relevant IAC and observing the relevant legal
rules on neutrality.[70] For third-state foreign fighters, this would mean that, if they fail
to qualify as combatants in accordance with the criteria set out above, they risk being
deprived of protection under GC IV if there is "normal diplomatic representation"
of their home country in the state party to the conflict, on whose territory they are.
The list of third states having diplomatic representation in both Russia and Ukraine
is relatively long and includes all the countries whose nationals have been reported

---

[67] GC IV (see fn. 23), Article 45.

[68] See Vienna Convention on Diplomatic Relations, Vienna, 18 April 1961, 500 UNTS 95.

[69] Pictet 1958, p. 49.

[70] Salmón 2015, p. 1147; Hague Convention (V) (see fn. 60). Convention (XIII) Concerning the
Rights and Duties of Neutral Powers in Naval War, The Hague, 18 October 1907, 36 Stat. 2415.

to have taken part in the armed conflict in Ukraine as foreign fighters,[71] while there is no evidence that either Russia or Ukraine has broken off diplomatic relations (*de jure* or *de facto*) with any of these third states. Therefore, it seems that relatively few foreign fighters (i.e., nationals of third states) will qualify as "protected persons" under GC IV. This could be the case, for example, for members of the Georgian National Legion, who possess Georgian nationality, when captured by Russia. After the Russian intervention in Georgia in 2008, diplomatic relations between the two countries were cut off;[72] therefore Georgian nationals, when captured by Russia, must be qualified as "protected persons" under GC IV. This does not mean, however, that foreign fighters who do not enjoy the "protected persons" status are left to the mercy of the capturing power, as will be shown below.

11.6.4 Foreign Fighters not Enjoying the "Protected Persons" Status

Foreign fighters who do not qualify as "protected persons" in accordance with Article 4 of GC IV (which, as shown above, will most likely be the case) can only rely on subsidiary protection under IHL. This could be relevant, for example, in the case of Belarusian nationals who are members of the "Pahonia" unit when captured by Russia. Given that Belarus allegedly has "normal diplomatic representation" in Russia, Belarusian nationals will not be considered as "protected persons" in the sense of GC IV. Article 13 of GC IV expressly provides that the provisions in Part II of the convention shall be applied "without any adverse distinction, based, in particular, on… nationality".[73] However, these provisions are mostly of a general character and in particular concern the protection of hospitals and their personnel, establishing neutralized zones, the protection of the wounded, sick, children under 15 and expectant mothers, as well as the passage of humanitarian assistance and facilitating the maintenance of family links.

Foreign fighters who fail to qualifying as "protected persons" under GC IV are also protected by Articles 72–9 in AP I, which relates to all persons "in the power of a Party to the conflict". Of these, Article 75 of AP I is of particular importance. It is deals with "fundamental guarantees" and states, that "persons who are in the power of a Party to the conflict and who do not benefit from more favourable treatment under the Conventions or under this Protocol shall be treated humanely in all circumstances… without any adverse distinction based on… nationality… national

---

[71] See official websites of the Russian Ministry of Foreign Affairs (http://www.mid.ru/en/maps) and the Ukrainian Ministry of Foreign Affairs (http://mfa.gov.ua/en/about-ukraine/dip-in-ukraine/missions-list). Both accessed 28 February 2017.

[72] Official website of the Georgian Ministry of Foreign Affairs 2017. http://www.mfa.gov.ge/MainNav/ForeignPolicy/BilateralRelations/რუსეთის-ფედერაცია.aspx. Accessed 28 February 2017.

[73] GC IV (see fn. 23), Article 13.

or social origin… or on any other similar criteria". The fundamental guarantees provided for in Article 75 include, *inter alia*, the prohibition of murder, torture, corporal punishment, mutilation, outrages upon personal dignity and judicial guarantees, such as the right to be informed about the particulars of an offence, the principle of individual criminal responsibility and the presumption of innocence. Furthermore, those civilians, not enjoying the "protected persons" status can also rely on the guarantees provided for in Common Article 3 of all iterations of the GC, which has been recognized as being applicable in both IACs and NIACs[74] and includes the prohibition of violence, outrages upon personal dignity, and humiliating and degrading treatment.

However, the above provisions are definitely not enough to provide effective protection to individuals not enjoying the protected persons status, as they are not protected from being transferred to any other state (subject, however, to the *non-refoulement* principle), which sadly made the infamous "renditions" possible.

Concluding the discussion on the status of foreign fighters who are civilians under IHL, we would like to stress that most foreign fighters who are nationals of neutral states with regard to the conflict in question are likely to receive no more than the "safety net" protection of the general provisions of GC IV, Common Article 3 of all iterations of the GC and the fundamental guarantees listed in Article 75 of AP I. However, does this really mean that the status of a foreign fighter is of relevance for the purposes of IHL? We would again answer in the negative. While the criterion of nationality has a decisive influence on the scope of the guarantees provided to the person, the status of a foreign *fighter* does not differ from the status of any other foreign national, whether he is a "fighter" or not. We do not see any grounds that could justify special treatment for a "foreign fighter" who is a civilian, compared to any other civilian of the same nationality. Both enjoy immunity from attack, and both can be prosecuted in cases of direction participation in hostilities; therefore, we have to argue that the status of the "foreign fighter" should also be considered as irrelevant under IHL when applied to civilians.

11.7   The Status of Foreign Fighters: Civilians Under IHRL

The provisions of IHL mentioned above do not exclude the application of other branches of international law, including human rights law. To the contrary, Article 75(8) of AP I expressly provides that "no provision of this article may be construed as limiting or infringing any other more favourable provision, granting greater protection, under applicable rules of international law". Other "applicable rules of international law", first and foremost, include the provisions of IHRL. The applicability of IHRL in times of armed conflict has already been recognized by judicial bodies[75] and most scholars.[76] IHRL norms can be particularly important for foreign fighters – where they are nationals of neutral states having normal diplomatic representation in

---

[74] *Nicaragua* case (see fn. 33), para 218.

[75] *The Wall* case, paras 105–9.

[76] See, e.g., Droege 2007, pp. 310–55; Meron 2000, pp. 239–78.

the respective state – who are party to the conflict and do not fall under the category of "protected persons". In this case, IHRL norms can significantly plug the holes in the so-called "safety net" (Articles 3 of the GC and 75 of AP I), especially those related to procedural guarantees, judicial guarantees in the case of trials, the use of firearms by law enforcement officials, medical ethics and the definition of torture, among others. Both Russia and Ukraine are parties to a number of IHRL treaties,[77] including, in particular, the European Convention on Human Rights,[78] and obliged to comply with the provisions of relevant treaties in relation to foreign fighters. Besides the provisions of the treaties, both Ukraine and Russia are bound by the rules of customary IHRL.

11.8 The Status of Foreign Fighters Under International and National Criminal Law

The status of foreign fighters under international criminal law is also no different from that of nationals of the belligerent parties. Firstly, as is rightly recognized in the relevant literature, there is no crime under international law concerned with being a foreign fighter in general.[79] Researchers agree that the provisions of international criminal law apply to foreign fighters in the same manner as to other participants in the armed conflict, and thus do not enjoy any particular status under international criminal law.[80] Some researchers find that, in some cases, foreign fighters may not share the motives of nationals of the party to the conflict, or that it could be more problematic to establish the subjective elements of a crime;[81] however, these considerations, even if true, do not influence the status of foreign fighters under international criminal law *per se*. International criminal law also does not seem to provide for any specific crimes or any specific treatment for foreign fighters; therefore, in accordance with international criminal law, if they commit international crimes, such as war crimes or crimes against humanity, they should be prosecuted under the same conditions as nationals of the parties to the conflict. However, the nationality of a foreign fighter may trigger the jurisdiction of the ICC, provided that other criteria are complied with.[82]

---

[77] For example: International Covenant on Civil and Political Rights, 16 December 1966, 999 UNTS 171; Convention on the Rights of the Child, 2 September 1990, 1577 UNTS 3; Convention Against Torture and Other Cruel, Inhuman or Degrading Treatment or Punishment, 26 June 1987, 1465 UNTS 85. Ukraine is also a party to the International Convention for the Protection of All Persons from Enforced Disappearance, 23 December 2010, adopted by General Assembly Resolution 61/177 on 12 January 2007.

[78] European Convention for the Protection of Human Rights and Fundamental Freedoms, 4 November 1950, 1108 UNTS 151.

[79] Heinsch 2016, p. 163.

[80] Ibid., pp. 167–77.

[81] Ibid., pp. 176–8.

[82] Rome Statute of the ICC, 1 July 2002, ISBN No. 92-9227-227-6, Article 12(2)(b).

While being a foreign fighter is not criminalized at an international level, the situation is, in most cases, completely different under the national law of the states. Given that the detailed analysis of the national criminal legislation relating to foreign fighters is outside of the scope of the present chapter, we will only make brief remarks. The status of a foreign fighter (in an IAC framework) can be potentially relevant to prosecution at the national level due to (1) the criminalization of enlistment in foreign armed forces or armed groups or connected actions, or (2) the different treatment of foreign nationals by criminal law if prosecuted for crimes committed in the course of armed conflict,[83] although the latter does not seem not to be the case in either Russia or Ukraine.[84] Thus, some countries punish at least certain categories of their nationals for enlistment in foreign armed forces (for example, Switzerland).[85] Russian criminal law does not criminalize enlistment in foreign armed forces as such; however, under Article 208 of the Russian Criminal Code, participation (including by a foreign national)[86] in an armed group not authorized by legislation of the relevant foreign state on foreign territory, when contrary to the interests of the Russian Federation, is punishable by an eight- to 15-year prison sentence with a one- to two-year period of limited freedom. In the case of foreign fighters, this article could be applicable to the nationals of third states fighting on the Ukrainian side, for example, Belarusian nationals in the Pahonia unit. Article 114–1 of the Ukrainian Criminal Code penalizes "resistance to the legal actions of the Ukrainian armed forces and other military formations during the special period", for which the punishment is a five- to 15-year prison sentence. One could argue that (leaving aside arguable terminological aspects), this article could also be applicable to foreign fighters who are nationals of third states, having a relevant nexus to Russia and not enjoying combatant status.

11.9 Conclusion

Given the (unfortunate) but constant development of the modes of states' engagement in armed conflicts, it is always difficult to strike a proper balance between the conservative position of showing resistance to any change in existing law and

---

[83] The possibility of treating foreign nationals in a more lenient manner than nationals of the detaining power is provided for in GC IV (see fn. 23), Article 118 in respect of internees who are protected persons.

[84] Criminal Code of the Russian Federation, 13 June 1996 No. 63-FZ, Article 12. http://www.consultant.ru/document/cons_doc_LAW_10699/. Accessed 28 February 2017. The Criminal Code of Ukraine, 5 April 2001, No. 2341–III Articles 7–8. http://ua.spinform.ru. Accessed 28 February 2017.

[85] Military Penal Law of Switzerland, 13 June 1927 [SR 321.0 Militärstrafgesetz (MStG) vom 13. Juni 1927], Article 94¹3. https://www.admin.ch/opc/de/classified-compilation/19270018/index.html#a94. Accessed 28 February 2017.

[86] Under Article 12 of the Russian Criminal Code (see fn. 84), foreign nationals not residing on the territory of the Russian Federation are subject to the Russian Criminal Code, as well as in cases when the crime is directed against the interests of the Russian Federation or against a Russian citizen.

a willingness to make all new phenomena fit existing frames, on the one hand, and the temptation to assign a separate status to any situation that is more or less new or not widely recognized, on the other. As we have demonstrated, so-called "foreign fighters" precisely represent this problem. While no one disputes the participation of foreign nationals in the armed conflict in Ukraine, we have tried to show that an additional status (*de lege ferenda*) of "foreign fighters" neither provides these persons with any further protection, nor would it deprive them of the rights that could have been conferred upon them in the absence of such a status. However, as we have seen, labelling individuals as "foreign fighters" in terms of a seemingly new category of persons can be (ab)used by states in order to try avoiding responsibility for their actions. This is the case, for example, when Russia sends members of its military forces without insignia, with painted-over signs on vehicles and weapons, and without documents, while seeking to categorize them as "foreign fighters" in the context of an NIAC and *de facto* refusing to have anything in common with them (which, if true, would have deprived them of combatant privileges and POW status upon capture). We showed, however, that, under IHL, these persons stay members of Russia's armed forces and, in most cases, must enjoy POW status upon capture. Consequently, it is Russia that bears responsibility for their actions. Another example of abusing the term *foreign fighter* was highlighted by ICRC representatives at the Bruges Colloquium. In particular, the ICRC noted that some states oppose the application of IHL rules to the detention of foreign fighters.[87] Therefore, creating a special category of persons, namely, "foreign fighters", is not useful either under IHL and HRL, nor under international criminal law.

We would agree with the majority of experts who state that inventing new categories or agreeing upon new international norms will not help to resolve non-compliance with existing rules,[88] as well as believe that the necessity of establishing a separate status of "foreign fighters" is at least worthy of reconsideration.

References

Beerli C (2016) Statement of the ICRC Vice-President at the 17th edition Bruges Colloquium. https://www.icrc.org/en/document/terrorism-counter-terrorism-and-international-humanitarian-law. Accessed 28 February 2017

Bellingcat (2016) Russia's 200th Motorized Infantry Brigade in the Donbass. https://www.bellingcat.com/news/uk-and-europe/2016/01/16/russias-200th-motorized-infantry-brigade-in-the-donbass/. Accessed 28 February 2017

Briggs R, Silvermann T (2014) Western foreign fighters: innovations in responding to the threat. http://www.strategicdialogue.org/wp-content/uploads/2016/02/ISDJ2784_Western_foreign_fighters_V7_WEB.pdf. Accessed 28 February 2017

Butusov Y (2014) The Volunteer Battalions – structure, fears, problems of use in the conflict situations, http://gazeta.zn.ua/internal/dobrovolcheskie-batalony-struktura-strahi-problemy-boevogo-primeneniya-.html. Accessed 28 February 2017

---

[87] Beerli 2016.

[88] See, e.g., ICRC 2016.

Centre for Research on Globalization (2016) War in Ukraine: Foreign Mercenaries Arrive in Donbass, from US, Canada, EU Countries. http://www.globalresearch.ca/war-in-ukraine-foreign-mercenaries-arrive-in-donbass-from-us-canada-eu-countries/5551803. Accessed 28 February 2017

Dearden L (2016) MH17: How investigators were able to prove rebels shot down plane with missile from Russia.

Ditcham BGH (1978) The employment of foreign mercenary troops in the French royal armies 1415–1470. http://deremilitari.org/wp-content/uploads/2013/07/ditcham.pdf. Accessed 28 February 2017

Droege C (2007) The interplay between international humanitarian law and international human rights law in situation of armed conflict. Israel Law Review, Vol. 40 No.2

ECHR (2016) Factsheet – Extra-territorial jurisdiction of States Parties, http://www.echr.coe.int/Documents/FS_Extra-territorial_jurisdiction_ENG.pdf. Accessed 28 February 2017

European Council (2014) Council Implementing Decision 2014/238/CFSP. http://eur-lex.europa.eu/legal-content/EN/TXT/HTML/?uri=CELEX:32014D0238&from=EN. Accessed 28 February 2017

Flores M (2016) Foreign fighters involvement in national and international wars: a historical survey. In: de Guttry A, Capone F, Paulussen C (eds) Foreign fighters under international law and beyond. TMC Asser Press, The Hague

Grzebyk P (2015) Classification of the conflict between Ukraine and Russia in international law (Ius ad bellum and Ius in bello). https://poseidon01.ssrn.com/delivery.php?ID=110099072074091025000072069089080070021078038028040067091087012081114025103002010087041045016000015111098003014125117122125093026059004029003112092098005084007087089070036030114001074064092114096091083077067074097086074092127064113090081122116094103029&EXT=pdf. Accessed 28 February 2017

Guz' I (2014) Отряд «Погоня»: тезисы о белорусских добровольцах [The "Pahonia" unit: theses on Belarus volunteers]

Heinsch R (2016) Foreign fighters and international criminal law. In: de Guttry A, Capone F, Paulussen C (eds) Foreign fighters under international law and beyond. TMC Asser Press, The Hague

ICC (2016) Report on Preliminary Examination Activities. https://www.icc-cpi.int/iccdocs/otp/161114-otp-rep-pe_eng.pdf. Accessed 28 February 2017

ICRC (1987) Commentary of 1987 to Protocol Additional to the Geneva Conventions of 12 August 1949, and relating to the Protection of Victims of International Armed Conflicts (Protocol I), 8 June 1977. https://ihl-databases.icrc.org/applic/ihl/ihl.nsf/Comment.xsp?action=openDocument&documentId=FFC84B7639B26F93C12563CD00434156. Accessed 28 February 2017

ICRC (2008) Opinion Paper "How is the Term "Armed Conflict" Defined in International Humanitarian Law?". https://www.icrc.org/eng/assets/files/other/opinion-paper-armed-conflict.pdf. Accessed 28 February 2017

ICRC (2015) Report "International humanitarian law and the challenges of contemporary armed conflicts", EN 32IC/15/11. https://www.google.ch/url?sa=t&rct=j&q=&esrc=s&source=web&cd=1&ved=0ahUKEwjlme792rXSAhUG8RQKHbwYAy4QFggcMAA&url=https%3A%2F%2Fwww.icrc.org%2Fen%2Fdownload%2Ffile%2F15061%2F32ic-report-on-ihl-and-challenges-of-armed-conflicts.pdf&usg=AFQjCNHl3zVDI6mk4WtU2TvA8H7caCfg1g&sig2=gcloNtjDkKtnGIjceGL7XQ&cad=rjt. Accessed 28 February 2017

ICRC (2016) Guidance Document for the Informal Meeting on strengthening compliance with International Humanitarian Law. https://www.icrc.org/en/document/initial-meeting-states-strengthening-compliance-ihl-july-2012. Accessed 28 February 2017

Kraechenmann S (2014) Geneva Academy of International Humanitarian Law and Human Rights "Foreign Fighters under International Law", Academy Briefing No. 7. https://www.geneva-academy.ch/joomlatools-files/docman-files/Publications/Academy%20Briefings/Foreign%20Fighters_2015_WEB.pdf. Accessed 28 February 2017

Kraechenmann S (2016) The obligations under international law of the foreign fighter's state of nationality or habitual residence, state of transit and state of destination. In: de Guttry A, Capone F, Paulussen C (eds) Foreign fighters under international law and beyond. TMC Asser Press, The Hague

Melzer N (2009) Interpretative guidance on the notion of direct participation in hostilities under international humanitarian law. https://www.icrc.org/eng/assets/files/other/icrc-002-0990.pdf. Accessed 28 February 2017

Meron T (2000) The humanization of international humanitarian law. AJIL, Vol. 94/4

Mir24.tv (2014) Главой СБ и министром обороны ДНР назначили Игоря Стрелкова [Igor Strelkov was appointed the head of the Security Council and DPR Minister of Defence]. http://mir24.tv/news/society/10482003. Accessed 28 February 2017

Nishat N (2015) The structure of Geneva Convention IV and the resulting gaps in that Convention. In: Clapham A, Gaeta P, Sassòli M (eds) The 1949 Geneva Conventions. A Commentary. Oxford University Press, Oxford

Openbaar Ministerie [The Netherlands Public Prosecution Service] (2016) JIT: Flight MH17 was shot down by a BUK missile from farmland near Pervomaiskyi. https://www.om.nl/onderwerpen/mh17-crash/@96068/jit-flight-mh17-shot/. Accessed 19 March 2017

OSCE (2014) Spot Report by the OSCE Special Monitoring Mission to Ukraine (SMM). http://www.osce.org/ukraine-smm/126483. Accessed 28 February 2017

Parliamentary Assembly of the Council of Europe (2016) Resolution 2132. http://assembly.coe.int/nw/xml/XRef/Xref-XML2HTML-en.asp?fileid=23166&lang=en. Accessed 19 March 2017

Pictet J (ed) (1958). The Geneva Conventions of 12 August 1949. Commentary. Volume IV. https://www.loc.gov/rr/frd/Military_Law/pdf/GC_1949-IV.pdf, Accessed 28 February 2017

Quinn A (2016) Vladimir Putin sent Russian mercenaries to 'fight in Syria and Ukraine'. http://www.telegraph.co.uk/news/2016/03/30/vladimir-putin-sent-russian-mercenaries-to-fight-in-syria-and-uk/. Accessed 28 February 2017

Robinson N (1953) Convention relating to the status of refugees: its history, contents and interpretation; a commentary. Institute of Jewish Affairs, World Jewish Congress

Salmón E (2015) Who is a protected civilian? In: Clapham A, Gaeta P, Sassòli M (eds) The 1949 Geneva Conventions. A Commentary. Oxford University Press, Oxford

Soldier of Fortune Magazine (2016) Norwegian mercenary killed in Ukraine. https://www.sofmag.com/norwegian-mercenary-killed-in-ukraine/. Accessed 28 February 2017

Tsybulenko E, Pakhomenko S (2016) The Ukrainian Crisis as a Challenge for the Eastern Partnership. In: Kerikmäe T, Chochia A (eds) Political and Legal Perspectives of the EU Eastern Partnership Policy. Springer, Switzerland

Ukrainian News Portal "112.ua" (2015) Ярош: Соглашения с боевиками противоречат Конституции, ДУК "ПС" не собирается прекращать огонь [Yarosh: The agreement with the rebels contradict the Constitution: the UVC ("RS") is not intending to apply the ceasefire]. http://112.ua/obshchestvo/yarosh-soglasheniya-s-boevikami-protivorechat-konstitucii-duk-ps-ne-sobiraetsya-prekraschat-ogon-189638.html. Accessed 28 February 2017

Ukrainian News Portal "Censor.Net" (2016) Грузинский национальный легион официально вошел в состав ВСУ [Georgian National Legion officially incorporated in the Ukrainian armed forces]

United Nations General Assembly (2014) Resolution 68/262, UN Doc. A/Res/68/262

Walker S (2015) Putin admits Russian military presence in Ukraine for first time. https://www.theguardian.com/world/2015/dec/17/vladimir-putin-admits-russian-military-presence-ukraine. Accessed 28 February 2017

Walker S, Grytsenko O, Ragozin L (2014) Russian soldier: 'You're better clueless because the truth is horrible' https://www.theguardian.com/world/2014/sep/03/ukraine-soldier-youre-better-clueless-because-truth-horrible-moscow-ilovaysk. Accessed 28 February 2017

Warrick J (2015) Black Flags: The Rise of ISIS. Anchor Books, New York NY

Chapter 12
Children and the Armed Conflict in Eastern Ukraine

Natalia Krestovska

Contents

Abstract This chapter investigates the legal problems relating to the status of children affected by the armed conflict in Eastern Ukraine, such as their involvement in hostilities, losing parents, being deprived of schooling, trafficking and other grave violations of children's rights in the combat zone and territory not controlled by the Ukrainian Government. The author analyses legislative measures that have been implemented in Ukraine in relation to the provisions of international humanitarian and human rights law relating to children affected by armed conflict, as well as reveals certain gaps in national juvenile and criminal legislation. The author's propositions are as follows: full implementation of the Optional Protocol to the Convention on the Rights of the Child on the Involvement of Children in Armed Conflict and ratification of the Rome Statute of the International Criminal Court, fundamental revision of the section of the Criminal Code of Ukraine dedicated to crimes against the peace and security of mankind, and appropriate amendments to juvenile legislation.

Natalia Krestovska, Doctor of Legal Science, Professor, Head of the Department of Theory and History of Law, International Humanitarian University, Odessa, Ukraine, email: nataliakrestovska@onua.edu.ua. The annexation of the Crimea, which resulted from the international armed conflict triggered by the Russian Federation, has also affected children's rights, but in other forms and ways than in Donbas. Considering this, the theme of the violation of children's rights in annexed Crimea is beyond the scope of this chapter.

N. Krestovska (✉)
Department of Theory and History of Law, International Humanitarian University,
Odessa, Ukraine
e-mail: nataliakrestovska@onua.edu.ua

© T.M.C. ASSER PRESS and the authors 2018
S. Sayapin and E. Tsybulenko (eds.), *The Use of Force against Ukraine and International Law*, https://doi.org/10.1007/978-94-6265-222-4_12

Keywords armed conflicts · children · Convention on the Rights of the Child ·
Optional Protocol to the Convention of the Rights of the Child on the Involvement
of Children in Armed Conflicts

12.1 Introduction

The issue of children's involvement in armed conflicts has been widely studied in the
context of international legal scholarship. At the same time, however it has not often
been discussed in relation to the armed conflict in the east of Ukraine. Furthermore,
the application of international humanitarian law (hereinafter "IHL") to the situation
in Ukraine could have been considered absurd a few years ago. The international
aspect of this situation has several dimensions: international standards and norms
of child protection that need to be applied to the current situation; an assessment of
recruiting children into the armed forces of combating parties under international law;
and the interaction between international and domestic law on children's rights in
relation to the armed conflict. Last but not least, the historical and social background
involving children in the armed conflict in Eastern Ukraine needs to be assessed.

The aim of the present chapter is to outline problems relative to the status of children affected by the armed conflict in Eastern Ukraine and, more precisely, contribute
to improvements in Ukrainian legislation and the legal practice of child protection.

12.2 Previous Relevant Research

There have been many scientific studies in the field of international legal regulations concerning children's involvement in armed conflicts, the influence of armed
conflicts on children, and various aspects of the protection of children during armed
conflicts. Among the most well-known studies are those by Van Bueren, Kuper,
Tiefenbrun and Happold.[1] These authors have mostly focused on the role of children
in armed conflicts in Africa, sometimes combining legal, anthropological and cultural
approaches in their research. The study by Denov is a good example in this context.[2]
The experience of African and Asian armed conflicts and the social conditions of
the countries in these parts of the world have led some authors to conclude that the
involvement of children in armed conflicts is almost inevitable.[3] Tiefenbrun notes the
following interrelated factors in the involvement of children in armed conflicts: the
impact of a child's parental and family background, peer groups, school, religious
community, social disruptions and governmental failures to protect children, military
advantages of using children as soldiers, serious and pervasive changes in family and

---

[1] Van Bueren 1995; Kuper 1997; Happold 2005.
[2] Denov 2010.
[3] Wagner 2012, p. 6.

ethical values, lack of respect, marginalization of children, changes in the nature of warfare (long, protracted states of mass violence and disorder), etc.[4]

The contribution of Ukrainian authors is relatively modest, inasmuch as the topic was far from urgent in our country prior to the war and hostilities starting in Crimea and Eastern Ukraine. That said, it is appropriate to acknowledge the work of Baymuratov, Opolska, Skrypnyuk, Chehovska, Nychytajlo, Grushko and Pshenichna.

12.3 Historical Background to Ukrainian Children's Involvement in Armed Conflicts

It is no secret that children have been participating in armed conflicts since the phenomenon of war emerged. Before the First World War, the protection of children became part of the protection of all civilians, as reflected in IHL. The Preambles to the 1899 Convention on the Laws and Customs of War on Land (hereinafter "The Hague II"), which included the Martens Clause, and to the 1907 Convention on the Laws and Customs of War on Land (hereinafter "The Hague IV") contained guarantees for civilians during wartime.

However, Ukrainian children did not escape the horrors of the First World War. First of all, children made up a vast proportion of refugees from areas of combat, primarily in Galicia and Volyn. Many children lost their parents, while some, influenced by patriotic or romantic ideas, fled to the theatre of war. Moreover, the deliberate involvement of children in hostilities (so-called "sons of the regiment") was well known. The increase in juvenile crimes was another unfortunate consequence of the First World War. As noted by prominent Ukrainian philosopher and educator Vasyl Zenkovsky, the moral education of children and the negative impact of military propaganda became acute problems.[5] Ukrainian children were also involved in both the Ukrainian National Revolution and the Russian Civil War (1917–1921).

The catastrophic consequences of the First World War raised the issue about special protection for children at the international level. Eglantine Jebb proposed a draft Universal Declaration of Children's Rights. Among others, it was signed by prominent educationalist and supporter of children's rights Janusz Korczak and by the President of the International Committee of the Red Cross, Gustave Ador, and approved by the League of Nations in 1924. By order of the declaration, a child should be the first to receive help in any emergency situation, including armed conflict. As the USSR did not participate in the League of Nations until 1934, this international declaration did not play any important role in the Soviet system for child protection.

During the Second Word Ware, Ukrainian children went through a much more bitter experience: millions lost either lives, parents and/or home, or were displaced or became combatants ("sons of the regiment", guerrilla warriors both on the Soviet

---

[4] Tiefenbrun 2007, pp. 426–32.

[5] For more information, see Cohen 2002, pp. 38–49.

side and on the side of the Ukrainian Insurgent Army).[6] It is necessary to emphasize, that children's participation in combat and guerrilla warfare on the Soviet side was included in Soviet propaganda, promoting a kind of cult around "pioneer heroes".

In conclusion, the experience of armed conflicts, especially during the two world wars, informed an ambivalent social attitude towards the military employment of children in Ukraine: on the one hand, strongly prohibiting children's involvement in, and approving the special protection of children affected by, wars; and, on the other hand, by often regarding some "child soldiers" as historical heroes (many Soviet schools, streets and pioneer squads were named after pioneer heroes, some of the which have been in use ever since).

12.4   Current Situation

According to current data, 68 children have been killed and 186 have been wounded in Eastern Ukraine since the beginning of the conflict masterminded by Russia. There are 215,000 children among the number of internally displaced persons (hereinafter "IDPs") in Ukraine, who were forced to leave their homes in war-affected regions (17 million IDPs altogether).[7] As UNICEF reports, the lives of 580,000 children living in non-government-controlled areas and along the contact line in Eastern Ukraine have been severely affected as a result of the continuing conflict. There are also 39 schools, kindergartens and other child facilities in the temporarily occupied territories of Eastern Ukraine being used for military purposes (barracks, fortified military outposts, and ammunition and weapons storage facilities). On numerous occasions, Russian-backed armed groups have used school grounds as artillery and mortar positions.[8] The Office of the UN High Commissioner for Human Rights noted in its report that both Ukrainian forces and Russian-backed armed groups continue to ignore the special protection of schools as civilian objects used for educational purposes.[9] Finally, at the end of 2015, 280 schools in the Donetsk and Luhansk regions were destroyed or damaged.[10]

Besides, the normal functioning of schools in the anti-terrorist operation area is problematic; and, as a result, the right of children to an education is severely violated.

As the hostilities continue, the number of children affected by the armed conflict tends to increase, as well as the number of children who become war victims.

The number of child soldiers in Ukraine has not been determined since the beginning of hostilities; moreover, it has not even been estimated. It must be noted that, unlike children in some African and Asian countries, Ukrainian children do not have

---

[6] For more information, see Kucherenko 2011; Gavryshko 2016.

[7] Statement by the Ukraine delegation at the UN Security Council's open debate on children and armed conflict, 2 August 2016.

[8] Ibid.

[9] Report on the Human Rights Situation in Ukraine, 16 May to 15 August 2016, para 35.

[10] Dity, yaki ne vidviduyut shkolu v Ukraini 2016, pp. 46–7.

any realistic reason to fight, and the number of child soldiers is thus probably not significant. Perhaps, it explains why the involvement of children in the armed conflict in Eastern Ukraine was not reflected in the UN Secretary-General's report, Children and Armed Conflict, from 20 April 2016.

Nevertheless, news about child soldiers in Eastern Ukraine appears from time to time.[11] For example, early in November 2014, Russian state TV broadcast a report about two "underage soldiers" serving alongside a Russian-backed armed group in Donetsk.[12] Minors have also taken part in the "Motorola" squad (led by Russian mercenary Arsen Pavlov), as well as in a severe battle near Savur Mohyla (2014).[13] The story about a young accomplice of the Russian-backed armed group Bogdanka Nescheret – "the regiment's daughter" of the "Prizrak" (Ghost) battalion – was widely publicized.[14] The Soviet pattern of heroism, reinforced by the image of government armed forces as fascists, plays a major role in the recruitment of young people by Russian-backed armed groups in the area of Donbas, which is not under governmental control. For example, illegal armed formations of the so-called Donetsk and Luhansk People's Republics have restored such Soviet organizations as the Leninist Communist Union of Youth and even pioneer squads,[15] which, among other purposes, trained children and young people to fight for the "communist idea" and restore the Soviet Union, and thus fight against the "Kyevan junta".

As the report of the US Department of State on trafficking in persons (June 2016) proves, the recruitment of children by militant groups has taken place on territory not under the control of the central government and in areas where the government has been unable to enforce national prohibitions against the use of children in armed conflict.[16] However, the Interior Ministry of Ukraine and the Donetsk Oblast Prosecutor's Office confirmed several criminal proceedings taking place involving children in illegal armed formations in the territory not under governmental control.[17] Meanwhile, in the territory under governmental control (Mariupol), a group of minors was identified in November 2014, who had carried out sabotage at the request of collaborators in the Russian-backed Donetsk authorities.[18]

It must be mentioned that violations of the rights of children have been committed by government armed forces as well. The President of Ukraine claimed that, at the end of 2015, 21 defenders of the motherland under the age of 18 were killed in the east of Ukraine.[19] The circumstances of such involvement by minors in the hostilities are not clear, but the announcement of the deaths probably referred to activity by volunteer

---

[11] For more cases, see Chehovska and Nychytajlo 2016, p. 152.

[12] Shevchenko 2014.

[13] Pshenichnaya 2015, p. 80.

[14] Skandal s 9-letnej "Docej" izbataliona "Pryzrak".

[15] V DNR reshyly vozrodyt komsomol.

[16] Trafficking in Persons Report, June 2016, p. 381.

[17] The conflict in the Donbas 2016.

[18] Pshenichnaya 2015, p. 79.

[19] Za vremya ATO v Ukrayne pohybly 2269 ukraynskykh voennykh, yz nykh 21 nesovershenno-letnyy.

battalions. We can cautiously assume that the motives behind minors' involvement in military activity were patriotic and thus were not assessed properly by adults.

Assessing the current situation, we can confidently claim that minors are not involved in hostilities on the side of Ukrainian armed forces. The most serious violation of the law relating the status of children is occasional training with arms.

In conclusion, we assume that the involvement of children in the armed conflict and hostilities in Eastern Ukraine occurs in territory both under and not under governmental control. Such violations of law relating to children are mostly due to extreme ignorance concerning IHL among military personnel on both sides of the conflict.

Much more complicated and severe is the problem of appropriate state policy provisions relating to the children affected by the armed conflict. Parliamentary hearings on the rights of the child in Ukraine (security, compliance, protection) from 12 October 2016 concluded the deterioration in the living standards of children, as a result of the armed conflict in Eastern Ukraine, and the obvious discrepancy between national legislation and international standards concerning the protection of children's rights have been affected by armed conflict.

12.5 International Law Applied to the Armed Conflict in Eastern Ukraine

The type of armed conflict in Eastern Ukraine has yet to be qualified. Two years ago, Heinsch proposed three possible means of qualification: (a) a classic international armed conflict, (b) a non-international armed conflict or (c) a non-international armed conflict, which is "internationalized" by the involvement of a third state (Russia). He concluded that it could be qualified as an internationalized non-international armed conflict, i.e., an original non-international armed conflict, which, through the indirect influence of Russia and the support it is providing to, and the control it is exercising over, pro-Russian separatists, has become an international armed conflict.[20] With all due respect to the authoritative scholar, his opinion is not fully acceptable. The armed conflict in Eastern Ukraine should be assessed as an integral part of the Russian aggression and annexation of Crimea, which started in February 2014.

After all, the situation both in Crimea and in Eastern Ukraine is considered by the Prosecutor of the International Criminal Court (hereinafter "ICC") as an international armed conflict in parallel with a non-international armed conflict.[21] The issue of the Russian Federation's role in the conflict has been discussed, and the result is still controversial. Some analysts consider it to be overall control, whereas others consider

---

[20] Heinsch 2015, pp. 354–360.

[21] Report on Preliminary Examination Activities, 14 November 2016, pp. 168–169.

it to be effective control. However, the Parliamentary Assembly of the Council of Europe operates with the term "effective control".[22]

Ukraine is a party to the main treaties in this branch of international law; to be specific:

- The Geneva Convention Relating to the Protection of Civilian Persons in Time of War (hereinafter "Geneva IV"), approved by the Ukrainian Soviet Socialist Republic (SSR) in 1954
- Additional Protocol to the Geneva Conventions of 12 August 1949, and Relating to the Protection of Victims of International Armed Conflicts, 8 June 1977 (hereinafter "AP I"), approved by the Ukrainian SSR in 1977
- Additional Protocol to the Geneva Conventions of 12 August 1949, and Relating to the Protection of Victims of Non-international Armed Conflicts, 8 June 1977 (hereinafter "AP II"), approved by the Ukrainian SSR in 1989

The effective control of the Russian Federation, which is also a party to these treaties, over some regions of the Donetsk and Luhansk Oblasts means that the it must bear the burden of obligations of the occupying state relating to the children who live on the occupied territory.

According to Articles 14, 17, 23, 24, 38, 50, 76, 82, 89, 94 and 132 of Geneva IV, Articles 70 and 77–78 of AP I, and Article 4 of AP II, children are protected persons as civilians and as a vulnerable group of persons. Article 50 of Geneva IV imposes on the occupying power responsibility for: the proper working of all institutions devoted to the care and education of children; maintaining and educating them, if possible by people of their own nationality, language and religion; taking all necessary steps to identify children whose identity is in doubt. Furthermore, the occupying power must not hinder the application of any preferential measures with regard to food, medical care and protection against the effects of war, which may have been adopted prior to the occupation in favour of children under 15 years, expectant mothers, and mothers of children under seven years.

Article 77(2) of AP I and Article 4(3)(c) of AP II prohibit the recruitment of children under the age of 15 years by the armed forces and their participation in hostilities. If children nevertheless participate in hostilities, they will still benefit, if captured, from preferential treatment. If they are members of armed forces, they benefit from "combatant" and "prisoner of war" statuses as well.[23]

In addition, some provisions in IHL apply in peacetime, for example, the prohibition on recruiting children into armed forces.

Considering the fact that the armed conflict in Eastern Ukraine combines features of both types of armed conflict, the provisions of Geneva IV, AP I and AP II should be applied.

Besides that, the armed conflict in Eastern Ukraine should be considered from the perspective of international human rights law (hereinafter "IHRL") relating to

---

[22] The Office of the Prosecutor of the ICC, Legal Remedies to Human Rights Violations on the Ukrainian Territories Outside the Control of the Ukrainian Authorities: Resolution 2133 (2016), 12 October 2016.

[23] Sassòli et al. 2011, Part I, Chapter 8(c).

the rights of the child. Conceptual provisions of such an approach in relation to IHL were elaborated on by Van Bueren.[24] Specifically, she noted differences between the treatment of child soldiers and children affected by armed conflict in the provisions of these branches of international law.

Ukraine is a party to the Convention on the Rights of the Child from 20 November 1989 (hereinafter "CRC") and the Optional Protocol to the Convention on the Rights of the Child on the Involvement of Children in Armed Conflict (hereinafter "OP") from 25 May 2000.

Article 38 of the CRC establishes minimum standards for state policy relating to children involved in armed conflict as follows: (a) application of provisions of international humanitarian law related to children; (b) obligation of the state party to take all feasible measures to prevent children under the age of 15 years from participation in hostilities; (c) prohibition of recruiting children under the age of 15 into the armed forces; (d) obligation of the state party to take all feasible measures for the protection and care of children who are affected by an armed conflict.

Further progress by Ukraine on the road to preventing the involvement of children in armed conflict was made by ratification of the International Labour Organization's Convention No. 182 on the Prohibition and Immediate Action for the Elimination of the Worst Forms of Child Labour (October 2000). Article 3(a) of this convention specifies that the military use of children is one of the worst forms of child labour and prohibits the forced or compulsory recruitment of children for use in armed conflict.

The OP was approved by Ukraine in 2004, while the initial report on the implementation of its provisions was presented to the UN Committee of the Rights of the Child on 28 January 2011. The OP contains three main provisions concerning children involved in armed conflict: (a) states shall take all feasible measures to ensure that members of their armed forces who have not attained the age of 18 years do not take a direct part in hostilities; (b) states shall ensure that children under the age of 18 years are not compulsorily recruited into their armed forces; (c) states shall raise the minimum age for voluntary recruitment, taking into account the principles contained in that article and recognizing that, under the CRC, children are entitled to special protection. (The requirement to raise the age of the voluntary recruitment does not apply to military schools.) Tiefenbrun considers this treaty as the main international legal instrument that specifically addresses the use of children as soldiers, the minimum age for compulsory recruitment and voluntary recruitment, and direct participation in hostilities.[25]

According to the OP, the voluntary recruitment of children under the age of 18 years may be permitted by national armed forces under the following conditions: (a) such recruitment is genuinely voluntary; (b) such recruitment is carried out with the informed consent of the person's parents or legal guardians; (c) such persons are fully informed of the duties involved in this kind of military service; (d) such persons provide reliable proof of age prior to acceptance into a national military service.

---

[24] Van Bueren 1995, pp. 332–43.

[25] Tiefenbrun 2007, p. 442.

It could be useful to mention that the Rome Statute of the ICC (hereinafter "Rome Statute") defines "conscripting or enlisting children under the age of fifteen years into the national armed forces or using them to participate actively in hostilities" as a crime under international law (8(2)(b)(xxvi) and 8(2)(e)(vii)). The terms *using* and *participate* cover both direct and indirect participation in hostilities, such as combat and activities linked to combat (scouting, spying, sabotage and use of children as decoys, couriers or at military checkpoints). Use of children in a direct support function, such as acting as bearers to take supplies to the front line, or activities at the front line itself, would be included within the scope of the terminology.[26]

Child soldiers can be both the victims and the perpetrators of international crimes. But they cannot be prosecuted under international law because of Article 26 of the Rome Statute, which excludes minors from the jurisdiction of the ICC. However, children as victims of crimes within the court's jurisdiction are entitled to have their views and concerns presented and considered during proceedings against their alleged persecutors.[27]

As with the OP, the Rome Statute addresses the prohibition of children's recruitment and use in hostilities in relation to armed forces both in state bodies and in non-state groups. But, to be realistic, non-state armed groups, as a rule, deny any international law obligations, while there are very limited legal tools to enforce them. As Frostad notes, such groups are not parties to the OP (or any other treaty) and their activity cannot therefore be monitored by the Committee on the Rights of the Child; thus, they are not motivated to abide by the law.[28] Moreover, we have to admit that the special protection of children by international law makes the recruitment of children and their use in various kinds of military actions very attractive to illegal armed groups. Thus, they may use children with a military purpose, at their pleasure, because of the lower accountability for child soldiers in cases of captivity and criminal proceedings. In conclusion, it puts such children in greater danger than adults.

Furthermore, there is a certain gap in the regulation of accountability for crimes against children under international criminal law. All human beings under the age of 18 years enjoy the right to be protected from the negative consequences of armed conflict, but the recruitment of children between the ages of 15 and 18 years and using them to participate actively in hostilities are not qualified as war crimes according to the Rome Statute. As Chaikel states, "in the worst case scenario it could provide an incentive for armed groups to recruit and use persons between the ages of 15 and 18, given their legal invisibility before the ICC, which renders their criminal activities neutral before the Court".[29]

---

[26] Schabas 2016, p. 287.

[27] Happold 2009, pp. 605–6.

[28] Frostad 2013, p. 76.

[29] Chaikel 2015.

12.6   National Implementation

On reviewing the Ukrainian Periodic Report in 2011, the Committee on the Rights of the Child noted positive and negative aspects of Ukraine's implementation of international law concerning the rights of the child with regard to the involvement of children in armed conflicts. To be specific, the committee made recommendations, such as the following:

- To incorporate all the provisions of the OP into domestic legislation
- To strengthen educational activity to make the principles and provisions of the OP widely known, especially for children, military personnel, teachers and social workers, judges, border control and immigration officials
- To include peace education in the school curricula and in teachers' training courses, with special reference to crimes under the OP
- To prohibit enrolling children under the age of 17 in military secondary schools (in my opinion, that reproach does not meet the provisions of the OP)
- To prohibit and criminalize the recruitment and involvement of children in hostilities
- To establish and exercise extraterritorial jurisdiction over war crimes related to the conscription and enlistment of children in hostilities; to be specific, to ratify the Rome Statute
- To strengthen assistance to all children who have, or may have been, recruited or used in hostilities, including refugee and asylum-seeking children

In the main, these recommendations have not been completely fulfilled to date. Moreover, the current situation has changed so much for the worse that these recommendations must be revised thoroughly. The report prepared by Global Rights Compliance considers Ukrainian legal measures related to children in armed conflicts as scarce,[30] which seems to be fair assessment to a certain extent. To be specific, the requirement to criminalize the recruitment and involvement of children in hostilities must be satisfied without delay. Current national criminal legislation only provides for penalties in the trafficking of children or other illegal agreements concerning child recruitment, transportation, harbouring, transferring or receiving a child for unlawful purposes (Criminal Code of Ukraine, Article 149(2)(3)). The note to this provision explains the term *unlawful purpose*, *inter alia*, as the military use of children. It seems, however, that such an important provision should be directly included in the text of the article. Meanwhile, these provisions, being unspecified, do not cover all the probable aspects of such an activity as the military use of children. Article 304 on engaging minors in criminal activity, from the Criminal Code of Ukraine, is partially appropriate to the prosecution of those who have involved a child in the armed conflict. It is not suitable for prosecuting governmental military personnel because the defence of the motherland cannot be qualified as a crime. Article 447 of the Criminal Code of Ukraine, which deals with mercenaries, does not include punishment for recruiting a child as a mercenary, while a minor over the age of 16

---

[30] The Domestic Implementation of International Humanitarian Law in Ukraine 2016, p. 61.

years is responsible for committing such crime. In this respect, Article 359 (2) of the Criminal Code of the Russian Federation is closer to provisions of the IHRL, as it includes punishment for recruiting a minor as a mercenary. However, there are no data about convictions on the grounds of this article.

This lack of regulation is confirmed by national legal practice. Recently, a few minors have been sentenced, accused of creating illegal armed formations and participating in their operations (Criminal Code of Ukraine, Article 260(2)). For example, on 20 April 2016, Krasnoarmiysk City Court of the Donetsk Oblast sentenced a minor, whose illegal activity included the following: military training in the so-called First Slavic Brigade of the Donetsk People's Republic, standing at checkpoints, and providing a security service to a military supply depot.[31] An analysis of this sentence and many others reveals the fact that no adult who has involved accused minors in that kind of criminality was accused of committing the crimes envisaged by Articles 149 and 304 of the Criminal Code of Ukraine.

However, some improvements to national legislation, caused by changed circumstances, were made on 26 January 2016. The Law of Ukraine on the Protection of Childhood was amended by the Law of Ukraine on Amendments to Some Legislative Acts of Ukraine to Enhance the Social Protection of Children and Support Families with Children. Article 30 of the former law, amended by Article 30^1, prohibits any participation by children in hostilities and armed conflicts, including recruitment, financing, material supply, training, involvement in illegal paramilitary or armed groups, and war propaganda aimed at children. It must be emphasized that such prohibition should be supplemented by an appropriate criminal sanction in order to create the possibility of sentencing violators of this prohibitive norm.

Article 30^1 of the Law of Ukraine on the Protection of Childhood imposes an obligation on the Ukrainian state to take all necessary (not only feasible) measures to protect children affected by the armed conflict, including family reunions, the freedom of captured children, the resettlement of children from the zone of hostilities to safe areas, the return of children illegally taken abroad to Ukraine, and the creation of conditions for the medical, psychological and educational rehabilitation and social reintegration of children affected by war and armed conflict. The Law on the Rights and Freedoms of Internally Displaced Persons of 20 October 2014 authorizes local administrations to provide accommodation to displaced children. It is essential to note that the state provides a special status to a child affected by the armed conflict. Necessary components of such a status and the mechanics of its assignment to a child are were approved by the decree No. 268 of the Cabinet of Ministry of Ukraine of 5 April 2017.

Thus, we conclude that some legislative measures have been implemented in Ukrainian legislation in relation to the provisions of IHL and IHRL on children affected by armed conflict. According to the opinion of Ukrainian scholars, the next steps for state policy in the regulation of children's involvement in the armed conflict in Eastern Ukraine should be the following:[32]

---

[31] Vyrok Krasnoarmiyskoho miskrayonnoho sudu Donetskoyi oblasti u spravi 1-kp/235/256/16.

[32] Artemenko 2015, p. 6; Chehovska and Nychytajlo 2016, p. 154; Kochemyrovska 2016; Skrypnyuk 2015, p. 24.

- To determine whether the OP is the law of direct action, and whether it can be applied directly by the national courts for the protection of rights of the child. This proposal should be regarded as not absolutely correct, whereas the international treaties, adopted by the Verkhovna Rada of Ukraine, should become part of national legislation. Nowadays, Ukrainian courts use norms of IHL to justify their decisions in cases connected with various issues concerning the occupied territories, but the above-mentioned treaty is not often used. Thus, the main problem is implementing the OP in the context of the legal practice of the courts and law enforcement bodies.
- To ratify the Rome Statute to ensure punishment of persons who commit crimes against children. This proposal is supported by the author without remarks.
- To precisely criminalize, in definite terms, the military use of children (persons under the age of 18 years) in armed conflict. It should be noted that relevant bills have been submitted by the Verkhovna Rada of Ukraine, but they have not been approved yet. As mentioned above, such an amendment is immediately required for the proper qualification of crimes committed against children during the armed conflict.
- To strengthen the criminal responsibility of minors under the age of 16 years for such actions as obstructing the Ukrainian armed forces and other military formations, illegal handling of weapons, ammunition or explosives, and rioting.
- To preclude the involvement of children in military formations, programmes, and activities related to the skills of operating arms and military service.
- To strengthen educational activity in the field of IHL and IHRL concerning the rights of the child among children, parents, educators and military personnel.

The two last proposals should be explained in more detail. The report prepared by the independent analyst Aleksei Lazarenko on the risk of involvement of minors in military action demonstrates that students both in the north and in the south of the Donetsk Oblast are practically unaware of the OP, while their teachers have limited awareness in this area, as do representatives of security and law enforcement agencies in relation to the OP and appropriate norms of national legislation relating to the protection of children during armed conflict.[33] Thus, strengthening educational activity on the rights of children, and especially on the means of child protection during armed conflict, is urgently required.

The Ministry of Education and Science of Ukraine recommends implementing the basic provisions of IHL in school programmes.[34] But the recommended programme does not include studying provisions relating to children affected by war and child soldiers, which undermines the proposed programme. More importantly, knowledge of IHL and IHRL standards relating to children must be disseminated among military personnel.

---

[33] Lazarenko 2016, pp. 11, 13, 15.

[34] Metodychni rekomendatsiyi shchodo vykladannya kursu za vyborom "Doslidzhuyemo humani-tarne pravo" dlya zahalnoosvitnikh navchalnykh zakladiv.

12.7 Conclusion

Nowadays, Ukrainian children are at real risk of involvement in the armed conflict and hostilities in Eastern Ukraine, aside from the fact that they are directly and indirectly affected by them. The involvement of children in armed conflict is prohibited by IHL and IHRL relating to children. Ukraine and the Russian Federation, which backs illegal armed formations and controls certain regions of the Donetsk and Luhansk Oblasts, are parties to the main international treaties dealing with the protection of the children during armed conflict.

However, the four-year conflict in the east of Ukraine, masterminded by and involving the Russian Federation, has resulted in a number of crimes committed by the combating parties against children and grave violations of children's rights, especially in the combat zone: violations of the right to life, to education, to healthcare, to normal living standards. Moreover, Ukrainian children are involved in hostilities, although, thankfully, not to a large degree.

Ukraine currently faces the task of preventing the military use of children by legal, political and social means. In the legal area, thus means fully implementing the OP, ratifying the Rome Statute, fundamentally revising the section of the Criminal Code of Ukraine dedicated to crimes against the peace and security of mankind, and appropriately amending juvenile legislation. To be specific, the involvement of children in the armed conflict must be criminalized and national legal instruments for the treatment and rehabilitation of former child soldiers must be established. In turn, In turn, children affected by the armed conflict in eastern Ukraine (children, who have been wounded and internally displaced, lost their families, and been schooling, healthcare and a normal way of life) should get amends for their various losses.

References

Artemenko I (2015) Okremi pytannya zakhystu prav ditey u zbroynykh konfliktakh: novi vyklyky dlya Ukrayiny. Visnyk Vyshchoyi kvalifikatsiynoyi komisiyi suddiv Ukrayiny. 1: 2–6
Chaikel D (2015) The ICC's child soldier provisions: time to close the three-year gap. In: International justice monitor: A project of the Open Society Justice Initiative. https://www.ijmonitor.org/2015/08/the-iccs-child-soldier-provisions-time-to-close-the-three-year-gap/. Accessed 20 January 2017
Chehovska M, Nychytajlo I (2016) Pravovi aspekty vtyagnennya nepovnolitnih do uchasti u bojovyh diyah. In: Pidpryyemnycztvo, gospodarstvo i pravo. 8: 150–154
Cohen A (2002) Flowers of evil. Mass media, child psychology, and the struggle for Russia's future during the First World War. In.: Children and war. A historical anthology. New York University Press. New York, pp. 38–49
Council of Europe (2016) Legal remedies to human rights violations on the Ukrainian territories outside the control of the Ukrainian authorities: Resolution 2133 (2016), 12 October 2016 http://assembly.coe.int/nw/xml/XRef/Xref-XML2HTML-EN.asp?fileid=23167&lang=en. Accessed 20 January 2017
Delegation of Ukraine at the UN Security Council (2016) Statement by the delegation of Ukraine at the UN Security Council open debate on children and armed conflict,

2 August 2016 http://ukraineun.org/press-center/138-vystup-delegatsiy-ukrayny-na-vidkrytyh-debatah-rb-oon-shchodo-ditey-ta-zbroynyh-konfliktiv/. Accessed 15 January 2017

Denov M (2010) Child Soldiers: Sierra Leone's Revolutionary United Front. Cambridge University Press. Cambridge

Department of State USA (2016) Trafficking in Persons Report, June 2016/ Department of State, USA. https://www.state.gov/documents/organization/258876.pdf. Accessed 15 January 2017

Diti, yaki ne vidviduyut shkolu v Ukraini: Doslidzhennya masshtabiv ta vimiru problemi z rekomendatsiyami dlya podal'shikh diy (2016). Kiev

Frostad M (2013) Child Soldiers: Recruitment, Use and Punishment. International Family Law, Policy and Practice, Vol. 1.1, Winter: 71–89

Gavryshko M (2016) Divchata zi zbroyeyu vs choloviky u spidnycyax. uamoderna.com/blogy/marta-havryshko/female-child-soldiers-upa. Accessed 25 December 2016

Global Rights Compliance LLP (2016) The Domestic Implementation of International Humanitarian Law in Ukraine. Report prepared by Global Rights Compliance LLP, Kiev

Happold M (2005) Child soldiers in International law. Manchester University Press, Manchester

Happold M (2009) Child recruitment as a crime under the Rome Statute of the International Criminal Court. In: Doria J, Gasser H-P, Cherif Bassiouni M (eds) The Legal regime of the International Criminal Court: Essays in memory of Igor Blischenko. Brill, Leiden, pp. 581–609

Heinsch R (2015) Conflict classification in Ukraine: the return of the "proxy war"? International Law Studies. Vol. 91(323): 323–360

International Criminal Court (2016) Report on Preliminary Examination Activities, 14 November 2016: The Office of the Prosecutor of the International Criminal Court. www.icc-cpi.int/iccdocs/otp/161114-otp-rep-pe_eng.pdf. Accessed 15 January 2017

Kochemyrovska OO (2016) Shhodo dotrymannya Ukrayinoyu mizhnarodnyh standartiv zahystu prav ditej u zbrojnyh konfliktah: Analitychna zapyska The National Institute for Strategic Studies. http://www.niss.gov.ua/articles/1660/. Accessed 20 December 2016

Kucherenko O (2011) Little Soldiers: How Soviet Children Went to War, 1941–1945. Oxford University Press, New York

Kuper J (1997) International law concerning child civilians in armed conflict. Clarendon Press, Oxford

Lazarenko A (2016) Risk of Involvement of the Students of Vocational Educational Institutions of the Region of Donetsk Located in the Immediate Proximity to the Area of Hostilities in Armed Forces and/or Groups: Case Study and Recommendations. Kiev

Metodychni rekomendatsiyi shchodo vykladannya kursu za vyborom "Doslidzhuyemo humanitarne pravo"dlya zahalnoosvitnikh navchalnykh zakladiv. Ministerstvo osvity i nauky Ukrayiny, Lyst 18.02.2015 N 1/9-83

Office of the United Nations High Commissioner for Human Rights (2016) Report on the human rights situation in Ukraine 16 May to 15 August 2016. http://www.ohchr.org/Documents/Countries/UA/Ukraine15thReport.pdf. Accessed 15 January 2017

Pshenichnaya A. (2015) Problemyi obespecheniya prav rebenka v usloviyah vooruzhennogo konflikta: sovremennyie vyizovyi dlya organov vlasti Ukrainy. Legeasiviata. Mai: 77–81

Sassòli M, Bouvier A, Quintin A (2011) How does law protect in war? Cases, documents and teaching materials on contemporary practice in international humanitarian law. Vol. I: Outline of International Humanitarian Law, 3rd edn. ICRC, Geneva

Schabas WA (2016) The International Criminal Court: A commentary on the Rome Statute. Oxford University Press, Oxford

Shevchenko V (2014) Ukraine conflict: Child soldiers join the fight. www.bbc.com/news/world-europe-30134421. Accessed 15 January 2017

Skandal s 9-letnej "Docej" iz bataliona "Pryzrak": v "LNR" trebuyut vernut devochke medaly (2016). http://www.segodnya.ua/regions/donetsk/skandal-s-9-letney-docey-iz-batalona-prizrak-glavarey-lnr-prosyat-vernut-devochke-medali-713486.html/. Accessed 15 January 2017

Skrypnyuk OV (2015) Problemy zabezpechennya prav i svobod ditej v umovah zbrojnogo konfliktu: novi vyklyky dlya Ukrayiny. Almanahprava. 6: 20–24

The conflict in Donbas: War and children (2016). http://dw.com/p/1IpyF. Accessed 20 January 2017

Tiefenbrun SW (2007) Child soldiers, slavery, and the trafficking of children. Fordham International Law Journal. Vol. 31, Issue 2, Article 6: 417–486

V DNR reshyly vozrodyt' komsomol (2015). http://korrespondent.net/ukraine/3524844-v-dnr-reshyly-vozrodyt-komsomol. Accessed 15 January 2017

Van Bueren G (1995) The international law on the rights of the child. Martinus Nijhoff, Norwell, MA/Dordrecht/Boston

Vyrok Krasnoarmiyskoho miskrayonnoho sudu Donetskoyi oblasti u spravi 1-kp/235/256/16, 20 kvitnya 2016 roku. http://www.reyestr.court.gov.ua/Review/57287047. Accessed 15 January 2017

Wagner NB (2012) Child soldiers. http://www.humanitaeres-voelkerrecht.de/PaperChildSoldiers.pdf. Accessed 20 January 2017

Za vremya ATO v Ukrayne pohybly 2269 ukraynskykh voennykh, yz nykh 21 nesovershennolet-nyy (2016). http://ru.golos.ua/suspilstvo/za_vremya_ato_v_ukraine_pogibli_2269_ukrainskih_voennyih_iz_nih_21_nesovershennoletn. Accessed 20 January 2017

Chapter 13
International Legal Dimensions of the Russian Occupation of Crimea

Evhen Tsybulenko and Bogdan Kelichavyi

Contents

Abstract This chapter analyses the main violations of public international law in the territory of Ukraine as a result of the military occupation of Crimea by the Russian Federation. The following study encompasses an evaluation of the human rights violations in Crimea and the establishment of a Russian regime on the peninsula, while drawing attention to repressions against some parts of the local population, such as the Crimean Tatars. An important focus is placed on the international legal status of the territory despite the fact that the Russian Government *de facto* controls Crimea politically and economically. There are numerous international legal acts that have already confirmed that Russia's actions in Crimea constitute military aggression, as well as declared the Crimean Peninsula as an integral part of the territory of Ukraine. Furthermore, this paper briefly analyses the legal mechanisms of responsibility currently in place, which could be used to punish perpetrators for violations of international treaties committed by the aggressor state.

Evhen Tsybulenko, Department of Law, School of Business and Governance, Tallinn University of Technology, Tallinn, Estonia, email: evhen.tsybulenko@ttu.ee.
Bogdan Kelichavyi, email: bogdan.kelichavyi@gmail.com.
This article contains material previously published by the authors in Tsybulenko and Kelichavyi 2016, 'Crimea under Russian occupation', *Juridical Journal*, Vol. 168, pp. 58–68.

E. Tsybulenko (✉) · B. Kelichavyi
Department of Law, School of Business and Governance, Tallinn University of Technology, Tallinn, Estonia
e-mail: evhen.tsybulenko@ttu.ee

B. Kelichavyi
e-mail: bogdan.kelichavyi@gmail.com

S. Sayapin and E. Tsybulenko (eds.), *The Use of Force against Ukraine and International Law*, https://doi.org/10.1007/978-94-6265-222-4_13

Keywords public international law · international legal responsibility · human rights · Ukraine · Crimea · Russian aggression

13.1 Social Background

The Autonomous Republic of Crimea is a peninsula in the southernmost part of Ukrainian territory, located on the northern coast of the Black Sea. According to the Ukrainian Constitution, the Autonomous Republic has its own parliament, which accords additional political power to people living in that region.[1]

During the period when the region was under the control of Ukraine, the population of Crimea comprised around 2.4 million inhabitants. It was reasonably referred to as the most "Russian" region of Ukraine, since the majority of its population, around 58%, identified themselves as ethnic Russians.[2]

However, according to the results of a survey conducted in 2011 by the Razumkov Centre, an independent political institution in Kiev, 71.3% of Crimean residents said they considered their homeland to be Ukraine. The survey also showed that 66.8% of ethnic Russians living on the Crimean Peninsula acknowledged Ukraine as their home. Among ethnic Ukrainian and Crimean Tatars, the figure was over 80%. Only 18.6% of respondents said they did not consider Ukraine to be their motherland, and 10% could not answer the question. Additionally, only 27% of ethnic Russians answered that they would like Crimea to be part of the Russian Federation.[3]

The results of this survey confirmed that, even if most of Crimea's residents were Russian speakers, its majority considered Ukraine to be their home and did not express a desire to become part of Russia.

13.2 Intervention in Crimea: Legal Status of the Peninsula

On 22 February 2014, after the end of the Euromaidan Revolution, the Ukrainian Parliament adopted a resolution, which declared that Viktor Yanukovych had stepped down from performing his duties.[4] As a result, on the next day, it was decided that the duties of the President were to be entrusted to the Speaker of Parliament, Oleksandr Turchynov, for the time being.[5]

Commencing on 27 February 2014, numerous armed groups were deployed in the territory of Crimea. One of these groups was the "Berkut" special riot police, comprising so-called "Cossacks" and Russian representatives of various non-governmental

---

[1] Constitution of Ukraine, Article 133.

[2] Voronko 2011, pp. 28–33.

[3] Tsentr Razumkova 2011, p. 27.

[4] Official website of the Verkhovna Rada of Ukraine 2014.

[5] Ibid.

organizations, who had arrived in Crimea. Another group consisted of well-armed and -equipped men in uniforms without insignia. They were acting autonomously upon the orders of their own leadership and not subordinated to local authorities. These military groupings took control over strategic targets and local authorities, including their security and functioning, and blocked Ukrainian military facilities, units and headquarters.

During the first few days, the Ukrainian authorities and the leadership of Western countries confidently stated that they were discussing the actions of the Russian forces' units, qualifying them as aggression on the basis of UN General Assembly Resolution 3314.[6] However, it was a year before Russia's President Vladimir Putin, in an interview for a Russian documentary film called *Crimea: The Way Home*, admitted that those military groupings were in fact his troops and had entered the territory of Ukraine.[7] Even at the beginning of the conflict, on 4 March 2014, during a press conference, Putin made an verbal statement, in which he briefly described the essence of Russian aggression in Ukraine:

> [Let] one of the numbers of troops try and shoot at his own people, behind which we will stand, not in front, but behind. Let them try and shoot at the women and children! And I will look at those, who will give such an order in Ukraine.

Using civilian shields is a method that has often been applied by Russian militants in Crimea, as well as during the Russian aggression in Ukraine's Donetsk and Luhansk regions.[8]

On 16 March 2014, a so-called "referendum" was held on the status of the Autonomous Republic of Crimea with significant violations of Ukrainian and international legal norms. Despite the numerous proposals submitted by political representatives of the international community, on 18 March 2014, Putin spoke to deputies in the Kremlin's State Duma, the Federation Council and representatives of regional leaders. He recognized the so-called "referendum" in Crimea and stated that it had taken place in full accordance with democratic procedures and international law. The annexation of Ukrainian territory was justified by a statement on common history, calling it the reunification of the divided Russian people and a correction of historical injustice. Ukrainian authorities and the international community, however, did not recognize the legitimacy of the referendum and its results. Only 11 UN members, including Cuba, Venezuela, Afghanistan, North Korea and Syria, voted on 27 March 2014 against the territorial integrity of Ukraine and Crimea as legitimately belonging to the Russian Federation.[9]

In accordance with UN General Assembly Resolution A/RES/68/262 on the Territorial Integrity of Ukraine, the Autonomous Republic of Crimea and the city of Sevastopol are part of the territory of Ukraine. The document states the following:

---

[6] UN Audiovisual Library of International Law, Definition of Aggression, General Assembly Resolution 3314 (XXIX), 14 December 1974.

[7] BBC News, 'Putin reveals secrets of Russia's Crimea takeover plot', 9 March 2015. http://www. bbc.com/news/world-europe-31796226. Accessed 27 February 2017.

[8] OSCE Plenary Statement by the Delegation of Ukraine 2014.

[9] UN 68th General Assembly Meeting Coverage 2014.

1. Affirms its commitment to the sovereignty, political independence, unity and territorial integrity of Ukraine within its internationally recognized borders; [...]

5. Underscores that the referendum held in the Autonomous Republic of Crimea and the city of Sevastopol on 16 March 2014, having no validity, cannot form the basis for any alteration of the status of the Autonomous Republic of Crimea or of the city of Sevastopol;

6. Calls upon all States, international organizations and specialized agencies not to recognize any alteration of the status of the Autonomous Republic of Crimea and the city of Sevastopol on the basis of the above-mentioned referendum and to refrain from any action or dealing that might be interpreted as recognizing any such altered status.[10]

The provisions of Resolution 68/262 contain substantial ramifications alluding to several pre-existing conventional sources, including several provisions of the UN Charter, which have been breached throughout the conflict.[11]

According to PACE Resolution 1990 on the Reconsideration on Substantive Grounds of the Previously Ratified Credentials of the Russian Delegation, Russia's actions in Crimea are qualified as a military occupation and, subsequently, an illegal annexation of Crimea. The resolution *inter alia* states:

3. The Assembly considers that the actions of the Russian Federation leading up to the annexation of Crimea, and in particular the military occupation of the Ukrainian territory and the threat of the use of military force, the recognition of the results of the illegal so-called referendum and subsequent annexation of Crimea into the Russian Federation constitute, beyond any doubt, a grave violation of international law, including of the United Nations Charter and the Organization for Security and Co-operation in Europe (OSCE) Helsinki Final Act.[12]

On 8 July 2015, an OSCE Parliamentary Assembly meeting in Helsinki approved a resolution condemning Russia's actions in Ukraine. The actions of the Russian Federation were clearly recognized as acts of military aggression. The Russian state was also requested to cease its destabilization in Eastern Ukraine and the supply of weapons, ammunition and troops, as well as fulfil its obligations under international agreements.[13] Parliamentarians voted by a margin of 96 in favour to seven against with 32 abstentions on the above-mentioned resolution. This international document condemned Russia's unilateral and unjustified assault on Ukraine's sovereignty and its territorial integrity. In particular, the resolution *inter alia* states:

21. Considers that the actions by the Russian Federation in the Autonomous Republic of Crimea and the city of Sevastopol, as well as in certain areas of the Donetsk and Luhansk regions of Ukraine, constitute acts of military aggression against Ukraine;

33. Urges the Russian Federation, as the Occupying Power in the Autonomous Republic of Crimea and the city of Sevastopol, to permit and facilitate the work in that region of international organizations and human rights non-governmental organizations, the OSCE

---

[10] UN General Assembly 2014, Resolution 68/262.

[11] Sayapin 2015.

[12] PACE 2014, Resolution 1990.

[13] OSCE Resolution on the Continuation of Clear, Gross and Uncorrected Violations of OSCE Commitments and International Norms by the Russian Federation 2016.

High Commissioner on National Minorities, the OSCE Office for Democratic Institutions and Human Rights and the OSCE Representative on Freedom of the Media.[14]

According to the Warsaw Summit communiqué issued by the heads of state and government participating in the meeting of the North Atlantic Council in Warsaw, 8–9 July 2016:

> Russia bears full responsibility for the serious deterioration of the human rights situation on the Crimean peninsula, in particular the discrimination against the Crimean Tatars and other members of local communities. We demand that the Russian de facto authorities take the necessary measures to ensure the safety, rights, and freedoms of everyone living on the peninsula. International monitoring structures must be allowed to carry out their essential work in view of the protection of human rights. We condemn Russia's ongoing and wide-ranging military build-up in Crimea, and are concerned by Russia's efforts and stated plans for further military build-up in the Black Sea region.[15]

Additionally, Russian military aggression in Crimea was officially recognized in two PACE resolutions: Resolution 2132 (2016) on the Political Consequences of the Russian Aggression in Ukraine,[16] and Resolution 2133 (2016) on Legal Remedies for Human Rights Violations on the Ukrainian Territories Outside the Control of the Ukrainian Authorities.[17] On 31 October 2016, the Third Committee of the UN General Assembly, dealing with humanitarian and social issues, proposed and, on 19 December 2016, the UN General Assembly adopted Resolution A/C.3/71/L.26 on the Situation of Human Rights in the Autonomous Republic of Crimea and the city of Sevastopol (Ukraine). In this resolution, Russia is directly referred to as a state occupier, while the Autonomous Republic of Crimea and the city of Sevastopol are recognized as temporarily occupied territory.[18]

According to the aforementioned arguments, the Autonomous Republic of Crimea and the city of Sevastopol are still part of the territory of Ukraine, but currently occupied and annexed by the Russian Federation by means of military aggression. Officially, this territory is recognized by Ukraine as temporarily occupied.[19] Russia's occupation of the Crimean Peninsula was organized at a very inconvenient time for Ukraine after the Euromaidan Revolution. There were almost no casualties in this clash of military forces, except for one ensign, who was mortally wounded during an assault by a military unit in Simferopol.[20] However, this intervention had a significant impact on forthcoming events in this region and its people, many of whom were affected by a number of human rights violations.

---

[14] Ibid.

[15] NATO Warsaw Summit Communiqué 2016.

[16] PACE 2016, Resolution 2133.

[17] PACE 2016, Resolution 2132.

[18] UN 2016, Resolution No. A/C.3/71/L.26.

[19] Official website of the Verkhovna Rada of Ukraine 2014.

[20] TSN 2014, 'Ukrainian warrant was killed during the storming of a military unit in Simferopol'. http://tsn.ua/politika/ukrayinskiy-oficer-zaginuv-pid-chas-shturmu-viyskovoyi-chastini-u-simferopoli-340502.html. Accessed 27 February 2017.

13.3 Establishment of Russian Order and Violations of Human Rights

Despite the prohibitions from the international community, the Crimean Peninsula was occupied by the Russian Federation. A number of international laws and regulations was broken, and the human rights of the residents living on this land were also violated in various ways. However, for the leaders, it was not enough to "restore" historical justice by proclaiming a piece of foreign land as their own. Crimea was waiting on the establishment of a new political, economic and legal order, which was causing hardship for many local citizens.

On 7 March 2014, the Crimean Parliament adopted a resolution on the independence of Crimea and the proclamation of an independent sovereign state, the Republic of Crimea. On 18 March 2014, a treaty between the Russian Federation and the Republic of Crimea was signed to facilitate the acceptance of Crimea into the composition of the Russian Federation and the formation of new constituent entities. The Russian Federation began an active "integration" on the territory of Crimea. With many changes being widespread, Crimean citizens were beginning to be automatically recognized as citizens of the Russian Federation. New legislation was also introduced, which, in comparison with Ukrainian laws, was oppressive and limited human rights in different spheres of life. In addition, during this process of integration, the authorities adopted a number of laws and regulations, which resulted in a significant deterioration of conditions and violations of human rights.

The effect of the Law of the Republic of Crimea on Peculiarities of Buying-out of Property in the Republic of Crimea, from 8 August 2014, was disguise seizures of private property.[21] Another example is the Law of the Republic of Crimea on the National Militia, the People's Army of the Republic of Crimea, from 12 June 2014.[22] This legalized the paramilitary formation that took part in the capture of the peninsula, the seizure of property, which involved kidnappings and murders, the dispersal of peaceful assemblies and the obstruction of journalistic activities.[23]

On 11 March 2014, a decision was made by the Verkhovna Rada of Crimea on combating the spread of extremism in Crimea, while the Russian Federation issued Federal Law No. 91 on the Application of the Provisions of the Criminal Code and the Criminal Procedure Code of the Republic of Crimea and the Federal city of Sevastopol on 5 May 2014.[24] According to these laws, it was established that there was a possibility to be criminally liable for acts committed in Crimea and the city of Sevastopol before 18 March 2014, when Crimea officially fell under the political and legal control of the Russian Federation. Following these newly established laws, there was an initiation of mass arrests, which had the aim of prosecuting pro-Ukrainian activists and leaders of the Crimean Tatar community.

---

[21] Law of the Republic of Crimea of 8 August 2014, No. 47.

[22] Law of the Republic of Crimea of 12 June 2014, No. 22-ZRK.

[23] Gorbunova 2014, pp. 328–40.

[24] Federal Law of the Russian Federation of 5 May 2014, No. 91-FZ.

As a result of the Russian forces occupying the Crimean Peninsula, the immediate changes covered all aspects of life, currency, legislation, paperwork, rules providing medical and social services. As a result, this led to confusion and violations of social relations, as well as negatively affected the personal lives of the vast majority of citizens. One such example was the forced cut-off of Ukrainian telephone operators on the Crimean Peninsula in August and September 2014, which severed contacts between Crimea's residents and the inhabitants of mainland Ukraine.[25] Instead, people had to buy services from Russian companies.

Pursuant to Article 46 of the Annexe to the Convention (IV) Regarding the Laws and Customs of War on Land:

family honour and rights, the lives of persons, and private property, as well as, religious convictions and practice, must be respected. Private property cannot be confiscated.

Article 56 of the same document specifies that:

the property of municipalities, that of institutions dedicated to religion, charity and education, the arts and sciences, even when State property, shall be treated as private property. All seizure of, destruction or wilful damage done to institutions of this character, historic monuments, works of art and science, is forbidden, and should be made the subject of legal proceedings.[26]

In violation of these norms, the actions of the Russian invaders led to massive violations of property rights. For example, at the beginning of the occupation, under the guise of so-called "nationalization", state property of Ukraine was seized because a decision was adopted to "nationalize" businesses, property, land, schools, monuments etc. This occurred without the consent of the Ukrainian authorities and without the provision for obtaining any compensation for damages. On 8 August 2014, the Law of the Republic of Crimea on Peculiarities of the Foreclosure of Property in the Republic of Crimea and its amendments were passed, which provide that, with the assistance of the new government of Crimea, one could buy historical monuments and cultural heritage sites that were privately owned. Most of these objects were socially and culturally meaningful to Crimea.[27]

Representatives of the new authority announced that this law allowed them to apply its provisions to former state or municipal buildings, which had previously passed into private ownership. In most cases, the seizure of property was conducted by the legalized paramilitary formations known as "Crimean Self-defence". Within 10 months of the annexation, with the help of owners and lawyers, it was calculated that the value of seized property and other assets was more than one billion US dollars.[28]

Dual jurisdiction in matters of residence caused many problems in the area. For instance, Russia enforced complicated legislation on the freedom of migration. This

---

[25] LB.ua 2015, 'Ukrtelecom stopped working in Crimea – communication on the peninsula completely disabled'. http://ukr.lb.ua/news/2015/02/10/295007_ukrtelekom_pripiniv_robotu_krimu.html. Accessed 27 February 2017.

[26] International Committee of the Red Cross 1907, Convention (IV).

[27] Law of the Republic of Crimea of 10 August 2014, No. 47-ZRK.

[28] MacFarquhar 2015.

legislation introduced mandatory provisions for citizens to report whether they possessed an existing second citizenship.[29] Since 1 January 2016, in accordance with the newest edition of the Criminal Code of Russia, individuals can be punished for failing to report the possession of a secondary passport of another country. This also applies if an individual owns a residence permit or another valid document confirming his right to permanent residence in a foreign country.[30] As a result, all those who were registered in Crimea during the period of the occupation had to inform the authorities about holding Ukrainian citizenship. If citizens informed the authorities after a certain term or provided incomplete or obviously inaccurate data, they faced administrative liability.

The invasion of the Crimean Peninsula by the Russian Federation and the establishment of a new order affected many local citizens in their freedom of expression and freedom of peaceful assembly. The Russian legislation established a number of changes and regulations in Crimea with significant restrictions on freedom of assembly, which cannot be interpreted as reasonable in a democratic society.

On 21 June 2014, Russia passed Law No. 258-FZ on Amendments to Certain Legislative Acts of the Russian Federation in Improving Legislation on Public Events, which established criminal responsibility for repeated violations of the order for the organization of large-scale events.[31] On 4 October 2014, Law No. 292-FZ on Amending Article 9 of the Federal Law on Meetings, Rallies, Demonstrations, Marches and Pickets was passed, whereby public events could no longer begin before 7:00 and after 22:00, local time, excluding public events dedicated to memorable dates in Russia.[32]

On 12 November 2014, the Council of Ministers of Crimea issued Resolution No. 452 on Approving the List of Places for Public Events in Crimea, Which Defines the Places for Peaceful Gatherings. For example, in Simferopol, it is only allowed to conduct peaceful assembly in four places.

Introducing repressive legislation, criminal liability for "appeals to separatism", systemic violations of the right to peaceful assembly, and the targeted persecution of pro-Ukrainian activists by the police and the so-called "Crimean Self-defence" are not the only flagrant violations of international law. Other forms of widespread breaches of international norms include pressure on the public, attempts to destroy civil society, and the intimidation of segments of the population that do not agree with the occupation of the peninsula.

The establishment of the Russian order in Crimea coincided with an unprecedented increase in human rights violations in this region. According to Crimea SOS, from the beginning of the intervention in February 2014 until recently, over 250 cases of human rights abuses have been reported. These include the deprivation of life, torture, kidnapping, violence, illegal detention, discrimination, restrictions on the freedom of movement, raids, pressure on the media, the prohibition of peaceful

---

[29] Federal Law of the Russian Federation of 4 June 2014, No. 142-FZ.

[30] Criminal Code of the Russian Federation, Article 330.2 N 63-FZ.

[31] Federal Law of Russian Federation of 13 July 2015, No. 258-FZ.

[32] Federal Law of Russian Federation of 4 October 2014, No. 292-FZ.

assembly, pressure on the Mejlis from the Crimean Tatar population, pressure on religious communities, and interrogations.[33]

In this context, it is important to acknowledge the difficult situation concerning political prisoners who have been arrested by the Russian regime in Crimea, which does not recognize the Ukrainian judicial system of their official location. During a press conference, Dmytro Kuleba, Ambassador-at-large for the Ministry of Foreign Affairs of Ukraine, stated that a total of 23 Ukrainians was officially imprisoned for political reasons on the territory of the Russian Federation.[34] Among those arrested was a Ukrainian filmmaker from Crimea, Oleg Sentsov, who supported the local protest movement during the Euromaidan Revolution. Several other individuals have been illegally imprisoned, including Alexander Kolchenko, a student activist, and Gennadiy Afanasyev, a photographer who recorded short videos to demonstrate his pro-Ukrainian views.[35] These cases are examples of the intent to deter active citizens who are suspected of not being loyal to the new regime and to spread fear among their supporters.

In June 2016, Gennadiy Afanasyev was sent back to Ukraine; however, a number of illegally imprisoned people still remain in Russia. Various mechanisms are involved in the process of releasing Ukrainian political prisoners, such as Sentsov, Kolchenko and Afanasyev. The biggest legal contrariety is the fact that Ukraine recognizes these persons as their citizens and transfer requests to their homeland. However, since Russia has recognized Crimea as its territory, it considers these convicted individuals as Russian citizens who committed crimes on territory under Russian jurisdiction.

13.4 Repression Directed at the Crimean Tatars

Crimean Tatars have historically resided on the territory of the peninsula. Unlike ethnic Ukrainians and Russians, who also inhabit this land today, Crimean Tatars do not have another territory that could be recognized as their home. Before the occupation, Crimean Tatars constituted more than 12% of the peninsula's population, which is around 300,000 inhabitants.[36] These individuals can be distinguished based on their appearance, language and religion. Most Crimean Tatars have a negative attitude towards the Russian regime since around 185,000 of them were deported by Stalin out of Crimea to different regions of Russia in 1944.[37]

---

[33] CrimeaSOS, 'Human rights in Crimea'. http://crimeamap.krymsos.com/eng/list.html. Accessed 27 February 2017.

[34] TSN.ua 2016, 'The Foreign Ministry confirmed the official number of Ukrainian political prisoners in Russia and occupied Crimea'. http://tsn.ua/ukrayina/u-mzs-nazvali-oficiynu-kilkist-politv-yazniv-ukrayinciv-u-rosiyi-ta-okupovanomu-krimu-617789.html. Accessed 27 February 2017.

[35] Ministry of Foreign Affairs of Ukraine, 'Ukrainians illegally detained in Russia and in the occupied Crimea'. http://mfa.gov.ua/en/page/open/id/4177. Accessed 27 February 2017.

[36] Bakalchuk 2007, pp. 69–75.

[37] Uehling 2004, p. 91.

When Ukraine restored its independence, the deported Crimean Tatars finally got a chance to return home. Despite cultural differences, they have good relations with Ukraine, especially after the Ukrainian Government officially recognized the deportation of Crimean Tatars as an act of genocide, which destroyed 46% of the Ukrainian population.[38]

Higher stakes concerning the future of this nation fell into place when Russia began to occupy the peninsula, which has caused Crimean Tatars to become victims of many human rights violations. As events began to unravel, the disappearance of members of the Crimean Tatar community was reported. One of the first was a Crimean Tatar activist, Reshat Ametov, who was found dead two weeks after he participated in a peaceful protest outside the occupied Crimean Parliament. According to witnesses, Ametov was kidnapped from the square by people in military uniform.[39] In October 2014, the national leader of the Crimean Tatars, Mustafa Dzhemilev, announced to the Parliamentary Assembly of the Council of Europe (PACE) session that 18 of his people had gone missing without trace.[40]

There is still no proper evidence to explain what happened to these missing individuals and where they are now. The official website of the local law enforcement agencies of Crimea is also devoid of any relevant information about their disappearance. Despite frequent kidnappings of Crimean Tatars, according to Rakhat Chubarov, the leader of Mejlis, there is limited information on those who have been killed.[41]

In relation to indigenous Crimean Tatars, the occupying authorities launched an offensive strategy to remove these individuals from their homeland. At the beginning of its implementation, a policy was introduced to ban, on entry into Crimea, the national leaders Mustafa Dzhemilev, Rakhat Chubarov and Hayana Uksel. The Russian occupying authorities forced Crimean Tatars to leave the peninsula using different methods, such as calling on them to serve in the armed forces of the Russian Federation, with refusal to serve resulting in criminal prosecution. This prompted Crimean Tatars to leave the peninsula; thus, there appeared to be organized "voluntary" deportation by the occupying authorities.[42]

Ten months later, around 20,000 people had to leave Crimea; half of these were Crimean Tatars.[43] According to Mustafa Dzhemilev, as of 15 December 2015, around 35,000 residents were forced to leave Crimea. A proportionally higher number of

---

[38] Resolution of the Verkhovna Rada of Ukraine on the Genocide of the Crimean Tatar People 2015.

[39] Human Rights Watch 2014, 'Crimea: disappeared man found killed'. www.hrw.org/news/2014/03/18/crimea-disappeared-man-found-killed. Accessed 27 February 2017.

[40] Crimean News Agency 2014, '18 Crimean Tatar already missing in Crimea: Jemilev'. http://qha.com.ua/en/politics/18-crimean-tatar-already-missing-in-crimea-jemilev/132375/. Accessed 27 February 2017.

[41] Liha.Biznes.Inform 2015, 'During the year of occupation in Crimea, up to 10 Crimean Tatars killed – Chubarov'. http://news.liga.net/news/politics/5150484-za_god_okkupatsii_v_krymu_Ubili_do_10_krymskikh_tatar_chubarov.htm. Accessed 27 February 2017.

[42] National Institute for Strategic Studies Under the President of Ukraine 2015.

[43] Krym.Realii 2015, '10,00 Crimean Tatars left Crimea – Jemilev'. http://ua.krymr.com/content/news/27165502.html. Accessed 27 February 2017.

Crimean Tatars was prosecuted. For example, among the approximately 100 searches that were conducted amongst local residents, 95% were carried out in the homes and mosques of Crimean Tatars.[44]

The dismantling of Crimean Tatars' organizations led to the suppression of their political identity. The Mejlis are a recognized organization and a representative body of the Crimean Tatar community worldwide. On 18 May 2014, in an interview as the head of the newly established Crimean administration, Sergei Aksenov said that the Mejlis would need to register in accordance with Russian legislation; otherwise, they would not receive any recognition from the authorities. The Crimean Government implemented policies aimed at eliminating the Mejlis. Bank accounts belonging to the "Fund of Crimea", which was supporting the activities of the Mejlis, were seized and closed down. The fund also faced forced evictions from its office buildings, which in turn have resulted in the suspension of any further activities by this organization.

On 26 April 2016, the Crimean Supreme Court granted the petition of Natalia Poklonskaya, a local public prosecutor, to recognize the Mejlis of the Crimean Tatars as an extremist organization and ban its activities on the territory of Russia. The main premise for this decision was that the Mejlis were supported by international terrorist organizations and their aim was to destroy Russia's territorial integrity. In reaction to those statements, the Ministry of Foreign Affairs of Ukraine expressed dissent regarding this decision, which was made by an illegal authority on Ukraine's occupied territory.[45]

The decision to recognize the Mejlis as an extremist organization placed the highest representative body of the Crimean Tatars into a difficult situation. This resulted in the relocation of their headquarters out of Crimea in order to avoid further prosecution. At a press conference, Rakhat Chubarov, the leader of the Mejlis, announced that, from 26 April 2016, the organization would relocate its headquarters and activity to Kiev.[46] In addition, Crimean Tatar language media outlets were forced to shut down their operations in order to avoid heavy fines and criminal prosecutions.[47]

The invasion of Crimea did not solely affect Ukrainians and Russians who refused to support with the occupation of the peninsula. This military and political campaign initiated by the Russian Federation has yet again put the nation of Crimean Tatars on the brink of extinction.

---

[44] Ukrainski Novyny 2015, '35,000 internally displaced persons from Crimea – Jemilev'. http://ukranews.com/news/192922.Krim-pokinulo-35-tis-vinuzhdennih-pereselentsev---Dzhemilev.ru. Accessed 27 February 2017.

[45] Ministry of Foreign Affairs of Ukraine 2016, Statement on the Decision of the Illegal Judicial Authority of the Occupied Autonomous Republic of Crimea to Ban the Mejlis of the Crimean Tatar People. http://mfa.gov.ua/en/press-center/news/46887-zajava-mzs-ukrajini-u-zvjazku-z-nezakonnoju-zaboronoju-okupacijnoju-vladoju-v-avtonomnij-respublici-krim-medzhlisu-krimsykotatarsykogo-narodu. Accessed 27 February 2017.

[46] Nechepurenko 2016.

[47] Amnesty International 2016, Annual Report: Ukraine 2015/2016.

13.5   Mechanisms of Responsibility

After the occupation of the Crimean Peninsula and the proclamation that it was part of the Russian Federation, the Ukrainian Government lost control and influence over a significant part of its country. This was attributed to the fact that this government was experiencing difficulties at the time in a most tumultuous climate. Moreover, it became increasingly difficult to effectively use any of the existing national legal mechanisms to prevent these events and bring the perpetrators of these actions to justice.

Before the full-blown occupation, numerous experts from around the world believed that the Budapest Memorandum of 5 December 1994, on security assurances in connection with Ukraine's accession to the Treaty on Non-proliferation of Nuclear Weapons, would provide sufficient guarantees to Ukraine regarding its security.[48] According to the aforementioned document, the US, Russia and the UK pledged to respect the independence, sovereignty and existing borders of Ukraine, never use force against the territorial integrity and political independence of Ukraine, and seek immediate action by the UN Security Council to assist Ukraine if it became a victim of an act of aggression.[49]

Despite the fact that the Russian Federation is party to this agreement, it still had the courage and political will to breach this international legal document. As a result, there were no consequences for the breaching party; moreover, there were no serious obligations for the other parties to the agreement. The Budapest Memorandum failed to deter Russian aggression because it imposed no immediate consequence or penalty on account of its violations. The political assurances it provided rested on the goodwill and self-restraint of the guarantors: an arrangement that can work between allies but not potential adversaries.[50]

Numerous incidents of human rights violations in Crimea created a legal possibility to appeal to the European Court of Human Rights (ECtHR). Its jurisdiction applies to all member states of the Council of Europe that have ratified the European Convention on Human Rights (ECHR). On 13 March 2014, the Ukrainian Government submitted an application to the ECtHR (No. 20958/14) under Article 33 of the ECHR, which initiated various other applications at a state level. This document outlined the violations of the provisions of the ECHR due to the military occupation and control of the Autonomous Republic of Crimea. Moreover, the Ukrainian Government relied on the following: Article 2 (the right to life); Article 3 (the prohibition of torture and inhuman or degrading treatment); Article 5 (the right to liberty and security); Article 6 (the right to a fair trial); Article 8 (the right to respect for a private life); Article 9 (freedom of religion); Article 10 (freedom of expression); Article 11 (freedom of assembly and association); Article 13 (the right to an effective remedy); Article 14 (the prohibition of discrimination of the convention); and Article 1 of

---

[48] Yost 2015.

[49] OSCE 1994, Budapest Memorandum on Security Assurances.

[50] Budjeryn 2014.

Protocol 1 on the protection of property and Article 2 of Protocol 4 on the freedom of movement.[51]

Due to the fact that the Russian Federation officially recognized Crimea as its own territory, submitting applications to the ECtHR regarding various abuses stemming from the occupation may be a convenient mechanism for Ukraine to fight for its territorial rights. Additionally, numerous cases have also been submitted to the ECtHR from Ukraine as a state, as well as on behalf of private individuals and companies regarding the violations of human rights by Russia in Crimea. According to a press release from the ECtHR, issued on 13 April 2015, more than 20 individual applications were filed in relation to events in Crimea, mainly in the context of the assumption of control over the peninsula. These complaints mostly concerned the right to respect for a private life, peaceful enjoyment of possessions, freedom of movement, deprivation of liberty, and several aspects of criminal proceedings undertaken by the Russian Federation.[52]

Concerns remain regarding the legal mechanisms that could be used by the ECtHR in order to compel Russia to enforce the court's decisions. The court has also faced challenges in enforcing judgements about the situation in Crimea. For instance, to avoid possible negative impacts, on 14 July 2015, the Constitutional Court of the Russian Federation issued a decision regarding the applicability of ECHR decisions.[53] Accordingly, in the case where provisions of the Constitution of the Russian Federation conflict with the provisions of the ECHR, the former must always prevail over the latter. This places Ukraine in an unfavourable position, in which the Russian Federation holds the trump card at an international level, enabling it to sidestep possible responsibilities for the extensive violations of human rights in occupied Crimea.

One of the international mechanisms of punishment for the Russian Federation regarding the occupation of Crimea is related to PACE Resolution 1990 (2014), entitled Reconsideration on Substantive Grounds of the Previously Ratified Credentials of the Russian Delegation. According to this resolution, the Council of Europe denied the Russian Federation its voting and representative rights within the Bureau of the PACE, the Committee of Ministers and the Committee of Permanent Representatives of the Council of Europe. Paragraph 16 of this resolution gives PACE the right to continue to revoke the Russian Federation's powers if it fails to take appropriate measures in the de-escalation of the conflict and return Crimea to Ukraine. The political stance of the Russian Federation towards Ukraine remains one of threating force and the violation of the sovereignty and territorial integrity of the nation. These facts in the documents and legal acts of the Council of Europe confirm the violations by Russia concerning its obligations. Furthermore, the confirmation of these violations, in terms of *de lege ferenda*, may become the basis for the deprivation of its membership of the Council of Europe.[54]

---

[51] ECHR 2014, *Ukraine v. Russia, Application No. 20958/14.*

[52] ECHR 2015, 296.

[53] Constitutional Court of the Russian Federation 2015.

[54] Antonovych et al. 2014, p. 286.

On 28 January 2015, PACE adopted Resolution 2034 (2015), which extended the existing restrictions by one more year.[55] As such, a growing tendency of Russian aggression was observed towards Ukraine. Careful international legal analysis of the Crimean situation in 2014–2015 indicates that the Russian Federation had violated almost all of the obligations of a state concerning territorial integrity. Russia did not acquire sovereignty over the peninsula legally under any international law on territorial acquisition. Instead, there was a military occupation and an annexation of the peninsula.

It would be fair to say that sanctions have been among the most effective international measures in the context of punishing the Russian Federation for its aggressive actions in Ukraine. This measure was imposed by the US, the EU, and several other countries and international organizations. The combined effect of these sanctions and the drop in oil prices has caused a significant downward pressure on the value of Russian currency and increased capital flight. At the same time, the sanctions on access to financing have forced Russia to use part of its foreign exchange reserves to prop up the economy. It is estimated that Russia's GDP declined 2.2% in the first quarter of 2015.[56] Although there is no official proof in relation to the drop in GDP, many suggest that economic sanctions have taken a toll on Russia. Nevertheless, this has not restrained Russian authorities from exhibiting further aggression.

Additionally, there is the possibility of an active role for International Criminal Court (ICC), which is based in The Hague, Netherlands. This is an international judicial institution with jurisdiction over international crimes and over countries that have signed the Treaty of Rome. The ICC is not part of the formal structure of the UN; however, it may prosecute proceedings at the request of the UN Security Council.

According to Article 7 of the Rome Statute, "the jurisdiction of the Court shall be limited to the most serious crimes of concern to the international community as a whole". Thus, in accordance with this statute, the ICC has jurisdiction with respect to the following crimes: crimes of genocide, crimes against humanity, war crimes and the crime of aggression.[57] It is important to note that several countries (including the US, China, India, Israel and Iran), are fundamentally opposed to the idea of the ICC, which restricts the sovereignty of states and provides a broad competence to the court.[58] The Russian Federation and Ukraine belong to that grouping of countries that have signed the Rome Statute but not ratified its provisions. In this case, the ICC does not have direct jurisdiction over these Russia and Ukraine, as they are not officially part of the Rome Statute.

On 8 September 2015, the Ukrainian Government drafted a second declaration under Article 12(3) of the statute, accepting ICC jurisdiction over alleged crimes

---

[55] PACE 2015, Resolution 2034.

[56] NATO Review 2015, 'Sanctions after Crimea: have they worked?'. http://www.nato.int/docu/Review/2015/Russia/sanctions-after-crimea-have-they-worked/EN/index.htm. Accessed 27 February 2017.

[57] Rome Statute of the ICC 2002.

[58] Coalition for the ICC 2006, 'Overview of the United States' opposition to the International Criminal Court'. http://www.iccnow.org/documents/CICCFS_US_Opposition_to_ICC_11Dec06_final.pdf. Accessed 27 February 2017.

committed on its territory from 20 February 2014 onwards.[59] This declaration guided the ICC to give attention to crimes committed by senior officials of the Russian Federation and leaders of the terrorist organizations known as the Donetsk People's Republic and the Luhansk People's Republic. As a result, the Office of the Prosecutor is now conducting a preliminary examination of the situation in Ukraine, as well as other countries such as Afghanistan, Colombia, Georgia, Guinea, Honduras, Iraq, Nigeria and Palestine.[60]

Another potentially powerful mechanism for protecting Ukraine's sovereign rights from an external aggressor consists of the compliance with obligations related to all international legal treaties ever signed by both countries. On 14 September 2016, Ukraine initiated legal proceedings against Russia under the UN Convention on the Law of the Sea (UNCLOS), with a notification of arbitration and statement of claim instituting *ad hoc* arbitral proceedings under Annex VII of the convention.[61]

Since the Black Sea surrounds the Crimean Peninsula, Ukraine has asked the arbitral tribunal to confirm its rights as a coastal state and oblige the Russian Federation to stop internationally wrongful acts in the respective marine waters. This would provide Ukraine with the appropriate assurances of non-repetition and compensation for all losses incurred by the Russian Federation. Specifically, the claim concerns the deposits of mineral resources and the illegal exploitation of gas and oil from the Ukrainian Black Sea continental shelf. Additionally, there are issues with illegal fishing by the Russians, with the inaccessibility of Ukrainian fishing companies to conduct those activities freely having been observed. Russia has also begun building industrial infrastructure and conducting scientific research in the Black Sea without any consent from Ukraine. In December 2016, a tribunal was created and, according to Ukraine's Deputy Minister of Foreign Affairs, Elena Zerkal, the first hearing took place on 12 May 2017.[62]

Additionally, it should be mentioned that, on 6 January 2016, Pavlo Petrenko, Minister of Justice of Ukraine, made a public statement that his country was preparing a claim against Russia with the International Court of Justice (ICJ).[63] By using this mechanism, the Ukrainian Government would seek to protect its sovereign rights

---

[59] Resolution of the Verkhovna Rada of Ukraine on the Ukraine Jurisdiction of the International Criminal Court.

[60] International Criminal Court, Preliminary Examinations List. https://www.icc-cpi.int/en_menus/icc/structure%20of%20the%20court/office%20of%20the%20prosecutor/comm%20and%20ref/Pages/communications%20and%20referrals.aspx. Accessed 27 February 2017.

[61] Ministry of Foreign Affairs of Ukraine 2016, Statement on the Initiation of Arbitration Against the Russian Federation Under the United Nations Convention on the Law of the Sea. http://mfa.gov.ua/en/press-center/comments/6313-statement-of-the-ministry-of-foreign-affairs-of-ukraine-on-the-initiation-of-arbitration-against-the-russian-federation-under-the-united-nations-convention-on-the-law-of-the-sea. Accessed 27 February 2017.

[62] Ukrainska Pravda 2017, 'Arbitration hearings about a violation of RF Convention on Marine Law will begin 12 May'. http://www.pravda.com.ua/news/2017/03/11/7137849/. Accessed 13 May 2017.

[63] UNIAN 2016, 'Ukraine plans to sue against Russia to the International Court of Justice'. http://www.unian.info/politics/1229978-ukraine-to-lodge-claim-against-russia-with-international-court-of-justice.html. Accessed 27 February 2017.

and the rights of its citizens. Due to the "jurisdiction clause" provision concerning the International Convention for the Suppression of the Financing of Terrorism,[64] it could be legally possible to lodge a claim with the ICJ where both parties would be involved. Consequently, on 17 January 2017, Ukraine submitted a claim to the ICJ against Russia, alleging violations of the aforementioned international convention, as well as the International Convention on the Elimination of All Forms of Racial Discrimination.[65] The court announced it would hold public hearings from 6 to 9 March 2017.[66] During the first stage of this claim, it was important to convince the ICJ that Ukraine had exhausted all means for the pretrial settlement of its disputes with Russia. This action may potentially become one of the most effective legal mechanisms to impose legal responsibility on Russia for its aggressive actions in Ukraine.

The issue of the unlawful occupation of the peninsula by Russia does not merely lie in the precedent of a new redistribution of national borders in Europe; rather, it must be taken in context along with the numerous human rights violations committed by the state aggressor. At the current stage of events, it is quite difficult to come up with effective, workable solutions to resolve this problem. An even more challenging task in practice is the use of existing legal mechanisms to punish perpetrators. However, an important task remains to try and find as many effective resolutions for punishment because the lack of responsibility unties the hands of the perpetrators and encourages them to commit new unlawful acts.

13.6   Conclusion

This chapter explored several international public law violations committed by Russia through aggressive actions of the intervention in Crimea and the establishment of Russian order over the territory of the peninsula.

Despite the international public order and legal regulations within the Budapest Memorandum of Security Assurances, which confirms Ukraine's territorial integrity and the obligations to uphold its territorial integrity, the High Command of the Russian Federation consciously invaded part of its neighbouring state. Russian troops blocked Ukrainian military bases in Crimea, seized administrative buildings and established control of infrastructure and other strategic facilities. This takeover led to numerous types of human rights violations against the citizens of Ukraine, especially in the form of repression against Crimean Tatars. The Budapest Memorandum failed to deter Russian aggression and imposed no immediate penalty for the violation of its terms. An appeal process to the ECtHR was almost rendered impossible after Russia made a judgement regarding the applicability of the ECHR, in which it gave

---

[64] International Convention for the Suppression of the Financing of Terrorism 1999.

[65] International Convention on the Elimination of All Forms of Racial Discrimination 1965.

[66] ICJ 2017, 2017/4.

primacy to the Russian Constitution and ultimately avoided potential responsibility for any aggressive actions against Ukraine and its people.

Ukraine is in the process of seeking legal mechanisms of defence by referring to international institutions and agreements. There have been numerous cases of aggression observed in Crimea, which could potentially be used as arguments to impose responsibility on perpetrators. However, it is difficult to find effective solutions to successfully restore justice. An important step that Ukraine recently accomplished was the submission of a claim against Russia to the ICJ on the basis of conventions on terrorism financing and the elimination of racial discrimination. At this first stage, it is crucial for Ukraine to prove that all means for a pretrial settlement of disputes with Russia have been exhausted. Finally, as events further unfold, new and unexpected turns should be expected in this case in the near future.

References

Antonovych M et al (2014) Ukrainska Revoliutsiia Hidnosti, ahresiia RF i mizhnarodne pravo [Ukrainian Revolution of Dignity, RF aggression and International Law]. - K.I.S., Kiev

Amnesty International. Annual Report (2017): UKRAINE 2016/2017. https://www.amnesty.org/en/countries/europe-and-central-asia/ukraine/report-ukraine/. Accessed 27 February 2017

Bakalchuk V (2007) Tendentsii etnokulturnoi tolerantnosti v ukrainskomu suspilstvi [Trends in ethnic and cultural tolerance in Ukrainian society]. Stratehichni Prioritety: Naukovo-Analitychnyi Shchokvartalnyi Zbirnyk. Kyiv: Natsionalnyi Instytut Stratehichnykh Doslidzhen. No. 4(5)

Budjeryn M (2014) The Breach: "Ukraine's Territorial Integrity and the Budapest Memorandum". Nuclear Proliferation International History Project, Issue Brief No. 3. https://www.wilsoncenter.org/sites/default/files/Issue%20Brief%20No%203–The%20Breach–Final4.pdf. Accessed 27 February 2017

Constitutional Court of Russian Federation: on 14 July 2015 the Russian Constitutional Court ruled that the ECHR decision should be executed based on the rule of the Constitution. http://www.ksrf.ru/ru/News/Pages/ViewItem.aspx?ParamId=3244. Accessed 27 February 2017

ECHR (2015) 296: Press release issued by registrar of the court "European Court of Human Rights extends time allowed for Russia's observations on admissibility of cases concerning Crimea and Eastern Ukraine"

European Court of Human Rights (application no. 20958/14) deals with cases concerning Crimea and Eastern Ukraine. Ukraine v. Russia.

Federal Law of Russian Federation from July 13, 2015 No. 258-FZ "On Amendments to Article 222 of the Civil Code of the Russian Federation and the Federal Law "On introduction of the first part of the Civil Code of the Russian Federation". www.rg.ru/2015/07/16/grazhdansky-codex-dok.html. Accessed 27 February 2017

Federal Law of Russian Federation from October 4, 2014 No. 292-FZ "On Amendments to Article 9 of the Federal Law "On Meetings, Rallies, Demonstrations, Processions and Picketing". http://www.rg.ru/2014/10/08/miting-dok.html. Accessed 27 February 2017

Federal Law of the Russian Federation from June 4, 2014 No. 142-FZ "On Introducing Amendments to Articles 6 and 30 of the Federal Law "On Citizenship of the Russian Federation 'and Certain Legislative Acts of the Russian Federation". http://www.rg.ru/2014/06/06/grajdanstvo-dok.html. Accessed 27 February 2017

Federal law of the Russian Federation from May 5, 2014 No. 91-FZ "On the application of the provisions of the Criminal Code and the Criminal Procedure Code of the Russian Federation on the territory of the Republic of Crimea and the federal city of Sevastopol". www.rg.ru/2014/05/07/primenenie-dok.html. Accessed 27 February 2017

Gorbunova Y (2014) Human Rights Abuses in Crimea under Russia's Occupation. Security and Human Rights, Volume 25, Issue 3, pp. 328–340

ICC (2006) Coalition for the International Criminal Court. Overview of the United States' Opposition to the International Criminal Court. http://www.iccnow.org/documents/CICCFS_US_Opposition_to_ICC_11Dec06_final.pdf. Accessed 27 February 2017

ICC (2015) Resolution of the Verkhovna Rada of Ukraine "On the Ukraine jurisdiction of the International Criminal Court" from 8 September 2015. www.icc-cpi.int/iccdocs/other/Ukraine_Art_12-3_declaration_08092015.pdf#search=ukraine. Accessed 27 February 2017

International Committee of the Red Cross (1907) Convention (IV) respecting the Laws and Customs of War on Land and its annexe: Regulations concerning the Laws and Customs of War on Land. The Hague, 18 October 1907. https://www.icrc.org/applic/ihl/ihl.nsf/Treaty.xsp?action=openDocument&documentId=4D47F92DF3966A7EC12563CD002D6788. Accessed 27 February 2017

International Court of Justice (2017) Press Release No. 2017/4 Application of the International Convention for the Suppression of the Financing of Terrorism and of the International Convention on the Elimination of All Forms of Racial Discrimination (Ukraine v. Russian Federation) http://www.icj-cij.org/docket/files/166/19322.pdf. Accessed 27 February 2017

MacFarquhar N (2015) The New York Times: "Seizing Assets in Crimea, From Shipyard to Film Studio." 10th November 2015. www.nytimes.com/2015/01/11/world/seizing-assets-in-crimea-from-shipyard-to-film-studio.html?_r=3. Accessed 27 February 2017

National Institute for Strategic Studies under the President of Ukraine (2015) Concerning the rights of the Crimean Tatar people in annexed Crimea (undated). http://www.niss.gov.ua/articles/1798/. Accessed 27 February 2017

NATO Official web-portal (2016) Warsaw Summit Communiqué Issued by the Heads of State and Government participating in the meeting of the North Atlantic Council in Warsaw 8–9 July 2016 http://www.nato.int/cps/en/natohq/official_texts_133169.htm?selectedLocale=en. Accessed 27 February 2017

NATO Review (2015) Sanctions after Crimea: Have they worked? http://www.nato.int/docu/Review/2015/Russia/sanctions-after-crimea-have-they-worked/EN/index.htm. Accessed 27 February 2017

OHCHR (1965) International Convention on the Elimination of All Forms of Racial Discrimination. Adopted and opened for signature and ratification by General Assembly resolution 2106 (XX) of 21 December 1965. http://www.ohchr.org/EN/ProfessionalInterest/Pages/CERD.aspx. Accessed 27 February 2017

OSCE (1994) Budapest memorandum on Security Assurances with Ukraine's accession to the Treaty on the Non-Proliferation of Nuclear Weapons, signed 5 Dec 1994. http://www.larouchepub.com/eiw/public/2014/eirv41n08-20140221/34-35_4108.pdf. Accessed 27 February 2017

OSCE Parliamentary Assembly (2015) Resolution on The Continuation of Clear, Gross and Uncorrected Violations of OSCE Commitments and International Norms by the Russian Federation (Helsinki, 5–9 July 2015), https://www.oscepa.org/meetings/annual-sessions/2015-annual-session-helsinki/2015-helsinki-final-declaration/2282-07. Accessed 27 February 2017

OSCE Parliamentary Assembly (2015) Resolution on The Continuation of Clear, Gross and Uncorrected Violations of OSCE Commitments and International Norms by the Russian Federation (Helsinki, 5–9 July 2015), https://www.oscepa.org/meetings/annual-sessions/2015-annual-session-helsinki/2015-helsinki-final-declaration/2282-07. Accessed 27 February 2017

OSCE Statement by the Delegation of Ukraine (2014) at the 771st FSC Plenary Statement by the Delegation of Ukraine at the 771st FSC plenary meeting. http://www.osce.org/fsc/128766?download=true. Accessed 27 February 2017

PACE Resolution 1990 (2014) on "Reconsideration on substantive grounds of the previously ratified credentials of the Russian delegation". http://assembly.coe.int/nw/xml/XRef/Xref-XML2HTML-EN.asp?fileid=20882&lang=en. Accessed 27 February 2017

PACE Resolution 2034 (2015) on "Challenge, on substantive grounds, of the still unratified credentials of the delegation of the Russian Federation". http://assembly.coe.int/nw/xml/XRef/Xref-XML2 HTML-EN.asp?fileid=21538&lang=en. Accessed 27 February 2017

PACE Resolution 2132 (2016) on "Political consequences of the Russian aggression in Ukraine". http://assembly.coe.int/nw/xml/XRef/Xref-XML2HTML-en.asp?fileid=23166&lang=en. Accessed 27 February 2017

PACE Resolution 2133 (2016) on "Legal remedies for human rights violations on the Ukrainian territories outside the control of the Ukrainian authorities". http://assembly.coe.int/nw/xml/XRef/Xref-XML2HTML-en.asp?fileid=23167&lang=en. Accessed 27 February 2017

Rome Statute of the International Criminal Court (2002). https://www.icc-cpi.int/nr/rdonlyres/ea9aeff7-5752-4f84-be94-0a655eb30e16/0/rome_statute_english.pdf. Accessed 27 Feb 2017.

Sayapin S (2015) The United Nations General Assembly Resolution 68/262 in the context of general international law. European Political and Law Discourse 2:19–30

State Council of Crimea Republic (2014) Law of the Republic of Crimea from August 10th, 2014 No. 47-ZRK "On peculiarities of foreclosure properties in the Republic of Crimea". http://www.rg.ru/2014/08/08/krim-proekt-vikup-reg-dok.html. Accessed 27 February 2017

State Council of Crimea Republic (2014) Law of the Republic of Crimea on August 8, 2014 No. 47 - "On peculiarities of foreclosure properties in The Republic of Crimea". August 10th, 2014. http://www.rg.ru/2014/08/08/krim-proekt-vikup-reg-dok.html. Accessed 27 February 2017

State Council of Crimea Republic (2014) Law of the Republic of Crimea on June 12, 2014, No. 22-ZRK - "On people's militia - citizen patrols of The Republic of Crimea". http://mirnoe.com/respublika_krym/zakonodatelsvo_rk/1465-zakon-respubliki-krym-o-narodnom-opolchenii-narodnoy-druzhine-respubliki-krym.html. Accessed 27 February 2017

The Criminal Code of the Russian Federation (Ed. on 11.28.2015) Article 330.2 N 63-FZ. http://base.consultant.ru/cons/cgi/online.cgi?req=doc;base=LAW;n=189580;fld=134;dst=1630,0;rnd=0.5052344263531268. Accessed 27 February 2017

Tsentr Razumkova (2011) Natsionalna bezpeka i oborona. Yakist zhyttia krymchan - prioritety rozvytku krymu: problemy realizatsii [National security and defence. The quality of life and priorities of development: problems and realisation] No. 4–5

Uehling G (2004) "Beyond memory the Crimean Tatars' deportation and return". Palgrave Macmillan, New York

UN (1999) International Convention for the Suppression of the Financing of Terrorism Adopted by the General Assembly of the United Nations in Resolution 54/109 of 9 December 1999. http://www.un.org/law/cod/finterr.htm. Accessed 27 February 2017

United Nations General Assembly. Resolution adopted by the General Assembly on 27 March 2014 68/262. Territorial integrity of Ukraine. April 1, 2015. http://www.un.org/en/ga/search/view_doc.asp?symbol=A/RES/68/262. Accessed 27 February 2017

United Nations Organization official web-portal. Sixty-eighth General Assembly meeting coverage: "General Assembly Adopts Resolution Calling upon States Not to Recognize Changes in Status of Crimea Region". http://www.un.org/press/en/2014/ga11493.doc.htm. Accessed 27 February 2017

United Nations Resolution A/C.3/71/L.26 on "Situation of human rights in the Autonomous Republic of Crimea and the city of Sevastopol (Ukraine)". 31 October 2016. http://www.un.org/ru/documents/ods.asp?m=A/C.3/71/L.26. Accessed 27 February 2017

Verkhovna Rada (1996) Constitution of Ukraine Adopted at the Fifth Session of the Verkhovna Rada of Ukraine on 28 June 1996, Article 133

Verkhovna Rada of Ukraine Official Web Portal. LAW OF UKRAINE from 15 April 2014 "On the rights and freedoms of citizens and legal regime in the temporarily occupied territory of Ukraine". http://zakon5.rada.gov.ua/laws/show/1207-18/page. Accessed 27 February 2017

Verkhovna Rada of Ukraine Official Web Portal. Resolution of the Verkhovna Rada of Ukraine number 764-VII from 23 February 2014 "On laying on the Head of Verkhovna Rada of Ukraine the duties of President of Ukraine in accordance with Article 112 of the Constitution of Ukraine". http://zakon3.rada.gov.ua/laws/show/764-18. Accessed 27 February 2017

Verkhovna Rada of Ukraine Official Web Portal. Resolution of the Verkhovna Rada of Ukraine from 12 November 2015 "On the genocide of the Crimean Tatar people". http://zakon4.rada.gov.ua/laws/show/792-19. Accessed 27 February 2017

Verkhovna Rada of Ukraine Official Web Portal (2014) The draft resolution of the Verkhovna Rada of withdrawal Viktor Yanukovych. 02/22/2014. http://w1.c1.rada.gov.ua/pls/zweb2/webproc4_1?pf3511=49853. Accessed 27 February 2017

Voronko O (2011) Osoblyvosti etnodemohrafichnykh protsesiv u Krymu v druhii polovyni XX st. Kultura narodov Prychernomoria [Features of ethnic and demographic processes in the Crimea in the second half of the twentieth century. The culture of the Black Sea] No. 198. st. 28–33

Yost DS (2015) The Budapest Memorandum and Russia's intervention in Ukraine. International Affairs 91(3)

Chapter 14
The Russian–Ukrainian War in Donbas: Historical Memory as an Instrument of Information Warfare

Sergii Pakhomenko, Kateryna Tryma and J'moul A. Francis

Contents

Sergii Pakhomenko, Associate Professor of International Relations and Foreign Policy Chair of Mariupol State University; Associate Professor of Public Communications Chair of Mariupol State University, 180-16, Metalurgiv Avenue, Mariupol, Ukraine, +38 067 931 83 74, email: spplus@ukr.net.
Kateryna Tryma, Mariupol State University, Senior Lecturer of the Chair of Sociology and Philosophy, 16 Kalugska Street, Mariupol, Ukraine, +38 098 367 04 30, email: katet@ukr.net; katerynatryma@gmail.com.
J'moul A. Francis, Tallinn University of Technology, Graduate of the Department of Law, PO Box 3034, St. John's, Antigua, +1268 720 8655, email: jmoulfrancis@icloud.com.

S. Pakhomenko
International Relations and Foreign Policy Chair, Mariupol State University, Mariupol State University, 180-16, Metalurgiv Avenue, Mariupol, Ukraine
e-mail: spplus@ukr.net

K. Tryma (✉)
Leading Researcher at the Department of policy and governance in higher education, Institute of Higher Education (NAESU), Kyiv, Ukraine
e-mail: katet@ukr.net; katerynatryma@gmail.com

J. A. Francis
Graduate of the Department of Law, Tallinn University of Technology,
PO Box 3034, St. John's, Antigua, Estonia
e-mail: jmoulfrancis@icloud.com

© T.M.C. ASSER PRESS and the authors 2018
S. Sayapin and E. Tsybulenko (eds.), *The Use of Force against Ukraine and International Law*, https://doi.org/10.1007/978-94-6265-222-4_14

Abstract This chapter reviews how historical memory and historical policy are used as tools in the information war in the Donbas conflict. Historical memory is regarded as part of a complex set of collective representations and oral traditions, which form a national identity. Within the hybrid aggression on the territory of Ukraine, the use of narratives provides the background that enables the continuation of the conflict. While Ukraine is re-establishing a Ukraine-centric (nation-centric) policy, the leaders of the so-called "Donetsk People's Republic" ("DPR") and "Luhansk People's Republic" ("LPR") are trying to use historical memory and dominant narratives found among the population in Donbas to form a new identity. Therefore, the authors analyse what methods are being used by the Russian aggressors and what consequences are possible in the case of the formation of a new identity in Donbas. Methods of information propaganda, such as creating new holidays, new heroes and new approaches to schooling, are considered in detail. Furthermore, attempts to use the events and heroes of the Second World War are similarly analysed, while tangible narratives, such as Soviet symbols and "The Great Patriotic War", are also considered. Lastly, the development of a new Ukrainian historical policy in response to the historical propaganda challenges of the de-communization law, renaming cities and streets and deconstructing monuments, are evidence of the implementation of a nation-centric paradigm of historical discourse within Ukrainian society. As such, it is believed that the Ukrainian nation-centric paradigm of historical discourse will contribute to the process of *nation-building* and the strengthening of state institutions and society.

Keywords historical memory · historical policy · information warfare · hybrid war · national identity · Donbas

14.1 Introduction

The possible destructive effects of Russia's hybrid aggression against Ukraine are more intense than those experienced in many previous conflicts in Europe in the second half of the 20th century. The peculiarity of the aggression is the large-scale use of various information and propaganda tools. Historical memory, defined as a complex set of collective representations that form a national identity, is used as one of the impactful instruments of the propaganda used to exert influence. Moreover, the media attention given to historical memory and its use for utilitarian purposes is not unique but reflects a trend in the current state of an information-driven society.

The so-called "post-truth" era is characterized by the fact that misinformation, manipulation and "fake news" are effective factors influencing social processes, the political behaviour of citizens, election results, among others, in the configuration of the general world order. In this context, history or, more specifically, the idea of it is a fertile ground for manipulation. It not only seeks to distort historical facts but also advance historical processes and phenomena that generate a loose interpretation, which has little to do with historical truth. This is reflected specifically in the Russian Federation's historical policy, which is copied by the separatist organizations, the "Donetsk People's Republic" ("DPR") and the "Luhansk People's Republic" ("LPR"). Namely, this is the historical idolization of imperial and communist heroics with a distinct militaristic component in order to restore what was the historical status quo.

"Post-truth" is also reflected in the embellished idea of "historical rights" for certain territories with deep historical ties to the Russian Federation, which is then used to justify territorial infringement. Such arguments have no importance in international law; however, they resonate within certain circles in the West and influence public opinion. Furthermore, the growing popularity of national-populist projects around the world, the crisis of neo-liberalism as a dominant ideology, the return to so-called "traditional values", and the shift in domestic policy, which seeks to strengthen the importance of national, ethnic and religious identity, are all major factors influencing the ideology to find one's historical roots and restore a form of those roots. Specifically, these factors play a crucial role in the value-shaping of the Donbas separatist movement, aimed at camouflaging Russian aggression. Hence, it is no surprise that regional identity and archaic ideologemes are reflected, in particular, in the "Russkii Mir" ("Russian world").

Thus, recognizing the fact that historical propaganda occupies an important place in the overall context of the modern information society, specific questions must be addressed to determine the features of our case. What historical memory is used for propaganda manipulation within an armed conflict? Why is the population of Donbas particularly vulnerable to Russian historical propaganda messages? Was there a favourable sociocultural and mental background to the propaganda's acceptance? How did the armed conflict influence the transformation of the policy of historical memory in Ukraine?

14.2   Historical Memory and Historical Policy

Historical memory is a phenomenon of social consciousness, which can be attributed to the fields of social psychology and ideology. It includes material remains of the past and corresponding images, symbols, myths, rituals and historiographical representation.[1] The content of historical memory does not contain much objective information about the events of the past; however, it contains the events of the past presented in a certain way according to subjective perceptions and evaluations. The subjectivity of historical memory, specifically its role in the formation of the national identity, is highlighted by Yakovenko. The researcher tackles a fictional image of the past and "collective experience", which united society into a coherent unit through joint "memories" of an alleged common ancestor, the joint development of the conquered territory, or experiences of collective victories, defeats etc.[2]

---

[1] Nagorna 2012, p. 21.

[2] Iakovenko 2007, p. 34.

This form of social determinism of memory was first noted by Halbwachs, a scientist who researched the phenomenon of memory and introduced the notion of "frameworks of the collective memory".[3] It should be noted that social determinism through history aids in constructing values, attitudes and dominant world views across society. In other words, when individuals begin to understand and interpret foregone events, their outlook on life as it is will be reconstructed. Furthermore, the application of a constructed historical memory subtly imposes limits on society, i.e., what society ought to recall as its history and in what way. Thus, social determinism through the use of a constructed historical memory is part and parcel of any historical policy.

The conceptions of the "politics of memory" or "historical policy" are closely correlated with historical memory, emphasizing its instrumentalist function. Moreover, the practice of ideological interference in the interpretation of historical events is as old as time, but it has become systemic in the formation of national states and the formation of national historiography and school systems. Terminologically, conceptually and organizationally (in the form of institutes of national remembrance), the politics of memory (or historical policy) was formed not so long ago, at the turn of the millennium, primarily in Central and Eastern Europe. Furthermore, its formation of the politics of memory was influenced by ideological transformation in the region, based on the public's understanding and fashioned by way of a recent totalitarian past.[4]

Therefore, historical memory, which has become an object of the policy and been used in accordance with ideological and political objectives, is being transformed into mass consciousness, creating or adjusting the collective representations of the past. Similarly, the content of historical memory consists largely of information constructed by the stakeholders of social and political processes and used in accordance with moralist rhetoric. Hence, historical memory is far from rational. Additionally, historical memory is found in the speeches of politicians, publications and general media discourse. It is also presented as a somewhat constant, monumental and sacred heritage of society, which is obliged to protect historical memory. Therefore, it is of no surprise that historical memory is also viewed as a kind of moral duty on the part of every citizen. For example, it is perceived that it is necessary to appreciate the Soviet Union, celebrate Soviet holidays, honour Soviet heroes etc. However, attempts to discuss any controversial aspects of the Soviet Union are unacceptable. Hence, any neglect or alteration of this duty is tantamount to a misdemeanour, requiring a form of conviction.

---

[3] Halbwachs 2007, p. 127.

[4] The term "historical policy" (Geschichtspolitik) emerged in the 1980s in Germany in the context of discussions about the country's Nazi past. See Miller and Lipman 2012, The convolutions of historical politics. http://www.urokiistorii.ru/memory/conf/51482. Accessed 4 January 2017.

14.3   Historical Narratives in Ukraine During the Pre-war Period: Coexistence and Competition

The indoctrination of a prejudiced recollection of history as an instrument of war seeks to establish a dominant national historical narrative into the public's consciousness. The narrative in scientific terms presents a conceptual and systematic vision of the country's past (which is especially important for young states, where there is a necessity to delineate the self-sufficiency of national history). However, for ideological and political reasons, the perpetuation of a dominant national historical narrative legitimizes the state and authority, and in turn the narrative must consolidate society.

Over the course of the 25 years of modern Ukraine's development as an independent state, two historical narratives have coexisted in understanding and assessing the country's past. The first is defined as the *Ukraine-centric narrative* (nation-centric). It is based on the perception that the nation state has basic social values, and the struggle for the restoration of those values, which is regarded as a historical process in Ukraine. The ideological core of the narrative is the idea of the unification of Ukraine with its European identity. Hence, when Ukrainian lands were part of the Russian Empire and the Soviet Union, there was a culture of Russian dependency, which resulted in varying degrees of national oppression (albeit during different historical periods).

The second narrative is defined as either the imperial, Soviet or, to put it in more neutral terms, the *East Slavic narrative*. This promotes the pre-Soviet vision of a "common Russian" history, transformed into the common history of three fraternal Slavic nations, led by Russians, during Soviet times.[5] One of the most controversial aspects of both visions of national history is the history of the Organization of Ukrainian Nationalists (OUN) and the Ukrainian Insurgent Army (UIA) during the Second World War and what they represented. According to the Ukraine-centric narrative, the history and representation of the OUN and UIA depict the struggle for national liberation; and, from the Soviet's perspective, they depict a collaborative struggle with the Nazis.[6] Therefore, the aforementioned pre-war undercurrents, alongside the sociocultural and political features of Donbas, is what contributed to this region of Eastern Ukraine being dubbed as the most durable "bastion" of post-Soviet ideas.

---

[5] Kulyk 2016.

[6] The OUN was a sociopolitical movement created in 1929 with the aim of restoring an independent Ukrainian nation state. The organization fought against the Polish administration in Western Ukraine, including with the use of terrorist methods. It hoped to exploit the Soviet-German conflict to achieve the goal of establishing an independent Ukraine and concluded an alliance with Germany. After the occupation of Lvov by the Germans on 30 June 1941, the OUN declared that an independent united Ukraine had been restored, which prompted Hitler's indignation. OUN leader Stepan Bandera was arrested and deported to Sachsenhausen concentration camp. The organization then went underground and began to fight the German occupation of Western Ukraine and later the Soviet regime in the region. The UPA comprised armed groups of the OUN and was active in the period 1942–54 within Western Ukraine.

14.4 "Donbas Identity"

Donbas is an example of one of the most-defined regional identities in Ukraine, which is based, on the one hand, on historical cultural, social and economic characteristics, and on the regional elites' hypertrophied aspirations to achieve some political purposes on the other. The Donetsk and Luhansk regions, constituting the focal parts of the Ukrainian Donbas, are located in the east of Ukraine within the historic territory of the Ukrainian–Russian ethnic borderland. The main contingent of the population was formed during two waves of industrialization – the imperial (at the turn of the 19th and 20th centuries) and the Soviet (1920-1930). However, labour migration was also an important factor influencing the structure of the population.

From the time of the earliest settlements in Donbas, there were two dominant ethnic groups: Ukrainians and Russians. Thus, the melting pot of industrialization and state unification policy merged into a kind of Ukrainian–Russian and Russian-speaking ethnic coalition with a double identity.[7] It must be noted that the dominant position of the Russian language in the Russian Empire and the Soviet Union increased with interethnic dialogue. During the Soviet era, the intensive industrial development of the region, the migration of people from different parts of the Soviet Union to work in industrial infrastructure, and urbanization led to a dominance of the local social structure by the proletariat and the engineering and technical intelligentsia (*clerisy*). These factors also created favourable conditions for the idea of internationalism and a new historical community comprising the Soviet people, on the one hand, and for the cult of the toiler region on the other, to be established in Donbas.

All the above-mentioned factors influenced the contemporary sociocultural and mental "face" of Donbas. The main features of the face of Donbas can be observed through the widespread Ukrainian–Russian bi-ethnicity (duality of identification, the blurred and fuzzy border between Ukrainian and Russian identities), the dominance of the Russian language, an industrial type of culture, territorial patriotism, and complimentary attitudes to Soviet history and its symbols.[8] These factors were collectively used by local and regional elites to promote their political interests. They imposed a kind of "cult" of an exaggerated "Donbas patriotism", together with its historical memory (based on Soviet propaganda).

A soft version of the introduction of the imagery of Donbas' regional patriotism into the public consciousness was expressed by emphasizing the uniqueness of this region, and its economic power and achievements in sport. As such, attempts to share the Ukraine-centric matrix in Donbas were heavily criticized. Any change to the status quo could have led to new political parties, whose leaders would have actively participated in the political process in the region and disrupted the established "cult". Seemingly, the prevailing rationale is not to allow new ideological ideas to appear in this territory. This led to the vulgarization of certain specifics of Donbas and led to the consolidation of a hypertrophied sense of regional identity in the regional

---

[7] Kononov 1999.

[8] Pakhomenko and Tryma 2016, p. 50.

consciousness, and faith in its leadership and its indispensability. Furthermore, the hypertrophied identity included the notion that "Donbas feeds all of Ukraine", especially the "backward nationalist western" area.[9] Although technology was used in a pragmatic sense during the pre-election campaign, it created a fertile basis for possible secession. This separatism became a reality because of the direct intervention of the Russian Federation, which, in addition to military force, actively used the tools of information warfare.

14.5　Ukrainian Crisis and Russian Information Policy

The propaganda of the manipulation of historical information forms part of Russia's information policy in its hybrid warfare against Ukraine. Firstly, a common ideological aspect of historical content was formed – this is the idea of "Novorossiya" ("New Russia") for every area of the south and east of Ukraine (from Kharkov to Odessa). This idea was positively integrated into propaganda and sabotage operations carried out by Russia when implementing its information policy. The signal for a large-scale popularization of this idea originated at a press conference given by Vladimir Putin when he said the following: "Kharkiv, Luhansk, Donetsk, Kherson, Mykolaiv, Odessa were not part of Ukraine during the tsarist times. These territories were given by the Soviet government during the 1920s. Why they did it − God knows."[10]

That statement does not correspond with historical reality. Firstly, those territories were not annexed to Ukraine by the Bolsheviks, but were officially incorporated into the Ukrainian People's Republic in November 1917, according to the III Universal of the Central Rada during the Ukrainian Revolution, when Ukrainian statehood was formed. They were also part of the Ukrainian State of Hetman, or the Hetmanate of Ukraine, under Pavlo Skoropadskyi (April-December 1918).[11]

Meanwhile, the Novorossiysk Governorate was the administrative and territorial unit of the Russian Empire during the periods 1764–83 and 1796–1802. Most of that territory comprised the lands of the Zaporozhian Nizovoye Army (the territory of Ukrainian/Zaporizhian Cossacks). According to the results of the first audit (census) in the Russian Empire, 85% of the inhabitants of those territories were Ukrainians.[12] The centre of the governorate in 1764–1783 was the city of Kremenchug, which was located in Central Ukraine (now the Poltava Region). Kharkov had never been part of the Novorossiysk Governorate, but it was in the centre of the Slobodsko-Ukrainian Province.[13]

---

[9] Pakhomenko 2011, pp. 127–45.

[10] Vystuplenie Pytina: Novorossia i druhie iarkie tsytaty. http://news.bigmir.net/world/809994-Vystuplenie-Putina---Novorossija--i-drugie-jarkie-citaty. Accessed 6 December 2016.

[11] Boiko 2009, p. 217.

[12] Kabuzan 1976, p. 248.

[13] An contentious debunking of the "myth" about "Novorossiya" in the format of popular exposition, while at the same time referring to authoritative sources, can be found in an article by Odessa

Thereafter, due to the efforts applied by Kremlin propagandists, as well as by representatives of the academic community, the 'thesis' of "Novorossiya" would go onto acquire specific local characteristics and qualities; however, all the relevant aspects were embodied in the statements of the president. Thus, Leontiev stated that:

> Novorossiya unites nine regions: Crimea, which is already Russian, is certainly also part of Novorossiya. Novorossiya is also Russia, where we have started; it has never been Ukraine. The Leninist-Stalinist national simulacra were not created with an aim to promote a Ukrainian independent state but to manipulate national movements – not with domestic aims, but with foreign aims.

Deputy Director of the Institute of Russian History, in the Russian Academy of Sciences, Viktor Zakharov, stressed that Russia had begun the process of colonizing the Black Sea lands.[14]

At the same time, the manipulation of propaganda, the amorphous content and the lack of significant markers of the Novorossiya identity became obvious to any impartial observer of Ukraine. That name was never used to identify the population of these territories, including in the 19th century, and even during the period when the lands were a homonymous administrative unit of the Russian Empire. It should also be noted that the titles of the self-proclaimed republics include territorial content – the DPR and the LPR – derived from geographic names, rather than being ethnonyms. The designation *People's* refers to a share of the social (not ethnic) populism of its ideologues.[15] Finally, the selected symbol (flag) of Novorossiya has no historical connection *per se*; it is more so associated with the flag of the Confederation of Southern States (during the civil war between the north and south in the US). However, it emphasizes the unconscious attraction of its creators to the most appropriate historical counterparts, namely, to a separatist insurgency in a certain area.

In addition, the concept of "Novorossiya" has not been sufficiently advantageous, because its military and political implementation has failed in most regions of Ukraine (except Crimea and part of Donbas). Moreover, it was never a universal ideology, even in the occupied areas. Sentiments, emphasized by the imperial history and heroics of the region, found a response in Crimea, but this was not rooted in the historical consciousness of Donbas residents. Therefore, the image of "Novorossiya" remains a common "showcase" for the "Russian world" in Ukraine in theory; however, in practice, manipulated ideas with historical memory were differentiated for Crimea and Donbas. In the first case, arguments were premised on "historical rights", namely, Crimea's historical belonging to Russia (Sevastopol is known as the City of Russian Military Glory), and the sacred significance of the Crimea, given that Prince Volodymyr of Kievan Rus (an ancient Ukrainian leader who ruled from Kiev) was baptized there.

---

historian, Oleg Gava. See Gava, 'Putin's lies, or the history of "New Russia" and its ethnic composition in the XIX century'. http://argumentua.com/stati/lozh-putina-ili-istoriya-novorossii-i-ee-etnicheskii-sostav-v-xix-veke. Accessed 20 December 2016.

[14] Sokolova 2014.

[15] Pakhomenko 2015, p. 99.

In the case of Donbas, images from the Second World War were used to a greater extent. They were successfully transformed into a psychological pattern, according to which the "war in Ukraine" was a kind of revival of the war against the Nazis. This reaffirmed the role of fighters against fascism being Russians, who had already gained the status of "victors over fascism" and could in no sense be regarded criminals or occupiers. In addition, the "Great Patriotic War" is interpreted in Russia as a grand mission of universal liberation from evil when the Red Army saved Europe and all of humanity.[16] Russian propaganda uses this narrative pattern in every way, trying to split the Ukrainian historical consciousness. Therefore, vivid narratives such as "Ukrainian military", "castigators", "war with Ukraine", "war against the Nazis", "tragedy in Odessa", "Odessa Khatyn" are being actively extended. The Euromaidan Revolution has also been interpreted as a true "fascist coup", while the current "Ukrainian authorities" are regarded as a "junta with an ultra-nationalist and fascist nature".[17] These narratives have found support among the population of Donbas. The historical consciousness of Donbas, as mentioned above, is hypertrophied by the Soviet vision of history, with its glorification of the Great Patriotic War. Thus, the conflict is presented as a moral or value-based issue. Separatists and the Russians who support them believe that they have truth on their side. This is because of their portrayal as "defenders of the local population", particularly in the phraseology of "punitive measures used by the Kiev junta".

14.6   Objects of Historical Propaganda

Information flows used by the Russian propaganda machine are actively directed at particularly sensitive groups of the population. The population in the conflict zone has turned out to be among the most susceptible to the propaganda campaign. The practical method of using historical memory (along with other signs of identity) characterized the early stages of the conflict. Fearmongering, threats of inevitable "cultural genocide" against the residents of Donbas, the formation of new associative connections between the Kiev authorities and images of fascism, nationalism and Bandera have been promoted in no small measure to mobilize people to protest and seize administrative buildings. The "castigators" have been rumoured to have constructed death camps and even conducted medical experiments on prisoners. All these absurd messages have encouraged the mass consciousness to draw analogies with Nazi crimes.

The messages have also been addressed to the aggressor country's population, which had to ready itself for an invasion of the neighbouring state's territory. To this end, the suffering of the "Russian people" in Donbas and the image of "compatriots", whose "truthful" history was being taken away, have been played up in the propaganda. During the first stage of the war, historical re-enactors, historical fiction

---

[16] Lozovyi 2015.

[17] Litvinenko 2015.

writers and others were widely involved in the ranks of the warmongers who went to fight in Donbas. The world community has also become an essential object of the propaganda.

The nature of the Ukrainian crisis as a "nationalist" and "fascist" revolution, accompanied by the glorification of "fascist hirelings" (Bandera, Shukhevych etc.), and the desire to put their ideas into practice, was promoted during the assessment this crisis. On the one hand, this interpretation of the events in Ukraine among the European public caused Ukraine to be perceived as nationalistic and hostile to European values. On the other hand, an emphasis upon Ukraine's civilization and sociocultural split, coupled with the impossibility of guaranteeing state unity peacefully, has led to the formation of an image of Ukraine as a failed state.

14.7 Historical Memory Policy Carried Out on the Occupied Areas of Donbas

The occupied areas of Donbas, *as per* Ukrainian legislation, are separate regions of the Donetsk and Luhansk regions (ORDLO). The unrecognized "republics" – the so-called DPR and LPR (not controlled by the Ukrainian authorities) – are situated there. The management of these quasi-public entities is carrying out a policy aimed at the further ideological and identical exclusion of these areas from Ukraine. The most important and essential element of this policy was the establishment of a historical memory that differs from the one in Ukraine, in particular, the establishment of other memory patterns.

The national or public holiday dates contribute to these "places of memory". They were either borrowed from the Russian Federation or established by the leadership of the terrorists, alongside the popularization of new heroes, changes in school curricula etc.

The following is an incomplete list of holidays that are celebrated on the territory of the quasi-states: 23 February – Day of Defender of the Fatherland; 8 March – International Women's Day; 1 May – Spring and Labour Day; 9 May – Victory Day; 11 May – Day of the DPR; 12 May –Day of the LPR; 4 November –National Unity Day.[18]

As one can observe from the list, one "innovation" has been the official celebration of the Defender of the Fatherland Day, which is a holiday that is celebrated on 23 February in Russia, Belarus and Kyrgyzstan. In the USSR, the holiday was called the Day of the Soviet Army. This date is not related to the "armed forces of the republic"; however, its establishment was one of the elements in the formation of an identity based on the sentiments of the Soviet past and correlated with contemporary Russian politics about the memory-controlled territories.

---

[18] V DNR opredeleni prazdnicnije dni [The holidays are established by the DPR]. http://reporter. dn.ua/news/society/v_dnr_opredeleny_prazdnichnye_dni/. Accessed 20 December 2016.

One of the most important holidays on the territory of the "republics" is Victory Day, which is pompously celebrated and accompanied by large-scale parades of military hardware. Furthermore, following the example of the Russian Federation, an event called "Immortal Regiment" (*Bezsmertnyi polk*) is held on the territories controlled by terrorists. During the event, participants march and carry banners with photographic portraits of their relatives who participated in the Second World War.[19] These activities are carried out to emphasize the "anti-fascist" orientation of the terrorist organizations.

On the territory of the terrorist republics, other events – used as tools for the construction of historical memory – have been organized as "successors" to Victory Day. The events include the historical and patriotic action of "Memory Watch" (*Vahta pamiati*), the Day of Donbas Liberation, St. George's Ribbon Day, the Day of Heroes of the Fatherland (celebrated in 2016 for the first time), the Day of the Unknown Soldier and the Day of Military Glory. A series of billboards with the slogan, "Being true to the glorious traditions", was issued on the occasion of the Day of Donbas (8 September). The exhibition, "Donbas in Focus", opened at a museum on 4 December 2016. There was also an exhibition of photographs taken by military correspondents in the region, coordinated with activists of the public movement of the DPR, who reportedly delivered 300 metres of St. George's ribbon to the regional museum etc.[20]

At the same time, the agenda of revising the memory of the "Great Patriotic War" is sometimes constructed in a completely twisted and immoral way. On 24 August 2014, between 50 and 100 captured Ukrainian soldiers were taken along the main street of Donetsk. Their capture came about when an angry mob threw eggs and tomatoes at the soldiers, screaming at them and ordering them to kneel. In another episode, after they marched along the streets, the asphalt was ostentatiously washed with water, as happened when German prisoners of war had marched through Moscow. This action historically symbolizes the expulsion of the German Army from Soviet territory in terms of water washing away the 'dirt'. Moreover, this action was undoubtedly aimed at strengthening historic associations between this march and the Victory Day parade in Moscow in 1945, as well as emphasize the difference between the inhabitants of Donbas, who are fighting against "neo-fascism", and the inhabitants of the rest of Ukraine once again.

The 'republic days' in the DPR and the LPR, on 11 and 12 May, respectively, hold a special place in those separatist areas. The timing of these celebrations is linked to the anniversaries of the pseudo-referendums held in 2014. Parades and concerts are characteristic features of these events, while presence at them is obligatory. As such, the terrorists often use this method to demonstrate large-scale involvement in these activities.

---

[19] "Bessmertnyi polk" (official site) 2016. http://moypolk.ru/ustav-polka. Accessed 21 December 2016.

[20] Kak zhiteley DNR uchat naslazhdatsya bedoy 2016. http://www.dsnews.ua/politics/dnr-27012 017220000. Accessed 21 December 2016.

Russian memorial symbols have appeared in the official celebrations for National Unity Day, a Russian state holiday, which has been celebrated on 4 November since 2005. This festival commemorates the liberation of Moscow from Polish invaders in 1612 and is timed to coincide with the Day of the Godmother of Kazan. However, the festival has no historic significance in Donbas; rather, the ideological influence is of a much more important character.

The creation of a "new identity" is impossible without creating a new pantheon of heroes. These heroes had the most problematic reputations, such as Arsen Pavlov (nicknamed Motorola and known for killing Ukrainian captives) and Mikhail Tolstykh (nicknamed Givi). The attempt to represent their deaths as martyrdoms with pompous funerals has become an ideological tool on the territory controlled by the terrorists. A comparison between the DPR's leader, Alexander Zakharchenko, with the famous Marshal of the Soviet Union, Georgy Zhukov, is highlighted in a number of promotional brochures. This is designed to draw a parallel between the defenders of Soviet Union during World War II and the current "generals" who are defending Donbas from the "fascists".[21]

An important tool in the formation of new historical memory is education. The indoctrination of children, along with the denial of the occupation of Ukraine, could, in the future, cause difficulties for the process of reintegrating these territories' populations into Ukrainian society. At this stage, it is used by leaders of the "republics" as a proven method for creating an enemy image during the formative years of the next generation.

A vital tool in establishing the concepts of national identity is the study of history. It is still too early to say which discipline is adopted in the DPR. However, a compulsory course on the history of Ukraine was renamed National History (History of the Fatherland). This change came about because of a crisis in reformatting the territorial boundaries of the notorious fatherland during the 2014–15 school year. As such, different teachers were moved far away from the standardized curriculum and taught the course from a local history rather than a history of Ukraine perspective.

As far as one can judge, the "Ministry of Education" of the DPR has ordered the production of a standardized programme. According to the "Minister of Education", Larisa Polyakova: "The curriculum is built in the following way: to teach a course on world history, and the history of the native land being integrated into it – what was happening in Donbas during the time to be studied. It will be exactly as in the history books, but not the 'History of Ukraine', 'History of Russia' and the 'History of Donbas'."[22] The logic of the curriculum, based on the global context of local events, seems rather progressive in methodological terms. However, given the plans of the Ministry of Patriotic Education, there is enormous fear that everything will be reduced to the cultivation of a new identity.

---

[21] Hlavaria «DNR» sravnili s Kutuzovym y Zhukovym, v seti smeiutsia 2016. http://newsyou.info/glavarya-dnr-sravnili-s-kutuzovym-i-zhukovym-v-seti-smeyutsya. Accessed 22 December 2016.

[22] Izuchenye istoryy po novoi prohramme nachnetsia v DNR s sentiabria – Ministr obrazovania 2016. https://dan-news.info/culture-ru/izuchenie-istorii-po-novoj-programme-nachnetsya-v-dnr-s-sentyabrya-ministr-obrazovaniya.html. Accessed 25 December 2016.

The lessons in "patriotic education" are held in schools across the region, which dovetails with the constant repetition from leaders and members of the DPR that "military-patriotic education is one of the priorities of the republic". Furthermore, one New Year's Eve, a master class entitled "Christmas Toy" was held on how Christmas trees were decorated during the Great Patriotic War, while Yasynuvata District's administration initiated a project called "Memory Book: War Through the Eyes of Children".

Thus, we can say that the manipulation of historical memory in the areas controlled by the terrorists is aimed at creating a new identity and denying Ukrainian identity. It involves the formation of new memory patterns, establishing new holidays, glorifying the militants, emphasizing what is important, and manipulating schooling. As a result, 18% of the population of the DPR identify themselves as "the people of Donbas".[23]

14.8   New Trends in the Historical Policy of Ukraine

The promotion of a historical policy is also taking place in Ukraine outside of Donbas. This is reflected in the high-profile enactment of de-communization laws. As a result, 2,389 monuments and memorials have been dismantled in Ukraine, while its parliament also renamed 25 districts and 987 towns (including 32 cities).[24] In the Law on the Legal Status of Fighters for Ukraine's Independence, among other organizations, the OUN and the UIA, were given legal privilege. The law also provides special status to all military and Ukrainian underground organizations established in the 20th century who fought for independence. As such, Ukraine provides social guarantees and benefits to all participants in the struggle for independence in the last century. However, the law does not specify what benefits are available to them. Parliament also adopted the Law on the Perpetuation of the Victory Over Nazism in the Second World War 1939–1945. Among other things, this law introduces a new holiday, the Day of Remembrance and Reconciliation, which is celebrated on 8 May. However, 9 May is Victory Day, which will continue to be an official holiday. Additionally, the term *Second World War* is to be used instead of "the Great Patriotic War" in formal documentation. The latter term is no longer used.[25]

On the one hand, it is observed that the nation-centric paradigm of the historical discourse is being fixed at the societal level, lacking consultation and public discussion. On the other hand, under the influence of the Russian aggression, Ukraine

---

[23] Analitychnyi zvit za rezultatamy sotsiolohichnoho doslidzhennia «Osoblyvosti svidomosti ta identychnosti zhyteliv pidkontrolnoi ta nepidkontrolnoi Ukraine terytorii Donetskoi oblasti»: vysnovky ta rekomendatsii 2016.

[24] Instytut natsionalnoi pamiati opryliudnyv rezultaty dekomunizatsii u 2016 rotsi 2016. http://gazeta.ua/articles/history/_institut-nacionalnoyi-pamyati-oprilyudniv-rezultati-dekomunizaciyi-u-2016-roci/743473. Accessed 24 December 2016.

[25] Verkhovna Rada Ukrainy pryiniala paket zakoniv pro dekomunizatsiiu 2016. http://www.memory.gov.ua/news/verkhovna-rada-ukraini-priinyala-paket-zakoniv-pro-dekomunizatsiyu. Accessed 26 December 2016.

is destined to pursue an active, even slightly hostile, promotion of nation-centric memory. It is a tool of self-defence for its humanitarian and identity space.

14.9   Conclusion

Therefore, historical memory has become an important object in the framework of Russia's aggression and hybrid warfare against Ukraine. In terms of Russian propaganda, historical memory is an important element of the contextual war. It also serves as a unique tool to offer reasons for Donbas being alien to Ukraine, and for its "natural" belonging to the so-called "Russian world". At the same time, in contrast to Crimea, the main historical "argument" has been the "restoration" of the so-called "historical right". In the case of Donbas, the most replicable ways have been references to a "struggle against fascism" and the portrayal of Ukraine as a "fascist state". Propaganda units in the so-called DPR and LPR are actively promoting these associations and simultaneously replicating memorable practices from the Soviet period, as well as those belonging to the new Russian historical memory. With the existence of a frozen conflict and the separatist territories being in another (non-Ukrainian) political and humanitarian reality, the process of forming a new identity may not be a complex one. Consequently, Ukrainian historical policy has taken a course towards the de-communization of the public space, which is seen as an important detachment of Ukrainian memorial relations from the imperial past. It must be recognized that the existing habitat of historical narratives in Ukraine has not exhausted its effects on Ukrainian society. The habitat of historical narratives has also become a ticking time bomb, which has been detonated with the support of Russia's information policy.

Today, the task is not so much about forming new concepts of historical policy (which must still rely on the national and state views about history). It is also not about creating a considered system of patriotic pro-Ukrainian propaganda: a kind of "soft power" for internal use. The historical component should be significantly reduced, whereas images of a pro-European democratic Ukraine should be the main focus. Other important factors include the ongoing de-communization policy and a gradual replacement of the memory of World War II (which, unfortunately, is inseparable from the Soviet narrative). The information warfare that is being waged in the Russian–Ukrainian War in Donbas proves that military tactics include not only tangible weaponry, but also intangible and psychological weaponry. Thus, this highlights another dimension to international law and its ability to settle non-traditional methods of warfare.

References

Analytical center Donbas factory of thought, IFAK Institut Analitychnyi zvit za rezultatamy sotsiolohichnoho doslidzhennia «Osoblyvosti svidomosti ta identychnosti zhyteliv pidkontrolnoi ta nepidkontrolnoi Ukraine terytorii Donetskoi oblasti»: vysnovky ta rekomendatsii (2016) [Analytical report of survey "Features consciousness and identity of the inhabitants of controlled and uncontrolled territories of Ukraine Donetsk region": conclusions and recommendations] "Bessmertnyi polk" Official site (2016). http://moypolk.ru/ustav-polka. Accessed 21 Dec 2016

Boiko O (2009) The area, borders and administrative divisions of the Hetmanate of Hetman of Ukraine Pavlo Skoropadskyi (1918). Regional History of Ukraine, Institute of History of Ukraine, Kiev. – pp. 217–232

DSNews (2016) Narodnoe mozgopravstvo. Kak zhiteley DNR uchat naslazhdatsya bedoy. http://www.dsnews.ua/politics/dnr-27012017220000. Accessed 21 December 2016 [People's shrink. As residents of the DNR are taught to enjoy trouble]

Gazeta (2016) Instytut natsionalnoi pamiati opryliudnyv rezultaty dekomunizatsii u 2016 rotsi. http://gazeta.ua/articles/history/_institut-nacionalnoyi-pamyati-oprilyudniv-rezultati-dekomunizaciyi-u-2016-roci/743473. Accessed 24 December 2016 [Institute of National Memory published the results of decommunization in 2016]

Halbwachs M (2007) Sotsialnye ramki pamyati. Novoe isdatelstvo, Moscow [Social frameworks of memory]

Iakovenko O (2007) Vstup do istorii. Kritika, Kiev [The introduction to History]

Izuchenye istoryy po novoi prohramme nachnetsia v DNR s sentiabria – ministr obrazovania (2016). https://dan-news.info/culture-ru/izuchenie-istorii-po-novoj-programme-nachnetsya-v-dnr-s-sentyabrya-ministr-obrazovaniya.html. Accessed 25 December 2016 [The study of history according to the new program will start in DPR from September – Minister of Education]

Kabuzan M (1976) Zaselenie Novorossii v kontse XVIII — per. pol. XIX v. (1719–1858 gg.). Nauka, Moscow [Settlement of Novorossia in the late XVIII – the early XIX century. (1719–1858)]

Kononov I (1999) Ukrainsko-russkaya dominiruyuschaya koalitsiya kak faktor razvitiya etnicheskoy strukturyi Ukrainyi. http://www.niurr.gov.ua/ukr/dialog_1999/Kononov.html. Accessed 9 January 2017 [The Ukrainian-Russian dominant coalition as a factor in the development of the ethnic structure of Ukraine]

Kulyk V (2016) Natsionalistychne proty radianskoho: istorychna pamiat u nezalezhnii Ukrainy. http://www.historians.in.ua/index.php/istoriya-i-pamyat-vazhki-pitannya/379-volodymyr-kulyk-natsionalistychne-proty-radianskoho-istorychna-pamiat-u-nezalezhnii-ukraini. Accessed 10 January 2017 [Nationalistical against Soviet: historical memory in Independent Ukraine]

Litvinenko O (2015) Vyklyky natsionalnii politytsi pamiati v chasy "hibrydnoi viiny. http://www.niss.gov.ua/articles/1818/. Accessed 10 December 2016 [The challenges to the national politics of memory during hybrid warfare]

Nagorna L (2012) Istorychna pamjat: teorii, discursy, refleksii. IPiEND im. I.F. Kurasa NAN Ukrajni, Kiev [Historical memory, theory, discussion, reflection]

Newsyou (2016) Hlavaria «DNR» sravnili s Kutuzovym y Zhukovym, v seti smeiutsia. http://newsyou.info/glavarya-dnr-sravnili-s-kutuzovym-i-zhukovym-v-seti-smeyutsya. Accessed 22 December 2016 [The leader of "DPR" was compared with Kutuzov and Zhukov, they are laughing on the Internet]

Pakhomenko S (2011) Ukrainska Povstanska Armiia v suchasnomu informatsiinomu prostori Donechchyny.National Library of the Czech Republic - Slavonic Library, Prague [Ukrainian Insurgent Army in the modern information space Donetsk]

Pakhomenko S (2015) Identity Factor in Terms of the Ukrainian Crisis (the Example of The Donbas Region). Bezpieczenstwo. Teoria i Praktyka. Kwartalnik Krakowskiej Akademii im. Andrzeja Frycza Modrzewsiego 3:95–105

Pakhomenko S, Tryma C (2016) Identity and propaganda in Russian-Ukrainian hybrid warfare. Sojatedlane. Estonian Journal of Military Studies. Cultural, peace and conflict studies series. The crisis in Ukraine and information operations of the Russian Federation 2:42–54

Sokolova M (2014) Ekspertyi: «Novorossiya imeet pravo na samoopredelenie». http://www.pnp. ru/news/detail/64849. Accessed 13 December 2016 [Experts: "New Russia has the right to self-determination]

V DNR opredeleni prazdnicnije dni. http://reporter.dn.ua/news/society/v_dnr_opredeleny_ prazdnichnye_dni/. Accessed 20 December 2016 [The holidays are established by DPR 2016]

Verkhovna Rada Ukrainy pryiniala paket zakoniv pro dekomunizatsiiu (2016). http://www.memory. gov.ua/news/verkhovna-rada-ukraini-priinyala-paket-zakoniv-pro-dekomunizatsiyu. Accessed 26 Dec 2016 [Verkhovna Rada of Ukraine adopted the law on decommunization]

Vystuplenie Putina: Novorossia i druhie iarkie tsytaty (2016). http://news.bigmir.net/world/809994-Vystuplenie-Putina—Novorossija–i-drugie-jarkie-citaty. Accessed 06 December 2016 [Putin's speech: Novorossia and other notable quotations]

Chapter 15
An Alleged "Genocide of Russian-Speaking Persons" in Eastern Ukraine: Some Observations on the "Hybrid" Application of International Criminal Law by the Investigative Committee of the Russian Federation

Sergey Sayapin

Contents

Abstract In 2014, the Investigative Committee of the Russian Federation instituted a criminal prosecution of a number of Ukrainian nationals of charges of genocide of "a national group of Russian-speaking persons" in eastern Ukraine. It appears that here, in addition to instituting prosecutions in the absence of jurisdiction with respect to such alleged acts committed on the territory of Ukraine, Russia also abused the notion of genocide in that it included within the range of groups protected by the Convention on the Prevention and Punishment of the Crime of Genocide, and by its own Criminal Code, a group that is not covered by the definition of genocide.

Sergey Sayapin, LLB, LLM, Dr. iur., Assistant Professor in International and Criminal Law and Director of the LLB in International Law programme, KIMEP University, Kazakhstan. e-mail: s.sayapin@kimep.kz

S. Sayapin (✉)
KIMEP University, Almaty, Kazakhstan
e-mail: s.sayapin@kimep.kz

It is submitted that both factors void the entire prosecution exercise, and make it a manifestation of "hybrid law enforcement".

Keywords Genocide · "hybrid law enforcement" · Investigative Committee of the Russian Federation · jurisdiction · mass media · national group · patriacide

15.1 Introduction

On 29 September 2014, the Investigative Committee of the Russian Federation reported[1] that a criminal case on charges of genocide of the "Russian-speaking population in southeastern Ukraine" was instituted. According to an official news release issued by the Investigative Committee:

> [D]uring the period between 12 April 2014 until present, in violation of the 1948 Convention "On the Prevention of the Crime of Genocide and of the Punishment therefor" (*sic!*), as well as of other international legal acts, which condemn genocide, unidentified persons from among Ukraine's supreme political and military leadership, Ukraine's Armed forces, Ukraine's National guard and the "Right Sector" issued orders aimed at a full destruction, specifically, of *Russian-speaking citizens* [who were] resident on the territory of the Donetsk and Luhansk republics (emphasis added).[2]

By 8 September 2016, the Investigative Committee identified individuals from among Ukraine's nationals who were to be indicted in the framework of the alleged genocide case:

> This case features former as well as present officials of the Ministry of Defence and the National Guard of Ukraine. Among them are the Minister of Defence Stepan Poltorak, Chief of the General Staff of Ukraine's Ministry of Defence Viktor Muzhenko, former commander of the Land forces Anatoliy Pushnyakov, present commander of the Land forces Sergey Popko, and commander of the National Guard Yury Allerov. According to the investigation's data, between January and August 2016 all of them issued criminal orders to [their] subordinates from among military servicemen of Ukraine's Armed forces and Ukraine's National guard to use heavy types of weapons with high destructive capacities, for the destruction of civil infrastructure objects, [and] residential localities of the self-proclaimed Donetsk People's Republic, as well as [for the] full or partial destruction of *a national group of Russian-speaking persons*, including [of] minors. As a result of the said criminal acts, no fewer than 9 persons were killed, no fewer than 110 persons were wounded, including 9 minors, no fewer than 279 residential houses and objects of infrastructure were destroyed partially and fully (emphasis added).[3]

In the same news release, the Investigative Committee reported, more generally, that:

---

[1] See Investigative Committee of the Russian Federation 2014.

[2] Ibid.

[3] See Investigative Committee of the Russian Federation 2016.

Presently, the Investigative Committee continues the investigation of a general criminal case on the commission, in Donbas, by representatives of Ukraine's power structures of grave and particularly grave crimes against the peace and security of Ukraine's mankind (*sic!*). The processing of the present criminal case combines 53 criminal cases [relative to] developments in southeastern Ukraine. Over 130 thousand persons were questioned as witnesses and victims, among them more than 22 thousand [persons] were recognised as victims.[4]

First of all, it is quite striking that both original news releases contained important errors of grammar (the errors are authentically reproduced in the English translations above), which distorted their meaning and, in this author's opinion, as such put in doubt their overall credibility as sources of official information. More importantly, in this case, the Investigative Committee misinterpreted the notion of genocide in that it included, respectively, "Russian-speaking citizens" and "a national group of Russian-speaking persons" within the range of groups protected by the Genocide Convention and Russia's own Criminal Code, and exceeded the limits of Russia's jurisdictional authority with respect to alleged acts. This chapter briefly discusses the Investigative Committee's faulty interpretation of groups protected by the definition of the crime of genocide, and Russia's abusive exercise of jurisdiction in the case at hand, to suggest that the prosecution exercise in question is one of "hybrid law enforcement", a part of the overall "hybrid warfare" effort. By contrast, the chapter does not consider allegations of war crimes, which are likewise present in the Investigative Committee's materials, for they are less manifestly representative of "hybrid law enforcement" in the ongoing international armed conflict: the Russian Federation *might* have jurisdiction with respect to war crimes committed in its armed conflict with Ukraine, as far as Donbas is concerned, but for this, Russia would have to officially acknowledge its participation in that part of the conflict.[5] Still, alleged war crimes committed in the armed conflict between Ukraine's authorities and non-State armed groups in the east of the country should remain, as a matter of law, outside Russia's criminal jurisdiction.[6]

15.2 Linguistic Groups Are Not Protected by the Definition of Genocide

At first glance, the Russian Federation's Investigative Committee's reference to "a national group of Russian-speaking persons" might appear both appropriate and creative. Russian language undeniably *is* an important social factor in Ukraine – it is widely spoken throughout the country, it is Ukraine's main minority language, and

---

[4] Ibid.

[5] Cf. First Geneva Convention, Article 49; Second Geneva Convention, Article 50; Third Geneva Convention, Article 129; Fourth Geneva Convention, Article 146; First Additional Protocol to the Geneva Conventions, Article 88.

[6] See this author's *amicus* memorandum in defence of Nadiya Savchenko, an English translation of which is reproduced in this volume.

is especially widespread in the east of the country: according to *Der Neue Fischer Weltalmanach 2017*, ethnic Russians constitute 17 per cent of Ukraine's population,[7] and 30 per cent of Ukraine's residents speak Russian as their first language.[8] Hence, showing convincingly that (the use of Russian) language was a ground for seeking to destroy, in whole or in part, a particular national group (Russians) within Ukraine could theoretically have been a sound ground for invoking "genocide", for language, along with religion, is an important (but not a decisive) factor in the construction of national identity.[9] In other words, the Investigative Committee might have potentially constructed a promising case on the linguistic factor, were it not for one considerable error: there is *no* such national group as "a national group of Russian-speaking persons".

Claiming otherwise would lead one to an outwardly absurd conclusion to the effect that anyone who speaks Russian as a first or second language belongs (or should belong) to the "national group of Russian-speaking persons". Indeed, Russian is used widely throughout the former Soviet Union,[10] it is an "official" language in some post-Soviet States,[11] and some nationals of such States (especially those who grew up in the Soviet Union) master Russian better than their own native languages – but none of these factors plausibly, let alone automatically, makes them or any other Russian speaker belong to "a national group of Russian-speaking persons". Werle recalls that "[t]he element that connects a national group, above all, is shared nationality. Additional elements to consider are a common history, customs, culture and *language*" (emphasis added, footnotes omitted).[12] Werle emphasises also, by reference to the *Kayishema and Ruzindana*, *Jelisić*, and *Krstić* Judgments, that a national group protected by the concept of genocide is defined by a combination of objective and subjective elements, including by such cumulative criteria as self-identification, and identification by others,[13] as well as by the relevant sociohistorical context.[14] An ethnic group would be defined by similar criteria[15] but we will not dwell upon them here, for reasons of space, since the Investigative Committee did not invoke the notion of "ethnic groups" in this case. Clearly, a reasonable interpretation of "national groups" should *not* embrace groups of ethnically different people who

---

[7] See Der Neue Fischer Weltalmanach 2017 (2016), p. 471.

[8] Ibid.

[9] See *passim* Joseph 2004.

[10] Cf. Article 13(2) of the Republic of Moldova: "The State shall acknowledge and protect the right to the preservation, development and use of the Russian language and other languages spoken within the territory of the State"; Article 2(2) of the Constitution of the Republic of Tajikistan: "Russian shall be the language of international communication".

[11] Cf. Article 7(2) of the Constitution of the Republic of Kazakhstan: "In state institutions and local self-administrative bodies the Russian language shall be officially used on equal grounds along with the Kazakh language"; Article 10(2) of the Constitution of the Kyrgyz Republic: "The Russian language shall be used as an official language in the Kyrgyz Republic".

[12] See Werle and Jessberger 2014, p. 298.

[13] Ibid., p. 296.

[14] Ibid., p. 297.

[15] Ibid., p. 299.

share the knowledge of a language, and employ it, more or less regularly, in their daily lives – in other words, the notions "national group" and "linguistic group" are not semantically equivalent, and the former may not be substituted by the latter. For this reason alone, the invocation of "genocide" with respect to a linguistic group must be deemed legally incorrect: if the Investigative Committee had, instead, limited itself to investigating allegations of "genocide" with respect of, for example, "a national or ethnic group of Russians resident in Ukraine", the qualification would arguably have been more appropriate in terms of Russia's domestic criminal law – it must be noted that Article 357 of Russia's Criminal Code does (appropriately) not list linguistic groups among the groups protected by the definition of genocide,[16] but it does list national groups, in line with the letter of the Convention on the Prevention and Punishment of the Crime of Genocide.[17] Hence, invoking the notion of "genocide" in this context was, at least, a professional mistake. Yet it is believed that "genocide" was brought into play more deliberately.

15.3 "Compatriots" as a Legal Notion in the Russian Federation

On 1 June 1999, the Russian Federation's Federal Law "On the State Policy with Respect to Compatriots Abroad" entered into force.[18] This Law introduced, in Article 1, the notion of "compatriots", which has ever since had increasingly significant implications:[19]

1. Compatriots are individuals born in the same State, who are or were resident in it, and having a common language, history, cultural heritage, traditions and customs, as well as the aforesaid individuals' direct descendants.

2. Compatriots abroad (hereinafter referred to as compatriots) are nationals of the Russian Federation, who are permanently resident outside the territory of the Russian Federation.

3. Recognised as compatriots are also individuals and their descendants who are resident outside the territory of the Russian Federation and belong, as a rule, to peoples historically resident in the territory of the Russian Federation, as well as those who have made a free choice in favour of a spiritual, cultural and legal link with the Russian Federation,

---

[16] Cf. Article 357 of Russia's Criminal Code ("Genocide"): "Actions aimed at the complete or partial extermination of a national, ethnic, racial or religious group as such by killing its members, inflicting grave injuries to their health, forcible prevention of childbirth, forcible transfer of children, forcible resettlement, or by any other method of creating living conditions meant for the physical destruction of the members of this group, shall be punishable by deprivation of liberty for a term of 12 to 20 years with restriction of liberty for a term of up to two years, or by deprivation of liberty for life, or by capital punishment".

[17] The text of the Convention is available at: http://www.ohchr.org/EN/ProfessionalInterest/Pages/CrimeOfGenocide.aspx. Accessed 31 July 2017. The Russian Federation succeeded to the Convention, which was ratified by the Soviet Union on 3 May 1954.

[18] For the text of the Law (in Russian), see: http://www.kremlin.ru/acts/bank/13875. Accessed 31 July 2017.

[19] Some of these implications are considered in this book, see Chap. 4 by Hassler and Quénivet.

whose direct ascendants were earlier resident in the territory of the Russian Federation, including:

persons who had the nationality of the USSR, are resident in States, which were members of the USSR, acquired the nationality of these States or became stateless persons;

natives (emigrants) of the Russian State, the Russian Republic, the RSFSR, the USSR and the Russian Federation, who had the respective national affiliation and became nationals of a foreign State or stateless persons.

As one can see, this Law's personal and functional reach potentially is quite far. Technically, it concerns virtually all nationals and permanent residents in each of fifteen States, of which the former Soviet Union was comprised, and creates ample opportunities for Russia's more or less direct interference in those States' domestic affairs under the formal pretexts of "the necessity to ensure compatriots' civil, political, social, economic, cultural and other rights and freedoms, as well as their lawful interests in the States of residence, in accordance with generally recognised principles and norms of international law" (Article 5(2)), of "ensuring the legal protection of their interests, as well as conditions whereby they could live, as citizens with equal rights, in foreign States, or return to the Russian Federation" (Article 5(3)), and in particular, "to use the Russian language and native languages of the peoples of the Russian Federation for the development of spiritual and intellectual potential" (Article 5(4)). A handy political invention, the notion of "compatriots" is convenient for its ambiguity, quasi-patriotic scent, potential to rally masses under populist slogans, and opportunities to retreat in case of failure. It also offers an arsenal of tools to test official and popular reactions in neighbouring States, and to promote several related agendas at a time. In this context, recent signals of discontent, in Russia, about Kazakhstan's gradual introduction of the Latin alphabet in the use of Kazakh language by 2025,[20] or the Russian Minister of Education and Science's call, made on 6 June 2017, to "return to a single alphabet in the CIS space",[21] are noteworthy. It appears fairly clear that such a use of the Russian language as a tool of "soft power"[22] goes, as a matter of principle, hand in hand with other – more direct and less delicate – calls, made by some high-ranking Russian officials, to the effect of

---

[20] See, for example, "Nazarbayev ob'yavil o perehode na latinitsu k 2025 godu" [Nazarbayev has announced a transition to the Latin alphabet by 2015], https://www.nur.kz/1463119-nazarbaev-obyavil-o-perekhode-na-latin.html. Accessed 31 July 2017.

[21] See, for example: "Vasilieva predlagayet ispolzovat kirillitsu v stranah byvshego SSSR" [Vasilieva suggests using the Cyrillic alphabet in the former USSR countries], http://ru.sputniknews-uz.com/society/20170606/5565742/vasileva-predlagaet-ispolzovat-kirillicy-v-stranah-sng.html. Accessed 31 July 2017. A direct quote attributed to Ms Vasilieva reads as follows: "So, now we have to return to a single alphabet in the CIS space – this is the Cyrillic alphabet, because, as surveys show, *our population, in the nearest abroad*, does speak of affiliation [with], and the necessity of the Cyrillic alphabet" (emphasis added). It is quite notable that Ms Vasilieva referred to the "population" of the "nearest abroad" (that is, the peoples of the former Soviet countries) as Russia's own population.

[22] See Mkrtchyan 2017.

restoring the territory of the former Soviet Union under Russia's authority.[23] Attempts at Ukraine's *patriacide*[24] since early 2014 – including the annexation of Crimea,[25] the military intervention in Donbas,[26] and repeated calls for Ukraine's "federalisation"[27] – with declared goals of "protecting the Russian population in Ukraine"[28] are links in the same chain of Russia's pursuing (some of) its foreign policy objectives not only by political means.[29] The "hybrid law enforcement" – such as the legally unsound prosecution of Ukrainian nationals on charges of genocide – must be a part of this policy.

15.4 "Hybrid Law Enforcement"

For the purpose of this chapter, "hybrid law enforcement" means a deliberately abusive application of substantive or procedural international criminal law by law enforcement agencies, with a view to attaining, or increasing, popular approval of overarching political undertakings, based on a lack of proper understanding of international criminal law and procedure among the general public. Of course, such a definition of "hybrid law enforcement" does not exclude, as a matter of principle, possible misunderstanding of international criminal law's nuances even by some law enforcement specialists – inaccuracies in the Investigative Committee's news releases quoted above testify to this – but as such, "hybrid law enforcement", like many other aspects in "hybrid warfare",[30] is calculated to contribute to producing popular reactions, and is remote from proper legal process.[31] Three essential factors proper to the "hybrid law enforcement" phenomenon are highlighted below.

---

[23] See "Deputat Gosdumy Fedorov: nasha tsel - vosstanovlenie istoricheskih granits russkogo gosudarstva po sostoyaniyu na 1945 god" [Member of the State Duma Fedorov: our goal is the reestablishment of the Russian State's historical borders as of 1945], http://gordonua.com/news/worldnews/deputat-gosdumy-fedorov-nasha-cel-vosstanovlenie-istoricheskih-granic-russkogo-gosudarstva-po-sostoyaniyu-na-1945-god-108253.html. Accessed 31 July 2017. A direct quote attributed to Mr Fedorov reads as follows: "The territory of the whole Soviet Union is, under international law, the territory of our Motherland, of our nation. And we have to return to those borders. And we will have to do this".

[24] This author has elsewhere defined *patriacide* as "the destruction of a State's constitutional, political, economic, or technical organisation inherent to its statehood". See Sayapin 2015, at 26; Sayapin 2014, at 75.

[25] See chapters by Azarova (Chap. 3), Bowring (Chap. 2), and Tsybulenko and Kelichavyi (Chap. 13) in this volume.

[26] See chapters by Merezhko (Chap. 5), and by Pakhomenko and Tryma (Chap. 14) in this volume.

[27] See Kendall 2014.

[28] See "Putin o zashchite russkogo naseleniya na Ukraine" [Putin on the protection of the Russian population in Ukraine], published at: https://www.youtube.com/watch?v=qLe0jTMnEfk. Accessed 31 July 2017.

[29] Cf. von Clausewitz 2002, p. 24.

[30] See Chap. 8 by Tóth in this volume.

[31] Cf. Marchenko 2013, pp. 684–691.

15.4.1 Principle of Legality

The principle of legality (*nullum crimen sine lege*), as understood in criminal law, means that the definition of a crime must be construed specifically and narrowly, and should not allow for analogy or any extensive interpretations.[32] As was shown above, Russia's Investigative Committee included in the notion of "genocide" a linguistic group, in plain violation of its own Criminal Code and the Genocide Convention. The utility of such a misplacement of concepts is quite obvious: one should not be surprised that an allegedly "fascist"[33] government is found engaged in "genocidal" activities, and if such an engagement is confirmed as a result of a "legal process", both the image and authority of such a government should suffer irreparable losses. "Genocide" is a label, like terrorism: once an individual or an entity has been labelled with participating in "genocide", one should become virtually excluded from any civilised political dialogue, and lose legitimacy as a political actor.[34] Of course, in order for a desired effect to be there, the mass media must do their job.

15.4.2 Media Coverage

Quite surprisingly, atrocity crimes – even genocide – did not always receive quick and massive popular attention. Even the Nazi death camps, as they were exposed in the Western media towards the end of the Second World War, did not become a sensation.[35] Since then, however, the role of the mass media in armed conflicts and other situations of violence became more significant.[36] In addition to reporting facts, as faithfully as they possibly can, the mass media are crucial in shaping public opinion – and, more often than not, in manipulating the collective conscience. In the ongoing "hybrid" conflict between Russia and Ukraine, both formal and informal mass media (such as bloggers and "trolls")[37] were instrumental from its very beginning. As far as the issue at stake is concerned, a Google search for "genocide in Ukraine 2014" (in Russian) produces about 3.300.000 results – professional and amateur articles, blogs, videos – published, chiefly, in the Russian segment of the Internet (and calculated to shape massive anti-Ukrainian sentiments within a rather short time span) but also

---

[32] See Werle and Jessberger 2014, pp. 39–40.

[33] The alleged "resurgence of fascism in Ukraine" is a popular topic in the contemporary political discourse in Russia. See, for example, "Mirovye uchenye: Zapad privel k vlasti na Ukraine fashistov" [World scholars: the West has brought fascists to power in Ukraine], https://www.pravda.ru/news/world/14-03-2017/1327295-ukraine-0/. Accessed 31 July 2017.

[34] Cf. *passim* Sayapin 2004.

[35] See Rees 2014, p. 355.

[36] For a collection of brilliant pieces of investigative journalism, see *passim* Pilger 2004.

[37] According to RBC, Russia's largest media holding emerged only within the two past years, see "V nedrah "fabriki trolley" vyros krupneyshiy v Rossii mediaholding" [The largest media holding in Russia grew out of a "troll factory"], http://www.rbc.ru/technology_and_media/23/03/2017/58d2c2df9a7947273ccb28e5. Accessed 31 July 2017.

on some Ukrainian and other websites. According to some professional opinions,[38] Russia was better prepared for the "media war" with Ukraine – not least, due to the involvement of the "expert community".

15.4.3 "Expert" Opinions

In order for a message to be successful, it should not be simply imparted but it must be imparted by an "expert". Of course, opinions expressed by laymen – such as witnesses of alleged crimes, friends and relatives who empathise with victims, new neighbours of refugees fleeing from the dangers of war, etc. – do appeal, especially emotionally, to audiences composed of like laymen. However, messages of particular importance should be imparted by experts (certainly, the higher the rank of an expert, the better) – this adds both to the credibility of and durability of messages, for, unlike a layman's singular opinion, an expert opinion can be reproduced many times and in different formats, such as interviews, comments, journalist articles, and the like, to achieve maximum impact. Thus, the "genocide of the Russian people in Ukraine" was invoked, among others, by the Deputy Chairman of the State Duma Committee for Constitutional Legislation and State Construction Vadim Soloviev,[39] and a well-known politician and political scientist Sergey Kurginyan.[40] As unsound as these allegations are in terms of applicable law, they certainly do reach out to laymen whose principal (if not exclusive) source of information is Russia's State-controlled television. "Genocide" is a label, which is easy to use and more difficult to wash away.

Notably, in addition to individuals claiming to have expert knowledge of (international) criminal law, Russian mass media were repeatedly spotted engaging professional actors and actresses – also experts in their respective field – in the propaganda effort. This approach was at least dually useful: actors are excellent at reproducing human emotions typical to situations of armed conflicts (such as anger, distress, sorrow, etc.) more vividly than non-professionals, and can be effectively employed in multiple scenarios, hence some actors were spotted on different occasions and on different TV channels, playing different roles.[41] As promising as the strategy of engaging professional actors potentially was, many instances of such a staged engagement were successfully exposed by volunteers.[42]

---

[38] See Danilenko 2015.

[39] See Soloviev 2015.

[40] See "Kurginyan: ideologiey "svidomyh i nesvidomyh" Kiev obyavlyaet genotsid russkih" [Kurginyan: Kyiv is calling for a genocide of Russians through the ideology of "conscious and not conscious [ones]"], http://rossaprimavera.ru/news/kurginyan-ideologiey-svidomyh-i-nesvidomyh-kiev-obyavlyaet-genocid. Accessed 31 July 2017.

[41] See, for example, "Top-10 feykov rossiskoy propagandy v 2016 godu" [Top 10 fakes of Russian propaganda in 2016], https://informnapalm.org/31645-top-10-fejkov-rossijskoj-propagandy-2016/ Accessed 31 July 2017.

[42] Ibid.

15.5 Russia Has No Jurisdiction with Respect to Alleged Individual Acts of "Genocide" Committed in the Territory of Ukraine

Finally, it remains to be shown that the prosecution exercise undertaken by the Investigative Committee is void, because the Russian Federation had no valid jurisdictional ground to institute criminal proceedings, on charges of genocide, against nationals of Ukraine either under international or under its own domestic law. Article VI of the Genocide Convention provides:

> Persons charged with genocide or any of the other acts enumerated in article III shall be tried by a competent tribunal of the State in the territory of which the act was committed, or by such international penal tribunal as may have jurisdiction with respect to those Contracting Parties which shall have accepted its jurisdiction.

Thus, even if any of the alleged acts could have been qualified as genocide, Russia should have had no jurisdiction with respect to any of them. In the given circumstances, in accordance with the Genocide Convention, such jurisdiction would have been reserved only to Ukraine itself, or, theoretically, to the International Criminal Court (ICC), under Article 5 of the Rome Statute, with due regard to Ukraine's declarations under Article 12(3) of the same Statute.[43] The principle of territorial jurisdiction is a fundamental principle of international criminal law, recognised universally as a manifestation of State sovereignty.[44] The principle of territorial jurisdiction is superior to any other principle of criminal jurisdiction in that other jurisdictional principles apply when a territorial State is unable or unwilling to prosecute an individual suspected or accused or a crime in question.[45] The relationship between the principle of territorial criminal jurisdiction is expressed, as far as the direct enforcement of international criminal law is concerned, in the rule of complementarity,[46] and as far as the indirect enforcement of international criminal law is concerned, in the rule to the effect that individuals should be tried for crimes committed abroad, if they were not tried in the State where the crimes in question were committed. In terms of domestic criminal law, Ukraine would have been well prepared to prosecute individuals charged with genocide committed within its territory: Ukraine's territorial jurisdiction would have derived from Article 6 of its Criminal Code,[47] whereas the elements of the crime are included in the Code's Article 442. Clearly, references made in the Investigative Committee's news release of 29 September 2014 to "the Donetsk and Luhansk republics", and, in the news release of 8 September 2016, to "the self-proclaimed Donetsk People's Republic", have no legal significance, since

---

[43] On Ukraine's declarations under Article 12(3), see: https://www.icc-cpi.int/ukraine. Accessed 31 July 2017.

[44] On the principle of territorial jurisdiction, see Cryer et al. 2014, pp. 52–53; Kittichaisaree 2001, p. 6; Paust et al. 2007, p. 175.

[45] See Cryer et al. 2014, p. 53.

[46] Cf. Article 17 of the ICC Statute.

[47] Cf. Article 6 of Ukraine's Criminal Code.

none of these so-called "republics" is a State in its own right.[48] Notably, despite the enactment of a "Criminal Code",[49] the "Donetsk People's Republic" did not itself institute any criminal proceedings on charges of genocide (under Article 428 of the "Code") – instead, the Russian Federation "took over" jurisdiction on dubious grounds.

In accordance with Article 12(3) the Criminal Code of the Russian Federation, "[f]oreign nationals and stateless persons who do not reside permanently in the Russian Federation and who have committed a crime outside the Russian Federation shall be held criminally responsible under this Code, *if the crime is directed against the interests of the Russian Federation or a citizen of the Russian Federation or a stateless person permanently residing in the Russian Federation, as well as in cases provided for in an international treaty of the Russian Federation, or in another document of an international character, which contains obligations recognised by the Russian Federation, in a field regulated by this Code*, unless the foreign citizens and stateless persons not residing permanently in the Russian Federation have been convicted in a foreign state and are held criminally responsible on the territory of the Russian Federation" (emphasis added). Hence Russia's extraterritorial jurisdiction with respect to the alleged "genocide" would have been appropriate in either of the three alternative scenarios: (1) the crime in question should have been directed against Russia's interests; (2) the crime in question should have been directed against a Russian national or permanent resident; and (3) jurisdiction should have been reserved, or permitted, to Russia by an applicable treaty or another international legal document. However, none of these alternatives were present since the beginning of the armed conflict in 2014: Russia did not claim that any harm was caused to its interests as a result of the alleged "genocide", no national or permanent resident of Russia became a victim of the alleged "genocide", and the Genocide Convention itself – in the language of Article 12(3) of Russia's Criminal Code, an applicable international treaty of the Russian Federation – provides clearly that jurisdiction over genocide is only due to a territorial State, or to an appropriate international penal tribunal. It does not provide for universal jurisdiction over the crime of genocide.[50] Hence the Russian Federation, in having instituted criminal prosecutions with respect to alleged genocide, clearly exceeded the limits of extraterritorial criminal jurisdiction delineated both in its own Criminal Code and in the Genocide Convention.

---

[48] Whereas the employment of these designations by the Investigative Committee and other organs of the Russian Federation, as well as by State-owned mass media could arguably testify to Russia's recognition of the so-called "Donetsk and Luhansk Peoples' Republics" *de facto*, not even Russia recognised them *de jure*, and they could not claim to be States under international law. On recognition of States in international law, see Crawford 2011, 12–28.

[49] For the text of the "Criminal Code" of the "Donetsk People's Republic" (as of 3 March 2015), see: http://advokaty.dn.ua/criminal-codex-dnr. Accessed 31 July 2017.

[50] On the principle of universal jurisdiction, see Cryer et al. 2014, pp. 56–68; Paust et al. 2007, pp. 155–174; Werle and Jessberger 2014, pp. 73–83.

As far as the jurisdiction of the ICC is concerned, the ICC Prosecutor, in her annual Report on Preliminary Examination Activities, which was published on 14 November 2016,[51] made no allegation of genocide (see paras 171 – 183), and only listed crimes against humanity and war crimes as alleged crimes within the jurisdiction of the Court, which had been potentially committed in Crimea and Eastern Ukraine since 21 November 2013.[52] No doubt, the Prosecutor would have mentioned genocide in her report, had there been sound legal grounds to do so. It should be recalled that the ICC Prosecutor investigates alleged crimes committed by all sides in a situation in question, and so, the absence of a reference to "genocide" in her report may not be regarded as simply a technical omission: if the Ukrainian side had pursued a genocidal policy with respect to an identifiable protected group, this would have certainly been appropriately mentioned in the report. The ICC Prosecutor did not refer to genocide, because, on the basis of facts, there was no evidence of the crime's distinct *corpus delicti*, as understood in international criminal law.

15.6   Conclusion

The institution of criminal proceedings on charges of "genocide of Russian-speaking persons" in Eastern Ukraine by the Russian Federation's Investigative Committee is far from proper legal process. The prosecution is manifestly inconsistent with applicable international criminal law and Russia's own domestic criminal law, and represents, along with other elements of "hybrid warfare" an instance of "hybrid law enforcement". In international and domestic criminal law, the principle of legality (*nullum crimen sine lege*) is fundamental. This principle does not allow for analogy or extensive interpretation of the elements of a crime. Since the *corpus delicti* of the crime of genocide does not cover linguistic groups, the invocation of this crime with respect to "Russian-speaking persons" in Ukraine is incorrect. Likewise, the Russian Federation has no criminal jurisdiction with respect to alleged genocide committed abroad, since such exclusive jurisdiction is limited to territorial States, and the International Criminal Court (ICC). Extending such jurisdiction extraterritorially, for the purpose of protecting "compatriots" abroad, is not in conformity with customary international law, and could be invoked by Ukraine as a violation of general international law.

---

[51] See the text of the Report at: https://www.icc-cpi.int/iccdocs/otp/161114-otp-rep-PE_ENG.pdf Accessed 31 July 2017.

[52] On the legal significance of the ICC Prosecutor's Report, see Chap. 18 by Atadjanov in this volume, and Sayapin 2016.

References

Crawford J (2011) The Creation of States in International Law, 2nd edn. Oxford University Press, Oxford

Cryer R, Friman H, Robinson D, Wilmshurst E (2014) An Introduction to International Criminal Law and Procedure, 3rd edn. Cambridge University Press, Cambridge

Danilenko S (2015) "Informatsionnaya voyna Rossii protiv Ukrainy: uroki dlya Evropy" [Russia's information war against Ukraine: lessons for Europe], https://delo.ua/opinions/informacionnaja-vojna-rossii-protiv-ukrainy-uroki-dlja-evropy-291526/. Accessed 31 July 2017

Der Neue Fischer Weltalmanach 2017 (2016) S. Fischer Verlag GmbH

International Criminal Court. Office of the Prosecutor (2016) Report on Preliminary Examination Activities. https://www.icc-cpi.int/iccdocs/otp/161114-otp-rep-PE_ENG.pdf. Accessed 31 July 2017

Investigative Committee of the Russian Federation (2014) Sledstvennyy komitet vozbudil ugolovnoye delo o genotside russkoyazychnogo naseleniya na yugo-vostoke Ukrainy "The Investigative Committee has instituted a criminal case on the genocide of the Russian-speaking population in the southeast of Ukraine]. http://sledcom.ru/news/item/523738/. Accessed 31 July 2017

Investigative Committee of the Russian Federation (2016) Vozbuzhdeny eshche dva ugolovnyh dela v svyazi s sobytiyami na yugo-vostoke Ukrainy [Two more criminal cases were instituted in connection with developments in the southeast of Ukraine]. http://sledcom.ru/news/item/106 5642/. Accessed 31 July 2017

Joseph JE (2004) Language and Identity: National, Ethnic, Religious. Palgrave Macmillan UK, London

Kendall B (2014) Federalizatsiya Ukrainy v voprosah i otvetah [The federalisation of Ukraine in questions and answers], http://www.bbc.com/russian/international/2014/04/140402_ukraine_federation_q_and_a. Accessed 31 July 2017

Kittichaisaree K (2001) International Criminal Law. Oxford University Press, Oxford

Marchenko MN (2013) Problemy teorii gosudarstva i prava [Issues in the theory of State and law]. Prospect, Moscow

Mkrtchyan A (2017) "Myagkaya sila" russkogo medvedya [The Russian bear's "soft power"], http://inosmi.ru/politic/20170720/239852604.html. Accessed 31 July 2017

Paust JJ, Bassiouni MC, Scharf M, Gurulé J, Sadat L, Zagaris B (2007) International Criminal Law: Cases and Materials, 3rd edn. Carolina Academic Press, Durham, North Carolina

Pilger J (2004) Tell Me No Lies: Investigative Journalism and Its Triumphs. Vintage, London

Rees L (2014) Osventsim: Natsisty i "okonchatelnoe reshenie evreyskogo voprosa" [Auschwitz: The Nazis and the "Final Solution"]. CoLibri, Moscow

Sayapin S (2004) The Application of the Fair Trial Guarantees to Alleged Terrorists in Non-International Armed Conflicts. Humanitäres Völkerrecht – Informationsschriften 17:152–159

Sayapin S (2014) Territorialnaya tselostnost Ukrainy v svete Rezolyutsii 68/262 Generalnoy Assamblei OON [The Territorial Integrity of Ukraine in the Light of the UN General Assembly Resolution 68/262]. Journal of Constitutionalism and Human Rights 5:66–80

Sayapin S (2015) The United Nations General Assembly Resolution 68/262 in the Context of General International Law. European Political and Law Discourse 2(1):19–30

Sayapin S (2016) Russia's Withdrawal of Signature from the Rome Statute Would not Shield its Nationals from Potential Prosecution at the ICC. EJIL: Talk! http://www.ejiltalk.org/russias-withdrawal-of-signature-from-the-rome-statute-would-not-shield-its-nationals-from-potential-prosecution-at-the-icc/. Accessed 31 July 2017

Soloviev V (2015) Ostanovit boynyu i genotsid russkogo naroda na Ukraine - eto ogromnoe delo [Stopping the slaughtering and genocide of the Russian people in Ukraine is a great deal], http://www.km.ru/world/2015/02/14/protivostoyanie-na-ukraine-2013-2015/754871 -v-solovev-prekratit-boinyu-i-genotsid-r. Accessed 31 July 2017

von Clausewitz C (2002) O voyne [On war], volume I. Terra Fantastica, Moscow
Werle G, Jessberger F (2014) Principles of International Criminal Law, 3rd edn. Oxford University
    Press, Oxford

Part III
Jus Post Bellum

Chapter 16
The Conflict in Ukrainian Donbas: International, Regional and Comparative Perspectives on the *Jus Post Bellum* Options

Gerhard Kemp and Igor Lyubashenko

Contents

Gerhard Kemp, Professor of Law, Stellenbosch University, and senior research fellow, Robert Bosch Academy, Berlin.
Igor Lyubashenko, Assistant Professor, SWPS University of Social Sciences and Humanities, Warsaw. Research for this contribution was made possible by grant no. 2016/23/D/HS5/02600 from the National Science Centre, Poland.

G. Kemp (✉)
Stellenbosch University, Stellenbosch, South Africa
e-mail: Gkemp@sun.ac.za

G. Kemp
Robert Bosch Academy, Berlin, Germany

I. Lyubashenko
SWPS University of Social Sciences and Humanities, Warsaw, Poland
e-mail: igor.lyubashenko@gmail.com

© T.M.C. ASSER PRESS and the authors 2018
S. Sayapin and E. Tsybulenko (eds.), *The Use of Force against Ukraine and International Law*, https://doi.org/10.1007/978-94-6265-222-4_16

Abstract The past two decades have produced a substantial body of theoretical and practical insights into the field collectively known as post-conflict studies. Various modalities, including criminal justice responses, truth commissions, and hybrid modalities are aimed at post-conflict peace, justice and reconciliation. This chapter explores, first of all, relevant theoretical frames in the context of post-conflict studies. Comparative national and regional insights are also considered. The chapter deals, in the second place, with the armed conflict in the east of Ukraine as a contemporary problem in flux. In conclusion, the theoretical insights gained from a consideration of the national, regional and international frameworks on post-conflict theories and modalities are applied to the situation in Ukraine, with due regard for the fact that the situation is, indeed, still very much fluid.

Keywords Post-conflict studies · Truth · Peace · Justice · Transitional justice modalities

> For some, the war is something terrible, something black, but at the same time something very distant and quite safe, if one doesn't approach it and doesn't think about it. It is bitter, but self-resolving. For others, it is a dark forest, where they try to orient themselves but fail, making their way through the thicket of agitation and wailing, through the fence of cynical lies and bashful half-truths.[1]
>
> Serhiy Rakhmanin

16.1 A Brief Primer on Transitional and Post-conflict Justice

Under the collective term *jus post bellum* we include the broad fields of post-conflict justice and transitional justice. These terms are sometimes used interchangeably. To complicate matters further it should be noted that there are a plethora of other terms that are used either as interchangeable alternatives to transitional justice and post-conflict studies, or as sub-categories of either field. One will therefore find in literature also references to terms such as restorative justice, post-conflict peacemaking, reconstruction, and peace-building.[2] Depending on the context and the situation at hand, one could certainly employ some or all of these terms and the considerable bodies of literature that underscore them.[3] For present purposes we will mainly use the terms post-conflict justice and transitional justice. *Post-conflict justice*, then, refers to 'policies and strategies aimed at addressing the immediate cessation of conflict, reconciliation, addressing victims' needs, and ideally ensuring accountability for the atrocities and crimes committed, directly or indirectly, from the individual

---

[1] Rakhmanin 2017 (translated from the Russian).

[2] Rothe and Maggard 2012, p. 193.

[3] Ibid., at 195–198, for a useful overview. For theoretical expositions, see Fischer 2011; Teitel 2000. On post-conflict justice, see Bassiouni 2002, and, more recently, Saul and Sweeney 2015.

perpetrators to those orchestrating the conditions and mandates associated with the crimes committed.'[4] By comparison, the interdisciplinary field of *transitional justice* can be described as 'a toolkit that facilitates the establishment of "justice" and rule of law in post-conflict societies. The specific goals are to bring about the right to "truth", access to "justice", victims' right to "reparation", and the right to recognition of their suffering and to have their dignity restored – but the goals are also social reconciliation and to secure the non-repetition of violations.'[5]

An important, but contentious aspect of *jus post bellum* is the question of inclusive or collective memory, and the concomitant need for public discourse on past events, history, the present situation, and the way forward. It is so that 'active forgetting' may very well be the best *post bellum* strategy of all, and that there should at least be the option of forgetting, without which we may end up being 'wounded monsters, unforgiving and unforgiven... and, assuming that we have been paying attention, inconsolable'.[6] But this view is, arguably, an outlier. Instead, truth commissions as exponents of *jus post bellum* are typically presented as appropriate fora to facilitate and record processes on collective memory as well as individual narratives about past atrocities. 'Truth' is in itself a contentious notion – especially in the context of post conflict settings. We therefore devote a section of this chapter to ponder the meaning of truth in the context of *jus post bellum* strategies.

Reparations for past injustices and human rights violations forms another key component of *jus post bellum* strategies.[7] But reparations is also one of the most controversial aspects of *jus post bellum*. Indeed, as Rodrigo Uprimny Yepes pointed out, 'reparation prompts difficult paradoxes and dilemmas for societies that are settling an armed conflict or an authoritarian regime, in which large-scale gross human rights violations were committed.'[8]

It is clear from the above explanation that *just post bellum* strategies can, and sometimes should, include criminal prosecutions of individuals responsible for serious human rights violations. However, an important principle of transitional justice is that the criminal justice response to atrocities, violence and strife, should really be the last resort. This approach aligns with the *ultima ratio* principle in criminal law theory, namely that criminal law should not be regarded as the first response to unacceptable human conduct, but as the last response, and only in cases of the most harmful conduct. Criminal punishment should therefore only be regarded as appropriate when other available remedies fail.[9] At any rate, the factual matrix informing a *jus post bellum* question often involves structural or collective issues not necessarily susceptible to assigning individual guilt via criminal trials.[10]

---

[4] Rothe and Maggard 2012, at 194. The authors pointed out that this definition is compatible with the 2004 United Nations definition of transitional justice (which we also deal with below).

[5] Bengoetxea 2013, p. 32.

[6] Rieff 2016, p. 145.

[7] For detailed discussions, see De Feyter et al. 2005; Du Plessis and Pete 2007.

[8] Yepes 2009, p. 626.

[9] Bengoetxea 2013, at 50; Fletcher 2005, p. 31.

[10] Bengoetxea 2013, at 50.

One of the key strategic aspects of post-conflict and transitional justice options that we will address in this chapter is the question of sequencing, or, the temporal element of *jus post bellum*. This aspect refers to the best or most suitable moment to implement a particular aspect of the chosen post conflict justice modality or modalities. This is important because *jus post bellum* is rarely a single event or process. It often involves multiple (and sequenced) processes. The particular facts on the ground and the historical context of the conflict will be important, as we will see. Also important in this regard is to recognize that transitional justice, as one of the main components of *jus post bellum* can be understood as 'justice in the context of transition after conflict' and as 'justice to facilitate transition'.[11] While these two meanings of transitional justice seem to suggest a clean separation between *conflict* and *post-conflict*, the reality is that many situations, including the current situation in Ukraine which forms the subject of this book, are often more complex and not neatly divisible between the era of the conflict and the era of the post-conflict. It is therefore preferable to view *jus post bellum* strategies as a *normative process* with perhaps three diachronic stages[12] that address aspects of the past, the present and the future. Concerning the latter aspect, it should be obvious that *jus post bellum* would be meaningless if it did not also entail a prognostic element, and the guarantee of non-repetition. This may involve various actions aimed at collective and individual cohesion, including the social inclusion of former perpetrators of human rights violations.[13]

16.2 A Note on Demarcation

As the title of this chapter suggests, our focus is on the conflict in Ukrainian Donbas. The choice of our focus is informed by several factors. First, the aim of this chapter is not to provide an all-encompassing discussion and roadmap for *all* post-conflict options regarding the *multifaceted* situation in Ukraine (Euromaidan, Eastern Ukraine/Donbas-conflict, and annexation of Crimea). The sheer scale and scope of the issues would make it difficult to fit into a chapter of this nature. Second, our aim is to use the conflict in Ukrainian Donbas specifically as factual matrix and situational frame for the exploration of theoretical post-conflict modalities. Our decision to focus on the Donbas should by no means be read as a suggestion that the annexation of Crimea or the Euromaidan-related violence are somehow irrelevant for purposes of a *jus post bellum* analysis. Indeed, we fully accept that all these issues fall within a broad factual complex, currently under consideration at two international tribunals – the International Court of Justice (ICJ) and the International Criminal Court (ICC). It is not our aim to consider the merits of the application before the ICJ in the matter of

---

[11] Ibid., at 34.

[12] Ibid., at 35–36.

[13] Ibid., at 51.

Ukraine v Russian Federation,[14] or of the preliminary examination into the situation in Ukraine by the Prosecutor[15] of the ICC. Both matters concern a range of factual allegations which encompass more than just the Donbas conflict. The outcomes (if any) of these legal processes will of course have direct consequences for whatever we consider in this chapter to be options *beyond* narrow curial-centered approaches to post-conflict situations. However, in a sense, the legal matters are both factually broader and conceptually narrower in terms of what we want to achieve in this chapter. Our focus on the conflict in Donbas should therefore be seen as a *case study* of *jus post bellum* options, considered against the background of an international, regional and comparative theoretical framework, and with a *realistic chance of application* in order to further the goals of peace and justice in Ukraine. Perhaps our proposals or suggestions would be applicable *mutatis mutandis* to the other situations (including illegally occupied Crimea); we certainly do not pretend that the Donbas conflict is not part of a whole.

16.3   *Jus Post Bellum* and the Sensibilities of the International Community

Post-conflict modalities of transitional justice are normally established within certain legal, geographical and political contexts; they are usually associated with conflicts within states; not so much with conflicts involving more than one state. This is not to say that post-conflict justice is a parochial matter, devoid of any cosmopolitan imperatives. It is clear that the establishment of national truth commissions, frameworks by international bodies, including the United Nations, as well as reports by eminent voices in the fields of international human rights law and conflict prevention, prefaced the arrival of the International Criminal Court, which is the only permanent post-conflict justice institution which focusses on criminal justice, even though the survivability of this institution is somewhat contentious.[16]

---

[14] Application of the International Convention for the Suppression of the Financing of Terrorism and the International Convention on the Elimination of All Forms of Racial Discrimination (*Ukraine v Russian Federation*). http://www.icj-cij.org/docket/files/166/19310.pdf. Last accessed 31 March 2017. The matter concerns a number of factual allegations, including the shoot-down of Malaysian Airlines Flight MH17, the shelling of civilians in various towns and regions of Ukraine, activities by the Russian armed forces in occupied Crimea, the financing by the Russian Federation of acts of terrorism in Ukraine, and the suppression of the political and cultural practices of the Crimean Tatar People by the Russian authorities in occupied Crimea.

[15] Report on Preliminary Examination Activities (2016). The Office of the Prosecutor, International Criminal Court. https://www.icc-cpi.int/iccdocs/otp/161114-otp-rep-PE_ENG.pdf. Last accessed 31 March 2017. The report deals with the factual situations regarding the Maidan events (p. 34), the events in Crimea and Eastern Ukraine from 20 February 2014 onwards (p. 34), Crimea (pp. 35–36), and Eastern Ukraine (pp. 36–38).

[16] Bassiouni 2010, p. 296.

Kofi Annan's 2004 report, The Rule of Law and Transitional Justice in Conflict and Post-conflict Societies,[17] can be viewed as a kind of *vade mecum* of lessons learnt, actualities and the way forward with regard to post-conflict justice. Indeed, post-conflict justice is defined in the former Secretary-General's report as 'the full range of processes and mechanisms associated with a society's attempts to come to terms with a legacy of large scale past abuses, in order to ensure accountability, serve justice and achieve reconciliation'.[18] This understanding of post-conflict justice provides for both judicial and non-judicial mechanisms, 'with differing levels of international involvement (or none at all) and individual prosecutions, reparation, truth-seeking, institutional reform, vetting and dismissals or a combination thereof'.[19]

The aforementioned understanding of post-conflict justice is premised on a law-centric approach that emphasizes the various legal mechanisms that enable the transition from conflict to peace; from authoritarian rule to democracy; from oppression to freedom. The notion of post-conflict justice articulated in the Annan report was followed in 2012 by a more concrete step when the UN Human Rights Council appointed the Special Rapporteur on the Promotion of Truth, Justice, Reparation and Guarantees of Non-recurrence. The mandate of the Special Rapporteur, which includes situations in which there have been gross violations of human rights and serious violations of international humanitarian law, was extended in 2014 for a further period of three years. The Human Rights Council resolution on the mandate of the Special Rapporteur stated the following broad goals: 'preventing the recurrence of crises and future violations of human rights, to ensure social cohesion, nation-building, ownership and inclusiveness at the national and local levels and to promote reconciliation'.[20]

Remedial action, in the context of post-conflict justice, is a function of collective, institutional and individual considerations. The Basic Principles and Guidelines on the Right to Remedy and Reparation for Victims of Gross Violations of International Human Rights Law and Serious Violations of International Humanitarian Law,[21] adopted by the UN General Assembly in 2005,[22] mentions a number of responses that would be suitable in a post-conflict context, namely prosecutions, truth commissions, reparations, memorials, and institutional reforms. Crucially, the General Assembly document also provides for a definition of 'victim' as

> persons who individually or collectively suffered hard, including physical or mental injury, emotional suffering, economic loss or substantial impairment of their fundamental rights,

---

[17] The rule of law and transitional justice in conflict and post-conflict societies, UN. https://www.un.org/ruleoflaw/files/2004%20report.pdf. Last accessed 23 March 2017.

[18] The rule of law and transitional justice in conflict and post-conflict societies, para 8.

[19] Ibid., para 8.

[20] Report by UN Human Rights Council Special Rapporteur. http://www.ohchr.org/EN/Issues/TruthJusticeReparation/Pages/Index.aspx. Last accessed 23 March 2017.

[21] For background and analysis, see Van Boven 2010.

[22] Basic Principles and Guidelines on the Right to a Remedy and Reparations for Victims of Gross Violations of International Human Rights law and Serious Violations of International Humanitarian Law, UNGA A/RES/60/147, 16 December 2005. http://www.un.org/en/ga/search/view_doc.asp?symbol=A/RES/60/147. Last accessed 23 March 2017.

through acts or omissions that constitute gross violations of international human rights law, or serious violations of international humanitarian law. Where appropriate, and in accordance with domestic law, the term 'victim' also includes the immediate family or dependents of the direct victim of persons who have suffered harm in intervening to assist victims in distress or to prevent victimization.[23]

From the above description we can deduce that the basic UN architecture on post-conflict justice include a variety of modalities, all of which are dependent on national will and national legal and political conditions.

16.4   Regional Responses to Post-conflict Justice Discourse

Two regional bodies, the European Union (EU) and the African Union (AU), have made considerable progress towards regional institutional commitments toward post conflict justice. Indeed, some would argue that, in the case of Europe, transitional justice strategies, such as responses to war, genocide, civil war, democratization efforts, reconstruction, and reunification in the aftermath of the Cold War, form the underlying normative drivers of the integration and peace project.[24]

16.4.1   EU Frameworks

In 2015 the EU adopted the Policy Framework on Support to Transitional Justice,[25] which forms part of the implementation of the EU Action Plan on Human Rights and Democracy 2015–2019.[26] Action 22(b) of this Plan[27] outlines the ongoing commitment to develop and implement an EU policy on Transitional Justice. To this end, provision should be made for a framework for EU support to transitional justice mechanisms and processes and enhance the EU's ability to play a more active and consistent role, both in terms of engagement with partner countries and with international and regional organisations. So the Policy Framework sets out more concretely steps that the EU can take in order to engage in post-conflict situations and situations of mass human rights violations and serious violations of international humanitarian law. Like the UN architecture referred to above, the EU Framework also foresees manifold responses that are context-specific and should be aimed at the promotion

---

[23] Ibid., para 8.

[24] Bengoetxea 2013, at 40.

[25] EU Policy Framework on Support to Transitional Justice. http://eeas.europa.eu/archives/docs/top_stories/pdf/the_eus_policy_framework_on_support_to_transitional_justice.pdf. Last accessed 23 March 2017.

[26] EU Action Plan on Human Rights and Democracy 2015–2019. https://eeas.europa.eu/human_rights/docs/eu_action_plan_on_human_rights_and_democracy_en.pdf. Last accessed 23 March 2017.

[27] P. 35.

of truth, justice, reparations and guarantees of non-recurrence. Crucially, the Framework does not envisage any grand institutional creations. Rather, it portends to be a continuation and complementary effort regarding the EU's existing strong policy in support of the International Criminal Court[28] and it also takes account of the UN framework and activities. The EU Policy Framework is decidedly decentralised and emphasises the roles that local and national stakeholders should play. It also underscores the objectives of inclusivity, gender sensitivity and state's obligations under international law. On the whole, it is clear that the Framework sees transitional justice as integral to state-and peace-building; and as embedded in crisis response modus operandi, conflict prevention, and security and developmental efforts of the EU.

16.4.2 African Union Frameworks

In Africa, wars of national liberation, civil wars, mass human rights violations, genocide and interstate armed conflicts prompted a plethora of post-conflict modalities and institutions. These include international criminal tribunals,[29] special courts,[30] truth commissions,[31] and the utilization of traditional courts.[32] It is not the aim here to assess the relative success or impact of these modalities. However, it is relevant to note the efforts of prominent individuals, civil society as well as the African Union to digest and to systematize the region's various approaches to post-conflict and transitional justice. The most important initiative resulted in the draft AU Transitional Justice Policy Framework (AU-TJPF).[33] The framework is yet to be adopted. The draft text is the result of various workshops and symposia under the auspices of the so-called AU Panel of the Wise. The original impetus for a systematic approach to post-conflict justice in Africa was provided by the 2009 AU High Level Panel Report on Darfur,[34] also known as the Mbeki-Report, after the former President of South Africa who chaired the panel on the conflict in Darfur. Indeed, the Mbeki Report contained the kernel of an African understanding of the importance and util-

---

[28] EU Policy Framework Ch II, para 1.

[29] First, the *ad hoc* international criminal tribunal for Rwanda (1995); later the International Criminal Court for a number of African situations, including the first so-called self-referrals (Central African Republic, Democratic Republic of Congo, and Uganda).

[30] Notably the Special Court for Sierra Leone.

[31] Notably the South African Truth and Reconciliation Commission. Numerous other truth commissions, fact-finding commissions and other variations of these modalities were established in countries such as Algeria, Liberia, Kenya, and Sudan, amongst others. For a summary of each of these, see Fombad (2008).

[32] Most prominently, the use of *gacaca* courts in Rwanda in the aftermath of the 1994 genocide.

[33] AU Transitional Justice Policy Framework. http://lawyersofafrica.org/wp-content/uploads/2014/11/AUTJF.pdf. Last accessed 23 March 2017.

[34] Report of the AU High Level Panel on Darfur, Peace and Security Council 207th meeting at the level of the Heads of State and Government, 29 Oct 2009, Abuja, Nigeria, PSG/AHG/2 (CCVII).

ity of post-conflict justice, and referred to 'comprehensive national processes and principles for the establishment of hybrid courts in parallel with truth seeking and reconciliation processes.'[35] The AU-TJPF is first and foremost a guide to national strategies, with the following outcomes:

- Help end violent conflicts and repressive rule and nurture sustainable peace with development, social justice, human and peoples' rights, democratic rule, and good governance.
- Consolidate peace, reconciliation, and justice in Africa and prevent impunity.
- Draw lessons from various experiences across Africa in articulating a set of common concepts and principles to constitute a reference point for developing peace agreements and transitional justice institutions and initiatives in Africa.
- Develop AU benchmarks for assessing the compliance with the need to combat impunity.[36]

The draft text also recognizes the contextual sensibilities of post-conflict and transitional justice modalities, and warns against the promotion of modalities that are oblivious to country and regional contexts.[37]

The AU-TJP is firmly rooted in the rule of law and security architecture of the AU. It therefore emphasizes the need for coherence between the policy frameworks dealing with good governance, peace and security, and post conflict justice.[38] What value does the AU-TJP adds? It certainly purports to add a richer understanding of 'justice' as a component of good governance; of the rule of law; indeed, as a factor in any post-conflict peace and security strategy. It emphasizes that justice is more than retribution. The tripartite imperatives of reconciliation, accountability and responsibility are linked to a notion of sustainable peace.[39]

To the extent that reconciliation can contribute to peace, and therefore to the precondition for any sustainable post-conflict strategy, it is necessary to briefly note some of the important prerequisites for political reconciliation.[40] It can be noted that interdependence, genuine dialogue, and a democratic attitude to create political space for free discussion are key requirements for political reconciliation.[41] If these requirements seem difficult to achieve in domestic post-conflict situations, they may very well be regarded as *extremely* difficult to achieve in international or regional post-conflict settings. A keyword to introduce, then, is the concept of 'regionalism'

---

[35] Wachira 2016, p. 4.

[36] AU-TJPF Section I, p. 6.

[37] Ibid., p. 6.

[38] This sentiment is also captured in the Decision of the AU Assembly on the Declaration of the Theme of the January 2011 Summit – Toward Greater Unity and Integration through Shared Values, Assembly/AU/Decl. 1 (XVI), paras 4, 11. http://www.au.int/ar/sites/default/files/Combined%20Files%20Assembly%20AU%20Dec1%28XVI%29.pdf). Last accessed 23 March 2017.

[39] AU-TJPF Section IV.3(b).

[40] We are obviously more interested here in *political* reconciliation, and not necessarily in the more generic understanding of reconciliation that could also involve highly individualized forms of reconciliation between two or more individuals.

[41] Murithi 2016, p. 124.

as employed by international relations experts. This is the notion that regionalism creates 'patterns and networks of interdependence' and 'interdependence', in turn, can be described as a cost-factor: it imposes costs on insiders and outsiders.[42] Proponents of regional reconciliation therefore suggest that processes of truth recovery, accountability and redress across borders are preliminary requirements for eventual regional reconciliation.[43] The existence and membership of regional bodies such as the EU or AU could help to formalize and legitimize reconciliation between sovereign states. Formal regional reconciliation via institutional mechanisms can be complemented with informal regional reconciliation processes, for instance via civil society initiatives, and through the engagement of population diasporas.[44]

16.4.3   Some Lessons from the Regional Frameworks on Post-conflict Modalities

All of the abovementioned imperatives are contentious. For instance, more than 20 years after the establishment of South Africa's Truth and Reconciliation Commission (TRC), there appears to be growing disagreement about the contribution of the TRC to *reconciliation* and *truth*. There is a general lack of empirical data on the subject, which may be a function of the under-explored relationship between truth and reconciliation as components of post-conflict efforts.[45] A narrow assessment of the TRC's impact is that it undoubtedly contributed to peace (and a measure of historical truth) in the sense that it formed part of a package of transitional arrangements (including an interim constitution and certain guarantees regarding the job security of civil servants) that helped to end the hostilities between the apartheid government and the liberation movements. That was the immediate and by no means trivial contribution of the TRC process.[46] The longer-term post-conflict assessment of the TRC is far more contentious. *Accountability* and *responsibility* as building blocks of a sustainable peace are equally contentious issues. Amnesty as an element of TRC-like processes is obviously relevant in this context. And so is the opposite of amnesty, namely the prosecution of individuals responsible for gross human rights violations.

It seems, therefore, that the key is to find some kind of balance between the overarching goals of peace and justice, with reconciliation as an integral byproduct. This sounds good in the abstract, but any workable policy must ensure to be concrete enough in order to realize the stated goals. The AU-TJP contains a pragmatic tool known as *sequencing*, which may be helpful regarding the implementation of workable policies in post-conflict situations. On sequencing, the AU-TJP states as follows:

---

[42] Ibid., at 125.

[43] Ibid., at 130.

[44] Ibid., at 132–133.

[45] Clark 2011, p. 260.

[46] Furlong 2000, p. 95.

'While it is widely understood that real peace cannot exist without justice, the UN and other bodies have acknowledged that the relentless pursuit of justice may sometimes be an obstacle to peace. However there is an emerging consensus that suggests that sensible peace-building strategies should combine elements of both peace and justice, whether by sequencing peace and justice activities (as in the case of some Latin American countries, such as Argentina and Chile, where justice/accountability issues were addressed decades after democratic transitions), or by undertaking peace and justice activities simultaneously (as in the case of Rwanda, Sierra Leone, Uganda, Timor Leste).

"Justice and peace" therefore, should not be seen as conflicting or contradictory forces. Rather, properly pursued, they promote and sustain one another. The question should not be: whether to pursue justice and accountability, but rather when and how. In reality, it is about keeping alive the possibility of justice and accountability and finding the right combination and the right sequence in each specific context.[47]

16.5 A Note on Sequencing, Truth and Justice

Sequencing refers, in short, to the temporal element in post-conflict and transitional justice strategies. While it is possible to point to some general guidelines and comparative lessons, it is important to note that the ultimate choice about the timing of the implementation of the chosen post-conflict modality or modalities, is informed by context-specific conditions.

Amnesia, blanket amnesty, and *de facto* or *de jure* impunity for past atrocities should not be moral, political or legal options in a post-conflict situation. We argue, as a point of departure, that both *truth* and *justice* should play some role, with sustainable peace as the baseline outcome. On this assumption, we can turn to the three broad approaches regarding sequencing, as identified by scholars. These approaches are: (i) truth first, justice later; (ii) trials first, truth later; and (iii) truth and justice in tandem.[48]

We will return to the question of sequencing, and how it could apply to Ukraine, later.[49] For now it is necessary to briefly discuss the notions of *truth* and *justice*. It should be clear that the two terms are not presented as antonyms. They are evidently not mutually exclusive. Truth is not the opposite of justice. They are related, albeit not quite the same in terms of content, process or outcome. Truth and justice accentuate different moral claims.

---

[47] AU-TJPF Section V.3.
[48] Randeny and Lassee 2016, at 5.
[49] See Conclusion, Sect. 16.8.

16.5.1 On Truth

Albie Sachs, the former South African Constitutional Court justice, anti-apartheid activist and himself a victim of gross human rights violations by the apartheid state,[50] articulated four categories of truth, which he presented on the occasion of the inaugural National Archives Lecture in London in 2005.[51] The first category, *microscopic truth*, entails the narrowing of a problem or a field to a certain frame from which all variables (except those to be measured) can be excluded. Lawyers do this on a daily basis in court, where a legal question is posed and then answered with respect to a defined field (for instance: 'did the accused possess the necessary criminal capacity at the time of the commission of the offence'). The question is about the capacity of a person to distinguish between right and wrong (psychological responsibility); the defined field is the general principles of criminal law, and more particularly the principles relating to criminal capacity, which can be answered with reference to well-established principles of law and psychology.[52] The second category of truth, according to Sachs, is *logical truth*. Again, this is something that lawyers do on a daily basis: conclusions reached by deductive and inferential processes. Language is employed to reflect what is typical in nature and as experienced by humanity. Indeed, legal reasoning to a large extent can be described as an attempt to find connections between microscopic truth and logical truth. The third category is described by Sachs as *experiential truth*, a concept that Sachs encountered in the works of Mohandas Gandhi, the Indian anti-colonial and independence icon who also spent part of his life practicing law in segregated South Africa.[53] Experiential truth (or 'lived truth') is, essentially, storytelling. It is also reflective, in the sense that one needs to analyse one's experience of a phenomenon in which one has participated.[54] Whether we realise it or not, this category of truth is what guides us in our lives: 'We act on our experience of life and we infer things from that'.[55] Finally, the fourth category, *dialogical truth*, can best be described as inchoate. It does not end. There is no final outcome or final answer. It is a mix of evidential, testimonial, and experiential truths; the truths of many people being interpreted in many ways. The work and process of the Truth and Reconciliation Commission in South Africa was par excellence about both experiential and dialogical truth. Sachs explained as follows:

> It was its emotion, it was seeing on television people you could identify with, hearing voices that sounded like voices of your neighbours, people you'd been to school with – which you

---

[50] For autobiographical background, see Sachs 2014.

[51] Sachs 2005. http://archivaria.ca/index.php/archivaria/article/view/12887/14138. Last accessed 23 March 2017.

[52] Kemp et al. 2015, at 153.

[53] For a comprehensive collection of biographical and intellectual outputs on the life and work of Gandhi, see Jack 1956. For a succinct argument on Gandhi's contribution to legal method, see Narrain 2013, at 273–300. The gist of the argument is that Gandhi's contribution to law and legal method is not only to be found in his writings, but also in his lived experience.

[54] Sachs 2005, at 8.

[55] Ibid.

can't get from a document, you don't get from a document. The strength of the document is its impersonality, its objectivity. Its weakness in this context is precisely that, the voice, the texture, the emotion, the rhythm, the relationship to other materials, its place in the context in the story get lost.[56]

The TRC-process, at least as it played out in South Africa, can best be described as a converter of truth in the form of *knowledge* (data, facts, information) into truth in the form of *acknowledgement*. This, according to Sachs, 'involved doing something with the information. Connecting it with the world you live in.'[57] There is the risk that a reliance on subjective memory only, independent from truth in the form of verifiable facts, will undo the potential of a TRC-process by making it into a 'kind of dream world'.[58] The problem with a dream world, of course, is that it is not real.[59] It therefore comes as no surprise that most people would probably view the truth in terms of the correspondence theory which defines a true proposition as 'one which corresponds with the reality, the facts, the world out there'.[60] The correspondence theory does not hold that the truth equals the world or reality; rather, truth refers to any statement's status as 'accurately reflecting how things really are'.[61] The assumption underpinning the correspondence theory is that language is capable of accurately representing the world.[62]

The correspondence theory of truth has its limitations. Nicolson pointed out that the reliance on language as an accurate vehicle to express the truth fails to accommodate evaluative, negative, and vague statements.[63] The fundamental criticism seems to be that the correspondence theory treats language and reality as essentially the same thing.[64]

The basic argument of the sceptical school, then, is that there is no apparent vantage point outside language and the world; outside a person's own biases, motives, interests, values and preconceptions, 'to inform the rest of us when we finally arrive at the truth'.[65] Whether truth is viewed as 'the most coherent account of things', or, pragmatically, 'as that which is good, congenial or useful to believe', adherents to the sceptical school will counter that there simply is no such thing as objective truth 'which enables knowledge to be distinguished from mere belief'.[66] The proponents of the correspondence theory, and of truth as objective fact, argue that sceptical and relativist views of truth can easily lead to a moral abyss. But the moral stride of adherents to the correspondence theory belies the historical tendency of dominant

---

[56] Ibid., at 9.
[57] Ibid.
[58] Sachs 2005, at 10.
[59] Ibid.
[60] Nicolson 2013, at 32.
[61] Ibid.
[62] Ibid.
[63] Nicolson 2013, at 32–33.
[64] Ibid., at 33.
[65] Ibid., at 37.
[66] Ibid.

or hegemonic groups leaning on the truth, reality, human nature, normality and so on to defend oppressive systems like segregation, apartheid and fascism.[67] A more humble approach to truth is therefore called for. And Sachs's category of dialogical truth could perhaps serve to soften the harder edges of objective truth. Institutionally speaking one should therefore take a serious look at truth commissions as potentially better vehicles for a comprehensive truth that goes beyond microscopic and logical truth, the preferred categories of judicial-centred modalities, in other words, courts of law, the fora normally associated with *justice*.

16.5.2 On How Truth Relates to the Peace/Justice Conundrum

Summing up, then, it can be stated that whenever decision-makers select a modality of *jus post bellum* applicable to a certain conflict, they should bear in mind that it should address a kind of two-level dilemma: the first (most fundamental one) is the potential tension between *peace* and *justice*. The applied approach to *jus post bellum* should first of all be to prevent recurrence of violence. Then, establishing justice in itself, may require an even more sophisticated balancing between *truth* and *justice* (which is to say, the restorative and retributive functions of justice must be balanced).

In the following parts, we will apply the presented theoretical considerations to the case of the Donbas conflict.

16.6 The Evolution, Costs and Nature of the Donbas Conflict

16.6.1 The Evolution and Scale of the Conflict

The armed conflict in the east of Ukraine started to evolve in the aftermath of probably the most remarkable event in the country's contemporary history – the Euromaidan uprising that took place towards the end of 2013 – beginning of 2014. The protests ended with the escape of President Viktor Yanukovych to Russia on 22 February 2014. Almost immediately, on 1 March, it was followed by meetings in the cities of Kharkiv, Odesa, Donetsk, Kherson and Mykolaiv (all situated in the south and east of Ukraine). The participants openly expressed their disagreement with the change of authorities in Kyiv. It should be clearly stressed here, that this should not be regarded

---

[67] Nicolson 2013, at 42. The author does not specifically refer to apartheid, Nazism, or fascism, but it is not difficult to see how these ideologies relied on 'objective facts' about human nature and race in order to justify the oppressive and criminal systems of bigotry and racism. For useful references to some of the main critical schools of thought (as opposed to the adherents of the 'objective' and correspondence schools), see Jones 2006, at 1–25.

as a proof that there was no support for post-Euromaidan transitional government in eastern oblasts of the country. Indeed, meetings in support of political change generated by Euromaidan took place in the Donbas region; there were instances of clashes between them and representatives of what can be called 'pro-Russian option'. It is not our goal to present the detailed picture of the development of events – this task has been accomplished elsewhere.[68] What is important for our further analysis is the fact that the clear majority of citizens supporting Euromaidan was concentrated in the western and central regions of Ukraine.[69] Thus, the narrative presenting the mentioned events and their outcome as an illegal *coup d'état*, widely spread by Russian media, gained fertile ground in the east and in the south of Ukraine. During March and April 2014, anti-government meetings intensified, especially in Donetsk and Luhansk *oblasts*, which together constitute the Donbas region.

Anti-government slogans were soon complemented with separatist ones. There were instances of occupation of official buildings throughout the region, accompanied by the proclamation of 'people's authorities'. On 13 April 2014, the Ukrainian government authorised the counter-terrorist operation (ATO) in order to oppose growing centrifugal tendencies. This step hasn't prevented the mentioned 'authorities' from conducting unconstitutional 'referendums' (according to Ukraine's constitution, issues of altering the territory of Ukraine are resolved exclusively by an all-Ukrainian referendum) on 11 May 2014 in the territories controlled by militants, thus providing the dubious basis for the so-called independence of self-proclaimed 'people's republics' of Donetsk ('DNR') and Luhansk ('LNR'). This eventually led to a new cycle of escalation of the conflict to a full-fledged armed conflict in the summer of 2014.

The Donbas conflict produced a significant number of human rights violations. First and foremost, by the end of 2016, the conflict resulted in 9,733 people killed and 22,720 injured.[70] For the first time since independence, Ukraine has faced the problem of internally displaced persons. The number is estimated to oscillate around 1.4 million persons.[71] About 26% of Ukrainians declared that either they or their close relatives participated in the ATO as a result of mobilisation that took place in 2013–2015[72] – a number that may serve as an indicator of how a significant proportion of the population is directly affected by the conflict. International organisations as well as NGOs dealing with human rights regularly report violations as a direct or indirect result of warfare, not only by militants of the 'people's republics', but also by Ukrainian governmental forces.[73] Last but not least, the conflict resulted in significant economic costs. The estimated GDP loss as a result of the conflict ranges from 8 to 15 percent,[74] which obviously does not remain without significance for the overall well-

---

[68] See Wilson 2014.

[69] Democratic Initiatives Foundation 2014.

[70] OHCHR 2016, p. 6.

[71] OHCHR 2015, p. 5.

[72] Yakymenko et al. 2016, at 52.

[73] For example FIDH 2015.

[74] Litra et al. 2016, at 11.

being of the community. At the time of writing, the conflict remains unresolved, with periodic waves of escalation and de-escalation taking place in the east of Ukraine. Therefore, the catalogue of injustices remains far from being closed.

16.6.2   The Issue of Hybridity of the Conflict

What should be clearly stressed, is that the Donbas conflict should be analysed not as a separate phenomenon, but as an element of a wider process, which also pertains to the annexation of Crimea by Russia. Along with the growing tension in the east of Ukraine, rallies against the post-Euromaidan change of authorities took place in Crimea. The latter were used by local pro-Russian groups, openly supported by the Russian military, to organise a 'referendum' on independence of Crimea on 16 March 2014. Two days later, on 18 March, an agreement was signed in Moscow on the joining of Crimea to the Russian Federation. Taking into account the legal and political circumstances of these events, one should underline that Crimea's 'secession' from Ukraine was inconsistent with the latter's legal order (for the same reason as the putative self-proclaimed secession of 'DNR' and 'LNR'). Neither is there a ground to claim that inhabitants of Crimea had a right for remedial secession, primarily due to the speed of events, and the fact that there was no search for effective remedies prior to the separation of Crimea from Ukraine (separation could be acceptable as a final resort when continued rule by an oppressive government has become intolerable and no other means helped to solve the situation).[75] Generally, 'the separation of Crimea from Ukraine was not exclusively, or even largely, the result of developments confined to Ukraine's legal order: the act of separation was a direct (and immediate) result of international acts of another State'.[76] In other words, these events should be regarded as an act of aggression against Ukraine, an aspect that is dealt with elsewhere in this book.[77]

Events in Donbas generally fit the same pattern – unconstitutional 'referendums' became the main argument supporting the emergence of the new putative states of 'DNR' and 'LNR'. Although Russia does not acknowledge its direct participation in the conflict, its support for both 'people's republics' is evident. Unlike in the case of Crimea, there is no official recognition by Russian authorities of the use of military force against Ukraine; nevertheless, presence of Russian troops in the territory of Ukraine is confirmed by a number of international organisations.[78] There are also no attempts to annex the secessionist territories. Although warfare in Donbas is an element of the same policy of Russia towards Ukraine as was the case with the annexation of Crimea, it happens according to a different *modus operandi*, widely referred to as a 'hybrid warfare'. It is not our goal here to analyse in detail the

---

[75] Grant 2015, at 26–33.

[76] Ibid., at 22.

[77] A reference to other chapters of the book may be included here.

[78] NATO 2014; PACE 2016; OSCEPA 2015.

concept of hybrid warfare. Some analysts argue that the use of the term may be counterproductive in terms of a proper understanding of the essence of modern conflicts.[79] We will nevertheless consider the *hybridity* of the Donbas conflict as its crucial feature.

We understand the conflict primarily as a legal uncertainty regarding the status of the conflict, of combatants and fighters[80] taking part in it as well as of political entities responsible for and able of conducting warfare and implementing peace agreements. In practical terms, symptoms of *hybridity* can be grouped into two categories. First, although, like in the case of Crimea's so-called independence, one can state without exaggeration that on an analytical level, there is general consensus regarding Russia's active role in the emergence of the putative states of 'DNR' and 'LNR'. On the other hand, Russia is not *de jure* in a state of war with Ukraine; indeed it participates in peace talks as an observer/mediator. At the same time, the existence of a measure of popular support for the self-proclaimed 'republics' also cannot be denied. As a result, one can argue that the Donbas conflict contains elements of both international and internal conflict. Second, although in political discourse Ukrainian authorities widely refer to the conflict as inter-state war, martial law was never introduced in Ukraine; all the operations undertaken by Ukraine's armed forces take place in the framework of a counter-terrorist operation. Nevertheless, a number of legal acts introduced by the Ukrainian authorities since March 2014 suggest that Ukraine is in a situation which is materially or *de facto* similar to a state of war.[81] All in all, we are dealing with a complex of uncertainties and dilemmas, none of which have been resolved three years after the beginning of the conflict. Peace is still elusive. Whither *post bellum* initiatives?

---

[79] Van Puyvelde 2015.

[80] Under international humanitarian law, and in the context of *international armed conflicts*, the term 'combatant' is employed in order to distinguish between civilians, on the one hand, and persons who do not enjoy 'the protection against attack accorded to civilians', on the other hand. Members of the armed forces of a party to the conflict (with the exception of medical and religious personnel) are normally regarded as combatants. A civilian, then, is 'a person who is not (or who is no longer) a member of the armed forces'. It is so that civilians who participate directly in the hostilities risk losing their protective status as civilians. In *non-international armed conflicts* no formal designation of combatant status exists. Thus, the usual view is that participants in a non-international armed conflict are treated as ordinary criminals. It is important to note, however, that international humanitarian law governs the treatment of participants in non-international armed conflict via the normative frameworks of Common Article 3 of the Geneva Conventions and Additional Protocol II, both of which provide for the minimum standard of treatment of fighters in non-international armed conflicts. For more on this, see Strydom 2016, at 378–379.

[81] Such opinion was expressed in several concurring opinions accompanying verdicts of the Constitutional Court of Ukraine on draft amendments of the constitution in the field of the judiciary system and decentralisation of the state. On the difference between *war in the technical sense* and *war in the material sense*, Dinstein writes as follows: 'War is a hostile interaction between two or more States, either in a technical or in a material sense. War in the technical sense is a formal status produced by a declaration of war. War in the material sense is generated by actual use of armed force, which must be comprehensive on the part of at least one party to the conflict.' See Dinstein 2005, at 15.

16.7 Tentative *Jus Post Bellum* Initiatives

16.7.1 Peace Process as a Constrain of Jus Post Bellum Initiatives

Attempts to find a peaceful resolution of the conflict were taken already at the early stages of its escalation. On 17 April 2014, a declaration was signed in Geneva by representatives of Ukraine, Russia, the EU and the US containing four points: (1) prevention of violence and provocations by all sides; (2) disarmament of all illegal armed groups and the release of illegally seized buildings and public offices; (3) amnesty for all protesters who agree to leave seized public buildings and surrender weapons, with the exception of those found guilty of capital crimes; (4) start of an inclusive constitutional process to be carried out through a broad national dialogue.[82]

As mentioned above, the Geneva declaration did not prevent the conflict from further escalation. In June 2014, the so-called Normandy format of negotiations was established, consisting of political leaders and senior diplomats representing Germany, France, Ukraine and Russia. Simultaneously, the Trilateral Contact Group was created as a kind of 'working tool' of the Normandy format, including the representatives of Ukraine, Russia and the Organisation for Security and Cooperation in Europe (OSCE). The Group is aimed at facilitating the diplomatic resolution of the conflict. The group drafted two ceasefire agreements signed in Minsk on 5 September 2014 (Minsk-1) and 12 February 2015 (Minsk-2) by representatives of the OSCE, Ukraine, Russia and leaders of the self-proclaimed 'republics' of 'DNR' and 'LNR'. Along with the obvious provisions on ceasefire, both protocols emphasised the need to conduct a 'national dialogue' which would eventually lead to the transformation of Ukraine's political system in a manner that would guarantee a degree of autonomy (and thus more rights) to the rebellious territories, and amnesty which would protect militants, collaborators and supporters of the 'people's republics' from criminal prosecutions.

16.7.2 Society's Expectations as a Constrain of Jus Post Bellum Initiatives

As things stand at the time of writing (early 2017), the most feasible modality of post-conflict justice, taking into account the logic of the agreements achieved within the framework of the Normandy format (thus far the only loosely institutionalised platform designed for the sake of finding an end to the conflict) is exclusively future-oriented. It does not look to the past, let alone *deals* with the past. In an arrangement

---

[82] Dzerkalo Tyzhnya, 'Povnyy tekst zayavy za pidsumkamy perehovoriv u Zhenevi z ukrayins'koho pytannya', 17 April 2014, http://dt.ua/POLITICS/povniy-tekst-zayavi-za-pidsumkami-peregovoriv-u-zhenevi-z-ukrayinskogo-pitannya-141885_.html. Last accessed 29 March 2017.

like this, peace is obviously preferred over justice. We would submit that this makes it rather unsustainable in the long run. One simply cannot turn a blind eye to the scale of the conflict and violence related to it. Indeed, one must assume that the question of justice will sooner or later reappear on the agenda. This proposition can be supported by available surveys. In December 2015 (that is approximately 1.5 years since the beginning of the conflict) an absolute majority of Ukrainians declared that they are not ready to 'forget and forgive' the ones who fight against Ukraine on the side of 'DNR/LNR' (65.9%) let alone the ones who tortured Ukrainian servicemen and civilians (72.1%).[83] What should also be noted is that there are clear regional disparities in this regard – the further from the theatre of conflict, the more uncompromising is the position of respondents. One can expect that the existence of such differences may very well be put to the fore by political actors, when the issue of dealing with the past replaces the more urgent need of achieving peace. The problem can become sharper with the passage of time, if violence continues.

16.7.3   Going Beyond Peace and Justice Dichotomy

Some tentative *jus post bellum* initiatives at the behest of the Ukraine government that go beyond the peace and justice dichotomy can be noted. These steps may have significant impact on the general shape of post-conflict modalities down the road.

Firstly, following the logic established by the Minsk-1 protocol, the law on Special Order of Local Self-government in Certain Areas of Donetsk and Luhansk Oblasts was adopted on 16 September 2014.[84] According to this law, territories controlled by the 'people's republics' were to obtain a unique (within the borders of Ukraine) regime for a period of three years, including far-reaching competences of local authorities in appointing heads of prosecutor's offices and courts, as well as a right to establish 'people's militia'. The law has also guaranteed avoidance of prosecution, criminal and administrative responsibility and punishment of persons involved in the events in the territory of Donetsk and Luhansk oblasts. Furthermore, it includes provisions that can be interpreted as touching upon the issue of reparations – Ukraine has expressed a commitment to formulate an agreement on economic, social and cultural development and establish a special regime for business and investments in order to facilitate the quick reconstruction of the destroyed infrastructure. We can thus note that the Ukrainian authorities have basically agreed not only to abandon requests from the rebellious territories to bear economic costs of post-conflict reconstruction, but to establish a kind of nation-wide solidarity in this field. These provisions were premised on the condition of local elections in accordance with the relevant Ukrainian legislative frameworks. However, these elections never happened. None of the mentioned provisions has come into force.

---

[83] Yakymenko et al. 2016, at 52.

[84] Law of Ukraine On special order of local self-government in certain areas of Donetsk and Luhansk oblasts, no. 1680-VII, adopted 16 September 2014.

Secondly, Ukrainian authorities have elaborated a constitutional reform aimed primarily at the decentralisation of the state, but also providing for a provision that establishes a special (although not clearly specified) status for some parts of Donetsk and Luhansk oblasts.[85] As with the abovementioned law, the process of amendment of the Constitution was not finalised, leaving space for political negotiations regarding the final shape of the peace settlement and, perhaps, some measure of justice that would be acceptable in the general sense.

Thirdly, in August 2016, the Ukrainian government adopted the Concept of the State Program on Peace-making and Peacebuilding in Eastern Regions of Ukraine[86] (the Program itself has not been elaborated at the time of writing). The concept emphasises the need of reconstruction of physical infrastructure in the first place, economic recovery is thus regarded as the principal means of stabilisation and a necessary precondition of building reconciliation. The issues of dealing with the past or justice *per se*, is not referred to directly in the text. Similar logic can be found in the Action Plan on the state policy towards territories occupied by self-proclaimed republics.[87] Priorities are defined with reference to a number of considerations: a need to deal with corruption, avoid economic exclusion, provide basic social services, avoid discrimination, and take steps to set up national dialogue. In other words, the logic of *jus post bellum* that can be deduced from these documents is the following: one can hardly expect that reconciliation will work, while basic needs of the population affected by the conflict are not addressed. This logic is generally correct in the light of theoretical considerations presented above: interdependence favours reconciliation, and one can hardly imagine deeper interdependence than the one between actors of a well-functioning modern national economic system. Nevertheless, we should conclude here, that the efforts conducted by Ukrainian authorities are aimed at creating the basis for potential reconciliation; the decision on any kind of 'superstructure' in the form of extraordinary institution focused on providing justice as such in the aftermath of the Donbas conflict is not yet made.

In the meantime, problems related to the discussed conflict are being addressed within the framework of regular judicial procedures. Between March 2014 and the end of 2016, Ukrainian courts have issued around 1200 verdicts in cases that concern the conflict to some degree.[88] It is impossible, however, to give an unequivocal qualitative assessment of Ukraine's approach to criminal prosecutions in terms of

---

[85] Draft law on amendments to the Constitution of Ukraine (on decentralisation), no. 2217a, registered 1 July 2015.

[86] Ordinance of the Cabinet of Ministers of Ukraine on adoption of the Concept of the State Program on Peace-making and Peacebuilding in Eastern Regions of Ukraine, no. 892-p, adopted 31 August 2016.

[87] Ordinance of the Cabinet of Ministers of Ukraine on adoption of the Action Plan of Implementation of some elements of state's internal policy towards some parts of Donetsk and Luhansk oblasts, where institutions of state power temporarily do not fulfil their authority, no. 8-p, adopted 11 January 2017.

[88] This number is an estimation based on a number of verdicts published in an online database of Ukraine's court decisions, http://www.reyestr.court.gov.ua. Last accessed 23 March 2017. According to this database, approximately 1200 verdicts have been issued between March 2014 and November 2016 on the basis of provisions of the Criminal Code of Ukraine that are relevant to circumstances

the Donbas conflict. Reliable data on this is not readily available. Additionally, the Ukrainian government has made an attempt to engage the International Criminal Court regarding an investigation of events related to the Donbas conflict by accepting jurisdiction of the ICC over alleged war crimes on the territory of Ukraine starting from 20 February 2014.[89] The role of the ICC in post-conflict justice strategy also remains unclear – at the time of writing, the investigation was in its preliminary phase.

16.7.4   The Importance of Truth Element

In summary, then, one can hardly see evidence that Ukrainian authorities have settled on a comprehensive plan for the systematic implementation of any modality of post-conflict justice. The first priority is (still) the achievement of *peace* as the primary goal. Fragmentary indicators signalling a more general goal of reconciliation can be noted.

As the conflict progresses, the primary focus should be on steps to bring an end to hostilities. The inability to go beyond this basic threshold is explained by the *hybridity* of the conflict: although formally it is Kyiv and 'DNR/LNR' who are the negotiating sides within the Normandy format, the 'DNR/LNR' position on sequencing the implementation of the Minsk protocols corresponds with Russia's, which, as it was mentioned above, formally plays the role of mediator. In his interview for Bild magazine on 11 January 2016, President Putin asserted that the process of conflict de-escalation should start with the organisation of local elections in certain oblasts of Donetsk and Luhansk oblasts, the results of which would be recognised by Kyiv.[90] On the other hand, representatives of Ukrainian authorities in their numerous public statements consequently underline, that no steps would be taken without a *complete ceasefire*.[91] This problem could theoretically be solved more easily, should there exist a kind of regional setting containing all parties directly or indirectly engaged in the conflict, which would make continuation of the conflict more politically costly than taking steps towards reconciliation. In the given circumstances, however, achieving the primary goal of peace lies within the domain of *realpolitik*.

---

of an armed conflict in Donbas (crimes against national security; crimes against peace, humanity and war crimes; some types of crimes against public security).

[89] Statement of the Verkhovna Rada of Ukraine on recognition by Ukraine of jurisdiction of the International Criminal Court on crimes against humanity and war crimes committed by the high officials of the Russian Federation and leaders of terrorist organisations 'DNR' and 'LNR', which have led to serious consequences, and mass murder of Ukrainian citizens, no. 145-VIII, adopted 4 February 2015.

[90] Blome et al. 2016.

[91] For example: Ukrayinska Pravda, 'Poroshenko: niyakyh paralelnyh procesiv, spochatku bezpeka', 23 October 2016, http://www.pravda.com.ua/news/2016/10/23/7124578/. Last accessed 29 March 2017.

The inability of getting out of this fundamental stalemate hampers any movement towards the establishment of post-conflict justice that would be considered as *just* by all sides engaged in the conflict. Therefore, we can only refer to Ukraine's unilateral efforts. These can be summarised with reference to a number of outcomes. Having no prospect to establish binding agreements directly with the rebellious territories, Ukrainian authorities focus on what is possible to achieve, namely criminal prosecutions under existing national law and tentative initiatives aimed at avoiding further deterioration of the social and economic situation of persons directly affected by the conflict as well as of Ukrainian society in general (the analysis of their effectiveness is beyond the scope of this chapter). As it was explained above, this can hardly become a basis for reconciliation. It is simply a continuation of a precarious *status quo*. At the same time, Ukrainian authorities have generally signalled their readiness to provide concessions to the 'people's republics', both in political and economic terms. This overture is being made despite the fact that almost every step described in the preceding paragraphs induces strong reactions from the general public in Ukraine. Furthermore, it is also clear that there is much space left for debates on what *justice* may look like after peace is achieved. And then there is also the question of *truth*, or at the very least, a baseline of truth that would serve rather than obstruct peace and justice.[92]

The triad of peace, justice and truth presents the usual frame within which post-bellum modularisation occurs. Choices regarding sequencing and layering are informed by context, culture, the facts on the ground and international and parochial inputs. But it is the *hybridity* of the conflict in Ukraine that stands out as a significant constraint on the goal of peace - a peace which will be accepted by all sides of the conflict. Any *post-bellum* strategy, and any modality, is contingent on the removal of the barrier caused by the conflict. For that to happen, some basic truths about the nature of the conflict need to be acknowledged by all sides. And yes, down the line demands for truth about what happened during the conflict may very well resurface, but then with a different goal in mind, namely the more nuanced and stratified forms of truth identified by Sachs, twinned with the demand for justice via agreed upon fora.

16.8   Conclusion

There is no clear post-conflict strategy currently referring to the Donbas conflict. To a significant extent, the lack of such strategy is caused by the specificity of the conflict, namely its *hybridity*. It effectively prevents engaged parties from achieving

---

[92] Available research suggests that a growing disproportion in perception of the essence of the conflict is observed among inhabitants of territories occupied by "people's republics" and the rest of Ukrainian citizens. See Rekhtman 2016.

the fundamental goal of peace. As a result, any considerations regarding a proper modality of post-conflict justice remain rather theoretical. At the same time, we believe that the Ukrainian situation constitutes a good opportunity to formulate some conclusions that may be useful from the perspective of other similar conflicts.

Ukrainian authorities focus on efforts that are supposed to prevent the deterioration of social and economic situation of persons affected by the conflict and criminal prosecutions against the ones responsible for its ignition (within the ordinary system of justice). Criminal prosecutions – under national law or at the ICC – are perfectly acceptable manifestations of *jus post bellum*, but the existing knowledge in this field suggests that they are not enough.

In particular, what is missing is the element of *truth*. In any given circumstance, it seems that establishment of some basic truth about the conflict accepted by all sides is a *sine qua non* for establishing any form of justice. However, this should not be seen as identical to the traditional 'truth first and justice later' approach.

From the perspective of our topic, the main problem with *hybridity* is that it effectively conceals the international dimension of the conflict. One may debate whether the rebellious territories faced some form of discrimination, (and if so, what was the extent of it)? These issues should be subject of separate analysis. What can be said for sure is that at the dawn of the conflict the ideas publicly expressed by political and military leaders of 'DNR/LNR' did not occur in a void. They were supported by a significant part of the population. The third state—Russia—utilizes it to gain its own political goals.

It is thus natural that achieving peace will continue to be the top priority. Within the described circumstances it is hard to expect that any working agreement referring to justice can be achieved between Kyiv and 'DNR/LNR' without some basic agreement about what happened (and what continues to be happening). From this perspective, *truth* may appear crucial for achieving the fundamental goal of peace.

The problem, however, is that at least in the initial phase, truth-seeking efforts can be rather unilateral (conducted by Ukrainian authorities). It is thus important that the whole process should be transparent and also effectively promoted to the wider public. For example, ongoing criminal prosecutions can be a tool to present the *microscopic/logical truths* about the conflict from the perspective of the Ukrainian state; but such prosecutions can also be the first steps toward establishing the *dialogical truth*. In turn, the wider the area of agreement, the better are the opportunities to calibrate properly the functioning of institutions (those already in existence as well as those eventually to be established) aimed at achieving *justice*.

In the circumstances of hybrid conflicts, it is not sequencing, but rather the more flexible approach based on sequencing *plus* proper scaling between truth and justice which seems to be the basic element of an effective *jus post bellum* strategy.

References

Application of the International Convention for the Suppression of the Financing of Terrorism and of the International Convention on the Elimination of All Forms of Racial Discrimination (*Ukraine v. Russian Federation*), International Court of Justice. http://www.icj-cij.org/docket/files/166/19310.pdf. Accessed 31 March 2017AU Transitional Justice Policy Framework (2014) http://lawyersofafrica.org/wp-content/uploads/2014/11/AUTJF.pdf. Accessed 23 March 2017

Basic Principles and Guidelines on the Right to a Remedy and Reparations for Victims of Gross Violations of International Human Rights law and Serious Violations of International Humanitarian Law, UNGA A/RES/60/147 (2005). http://www.un.org/en/ga/search/view_doc.asp?symbol=A/RES/60/147. Accessed 23 March 2017

Bassiouni MC (ed) (2002) Post-Conflict Justice. Brill-Nijhoff, Boston

Bassiouni MC (2010) Perspectives on international criminal justice. Virginia Journal of International Law 2: 269–323

Bengoetxea J (2013) Transitional justice versus Traditional justice: The Basque case. Journal on Ethnopolitics and Minority Issues in Europe 12: 30–58

Blome N, Diekmann K, Biskup D (2016) For me, it is not borders that matter. Bild, 11 January 2016, http://www.bild.de/politik/ausland/wladimir-putin/russian-president-vladimir-putin-the-interview-44092656.bild.html. Accessed 29 March 2017

Clark J (2011) Transitional justice, truth and reconciliation: An under-explored relationship. International Criminal Law Review 11: 241–261

Dawn Rothe D, Maggard S (2012) Factors that impede or facilitate post-conflict justice mechanisms? An empirical investigation. International Criminal Law Review 12: 193–217

De Feyter K, Parmentier S, Bossuyt M, Lemmens P (eds) (2005) Out of the ashes. Reparations for victims of gross and systematic human rights violations. Intersentia, Antwerp/Cambridge

Democratic Initiatives Foundation (2014) Vid Maidanu-taboru do Maidanu-sichi: shcho zminylosya? http://www.dif.org.ua/ua/polls/2014_polls/vid-maidanu-taboru-do-maidan.htm. Accessed 23 March 2017

Decision of the AU Assembly on the Declaration of the Theme of the January 2011 Summit – Toward Greater Unity and Integration through Shared Values. Assembly/AU/Decl. 1 (XVI). http://www.au.int/ar/sites/default/files/Combined%20Files%20Assembly%20AU%20Dec1%28XVI%29.pdf. Accessed 23 March 2017

Dinstein Y (2005) War, Aggression and Self-Defence. Cambridge University Press, Cambridge

Du Plessis M, Pete S (eds) (2007) Repairing the past? International perspectives on reparations for gross human rights abuses. Intersentia, Antwerp/Cambridge

EU Action Plan on Human Rights and Democracy 2015–2019. https://eeas.europa.eu/human_rights/docs/eu_action_plan_on_human_rights_and_democracy_en.pdf. Accessed 23 March 2017

EU Policy Framework on Support to Transitional Justice (2015) http://eeas.europa.eu/archives/docs/top_stories/pdf/the_eus_policy_framework_on_support_to_transitional_justice.pdf. Accessed 23 March 2017

FIDH (2015) Eastern Ukraine. Civilians caught in the crossfire. https://www.fidh.org/IMG/pdf/eastern_ukraine-ld.pdf. Accessed 23 March 2017

Fischer M (2011) Transitional Justice and Reconciliation: Theory and Practice. http://www.berghof-foundation.org/fileadmin/redaktion/Publications/Handbook/Articles/fischer_tj_and_rec_handbook.pdf. Accessed 23 March 2017

Fletcher G (2005) Parochial versus Universal Criminal Law. Journal of International Criminal Justice 3: 20–34

Fombad C (2008) Transitional Justice in Africa: The Experience with Truth Commissions. http://www.nyulawglobal.org/globalex/Africa_Truth_Commissions.html. Accessed 23 March 2017

Furlong K (2000) The law as peacemaker: A search for truth and reconciliation in South Africa. Hibernian Law Journal 1: 95–120

Grant T (2015) Aggression against Ukraine. Territory, Responsibility, and International Law. Palgrave Macmillan, New York

Jack H (ed) (1956) The Gandhi Reader. Grove Press, New York

Jones B (2006) When critical race theory meets legal history. Rutgers Race & The Law Review 8: 1–25

Kemp G et al. (2015) Criminal Law in South Africa, 2nd edn. Oxford University Press, Cape Town

Litra L, Mylovanov T, Sologoub I, Syzov V, Zamikula M, Zarembo K, Zholud O, Zolkina M (2016) Not So Quiet on the Eastern Front: An Audit of the Minsk Agreements and Ukraine's Reintegration Options. http://dif.org.ua/uploads/pdf/20029751515805fa9b0ea035.89434323.pdf. Accessed 23 March 2017

Murithi T (ed) (2016) The politics of transitional justice in the Great Lakes Region of Africa. Institute for Justice and Reconciliation, Cape Town

Narrain A (2013) My experiments with law: Gandhi's exploration of law's potential. NUJS Law Review 6: 273–300

NATO (2014) NATO releases satellite imagery showing Russian combat troops inside Ukraine. http://www.nato.int/cps/en/natohq/news_112193.htm?selectedLocale=en. Accessed 23 March 2017

Nicolson D (2013) Taking epistemology seriously: 'truth, reason and justice' revisited. The International Journal of Evidence & Proof 17: 1–46

OHCHR (2015) Report on the Human Rights situation in Ukraine 16 May to 15 August 2015

OHCHR (2016) Report on the Human Rights situation in Ukraine 16 August to 15 November 2016

OSCEPA (2015) Resolution on the Continuation of Clear, Gross and Uncorrected Violations of OSCE Commitments and International Norms by the Russian Federation, Helsinki, 5–9 July 2015

PACE (2016) Political consequences of the Russian aggression in Ukraine. Resolution 2132, adopted 12 October 2016

Rakhmanin S (2017) Zalesye. http://gazeta.zn.ua/internal/zalese-_.html. Accessed 23 March 2017

Randeny I, Lassee I (2016) The politics of sequencing: A threat to justice? South Asian Centre for Legal Studies 5 (http://sacls.org/images/publications/reports/THE_POLITICS_OF_SEQUENCING_A_THREAT_TO_JUSTICE.pdf. Accessed 23 March 2017

Rekhtman Y (2016) Komunikatsiya yak instrument reintehratsiyi Donbasu. http://dif.org.ua/uploads/pdf/86379800258500cc1acd5b9.29169737.pdf. Accessed 23 March 2017

Report on Preliminary Examination Activities (2016) The Office of the Prosecutor, International Criminal Court. https://www.icc-cpi.int/iccdocs/otp/161114-otp-rep-PE_ENG.pdf. Accessed 31 March 2017

Report by UN Human Rights Council Special Rapporteur (2016). http://www.ohchr.org/EN/Issues/TruthJusticeReparation/Pages/Index.aspx. Accessed 23 March 2017

Report of the AU High Level Panel on Darfur, Peace and Security Council 207th meeting at the level of the Heads of State and Government, 29 Oct 2009, Abuja, Nigeria, PSG/AHG/2 (CCVII). http://www.refworld.org/pdfid/4ccfde402.pdf. Accessed 23 March 2017

Rieff D (2016) In praise of forgetting – Historical memory and its ironies. Yale University Press, New Haven

Sachs A (2005) Archives, Truth, and Reconciliation. http://archivaria.ca/index.php/archivaria/article/view/12887/14138. Accessed 23 March 2017

Sachs A (2014) The Soft Vengeance of a Freedom Fighter. University of California Press, Oakland

Saul M, Sweeney J (eds) (2015) International Law and Post-conflict Reconstruction Policy. Routledge, London

Strydom H (ed) (2016) International Law. Oxford University Press, Cape Town

Teitel R (2000) Transitional Justice. Oxford University Press, Oxford

UN (2004) The rule of law and transitional justice in conflict and post-conflict societies (2004) UN S/2004/616, 23 August 2004. https://www.un.org/ruleoflaw/files/2004%20report.pdf. Accessed 23 March 2017

Van Boven T (2010) The Basic Principles and Guidelines on the Right to Remedy and Reparation for Victims of Gross Violations of International Human Rights Law and Serious Violations of International Humanitarian Law. http://legal.un.org/avl/pdf/ha/ga_60-147/ga_60-147_e.pdf. Accessed 23 March 2017

Van Puyvelde D (2015) Hybrid war – does it even exist? http://www.nato.int/docu/review/2015/also-in-2015/hybrid-modern-future-warfare-russia-ukraine/EN/index.htm. Accessed 23 March 2017.
Wachira G (2016) The African Union Transitional Justice Policy Framework: Promise and Prospects. http://www.africancourtresearch.com/wp-content/uploads/2016/07/The-African-Union-Transitional-Justice-Policy-Framework-Wachira-GM.pdf. Accessed 23 March 2017
Wilson A (2014) Ukraine Crisis: What It Means for the West. Yale University Press, New Haven/London
Yakymenko Y, Bychenko A, Zamiatin V, Mishchenko M, Stetskiv A, Lytvynenko O (2016) Identychnist hromadian Ukrayiny: zminy, tendentsiyi, rehionalni osoblyvosti. Natsionalna Bezpeka i Oborona 3–4 (161–162): 2–57
Yepes R (2009) Transformative reparations of massive gross human rights violations: Between corrective and distributive justice. Netherlands Quarterly of Human Rights 4: 625–647

Chapter 17
Triggering the International Criminal Court's Jurisdiction for Alleged Crimes Committed Across Ukraine, Including in Crimea and Donbas

Beatrice Onica Jarka

Contents

Abstract In 2017, the International Criminal Court (ICC) celebrated its 15th anniversary, by which point it had heard 24 cases (all relating to African countries, 40 defendants and only nine people of African origin convicted). In extending its territorial jurisdiction practice, based on an Article 12(3) of the Rome Statute, the ICC's Office of the Prosecutor (OTP) announced, on 25 April 2014, the opening of a preliminary examination of the situation in Ukraine, which, on 29 September

Beatrice Onica Jarka, Associate Professor of International Public and Humanitarian Law at University Nicolae Titulescu (Bucharest Romania), Attorney at Law and Coordinator of the Romania National/International Competition of International Humanitarian Law and Refugee Law, organized in cooperation with Romanian Red Cross Society, UNHCR – Romania, Romanian Army Centre for Humanitarian Law and National Commission of Humanitarian Law, www.concurstitulescu.ro, email: beatrice.onicajarka@cunescu.ro.

B. O. Jarka (✉)
University Nicolae Titulescu, Bucharest, Romania
e-mail: beatrice.onicajarka@cunescu.ro

2015, based on Ukraine's second declaration under the same article, was extended to include alleged crimes occurring after 20 February 2014. On 14 November 2016, the OTP released its Report on Preliminary Examination Activities on Ukraine, in which it concluded that it would continue with Phase 2 (subject-matter jurisdiction), as the declaration on jurisdiction made by Ukraine was open-ended. An assessment of the ICC's jurisdiction will be a long-lasting process, statement supported by the release of the 2017 OTP Report on Preliminary Examinations which does not bring much progress, if any. If it succeeds in meeting the Phase 2 requirements, the assessment will need to undergo admissibility and interests of justice tests before the OTP decides whether or not to investigate. There are challenges to be addressed at this stage, derived from both the particular nature of the ICC and the novelty and peculiarities of Ukraine's situation in respect of subject-matter jurisdiction, admissibility and interests of justice assessment. Such an overview of challenges forms the subject matter of this article with a view to looking for possible solutions to overcome them and until the ICC's jurisdiction over Ukraine is triggered.

Keywords Ukraine · International Criminal Court's (ICC's) jurisdiction · Office of the Prosecutor (OTP) · preliminary examination · subject-matter jurisdiction · admissibility · interests of justice · gravity of crimes · decision to investigate · decision to prosecute

17.1 Preconditions for Triggering the International Criminal Court's Jurisdiction

The ICC's jurisdiction was particularly designed to make this institution the ultimate deterrent for perpetrators of the most heinous international crimes ever committed: genocide, crimes against humanity, war crimes and further crime of aggression, once 30 states parties ratified the Kampala amendment (see below) and once states parties decided by a two-thirds majority to activate the ICC's jurisdiction regarding crime of aggression. While the ICC was established to have global jurisdiction, as a court of last resort, it can only intervene when national authorities cannot or will not prosecute.

17.1.1 The International Criminal Court's Material Jurisdiction

According to the Rome Statute (Articles 6–8), the ICC has jurisdiction *ratione materiae* over crimes of genocide, crimes against humanity and war crimes. The elements of these crimes were defined in the Rome Statute and comprehensively completed in the form of the Elements of Crimes, adopted by the Assembly of State Parties to the Rome Statute.[1]

In Kampala, Uganda, in 2010, at the ICC Review Conference, an amendment to the Rome Statute was adopted, defining the crime of aggression, over which the court only has jurisdiction after two additional conditions are met. The amendment was supported by 30 states parties and, on 1 January 2017, the Assembly of States Parties voted in favour of allowing the court to exercise jurisdiction in this regard. At the time of both of Ukraine's declarations, the court was unable to address the crime of aggression, which could have been relevant in the context of determining criminal responsibility for eventual Russian aggression against Ukraine in Crimea. As the current situation stands, even if Putin were to stand trial, he could not be prosecuted for the Russian aggression against Ukraine.

17.1.2   The International Criminal Court's Personal Jurisdiction

The ICC only has *ratione personae* jurisdiction (i.e., only over individuals). While Article 1 of the Rome Statute does not expressly refer to natural persons, Article 25(3) provides that the court shall have jurisdiction over them. The Rome Statute makes clear that, regarding its *ratione personae* jurisdiction, which applies the principle of personality, the ICC can only exercise its jurisdiction if the alleged perpetrator is a national of a state party or a national of a state that has accepted this jurisdiction. In addition, the ICC has unlimited personal jurisdiction over those situations that have been referred by the UN Security Council under Article 13(b) of the Rome Statute.

In this context, one should note the ability of the ICC to prosecute nationals of non-state parties if the alleged crimes are committed on the territory of a state party or a state that has accepted the court's jurisdiction.

To the same extent, with less relevance to the Ukraine situation according to the assessment of the OTP, Article 26 of the Rome Statute bars the prosecution of persons under the age of 18.

17.1.3   The International Criminal Court's Territorial Jurisdiction

Under Article 12(2)(a) of the Rome Statute, the ICC may exercise its jurisdiction over a crime if the state on the territory of which the conduct in question occurred is a party to the statute or has accepted the court's jurisdiction by declaration.

When it comes to the ICC's position regarding territoriality, one should consider the determination of "the precise scope of the territorial parameter of the Court's

---

[1] ICC 2002.

jurisdiction",[2] which, in terms of analysing Ukraine's situation, could become pertinent, considering both the way that Ukraine chose to accept the ICC's jurisdiction and the particularities of this situation (i.e., Ukraine's decision to delay its acceptance of this jurisdiction).

Article 12(2)(a), when read literally, points out that the ICC has jurisdiction over a crime when the *conduct* of this crime occurred on the territory of a state party, which could pose challenges in the case of certain cross-border crimes. The *commission* of a crime essentially requires two elements: criminal conduct and a result; a crime is considered as having been *committed* on the territory of a state when either of these two elements has taken place there. In the traditional[3] interpretation of these terms, the conduct and the result may be considered to be two disconnected chronological moments (albeit still very close in absolute time). Based on this interpretation, Article 12(2) (a) could[4] mean that the court only has jurisdiction over crimes for which the criminal conduct took place within the territory of a state party, irrespective of whether the result took place within that territory.

The precise scope of a "territorial parameter" also covers the localization of criminal activity under the ICC's material jurisdiction and the application of the notorious territorial fictions or the use of the effects doctrine by the court in the exercise of its territorial jurisdiction, as well as in relation to crimes committed by means of electronic systems, particularly the Internet.

Last but not least, the exercise of the ICC's territorial jurisdiction in cases of belligerent occupation may be controversial when analysing the "territorial parameter" concept. Such an exercise could further include situations in which a state loses control over its territory and the impact of this situation would fall under the ICC's territorial jurisdiction. This kind of controversy refers to the interpretation of 'territory' within the meaning of 'effective control' for the purposes of Article 12(2)(a) of the Rome Statute.

Such aspects could pose a real challenge for a decision to seek an investigation by the ICC in situations concerning Donbas and Crimea.

17.1.4 The International Criminal Court's Temporal Jurisdiction

According to Articles 11 and 126 of the Rome Statute, the ICC has had the power to exercise its jurisdiction since 1 July 2002, when the Rome Statute was ratified by 60 states and thus entered into force. At an immediate level, the Rome Statute is based on the non-retroactivity principle and the temporal jurisdiction of the court is prospective (Article 24(1)).

---

[2] Vagias 2011, p. 15.

[3] Maillard 2014.

[4] Ibid.

Furthermore, *as per* Article 11(2) of the Rome Statute, "if a State becomes a Party to this Statute after its entry into force, the Court may exercise its jurisdiction only with respect to crimes committed after the entry into force of this Statute for that State, unless that State has made a declaration under Article 12, para 3".

Acceptance of the court's exercise of its jurisdiction is a precondition to such an exercise. However, Article 12(3) of the Rome Statute concerns non-party states. In such cases, the ICC may still exercise jurisdiction provided that the territorial state and/or the nationality state (being a non-state party), on an *ad hoc* basis, accepts the exercise of jurisdiction by the ICC. The declaration by which the approval of the court's jurisdiction is affirmed "must be express, unequivocal, and precise as to the crime(s) or situation it applies to".[5]

It is important to emphasize that, when a declaration is lodged with the Registrar of the ICC, according to Article 12(3) of the Rome Statute, the state commits itself to cooperate with the court as if it were a state party for the crimes covered by the declaration. The obligation to cooperate[6] is in line with Article 34 Vienna Convention on the Law of Treaties, according to which a "treaty does not create either obligations or rights for a third State without its consent".

The wording *the crime in question*, contained in Article 12(3), must furthermore be interpreted in accordance with Rule 4 from the ICC Rules of Procedure and Evidence.[7] Accordingly, an Article 12(3) declaration made by a non-state party implies the "acceptance of jurisdiction with respect to the crimes referred to in Article 5 of relevance to the situation" rather than individual crimes or specific incidents.

Concerning the situation in Ukraine, on 17 April 2014, the Ukrainian Government lodged a declaration under Article 12(3) of the Rome Statute, accepting the ICC's jurisdiction over alleged crimes committed on its territory from 21 November 2013 to 22 February 2014. Further, on 8 September 2015, the Ukrainian Government lodged a second declaration under Article 12(3) of the statute accepting the exercise of jurisdiction by the ICC in relation to alleged crimes committed on its territory from 20 February 2014 onwards, with no end date. The court has therefore been able to exercise its jurisdiction over crimes, as defined by the Rome Statute, committed on the territory of Ukraine since 21 November 2013.[8]

Due to its facultative character, Article 12(3) is in line with the overall state sovereignty-friendliness[9] of Article 12; and, as seen in the case of Ukraine, it does not exclusively provide for the possibility for states to extend the *ratione temporis* jurisdiction of the court. In this context, it cannot be denied that the ICC may also consider facts that relate to a period before the time specified in the Article 12(3) declaration, at least for the purpose of securing evidence or uncovering acts of a

---

[5] Ibid.

[6] Ibid.

[7] See ICC Rules of Procedure and Evidence 2002.

[8] ICC OTP Report on Preliminary Examination Activities 2016, p. 33 and subsequent pages.

[9] Ibid.

continuing nature, provided that these facts were linked to events that occurred after that time.[10]

17.1.5   Gravity of Crimes

The Prosecutor may only prosecute serious crimes of sufficient gravity within the jurisdiction of the ICC. The Prosecutor has to be certain[11] that a case is "of such gravity to justify further action by the Court". Such a degree of gravity required to justify the Court's further action is called the "gravity threshold".

The term *gravity* may be observed[12] in many provisions of the ICC's statute and reflects the purpose and scope of the court in prosecuting and punishing the most serious crimes that concern the entire international community.

On the other hand, the so-called "gravity threshold" appears as a precondition that is included in Article 17(1)(d) of the Rome Statute, which provides that the court shall determine a case to be inadmissible where the case does not have sufficient gravity to justify further action by the court. Practical reasoning[13] stands behind such a precondition, which ensures not only that the ICC limits its focus to the most serious crimes, but also that it can manage its caseload. In the absence of such a precondition, the ICC would likely be flooded with cases and become ineffective due to an excessive workload.[14]

The concept of gravity plays an important role in the selection of cases and situations that appear before the ICC. The identification of the object of ICC proceedings takes place in two essential stages. The first involves the selection of "situations", which is normally the identification of a certain period of time and place[15] for which the Prosecutor conducts an investigation. There are three ways of selecting situations, which represent, at the same time, mechanisms for triggering the ICC's jurisdiction: through either a Security Council referral (Article 13), a state party referral (Article 14) or a *proprio motu* investigation by the Prosecutor (Article 15). The second stage covers the selection of "cases". Briefly, the OTP conducts its investigation into a situation that is referred by any of the ways mentioned above and chooses cases by identifying the suspected persons who have allegedly committed crimes under the ICC's jurisdiction.

During both stages, the Prosecutor makes a final decision on the gravity of the objects. *As per* Article 53(1) of the ICC's statute, the OTP shall, after fully evaluating the information that is available to it, initiate an investigation unless it determines that there is no reasonable basis to proceed under the said statute. In such an evaluation,

---

[10] Ibid.

[11] Ochi 2016.

[12] Ibid., p. 2.

[13] Ibid.

[14] Ibid.

[15] Ibid.

the Prosecutor shall consider, according to Article 53(1)(b), among other things, the admissibility of possible cases under Article 17, which includes an assessment of the sufficiency of gravity.

Further, during the judicial review process for case or situation selection, there are several guarantee mechanisms, in which an assessment of the gravity may be considered: a determination of admissibility under Article 19; a review by the Preliminary Trial Chamber of the decision of the Prosecutor not to proceed under Article 53(3); or authorization by the same chamber to initiate an investigation according to Article 15(3), based on the *proprio motu* powers of the Prosecutor.

Criteria for situation and case selection are also provided in Regulation 29[16] of the OTP, which entered into force on 23 April 2009, according to which, in order to assess the gravity of crimes that were allegedly committed in a situation, the Prosecutor "shall consider various factors including their scale, nature, manner of commission, and impact".

Through its practice,[17] the ICC has so far not provided standards or a definition of sufficient gravity, only factors, criteria or elements to be taken into account. All these factors are nevertheless only topics to be considered, and an actual standard, such as the degree of scale, brutality or impact or the rank or level of involvement of relevant persons, has not yet been defined, leaving room for a case-by-case assessment of the gravity.

17.2 Mechanisms for Triggering the International Criminal Court's Jurisdiction

The Rome Statute provides for the mechanisms of triggering the ICC's jurisdiction: in light of a proprio motu investigation by *the Prosecutor* (according to the Rome Statute, Articles 13(c) and 15), referrals by the UN Security Council (according to the Rome Statute, Article 13(b)), and finally by state referrals (Article 13(a)).

17.3 Stages of the International Criminal Court's Legal Process

The legal process involving the ICC consists of different stages and finally triggers jurisdiction, which brings defendants to trial.

The triggering process for jurisdiction, besides being framed by the three clearly determined mechanisms, also contains several checks, reviews and safeguards specific to nature of the ICC. These are intended to take into account all the preconditions mentioned above and thoroughly consider all the factors, as well as characterize each

---

[16] See ICC Regulations of the Office of the Prosecutor 2009.

[17] See Ochi 2016.

of the preconditions until the jurisdiction of the ICC is finally triggered. At this point, an investigation is opened by the Prosecutor, and, if there is a case to answer, a trial is organized. Such a process is initiated at the preliminary examination stage, during which the OTP evaluates whether there is sufficient evidence of crimes of sufficient gravity that fall within the ICC's jurisdiction, whether there are genuine national proceedings, and whether opening an investigation would serve the interests of justice and victims. If the Prosecutor is not satisfied that there is a reasonable basis to proceed, s/he will inform the Pre-Trial Chamber (Article 53(1), last paragraph, of the Rome Statute).

Based on the results of the preliminary investigation, the Prosecutor may decide to open an investigation (Article 53(2) of the Rome Statute). During the investigation stage, the Prosecutor may further determine, within his/her investigative powers under Article 54, that there is no sufficient basis for prosecution and inform the Pre-Trial Chamber of this decision.

Following the Prosecutor's decision under Article 53(1) or 53(2), the Pre-Trial Chamber may, at the request of the referral state or the UN Security Council, when a referral is forthcoming, review the decision of the Prosecutor not to investigate or not to prosecute, as well as ask him/her to reconsider the decision. If the decision of the Prosecutor not to investigate or not to prosecute is grounded on the fact that the interests of justice would not be served by either an investigation or a prosecution, the Pre-Trial Chamber may review, on its own initiative, the decision of the Prosecutor, which becomes final only after confirmation by Pre-Trial Chamber.

Following the investigation, if the Prosecutor decides to proceed with the prosecution, then the process enters into the pretrial stage, when an initial appearance by the suspect may take place and three pretrial judges confirm his/her identity and ensure that s/he understands the charges.

After hearing from the prosecution, the defence and the legal representative of the victims, the judges decide (usually within 60 days), when hearing the confirmation of charges, whether there is enough evidence for the case to go to trial (Articles 60–61 of the Rome Statute). It should be noted that, at this stage, if the suspect is not arrested or does not appear in front of the court, the hearing cannot begin, even if submissions can still be made.

During the trial stage, the prosecution has to prove beyond a reasonable doubt the guilt of the accused in front of the Trial Chamber, which consists of three judges (Article 61 and subsequent articles from the Rome Statute). After considering the evidence, the judges issue a verdict; if the verdict is a guilty one, they issue a sentence, by which they may sentence a person to up to 30 years of imprisonment or, under exceptional circumstances, to life imprisonment.

Verdicts are subject to appeal by the defence and by the prosecution, according to Article 81 and subsequent articles of the Rome Statute.

Finally, the sentences, after being issued, are enforced.

From the brief overview of the ICC legal process, one may notice that the ICC system is based on states interacting with an independent and permanent court dealing with international crimes, supported by international organizations and a global civil society. While there is an expectation that states will punish such crimes themselves, the independent work of the ICC complements national criminal jurisdictions, but only if a state remains inactive or is otherwise unwilling or genuinely unable to investigate and prosecute crimes that fall within the court's jurisdiction.

Such an independent intervention by the ICC in cases where a state does not or cannot investigate and prosecute crimes under the court's jurisdiction turns into a long process with several checks and reviews, and involving the entire judicial mechanism created under the Rome Statute to end impunity for the most serious crimes under ICC jurisdiction and prevent the commission of such crimes. Until suspects are identified and situations becomes cases, and suspects prosecuted, given the existing checks, reviews, safeguards and factors to be considered, the process is thoroughly accurate in respect of the decision about whether or not to prosecute. In this sense, a double check of the factors that are determinable by ICC jurisdiction within a preliminary investigation under Article 53(1)(a)–(c) of the Rome Statute and also within the investigation stage, until a decision whether to prosecute or not is made, becomes essential.

17.3.1 Preliminary Examination

According to an OTP Policy Paper from 2013,[18] once a situation has been identified for a preliminary examination, the OTP will consider, in accordance with the factors set out in Article 53(1)(a)–(c) (so-called statutory factors), whether: (a) the information available provides a reasonable basis to believe that a crime within the jurisdiction of the court has been, or is being, committed; (b) the case is, or would be, admissible under Article 17; and (c) an investigation would serve the interests of justice.

The factors indicated in Article 53(1)(a)–(c) are to be analysed, according to the same quoted document, by considering the ICC jurisdiction preconditions, followed by admissibility, which includes an assessment under Article 17 of the gravity of the crimes and complementarity. If the admissibility factor is satisfactory, an assessment of the interests of justice is made by the opening of an investigation into the respective case.

The standard of proof required for the assessment of the factors by a preliminary investigation is 'reasonable basis'. This has been interpreted by the Chambers of the Court as requiring "a sensible or reasonable justification for a belief that a crime falling within the jurisdiction of the Court 'has been or is being committed'".[19]

---

[18] See at https://www.icc-cpi.int/iccdocs/otp/OTP-Policy_Paper_Preliminary_Examinations_2013 -ENG.pdf. Accessed 9 July 2017.

[19] *Situation in the Republic of Kenya, Decision Pursuant to Article 15 of the Rome Statute on the Authorization of an Investigation into the Situation in the Republic of Kenya, ICC-01/09-19- Corr, 31 March2010*, para 35. See www.icc-cpi.int/iccdocs/otp/OTP-Policy_Paper_Preliminary_ Examinations_2013-ENG.pdf, p. 8. Accessed 12 July 2017.

17.4   Preliminary Examination – Four Phases Peculiar to the Ukraine Situation

17.4.1   The Office of the Prosecutor's Approach to Situations Falling Under the International Criminal Court's Jurisdiction

In order to methodologically approach the statutory factors stated under Article 53(1)(a)–(c), the OTP has developed a four-phase filter for the assessment of information on alleged crimes received under Article 15 communications. Each phase focuses on a distinct statutory factor for analytical purposes as part of a holistic approach[20] of the part of the Prosecutor throughout the preliminary examination process.

Phase 1 considers the initial assessment of the seriousness of the information received under Article 15, filters out information on crimes that are outside the jurisdiction of the court and identifies those that appear to fall within this jurisdiction.

The OTP uses the information that has been identified under Phase 1 as being within the jurisdiction of the court in Phase 2, which represents the formal commencement[21] of a preliminary examination and focuses on whether the preconditions for the exercise of jurisdiction under Article 12 are satisfied and whether there is a reasonable basis to believe that the alleged crimes fall within the subject-matter jurisdiction of the Court. During Phase 2, the OTP performs a factual and legal assessment of the alleged crimes with the scope to identify, within the situation under preliminary investigation, the potential cases that would fall under ICC jurisdiction. Information about the national proceedings that exist with regard to the situation under preliminary investigation may also be gathered during this phase.[22]

If, on account of the legal and factual analysis performed on the situation in Phase 2, sufficient information is gathered as to the incidence of the subject-matter jurisdiction of the ICC and the potential cases, the OTP takes the assessment to Phase 3, where the analysis is focused on the admissibility of potential cases from the point of view of complementarity and gravity. In this phase, the OTP may also continue to collect[23] information on subject-matter jurisdiction, in particular, when new or ongoing crimes are alleged to have been committed in the situation.

Determining the admissibility of the potential cases, the OTP may take the analysis to Phase 4, where the interests of justice are considered, before finally recommending to the Prosecutor whether there is a reasonable basis to initiate an investigation.

---

[20] Ibid., p. 18.

[21] Ibid., para 80, p. 19.

[22] Ibid., para 82, p. 19.

[23] Ibid.

17.4.2 Ukraine Situation in Relation to the Office of the Prosecutor's Preliminary Investigation

17.4.2.1 Accepting ICC Jurisdiction by Ukraine

Ukraine has lodged two declarations under Article 12(3) of the Rome Statute. The first was lodged on 7 April 2014, in which the Ukrainian Government's declaration accepted the ICC's jurisdiction over alleged crimes committed on its territory from 21 November 2013 to 22 February 2014.

A second declaration was lodged on 8 September 2015, by which the Ukrainian Government accepted the exercise of jurisdiction by the ICC in relation to alleged crimes committed on its territory from 20 February 2014 onwards, with no end date.

17.4.2.2 Opening Preliminary Examination on Ukraine – Phases 1 and 2

The preliminary examination was announced by the OTP on 25 April 2014, based on the first declaration lodged by Ukraine.

When initiated, the preliminary examination focused on alleged crimes against humanity committed in the context of the "Maidan" protests which took place in Kiev and other regions of Ukraine between 21 November 2013 and 22 February 2014, including murder, torture and/or other inhumane acts.

The first OTP Report on Preliminary Examinations Activities, released on 2 December 2014,[24] examined the context of the Maidan protests, which took place against the decision, on 21 November 2013, by the Ukrainian Government not to sign an Association Agreement with the EU. At the time of the events that were the subject of the OTP's preliminary examination, the democratically elected government of Ukraine was dominated by the Party of Regions, which was also the party of then President Yanukovych.[25] The mass protests began in Independence Square, Kiev, with clashes between the demonstrators and security forces increasing,[26] while protesters grew dissatisfied with Yanukovych's government and demanded his removal from office.[27]

Following the adoption, on 16 January 2014, by the Ukrainian Parliament of laws that imposed tighter restrictions on the freedom of expression, assembly and association, relations between the protesters and the authorities deteriorated further. Furthermore, from 23 January 2014, protests also erupted in other Ukrainian cities, such as Kharkiv, Luhansk, Donetsk, Rivne, Ivano-Frankivsk, Dnipropetrovsk, Vin-

---

[24] OTP Report on Preliminary Examinations Activities 2014.

[25] Ibid., para 62.

[26] Ibid., para 63.

[27] Ibid., para 62.

nytsya, Zhytomyr, Zaporizhzhya, Lviv, Odessa, Poltava, Sumy, Ternopil, Cherkasy and Sevastopol, while in some cities, protesters forcibly occupied state buildings.[28]

Violent clashes in the context of the Maidan protests continued over the following weeks, causing injuries both to protesters and to members of the security forces, as well as the deaths of some protesters. On the evening of 18 February, the authorities reportedly initiated an operation to try to clear the square of protesters. The violence escalated sharply from that time onwards, causing several fatalities and hundreds of injuries during the following three days. On 21 February 2014, with EU mediation, President Yanukovych and opposition representatives agreed on a new government and fixed presidential elections for May 2014. On 22 February, the Ukrainian Parliament voted to remove President Yanukovych, who left the country the same day. Alleged crimes (injuries and killings of both protesters and members of the security forces) were reported in the context of the Maidan events from 24 November 2013 onwards.

In the context of the Maidan protests, the OTP identified[29] several alleged crimes, which appear to have resulted from an excessive use of force by security forces against protesters, as follows:

- Killings (at least 118 people were killed in the context of the Maidan events between 21 November 2013 and 22 February 2014 by both the security forces and protesters)
- Injuries (approximately 1,890 people were treated in hospitals in Kiev in the context of the Maidan events)
- Disappearances (some 39 people reportedly went missing during the Maidan events, some or all of whom may have been amongst those killed or arrested during the events)
- Torture and or other inhumane acts (a number of incidents of alleged ill-treatment in the course of arrest, during detention and/or following abduction was also reported in the context of the Maidan protests)

For its first report on Ukraine, the OTP focused mainly on gathering available information from reliable sources in order to assess whether the alleged crimes fell within the subject-matter jurisdiction of the court, as well as met with different Ukrainian authorities.

17.4.2.3   Continuing Preliminary Examination on Ukraine – Phase 2 – Subject-Matter Jurisdiction Following the Second Ukraine Declaration Under Article 12(3) of the Rome Statute

On 29 September 2015, following the second declaration lodged on 8 September by the Ukrainian Government, and bearing its legal effect in mind as well as the

---

[28] Ibid.

[29] Ibid., paras 65–9.

interconnected nature of the events in Ukraine, the OTP agreed[30] to extend the temporal scope of the existing preliminary examination to include any alleged crimes committed on the territory of Ukraine from 20 February 2014 onwards.

Extension of the Context Analysed Under Subject-Matter Jurisdiction – Phase 2 – to Events in Crimea and Eastern Ukraine

In its Report on Preliminary Examinations Activities released on 12 November 2015,[31] the OTP added more filtered information in addition to that on the Maidan protests by considering the seizure and control by armed individuals on 27 February 2014 of government buildings in Simferopol, the capital of the Autonomous Republic of Crimea, followed on March 2014 by the integration of Crimea and the city of Sevastopol into the Russian Federation as a consequence of an referendum that was declared invalid by the interim Ukrainian Government, led by Arseniy Yatsenyuk, and by a majority of states at the UN General Assembly.[32]

Furthermore, in the context under analysis, the OTP looked into information on pro-Russian demonstrators' seizure of government buildings in April and May 2014 in the Eastern Ukrainian oblasts of Donetsk and Luhansk and the alleged declaration, following referenda that were deemed illegitimate by the Ukrainian Government, of the Donetsk and Luhansk People's Republics. The report also referred to the announcement on 15 April 2014 by the Ukrainian Government of an "anti-terrorist operation" and the deployment of armed forces to the regions of Donetsk and Luhansk, (collectively referred to as "Donbas"), and stated that the continuation of fighting to varying degrees of intensity continued in Donbas between Ukrainian Government forces and separatist groups.[33]

Legal Analysis of Maidan Events (21 November 2013 to 22 February 2014)

The OTP Report on Preliminary Examination Activities continued with a legal analysis of the Maidan protests from the point of view of the subject-matter material jurisdiction of the ICC over such events.

The analysis focused on whether the crimes allegedly committed during the protests amounted to crimes against humanity under Article 7 of the Rome Statute. Any other crime under the ICC's material jurisdiction was considered inapplicable in the case of the Maidan protests.

---

[30] See 'ICC Prosecutor extends preliminary examination of the situation in Ukraine following second article 12(3) declaration, ICC-OTP-20150929-PR1156'. https://www.icc-cpi.int/legalAidConsultations?name=pr1156. Accessed 12 July 2017.

[31] See OTP Report on Preliminary Examinations Activities 2015.

[32] Ibid., para 85.

[33] Ibid., para 86.

Several elements of crimes against humanity were identified on a preliminary basis by the OTP in its report,[34] as follows:

- Violent acts allegedly carried out by members of the Ukrainian security forces and associated unidentified private individuals (*titushky*), which were directed against a civilian population within the meaning of Article 7 of the Rome Statute. Such acts were committed, according to OTP findings, against civilians participating in, or otherwise associated with, the Maidan protest movement in Kiev, as well as other regions in Ukraine. This collective comprised a large number of individuals, generally linked by their dissatisfaction with and opposition to the Yanukovych administration and its policies.
- The commission of violence against protesters, including the excessive use of force causing death and serious injury as well as other forms of ill-treatment, was found by the OTP to be actively promoted or encouraged by the Ukrainian authorities. In this respect, the OTP considers that it is possible to infer the existence of a state policy to attack the civilian population, within the meaning of Article 7(2)(a) of the Rome Statute, from the available information, namely: coordination of and cooperation with anti-Maidan citizen volunteers (i.e., *titushky*, or groups of unidentified private individuals) who violently targeted protesters; the consistent failure of state authorities (at multiple levels) to take any meaningful or effective action to prevent or deter the repetition of incidents of violence (including to genuinely pursue or investigate complaints or otherwise take measures to manage or hold accountable the law enforcement units alleged to be responsible for the serious ill-treatment of protest participants); and the apparent efforts to conceal or cover up alleged crimes.

As a preliminary conclusion, the OTP stated in its report[35] that the acts of violence allegedly committed by the Ukrainian authorities between 30 November 2013 and 20 February 2014 could constitute an "attack directed against a civilian population" under Article 7(2)(a) of the Rome Statute.

On the other hand, the legal analysis concluded that there was limited information available at that stage to support the conclusion that alleged attacks carried out in the context of the Maidan protests were either widespread or systematic, within the scope of Article 7 of the Rome Statute.[36] In its Report on Preliminary Examination Activities, issued on 14 of November 2016,[37] the OTP announced that it had received new information in October 2016, which would be subject to close examination for an eventual possible reassessment of its preliminary analysis of the Maidan protests in light of any new information. In its most recent report, [38] the OTP stated that it was analysing additional information related to the Maidan events, and that crimes

---

[34] Ibid., paras 89–90.

[35] Ibid., para 91.

[36] Ibid., para 100.

[37] See OTP Report on Preliminary Examination Activities 2016.

[38] See OTP Report on Preliminary Activities 2017.

allegedly committed during the period from 21 November 2013 to 22 February 2014 would not amount to crimes against humanity under the Statute.

More Filtered Information and Factual Analysis Following the Extended Examination of Events in Crimea and Eastern Ukraine Under Subject-Matter Jurisdiction – Phase 2

The Report on Preliminary Examination Activities, issued by the OTP on 14 of November 2016,[39] added more information on the situation in Crimea and Eastern Ukraine to inform the factual analysis of such events in order to identify potential cases from this situation.

On the Crimea Situation

Factual Identification of Events to Possibly Trigger the ICC's Jurisdiction

The report further processed the available information by adding a developed circumvention to the context in which, during the last days of February 2014, protests against the new government in Kiev began to build, notably in eastern regions of the country and in Simferopol, the capital of the Autonomous Republic of Crimea.

The report notes[40] that, on 27 February 2014, armed and mostly uniformed individuals wearing no identifying insignia seized control of government buildings in Simferopol, including the Crimean Parliament building. Such events were followed on the same day, in the reported presence of armed men, by the decision of the Crimean Regional Parliament to appoint a new prime minister and hold a referendum on the status of Crimea.

The OTP records,[41] for the first time within the Crimea context, the Russian Federation's admission that its military personnel had been involved in taking control of the Crimean Peninsula, justified by an intervention on the basis *inter alia* of alleged threats to Russian citizens, the alleged decision of residents of Crimea to join the Russian Federation, and an alleged request for Russian intervention by (former) President Yanukovych, whom the Russian Federation still considered as the legitimate leader of Ukraine.

The OTP Report on Preliminary Examination Activities factually stated[42] that the incorporation of Crimea and the city of Sevastopol into the Russian Federation was announced on 18 March 2014, following a referendum held two days earlier, which was declared invalid by the interim Ukrainian Government and by a majority of states at the UN General Assembly. The report also confirms the signing of the Treaty on the Adoption of the Republic of Crimea into Russia by the Crimean *de facto* authorities and the Russian Federation on 20 March 2014, followed by the adoption

---

[39] Ibid., paras 155–70.

[40] Ibid., para 155.

[41] Ibid.

[42] Ibid., para 156.

by the Russian State Duma of the Law on the Acceptance of the Republic of Crimea into the Russian Federation and the Creation of New Federal Subjects, paving the way for the application of Russian legislation and policy in Crimea. Furthermore, the report[43] acknowledged the consequences of the referendum, agreements and legislation passed by the Russian Duma in relation to Crimea, stating that Crimean residents were automatically declared Russian citizens, while those wishing to retain their Ukrainian citizenship were required to notify the authorities within a one-month deadline.

Thus, the assumption of control over Crimea by the Russian Federation occurred, for the most part, without an exchange of fire in mid-March, when the Ukrainian Government began withdrawing its troops stationed in bases on Crimea to the mainland.[44]

Legal Qualification of the Context of the Crimea Events

The report proceeded with a legal qualification of the situation within the territory of Crimea and Sevastopol, which, based on the information available, has been considered to be an international armed conflict between Ukraine and the Russian Federation, beginning at the latest on 26 February 2017, when the Russian Federation deployed members of its armed forces to gain control over parts of the Ukrainian territory without the consent of the Ukraine's government. The law of international armed conflict continued to apply after 18 March 2014 to the extent that the situation within the territory of Crimea and Sevastopol factually amounted to an ongoing state of occupation. A determination of whether or not the initial intervention, which led to the occupation, can be considered lawful is not required.

Alleged Crimes

Concerning alleged crimes committed in Crimea, the OTP put together a preliminary summary of alleged crimes based on publicly available reports and information it had received, leaving open the possibility that the office might identify any further alleged crimes in the course of its analysis. That said, this was not taken to be indicative of or implying any particular legal qualifications or factual determinations regarding the alleged conduct.

For Crimea, the OTP indicated[45] the following as alleged crimes:

- The harassment of the Crimean Tatar population–Since the assumption of control by the Russian Federation over the territory of Crimea, some 19,000 residents of the region have reportedly become internally displaced within mainland Ukraine. A large proportion of this number of internally displaced persons is believed to be of Crimean Tatar ethnicity. Under the application of Russian law throughout the territory, members of the Crimean Tatar population and other Muslims residents in

---

[43] Ibid.

[44] Ibid., para 157.

[45] Ibid., paras 172–6.

Crimea have also reportedly been subjected to harassment or intimidation, including a variety of measures such as entry bans to the territory, house searches, and restrictions on their freedom of expression, assembly and association.

- Killing and abduction: At least 10 people have been reported missing since March 2014 in the context of the situation in Crimea. In most instances, the alleged victims were known to oppose the occupation of Crimea and their abductions were attributed to the "Crimean Self-Defence" paramilitary group. The OTP is also analysing two incidents of alleged abduction and killing of Crimean Tatar activists in March and September of 2014.
- Ill-treatment: Several incidents of alleged ill-treatment in the context of detention or abduction were also reported, including beatings, choking, and, in at least one instance, threats of sexual violence.
- Detention and fair trial: A number of civilians who opposed the 16 March referendum have reportedly been arrested and held in detention since March 2014 with the information available pointing to the non-respect of a number of due process and fair trial rights. Some 179 persons deprived of their liberty have reportedly been forcibly transferred from prisons in Crimea to prisons in the territory of the Russian Federation.
- Compulsory military service: As a consequence of the imposed change in citizenship, men of conscription age residing in Crimea became subject to mandatory Russian military service requirements. There were reports of a number of young men leaving for mainland Ukraine to escape forced conscription notices from the *de facto* authorities.

Eastern Ukraine

Factual Identification of Events to Possibly Trigger the ICC's Jurisdiction

For Eastern Ukraine, the most current OTP report notes[46] that anti-government protests continued in other regions of Ukraine, but most notably in the east of the country, while, during April and May 2014, anti-government demonstrators seized government buildings in the Eastern Ukrainian provinces of Kharkiv, Donetsk and Luhansk. The report identifies an anti-government group calling itself the "Donbas People's Militia", which emerged and has attempted by law enforcement to regain control of areas thwarted by reoccupations by anti-government elements.

The factual situation in Eastern Ukraine is further detailed[47] with elements of violence and the reaction of the Ukrainian Government on 15 April 2014, which announced the start of an "anti-terror operation" and deployed its armed forces to Donetsk and Luhansk. The report also states that, at the end of April 2014, the then acting Ukrainian President announced that the Ukrainian Government was no longer in full control of Donetsk and Luhansk, and that country was on "full combat alert", as well as reinstating conscription into the armed forces by decree.

---

[46] Ibid., para 159.
[47] Ibid., para 160.

In addition, the OTP reports[48] on the events of 2 May 2014 in Odessa, Southern Ukraine, which further exacerbated anti-government feeling in the eastern areas and turned the protests in the city, between pro-unity and pro-federalist supporters violent, resulting in more than 40 deaths, mainly among the pro-federalist protesters who had taken refuge inside a trade union building, in which a fire then started.

The OTP also refers to the "referenda" held on 11 May 2014, which were deemed illegitimate by the Ukrainian Government, and the declarations of "independence" from Ukraine by representatives of the self-proclaimed DPR and LPR. Both "people's republics" appealed to be incorporated into the Russian Federation, but remain unrecognized by almost all states, including the Russian Federation.

More elements of the increased intensity of hostilities in Eastern Ukraine in April and May 2014 have been added to the OTP's factual analysis. Included as significant in terms of triggering the ICC's jurisdiction was on the shooting down of two Ukrainian military helicopters over the eastern city of Sloviansk by anti-government armed elements on 2 May,[49] intense battles for control of Donetsk International Airport at the end of May, and the shooting down of a Ukrainian military transport plane as it approached Luhansk Airport on 14 June.

The OTP has considered the Russian Federation's claim from mid-July 2014 that Ukrainian armed forces shelled the Russian border town of Donets, as well as Kiev's claim that rockets were fired at Ukrainian military positions over several days in July and August 2014, which had been launched from positions in the Russian Federation, along with the shooting-down of a Ukrainian military aircraft by the Russian Air Force on 16 July 2014.[50]

A further event considered within the context of the Eastern Ukraine situation and the factual identification of potential cases elements is the shooting-down on 17 July 2014[51] of a civilian aircraft (Malaysian Airlines flight MH17) *en route* from Amsterdam to Kuala Lumpur, carrying 298 passengers and crew, over Eastern Ukraine, in which everyone on board was killed. According to the OTP, a joint investigation team has been formed to look into the incident, following an agreement between Ukraine, Malaysia, the Netherlands (whose nationals represented the majority of victims) and the other states whose nationals had been on board. The OTP also reports that this team alleges that the aircraft as shot down from a location near Pervomaisk, Donetsk, in the territory controlled by anti-government armed groups.

Legal Qualification of the Context of the Events

The report focuses on identifying whether the threshold of an internal armed conflict, in terms of intensity and organization, has been reached in Eastern Ukraine.

In this sense, the OTP has identified[52] persistent fighting, to varying degrees of intensity and involving the use of military weaponry on both sides, for more than two

---

[48] Ibid., para 161.

[49] Ibid., para 164.

[50] Ibid.

[51] Ibid., para 165.

[52] Ibid., para 168.

years in Eastern Ukraine between Ukrainian Government forces and anti-government elements, allegedly supported by the Russian Federation.

Two periods of particularly intense battles are recorded in relation to Ilovaisk (Donetsk Oblast) in late August 2014 and in Debaltseve (Donetsk) from January to February 2015. The increased intensity of fighting during these periods is attributed to alleged corresponding influxes of troops, vehicles and weaponry from the Russian Federation to reinforce the positions of the armed groups.

The report also highlights[53] the effects of the two attempted ceasefire agreements, the Minsk Protocol, signed on 5 September 2014, and a second agreement within the same framework, known as "Minsk II", in February 2015, both of which failed to achieve a cessation of hostilities.

The second agreement, monitored by the OSCE, appears to have reduced the intensity of fighting to some extent, but daily violations of the ceasefire, including the use of heavy weapons, and detentions by both sides have continued.

Based on the information available, the OTP has reached a preliminary conclusion[54] that, by 30 April 2014, the level of intensity of hostilities between Ukrainian Government forces and anti-government armed elements in Eastern Ukraine reached a level that would trigger the application of the law of armed conflict.

Regarding the level of organization, the OTP considers that the information available indicates that the level of organization among armed groups operating in Eastern Ukraine, including the DPR and the LPR, had by the same time reached a degree that was sufficient[55] for them to be parties to a non-international armed conflict.

The report also considers additional information, such as the reported shelling by both states of each other's military positions, and the detention of Russian military personnel by Ukraine, and *vice versa*, concluding that such information points to direct military engagement between Russian armed forces and Ukrainian Government forces, which would suggest the existence of an international armed conflict in the context of armed hostilities in Eastern Ukraine since 14 July 2014 at the latest, in parallel to the non-international armed conflict.

For the purpose of determining whether the otherwise non-international armed conflict could, in fact, be international in character, the OTP is examining allegations that the Russian Federation has exercised overall control over armed groups in Eastern Ukraine. In conducting its analysis, the OTP[56] must assess whether the information available indicates that Russian authorities have provided support to the armed groups in the form of equipment, financing and personnel, and also whether they have generally directed or helped in planning actions of the armed groups in a manner indicating that they exercised genuine control over them.

---

[53] Ibid., para 167.

[54] Ibid., para 168.

[55] Ibid., para 168.

[56] Ibid., para 170.

Alleged Crimes

Concerning alleged crimes committed in Eastern Ukraine, the OTP has put together a preliminary summary of alleged crimes, based on publicly available reports and information received by the OTP, leaving open the possible identification of any further alleged crimes that could be further made by the office in the course of its analysis. This should not be taken as being indicative of or implying any particular legal qualifications or factual determinations regarding the alleged conduct.

For Eastern Ukraine, the OTP has documented[57] more than 800 incidents involving crimes allegedly committed since 20 February 2014 in the context of events in Eastern Ukraine, as follows:

- Killing: Since the start of the conflict, according to the UN Office of the High Commissioner for Human Rights, some 9,578 people have been killed and 22,236 injured, including members of the armed forces and armed groups and civilians. Between April 2014 and June 2016, up to 2,000 civilians were killed in armed hostilities, mostly (85–90%) as a result of the shelling of populated areas in both government-controlled territory and areas controlled by armed groups. Other incidents reported include several civilians allegedly killed or injured by firearms, attributed to both pro-government forces and armed groups. A smaller number of summary executions of persons who were *hors de combat*, including members of armed groups and Ukrainian forces, are also alleged.
- Destruction of civilian objects: In the course of the conflict, hundreds of civilian objects, including residential properties, schools and kindergartens, have allegedly been destroyed or damaged, largely by shelling, in both government-controlled territory and in areas controlled by armed groups. In some cases, it is alleged that the shelling of such objects was deliberate or indiscriminate, or that civilian buildings including schools have been improperly used for military purposes.
- Detention: All sides have also allegedly captured and detained both civilians and fighters of the opposing side in the context of the conflict in Eastern Ukraine. Ukrainian security forces are alleged to have held both civilians and alleged armed group members without due process, while DPR and LPR forces are alleged to have arbitrarily detained civilians suspected of being pro-Ukrainian and members of Ukrainian armed forces, and in many cases ill-treated them. Several hundred detentions have occurred during the conflict and, in many instances, those detained have been exchanged in mutual prisoner releases by both sides, although often after long periods of detention.
- Disappearance: More than 400 people have been registered as "missing" in the context of the conflict in Eastern Ukraine, although it remains unclear as to how many of these individuals were forcibly disappeared. Some are believed to be alive and in detention, while others may be among the large number of bodies that remain unidentified by the relevant authorities. Some documented instances of alleged forced disappearance have, however, been reported and are mainly attributed to pro-government forces.

---

[57] Ibid., paras 177–83.

- Torture/ill-treatment: Torture or ill-treatment has reportedly been perpetrated by both sides in the context of the conflict, involving several hundred alleged victims. Beatings, the use of electric shocks and other physical abuse are widely documented in both government-controlled territory and in areas outside the government's control, allegedly targeted at civilians and members of both Ukrainian armed forces and armed groups. In the majority of the reported incidents, the torture or ill-treatment occurred in the context of detention, frequently in "irregular" detention facilities and often during interrogation.
- Sexual and gender-based crimes: While there are some documented instances of alleged sexual and gender-based crimes in the context of the conflict in Eastern Ukraine, the OTP acknowledges that the information available could suffer from under-reporting due to social and cultural taboos, and a lack of support services for victims in conflict-affected areas, among other factors. The majority of documented instances allegedly occurred in the context of detention and targeted male and female victims, including civilians and members of the armed forces or armed groups. These alleged crimes can be attributed to both state and non-state forces. In several documented cases, sexual violence, including rape, threats of rape, the beating of genitals and forced nudity were perpetrated in the context of interrogations.

The 2017 OTP Report takes account of additional information with respect to the qualification of the situation in Crimea and Eastern Ukraine under international law. The OTP database was extended to over 1,200 reported incidents alleged to have occurred in the context of the situation in Eastern Ukraine.

The preliminary examination is slowly moving in the case of Ukraine's two declarations of acceptance of the ICC's jurisdiction. Based on the information received under Article 15, the OTP has identified, in more detail, the context of the situation in Ukraine, with a particular focus on three events, the Maidan protests, Crimea and Eastern Ukraine, which are also the three territorial delimitations of the eventual ICC's jurisdiction exercise.

The four Reports on Preliminary Examination Activities from 2014, 2015, 2016 and 2017 have kept such activities at the beginning of Phase 2 – subject-matter jurisdiction. Concerning the Maidan protests, the OTP has reached preliminary conclusions given the actual absence of factual and legal elements for triggering the material jurisdiction of the ICC, while, in the case of Crimea and Eastern Ukraine, more concrete elements for determining the ICC's material jurisdiction are required.

The peculiarities of Ukraine's situation, given the OTP's preliminary examination filter, have been triggered by the way in which Ukraine decided to accept the ICC's jurisdiction, i.e., by making declarations under Article 12(3) of the Rome Statute, rather than by way of ratifying the Rome Statute, which would have conferred on Ukraine the rights and obligations of a state party to the statute. Ukraine has put itself into an awkward position:[58] on the one hand, the ICC potentially has full jurisdiction over any international crimes committed in Ukraine after 21 November 2013 (the beginning of the Maidan protests); on the other, Ukraine does not enjoy all the privileges of a member state.

Ukraine's delay in ratifying the Rome Statute is not going to serve any purpose in terms of protecting its own military involved in the situation, in deference to the ICC, but rather generates[59] an international misperception that Ukraine has something to hide.

Moreover, the acceptance of jurisdiction in two stages – the first declaration, involving specific subject matter limited in time to the Maidan protests situation, and the second declaration, in relation to alleged crimes committed on Ukrainian territory from 20 February 2014 onwards, with no end date, issued by the Ukrainian Government on 8 September 2015, after Ukraine lost full control over Crimea and Eastern Ukraine (i.e., Donetsk and Luhansk) – would create further challenges for the Phase 2 assessment by the OTP of the subject-matter jurisdiction, which, if successfully passed, would lead to Phases 3 and 4 of the preliminary investigation.

Maidan Protests

The three OTP reports focused on the Maidan protests in terms of gathering and processing information on these events and determining the eventual case for ICC jurisdiction.

The OTP ruled out the possibility that, in relation to the Maidan protests, either a non-international or an international armed conflict existed, while limiting its preliminary conclusion on the material jurisdiction of the ICC as being not applicable to these protests, which did involve some, but not all, elements of crimes against humanity. It was found that, with regard to the Maidan protests, the widespread or systematic nature of the attack against the civilian population cannot be assessed on the basis of existing information, although the OTP did not reach any conclusions while awaiting and analysing possible new information.

While this article is centred on determining the challenges for the OTP in triggering the ICC's jurisdiction, and not on the analysis of possible crimes in Ukraine[60] under such jurisdiction, given the ongoing findings of the OTP on this subject, one may infer that the Maidan protests were unlikely to pass the OTP's Phase 2 filter, i.e., subject-matter jurisdiction.

When any information received and processed by the OTP does not at least cover the basic elements of the crimes under the ICC's material jurisdiction, there is little room left to consider whether the other preconditions of its jurisdiction can be met in terms of a reasonable basis for determining the opening of an investigation by the Prosecutor.

---

[58] Polunina and Umland 2016.

[59] Ibid.

[60] An analysis of the crimes committed on the territory of Ukraine from November 2013 onward can be found in Chapter 18 *infra*.

Although the temporal and territorial jurisdiction checks on the Maidan protests would likely have, given the information processed by the OTP so far, positive results, the *ratione personae* jurisdiction could pose several challenges in the identification of the perpetrators and making charges against them. In Ukraine, there is an ongoing criminal investigation against former President Yanukovych for actions against the Maidan protesters; indeed, in 2014, the country requested an international arrest warrant for genocide against Yanukovych. It is a well-known fact that Yanukovych, as recorded in the OTP's reports, left Ukraine on 22 February 2014 and now lives in Russia. From this perspective, one may consider that the ICC cannot address Ukraine's public demand for justice in full, as it typically only focuses on high-ranking perpetrators of crimes against international law.

Further, the gravity of crimes precondition could also be viewed as challenging, in passing, the Maidan protests. While the OTP noted[61] that "serious human rights abuses had occurred in the context of the Maidan events", the "gravity threshold" requires the assessment of the scale, nature, manner of commission and impact that such acts would have had, if falling under Article 5 crimes.

If the Maidan protests are satisfactory in terms of the Phase 2 assessment, thereby initiating Phases 3 and 4, further challenges would appear from the point of view of the admissibility assessment under the complementarity requirement of the ICC's jurisdiction. Prosecutions in relations to Maidan protest in terms of repressions against the protesters are currently taking place in Ukraine.

Last but not least, the interests of justice assessment, which can only be considered where positive determinations have been made on both jurisdiction and admissibility, is going to be challenging in the context of the Maidan protests. The interests of justice test is a potential countervailing consideration, which could produce a reason not to proceed, even where both jurisdiction and admissibility are positive.

Under Article 53(2)(c) of the Rome Statute, the Prosecutor[62] is required to consider whether a prosecution is not in the interests of justice by taking into account all of the circumstances, including the gravity of the crime, the interests of the victims, the age or infirmity of the accused, and his or her role in the accused crime. Considering again the targeting by ICC jurisdiction of high-ranking perpetrators of crimes against international law, and the role played by former President Yanukovych in the repression of the Maidan protests, one may conclude that it is likely that the Prosecutor might conclude that the interests of justice regarding the Maidan protests would not justify opening an investigation.

Crimea

An assessment of the Crimea situation is further advanced under Phase 2 (subject-matter jurisdiction) of the OTP report, which reveals a thorough factual and legal analysis of information received in relation to the conflict in order to establish whether

---

[61] Report on Preliminary Examination Activities 2016.

[62] Policy Papers on Interests of Justice, September 2007. https://www.icc-cpi.int/NR/rdonlyres/772C95C9-F54D-4321-BF09-73422BB23528/143640/ICCOTPInterestsOfJustice.pdf. Accessed 12 July 2017.

there is a reasonable basis to believe that the alleged crimes fall within the subject-matter jurisdiction of the ICC.

The situation in Ukraine concerning Crimea in this phase has been focused on both the examination and the evaluation of information relevant to determining the existence (or otherwise) of an international armed conflict in Crimea and an analysis the more specific alleged acts that may constitute crimes under Article 5 of the Rome Statute.

The OTP reached the conclusion that, on the information available regarding Crimea, an international armed conflict exists between Ukraine and the Russian Federation, which began no later than 26 February 2014, when the Russian Federation deployed members of its armed forces to gain control over parts of Ukrainian territory without the consent of the Ukrainian Government.

The law of international armed conflict would continue to apply after 18 March 2014 to the extent that the situation within the territory of Crimea and Sevastopol factually amounts to an ongoing state of occupation.

Further, the OTP states[63] that a determination of whether or not the initial intervention, which led to the occupation, is considered lawful is not required. The statement from the OTP gives a clear indication that the state of ongoing occupation and the existence of an international armed conflict are going to be considered as the contextual element of war crimes under the Rome Statute. Such a conclusion is also supported by the indication of alleged crimes, which may fall within the nexus of international armed conflict material elements of war crimes under Article 8 of the Rome Statute.

While the preliminary conclusions on an eventual ICC *ratione materiae* jurisdiction are positive regarding Crimea, the personal and territorial jurisdiction assessment may encounter several problems.

The OTP, according to its most recent report, notes that Ukraine lost full control over Crimea, while the Russian Federation admitted that its military personnel had been involved in taking control of the Crimean Peninsula.

It is indicative that the eventual ICC jurisdiction over the Crimea events starting in February 2014 is supported by the second Ukraine declaration under Article 12(3) of Rome Statute, dated 8 September 2015. Lodging such a declaration does not automatically trigger the jurisdiction of the ICC, as stated in the Agenda for the Appeal of the Pre-Trial Chamber's Decision, whose only purpose was to broaden the temporal and territorial jurisdiction of the court.[64]

In accordance with Article 12 of the ICC's statute, the court shall have territorial jurisdiction over the crimes referred to in Article 5, provided that the state in which the crime was conducted (a territorial state or the state of which the accused is a national, i.e., the nationality state) is a party to the statute or has lodged a declaration accepting the court's jurisdiction on an *ad hoc* basis. Consequently, it may be inferred that only a territorial state or a nationality state is competent to lodge a declaration pursuant to Article 12(3) of the statute.

---

[63] Report on Preliminary Examination Activities 2016.

[64] Stahn and Sluiter 2009, p. 76.

In this situation, Ukraine has lodged the said declaration as a territorial state, despite the fact that it lost its effective control over Crimea from February 2014 onwards and the alleged crimes preliminarily identified by the OTP appear to have been committed after this date. Moreover, not only did Ukraine have no effective control over Crimea at the time of commissioning the alleged crimes, but Ukraine also had no effective control over Crimea at the moment the declaration was lodged (8 September 2015).

Although effective control over the territory in which alleged crimes were committed is not necessarily a precondition for lodging a declaration under Article 12(3), the loss of effective control by Ukraine over Crimea, in the context of alleged war crimes committed on this territory from February 2015 onwards, is going to have consequences in triggering the ICC's jurisdiction in the preliminary examination phase.

The application of effective control must meet two conditions: "[a] willingness of implementing or continuing to implement the acts of control" and "[that] the acts actually show the purpose of control".[65] The acts of effective control (i) should be the acts of a sovereign state related to the disputed territory.[66] Acts of sovereignty are, but not limited to, legislative acts or acts of administrative control, taking taxes from the population, and regulating fishing and other economic activities.[67] The public character of the acts, by necessity,[68] (ii) should be sustained and stable. "Sustained" means no interruption, while "stable" stresses that there should be no state making competing sovereignty claims[69] over disputed territory over a long period of time. Meanwhile, there is the issue of (iii) relativity, which is the consequence of the measurement in relation to state parties' acts.[70]

In the Crimea situation, most of these criteria are fulfilled in terms of the Russian Federation's effective control over Crimea at the point when the alleged crimes under the ICC's material jurisdiction were committed and the point when Ukraine's declaration under Article 12(3) of the Rome Statute was lodged.

It is of great importance that the Crimea situation was qualified by the OTP as being an ongoing occupation by the Russian Federation from 2014 onwards, meaning that international humanitarian law would apply. Nevertheless, if such a qualification is of strong relevance from the point of view of war crimes allegedly committed on Crimea's territory, for which a nexus involving an ongoing armed conflict is essential, would the same qualification serve the purpose of determining the "precise scope of the territorial parameter of the Court's jurisdiction"?[71]

---

[65] Legal Status of Eastern Greenland (Denmark v. Norway) PCIJ. Series A/B No.3, p. 45.

[66] Ibid. 23, para 136.

[67] Ibid., pp. 713–22, paras 176–208; see also Minquiers and Ecrehos, 1953 ICJ, p. 54.

[68] Sovereignty over Pedra Branca/Pulau Batu Puteh, Middle Rocksand South Ledge (Malaysia/Singapore). ICJ. Judgment of 23 May 2008. paras 285, 290.

[69] Dixon and McCorquodale 2003, p. 245.

[70] Munkman 1972–73, p. 104.

[71] See Vagias 2011, p. 15.

The application[72] submitted by Ukraine against the Russian Federation to the International Court of Justice (ICJ), by which the court is requested to deliver a judgement as to the breach by the Russian Federation concerning the International Convention for the Suppression of the Financing of Terrorism and of the International Convention on the Elimination of All Forms of Racial Discrimination, as well as the request for a provisional measures order,[73] somewhat weakens the support of Ukraine as a full territorial state, which is entitled to lodge a declaration under Article 12(3). Such an ICJ application recognizes implicitly that, in respect of the alleged crimes in relation to the discrimination of the Tatar population in Crimea, the effective control, on the commission of such crimes, lies with the Russian Federation, which was in effective control of Crimea.

There are certainly still several powerful arguments that would support an interpretation of Ukraine's right to lodge a declaration under Article 12(3) of the Rome Statute in support of the ICC's jurisdiction over Crimea.

The illegitimacy of the Crimea referendum, according to the Ukraine Government, would illegalize all subsequent legislative acts in Crimea and the Russian Federation, on the basis of the Treaty on the Adoption of the Republic of Crimea into Russia, between the Crimean de facto authorities and the Russian Federation on 20 March 2014, followed by the adoption by the Russian State Duma of the Law on the Acceptance of the Republic of Crimea into the Russian Federation and the Creation of New Federal Subjects, paving the way for the application of Russian legislation and policy in Crimea.

Moreover, the negative attitude of the international community towards the result of the referendum is of vital significance in deciding the legitimacy of a referendum. Currently, very few UN states have recognized Crimea as federal subject of the Russian Federation, while the majority of UN states have declared non-recognition. The lack of international recognition further justifies the illegitimacy of the referendum and supports the ongoing sovereignty of Ukraine over Crimea.

The context of establishing territorial and personal ICC jurisdiction over Crimea should not be neglected in relation to alleged crimes on the part of the Russian Federation following qualification of the Crimea situation as an ongoing occupation. On 16 November 2016, Russia announced that it was formally withdrawing its signature from the founding statute of the ICC, a day after the court published a report classifying the Russian annexation of Crimea as an occupation.[74]

Beyond the passions surrounding the subject of Crimea's annexation by the Russian Federation, one cannot ignore the debatable legal and practical aspects of determining the ICC's territorial and personal jurisdiction. One of the implications of Ukraine's declaration under Article 12(3) concerns its cooperation with the ICC in

---

[72] Application of the International Convention for the Suppression of the Financing of Terrorism and of the International Convention on the Elimination of All Forms of Racial Discrimination (Ukraine V. Russian Federation). http://www.icj-cij.org/files/case-related/166/19394.pdf. Accessed 12 July 2017.

[73] Ibid.

[74] See: https://www.theguardian.com/world/2016/nov/16/russia-withdraws-signature-from-international-criminal-court-statute. Accessed 12 July 2017.

determining and exercising its jurisdiction over crimes that are materially, personally, territorially and temporally covered by such a declaration.

Considering the actual ongoing situation of Crimea as an autonomous republic within the Russian Federation and the position of Russia towards the ICC, it is to be expected Russia does not support the OTP's preliminary examination activities concerning alleged war crimes committed on Crimean territory after Ukraine's loss of control.

The gravity of crimes and complementarity criteria, under the admissibility assessment of the OTP's Phase 3 filter, should also pose further challenges for the analysis of Crimea situation. From the information analysed by the OTP in its most recent report, the alleged crimes are indicated in the possible context of, and armed conflict as, eventual war crimes with consequences in terms of the numbers of victims, which are not necessarily significant in terms of scale, nature, manner of commission and eventual impact.

Last but not least, the interests of justice assessment should play a decisive role in the Prosecutor's decision about whether or not to open an investigation into Crimea and finally in triggering the ICC's jurisdiction over Crimea.

Eastern Ukraine

For Eastern Ukraine, the Donbas area and the self-proclaimed DPR and LPR, the 2016 OTP's report[75] offers a coherent and pertinent analysis of the situation, which is most likely to lead to the actual triggering of the ICC's jurisdiction.

In its analysis, the OTP identifies the context of the events in Eastern Ukraine: i.e., the existence of an armed conflict, whether internal and/or international, and whether Russia's support for anti-governmental militia was in the form of direction or help in planning actions by armed groups in a manner that indicated it was exercising genuine control over them.

On alleged crimes committed in Eastern Ukraine, the OTP has put together a preliminary summary of alleged crimes, based on publicly available reports and information received by the ICC concerning more than 800 incidents, which involve crimes allegedly committed since 20 February 2014 in the context of events in Eastern Ukraine, which in general amount to material elements of war crimes.

The preconditions of territorial, temporal and personal jurisdiction for the ICC are easily configurable by the information processed by the OTP in the case of Eastern Ukraine for the Phase 2 filter. Ukraine's loss of control in the east of the country and Russian support for anti-governmental forces could pose in this case challenges for determining territorial and personal jurisdiction, given that cooperation between the ICC, Ukraine and/or Russian Federation is unlikely.

On meeting the requirements of Phase 2, the Eastern Ukraine situation is likely to reach Phase 3, making admissibility (gravity of crimes and complementarity) factors more assessable.

In Phase 4, the OTP filter concerning interests of justice may also be more justifiable in the case of events in Eastern Ukraine.

---

[75] Report on Preliminary Examination Activities 2016.

A preliminary examination in the case of Eastern Ukraine could potentially end with a decision by the Prosecutor to open an investigation into this situation and turn it into a potential case, which in turn triggers the ICC's jurisdiction.

17.5 Conclusion

Triggering the ICC's jurisdiction is a complex process, which is also costly and time-consuming. In the case of Ukraine, the process is even more complex and faces more challenges, mainly due to the way in which Ukraine decided to accept the ICC's jurisdiction, instead of becoming a state party to the Rome Statute.

In addition, Ukraine's situation is complicated given Russia's formal intervention in Crimea and its informal support of the self-proclaimed DPR and LPR, which will definitely impact on the legal process pursued by the ICC, especially in the early preliminary examination.

As explained above, although the conduct of the OTP is not completely predictable, the evolution of its findings in the factual and legal analysis of the Ukraine situation could be considered indicative of the finally triggering of the ICC's jurisdiction concerning the Ukraine events, which are part of this country's situation.

Although the overall political situation is strongly impacting the OTP's findings, the practical legal factors, as presented, will finally support the decision of the Prosecutor to open an investigation into the Ukraine case.

It should not be forgotten that, in this process, the role that the ICC is seeking to play is that of an independent and professional court of justice, intervening only to complement national jurisdictions in those very specific cases when such national jurisdictions are not functioning or willing to function and to prosecute those most heinous crimes committed by high-ranking perpetrators under international law.

Ukraine's expectations that the ICC will act as a substitute for the Ukrainian authorities are not going to be fulfilled. The ICC will not carry out all the work of the Ukrainian national authorities on their behalf, nor will it usurp the role of national courts in prosecuting international crimes.

To conclude, the Ukraine situation, in relation to all three events discussed above, should be seen as a splendid opportunity for the ICC to unroll its statutory professional checks, reviews and safeguards and reveal its commitment to act as a powerful deterrent against impunity.

References

Application of The International Convention for The Suppression of The Financing Of Terrorism and of The International Convention on The Elimination of All Forms Of Racial Discrimination (Ukraine v. Russian Federation), http://www.icj-cij.org/files/case-related/166/19394.pdf. Accessed 12 July 2017.

Dixon M, McCorquodale R (2003) Cases & Materials on International Law, 4th edn. Oxford University Press, Oxford

ICC (2002) Elements of Crimes replicated from the Official Records of the Assembly of States Parties to the Rome Statute of the International Criminal Court, First session, New York, 3-10 September 2002 (United Nations publication, Sales No.E.03.V.2 and corrigendum), part II.B. The Elements of Crimes adopted at the 2010 Review Conference are replicated from the Official Records of the Review Conference of the Rome Statute of the International Criminal Court, Kampala, 31 May - 11 June 2010 (International Criminal Court publication, RC/11), https://www.icc-cpi.int/NR/rdonlyres/336923D8-A6AD-40EC-AD7B-45BF9DE7 3D56/0/ElementsOfCrimesEng.pdf. Accessed 12 July 2017.

ICC (2002) Rules of Procedure and Evidence, https://www.casematrixnetwork.org/cmn-knowledge-hub/icc-commentary-clicc/rules-of-procedure-and-evidence/#c1569. Accessed 12 July 2017.

ICC (2007) Policy Papers on Interests of Justice, September 2007, https://www.icc-cpi.int/NR/rdonlyres/772C95C9-F54D-4321-BF09-73422BB23528/143640/ICCOTPInterestsOfJustice.pdf. Accessed 12 July 2017

ICC (2009) Regulations of the Office of the Prosecutor ICC-BD/05-01-09, 23 April 2009, https://www.icc-cpi.int/NR/rdonlyres/FFF97111-ECD6-40B5-9CDA-792BCBE1E695/2 80253/ICCBD050109ENG.pdf. Accessed 9 July 2017

ICC (2014) OTP Report on Preliminary Examinations Activities, 2 December 2014, https://www.icc-cpi.int/iccdocs/otp/OTP-Pre-Exam-2014.pdf. Accessed 9 July 2017.

ICC (2015) OTP Report on Preliminary Examinations Activities, 12 November 2015, https://www.icc-cpi.int//Pages/item.aspx?name=otp-rep-pe-activities-2015. Accessed 12 July 2017

ICC (2016) OTP Report on Preliminary Examination Activities 2016, https://www.icc-cpi.int/iccdocs/otp/161114-otp-rep-PE_ENG.pdf. Accessed 10 July 2017

ICC (2017) OTP Report on Preliminary Examination Activities 2017, https://www.icc-cpi.int/itemsDocuments/2017-PE-rep/2017-otp-rep-PE_ENG.pdf. Accessed 10 July 2018.

ICC (2017) ICC Prosecutor extends preliminary examination of the situation in Ukraine following second article 12(3) declaration, https://www.icc-cpi.int/legalAidConsultations?name=pr1156. Accessed 12 July 2017

ICJ (2008) Sovereignty over Pedra Branca/Pulau Batu Puteh, Middle Rocks and South Ledge (Malaysia/ Singapore). Judgment of 23 May 2008

Maillard J-B (2014) Article 12(2)(a) Rome Statute: The Missing Piece of the Jurisdictional Puzzle, https://www.ejiltalk.org/article-122a-rome-statute-the-missing-piece-of-the-jurisdictional-puzzle/. Accessed 15 June 2017

Munkman ALW (1972–1973) Adjudication and Adjustment-International Judicial Decision and the Settlement of Territorial and Boundary Disputes, British Yearbook of International Law, Vol 46, 1972–1973

Ochi M (2016) Gravity threshold before the International Criminal Court: an overview of the Court's practice at http://www.internationalcrimesdatabase.org/upload/documents/20160111T1 15040-Ochi%20ICD%20Format.pdf Accessed 9 July 2017

PCIJ, Legal Status of Eastern Greenland (Denmark v. Norway). Series A/B No.3.

Polunina V, Umland A (2016) If Ukraine Wants the ICC's Help, It Must Play by the ICC's Rules, at http://nationalinterest.org/feature/if-ukraine-wants-the-iccs-help-it-must-play-by-its-rules-17 089. Accessed at 12 July 2017

Sluiter G (2009) The Emerging Practice of the International Criminal Court. Martinus Nijhoff Publishers, Leiden/Boston, p. 76

Vagias M (2011) The Territorial Jurisdiction of the International Criminal Court, Certain Contested Issues. Bykers Hoek Publishing https://openaccess.leidenuniv.nl/bitstream/handle/1887/17669/ Kopie%20van%2015976970002-bw.pdf?sequence=3 Accessed 1 July 2017

Chapter 18
War Crimes Committed During the Armed Conflict in Ukraine: What Should the ICC Focus On?

Rustam Atadjanov

Contents

Abstract Despite the claims that the ongoing armed conflict in Ukraine has become a "frozen zone", the reality demonstrates such a characterization runs afoul of the facts: hostilities continue on, with the increasing number of cases of massive human rights violations following the use of force by the Russian Federation in Crimea and its participation in the conflict in Eastern Ukraine. According to multiple reports, those violations in many cases amount to war crimes. It is thus necessary to ensure a proper compliance with legal rules applicable in the course of armed conflict, i.e., rules of international humanitarian law. Making sure the perpetrators of such crimes are brought under proper responsibility in accordance with relevant international criminal law standards is of equal importance. The matter of analysing and properly qualifying the human rights violations as crimes under the jurisdiction of the ICC

The author is Dr. jur. (Ph.D.) Candidate in International Criminal Law, Faculty of Law, University of Hamburg.
Rustam B. Atadjanov, Universität Hamburg, Fakultät für Rechtswissenschaft, Rothenbaumchaussee 33, 20148 Hamburg, Germany. e-mail: rustamatadjanov1@gmail.com.

R. Atadjanov (✉)
Fakultät für Rechtswissenschaft, Universität Hamburg, Rothenbaumchaussee 33,
20148 Hamburg, Germany
e-mail: rustamatadjanov1@gmail.com

© T.M.C. ASSER PRESS and the authors 2018
S. Sayapin and E. Tsybulenko (eds.), *The Use of Force against Ukraine
and International Law*, https://doi.org/10.1007/978-94-6265-222-4_18

will be a central substantive task of the Prosecution team and the Court if the situation makes it to the case. This Chapter deals with the qualification of war crimes as pertains to the armed conflict in Ukraine. Its main aim is to consider the relevant IHL norms and apply them to the alleged acts. This is instrumental in a proper determination of what criteria could be helpful for the ICC in ensuring the criminal responsibility of those who committed – and continue to commit, the horrible acts on both sides of the conflict. Eventually, the Chapter will argue that adjudicating war crimes committed in Ukraine by all parties at the ICC level represents an imperative task if the claimed purpose of international criminal law to bring the perpetrators of international crimes to justice is viable at all.

Keywords War crimes · Ukraine · Types of armed conflict · International humanitarian law · International Criminal Court · Case selection and evaluation criteria

18.1 Introduction

The ongoing situation in Ukraine has recently come to be referred to in the popular news as a "frozen zone" or "forgotten war", along with other regions where Russia used force or intervened – such as South Ossetia and Abkhazia, Transnistria and Nagorno-Karabach.[1] It has been claimed that because of the indifference and waning interest on the side of the Western news media towards the armed conflict in Ukraine – in Donbass in particular, and the ensuing dire situation the civilian population of the region finds itself in, it may be doomed to become a so-called "long-term frozen zone" – an area where the living standards are inferior, virtually no government support for the population can be found and no normal societal development is possible.[2]

However, the most recent events in the city of Avdiivka in the Donetsk region have demonstrated that the hostilities in Eastern Ukraine had not gone into a dormant or frozen state. The battle of Avdiivka between the Ukrainian government forces and pro-Russian separatists has been acknowledged as the deadliest one in weeks[3] and it may have been the most intense fighting episode so far in 2017. Moreover, if one looks at the overall numbers of victims and casualties since the armed conflict in Eastern Ukraine started (April 2014), it becomes clear that this conflict is anything but frozen or ordinary: according to the United Nations Human Rights Monitoring Mission in Ukraine (UNHRMMU), mortar, rocket, and artillery attacks between April 2014 and May 2016 claimed lives of over 9,000 people and injured more than

---

[1] Altshuller 2017, at 8.

[2] Ibid.

[3] A. Prentice, 'Ukraine Says More Soldiers Killed In Deadliest Clashes In Weeks', *Reuters* (*US edition*), 30 January 2017.

21,000 — including civilians and combatants on all sides — in Donetsk and Luhansk regions.[4]

What is also troubling is that the available reports indicate towards a stable increase in these casualty numbers.[5] The killings, harassment, mistreatment, persecutions, unlawful detention and other types of what is often called both individual and collective human rights breaches have all been made possible due to a critical violation of international law, namely, use of force against Ukraine and the resulting annexation of Crimea as well as the continuous support of and participation in the armed conflict in Eastern Ukraine.

It is therefore imperative to ensure a proper compliance with legal rules applicable in the course of armed conflict, i.e., rules of international humanitarian law (IHL). Unfortunately, allegations that those have been repeatedly – and grossly, violated by both sides to the conflict, are abundant. We will look closer at those allegations of war crimes in the next sections of the Chapter. The question of making sure the perpetrators of such crimes are brought under proper responsibility in accordance with relevant international criminal law (ICL) standards is of equal importance. For this reason, the ongoing preliminary examination of the situation in Ukraine (in both Crimea and Eastern Ukraine) being carried out by the Office of the Prosecutor (OTP) of the International Criminal Court (ICC) since 25 April 2014 is to be welcomed. It has already started to bear positive fruits, from the point of view of legal developments: the OTP report on Preliminary Examination Activities in 2016 provides a first-ever preliminary indication of how the types of armed conflict in both Crimea and Eastern Ukraine will supposedly be qualified at the level of representatives of the contemporary international criminal justice system.[6]

Although Ukraine is not a State Party to the Rome Statute of the ICC,[7] it has lodged two declarations with the Court thereby accepting its jurisdiction over the alleged crimes committed on the territory of Ukraine from 21 November 2013 to 22 February 2014 (first declaration) and from 20 February onwards (second declaration). This has allowed the ICC Prosecutor to open her preliminary examination of the situation in Ukraine on 25 April 2014 and further extend it to include the alleged crimes which occurred after 20 February 2014. The matter of analysing and properly qualifying the human rights violations as crimes under the jurisdiction of the ICC will be a central substantive task of the Prosecution team, and subsequently, of the Court's relevant Chambers – if the ongoing examination makes it to the full-fledged investigation and further on to an accepted case before the judges, in accordance with the relevant provisions of the Rome Statute. Given the vast informative material, the task is in no way easy.

---

[4] Human Rights Watch 2017, at 621.

[5] The UNHRMMU reported a 66 percent increase in civilian casualties from May to August compared to earlier in 2016, and documented 28 civilian deaths in the summer, many of which resulted from shelling and land mines. Ibid.

[6] International Criminal Court, Office of the Prosecutor 2016, at 35, 37, paras 158, 168.

[7] See the most recent list of State Parties to the ICC available at https://asp.icc-cpi.int/en_menus/asp/states%20parties/Pages/the%20states%20parties%20to%20the%20rome%20statute.aspx Accessed 25 February 2017. Russia is not a State Party either.

The present Chapter will deal with the question of qualification of war crimes as pertains to the armed conflict in Ukraine. The determination of exact types of conflict is an important part in the beginning of the qualification process for any judicial body that has to adjudicate war crimes. Furthermore, the relevant substantive rules of IHL will be considered, from treaty law and sometimes customary law perspectives, in order to categorize the alleged violations of the law as war crimes. All this will be helpful in answering the question of what possible criteria the ICC/OTP will have to apply in the analysis of the situation in Ukraine, in accordance with applicable provisions of its material and procedural law, and what possible hurdles it might have to overcome in the process. Those criteria – both legal and relative, are key in the determination of whether the "situation of Ukraine" will turn eventually into the "case of Ukraine" in the Court's jurisprudence.

That being said, the Chapter in no way purports to predict how exactly the OTP or ICC will qualify the alleged violations of human rights in Crimea and Eastern Ukraine as war crimes, or any other core crimes under international law for that matter. That remains to be seen. Rather, its main aim is to consider the relevant IHL norms and apply them to the acts that are said to be amounting to war crimes. This would then assist in a proper determination of what criteria could be helpful for the main judicial body of the modern international criminal justice in ensuring the criminal responsibility of those who committed – and continue to commit, the horrible acts on both sides of the conflict.

18.2 Types of Armed Conflict in Ukraine

When dealing with acts which may constitute war crimes the first step in the determination process is the classification of the armed conflict by its typology – as IHL whose most serious breaches amount to war crimes applies in two different types of situations of armed conflict: international and non-international armed conflict (or IAC and NIAC). Moreover, it is this basic distinction that serves as an organizing principle of Article 8 of the Rome Statute (the one dealing with war crimes).[8]

Distinguishing between IAC and NIAC (or, to use a technical term for the latter, "armed conflicts not of an international character") has become somewhat outdated due to the ever-increasing tendency to reduce the difference between the two types and to converge the rules which apply to IAC and NIAC.[9] The rationale for such a convergence may be supported by the conclusion made by the International Committee of the Red Cross (ICRC) in its comprehensive study on customary IHL that

---

[8] Rome Statute of the International Criminal Court, 17 July 1998, 2187 U.N.T.S. 90, Article 8 (hereinafter: Rome Statute).

[9] See, for example, Werle and Jessberger 2014, at 410, para 1076.

out of 161 rules of customary IHL arguably more than 136 apply to both IAC and NIAC.[10]

Furthermore, in the categorization of different acts which were carried out on the territory of Ukraine – in both Crimea and Eastern Ukraine as war crimes, it will make more logical sense to look at them from a substantive point of view, i.e., by looking at separate groups of acts, their targeted objects and the manner in which they were committed, not by primarily distinguishing between those which took place in the context of either IAC and NIAC.

However, the contemporary IHL treaty law – first of all, the Geneva Conventions and their Additional Protocols of 1977, continues operating based on this distinction. The Rome Statute's stipulation on war crimes divides the *corpus delicti* of war crimes by the two types of armed conflict. The distinction is important because it determines the applicable legal regime, i.e., the pertaining set of IHL rules, in a particular conflict. The OTP's Preliminary Examination Report classifies the types of conflict in Ukraine precisely based on this distinction.[11] Thus, the Chapter will also start with the conflict qualification.

18.2.1   Crimea

According to the Report of the ICC Prosecutor, the situation on the territory of Crimea and the city of Sevastopol amounts to an IAC between Ukraine and Russian Federation.[12] The start of the conflict is assumed to be 26 February 2014 (the latest) when Russian armed forces were deployed on Ukraine to gain control of the land without the Ukrainian Government's consent.[13] The Prosecutor has not provided her legal argumentation on how this conclusion was arrived at – and she was not required

---

[10] Henckaerts and Doswald Beck 2005. The gradual merging of two regimes can also be supported by the jurisprudence of international criminal tribunals, the influence of human rights law as well as some treaty rules adopted by States which may be said to have moved the law of armed conflicts not of an international character closer to the law of international armed conflicts.

[11] The leading international case law has long found that, despite the overall lower number of provisions of Common Article 3 of the Geneva Conventions and their Additional Protocol II, IHL extends further in NIAC than the written law. The famous *Tadic* decision of the ICTY concluded that a large number of prohibited acts under IHL are covered by customary law and apply in NIAC as well. Moreover, the Tribunal determined that IHL violations applicable to NIAC can be criminal under customary international law. *Prosecutor v. Duško Tadić*, Appeals Chamber, Decision on the Defence Motion for Interlocutory Appeal on Jurisdiction, Case No. IT-94-1, 2 October 1995, paras 119–120, 128 et seq. Also Werle and Jessberger 2014, at 406–408, paras 1069–1070.

[12] International Criminal Court, Office of the Prosecutor 2016, at 35, para 158. Concerning the status of the city of Sevastopol and the legal contradiction between this status and the constitutional law of the Russian Federation, see the excellent argumentation (in Russian) in Luk'janova E 2015.

[13] For a succinct overview of the events related to Maidan as well as events in Crimea and Eastern Ukraine from 20 February onwards, see International Criminal Court, Office of the Prosecutor 2016, at 34–38.

to, in fact, for this report which is an informative document on facts, activities and contextual background.

The OTP Report further states that the situation within the territory of Crimea and Sevastopol factually amounts to an ongoing state of occupation; it further establishes that "... for purposes of the Rome Statute an armed conflict may be international in nature if one or more States partially or totally occupies the territory of another State, whether or not the occupation meets with armed resistance."[14] The notion of occupation has not been yet exhaustively defined in contemporary treaty law, in neither the Geneva Conventions nor their Additional Protocol I.[15] The existing simplistic and short definition found in the Hague Regulations of 1907[16] does not provide all the answers which are caused by often complicated contexts of modern armed conflicts. But using this definition, one can arrive at the elements which could help in establishing the state of occupation. In order to determine, if the law of IAC applies to the violations of human rights which occurred in Crimea since the Russian use of force in February 2014, one first has to answer the question of whether the situation there amounts to the state of occupation as understood under acting international law (law of occupation).

The law of occupation is a normative construction essentially made up of the Hague Regulations, the Geneva Convention IV and, when applicable, Additional Protocol I.[17] The definition of occupation in the Regulations goes as follows: "Territory is considered occupied when it is actually placed under the authority of the hostile army. The occupation extends only to the territory where such authority has been established and can be exercised."[18]

Any determination of the state of occupation must be based fully and solely on the established facts. Only based on the prevailing facts we can confirm (or refute) the existence of the state of occupation based on the use of the so-called notion of "effective control" which has become popular in contemporary legal discourse. In my understanding, any judicial body dealing with the issue at hand, will have to use the "effective control test" which consists of three fundamental conditions:

---

[14] Ibid., at 35, para 158.

[15] Geneva Convention Relative to the Protection of Civilian Persons in Time of War, Aug. 12, 1949, 75 U.N.T.S. 287–417, Articles 2, 6, 47–78, hereinafter Geneva Convention IV; Protocol I Additional to the Geneva Conventions of 12 Aug. 1949 and Relating to the Protection of Victims of International Armed Conflicts, Dec. 12, 1977, 1125 U.N.T.S. 3–434, reprinted in 16 I.L.M. 1391 (1977), Articles 1, 3–4, 33–34, 59, and 99; hereinafter Protocol I.

[16] Hague Convention (IV) Respecting the Laws and Customs of War on Land and Its Annex: Regulations Concerning the Laws and Customs of War on Land (Hague Regulations), The Hague, 18 October 1907, reprinted in Roberts and Guelff 2000; hereinafter Hague Regulations (referring to the articles in the Annex).

[17] See International Committee of the Red Cross 2016, Common Article 2, para 297.

[18] Hague Regulations, Article 42. The view that there exists only one confirmed definition of occupation in the existing treaty law has been confirmed by the case law of the International Court of Justice (ICJ) and International Criminal Tribunal for the Former Yugoslavia (ICTY), see ICRC 2016, para 298.

(1) *The armed forces of a State are physically present in a foreign territory without the consent of the effective local government in place at the time of the invasion.* The invasion point – to meet the first requirement of the control test – has started when Russia deployed members of its armed forces to gain control over Crimea without the consent of the Ukrainian government. They have been physically present on the territory since at least 26 February 2014, and by "local government" one should understand the government of the State to whom the territory belongs in accordance with acting international law, not the local municipal authorities;

(2) *The effective local government in place at the time of the invasion has been or can be rendered substantially or completely incapable of exerting its powers by virtue of the foreign forces' unconsented-to presence.* The Ukrainian forces have been, indeed, rendered "incapable" to ascertain their territory due to, first, a completely unexpected nature of the use of force by the Russian Federation, and, second, armed resistance would not have led to efficient results but to unnecessary death and suffering of the military personnel because of the overwhelming superiority of the Russian troops;

(3) *The foreign forces are in a position to exercise authority over the territory concerned (or parts thereof) in lieu of the local government.*[19] Russian forces have established a factual control of the Ukrainian military installations and facilities located on the territory of Crimea as well as the governmental buildings while the Ukrainian government withdrew its troops to the mainland.[20] The whole peninsula has been overtaken; thus, the occupation appears to be total in character.

Even if there was no extensive exchange of fire between the belligerents, the Russian Federation used its military personnel to establish a firm control over the territory of Crimea. Each condition has been met. The state of occupation, as implied within the meaning of the Hague Regulations, has been and is present.

If we look at the relevant treaty law and compare it to the facts, it becomes clear that IHL rules are fully applicable to the situation in Crimea. The governing law here would be the Geneva Conventions of 1949 on the Protection of Victims of War and the Additional Protocol I of 1977 which deal with IAC.[21] Both Ukraine and the Russian Federation are State Parties to all four Conventions and the Protocol I.[22] Common Article 2 to all four Conventions states: "... The Convention shall also apply

---

[19] See International Committee of the Red Cross 2016, para 304.

[20] International Criminal Court, Office of the Prosecutor 2016, at 35, para 157.

[21] Geneva Convention for the Amelioration of the Condition of the Wounded and Sick in Armed Forces in the Field, Aug. 12, 1949, 75 U.N.T.S. 31–83 (Geneva Convention I); Geneva Convention for the Amelioration of the Condition of Wounded, Sick and Shipwrecked Members of the Armed Forces at Sea, Aug. 12, 1949, 75 U.N.T.S. 85–133 (Geneva Convention II); Geneva Convention Relative to the Treatment of Prisoners of War, Aug. 12, 1949, 75 U.N.T.S. 135–285 (Geneva Convention III); Geneva Convention IV; hereinafter Geneva Conventions, or a specific numbered Convention; Protocol I.

[22] See ICRC, 'States Party to the Following International Humanitarian Law and Other Related Treaties as of 14 February 2017' (listing all the four Geneva Conventions and their Additional

to all cases of partial or total occupation of the territory of a High Contracting Party, even if the said occupation meets with no armed resistance. ...".[23] That is clearly the situation of Crimea where the minimal clashes between Russian and Ukrainian forces have met the threshold to trigger the application of IHL rules in IAC.

18.2.2   Eastern Ukraine

Unlike the situation of Crimea, the armed conflict in Eastern Ukraine does not involve the element of occupation, as understood in accordance with existing law of IAC.[24] But the conflict in this part of Ukraine is of even more complicated character due to the existence of two parallel conflicts – both NIAC and IAC.

18.2.2.1   Non-International Armed Conflict

With regard to the former, the ICC Prosecutor states in her preliminary report that the degree of intensity of hostilities between Ukrainian forces and anti-governmental armed elements in Eastern Ukraine reached by 30 April 2014 a level that triggers the application of the law of armed conflict.[25] She further specifies the nature of the conflict by maintaining – correctly – that the level of organization of armed groups (including so-called "LPR" and "DPR") shows they are parties to a NIAC.[26]

The IHL treaty law governing this type of conflict is Common Article 3 of the Geneva Conventions and their Additional Protocol II of 1977.[27] The latter sets up quite a high threshold of application for a conflict to qualify as non-international: the Protocol

> [s]hall apply to all armed conflicts not covered by Article 1 [...] of Protocol I and which take place in the territory of a High Contracting Party between its armed forces and dissident armed forces or other organized armed groups which, under responsible command, exercise such control over a part of its territory as to enable them to carry out sustained and concerted military operations and to implement this Protocol [...].[28]

Protocols), https://ihl-databases.icrc.org/applic/ihl/ihl.nsf/vwTreatiesByCountry.xsp Accessed 25 February 2017.

[23] Geneva Conventions, Common Article 2.

[24] The presence of the Russian armed forces in Eastern Ukraine amounts to the participation of the Russian Federation as a full party to the conflict and proves the nature of this conflict being an IAC as argued below.

[25] International Criminal Court, Office of the Prosecutor 2016, at 37, para 168.

[26] Ibid.

[27] Geneva Conventions, Common Article 3; Protocol II Additional to the Geneva Conventions of 12 Aug. 1949 and Relating to the Protection of Victims of Non-International Armed Conflicts, Dec. 12, 1977, 1125 U.N.T.S. 609–699; hereinafter Protocol II.

[28] Protocol II, Article 1.

No matter whether the restrictive provision of Protocol II applies to the situation in Eastern Ukraine or not, it will remain covered by common Article 3 of the Geneva Conventions (the so-called "mini-Convention"). If one looks at the way the ICC Prosecutor dealt with qualifying the conflict as non-international, it becomes clear that her rationale was guided not by the language of the Protocol II but by a more intermediary threshold of application provided in the Rome Statute of the ICC. The latter does not require the following elements of the Protocol's Article 1: that the conflict be between governmental forces and rebel forces, that the rebel forces control part of the territory, or that there has to be a responsible command.[29] The only two requirements would be that the conflict is protracted and the armed groups are acting in an organized manner.

Both elements are satisfied in the case of Eastern Ukraine. First, by the time the Report was submitted the conflict has been continuing for more than two and a half years (April 2015–November 2016).[30] Second, the separatist groups would not have been able to fight for such a long time if they had not been acting in an organized manner. But the element of intensity is of even more importance for the purpose of qualification.

The Prosecutor's preliminary analysis is consistent with the relevant case-law of the ICTY where the conflict's protracted character is replaced by a requirement of intensity: a high degree of organization and violence for any situation to be classified as an armed conflict not of an international character, must be present.[31]

18.2.2.2 International Armed Conflict

With regard to the second type of conflict, it appears the OTP has started its factual and legal analysis on determining if the otherwise non-international armed conflict in Donbass could in fact be said to be international in nature.[32] The implications of such a conclusion are important for this Chapter because the provisions in the treaty law on international conflicts which are relevant for war crimes are more detailed than the ones on non-international conflicts. It is important because, as correctly argued by the Prosecutor, the existence of a single international conflict in Eastern Ukraine would entail the application of articles of the Rome Statute relevant to armed conflict of an international character for the relevant period.[33]

The Prosecutor further indicates towards the analytical direction the Office is going to take to prove the existence of IAC: it will assess the level of support Russian authorities have provided to the armed groups in the form of equipment, financing and personnel, and also whether they have generally directed or helped in planning actions of the armed groups in a manner that indicates they exercised genuine control

---

[29] Rome Statute, Article 8(2)(f).

[30] The element of protracted time can also be a clear sign of the intensity of the conflict.

[31] Marco Sassòli et al. 2011, Part I, Chapter 2, Section III, at 22–23, n. 38.

[32] International Criminal Court, Office of the Prosecutor 2016, at 38, para 170.

[33] Ibid.

over them.[34] That is fully in line with the gradually waning line between IAC and NIACs, as well as with the fact that several partial conflicts of different natures may take place on a single territory (leading one to name them as "mixed conflicts").[35]

There is a certain danger in characterizing an overall situation as either exclusively international or internal since it might lead to gaps and inconsistencies in assigning the responsibilities of the Parties to the conflict.[36] This danger was also confirmed in ICC's case law.[37] To avoid the risk of gaps, the qualification analysis, both by the Prosecutor and the Court, must bear a functional/contextual character, meaning, the acts under question as well as their contexts need to be assessed, to decide whether those acts were committed as part of a IAC or NIAC (for the purposes of Rome Statute's Article 8's distinction). It presupposes the analysis done according to the belligerent parties involved, not based on purely other aspects such as the territorial scope, for example. This rationale accords with the logic – as there exists no general test to apply in such analysis. The OTP Report's reasoning indicates that the Prosecutor intends to take precisely this approach.

It would be corresponding to the rationale of the ICTY jurisprudence, e.g., *Tadic* case, where the Appeals Chamber dismisses the ICJ's effective control test elaborated in its famous *Nicaragua* case stating that it is not consonant with the logic of the law of state responsibility and is at variance with the judicial and state practice. Instead, it proposed a so-called "overall control test" whereby it has to be established that the participation of another State in an otherwise NIAC went beyond mere financing and equipping the armed groups and also involved participation in the planning and supervising of the military operations.[38]

Applying this test to Eastern Ukraine, it becomes clear that the situation there would pass it: not only the Russian Federation provided, and continues to provide a substantial material, financial and military assistance to the separatist groups (it would be naive to think that those groups could have effectively been able to fight alone against the regular and well-trained military forces of the Ukrainian government) but it has also been factually admitted that the rebel groups were carrying out military tasks.[39] Carrying such tasks implies there have been certain exact instructions to the belligerents which must be a strategic part of the planning and overall supervision of the military operations in Donbass.[40] Moreover, the direct military confrontation

---

[34] Ibid.

[35] See Werle and Jessberger 2014, at 420, para 1104, citing the ICTY case law (*Tadic*).

[36] Ibid.

[37] *The Prosecutor v. Thomas Lubanga Dyilo*, Trial Chamber, Judgement pursuant to Article 74 of the Statute, Case No. ICC-01/04-01/06, 14 March 2012, para 540; also Werle and Jessberger 2014, at 420, para 1104.

[38] *Prosecutor v. Duško Tadić*, Appeals Chamber, Judgement, Case No. IT-94-1-A, 15 July 1999, paras 116–145.

[39] S. Walker, 'Putin admits Russian military presence in Ukraine for first time', *The Guardian*, 17 December 2015; https://www.theguardian.com/world/2015/dec/17/vladimir-putin-admits-russian-military-presence-ukraine Accessed 24 February 2017.

[40] For a more detailed analysis of the Russian involvement (including Crimea) affecting the conflict qualification, see International Partnership for Human Rights 2015 at 21–26.

between Ukrainian and Russian armed forces (by way of shelling military positions) indicates the existence of IAC, in parallel to NIAC.

18.3 Alleged War Crimes Committed in the Conflict in Ukraine

Now, after having established the nature of the armed conflict taking place in Ukraine – IAC and the state of occupation in Crimea and NIAC in parallel to IAC in Eastern Ukraine (while the ICC's Prosecutor has yet to legally arrive at such a conclusion, I believe that this is a correct characterization which corresponds to current international law), we can move to the task of categorizing the alleged acts of human rights violations in Ukraine during the conflict as war crimes.

Due to the increasing convergence between the rules of IAC and NIAC in international law, it makes sense to classify war crimes based not on the principal two-type conflict distinction but rather on the crimes' substance, attacked object and nature. Accordingly, they can be divided into five main categories: war crimes against persons, war crimes against property and other rights, employing prohibited methods of warfare, use of prohibited means of warfare and war crimes against humanitarian operations.[41] The first two groups of crimes constitute the so-called "Law of Geneva" while the third and fourth belong to the "Law of the Hague". Based on the available materials, the first three out of five categories of war crimes appear to have been committed in Ukraine.

Before moving on, it makes sense to provide a proper definition of war crimes. In order to avoid the confusion which sometimes happens in defining this type of crimes against international law (for example, labelling all violations of IHL as war crimes even if those violations are not criminal and do not entail criminal responsibility), the following short and more narrow definition seems best fitting the concept in accordance with modern ICL: war crimes are violations of rules of IHL which create direct criminal responsibility under international law.[42] This definition also allows one to see the existing link between IHL and ICL. Furthermore, the alleged conduct would fall under the above definition only if it is functionally connected to the armed

---

[41] This content-based categorization is borrowed from a useful description in Werle and Jessberger 2014, at 427–526, also p. 410, para 1076. It is also similar to the logic of the German Code of Crimes Against International Law [Völkerstrafgesetzbuch, oder VStGB]. Ibid., n.142.

[42] Ibid., at 391–392, para 1029. ICC in its work is applying a long and complicated definition established in the Rome Statute's Article 8 which names as war crimes the grave breaches of the 1949 Geneva Conventions and other serious violations of the laws and customs applicable in IAC as well as serious violations of the laws and customs applicable in NIAC, with the ensuing detailed list of individual acts constituting the crimes. Rome Statute, Article 8. As we will see, not all of the said acts may be found in the contexts of the armed conflict in Ukraine which certainly in no way diminishes the necessity of investigating and prosecuting those responsible for their commission. It is important to note here that due to the limited space, the present Chapter will not be able to consider in detail all the alleged acts or to analyse all the important aspects of the gave breaches of IHL related to qualifying those acts as war crimes.

conflict and took place in its context;[43] this is a task to be carried out by a judicial body as well in the qualification process of war crimes.

The sources of information used in the subsequent sub-sections include the OTP Report (which itself relies on multiple abundant and publicly available sources including the Ukrainian government, NGOs and other organizations as well as individuals)[44] and reports from independent sources – the UN agencies and human rights protection organizations such as Amnesty International and Human Rights Watch. While there are claims that it is difficult to find reliable up-to-date accounts and/or descriptions of what happened/happens in the conflict zones,[45] I think otherwise. There is plenty of trustworthy material documenting various cases and incidents alleged to have occurred in both Crimea and Eastern Ukraine since 20 February 2014.[46]

18.3.1   War Crimes Against Persons

18.3.1.1   Crimea

For the context of Crimea, the law of IAC and occupation applies, i.e., the Geneva Conventions of 1949, their Additional Protocol I of 1977 and the Hague Regulations of 1907. A majority of this law is also part of customary IHL.

Killing: this act constitutes a grave breach of all four 1949 Geneva Conventions ("wilful killing").[47] Article 8(2)(a)(i) of the Rome Statute establishes a criminal responsibility for the commission of this breach. The crime's material elements require killing a person who is under the protection of the Geneva Conventions or causing his/her death.[48] Typical examples would include, among others, killing of prisoners of war (PoWs) or interned civilians without a prior fair trial or mistreatment of PoWs which led to their death.[49] In case of Crimea, the alleged incidents of killing the Crimean Tatar activists in March and September 2014 (alleged 14 and confirmed 2 cases) would amount to war crimes. The link to the conflict consists in the victims'

---

[43] See Werle and Jessberger 2014, at 422, paras 1109 et al.

[44] International Criminal Court, Office of the Prosecutor 2016, at 40–41, paras 185–188.

[45] Naming the available news sources as "partisan sources". Altshuller 2017, at 8.

[46] The OTP Report states that the Office has compiled a comprehensive database of over 800 incidents of violations in Eastern Ukraine alone since February 2014 while the overall number of pages of the documented accounts from witnesses and victims amounts to more than 7000 (!). International Criminal Court, Office of the Prosecutor 2016, at 40–41, paras 185–186.

[47] Geneva Conventions: Geneva Convention I, Article 50; Geneva Convention II, Article 51; Geneva Convention III, Article 130; Geneva Convention IV, Article 147.

[48] ICC Elements of Crimes, reproduced from the Official Records of the Assembly of States Parties to the Rome Statute of the International Criminal Court, 1st session, New York, 3–10 September 2002 (UN publication, Sales No. E.03.V.2 and corrigendum), part II.B. Article 8(2)(a)(i) of the Rome Statute, num.1; hereinafter Elements of Crimes.

[49] Werle and Jessberger 2014, at 432, para 1140.

opposition to Crimea's occupation, and in their abductions and subsequent killings' being attributed to a paramilitary group called "Crimean self-defense".[50]

Mistreatment: the offences of mistreatment constituting war crimes include several groups of acts – torture; wilfully causing great suffering or serious injury to health; inhuman or cruel treatment; mutilation; and performing biological, medical or scientific experiments. For the context of Crimean occupation, three of these five groups appear to be relevant: torture, wilfully causing great suffering or serious injury to body or health, and inhuman or cruel treatment. All three constitute grave breaches of the four Geneva Conventions of 1949.[51] For IAC, the Rome Statute proscribes torture as well as inhuman treatment in its Article 8(2)(a)(ii). Although the OTP Report does not expressly mention torture – carefully avoiding any potential implication of legal qualification at this stage,[52] another report indicates at least one case of torture.[53] The reported instances of beatings and chokings of Crimean pro-Ukraine activists in the context of detention by the armed paramilitary groups (so-called "self-defense units")[54] suggest the occurrences of either inhuman or cruel treatment – that requires a lesser degree of physical or psychological suffering than torture,[55] or causing suffering or injury to health – which does not require any particular purpose in the infliction of such suffering as, again, compared to torture.[56]

Unlawful confinement or transfer: these types of acts are grave breaches under Geneva Convention IV's Article 147. According to the ICTY, under no circumstance a civilian may be interned (confined, detained) solely because of his/her political opinion, nationality or gender.[57] The relevant provision in the Rome Statute for both acts is its Article 8(2)(a)(vii).[58] Judging by the available report information, illegal arrests, detention and transfers of the civilians, namely, Tatar activists as well as pro-

---

[50] International Criminal Court, Office of the Prosecutor 2016, at 38, para 173; Human Rights Watch 2014, at 7–8; see also Amnesty International 2015–2016, at 381–382.

[51] Geneva Conventions: Geneva Convention I, Article 50; Geneva Convention II, Article 51; Geneva Convention III, Article 130; Geneva Convention IV, Article 147.

[52] International Criminal Court, Office of the Prosecutor 2016, at 38, paras 171, 174.

[53] Human Rights Watch 2014, at 2, 20, n.1; see also Amnesty International 2015–2016, at 381–382. It will be important for the ICC to note the significant overlaps/differences between the war crime of torture and torture as a crime against humanity (Article 7(1)(f) of the Rome Statute) as well as the requirements for torture in accordance with international human rights law (IHRL), e.g., the necessity to act in an official capacity. See *Prosecutor v. Kunarac et al.*, Appeals Chamber, Judgement, Case No. IT-96-23 & IT-96-23/1-A, 12 June 2002, para 148.

[54] Ibid.

[55] See, e.g., the relevant case-law of the ICTY such as *Prosecutor v. Milan Lukić and Sredoje Lukić*, Appeals Chamber, Judgement, Case No. IT-98-32/1-A, 4 December 2012, para 634.

[56] *Prosecutor v. Mucić et al.*, Trial Chamber, Judgement, Case No. IT-96-21-T, 16 November 1998, para 442.

[57] Ibid., paras 567, 577; see also Dörmann, in Triffterer 2008, Article 8, at 318, para 28.

[58] The ICC will need to carefully distinguish between war crime of deportation or forcible transfer and the corresponding crime against humanity of deportation or forcible transfer of the population (Article 7(1)(d) of the Rome Statute) as the law of crimes against humanity can apply in times of both peace and armed conflict. There are some notable differences in *corpus delicti* to be kept in mind (e.g., the requirement of prior legal residence).

Ukrainian oppositioners, have taken place since March 2014; approximately 180 confined people were reportedly transferred from Crimea to Russian Federation's prisons.[59] Both acts appear to fall under the definitions of the Geneva Convention IV.

Deprivation of the right to fair trial: the deprivation of the rights to fair and regular trial constitutes a grave breach of the Geneva Conventions III (Article 130) and IV (Article 147). Those rights are described in the Conventions as "judicial guarantees".[60] Article 8(2)(a)(vi) of the Rome Statute ensures the right of the protected persons under the Geneva Conventions to a fair and regular trial. The manner in which court hearings were conducted in Simferopol against some Crimean activists (e.g., the defendant's right to call and present witnesses completely denied) suggests that this conduct violates the proscribed definitions in IHL regarding the grave breaches.[61]

Compelled service in military forces: the war crime of compelling to serve in military forces and military operations in IAC consists of two distinct acts: compelled service in the forces of a hostile power and compelled participation in operations of war; the two are overlapping. Both are based on a particular provision in the Hague Regulations which provides that the belligerents are "… forbidden to compel the nationals of the hostile party to take part in the operations of war directed against their own country, …"[62] The former act, i.e., compelling to serve in the forces of a hostile power represents grave breaches of the Geneva Conventions III (under Article 130) and IV (under Article 147). As a result of the imposed change of citizenship, the male residents of Crimea eligible for conscription (age) have become subject to mandatory Russian military service requirements.[63]

18.3.1.2   Eastern Ukraine

The law of armed conflict applicable to the situation in Eastern Ukraine would be IHL rules pertaining to both NIAC and IAC, as argued in the previous section, i.e., Common Article 3 of the Geneva Conventions, their Additional Protocol II of 1977 (NIAC) and the Geneva Conventions of 1949 and their Additional Protocol I of 1977 (IAC).

Murder/Killing: the war crime of murder in NIAC is established in the Common Article 3(1)(a) of the Geneva Conventions. The different wording ("murder" instead of "killing") does not affect the meaning: the substance of the crime is the same as

---

[59] International Criminal Court, Office of the Prosecutor 2016, at 39, para 175; Human Rights Watch 2014, at 11–12.

[60] Elements of Crimes, Article 8(2)(a)(vi), at 11, num. 1. For a detailed and comprehensive list of those guarantees, see Werle and Jessberger 2014, pp. 450–451, para 1203.

[61] Human Rights Watch 2014, at 11–12.

[62] Hague Regulations, Article 23(h).

[63] International Criminal Court, Office of the Prosecutor 2016, at 39, para 176; Human Rights Watch 2014, at 28.

in killing in IAC.[64] Article 8(2)(c)(i) of the Rome Statute contains the corresponding crime for NIAC. As for the international conflict, see the sub-section for Crimea above. High numbers have been reported for the incidents of killings during the conflict in Eastern Ukraine since it started: the OTP Report and UN OHCHR Report provide the number of 9578 killed persons including both members of armed forces (Ukrainian)/armed groups and civilians.[65] The killings – on the side of both pro-governmental forces and armed groups, were a result of the shelling of civilian-populated areas (up to 2000 people), firearms and summary executions.[66] All acts appear to be falling under the category of war crimes for both types of conflicts, including the shelling: bombardment of towns which has caused the death of civilians – that's what happened in both government-controlled and separatist-controlled areas of Eastern Ukraine, falls under the definition of Article 8(2)(c)(i) for NIAC.[67]

Unlawful confinement/Arbitrary detention: Concerning this type of acts, it needs to be considered from the perspective of IAC, as unlawful confinement in NIAC does not constitute a war crime either under the Rome Statute or customary law. Therefore, the relevant treaty law would be Article 147 of the Geneva Convention IV; as regards the Rome Statute, its Article 8(2)(a)(vii) contains the disposition of unlawful confinement. It is alleged that both sides – Ukrainian armed, security and law enforcement forces and "DPR"/"LPR" forces backed by Russian Federation, have engaged in arbitrary (unlawful) detention.[68] While under the current IHL/ICL framework the non-state perpetrators may not be said to be committing war crimes of unlawful confinement – which nevertheless remains a violation of human rights law, they could be brought under responsibility for the cases of ill-treatment.

Deprivation of the right to fair trial: The pertaining treaty law provisions for violation of the rights to fair and regular trial in IAC have earlier been indicated above, for Crimean context. As concerns the internal armed conflict, Common Article 3(1)(d) of the 1949 Geneva Conventions prohibits "the passing of sentences and the carrying out of executions without previous judgement pronounced by a regularly constituted court, affording all the judicial guarantees which are recognized as indispensable by civilized peoples". This language is almost completely mirrored by Article 8(2)(c)(iv) of the Rome Statute. The multitude of the reported cases of

---

[64] The primary purpose of Common Article 3 is to extend the "elementary considerations of humanity" to NIAC; thus, the differing terminology bears no major significance. *Prosecutor v. Mucić et al,* Trial Chamber, Judgement, Case No. IT-96-21-T, 16 November 1998, paras 420 et seq.; Werle and Jessberger 2014, at 431, para 1138.

[65] International Criminal Court, Office of the Prosecutor 2016, at 39, para 178; United Nations Office of the High Commissioner for Human Rights September 2016.

[66] International Criminal Court, Office of the Prosecutor 2016, at 39, para 178.

[67] See Werle and Jessberger 2014, at 432, para 1140; *Prosecutor v. Pavle Strugar*, Trial Chamber, Judgement, Case No. IT-01-42-T, 31 January 2005, paras 237 et seq.

[68] According to the ICC Prosecutor, several hundred acts of detention occurred overall in the course of the conflict. International Criminal Court, Office of the Prosecutor 2016, at 39, para 180; United Nations Office of the High Commissioner for Human Rights 2016, May 2016, United Nations Office of the High Commissioner for Human Rights 2016, September 2016, at 13–16, 21–22; International Partnership for Human Rights 2015, at 50–75; also Bielousov et al. 2015, at 26–37.

due process and fair/regular trial rights' violations on the side of the Ukrainian government (law enforcement and security forces) suggests the repeated commission of war crimes against civilians. Those violations may be called "conflict-related abuse of process".[69]

Mistreatment: offences of mistreatment including torture all represent grave breaches of the four Geneva Conventions of 1949 in IAC (see above for Crimea), while not all of them amount to war crimes in the context of NIAC such as causing suffering or injury to body or health. The NIAC prohibition of torture and cruel treatment is found in the Common Article 3 of the Geneva Conventions. The Rome Statute's relevant textual provision in internal armed conflict is Article 8(2)(c)(i) for both torture and cruel treatment. All the available report sources contain references to the abundance of cases of torture and other forms of mistreatment related to the conflict in Eastern Ukraine, on both sides.[70] In many cases, they appear to be amounting to war crimes.

Sexual and gender-based offences: although this group of offences which includes rape, sexual slavery, forced prostitution, forced pregnancy, enforced sterilization and other forms of sexual violence (Article 8(2)(b)(xxii) of the Rome Statute for IAC and Article 8(2)(e)(vi) for NIAC) are not listed as grave breaches in the Geneva Conventions of 1949 or their Additional Protocols of 1977, they are recognized as such under the Rome Statute.[71] The corresponding provisions in the Conventions and Protocols treat this class of offences as "attacks on the victim's honour".[72] The majority of the documented and reported cases (both in the territory controlled by the Government of Ukraine and in the areas held by separatist groups) demonstrate that sexual violence in Eastern Ukraine has been used in the context of detention related to the armed conflict.[73] Under the current prevailing interpretation of IHL/ICL, sexual offences committed in both IAC and NIAC constitute war crimes.[74]

---

[69] See United Nations Office of the High Commissioner for Human Rights 2016 September 2016, at 20–21; Bielousov et al. 2015, at 26–37.

[70] United Nations Office of the High Commissioner for Human Rights 2016, September 2016, at 13–16; International Criminal Court, Office of the Prosecutor 2016, at 40, para 182; Amnesty International 2015–2016, at 379–380; Human Rights Watch 2017, at 621–622; a rather scrupulous report details the instances of torture and other forms of mistreatment by both Ukraine and separatists: see Amnesty International, Human Rights Watch 2016; International Partnership for Human Rights 2015, at 50–75; Bielousov et al. 2015, pp. 55–74.

[71] Werle and Jessberger 2014, at 442, para 1173–1176.

[72] Geneva Conventions: Geneva Convention IV, Article 27(2); Protocol I, articles 75(2) and 76(1); Protocol II, Article 4(2)(e).

[73] International Criminal Court, Office of the Prosecutor 2016, at 40, para 183; United Nations Office of the High Commissioner for Human Rights 2017.

[74] For a corresponding international case-law supporting this view, see Werle and Jessberger 2014, at 441–443, paras 1173–1180.

18.3.2 War Crimes Against Property and Other Rights

Expropriation and destruction of property/Pillage: It appears, judging by the available information, that the offences targeting the property have taken place in the conflict in Eastern Ukraine. The provisions of the Rome Statute which concern war crimes against property criminalize the expropriation or destruction of property as well as acts of pillage (Article 8(2)(a)(iv) in IAC, Article 8(2)(b)(xiii) in IAC and Article 8(2)(e)(xii) in NIAC, Article 8(2)(b)(xvi) in IAC and Article 8(2)(e)(v) in NIAC and Article 8(2)(b)(xiv)). These offences (appropriation/seizure, extensive destruction of property not justified by military necessity and carried out unlawfully and wantonly, and pillaging) are of direct relevance for the context of hostilities in Donbass. They represent serious violations of IHL and they have accompanied the carrying out of other war crimes described above and below. At least two reports include the information that war crimes against property have occurred in Eastern Ukraine.[75]

18.3.3 Employing Prohibited Methods of Warfare

Attacks against the civilian population and civilian objects: The category, again, concerns the belligerents' conduct in Eastern Ukraine. The offence of attacking civilians is dealt with in Rome Statute's Article 8(2)(b)(i) for IAC and Article 8(2)(e)(i) for NIAC. These provisions are based on two Additional Protocols of 1977 to the Geneva Conventions (Article 51(2) of the Protocol I and Article 13(2) of the Protocol II). There is a serious evidence of the multitude of attacks against civilians which violate IHL and must entail individual criminal liability under ICL.[76] The same is true with regard to some other offences that make up this category, i.e., intentionally directing attacks against civilian (non-military) objects (Article 8(2)(b)(ii) of the Rome Statute and Article 52(1) of Protocol I), attacks on undefended non-military objects (Articles 8(2)(b)(v) of the Rome Statute and 59(1) of the Protocol I) as well as attacks against specially protected objects such as hospitals, schools, historic monuments, religious cites, etc (Article 8(2)(b)(ix) of the Rome Statute and relevant provisions of the Geneva Conventions and Additional Protocol I).[77] Perhaps, the biggest example of the last class of acts in this category of crimes are the indiscriminate or deliberate attacks on schools by both Ukrainian government forces and Russia-backed militants who used heavy artillery, mortar, and in some cases unguided rockets; the schools

---

[75] International Criminal Court, Office of the Prosecutor 2016, at 39, para 179; International Partnership for Human Rights 2015, at 86–95.

[76] For an exemplary analysis of that evidence and corresponding factual/legal conclusions, see International Partnership for Human Rights 2015, at 34–49.

[77] Geneva Conventions: Convention I, Articles 19–23; Convention II, Articles 22–24, 35; Convention IV, Articles 14, 18–19; Protocol I, Articles 12, 85(4).

were also used for military purposes, with military forces being deployed in and near schools.[78]

The preceding preliminary overview does not pretend to be exhaustive and encompassing. Given the Chapter's limited space and the vast documented information, it was not possible to carry out a detailed factual and legal analysis (for example, it excluded the consideration of the role of customary law and relevant international case law, for the most part)[79] on war crimes in the context of both Crimea and Donbass in this format. The overview was intended to provide a useful picture of the law applicable to the situation of armed conflict in Ukraine (IHL/ICL) with respect to war crimes. It will help in the subsequent explanation of the elements – legal, factual, substantive, which will have to be considered by the Office of the Prosecutor and ICC Chambers in the investigation and adjudication of war crimes committed since the start in February 2014 of the overall armed conflict in Ukraine. It will be followed by the indication of what criteria (objective, legal) would be important to deal with if the preliminary examination is ever to make to the full-fledged investigation and ensuing trial.

18.4 Criteria for the ICC

18.4.1 Substantive Evaluation

According to Article 21 of the Rome Statute, the ICC shall apply in deciding its cases, first, the Rome Statute, its Elements of Crimes and Rules of Procedure and Evidence, second, applicable treaties and the principles and rules of international law, including the established principles of the international law of armed conflict, and third, general principles of law. The Court may also apply principles and rules of law as interpreted in its previous decisions.[80] This range of legal sources cover all the applicable law that the ICC is allowed to use by its principal establishing instrument.

When dealing with war crimes from a substantive point of view, i.e., in the analysis of whether a particular conduct qualifies as a war crime for the purposes of the Rome Statute, the Court will need to consider the following important aspects:

- nexus with the armed conflict: in order for a certain conduct to qualify as a war crime it must have a functional relationship (or "nexus") to the armed conflict;[81]
- relevant principles of IHL: the Court will have to assess in what way the principles of humanity, military necessity, distinction and proportionality were violated in the commission of the offences by all parties to the conflicts in Ukraine (e.g., for

---

[78] Human Rights Watch 2016.

[79] For an encompassing overview of that case law, see in general Werle and Jessberger 2014.

[80] Rome Statute, Article 21(2).

[81] See for more detail on this point Werle and Jessberger 2014, at 422–425, paras 1109–1115.

the offences constituting attacks against civilians and civilian objects, the question of how exactly the principle of distinction was breached must be answered);
- material elements of the crimes: material acts which constitute a certain conduct that may amount to war crimes. In the consideration process, it will be important to clarify some significant aspects without which the conduct cannot be said to be the crimes under the Court's material jurisdiction (e.g., in deciding on the attacks against civilian population the question of whether the victims represent the civilian population must be answered);
- mental element of the crimes: in determining whether the material elements of a crime have been committed with "intent" and "knowledge", Rome Statute's Article 30 will have to be guiding.

It is also important that the ICC follows the progressive decisions which have been made in the previous case law of other international tribunals (even if it is not required to do so by the Rome Statute), such as the ICTY and ICTR, for example, when qualifying the nature of the armed conflict in Eastern Ukraine as IAC.

18.4.2 Selection Criteria

The armed conflict in Ukraine is now being considered at the pre-investigation stage of the ICC by the Office of the Prosecutor.[82] While it initially focused on the alleged commission of crimes against humanity in the context of "Euromaidan" events, it was then extended to include any alleged crimes committed on Ukraine's territory (both Crimea and Eastern Ukraine) from 20 February 2014 up to now. That includes the alleged war crimes concerned with in the Chapter.

The evaluation criteria for the Prosecutor in deciding whether to initiate a full formal investigation or not, are laid out in Article 53(1) of the Rome Statute. Those include: (1) the applicability of ICC's jurisdiction to the particular situation; (2) admissibility of the investigation (in accordance with Article 17); and (3) whether or not an investigation would be in the interests of justice and of the victims, regardless of the situation's jurisdiction and admissibility.

The principal challenge for the Prosecutor to overcome would be how to define and apply exactly those main criteria which are left undefined in the Statute. The task is of an utmost importance as it cuts into the substantive matters regulated by the Rome Statute. This author believes that the main selection criteria as concerns the situation in Ukraine have been satisfied and the preliminary examination must move to the stage of full-fledged formal investigation. That is so for the following reasons:[83]

---

[82] For an exemplary overview of ICC's pre-investigation and investigation stages as well as an exhaustive analysis of the situation/case selection criteria by the Court, see in general Stegmiller 2011.

[83] These reasons are only briefly sketched here due to limited space.

(1) with regard to the first criteria, i.e., jurisdiction, the temporal jurisdiction requirement is met as the alleged crimes in Ukraine have all occurred after the 1 July
2002 (the date of the Statute's entry into force). As Ukraine has lodged an *ad hoc*
acceptance declaration with the Court, these crimes fall within *ratione temporis*.
Numerous reports from various actors and a number of interviews conducted
by the OTP indicate that the alleged crimes took place in the territory of the
State which made the acceptance declaration. Crimean peninsula and Eastern
Ukraine constitute an integral part of the country's territory, thus, the territorial
jurisdiction (or *ratione loci*) requirement is satisfied, too.

Furthermore, the "reasonable basis to believe" that a crime exists is a rather
low threshold which still requires that OTP must assess the available evidence
objectively and only based on the facts. The factors to consider are: availability
of evidence (in most cases, the evidence is more than abundant for the conflict
in Ukraine), the credibility and reliability of information (which comes from
multiple sources including the governmental and UN agencies as well as the
respected and competent organizations), and incriminating weight of the materials (each analysed fact in the reported documentation almost always explicitly
indicates the commission of the offences by one or all parties to the conflict –
Russia, Ukraine and separatists).

(2) with regards to admissibility (Article 17), the OTP must decide on two aspects:
gravity of the case and complementarity of the Court's regime to the State in
question. According to the OTP Policy Paper on Case Selection and Prioritization, the Office will select cases for investigation and prosecution in light of
the gravity of the crimes, the degree of responsibility of the alleged perpetrators
and the potential charges; the assessment of gravity must logically include both
quantitative and qualitative considerations, and the important aspects in such
assessment would be the scale, nature, manner of commission, and impact of
the crimes.[84]

The available reports on Ukraine indicate that for each of the aspects, the conflict in Ukraine tends to suggest the case is admissible: the number of victims
of atrocities is high, the degree of the damage caused by the alleged crimes
seems to be extensive, so is their geographical and temporal spread (scale);
specific factual elements of each offence all indicate towards the nature of their
nature of being war crimes (nature); the means employed to execute the crimes,
discriminating motives, particular cruelty against the victims especially in the
mistreatment cases (manner of commission); the increased vulnerability of victims, the terror subsequently instilled, or the social, economic and environmental
damage inflicted on the affected communities (crimes' impact). When studied
carefully, the available material reveals the presence of each of these aspects for
all groups of offences considered in the previous section.

(3) Even if the OTP itself states that "[c]onsiderations relating to the interests of justice will continue to be assessed on a case by case basis by the Office as a matter

---

[84] International Criminal Court, Office of the Prosecutor 2016, Paper, at 12–14, paras 34–41.

of best practice …",[85] my opinion is that the concept of interests of justice must be interpreted in a way that does not preclude the Prosecutor from pursuing the case in Ukraine. This is because the absence of a proper international investigation and ensuing trial would leave a huge number of victims of the conflict in both Crimea and Eastern Ukraine without redress and the perpetrators – with impunity. That is clearly not the purpose of rendering justice. War crimes as well as their other counterpart core crimes in the Rome Statute, represent a serious threat to the peace, security and well-being of the world. If they are left with no response from the most important existing judicial mechanism of international criminal justice, then the purported aims of the Statute's Preamble are void of meaning.

18.5 Conclusion

It is hard to argue against stating that the armed conflict in Ukraine represents a serious challenge to the contemporary system of international law – along with other negative phenomena which have been occurring at a fast pace such as violations of international law committed by the Islamic State and armed conflict in Syria, just to name some. That is so not because it constitutes an argumentative statement but because it is a matter of fact. International community must respond to the challenge and strive to bring those responsible for war crimes in Ukraine under responsibility in accordance with existing mechanisms of international criminal law.

ICC nowadays is experiencing a big setback due to decisions of some African states such as South Africa and Burundi to withdraw from the Court. It was exacerbated by a recent announcement of a planned mass withdrawal by members of the African Union from the ICC.[86] This angered move has been caused, among others, by a perception that ICC is unfairly focused on trying cases only coming from the African continent.[87] Opening a case in Ukraine would, in addition to the main rationale of bringing justice to the now long-troubled region, help in dispelling this kind of accusations against the ICC.

While this Chapter focused on the rules of IHL and thus what is known by international lawyers as *jus in bello* (or "laws of war") as well as the law to be applied after the cessation of hostilities (*jus post bellum*), it is not always easy to separate the different *corpora* of law, especially when it comes to matters related to the use of force (*jus ad bellum*) and regulation of war (*jus in bello*). This is equally true for the case of Ukrainian conflict. Has it not been for the use of force by Russia in the first place back in February 2014 to occupy Crimea, all those massive human rights

---

[85] Ibid., at 12, para 33.

[86] E. Igunza, 'African Union Backs Mass Withdrawal from ICC', *BBC News*, 1 February 2017; but see also G. York, 'New Setback for African Rebellion Against International Court', *The Globe and Mail*, 22 February 2017.

[87] For a convincing argumentation against such allegations, see Mendes 2010, at 168.

violations in Crimea and Eastern Ukraine which – in my firm opinion – constitute war crimes and crimes against humanity, would not have occurred. Despite Russia's recent signature withdrawal from the Rome Statute[88] and given Ukraine's current willingness to cooperate, the ICC is in the position to legally pronounce on the proper qualification of those violations of law as crimes against international law and bring those responsible to answer for their atrocities. It has the potential, and that potential must be seized.

References

Altshuller M (2017) Another Forgotten War: The Lack of A Western Response to the Ukrainian Conflict. Harvard Int'l Rev. 38:7–8

Amnesty International (2015–2016) The State of the World's Human Rights: Report https://www.amnesty.org/en/documents/pol10/2552/2016/en/. Accessed 26 February 2017

Amnesty International, Human Rights Watch (2016) You Don't Exist: Arbitrary Detentions, Enforced Disappearances, and Torture in Eastern Ukraine https://www.hrw.org/sites/default/files/report_pdf/ukraine0716web_2.pdf. Accessed 23 February 2017

Bielousov I, Korynevych A, Martynenko O, Matviychuk O, Pavlichenko O, Romensky Y, Shvets S (2015) Surviving Hell: Testimonies of Victims on Places of Illegal Detention in Donbas. Monitoring Report. TsP Komprint. https://jfp.org.ua/system/reports/files/2/en/SURVIVING_HELL_eng_web.pdf Accessed 26 February 2017

Henckaerts J-M, Doswald Beck L (2005) Customary International Humanitarian Law. Cambridge University Press, Cambridge

Human Rights Watch (2014) Rights In Retreat: Abuses In Crimea. https://www.hrw.org/sites/default/files/report_pdf/russia1114web.pdf. Accessed 26 February 2017

Human Rights Watch (2016) Studying under Fire: Attacks on Schools, Military Use of Schools During the Armed Conflict in Eastern Ukraine https://www.hrw.org/report/2016/02/11/studyingunder-fire/attacks-schools-military-use-schoolsduring-armed-conflict. Accessed 24 February 2017

Human Rights Watch (2017) World Report 2017: Events of 2016. https://www.hrw.org/sites/default/files/world_report_download/wr2017-web.pdf. Accessed 18 February 2017

International Committee of the Red Cross (2016) Commentary on the First Geneva Convention: Convention (I) for the Amelioration of the Condition of the Wounded and Sick in Armed Forces in the Field. Cambridge University Press, Cambridge

International Criminal Court, Office of the Prosecutor (2016) Policy Paper on Case Selection and Prioritization. https://www.icc-cpi.int/itemsDocuments/20160915_OTP-Policy_Case-Selection_Eng.pdf. Accessed 26 February 2017

International Criminal Court, Office of the Prosecutor (2016) Report on Preliminary Examination Activities. https://www.icc-cpi.int/iccdocs/otp/161114-otp-rep-PE_ENG.pdf. Accessed 18 February 2017

International Partnership for Human Rights (2015) Fighting Impunity in Eastern Ukraine: Violations of International Humanitarian Law and International Crimes in Eastern Ukraine. Report prepared by International Partnership for Human Rights in the framework of the Civic Solidarity Platform. http://iphronline.org/wp-content/uploads/2016/05/Fighting-impunity-in-Eastern-Ukraine-October-2015.pdf. Accessed 24 February 2017

---

[88] For an exemplary analysis of why Russia's withdrawal would not protect it from ICC's prosecution, see Sayapin 2016.

Luk'janova E (2015) O prave nalevo. Novaja gazeta [Luk'yanova E (2015) On the Law to the Left. New Journal]. https://www.novayagazeta.ru/articles/2015/03/19/63473-o-prave-nalevo. Accessed 20 February 2017

Mendes E (2010) Peace and Justice at the International Criminal Court: A Court of Last Resort. Edward Elgar, Cheltenham

Roberts A, Guelff R (2000) Documents on the Laws of War. Oxford University Press, Oxford

Sassòli M, Bouvier A, Quintin A (2011) How Does Law Protect in War? ICRC, Geneva

Sayapin S (2016) Russia's Withdrawal of Signature from the Rome Statute Would not Shield its Nationals from Potential Prosecution at the ICC. EJIL: Talk! http://www.ejiltalk.org/russias-withdrawal-of-signature-from-the-rome-statute-would-not-shield-its-nationals-from-potential-prosecution-at-the-icc/. Accessed 26 February 2017

Stegmiller I (2011) The Pre-Investigation Stage of the ICC: Criteria for Situation Selection. Duncker & Humblot, Berlin

Triffterer O (2008) Commentary on the Rome Statute of the International Criminal Court. Beck/Hart Publishing, Munich

United Nations Office of the High Commissioner for Human Rights (2016) Report on the Human Rights Situation in Ukraine: 16 February to 15 May 2016 http://www.ohchr.org/Documents/Countries/UA/Ukraine_14th_HRMMU_Report.pdf. Accessed 23 February 2017

United Nations Office of the High Commissioner for Human Rights (2016) Report on the Human Rights Situation in Ukraine: 16 May to 15 August 2016 http://www.ohchr.org/Documents/Countries/UkUkraine15thReport.pdf. Accessed 23 February 2017

United Nations Office of the High Commissioner for Human Rights (2017) Conflict-Related Sexual Violence in Ukraine: 14 March 2014 to 31 January 2017 http://www.ohchr.org/Documents/Countries/UA/ReportCRSV_EN.pdf. Accessed 24 February 2017

Werle G, Jessberger F (2014) Principles of International Criminal Law, 3rd edition. Oxford University Press, Oxford

Chapter 19
Sexual Violence in War-Torn Ukraine: A Challenge for International Criminal Justice

Ioannis P. Tzivaras

Contents

Abstract Sexual violence constitutes a set of offences established by international law, particularly after the establishment of the *ad hoc* International Criminal Tribunals and the permanent International Criminal Court. This chapter presents an overview of the situation regarding gender-based violence in the recent and ongoing Russian-Ukrainian dispute over Crimea. Especially in the regions of Eastern Ukraine, many

Ioannis P. Tzivaras, LLM., Dr. Jur., Faculty of Law, Democritus University of Thrace, Komotini, Greece, e-mail: jtzivaras@gmail.com; Department of Economics and Administration, Open University of Cyprus, Nicosia, Republic of Cyprus, email: ioannis.tzivaras@ouc.ac.cy; Department of Social Sciences, Hellenic Open University, Patras, Greece, email: tzivaras.ioannis@ac.eap.gr; Deputy Director of Hellenic Institute for United Nations Affairs, Thessaloniki, Greece, email: tzivaras@hapsc.org.

I. P. Tzivaras (✉)
Faculty of Law, Democritus University of Thrace, Komotini, Greece
e-mail: jtzivaras@gmail.com; ioannis.tzivaras@ouc.ac.cy; tzivaras.ioannis@ac.eap.gr;
tzivaras@hapsc.org

I. P. Tzivaras
Department of Economics and Administration, Open University of Cyprus, Nicosia, Republic of Cyprus

I. P. Tzivaras
Department of Social Sciences, Hellenic Open University, Patras, Greece

I. P. Tzivaras
Deputy Director of Hellenic Institute for United Nations Affairs, Thessaloniki, Greece

© T.M.C. ASSER PRESS and the authors 2018
S. Sayapin and E. Tsybulenko (eds.), *The Use of Force against Ukraine and International Law*, https://doi.org/10.1007/978-94-6265-222-4_19

cases of human rights violations, including evidence of sexual violence in the areas affected by military operations, are recorded in the reports of various international bodies. Meanwhile, Ukrainian non-governmental organizations (NGOs) working for gender equality have presented findings highlighting incidents of sexual violence that are punishable under the International Criminal Court's statute, including threats of rape and other forms of sexual violence, as well as methods of ill-treatment and torture in the context of sexual abuse, primarily against women and men. Considering that the Russian-Ukrainian war is still under preliminary examination by the International Criminal Court, the breakdown in the rule of law in conflict-affected areas in Ukraine has increased the vulnerability towards sexual and gender-based violence, including both crimes related to the jurisdiction of the Court, and also domestic sexual violence. The related reports have shown that there is not much information on the armed conflict situation in Ukraine in which sexual violence has been widely or systematically employed against civilians in general. As documented, most incidents of sexual violence have taken place under a regime of the illegal detention of women, often followed by various forms of sexual violence against them by members of illegal armed forces. The International Criminal Court is conducting an in-depth analysis of received information related to this conflict in order to establish a reasonable connection between the alleged crimes and the jurisdiction of the court. The main question in the case of the Russian-Ukrainian war is whether the International Criminal Court, as a permanent and established holdover of international criminal justice will continue to face, in addition to its statutory provision, crimes against sexual violence to the extent they deserve, given their heinous nature and the particular and growing needs of the victims.

Keywords sexual violence · gender-based violence · crimes against sexual dignity · women · International Criminal Court · international criminal justice

19.1 Introduction

Sexual violence in the context of armed conflicts is an issue as old as the armed conflicts themselves. Violence against women and children and all forms of sexual violence, including all forms of crimes against sexual dignity, are increasingly recognized as facets of many armed conflicts, often as practices rather than as strategies, and regarded among the most common human rights violations.[1] The Russian-Ukrainian armed conflict and, especially, the Russian aggression violate the general principles of international law and constitute a major factor in the transformation of the international legal order.[2]

---

[1] Leatherman 2011, p. 2, pp. 13–4.

[2] OSCE Parliamentary Assembly, 2015, Resolution on the Continuation of Clear, Gross and Uncorrected Violations of OSCE Commitments and International Norms by the Russian Federation. https://www.oscepa.org/meetings/annual-sessions/2015-annual-session-helsinki/2015-helsinki-final-declaration/2282-07. Accessed 17 March 2017. See Tsybulenko and Pakhomenko 2016, pp. 167–8; Grant 2015, pp. 43–5.

The risk of gender-based violence and humanitarian crises and the vulnerability of sexual violence survivors increase in times of armed conflict.[3] The ongoing military conflict in Eastern Ukraine and its destructive effects have been accompanied by many cases of human rights violations, including evidence of sexual violence in the areas affected by the military operations, and the creation of large-scale flows of internally displaced persons.[4]

Generally, the conflict over Crimea has led to many incidents of sexual and gender-based violence; but, until now, many of them have been difficult to verify. Given that there is a total collapse of law and order in the conflict-affected areas, sexual crimes are the "tip of the iceberg", in general, as only a few victims ask for help given the social barriers in place and failing legislation, which in turn lead to an underreporting of sexual and gender-based violence.[5]

After some preliminary reflections on the concept of sexual violence during the armed conflict in Ukraine (Sect. 19.2) and introducing the concept in the context of reported sexual crimes, especially in areas of Eastern Ukraine (Sect. 19.3), the chapter focuses on the International Criminal Court. Especially, it cites the role of the court in the Russian-Ukrainian war and the investigation of alleged crimes, including sexual crimes (Sect. 19.4) and how the court upholds the legal basis of and jurisdiction over the prosecution and punishment of those who are responsible for committing sexual crimes (Sect. 19.5).

19.2   Sexual Violence in the Temporarily Occupied Territories in Ukraine

The Russian-Ukrainian war has generated much evidence of gender-based crimes, which have taken place during the period of the armed conflict and the Russian occupation. In the early stages of the conflict, many cases of conflict and reports were produced, documenting sexual and gender-based crimes, including threats of rape and other forms of sexual violence, as well as methods of ill-treatment and torture in the context of sexual abuse against both women and men. The temporary occupation of part of the territory in Eastern Ukraine has been a topic of research among various international bodies and Ukrainian NGOs working for gender equality,[6] whose findings have highlighted incidents of sexual violence punishable under the International Criminal Court's statute.

Armed conflicts exacerbate existing gender inequalities, placing women, in particular, at a heightened risk of various forms of sexual violence by both state and non-state actors,[7] alongside the wide-ranging effects of war on women and the impor-

---

[3] Segal 2008, pp. 21–35.

[4] Ukrainian Centre for Social Reforms 2015, p. 8.

[5] Volosevych et al. 2014, pp. 17–47.

[6] Onuch and Martsenyuk 2014, pp. 110–1.

[7] Committee on the Elimination of Discrimination Against Women 2013.

tance of ensuring women's rights in times of national crisis. Against this backdrop, sufficient information cannot be provided to prove the real situation concerning the commission of such crimes, given the lack of statistics, as well as ineffective nature of investigations into sexual violence. Considering that the Russian-Ukrainian war is still under preliminary examination by the International Criminal Court, the breakdown in the rule of law in conflict-affected areas in Ukraine has increased the vulnerability towards sexual and gender-based violence, including crimes related to the jurisdiction of the court, and also domestic sexual violence and trafficking for the purposes of sexual exploitation in areas with a high concentration of military and armed groups.[8]

Bearing in mind that the armed conflict in Ukraine has led to the existence of many internally displaced people,[9] women are increasingly vulnerable to sexual violence and other heinous human rights violations and abuses, and severely victimized by wartime displacement, both in governmental and non-governmental controlled areas.[10] The prevalence of sexual violence, especially against women, and other forms of degrading treatment against women, including increased exposure to sexual and other forms of gender-based violence, has been recognized as a major concern in the context of this crisis and remains a predominant risk, particularly in conflict-affected areas of Ukraine.

In general, the conflict, especially in the eastern part of Ukraine, has had a major impact on the lives of women and girls. As a significant part of the internally displaced population, women, forced from their communities or trapped in conflict-affected areas, are at risk of intensified uses of, or threats to use, sexual violence, as well trading sex as a means of providing the most basic needs, in the meaning of "survival sex".[11] It must be said that, when it comes to assessing situations involving the use of sexual violence in the temporarily occupied territory of Ukraine, it is difficult to provide detailed and concrete data because neither the government nor civil society nor other organizations have access to that territory.

---

[8] CSO's Shadow Report 2016 on Ukraine 2016, Implementation of the Recommendations of the Committee on the Elimination of Discrimination Against Women No. 30 on Women in Conflict Prevention, Conflict and Post-conflict Situations and UN Resolution 1325 Women, Peace and Security of the UN Convention on the Elimination of All Forms of Discrimination against Women, pp. 5–8. http://tbinternet.ohchr.org/Treaties/CEDAW/Shared%20Documents/UKR/INT_CEDAW_NGO_UKR_24435_E.pdf. Accessed 11 March 2017.

[9] Maiorova 2017, pp. 50–2.

[10] OSCE, Chief Monitor Apakan condemns sexual harassment of special monitoring mission to Ukraine patrol member in Donetsk Region'. http://www.osce.org/special-monitoring-mission-to-ukraine/315891. Accessed 28 May 2017. As stated: "This latest incident, in which a man, armed with an assault rifle, intimidated an unarmed civilian female member of an SMM patrol by making comments of a sexual nature, demands a swift and unequivocal response by the so-called 'Donetsk People's Republic'. This must include identification of the individual responsible, and full application of appropriate measures to ensure that such incidents are not repeated."

[11] OSCE Special Monitoring Mission to Ukraine 2012, Thematic Report: Internal Displacement in Ukraine. SEC.FR/473/14/Corr.1. http://www.osce.org/ukraine-smm/122620?download=true. Accessed 2 February 2017.

19.3 Reported Sexual Violence in Ukraine

Since the beginning of the armed conflict, human rights protection organizations, including women's organizations, have collected data with the aim of informing Ukrainian law enforcement authorities and international organizations on human rights violations, as well as providing social and legal support to victims. From the various reports on the use or threat of sexual violence, and given that there are still no official data on this issue, the surveys of international bodies and NGOs, in general, have shown that, in the conflict area and neighbouring territories, there have been cases of gender-based violence, including rapes, both collective and against girls, sending women to satisfy the sexual needs of soldiers in the war zones, coercion to perform sexual acts, touching of sexual organs, harassment, stripping women, threats of rape, sharing of shells and toilets by women and men, forced nudity for the purpose of psychological pressure, and kidnappings of young women.[12] Moreover, related reports have shown that there little information on the armed conflict situation in Ukraine in which sexual violence has been widely or systematically employed against civilians in general.

As documented, most incidents of sexual violence have taken place under a regime of the illegal detention of women, often followed by various forms of sexual violence against them by members of illegal armed forces, especially in the areas of Luhansk and Donetsk. In particular, there is evidence of cruel and inhuman treatment against women by the militants of illegal armed groups and representatives of quasi-state agencies as a widespread and systematic practice in relation to detainees.[13] Furthermore, increased levels of sexual violence against women have been reported by both non-combatant men and returning fighters, who find themselves idle in displacement, as well as intimidation, harassment and violence against non-combatants. There are also high levels of sexual violence in the conflict areas, which require substantiation and legal redress, with exposure to HIV as a real threat in this context.[14]

In particular, many human rights organizations have highlighted the extremely poor conditions experienced by illegally detained civilians in the occupied territories, in the meaning of the use of undue force during detention, no separation between civilian women and men in illegal detention units, no access to sanitation, water and food, and torture and trafficking, especially of women and girls, for sexual purposes. Moreover, as noted, the armed conflict in Ukraine has led to many incidents of gender-based violence, namely, in relation to special survival needs in the conflict, i.e., sex work in exchange for ensuring basic human needs. In general, there are no reports from the Ukrainian-Russian conflict indicating mass rapes and incidents of

---

[12] Justice for Peace in Donbass 2016, Report on the Issue of Sexual Violence in the Conflict Zone in Donbas to Be Presented at the 66th CEDAW Session. https://jfp.org.ua/coalition/novyny-koalicii/articles/submission-cedaw?locale=en. Accessed 12 January 2017.

[13] Bielousov et al. 2015, pp. 32, 57.

[14] Protection Cluster Ukraine 2016, Ukraine: Protection Cluster Strategy, p. 4. http://www.globalprotectioncluster.org/_assets/files/field_protection_clusters/Ukraine/2016_protection_cluster_strategy.pdf. Accessed 13 January 2017.

sexual violence on a large scale, used as a "tool of war", as occurred in many recent conflict zones around the world. Nevertheless, there is evidence to the contrary in the territories not under Ukrainian control, in which many human rights violations and acts that especially constitute brutal and frequent sexual violence have occurred.

In its report on the human rights situation in Ukraine of November 2014, the Office of the UN High Commissioner for Human Rights noted, with regard to the eastern regions of Ukraine:[15]

[Those] trapped in areas of fighting are at a heightened threat of sexual violence. Information from NGOs and IDPs that young women and men are being taken off buses leaving the conflict zone require further investigation. The HRMU is concerned that cases of violence against women may go unreported... Women, including those internally displaced, and may be at heightened risk of being exposed to trafficking, sexual violence and resorting to prostitution as a means of survival.

Furthermore, the UN High Commissioner for Refugees stated that:[16]

[There] are increasing reports of violence against women in this area including harassment, forced labour and sexual violence; there are also reports of sexual harassment at checkpoints whilst leaving the non-government controlled areas.

The General Assembly of the UN, in its 71st session on 31 October 2016, making reference to Resolution 68/262,[17] and in accordance with Resolution 2202/2015,[18] noted that, in the territory of Ukraine, and especially in the eastern part, serious violations against civilians have been committed, in particular, abuses of fundamental freedoms and measures and practices of discrimination against civilians, Crimean Tatars and people belonging to other ethnic and religious groups by the Russian occupation authorities.[19]

Furthermore, the Council of Europe, in many of its resolutions, has stated the flagrant violations and actions on the part of the Russian Federation, the military occupation of Ukrainian territory, and the use and threat of military force constitute a grave violation of international law, including heinous human rights violations, as documented in various reports.[20] Especially in Resolution 2112 (2016), the council's Parliamentary Assembly noted the numerous reports of the inhumane and degrading treatment of captured people who have been subjected to torture, ill-treatment and sexual violence, violating further the Geneva Conventions of 1949 and its two Additional Protocols from 1977.[21]

---

[15] Office of the UN High Commissioner for Human Rights 2016.

[16] UN High Commissioner for Refugees 2015.

[17] UN General Assembly 2014.

[18] UN Security Council 2015.

[19] UN General Assembly 2016.

[20] Council of Europe Parliamentary Assembly 2014, Resolution 1990 (2014) Reconsideration on Substantive Grounds of the Previously Ratified Credentials of the Russian Delegation. http://assembly.coe.int/nw/xml/XRef/Xref-XML2HTML-en.asp?fileid=20882&lang=en. Accessed 13 January 2017.

[21] Council of Europe Parliamentary Assembly 2016, Resolution 2112 (2016) The Humanitarian Concerns with Regard to People Captured during the War in Ukraine. http://assembly.coe.int/nw/xml/XRef/Xref-XML2HTML-en.asp?fileid=22750&lang=en. Accessed 19 January 2017.

Meanwhile, the Council of Europe's Resolution 2132 (2016) states that 1.5 million people have left their homes as a result of the conflict, with hundreds held captive or reported missing.[22] In addition, as stated in Resolution 2133 (2016), both in Crimea and in the conflict zone in the Donbas region, serious human rights violations, including sexual violence, are still occurring, as documented by numerous reports from, *inter alia*, the council's Commissioner for Human Rights, the UN Human Rights Monitoring Mission in Ukraine, the Special Monitoring Mission to Ukraine of the Office for Democratic Institutions and Human Rights of the Organization for Security and Co-operation in Europe, and international and Ukrainian NGOs.[23]

In particular, the Office of the UN High Commissioner for Human Rights, in relation to the human rights situation in Ukraine, noted that both methods and threats of sexual violence have been used, in many situations, as means to compel male detainees to confess or perform other actions as human rights violations, involving an explicit condition for their safety in general. Cases documented by the UN High Commissioner for Human Rights indicate that threats of sexual violence are employed in connection with charges of terrorism, ill-treatment and torture, especially during interrogations. These documents highlight the coercion of victims to confess involving the threat and use of sexual violence, both against women and men. Other documented cases are linked to military status, in civilian areas, where members of battalions have used sexual violence against women, men and civilians with physical and mental disabilities in order to cause serious physical and mental harm to them.

It must be said is that, in the armed conflict in Ukraine, proper statistical data on instances of sexual violence are lacking, due, especially, to the under-reporting of such crimes because of the fear and trauma experienced by victims, as well the unreliable information on violations related to gender-based violence, which appears in connection with the military conflict itself. The limited number of effective investigations into cases of sexual crimes, especially in the territories within the conflict zone under governmental control, is a particular concern, as it is preventing the collection of reliable data on sexual crimes that have taken place during the armed conflict in Ukraine.

---

[22] Council of Europe Parliamentary Assembly 2016, Resolution 2132 (2016) Political Consequences of the Russian Aggression in Ukraine. http://assembly.coe.int/nw/xml/XRef/Xref-XML2 HTML-en.asp?fileid=23166&lang=en. Accessed 17 January 2017.

[23] Council of Europe Parliamentary Assembly 2016, Resolution 2133 (2016) Legal Remedies for Human Rights Violations on the Ukrainian Territories Outside the Control of the Ukrainian Authorities. http://assembly.coe.int/nw/xml/XRef/Xref-XML2HTML-en.asp?fileid=23167&lang= en. Accessed 12 January 2017.

19.4   Gender-Based Violence, the International Criminal Court and the Ukrainian Situation

As is known, a real breakthrough came with the establishment of the International Criminal Court in terms of the supranational criminal prosecution of sexual violence. The court, whose remit, through its statutory jurisdiction, covers the prosecution of the crime of genocide, crimes against humanity and war crimes,[24] also provides for the prosecution of crimes against sexual dignity in a more extended form, in correspondence with the statutes of the International Criminal Tribunal for former Yugoslavia and Rwanda and the Special Court for Sierra Leone,[25] under the broader term of *gender-based violence*.[26] The Rome Statute refer to the explicit stipulation of a list of sexual crimes as crimes against humanity and war crimes, as well as takes gender issues in the legal process into account.[27] Furthermore, Articles 7 and 8 of the court's statute establish those crimes and include, *inter alia*, the direct punishment of sexual violence.[28]

Gender-based violence in international criminal law constitutes a major form of sexual violence. This does not only involve rape; other forms of sexual violence and many acts that do not involve physical contact can constitute sexual violence. In general, a sexual crime has been defined as an act of a sexual nature, which is committed on a person under coercive circumstances. Furthermore, based on the *ad hoc* International Criminal Tribunals' practice,[29] sexual assault is similarly defined as all serious abuses of a sexual nature inflicted upon the physical and moral integrity of a person by means of coercion.

Sexual violence has been defined in various cases that have come before the *ad hoc* International Criminal Tribunals for former Yugoslavia and Rwanda, the Special Court for Sierra Leone and the International Criminal Court. In particular, it has been determined as an act of a sexual nature, which is committed on a person under coercive circumstances. Sexual assault has been similarly defined as all serious abuses of a sexual nature inflicted upon the physical and moral integrity of a person by a means of coercion, threat of force or intimidation in a way that is both degrading and humiliating for the victim's dignity.[30]

Furthermore, the International Criminal Court defines "sexual violence", in Articles 7(1)(g)-6, 8(2)(b)(xxii)-6 and (e)(vi)-6 (Elements of Crimes), as follows:

---

[24] Carden and Sadat 2000, pp. 434–6; Beresford 2001, pp. 33–50; Boas 2000, pp. 268–72.

[25] McDonald 2000, pp. 2–16.

[26] Dieng 2002, pp. 688–707; Bedont and Hall-Martinez 1999, pp. 65–85; Oosterveld 2013, pp. 66–70.

[27] Hagay-Frey 2011, p. 104.

[28] De Brouwer 2005, pp. 19–22.

[29] International Criminal Tribunal for Rwanda, *Prosecutor v. Jean-Paul Akayesu, Judgment, 02 September 1998, ICTR-96-4-T*, Para 688, International Criminal Tribunal for Former Yugoslavia, *Prosecutor v. Miroslav Kvocka, Milojica Kos, Mlado Radic, Zoran Zigic and Dragoljub Prcac, Judgment, 02 November 2001, IT-98-30/1-T*, Paras 180, 559.

[30] De Ruiter 2011, p. 7.

> The perpetrator committed an act of a sexual nature against one or more persons or caused such person or persons to engage in an act of a sexual nature by force, or by threat of force or coercion, such as that caused by fear of violence, duress, detention, psychological oppression or abuse of power, against such person or persons or another person or by taking advantage of a coercive environment or such person's or persons' incapacity to give genuine consent.

Sexual violence can be found in many forms, with gender-based offences, such as rape, sexual slavery, forced marriage, sexual mutilation, enforced prostitution, forced abortion, forced pregnancy,[31] forced sterilization,[32] slavery and torture and, based on the case law of the International Criminal Tribunals, and other inhuman acts, outrages upon personal dignity and cruel treatment, considered as violations of the Common Article 3 of the Geneva Conventions.[33] Wilfully causing great suffering or serious injury to a person's body or health and inhuman treatment are also grave breaches of the Geneva Conventions.[34]

The need to include sexual violence in criminal acts that are not expressly sexual in nature has been obviated by the International Criminal Court, whose statute includes other inhuman acts as crimes against humanity,[35] war crimes applicable both in internal and international armed conflicts, causing serious bodily and mental harm,[36] and imposing measures intended to prevent births within the group of acts that constitute genocide.

As is known, on 17 April 2014, the Ukrainian Government lodged a declaration under Article 12(3) of the Rome Statute, accepting the jurisdiction of the International Criminal Court over alleged crimes committed in the context of the "Maidan" protests on its territory from 21 November 2013 to 22 February 2014 and onwards, on the basis of the Declaration of the Parliament of Ukraine. In turn, the International Criminal Court has exercised its jurisdiction its statute for crimes committed on the territory of Ukraine since 21 November 2013.

Based on the communications that the court received, the preliminary examination focused on events in Crimea and Eastern Ukraine and concluded that the alleged crimes against humanity committed in the context of the "Maidan" protests included murder, torture and other inhuman acts. Given that these crimes were allegedly committed in the context of armed hostilities, the International Criminal Court's jurisdiction has entailed further analysis of whether they occurred in the context of an international or a non-international armed conflict.

---

[31] Boon 2001, pp. 625–6.

[32] *Kvocka, Kos, Radic, Zigic and Prcac* 2001 (see fn. 202), Paras 180–1.

[33] *Akayesu* 1998 (see fn. 28), Para 688; International Criminal Tribunal for Former Yugoslavia, *Prosecutor v. Zejnil Delalic, Zdravko Mucic, Hazim Delic and Esad Landzo, Judgment, 16 November 1998, IT-96-21-T*, Paras 1040–1, 1066, *Prosecutor v. Dragoljub Kunarac, Radomir Kovac and Zoran Vukovic, Judgment, 22 February 2001, IT-96-23* and *IT-96-23/1*, Paras 773–774.

[34] *Delalic, Mucic, Delic and Landzo* 1998 (see fn. 32), Paras 1040, 1066.

[35] *Kvocka, Kos, Radic, Zigic and Prcac* (see fn. 28), Paras 208–9, *Akayesu* 1998 (see fn. 28), Para 688. See Askin 2003, pp. 288–9.

[36] International Criminal Tribunal for Former Yugoslavia, *Prosecutor v. Vidoje Blagojevic and Dragan Jokic, Transcripts, 22 July 2003, IT-02-60*, Para 646.

The summary of alleged crimes in the Report on Preliminary Examination Activities of 2016[37] concerning, especially, Crimea and Eastern Ukraine, is based on reports and publicly received information by the Office of the Prosecutor. As indicated, in Crimea, there have been many incidents concerning the harassment of the Crimean Tatar population and a significant number of internally or non-internally displaced persons, killings and abduction of members of the Crimean Tatar population, ill-treatment in the context of detention or abduction, including, among others, threats of sexual violence, detention and fair trial rights, and issues concerning compulsory military service.

In the area of Eastern Ukraine, the International Criminal Court, according to the aforementioned report, has evidence of killings of and injuries to civilians, members of the armed forces and other armed groups, the destruction of civilian objects, including residential properties, schools and kindergartens in both governmental and non-governmental territories, cases of the detention of civilians and alleged armed group members, which have often been accompanied with ill-treatment, including the use or threat of sexual violence and disappearances. It is unclear how many individuals have been forcibly disappeared, tortured and ill-treated, although there are several hundred alleged victims, including victims of sexual violence, sexual and gender-based violence, especially in the context of detention, against both female and male victims, including civilians and members of the armed forces and armed groups.

These alleged crimes have been attributed to both state and non-state forces. In several documented cases, sexual violence has been perpetrated in the context of interrogations. Specifically, the International Criminal Court's findings on Crimea refer to harassment and abuse, and possible abuse of a sexual nature, and internally displaced persons, with a large proportion of these believed to be of Crimean Tatar ethnicity, within mainland Ukraine. The court has also highlighted cases of ill-treatment Crimea, including several incidents in the context of detention, abduction or forcible transfer from prisons in Crimea to prisons in the territory of the Russian Federation; these reports also refer to the use and threat of sexual violence.

In Eastern Ukraine, the International Criminal Court notes that, apart from a large number of civilians who have been killed or injured in armed hostilities, all sides have allegedly detained both civilians and members of armed groups, while DPR and LPR forces are alleged to have detained suspected civilians and ill-treated them, including with sexual violence. Torture and ill-treatment have been reportedly perpetrated by both sides, involving several alleged victims, while many cases of sexual abuse in both government-controlled territory and in many areas outside the government's control have been documented.

The Office of the Prosecutor notes that, while there are many documented instances of gender-based violence in the context of the armed conflict in Eastern Ukraine, there is an acknowledgement that the limited information available is

---

[37] International Criminal Court, Office of the Prosecutor 2016, Report on Preliminary Examination Activities 2016, pp. 36–41. https://www.icc-cpi.int/iccdocs/otp/161114-otp-rep-pe_eng.pdf. Accessed 19 January 2017.

due to underreporting on account of social barrier and a lack of support services in armed conflict-affected areas. As indicated, the majority of these instances have occurred during the illegal detention of civilians and members of the armed groups for crimes committed by both state and non-state actors. Based on the findings, the sexual crimes committed include rape, threats of rape, forced nudity and beating genitals, especially during interrogations.

19.5 Relation Between Sexual Crimes in Ukraine and the International Criminal Court's Jurisdiction

The International Criminal Court is conducting an in-depth analysis of received information related to the Russian-Ukrainian conflict in order to establish a reasonable relation between the alleged crimes and the jurisdiction of the court. Given that the court's analysis is based on the examination of information relevant to determining the existence of international and/or non-international armed conflict in the areas of Eastern Ukraine, and the jurisdictional analysis of the related criminal acts or omissions, the court has proceeded to analyse documented information and materials provided by international organizations, various NGOs, the Ukrainian Government and many individuals. The database of incidents that occurred in Ukraine since 20 February 2014 facilitates a crime pattern analysis on the alleged crimes committed by both sides in the armed conflict through communications with national and international organizations, as well as the Ukrainian Government.

While the Russian-Ukrainian War does not constitute genocide, the International Criminal Court does have jurisdiction over crimes against humanity, where Article 7(1)(g) makes direct reference to sexual crimes, such as "rape, sexual slavery, enforced prostitution, forced pregnancy, enforced sterilization, or any other form of sexual violence of comparable gravity". Furthermore, sexual crimes can be related to acts of enslavement, displacement, torture, persecution and segregation, which, through other inhumane acts, can intentionally cause great suffering or serious injury to mental or physical health. More specifically, Article 7(3) further states that:

> For the purpose of this Statute, it is understood that the term 'gender' refers to the two sexes, male and female, within the context of society. The term 'gender' does not indicate any meaning different from the above.

Regarding the provisions of the International Criminal Court's statute concerning war crimes, sexual crimes are initially referred to in Article 8(2)(b)(xxi)–(xxii), which covers specific provisions for major violations of laws and customs applicable in international armed conflicts, in particular:[38]

> 1… 2. For the purpose of this Statute, 'war crimes' means: (a)… (b) Other serious violations of the laws and customs applicable in international armed conflict, within the established framework of international law, namely, any of the following acts:… (i)… (xxi) Committing

---

[38] Wagner 2003, pp. 409–512.

outrages upon personal dignity, in particular humiliating and degrading treatment; (xxii) Committing rape, sexual slavery, enforced prostitution, forced pregnancy, as defined in Article 7, para 2(f), enforced sterilization, or any other form of sexual violence also constituting a grave breach of the Geneva Conventions.

Article 8 also refers to the commission of sexual offenses during an armed conflict that is not of an international character,[39] which in turn refers to the aforementioned offenses and, in particular, Article 8(2)(c)(ii) and Article 8(2)(e)(vi), respectively.[40] Still, the impact of armed conflict upon victims, in particular, those of sexual violence, is a matter of special interest for the International Criminal Court, in light of Articles 42(9) and 43(6).[41] In Article 42(9), concerning the Office of the Prosecutor, it is noted that:[42]

The Prosecutor shall appoint advisers with legal expertise on specific issues, including, but not limited to, sexual and gender violence and violence against children.

Meanwhile, according to the Registry of the International Criminal Court, Article 43(6) refers to the operation of the Special Unit for Victims and Witnesses.[43] As such:[44]

The Registrar shall set up a Victims and Witnesses Unit within the Registry. This Unit shall provide, in consultation with the Office of the Prosecutor, protective measures and security arrangements, counselling and other appropriate assistance for witnesses, victims who appear before the Court, and others who are at risk on account of testimony given by such witnesses. The Unit shall include staff with expertise in trauma, including trauma related to crimes of sexual violence.

Particular reference to sexual crimes is made in Article 54(1)(b) in terms of the duties and the powers of the Prosecutor with respect to investigations. According to this article:

1. The Prosecutor shall: (a)… (b) Take appropriate measures to ensure the effective investigation and prosecution of crimes within the jurisdiction of the Court, and in doing so, respect the interests and personal circumstances of victims and witnesses, including age, gender as defined in Article 7, para 3, and health, and take into account the nature of the crime, in particular where it involves sexual violence, gender violence or violence against children.

Finally, special mention is made in Article 68(1) of the International Criminal Court's statute, combined with the provisions in Articles 43(6) and 75, to the protection of victims and witnesses involved in the proceedings before the court:[45]

---

[39] West 1987, pp. 3–5; Katz and Mazur 1979, pp. 11–3; Van Boven 1999, pp. 77–89.

[40] Flores-Acuna 2006, pp. 39–51; Pillay 2003, pp. 685–92.

[41] Garkawe 2003, pp. 345–67.

[42] Roben 2003, pp. 513–52.

[43] Ingadottir et al. Ingadottir T 2003, pp. 2–45; Jones 2002, pp. 1355–70.

[44] Garkawe 2001, pp. 269–89.

[45] Donat-Cattin 1999, pp. 869–88.

The Court shall take appropriate measures to protect the safety, physical and psychological well-being, dignity and privacy of victims and witnesses. In so doing, the Court shall have regard to all relevant factors, including age, gender as defined in article 7, paragraph 3, and health, and the nature of the crime, in particular, but not limited to, where the crime involves sexual or gender violence or violence against children. The Prosecutor shall take such measures particularly during the investigation and prosecution of such crimes. These measures shall not be prejudicial to or inconsistent with the rights of the accused and a fair and impartial trial.

Taking into consideration all the above, and given the situation related to the various reports before the court and the fact that it can exercise jurisdiction over Rome Statute crimes committed in the Ukrainian territory during the relevant periods, it has stated that there are many incidents of attacks directed against the civilian population under Article 7(2)(a) of the statute, which constitute serious human rights abuses, but they are not systematic and widespread under the general provisions of Article 7.

Given the humanitarian situation in conflict-affected areas in Ukraine, and the fact that the civilian population, as well as a large number of combatants, have been subjected to human rights violations, which constitute war crimes and crimes against humanity, in a climate of impunity and general lawlessness, it can be argued that crimes against humanity are connected to crimes against sexual dignity in many cases. Within this framework, relevant case law is available from the *ad hoc* International Criminal Tribunals and the International Criminal Court, as follows: the enslavement (Article 7(1)(c)), deportation or forcible transfer of populations (Article 7(1)(d)), primarily from the perspective of internally displaced persons in Ukrainian territory; imprisonment or other severe deprivation of physical liberty in violation of fundamental rules of international law (Article 7(1)(e)); torture (Article 7(1)(f)); rape, sexual slavery, enforced prostitution, forced pregnancy, enforced sterilization or any other form of sexual violence of comparable gravity (Article 7(1)(g)); persecution against any identifiable group or collective on political, racial, national, ethnic, cultural, religious, gender or other grounds, which are universally recognized as impermissible under international law (Article 7(1)(h)); and, finally, other inhumane acts of a similar character, which intentionally cause great suffering, or serious injury to the body or to mental or physical health (Article 7(1)(k)).

If the International Criminal Court concludes that the armed conflict in Ukraine is of a non-international character, sexual crimes, depending on the interpretation, can be connected with grave breaches of the Geneva Convention of 12 August 1949, other serious violations of laws and customs applicable in an international armed conflict within the established framework of international law, serious violations of Article 3 common to the four Geneva Conventions of 12 August 1949.

Specifically, sexual crimes can be found under the general provisions of grave breaches of the Geneva Conventions of 12 August 1949, and especially in Article 8(2)(a)(ii) concerning torture or inhuman treatment and in Article 8(2)(a)(iii) on wilfully causing great suffering or serious injury to a person's body or health. Given the provisions regarding other serious violations of laws and customs applicable to international armed conflict, sexual crimes can be connected to Article 8(2)(b)(xxi) on committing outrages upon personal dignity, in particular, in the form of humiliating and degrading treatment, and Article 8(2)(b)(xxii) on committing rape, sexual slavery, enforced prostitution, forced pregnancy, enforced sterilization, or any other form of sexual violence that constitutes a grave breach of the Geneva Conventions.

Finally, taking into account the reported crimes from the Russian-Ukrainian war, sexual violence can be connected to Article 8(2)(c)(i) on violence against a person, in particular, murder of all kinds, mutilation, cruel treatment and torture, which are serious violations of Article 3 common to the four Geneva Conventions of 12 August 1949, in the case of an armed conflict not of an international character, as well as Article 8(2)(3)(vi) on committing rape, sexual slavery, enforced prostitution, forced pregnancy, enforced sterilization and any other form of sexual violence, which again constitute a serious violation of Article 3 common to the four Geneva Conventions, as well as other serious violations of the laws and customs applicable in armed conflicts that are not of an international character.

19.6   Conclusion

It is obvious that the commission of sexual crimes as violations of human rights on a large scale and armed conflict are an inseparable and real issue. Over the last 20 years, the high productivity of international criminal law on the internationalization of sexual violence has indeed been demonstrated, in addition to the prosecution of established international crimes and their transformation into war crimes, crimes against humanity and crimes that constitute genocide.

The contribution, in particular, of the *ad hoc* International Criminal Tribunals, the Special Court for Sierra Leone and the International Criminal Court has been subversive, given that the previously unclear legal framework on sexual violence has been clarified, while there is universal acceptance that crimes against sexual dignity are international crimes, which has in turn marginalized the effect of the historic concept of unpunished attacks on the sexual dignity of the victim. It therefore becomes important that, beyond the provision of sexual violence as a collection of criminal crimes of international concern, particular attention is given to the protection of victims of sexual crimes, given the specificity of the scheme in which they are vested.

The main question in the case of the Russian-Ukrainian war is whether the International Criminal Court, as a permanent and established holdover of international criminal justice, will continue to tackle, in addition to its statutory provision, crimes against sexual violence to the extent they deserve, given their heinous nature and the particular and growing needs of victims. It must be said that the court must continue to engage with the Ukrainian authorities, international and national NGOs, civil society and other stakeholders on all matters that are relevant to the examination of the situation in Ukrainian territory. Given that the Office of the Prosecutor is continuing its analysis of alleged sexual crimes, among other relevant crimes, and the open-ended Ukrainian acceptance of the International Criminal Court's jurisdiction, it must be said that, in the case of Ukraine, sexual violence will play a significant role in the proceedings before the court. What should be noted, finally, is that the court must rely on the significant amount of available case law, as well as the jurisprudence of the *ad hoc* International Criminal Tribunals, in order to establish and strengthen the view that sexual violence, especially in armed conflicts, involves heinous crimes, which are committed under the cruellest conditions.

References

Askin K (2003) Prosecuting Wartime Rape and other Gender-Related Crimes under International Law: Extraordinary Advances, Enduring Obstacles. Berkeley Journal of International Law 21: 288–349

Bedont B, Hall-Martinez K (1999) Ending Impunity for Gender Crimes under the International Criminal Court. Brown Journal of World Affairs 6(1): 65–85

Beresford S (2001) Unshackling the Paper Tiger: The Sentencing Practices of the *Ad Hoc* International Criminal Tribunals for the Former Yugoslavia and Rwanda. International Criminal Law Review 1: 33–50

Bielousov I et al. (2015) Surviving Hell: Testimonies of Victims on Places of Illegal Detention in Donbas. TsP Komprint, Kiev

Boas G (2000) Comparing the ICTY and the ICC: Some Procedural and Substantive Issues. Netherlands International Law Review 47(3): 267–291

Boon K (2001) Rape and Forced Pregnancy under the ICC Statute: Human Dignity, Autonomy and Consent. Columbia Human Rights Law Review 32: 625–675

Carden SR, Sadat LN (2000) The New International Criminal Court: An Uneasy Revolution. Georgetown Law Journal 88(3): 381–474

Committee on the Elimination of Discrimination against Women (2013) General Recommendation no. 30 on Women in Conflict Prevention, Conflict and Post-Conflict Situations, CEDAW/C/GC/30

De Brouwer AM (2005) Supranational Criminal Prosecution of Sexual Violence: The ICC and the Practice of the ICTY and the ICTR. Intersentia, Antwerp/Oxford

De Ruiter D (2011) Sexual Offences in International Criminal Law. International Courts Association, The Hague

Dieng A (2002) Other Preparations for the Establishment of the Court: International Criminal Justice. From Paper to Practice: A Contribution from the International Criminal Tribunal for Rwanda to the Establishment of the International Criminal Court. Fordham International Law Journal 25: 688–707

Donat-Cattin D (1999) Article 68: Protection of Victims and Witnesses and their Participation in the Proceedings. In: Triffterer O (ed) Commentary on the Rome Statute of the International Criminal Court: Observer's Notes, Article by Article. Nomos, Baden-Baden, pp 869–888

Flores-Acuna T (2006) The Rome Statute's Sexual Related Crimes: An Appraisal under the Light of International Humanitarian Law. Humanitäres Völkerrecht 19(1): 39–59

Garkawe S (2001) The Victim-Related Provisions of the Statute of the International Criminal Court: A Victimological Analysis. International Review of Victimology 8: 269–289

Garkawe S (2003) Victims and the International Criminal Court: Three Major Issues. International Criminal Law Review 3(4): 345–367

Grant T (2015) Aggression against Ukraine: Territory, Responsibility and International Law. Palgrave Macmillan, London/New York/Shanghai

Hagay-Frey A (2011) Sex and Gender Crimes in the New International Law. Past, Present, Future. Martinus Nijhoff, Leiden/Boston

Ingadottir T (ed) The International Criminal Court - Recommendations on Policy and Practice: Financing, Victims, Judges and Immunities. Transnational Publishers, Ardsley, New York, pp 2–45

Ingadottir T et al. (2003) The Victims and Witnesses Unit (Article 43.6 of the Rome Statute). In: Jones JRWD (2002) Protection of Victims and Witnesses. In: Cassese A et al. (ed) The Rome Statute of the International Criminal Court: A Commentary. Oxford University Press, Oxford, pp 1355–1370

Katz S, Mazur MM (1979) Understanding the Rape Victim. John Willey and Sons, New York

Leatherman LJ (2011) Sexual Violence and Armed Conflict. Polity Press, Cambridge

Maiorova A (2017) Donbas in Flames: Guide to the Conflict Zone. Lviv

McDonald GK (2000) Friedmann Award Address Crimes of Sexual Violence: The Experience of the International Criminal Tribunal. Columbia Journal of Transnational Law 39(1): 2–16

Office of the United Nations High Commissioner for Human Rights (2016) Report on the Human Rights Situation in Ukraine 16 February to 15 May 2016. http://www.ohchr.org/Documents/Countries/UA/Ukraine_14th_HRMMU_Report.pdf. Accessed 10 January 2017

Onuch O, Martsenyuk T (2014) Mothers and Daughters of the Maidan: Gender Repertoires of Violence and the Division of Labour in Ukrainian Protests. Social, Health and Communication Studies Journal 1(1): 105–126

Oosterveld V (2013) Prosecuting Gender-Based Persecution as an International Crime. In: De Brouwer et al. (eds) Sexual Violence as an International Crime: Interdisciplinary Approaches. Intersentia, Antwerp/Oxford, pp 57–78

Pillay N (2003) The Rule of International Jurisprudence in Redressing Crimes of Sexual Violence. In: Vohrah LC et al. (eds) Man's Inhumanity to Man. Essays on International Law in Honor of Antonio Cassese. Kluwer Law International, The Hague, pp 685–692

Roben V (2003) The Procedure of the ICC: Status and Function of the Prosecutor. Max Planck Yearbook of United Nations Law 7: 513–552

Segal L (2008) Gender, War and Militarism: Making and Questioning the Links. Feminist Review 88(1): 21–35

Tsybulenko E, Pakhomenko S (2016) The Ukrainian Crisis as a Challenge for the Eastern Partnership. In: Kerikmae T, Chochia A (eds) Political and Legal Perspectives of the EU Eastern Partnership Policy. Springer, Cham/Heidelberg/New York/Dordrecht/London, pp 167–168

Ukrainian Centre for Social Reforms (2015) Gender-Based Violence in the Conflict-Affected Regions of Ukraine: Analytical Report. Kiev

United Nations General Assembly (2014) Resolution 28/262 Adopted by the General Assembly on 27 March 2014, Territorial Integrity of Ukraine, A/RES/28/262 (2014)

United Nations General Assembly (2016) Situation of Human rights in the Autonomous Republic of Crimea and the City of Sevastopol (Ukraine), A/C.3/71/L.26 (2016)

United Nations High Commissioner for Refugees (2015) International Protection Considerations Related to the Developments in Ukraine-Update II. http://www.refworld.org/docid/54c639474.html. Accessed 14 February 2017

United Nations Security Council (2015) Resolution 2202/2015 adopted at its 7384th meeting on 17 February 2015, S/RES/2202 (2015)

Van Boven T (1999) The Position of the Victim in the Statute of the ICC. In Von Hebel H et al. (eds) Reflections on the International Criminal Court: Essays in Honor of Adrian Bos. T.M.C. Asser Press, The Hague, pp 77–89

Volosevych I et al. (2014) The Prevalence of Violence against Women and Girls. Kiev

Wagner M (2003) The ICC and its Jurisdiction: Myths, Misperceptions and Realities. Max Planck Yearbook of United Nations Law 7: 409–512

West DJ (1987) Sexual Crimes and Confrontation: A Study of Victims and Offences. Aldershot, Gower

Chapter 20
Post-conflict Reconstruction of Trust in the Media

Katrin Nyman Metcalf

Contents

Abstract The media landscape and the consumption of media have recently changed significantly, challenging traditional ways to promote trust in media. "Gatekeepers" in the shape of journalists, editors or owners of media houses have to a large extent lost their role. Traditional communications law developed ways to deal with media in societies with freedom of expression: some possible intervention but strong protection for free media. New technologies challenge the established understanding of regulation. Against this background, there is more than ever a struggle via information channels for the hearts and minds of people, with increasing amounts of propaganda. This is one aspect of cyber warfare. In times of crisis media has an important role but it is also in such a time when there will be extra much propaganda,

Professor Katrin Nyman Metcalf is visiting professor at Tallinn University of Technology, Head of Research at the Estonian e-Governance Academy as well as active as independent consultant on communications issues. Katrin.nyman-metcalf@ttu.ee.

K. N. Metcalf (✉)
Tallinn University of Technology, Tallinn, Estonia
e-mail: Katrin.nyman-metcalf@ttu.ee

© T.M.C. ASSER PRESS and the authors 2018
S. Sayapin and E. Tsybulenko (eds.), *The Use of Force against Ukraine and International Law*, https://doi.org/10.1007/978-94-6265-222-4_20

attempts to limit expressions and exercise governmental control. It is a challenge to maintain or recreate trust in media. The situation in Ukraine shows examples of the challenges, of ways to meet them and what to avoid in this work. Comparisons with situations like the post-war Bosnia Herzegovina or the ongoing occupation of Palestine provide lessons but also examples of lessons that have not been learnt.

Keywords Media law · Broadcasting · Internet · Cyberwar · Social media · Regulation · Post-conflict · Censorship

20.1   Introduction

The media landscape has changed significantly and our consumption of media is quite different compared even with only a decade ago. The statement that information and communications technologies (ICT) have dramatically influenced the lives of people in most of the world and changed the way we see reality is so ubiquitous that it is easy to get tired of it. Nevertheless, it is difficult to deny the importance of the changes to the information environment: anyone can reach a large audience almost immediately to spread their views, observations and interpretation of events. The traditional "gatekeepers" in the shape of journalists, editors or owners of media houses – who would decide what content should be made available to the public and hopefully verify its veracity and quality – have to a large extent lost their role. However, the struggle via media and other information channels for the hearts and minds of people goes on. Propaganda is as prevalent as ever before, or more so. Combating it is more difficult as there are so many channels through which it reaches people. Modern ways of consuming media mean that we can select content in a much narrower way than only some decades ago and safely stay in our selected bubble, ignoring attempts to provide us with a variety of facts and opinions. Maybe we are reaching a situation where there is no trust in media in any situation? The debate around the election of President Trump in the USA in November 2016 or the Brexit referendum campaign in the first half of 2016 point in that direction: even in democratic states with freedom of expression, politicians as well as media outlets do not hesitate to express blatant lies as well as negate evident facts. It is easy to question if and how quality media can still play a role to create or maintain a successful democratic state with respect for the rule of law. At the same time, the importance of providing information, of ensuring that people have a basis for understanding society, remains as relevant as ever.

This article examines the role of media in times of crisis and more specifically the question of trust in media – how to create such trust in our times of "post-truth" and "fake news". We look particularly at rebuilding confidence in media in a post-conflict situation or even during an ongoing crisis. Any crisis of society, whether armed conflict or serious political instability quite naturally entails a lack of confidence in institutions. There will be challenges to freedom of expression and access to information, propaganda and counter-propaganda, leading to a loss of confidence in channels of communication. In a post-conflict situation, it is important to recreate a feeling of trust in society – without this it is very difficult to proceed with rebuilding the state. This chapter looks at different examples with the situation in Ukraine as inspiration for the discussion.

After the introduction, we give a theoretical background about the legal environment for media in democratic rule of law states, discussing regulation, including recent initiatives to deal with the internet. This leads into the discussion about legitimate restrictions on freedom of expression in times of crises and how to avoid the temptation to fight propaganda with counter-propaganda or excessively restrictive measures. Examples from Bosnia Herzegovina as well as Palestine illustrate quite different issues related to the importance of media in societies in crisis and the difficulties in dealing with it, that in different ways may be relevant for Ukraine – unfortunately, as these are not positive examples. Finally, we will answer the question indirectly posed by the title: how can we rebuild trust in media in a situation like, for example, the one in Ukraine today?

20.2   Regulating – Not Restricting: The Regulation of Media in Societies with Freedom of Expression

20.2.1   Different Media – Different Regulation

Freedom of expression is not an absolute right. Article 10 of the European Convention on Human Rights (ECHR) allows limitations like formalities, conditions, restrictions or penalties, prescribed by law and necessary in a democratic society to protect valuable interests. There is considerable case law from the European Court on Human Rights (ECtHR) on the interpretation of limitations and the legitimacy of restrictions.[1]

In societies that respect freedom of expression, rules about media have as their task to make sense of the reasons and situations that necessitate limitations, to avoid that such considerations are arbitrary. Media regulation and self-regulation see as one of their tasks to provide a basis for trust, through stipulations on how to separate facts and opinion, on how to ensure transparency of ownership of media and of sponsored content, by permitting a right of reply and through other means.

The watchdog role of media –to be critical of governments or other institutions, to investigate suspected or alleged wrongdoing and to otherwise be "uncomfortable" - is recognised as a sign of a democratic and free country. Regulation needs to act in this environment, in which the authorities do not try to influence the message but rather to provide conditions for a plurality of messages, albeit within some limits. Weaver presents examples of satirical and critical press already in the eighteenth

---

[1] The ECtHR produces regular reports on its case law related to different Articles of the ECHR, see e.g. http://www.echr.coe.int/Documents/Research_report_internet_ENG.pdf.

century.[2] People must be able to participate in the public discourse if democracy is to function.[3]

Briefly, communications regulation used to be divided into categories of rules, for different types of communication. If a message is transmitted from one known point (person) to another - point-to-point - like a telephone call, a letter or an e-mail, there is no reason for the state to regulate the content of the message. If something illegal is discussed, such as planning a crime, the message as such or the company and technology making it possible to communicate are not elements of the crime but incidental to other things. In some cases, the actual content may be illegal, for example libel and slander or incitement to hatred and violence, but most often a private message does not meet other criteria for such statements to be infringements of the law, as they are not likely to have any effect of causing harm to the person´s reputation or leading to violence. Simply put – if we get offended or upset by a private message we should deal with it privately. The legislation that exists for point-to-point communication deals with practical and technical issues for telecommunications operators.

A different view is posed on point-to-multipoint messages: such that can be seen or heard by an unknown audience, typically broadcasting or newspapers and other publications. Even in societies with freedom of expression, it may be legitimate to have rules on content. This does not mean detailed rules on what can be said or shown, and it most definitely does not mean prior control of broadcasts or publications, which is censorship and thus incompatible with freedom of expression. The kind of rules that can be proportional and legitimate are those mentioned above – libel and slander as well as prohibition of incitement – as the fact that the message can reach a larger and unknown audience may pose risks of negative effects. Incitement is criminalised in many national legislations and some forms of incitement – like to genocide – are criminal also under international law. Hate speech may be criminalised under national law, although it is quite often dealt with as a regulatory issue if it does not amount to incitement.[4] There may also be other rules, including positive requirements, like the need to broadcast news, the requirement to make a distinction between opinion and facts as well as restrictions on violence or pornography during certain hours. The philosophical motivation for such rules is that the state has a responsibility to the population; it should protect children and vulnerable people as well as ensure that people are informed about important events.

It is quite possible that the reader wonders by now if and how internet will fit in this context. Clearly, it disturbs these categories, as it can be point-to-point (like e-mail, internet telephony) or point-to-multipoint (using internet as the transmission technology for broadcasting). Even more importantly, it can be something entirely different, multipoint-to-multipoint, with any number of possibilities for interaction, for degrees of publicity of content and so on. Indeed, although there have been

---

[2] Weaver 2014, p. 32.

[3] Weinstein 2009, p. 29.

[4] Burri makes the distinction that hate speech is prohibited but not criminalised under international criminal law. Burri 2015, p. 172.

important changes of terminology in communications regulation in recent years, legislators, regulators and the industry are still coming to terms with the new means of communicating.[5]

Generally, the principle of technology neutrality[6] should help to deal with the rapidly changing technical environment, by providing that rules and regulations do not focus on the technology used to deliver a message or service, but rather on what the activity is: is it sending a message to a large, unknown group of people (resembling broadcasting) or is it a closed communication between parties? This and not technology should decide which laws and regulations are applicable. In this way, rules do not date too quickly and a level playing field can hopefully be achieved for different players, using different means to do essentially the same thing. In practice, this is easier said than done for many reasons. One such reason is jurisdiction. It is easy for internet-based content to move to a different jurisdiction and still be equally accessible, so restrictions in one country would just lead to the content being administered from elsewhere, with the users normally not even noticing. The difficulty in using traditional regulatory tools has led to rather creative thinking on what could replace it, like different multi-stakeholder fora for internet regulation.[7] These fora use interaction of different groups like governments, regulators, academia but also private firms, pressure groups and so on to discuss and draft codes of conduct, self-regulatory rules and other instruments to encourage an organised form of voluntary regulation.

If the critical role of media is not new, the idea that new technologies that enable communication should be regulated also has a long history. Many governments sought to ensure governmental control over the printing press soon after Gutenberg had invented it.[8] What has changed is essentially the importance of communication technology in our lives and the speed of change. The "soft law" approach of multi-stakeholderism may be a solution to the need for rapidly reaching at least some common understanding of what applies. In any event, given the difficulty to fit internet into the traditional model of communications law, it may be the only solution.

20.2.2 The State Will Look After You

Ideas on the extent to which states should look after their populations by providing trustworthy news, quality entertainment or educational programmes, differ in time and place. In Europe, from the early days of television, there was an understanding

---

[5] Van Eijk 2008, p. 1116.

[6] See for example https://ec.europa.eu/digital-agenda/en/easier-access-radio-spectrum-eus-electroniccommunications-framework. Van Eijk 2008, p. 1117.

[7] Weber and Heinrich, 2014 p. 97. For an example, see the Freedom Online Coalition, www.freedomonlinecoalition.com.

[8] Weaver 2014, p. 33.

that such a medium was too important to be left to the private sector.[9] When new means of transmission arrived, the idea of special public responsibility was underlined by must-carry provisions, meaning that cable and satellite (and more recently digital)[10] operators have to include public service broadcasting in their packages.[11] Similar ideas were adopted in slightly different forms by many countries in other parts of the world, like Africa and Australia. Best practices developed on what came to be called public service broadcasting.[12] For societies that supported this idea, in the words of Keller paternalistic assumptions made by the state were better than the collective outcomes of individual choices.[13] Although this idea spread to many parts of the world, it had very little impact in others, like the US but also parts of Asia. After the fall of communism, there were discussions in Eastern and Central Europe on whether it was best to follow the European model or to regard it as outdated. Eventually state broadcasters were transformed into public service broadcasters rather than privatised (or just closed).[14]

The discussion about the obsolescence of the idea of public involvement in media content has gone on for some time. In Europe for many years, public service broadcasting was the only available offering but when especially in the 1980s private channels started appearing in many countries, the question arose if and what role public broadcasting should have in the future. The debate took on another aspect and urgency with technologies like satellite and cable, which not only made many more channels possible but also led to content easily crossing national borders. However, decisions about allowing or prohibiting satellite signals were strategic business decisions rather than being based on national interests and free-expression values.[15] Internet is a prolongation of this same debate with the difference that interactivity and possibilities for personal choices have made the choice of what media content to access even more personal.

Although it is still possible to argue that it is important that at least some media content is provided not for profit but in the public interest, in a market with very many players it is difficult to ensure that the content will be able to reach the audience. Even if it does, it may be unlikely that a few channels have much impact when there is so much to choose from. To ensure any effect of public service broadcasting it must be seen that this is something else than just another channel. Such broadcasters

---

[9] This author has discussed this from the viewpoint of digitalisation. Nyman Metcalf 2014, p. 70.

[10] See e.g. the European Broadcasting Union (EBU) 2006 EBU contribution to the European Commission calls for input on the forthcoming review of the EU regulatory framework for electronic communications and services, 30 January 2006 – at a time when this issue was topical all over Europe.

[11] Article 31 Directive 2002/22/EC of the European Parliament and of the Council of 7 March 2002 on universal service and users' rights relating to electronic communications networks and services (Universal Service Directive);

[12] Jakubowicz 2003, p. 46.

[13] Keller 2011, pp. 49 and 84.

[14] IRIS Legal Observations of the European Audiovisual Observatory 2000–6. Report: The Financing of Public Service Broadcasting in Selected Central and Eastern European States.

[15] Price 2012, p. 514.

in most states start out with a competitive advantage as a known and recognisable media outlet. However, in post-communist states this does not equate trustworthiness. The transition from state broadcasting to public service has met challenges in many countries. Governments are reluctant to let go of a vehicle for their political message and the broadcasters struggle with quality and attractiveness.

While regulation continued to favour the idea of a role for publicly supported (tax funded or through a compulsory subscription fee) broadcasting content, commentators have pointed out since more than a decade that this idea will grow all the more arcane when the amount of available content just keeps growing.[16] More than just the number of additional broadcasting channels, in recent years the way media content is accessed has changed traditional presumptions upon which the popular trust in media were construed.

20.2.3 *If I Know Who Is Talking, I Understand What They Say*

It is illusory to think that all available media would be trustworthy and perfectly objective in every circumstance – and even more illusory to pretend that legislation can ensure this optimal situation without interfering too much in the editorial work of media. Instead, media law and regulation focuses on other ways to achieve a good level of objectivity, plurality and trustworthiness. One tool is regulation of media ownership. By preventing concentrations, there will be more than one source available and hopefully more than one message. With a pluralistic and dynamic media sector, people will be able to compare messages and to temper especially outrageous statements. The transparency of media ownership is an important corollary to the ownership rules, as often if the audience is aware of where a certain message comes from, it will be able to judge its veracity and credibility.

In countries in the process of transition to democracy and market economy, excessive public sector involvement in media ownership is a common problem. It is not surprising that the instinct is for the government to be reluctant to cede control over a tool through which it can get its message out, in the shape and form that it selects. Not just public sector involvement causes problems regarding ownership but concentration in too few private hands will also hamper plurality and diversity. Even if there are few restrictions for anyone to start a new media outlet, it usually takes time and effort to reach an important audience – even with modern technologies. That certain content is available or that it is actually seen are two different things. The ubiquity of content thanks to modern ICT has underlined this difference.[17]

Recent examples of the problems created by excessive media concentration can be seen in the United Kingdom, where violation of ethical rules by privately owned

---

[16] Jakubowicz 2003, p. 48.

[17] As for example discussed in *The Economist* special report on Mass Entertainment, 11 February 2017.

press led to a major inquiry at different levels, in Parliament, by the Press Complaints Commission and with a special inquiry.[18] The issue was exacerbated by the fact that one owner held so many different publications with such important reach that the content had an important impact on society. Also the aggressive style of reporting influenced the general media sector. The various investigations could all conclude this but what if anything to do without sacrificing freedom of expression is a more challenging issue. It needs little imagination to see what effect a more or less covert dominance by a certain political view or even a certain individual over important media groups can have. If this dominance is indeed covert and perhaps exercised for the benefit of a hostile state, the consequences are potentially even more dire. Against this background, being able to know who is actually the owner of a media house is very important.

Russia is an example of a country that openly has admitted the importance to use the state to ensure that the appropriate message gets out. In the National Security Strategy 2020 it is said that as there is a global information struggle, it is important to ensure that truthful information – meaning such that the Russian government finds truthful – gets out to people, for example by ensuring native internet platforms and social media.[19] It is more surprising and for this reason also more saddening that the US President has taken to selecting media who gets access to presidential briefings depending on whether they support presidential policies and calling for an end to journalistic protection of sources.[20] For a country that traditionally has not supported a public media message but a plurality of private sources, such tendencies are worrying.

20.3   Trusting the Messenger in Times of Crisis

20.3.1   Truth in Crisis

Although it is disputed who was the first to say it and exactly how, it is a well-known statement that truth is the first casualty of war.[21] At a time of crisis even governments that normally accept freedom of expression, including criticism of authority, will be tempted to ban propaganda from the "other side" as well as engage in it itself. Lasswell defines propaganda as the technique of influencing human action by the manipulation of representations, in the form of spoken or written words, pictures, films or any other

---

[18] Leyland 2014, pp. 160–161.

[19] Levin Jaitner 2015, p. 88. See also http://www.bbc.com/news/world-europe-39062663 for an (23 February 2017) admittance by the Russian Defence Minister Sergei Shoigu that Russian "information troops" are involved in "intelligent, effective propaganda".

[20] For example: https://www.theguardian.com/us-news/2017/feb/24/media-blocked-white-house-briefing-sean-spicer.

[21] https://www.theguardian.com/notesandqueries/query/0,5753,-21510,00.html.

form.[22] Propaganda has probably existed since humans started communicating, but the term in its political meaning together with a deeper understanding of it date from the early 20th century.[23] Propaganda may be used to try to influence the other side in a war or conflict, but it may equally be mainly for the domestic audience, which does not make it less important. Actions in information space aim at creating confusion, shaping opinion and inflicting damage on data, as Lewis says.[24] In an increasingly data-dependent world, these aims go beyond just spreading messages. It is telling that Russia prefers the term "information security" over "cyber security" as they see cyber as narrower and technical, while the key is the information area in its entirety: from passwords to content of the message. This fits with their cyberattacks being elements of information warfare rather than something new and entirely "cyber" dependent.[25]

Propaganda is banned by Article 20 of the International Covenant on Civil and Political Rights (ICCPR), mentioning war propaganda and incitement to hatred. There is rarely consensus about propaganda having been used. During the Nuremberg trials after the Second World War, the Soviet judge Nikitchenko stated: *"The dissemination of provocative lies and the systematic deception of public opinion were as necessary to Hitlerites for the realisation of their plans as were the production of armaments and the drafting of military plans"*.[26] This lesson was well learnt by the Soviets and taken over by Russia after the fall of the Soviet Union.

Cyberattacks may target physical infrastructure via attacks on ICT systems controlling these[27] or be aimed at the data itself. Shaping opinion may be done through destroying data. How international law should be applied to data destruction is still a matter of discussion. There is broad agreement that international law applies also in cyberspace,[28] but what is not clear is when an armed attack occurs when only (intangible) data is targeted, how data in a cloud should be assessed jurisdictionally, etc. Manipulation of information, spreading fear and distrust and obtaining a psychological effect on people are possible aims of cyberattacks. As Lewis says, to introduce uncertainty in the minds of leaders to make them hesitate or make mistakes are worthwhile military goals.[29] Levin Jaitner points to Russian military academic debate in which it is openly discussed that organising anti-government protests, deluding adversaries and influencing public opinion are important tools of warfare in any zone of influence, like in the Crimea conflict.[30]

---

[22] Laswell 1934/1995, p. 13.

[23] Richter 2015, p. 489.

[24] Lewis 2015, pp. 39–40.

[25] Levin Jaitner, 2015 p. 88.

[26] Quote taken from Burri 2015, p. 266.

[27] Like the suspected attack on the Kiev power grid at the end of 2016. http://www.reuters.com/article/us-ukraine-crisis-cyber-attacks-idUSKBN1491ZF.

[28] As set out in the Tallinn Manual https://ccdcoe.org/tallinn-manual.html.

[29] Lewis 2015, p. 40.

[30] Levin Jaitner 2015, p. 89.

20.3.2   Lessons Learnt – or Not Learnt – from Bosnia Herzegovina

The balancing on the often thin line between legitimate regulation and censorship is especially precarious in times of crisis. Perhaps this is one reason why the international community, despite getting increasingly active in intervening in different ways to monitor or even enforce peace, is reluctant to deal with media issues. Sadly, we have many recent wars to use as examples. The conflicts in the former Yugoslavia show examples of significant international involvement, most of all in Bosnia Herzegovina. The General Framework Agreement for Peace (GFAP),[31] better known as the Dayton Agreement, made by international guarantors for peace, basically created the country. Despite the recognised role of media during and after the conflict, inciting to violence and hatred often in very direct ways, the GFAP did not say anything about media. This was rectified by the organ set up by GFAP – the High Representative – through creating e.g. a broadcast regulator. This decision came after the international troops active in the country had used military force to close down a broadcaster that was disrupting the peace process and inciting violence.[32] This event was used as an explanation for expanding the powers of the High Representative, not just over media.[33]

The muscular international intervention in building up a country has been criticised[34] and the fact that the idea of a representative of the international community with a very wide mandate – including to adopt laws or disqualify appointments of officials and politicians – has not been followed elsewhere does indicate that such a solution may appear simpler than what it is in practice. The intervention in media regulation was more successful. Despite problems of political pressure and the same kind of ethnicity-based obstacles to appointments that affect all levels of Bosnia Herzegovina, the Communications Regulatory Agency[35] is generally regarded as successful and has been used as a model in the region and elsewhere.[36] The secret behind its success was a firm rule-based and transparent way to work. In a tense situation, it is inevitable that there will be allegations of bias or even corruption, but if all decision-making processes are open and traceable with every decision motivated objectively, it is more difficult to allege wrongdoing. The regulator had to draft most of its own rules, as the legislation of Bosnia Herzegovina was only in the process of creation at the time the agency was set up. Rules were kept as objective as possible, avoiding any subjective language and ensuring that decisions were made by a group of professionals that involved different ethnicities and backgrounds, but was selected

---

[31] https://www.osce.org/bih/126173?download=true.

[32] Nyman Metcalf and Thelin 2000, p. 583.

[33] Knaus and Martin 2003, p. 64.

[34] Ibid. pp. 64–66.

[35] http://rak.ba/eng/.

[36] Nyman Metcalf and Thelin 2000, p. 590. This author was the first Head of the Legal Department of the Independent Media Commission, as the regulator was first known, and later advisor to the Communications Regulatory Authority.

on merit only. By relying on international instruments such as those of the Council of Europe even before the country was a member of the ECHR ensured that rules were not seen as arbitrary.[37]

In this context it should be recalled that Bosnia Herzegovina came from a system without protection for freedom of expression and the rule of law and while other countries in East and Central Europe were able in the 1990s to start constructing democratic societies, Bosnia Herzegovina descended into war. Thus, it was not a *re-creation* of guarantees for free media but a *creation*. This is to some extent similar in Ukraine where the process of creating a modern media regulatory environment is ongoing while the country has to struggle with the war in parts of its territory. What can be learnt from Bosnia Herzegovina is the importance of a proper regulatory system with transparent and objective rules, to create order in the broadcasting system even while the situation in the country may be far from optimal.

20.3.3 Lessons Learnt – or Not Learnt – from Palestine

Occupation should be a temporary situation that carries with it rights and duties under humanitarian law, including to respect freedom of the media with possibilities to restrict this in a proportional manner if it is necessary in order to maintain public order in the occupied territory. This however requires an important degree of acceptance by the occupying power of its status and obligations. Due to the length of time that the Israeli occupation of Palestine has gone on, this situation provides numerous examples of the challenges to this.[38] Israeli obstruction of Palestinian communications is interesting to observe as it includes not just (or even mainly) prohibition of media content, but rather other element. Israel can thus claim to allow freedom of expression as there is not widespread censorship, while using other means of restriction. There are physical attacks and limited freedom of movement for media professionals.[39] Palestinian journalists are only granted freedom of movement if they obtain an Israeli press card, but this is extremely difficult to get.[40] It is regrettably not impossible that Russia will learn from the Israelis when it comes to restricting free media over the course of the occupation of Crimea and what can be a *de facto* occupation of parts of Eastern Ukraine. Until now, Russia has been more crude but especially if the promised warming of relations with the US really does happen, Russia may have an interest in masking its worst behaviour in order to minimise opposition internationally and in the US to friendly relations. In such a situation, less blatant media restriction can be useful.

Perhaps the most important restrictions that Israel imposes are regarding technical aspects of communication. Since at least 1967 Israel has controlled the fre-

---

[37] Topic 2007, pp. 164–165.

[38] Quigley 2010, p. 219.

[39] Called the *Silencing the Press* Reports, http://pchrgaza.org/en/?cat=59.

[40] Nasser et. al. 2011; Kuntsman and Stein 2015.

quency spectrum and the telecommunications networks of Palestine. In 1995 some infrastructure was handed over to the Palestinian Authority but East Jerusalem was excluded. Telephony was privatised in Palestine in 1997, the private firm created (Paltel) in 1999 set up a mobile operator Jawwal. Israel released limited frequencies to Jawwal, obliging sharing with Israel. In 2007 a second Palestinian operator was created, Watanyia, which received limited frequencies only in 2009. Israel prevents 3G and 4G for Palestinian operators, while granting Israeli operators frequency allocation for 4G, including to operators that cover Palestine (West Bank and Gaza, not just East Jerusalem). Some Israeli operators sell SIM-cards in the West Bank and as only these operators can offer services like GPS or others in need of significant bandwidth they have a clear competitive advantage.[41]

The proportionality of many different Israeli actions undertaken during the long occupation has been questioned on many occasions. This includes acts of violence but also restriction of economic rights. It is clear that humanitarian law, which is intended to deal with short-term protection of civilians while safeguarding military necessities of the occupier, is not suited for every-day questions arising over a long period.[42] The legal situation for territories under the dominance of another county remains very problematic in international law. It is illegal to annex territory by force[43] and occupation, or correctly referred to as belligerent occupation, should not be seen as a first step to a territorial change but as a temporary state of affairs.[44]

To search for some analogies in Europe, with statements on occupation and annexation we find some cases from the ECtHR related to Transnistria.[45] Russia denies jurisdiction[46] and claim to have no role in the territory. Even if "everybody knows" what the real situation is, we cannot resort to this kind of vague notions if we are not to fall into the trap of imprecise and unsubstantiated accusations of non-democratic leaders with no respect for correct information. There has to be a proper basis for legal responsibility and unfortunately it may be very difficult to assign such responsibility. Another Transnistria case, Ilascu and others v. Moldova and Russia,[47] contains an interesting discussion on jurisdiction and responsibility of states for violations of the ECHR in situations of occupation.[48] The need for functioning of media is mentioned.[49] In situations like the ones mentioned, a problem for case law is that *de facto*

---

[41] Arafeh et al. 2015.

[42] Gross 2006, p. 839.

[43] Roberts points out that the concept of occupation is a victory for international law, as it replaces the idea that a state can just annex the territory of another state by force. Instead there is now this temporary instrument. Roberts 1989/2008, p. 393.

[44] Shah 1997–98/2008, p. 451.

[45] *Catan and others v. Moldovia and Russia* (Grand Chamber), Applications nos. 43370/04, 8252/05 and 18454/06, Judgement of 19 October 2012.

[46] Ibid., para 96.

[47] Application no. 48787/99, Judgement 8 July 2004.

[48] Ibid., especially paras 312 and 333.

[49] Ibid., para 234.

occupying powers will often deny that they have any such role and thus also deny any responsibility to apply laws and protect rights.

Russia claims that Crimea has selected to join Russia, although the international opinion is that this is an annexation and thus illegal. Eastern Ukraine is *de jure* neither annexed or occupied. Such situations rely on the parties stating intent and admitting the real situation. As for Palestine, Israel has officially not claimed to have annexed the territory of Palestine, even if East Jerusalem for local administration purposes has been included in the Western Jerusalem and recently there are also other signs of *de facto* claiming annexation of parts of Palestinian territory. Akehurst, a well-known authority on international law, in 1973[50] claimed that even if it may be reasonable to maintain that Israel could remain in control over Palestinian territories until a peace settlement, he reminded that occupation gives much fewer rights than annexation (and found that Israel did not respect this). Israel also disputes the application of the Geneva Conventions (with rules of occupation), referring to the special nature of the situation.[51] Claims that a situation is too specific to fall under the established law are always difficult as every situation in international law is special and this cannot mean that law does not apply. It is to be sincerely hoped that Russian activities in Ukraine will not be of the same kind of length and intensity as Israeli ones in Palestine.

20.3.4   Ukraine

Ukraine is experiencing a crisis with many ingredients. The Russian annexation of Crimea in 2014 violated international law and has been condemned by a large number of states as well as the European Union (EU). Russia has used bogus referenda and similar to support its claim that the territory of Crimea is now a legitimate part of Russia. As for the situation in Eastern Ukraine, the official Russian line has been to claim that it is not (officially) involved. Instead, Russia sees the situation as an uprising by parts of the population in the areas, looking for independence or greater autonomy – not unlike Bosnia Herzegovina during the war there. This gives a good excuse for other countries that want to avoid having to take a firm stance against Russia. Anna Jonsson Cornell already in 2011 wrote that EU policy toward Russia had moved from being value-driven to being dictated by realism.[52] This changed somewhat with the annexation of Crimea but quite soon some European states were looking for something to latch onto to explain a softer approach toward Russia.

Regarding media, the situation in Ukraine today is to some extent similar to that described above for Bosnia Herzegovina after the war. The country is going through a period of reform as a result of the democratisation after the fall of the Yanukovych regime, while at the same time the country is at war. Ukraine has not had strong or well-functioning guarantees for a free media. Comparing with other

---

[50] Akehurst 1973/2008, p. 30.

[51] Roberts 1989/2008, p. 395; Imseis 2003/2008, p. 533.

[52] Jonsson 2011, p. 444.

Eastern Partnership countries, Ukraine comes in the middle of the list of media freedom, after Georgia and Moldova but ahead of Armenia, Azerbaijan and Belarus. The situation in Eastern Ukraine is much worse than the overall situation in the country.[53] As regards ICT, there has been and still is a dependence on Russia (for internet service provision for example) that resembles the situation Palestine finds itself in. Giles points out that Ukraine gives Russia an advantage in any cyberattack situation, as Russian firms own infrastructure and even government officials (at least until recently) use Russian e-mail services.[54]

Among the ways Russia has used information warfare in Ukraine is the use of internet trolls[55] to help support the spreading of the propaganda message, like Ukrainians being fascists, of atrocities committed by Ukrainian forces or civilians and similar. Lewis in 2015 wrote that he found these attempts annoying rather than important[56] but effects of such actions are difficult to measure objectively and may be seen only over time. Any occupying power has an interest in limiting access to alternative sources of information in order to exacerbate the effect of its propaganda. As this is potentially difficult because of the nature of modern social media it is not enough to just try to stop some media outlets. Proactivity is needed.

At the time of the Russian annexation of Crimea, there were severe restrictions of access to information. This was one of many factors that meant that the so-called referendum did not meet international standards, even if it were to have been legitimate (which it was not).[57] Russia was aware that it needed to occupy the information space before moving on with the physical occupation. In Eastern Ukraine the access to information as well as the possibility for journalists to move freely is severely restricted. Ukrainian authorities are taking measure to ensure the availability of Ukrainian media in the area but there have been numerous actions to prevent this over the course of the conflict, so the work to make the media available is constant.[58] Thus Ukrainian authorities have difficulties exercising control, Russia does not admit to being an occupying power and thus denies any responsibility and the separatists lack legitimacy as well as actual control so in practice there is no rule of law for media.

However, as Ukraine does not have strong and well-established guarantees for freedom of expression there are concerns not just in the areas that are outside of

---

[53] http://euukrainecoop.com/2015/02/25/media/ The ranking was made based on monitoring through the EU-funded Eastern Partnership Media Freedom Watch project, presented February 2015.

[54] Giles 2015, p. 24.

[55] Lange-Ionatamishvili and Svetoka 2015, p. 110.

[56] Lewis 2015, p. 45.

[57] Jonsson Cornell 2016, p. x.

[58] For example, 5 January 2016 Ministry of Information Policy of Ukraine - *MIP: broadcasting of the First channel of Ukrainian radio in Donetsk and Luhansk regions was renewed* (http://mip. gov.ua/en/news/874.html); 29 December 2015 - *MIP: In Starobilsk Luhansk region broadcasting of one more Ukrainian TV channel was renewed* (http://mip.gov.ua/en/news/872.html); 1 December 2015 - *MIP: Latvia will provide three powerful transmitters to restore broadcasting in the east of Ukraine* (http://mip.gov.ua/en/news/821.html).

the control of the Ukrainian authorities. Among negative events are a decree of the
Ukrainian President in September 2015 banning over 30 international journalists
and bloggers from Ukraine for one year for being a threat to national interest and
national security[59] and actions by the regulator the National Television and Radio
Broadcasting Council (NTRBC) in February 2016 with an unscheduled inspection
of a channel, Inter TV, that broadcast Russian movies.[60] Even if such measures
can be taken in extreme circumstances, they should be very last resort. As the OSCE
Representative on Freedom of the Media, Dunja Mijatovic said in a statement related
to proposals introducing legislation to restrict access to Russian films: *Even under the
state of hostilities democratic countries have a responsibility to carefully address the
potentially problematic content, for example through the use of appropriate judicial
mechanisms, in order to avoid overbroad steps and introduction of censorship-like
provisions.*[61]

There are also positive signs. In November 2015, the Parliament adopted a law (in
force 1 January 2016) regarding reforming state and communal print mass media.[62]
It is a step in the process of reforming media ownership and it aims to facilitate for
private owners to take over state and communal print media. Such media ownership
should contribute to plurality of the media scene, but it needs to be considered
that the economic situation of the country and the level of profitability or potential
profitability of the media outlets is such that it will not be easy to find buyers for all
media. There is thus a risk that the number of publications actually goes down when
a reform is introduced.

Another positive step toward plurality and transparency was a law ensuring transparency of media ownership, which entered into force in October 2015.[63] The law
amends a number of other laws and obliges broadcast companies and programme
service providers to disclose detailed information about their ownership structure
and end beneficiaries. The law also bans entities registered in offshore economic
zones to establish and own broadcast companies and programme service providers.
Further, the amendments aim to enhance the transparency of the licensing activities
of the regulator NTRBC.

Thus, the impression of the communications landscape in Ukraine is somewhat
complex and even contradictory, with moves towards proper respect for freedom
of expression and information but occasional backward steps as well. The more
complex and untransparent a situation is, the easier it is to exploit it for propaganda.
There is a need to fabricate a discourse, to create the criteria by which success is
measured.[64] When the popular opinion is ambiguous, as is often especially the case
when a conflict has aspects of civil war, it becomes extra important to manipulate

---

[59] https://www.indexoncensorship.org/2015/09/ukraine-serious-blow-to-media-freedom/.

[60] http://www.osce.org/fom/224676 26 February 2016.

[61] http://www.osce.org/fom/235681 22 April 2016.

[62] http://www.osce.org/fom/203431 24 November 2015.

[63] http://www.osce.org/fom/187956 1 October 2015.

[64] In literature the Vietnam war is often mentioned as the first war when it was necessary to pay
attention to creating the narrative of success. Altheide and Johnson 1980/1995, p. 300.

opinion. The propaganda battle is not just against an external enemy but also against "the enemy in our midst" as Haste explains from the First World War and the hatred against pacifists or other opponents of the official message.[65]

For Russia, information has been seen as an important element of power also before the current information dependent era. Instead of seeing cyber security and information security as separate things, as is done by NATO and generally in the West, with one being the technical and the other the content related aspect, Russian discourse sees them as different aspects of the same thing. There is still a great fear of content (just as for the Soviet Union, witnessed e.g. in discussions around direct broadcasting satellites in the 1970s and 1980s) and thus defending information space becomes a major issue[66] – and as a corollary also attacking information space. The situation for Russian media was restricted already before the war in Ukraine but state control of media content has increased lately. One aspect of this is to ensure that at least the vast majority of Russian people do not get anything but the official Kremlin version of the Ukraine crisis. This applies even more to people in the territories of Eastern Ukraine where the pro-Russia forces have made attacks and limitations on media a major tool.

20.4 To Fight Fire with Fire?

20.4.1 Special Rules for Crisis or Not?

There has been an interest in influencing and controlling people´s minds and thoughts, ever since humans started interacting. Especially in times of war, hostilities and other crises, the possibility of impacting information flows becomes a priority. What is new in our modern information society is how important ICT is for society – we do so much more through ICT than just exchange messages. Consequently, control over information space in a time of war becomes extremely important. At the same time, modern information systems make such control more difficult. There are so many different ways to communicate, the information market can be global and it is to a large extent privately handled.

Media regulation in societies with freedom of expression attempts to set standards that protect against the worst kinds of hate speech and incitement, while maintaining the right for people to say even offensive and hurtful things. This is in order to permit the watchdog role of media as well as the operation of the marketplace of ideas – both valued elements of public discussion. There are different methods of dealing with undesirable speech. One way to do it is to introduce bans on certain messages that are pre-determined to be harmful. The most famous may be holocaust denial legislation in a number of European countries but examples exist also from US jurisprudence of

---

[65] Haste 1977/1995, p. 105.
[66] Levin Jaitner 2015, p. 88.

statements that Ku Klux Klan cross-burning is per se offensive.[67] The problem with such bans is that someone has to decide that certain things cannot be said. It differs from relying on incitement rules, where the context is relevant and the real risk of a negative consequence of some speech is considered rather than just what it is that is said.

Recognising that society is more vulnerable in a time of crisis can justify to make the determination of potential harm in a generalised manner by introducing special rules for media in such times. This can be done in what may be seen as a preventive fashion by reacting against propaganda, if this is a feature of society and contributes to creating, worsening of maintaining crises. However, even if such considerations appear legitimate and justifiable, they still carry risks. Trying to legislate against propaganda risks bringing in excessive restrictions. This will quickly erode trust.

It is better to emphasize the proper and proportional application of existing rules on media. At the same time, it may be recognised that such existing tools are often slow and diffuse and do not provide the kind of immediate satisfaction that adopting a new law, decision or even international convention appear to give. What has been shown by ECtHR case law is that even a crisis situation does not mean that restrictions on freedom of expression should be excessive.[68] This applies also in situations of occupation or annexation (which in itself is often difficult to conclusively agree upon) as authorities in control of a disputed territory are not permitted to limit freedom of expression because the substance of the expression is against the views of this power.[69]

One reason for not adopting special rules on propaganda but rather using existing rules that are not made specifically for this, is that it is very difficult to define propaganda. We are all guilty of more readily finding a message which we disagree with to be propaganda. This is not to claim that there is no truth, but it is a recognition of the fact that as soon as a message moves beyond the statement of facts to include an interpretation or discussion, we fall into a territory in which our views will colour how likely we are to suspect bias. The feeling that someone is making distinctions of messages based on their content without clear and objective criteria for this will be negative for trust.

20.4.2 If You Shout, I Shout Louder

Fighting back with counter-propaganda is often the first and quite natural reaction to enemy propaganda attacks. The justification will be that what the "good side" is doing is not propaganda – it is information and facts. In practice, it may not be so easy. This is most definitely not a "Trumpian" claim that there is no truth, but it is a recognition of the fact that in a complex situation it is hard to distinguish between

---

[67] In the dissenting opinion of *Virginia v. Black* 538 US 343 (2003). Kahn 2014, p. 444.

[68] *Cyprus v. Turkey*, Application no. 25781/94, Judgment on 10 May 2001.

[69] Ibid., para 248 onwards.

opinion and fact, news and commentary. Media regulation and self-regulation as well as guidelines for public service broadcasting often contain provisions on how to make the distinctions between basic facts and reporting coloured by opinion. This is not easy even in calm situations, and in a heated debate climate it is likely to be even harder. Most often, the factual reporting of a situation is less "attractive" to the broad public than the exaggerated and dramatic claims that are made based on partisan opinion. Thus, there is a temptation to give back with the same tool, to compete for attention in the same manner. This may however be a dangerous trap.

Meeting propaganda with propaganda leads to an escalation, where both sides have to provide more and more propaganda and people in any case end up believing only what comes from "their" side. With the kind of media sector that we have today with so many sources, possibilities to pick and choose, all that is likely to happen is that any objective and reasonable message drowns in the floods of propaganda from different sides – while anyway the messages mainly reach only those who are already converted to one or other side. Before engaging in propaganda, those behind it should also consider that educated and active people with an interest in a matter will seek alternative information and if they see media outlets engaged in propaganda they will just not believe these outlets any more.

Banning propaganda is as mentioned not easy as it would have to be properly defined before we know what to ban. Real or perceived censorship will erode trust. Haste says that censorship is a form of negative propaganda.[70] By depriving people from access to information a false impression of reality can be constructed. Authorities have been known to exaggerate their victories or vilify enemies but nowadays with social media people can transmit eyewitness reports that challenge the public control of the image spread. Although it is often almost impossible to know what to believe (as manipulation is so simple), if it appears that supposedly reputable media outlets block information or spread falsehoods, these will lose any trust vested in them. Russian media has been strongly advocating the official narrative on heroic warfare as well as Russian victimhood in relation to the war in Ukraine.[71] This has to be part of an important effort to block differing views and make people dependent on the official message, if it is to be effective, but creating that kind of unfree media environment is not something desirable to copy.

The only way to maintain real freedom of expression is to stay on the moral high ground of not doing the same as those one wants to oppose. By setting out to defend certain interests that are being attacked by propaganda, there is a danger that legitimate discussions in media are endangered. Creating media content should not be a state task. A pluralistic and free media market shall cater for content, with public service media complementing private media and in addition access to international media. Even in times of crisis, proportionality and necessity of restrictions to freedom of expression are essential.

---

[70] Haste 1977/1995, p. 114. She mentions how even weather reports were banned as they could be useful for the enemy and chess problems (unless sent by perfectly reliable British nationals) as they could be hidden code, ibid., p. 116.

[71] Giles 2015, p. 21.

It is difficult to convince states to abide by this, especially if one side of a conflict is a state that does not respect such rules (as is the case in the Ukrainian war, as Russia has severely limited freedom of expression). In such a case the battle of the information space will be fought without equality of arms. However, the option of sacrificing freedom of expression in what should be a fight for freedom and democracy would be a Pyrrhic victory indeed. The only way to maintain real freedom of expression is to stay on the moral high ground and not doing the same as those one wants to oppose.

20.4.3   The Moral High Ground: Concluding Remarks

There are so many conditions and unknowns related to the topic that it is not easy to draw conclusions. We do not know if it is correct to speak about trust in media in the first place. Even just defining media is a challenge, with social media being a mix between the communication with the public or with a closed circle. Furthermore, we cannot easily determine what is post-conflict, as modern-day crises are often hybrid conflicts, frozen conflicts or other situations without clear beginning and end.

However, despite all these qualifications, we will make some concluding remarks to highlight that there is something to do: that those of us who care about plurality, diversity and quality of media should not give up already beforehand. We recognise that there are no magic wands or infallible tools: quite the opposite. The weapons with which to fight back against propaganda, threats and limitations to freedom of expression and so on are rather blunt and the effect of measures taken may be slow and uncertain.

Even in this situation, states should have the courage to not attempt to fight propaganda with more propaganda, but instead to stick to such media legislation that exists in democratic rule of law societies, where the careful balancing of what restrictions are needed while still preserving maximum freedom of expression has been made over the years, through practice and discussions. If something is incitement to hatred or violence, there are tools with which to fight back. An essential ingredient of a free media environment is transparency: it should be known who is behind certain media as such information can go a long way toward showing how trustworthy the message can be expected to be. Ownership rules will help avoid undesirable concentration or excessive state influence. Public interests can be served by public service broadcasting, which should be non-political. Examples of legislation and best practices exist also on issues such as how to make a distinction between opinion and fact or how to allow the right of reply.

Propaganda is not new. Trying to gain control over the minds of people has been a feature of conflict since time immemorial. What has changed is the multitude of tools and situations in which this can be exercised. It is not easy to resign to having to use the blunt weapons mentioned above but in a long-term perspective, staying on the moral high ground will pay off and trust can be built or rebuilt in society in general and in media.

There is no question that Ukraine is facing challenges concerning trust in media - struggling with propaganda, intimidation of journalists, lack of access to information and many other ills. It may not be much of comfort in knowing that it is not alone, not the first (and regrettably almost certainly not the last) state to face this. The only way to conquer these difficulties is to ensure that respect for freedom of expression remains paramount.

References

Akehurst M (2008) The Arab-Israeli Conflict and International Law. In: Kattan V (ed) The Palestine Question in International Law. British Institute of International and Comparative Law, London (reprinted from 5 New Zealand Universities Law Review 1973), pp. 19–37

Altheide DL, Johnson JM (1995) Bureaucratic Propaganda: The Case of Battle Efficiency Reports. In: Jackall R (ed) Propaganda. New York University Press, New York (reprinted from Altheide DL, Johnson JM (1980) Bureaucratic Propaganda. Boston), pp. 299–328

Arafeh N, Abdullah WF, Bahour S (2015) ICT: The Shackled Engine of Palestine´s Development https://al-shabaka.org/briefs/ict-the-shackled-engine-of-palestines-development/?utm_source

Burri N (2015) Bravery or Bravado? The Protection of News Providers in Armed Conflict. Brill/Nijhoff, Leiden/Boston

Giles K (2015) Russia and its Neighbours: Old Attitudes, New Capabilities. In: Geers K (ed) Cyber War in Perspective: Russian Aggression against Ukraine. NATO Cooperative Cyber Defence Centre of Excellence, Tallinn, pp. 19–28

Gross AM (2008) The Construction of a Wall between the Hague and Jerusalem: The Enforcement and Limits of Humanitarian Law and the Structure of Occupation. In: Kattan V (ed) (2008) The Palestinian Question in International Law. British Institute of International and Comparative Law, London (reprinted from Leiden Journal of International Law 19 2006), pp. 833–880

Haste C (1995) The Machinery of Propaganda in Jackall R (ed) (1995) Propaganda. New York University Press, New York (reprinted from Haste C (1977) Keep the Home Fires Burning, Allen Lane), pp. 105–136

Imseis A (2008) On the Fourth Geneva Convention and the Occupied Palestinian Territory. In: Kattan V (ed) The Palestinian Question in International Law. British Institute of International and Comparative Law, London (reprinted from Harvard International Law Journal 44, No 1, Winter 2003), pp. 499–572

Jakubowicz K (2003) Endgame? Contracts, Audits, and the Future of Public Service Broadcasting. 10 The Public, pp. 45–62

Jonsson A (2011) Russia and Europe. In: Gill G, Young J (eds) Routledge Handbook of Russian Politics and Society. Routledge, London, pp. 444–453

Jonsson Cornell A (2016) Russia´s Annexation of Crimea – A Violation of Russian Constitutional Law? In: Russia´s War in Ukraine – a Russian Constitutional Law Analysis, Uppsala University Yearbook on Eurasian Studies I, Simmonds and Hill, London, pp. 263–268

Kahn RA (2014) Offensive symbols and hate speech law: Where to draw the line? In: Koltay A Media (ed) Freedom and Regulation in the New Media World, CompLex. Wolters Kluwer, Budapest, pp. 441–457

Keller P (2011) European and International Media Law. Oxford University Press, Oxford

Knaus G, Martin F (2003) Travails of the European Raj. Lessons from Bosnia and Herzegovina. Journal of Democracy Volume 14, Number 3, July 2003, pp. 60–74

Kuntsman A, Stein R (2015) Digital Militarism: Israel's Occupation in the Social Media Age. Stanford University Press, Stanford

Lange-Ionatamishvili E, Svetoka S (2015) Strategic Communications and Social Media in the Russia Ukraine Conflict. In: Geers K (ed) Cyber War in Perspective: Russian Aggression against Ukraine. NATO Cooperative Cyber Defence Centre of Excellence, Tallinn, pp. 103–111

Laswell HD (1995) Propaganda. In: Jackall R (ed) Propaganda. New York University Press, New York (reprinted from Seligman ERA (ed) (1934) Encyclopaedia of the Social Sciences, Macmillan, London), pp. 13–25

Levin Jaitner M (2015) Russian Information Warfare: Lessons from Ukraine. In: Geers K (ed) Cyber War in Perspective: Russian Aggression against Ukraine. NATO Cooperative Cyber Defence Centre of Excellence, Tallinn, pp. 87–94

Lewis JA (2015) "Compelling opponents to our will": The role of cyber warfare in Ukraine. In: Geers K (ed) Cyber War in Perspective: Russian Aggression against Ukraine. NATO Cooperative Cyber Defence Centre of Excellence, Tallinn, pp. 39–47

Leyland P (2014) Regulating press freedom in the United Kingdom and the constitutional response to the phone-hacking scandal. In: Koltay A Media (ed) Freedom and Regulation in the New Media World. CompLex, Wolters Kluwer, Budapest, pp. 157–176

Nasser I, Lawrence PH, Berlin N (eds) (2011) Examining Education, Media, and Dialogue under Occupation. Multilingual Matters, Bristol/Buffalo/Toronto

Nyman Metcalf K (2014) Digitalisation and beyond: Media freedom in a new reality. In: Koltay A Media (ed) Freedom and Regulation in the New Media World. CompLex, Wolters Kluwer, Budapest, pp. 65–83

Nyman Metcalf K, Thelin K (2000) Media and the Rule of Law. The Importance of Media Regulation for the Peace Process in Bosnia and Herzegovina. Juridisk Tidskrift 11, 1999–2000 No.3, pp. 579–590

Price ME (2012) Orbiting Hate? Satellite Transponders and Free Expression. In: Herz M, Molnar P (eds) The Content and Context of Hate Speech. Rethinking Regulation and Responses. Cambridge University Press, Cambridge, pp. 514–37

Quigley J (2010) The Statehood of Palestine. Cambridge University Press, Cambridge

Richter A (2015) The Relationship between Freedom of Expression and the Ban on Propaganda for War. In: Benedek W, Benoît-Rohmer F, Kettemann MC, Kneihs B, Nowak M (eds) European Yearbook on Human Rights. Intersentia, Antwerp, pp. 489–505

Roberts A (2008) Palestinians, the Uprising and International Law. In: Kattan V (ed) The Palestinian Question in International Law. British Institute of International and Comparative Law, London (reprinted from 2:1989 Journal of Refugee Studies), pp. 391–404

Shah S (2008) On the Road to Apartheid: The Bypass Road Network in the West Bank. In: Kattan V (ed) The Palestine Question in International Law. British Institute of International and Comparative Law, London (reprinted from 29 Columbia Human Rights Review 1997–8), pp. 429–498

Topic T (2007) Electronic media: Regulation Efforts in a Semi-Protectorate. In: Fischer M (ed) Peacebuilding and Civil Society in Bosnia Herzegovina, 2nd edn. LIT, Berlin, pp. 157–184

Van Eijk N (2008) The New European Framework for the Communications Sector. In: Castendyk O, Dommering E, Scheuer A (eds) European Media Law. Wolters Kluwer, Alphen aan den Rijn, pp. 1109–1125

Weaver R (2014) The press and freedom of expression. In: Koltay A Media (ed) Freedom and Regulation in the New Media World. CompLex, Wolters Kluwer, Budapest, pp. 29–43

Weber RH, Heinrich UI (2014) Governance issues of the new media environment. In: Koltay A Media (ed) Freedom and Regulation in the New Media World. CompLex, Wolters Kluwer, Budapest, pp. 85–101

Weinstein J (2009) Extreme Speech, Public Order, and Democracy: Lessons from *The Masses*. In: Hare I, Weinstein J (eds) Extreme Speech and Democracy. Oxford University Press, Oxford, pp. 23–61 (Chapter 2)

Appendices

Appendix 1: Resolutions Adopted by International Organisations

General Assembly of the United Nations:

"Territorial integrity of Ukraine", A/RES/68/262, Resolution adopted by the General Assembly on 27 March 2014: http://undocs.org/A/RES/68/262.

"Situation of human rights in the Autonomous Republic of Crimea and the city of Sevastopol (Ukraine)", A/RES/71/205, Resolution adopted by the General Assembly on 19 December 2016: http://undocs.org/A/RES/71/205.

"Situation of human rights in the Autonomous Republic of Crimea and the city of Sevastopol, Ukraine", A/RES/72/190, Resolution adopted by the General Assembly on 19 December 2017: http://undocs.org/A/RES/72/190.

Office of the United Nations High Commissioner for Human Rights:

"Situation of human rights in the temporarily occupied Autonomous Republic of Crimea and the city of Sevastopol (Ukraine), 22 February 2014–12 September 2017": http://www.ohchr.org/Documents/Countries/UA/Crimea2014_2017_EN.pdf.

Parliamentary Assembly of the Council of Europe:

"Recent developments in Ukraine: threats to the functioning of democratic institutions", Resolution 1988 (2014): http://assembly.coe.int/nw/xml/XRef/Xref-XML2HTML-en.asp?fileid=20873&lang=en.

"Reconsideration on substantive grounds of the previously ratified credentials of the Russian delegation", Resolution 1990 (2014): http://assembly.coe.int/nw/xml/XRef/Xref-XML2HTML-EN.asp?fileid=20882&lang=en.

© T.M.C. ASSER PRESS and the authors 2018
S. Sayapin and E. Tsybulenko (eds.), *The Use of Force against Ukraine and International Law*, https://doi.org/10.1007/978-94-6265-222-4

"The progress of the Assembly's monitoring procedure (October 2013–September 2014)", Resolution 2018 (2014): http://assembly.coe.int/nw/xml/XRef/Xref-XML2HTML-en.asp?fileid=21293&lang=en.

"Challenge, on substantive grounds, of the still unratified credentials of the delegation of the Russian Federation", Resolution 2034 (2015): http://assembly.coe.int/nw/xml/XRef/Xref-XML2HTML-EN.asp?fileid=21538&lang=en.

"Missing persons during the conflict in Ukraine", Resolution 2067 (2015): http://assembly.coe.int/nw/xml/XRef/Xref-XML2HTML-EN.asp?fileid=21970&lang=en.

"The humanitarian concerns with regard to people captured during the war in Ukraine", Resolution 2112 (2016): http://assembly.coe.int/nw/xml/XRef/Xref-XML2HTML-EN.asp?fileid=22750&lang=en.

"Political consequences of the Russian aggression in Ukraine", Resolution 2132 (2016): http://assembly.coe.int/nw/xml/XRef/Xref-XML2HTML-en.asp?fileid=23166&lang=en.

"Legal remedies for human rights violations on the Ukrainian territories outside the control of the Ukrainian authorities", Resolution 2133 (2016): http://assembly.coe.int/nw/xml/XRef/Xref-XML2HTML-en.asp?fileid=23167&lang=en.

"Humanitarian consequences of the war in Ukraine", Resolution 2198 (2018): http://assembly.coe.int/nw/xml/XRef/Xref-XML2HTML-en.asp?fileid=24432&lang=en.

Parliamentary Assembly of the Organization for Security and Cooperation in Europe:

Resolution on clear, gross and uncorrected violations of Helsinki Principles by the Russian Federation: http://www.oscepa.org/documents/all-documents/annual-sessions/2014-baku/declaration-2/2540-2014-baku-declaration-eng/file.

Resolution on the continuation of clear, gross and uncorrected violations of OSCE commitments and international norms by the Russian Federation: https://www.oscepa.org/meetings/annual-sessions/2015-annual-session-helsinki/2015-helsinki-final-declaration/2282-07.

European Union:

EU statement on "Russia's Ongoing Aggression against Ukraine and Illegal Occupation of Crimea", PC.DEL/1558/16, 11 November 2016: https://eeas.europa.eu/sites/eeas/files/pc_1118_eu_on_ukraine.pdf.

International Criminal Court:

Office of the Prosecutor, Report on Preliminary Examination Activities 2016: https://www.icc-cpi.int/iccdocs/otp/161114-otp-rep-PE_ENG.pdf.

Office of the Prosecutor, Report on Preliminary Examination Activities 2017: https://www.icc-cpi.int/itemsDocuments/2017-PE-rep/2017-otp-rep-PE_ENG.pdf.

International Court of Justice:

Application of the International Convention for the Suppression of the Financing of Terrorism and of the International Convention on the Elimination of All Forms of Racial Discrimination (*Ukraine v. Russian Federation*), Order of 19 April 2017: http://www.icj-cij.org/docket/files/166/19394.pdf.

Permanent Court of Arbitration:

Arbitration between Everest Estate LLC and Others as Claimants and The Russian Federation as Respondent, Press Release of 9 May 2018: https://www.pcacases.com/web/view/133.

Government of The Netherlands:

MH17: The Netherlands and Australia hold Russia responsible, News Item of 25 May 2018: https://www.government.nl/latest/news/2018/05/25/mh17-the-netherlands-and-australia-hold-russia-responsible.

G7:

The Charlevoix G7 Summit Communiqué of 9 June 2018: https://g7.gc.ca/en/official-documents/charlevoix-g7-summit-communique/.

Appendix 2

Amicus **Memorandum**[1]
on certain international legal aspects of criminal case № 201/404091-15
regarding the charging of Nadezhda Viktorovna Savchenko
with the commission of crimes provided under subparagraphs
«a», «e»,«zh»,«l» of Article 105(2);
Article 30(3), subparagraphs «a», «e»,«zh»,«l» of Article 105(2);
Article 322(1) of the Criminal Code of the Russian Federation

1. Nadezhda Victorovna Savchenko, a national of Ukraine, born on 11 May 1981, is charged with the commission of crimes provided under subparagraphs «a», «e»,«zh»,«l» of Article 105(2); Article 30(3), subparagraphs «a», «e»,«zh»,«l» of Article 105(2); Article 322(1) of the Criminal Code of the Russian Federation in the course of a non-international armed conflict in the territory of Ukraine.

---

[1] Dr. Sergey Sayapin drafted this *amicus* memorandum in early 2016, upon request from N. Savchenko's Russian lawyers. Their final speech in the trial was largely based upon the memorandum's substance. The text reproduced here is an unofficial translation from the Russian original. The armed conflict's non-international aspect was emphasized specifically for the purpose of Ms Savchenko's defence, and should not be interpreted as Dr. Sayapin's scholarly disagreement with the legal qualification of the international dimension of the armed conflict.

2. It should thereby be noted that N.V. Savchenko is incorrectly charged under Article 105 («Murder»), and not under Article 365[2] («Use of prohibited means and methods of warfare») of the Criminal Code of the Russian Federation. Acts imputed to N.V. Savchenko were committed during a non-international armed conflict in Ukraine, and in connection with it, and therefore, they should be qualified not as common premeditated murders in the sense of Article 105 of the Criminal Code of the Russian Federation, but specifically as *war crimes* in the sense of Article 356 of the Criminal Code of the Russian Federation («[…] use in an armed conflict of means and methods prohibited by a treaty of the Russian Federation»).

3. War crimes are acts (1) violating international humanitarian law, committed (2) during an international and non-international armed conflict, and in connection with it, (3) by a subject related to a party to the armed conflict (4) against persons or objects related to another party to the armed conflict.[3] It is clear from the context of the indictment that the *circumstances of acts imputed to N.V. Savchenko included all of the abovementioned attributes of war crimes.* However, the qualification of offences was carried out incorrectly under Article 105 of the Criminal Code of the Russian Federation – with no regard for the circumstances of a non-international armed conflict in Ukraine, in which they were committed.

4. Article 4(2)(a) of Additional Protocol II to the Geneva Conventions of 12 August 1949 provides an unambiguous definition of a war crime, which is imputed to N.V. Savchenko: «[…] violence to the life, health and physical or mental well-being of persons, in particular *murder*» (emphasis added – S. S.). Thereby, Article 4(1) of the same Additional Protocol defines the victims of this crime as « [a]ll persons who do not take a direct part or who have ceased to take part in hostilities» – that is, as *civilians* in accordance with international humanitarian law.

5. Thereby, the indictment does not mention international humanitarian law, and does not employ the term «armed conflict», but instead employs phrases not having any technical legal significance under international law: «armed confrontations» (p. 2), «armed opposition» (pp. 3, 4). From the perspective of applicable international humanitarian law, the employment of the term «armed conflict» would be of a principal significance in the given context, since charging N.V. Savchenko with the «murder of civilians» (pp. 3, 4 of the

---

[2] See Article 356 of the Criminal Code of the Russian Federation («Use of Banned Means and Methods of Warfare»): "1. Cruel treatment of prisoners of war or civilians, deportation of civilian populations, plunder of national property in occupied territories, and use in a military conflict of means and methods of warfare, banned by an international treaty of the Russian Federation,shall be punishable by deprivation of liberty for a term of up to 20 years. 2. Use of weapons of mass destruction, banned by an international treaty of the Russian Federation, shall be punishable by deprivation of liberty for a term of 10 to 20 years».

[3] See: A. Cassese, P. Gaeta, L. Baig, M. Fan, C. Gosnell, and L. Whiting, *Cassese's International Criminal Law*, 3rd edition (Oxford University Press, 2013), pp. 63–65; G. Werle, F. Jessberger, *Principles of International Criminal Law*, 3rd edition (Oxford University Press, 2014), pp. 391–427.

indictment) *would not otherwise make any sense in terms of law*, since distinguishing between persons taking a direct part in hostilities and persons not taking a direct part in hostilities (civilians) would make sense *only in the circumstances of a non-international armed conflict.* Situations that do not reach the intensity threshold of a non-international armed conflict («armed confrontations», «armed opposition») are not armed conflicts,[4] and international humanitarian law does not apply in such situations. In such situations, the term «civilians» is not employed either. The presence of this special term in the indictment confirms that the investigativ authorities of the Russian Federation considered the relevant circumstances as a non-international armed conflict.

6. In accordance with applicable international humanitarian law, the situation in Ukraine should *certainly be qualified as a non-international armed conflict.* In the sense of Article 1(1) of Protocol Additional to the Geneva Conventions of 12 August 1949, and relating to the Protection of Victims of Non-International Armed Conflicts (Protocol II) of 8 June 1977, a non-international armed conflict is:

[an] armed conflic[t ...] which take[s] place in the territory of a High Contracting Party between its armed forces and dissident armed forces or other organized armed groups which, under responsible command, exercise such control over a part of its territory as to enable them to carry out sustained and concerted military operations and to implement this Protocol.

Page 5 of the indictment refers to the arrival of N.V. Savchenko in the vicinity of positions of «the self-proclaimed Luhank People's Republic's national militia» – that is, of «dissident armed forces» in the sense of Article 1(1) of Additional Protocol II of 8 June 1977. Accordingly, *the indictment admits the existence of a non-international armed conflict in the territory of Ukraine* at the time the acts imputed to N. V. Savchenko were committed.

7. It is thereby clear that, in accordance with Article 3(1) of Additional Protocol II of 8 June 1977, the Government of Ukraine was responsible «by all legitimate means, to maintain or re-establish law and order in the State or to defend the national unity and territorial integrity of the State». It follows that N.V. Savchenko *should not be criminally liable for the mere fact of participation in hostilities as such*, because the re-establishment of law and order in the State and the defence of national unity and territorial integrity of the State – implemented through the use of armed or security forces – are legitimate functions of any State.

8. Persons who commit criminal offences in non-international armed conflict are subjects to prosecution and punishment under Article 6 of Additional

---

[4] See Protocol Additional to the Geneva Conventions of 12 August 1949, and Relating to the Protection of Victims of Non-international Armed Conflict (Protocol II), of 8 June 1977, Article 1 (2): «This Protocol shall not apply to situations of internal disturbances and tensions, such as riots, isolated and sporadic acts of violence and other acts of a similar nature, as not being armed conflicts".

Protocol II of 8 June 1977.[5] Thus, persons who caused death *in the circumstances of a non-international armed conflict in violation of international humanitarian law* should be held criminally responsible.

9. However, in accordance with international law, jurisdiction over criminal violations of international humanitarian law in situations of non-international armed conflicts *is due to the State in whose territory the non-international armed conflict in question took place.* In this case, jurisdiction over the acts imputed to N.V. Savchenko is due to Ukraine. This conclusion follows from the corresponding provisions of applicable treaties as well as from the Criminal and Criminal Procedural Codes of the Russian Federation.

10. Thus, Article 12(3) of the the Criminal Code of the Russian Federation provides that «[f]oreign nationals and stateless persons who do not reside permanently in the Russian Federation and who have committed crimes outside the boundaries of the Russian Federation shall be brought to criminal liability under this Code in cases where the crimes run against the interests of the Russian Federation or a citizen of the Russian Federation or a stateless person permanently residing in the Russian Federation, and also in the cases provided for by international agreements of the Russian Federation, and unless the foreign citizens and stateless persons not residing permanently in the Russian Federation have been

---

[5] See Protocol Additional to the Geneva Conventions of 12 August 1949, and Relating to the Protection of Victims of Non-international Armed Conflict (Protocol II), of 8 June 1977, Article 6: "1. This Article applies to the prosecution and punishment of criminal offences related to the armed conflict.

2. No sentence shall be passed and no penalty shall be executed on a person found guilty of an offence except pursuant to a conviction pronounced by a court offering the essential guarantees of independence and impartiality. In particular:

(a) the procedure shall provide for an accused to be informed without delay of the particulars of the offence alleged against him and shall afford the accused before and during his trial all necessary rights and means of defence;

(b) no one shall be convicted of an offence except on the basis of individual penal responsibility;

(c) no one shall be held guilty of any criminal offence on account of any act or omission which did not constitute a criminal offence, under the law, at the time when it was committed; nor shall a heavier penalty be imposed than that which was applicable at the time when the criminal offence was committed; if, after the commission of the offence, provision is made by law for the imposition of a lighter penalty, the offender shall benefit thereby;

(d) anyone charged with an offence is presumed innocent until proved guilty according to law;

(e) anyone charged with an offence shall have the right to be tried in his presence;

(f) no one shall be compelled to testify against himself or to confess guilt.

3. A convicted person shall be advised on conviction of his judicial and other remedies and of the time limits within which they may be exercised.

4. The death penalty shall not be pronounced on persons who were under the age of eighteen years at the time of the offence and shall not be carried out on pregnant women or mothers of young children.

5. At the end of hostilities, the authorities in power shall endeavour to grant the broadest-possible amnesty to persons who have participated in the armed conflict, or those deprived of their liberty for reasons related to the armed conflict, whether they are interned or detained".

convicted in a foreign state and are brought to criminal liability on the territory of the Russian Federation».

11. In the case under consideration, if the acts imputed to N.V. Savchenko were qualified correctly under Article 105 of the Criminal Code of the Russian Federation as common premeditated murders, the exclusive ground for the *Russian Federation's jurisdiction* would be Article 12(3) of the Criminal Code of the Russian Federation. However, since the acts imputed to N.V. in the criminal case № 201/404091-15 are war crimes, jurisdictional grounds for their criminal prosecution are contained in a treaty to which the Russian Federation is party as well – that is, in Additional Protocol II of 8 June 1977.

12. Unlike the Geneva Conventions of 8 August 1949,[6] Additional Protocol II from the 8th of June 1977 *does not contain provisions on universal jurisdiction with regard to criminal violations of international humanitarian law (war crimes).* Article 6 of Additional Protocol II of 8 June 1977, which regulates criminal prosecution for war crimes committed in a non-international armed conflict, does not contain provisions on the jurisdiction of a foreign State with regard to such crimes. In other words, according to Additional Protocol II of 8 June 1977, *persons who committed criminal violations of international humanitarian law in a non-international armed conflict should be criminally prosecuted exclusively in the State in whose territory such crimes were committed.* That is, in the sense of an applicable treaty of the Russian Federation,[7] exclusive jurisdiction with respect to war crimes, which were committed in the course of the non-international armed conflict in Ukraine and are imputed to N.V. Savchenko, is due to Ukraine but not the Russian Federation.

13. The same conclusion follows from Article 1(3) of the Criminal Procedural Code of Russian Federation: «If a treaty of the Russian Federation has laid down the rules different from those stipulated by the present Code, the rules of the international treaty shall be applied». Since Additional Protocol II of 8 June 1977 – a treaty of the Russian Federation – excludes the Russian Federation's jurisdiction with respect to war crimes imputed to N.V. Savchenko, her criminal prosecution in the Russian Federation should be regarded as incompatible with the Russian Federation's obligations under international law.

---

[6] See for example the second paragraph of Article 49 of the First Geneva Convention of 8 August 1949: "Each High Contracting Party shall be under the obligation to search for persons alleged to have committed, or to have ordered to be committed, such grave breaches, and shall bring such persons, regardless of their nationality, before its own courts. It may also, if it prefers, and in accordance with the provisions of its own legislation, hand such persons over for trial to another High Contracting Party concerned, provided such High Contracting Party has made out a *prima facie* case".

[7] The Additional Protocol of the 8th of June 1977 was ratified by USSR on the 29th of September 1989. The Russian Federation takes part in the Additional Protocol II under the right of succession.

14. Consequently, Ukraine's national N.V. Savchenko should be transferred to Ukraine, in accordance with applicable treaties on mutual legal assistance, in order for the matter of N.V. Savchenko's criminal liability to be resolved under Ukraine's criminal and criminal procedure legislation.

Respectfully,

Sergey Sayapin LLB, LLM, Dr. iur.

Assistant-Professor
School of Law
KIMEP University
Almaty
Republic of Kazakhstan